Toward a Comparative Institutional Analysis

Toward a Comparative Institutional Analysis

Masahiko Aoki

The MIT Press
Cambridge, Massachusetts
London, England

This book was set in Times New Roman on 3B2 by Asco Typesetters, Hong Kong.

Library of Congress Cataloging-in-Publication Data

Aoki, Masahiko, 1938–
    Toward a comparative institutional analysis / Masahiko Aoki.
        p.   cm. — (Comparative institutional analysis ; 2)
    Includes bibliographical references and index.
    ISBN 978-0-262-01187-7 (hc), 978-0-262-55083-3 (pb)
    1. Institutional economics. 2. Game theory. I. Title. II. Series.
HB99.5 .A63   2001
3330—dc21   2001032633

Contents

Acknowledgments

This is the first volume in the Comparative Institutional Analysis series. The intent of this book is to present a general introduction to an emergent field of economics, with some original contributions in the application of a methodology to salient institutional issues.

In the writing of the book I benefited from two exceptionally favorable work environments. First, in 1990 the Stanford Economics Department inaugurated a new graduate field, comparative institutional analysis (CIA). I have been its active faculty member since its inception. The idea originated in conversations among Paul Milgrom, Avner Greif, Yingyi Qian, John Litwack, and myself. Later we were joined by Marcel Fafchamps, Steven Tadelis, Ilya Segal, and Jonathan Levin. I have learned a great deal from these colleagues in workshops, casual conversations, and in the joint supervision of students. Although the contents of the book are organized, and interpreted, according to my own views, their intellectual imprints on the development of my thinking are beyond what I am able to specifically acknowledge in this book.

Further I have learned from many former and current graduate students in the field. For the last ten years I have been teaching a course entitled "Comparative Organizations and Institutions." This book has evolved from successive lecture notes prepared for the course. Over the years I was able to improve on these notes from students' active discussions, embarrassing questions, and enthusiasm for the subject matter. In this book I even draw upon a number of theses written by my students to illustrate important analytical points. In particular, I would like to acknowledge contributions by Jiahua Che, Serdar Dinç, Thomas Hellmann, Christopher Kingston, Kevin Murdonck, Tetsuro Toya, Andreas Prat and Ayako Yasuda.

Second, the Economic Development Institute of the World Bank (now the World Bank Institute) allowed me and co-organizers to conduct four international projects with generous support from the Policy and Human Resource Fund established at the Bank by the Government of Japan. These projects were managed under the co-sponsorship of the Stanford Institute of Economic Policy Research. The themes of the projects ranged from the role of (main) banks in developing and transforming economies (Aoki and Patrick 1994) to corporate governance in transitional economies (Aoki and Kim 1995), to the role of government in East Asian economic development (Aoki, Kim, and Okuno-Fujiwara 1996), and to communities and markets in economic development (Aoki and Hayami 2001). Sixty-two papers from fourteen countries were presented. Through intensive interactions with participants of diverse academic backgrounds, I was able to gain wide-ranging comparative and historical knowledge, as well as to learn methods of applying comparative analytical insights. My exposition in this book is enriched in my borrowing from the writings of some of these participants, taking me far beyond what I could have done alone.

Because my intellectual indebtedness in writing this book is so widespread and extensive, I could not do justice to all the scholars who helped me just by acknowledging their names. Therefore I will limit myself mentioning the names of those who kindly read parts or all of earlier manuscripts and provided comments for improving them. They are Pranab Bardhan, Kausik Basu, Hans Binswanger, Samuel Bowles, Robert Boyer, Jiahua Che, Serdar Dinç, Richard Freeman, Miguel Garcia-Cestona, Avner Greif, Yujiro Hayami, Thomas Hellmann, Geoffrey Hodgson, Tarun Khanna, Stephen Krasner, Bentley McLeod, Claude Ménard, Hiroyuki Nakata, Tetsuji Okazaki, Douglass North, Ugo Pagano, John Roberts, AnnaLee Saxenian, Stephen Tadelis, Tetsuro Toya, Jean-Philippe Touffut, Kotaro Tsuru, Meredith Woo-Cummings, Erik Wright, and Peyton Young. Also I benefited from the kind instructions of Robert Allen, Yasumasa Koga, and Hiroshi Miyajima on some historical facts and interpretations. Christopher Kingston gave me his valuable assistance throughout by discussing material, suggesting improvements for manuscripts, and searching for relevant literature. Also Christopher Clatterbuck and Naoki Ohishi assisted me in collecting needed information and data with competence and efficiency. Deborah Johnston patiently edited the many versions of my manuscript. Hirokazu Takizawa and Kazuhiro Taniguchi undertook the Japanese translation of the book, while Li-an Zhou did the Chinese translation. Because their enthusiasm enabled them to complete the translations before the current English version was edited, I was able to benefit from their queries, comments, reference preparation, and correct the errors they found.

Writing this book was financially supported by the Stanford Institute of Economic Policy Research. Also I would like to express my gratitude to several institutions and their hosts who allowed me to escape from the normal duties of teaching and concentrate on writing and thinking in stimulating academic environments. They are the Suntory and Toyota International Centres for Economic and Related Disciplines (STICERD) at the London School of Economics and Political Science and Dr. Athar Hussain; the Havens Center for Study in Social Structure and Social Change at the University of Wisconsin and Professor Erik Wright; Max Planck Institut für Gesellschaftsforschung in Köln and Professor Wolfgang Streeck; Università di Siena and Professor Ugo Pagano; and Centre Saint-Gobain pour la recherche en économie and Jean-Louis Beffa. Also the International Joseph Schumpeter Society provided an impetus for the completion of the book project by awarding me the Schumpeter Prize 1998 for an earlier manuscript.

Terry Vaughn and Victoria Warneck, both formerly of The MIT Press showed a kind interest in comparative institutional analysis from its early stage and were instrumental in conceptualizing the CIA series from The Press. John S. Covell took over the responsibility for the project from them and has skillfully engineered its launching. Dana Andrus did an excellent job editing and improving the final manuscript. I am grateful to these people and many others at The Press who contributed to the production of the book.

Writing a book generally forces an author's family members to bear burdens and sacrifices by forgoing shared time, dealing with the author's absorbed mind, tolerating numerous breaches of promise on the data of completion, and so on and on. In my case these burdens were heightened by my frequent trans-Pacific trips to fulfill my civil duties as the part-time director of a government research institute in Japan. At last, however, I am done with this book project, for which I am sure my wife, Reiko, is the happiest. My deepest gratitude goes to her.

February 9, 2001
at Stanford, California

Toward a Comparative Institutional Analysis

1 What Are Institutions? How Should We Approach Them?

[I]n the great chessboard of human society, every single piece has a principle of motion of its own, altogether different from that which the legislature might chuse to impress upon it. If those two principles coincide and act in the same direction, the game of human society will go on easily and harmoniously, and is very likely to be happy and successful. If they are opposite or different, the game will go on miserably, and the society must be at all times in the highest degree of disorder.
—Adam Smith, *The Theory of Moral Sentiments* (1759:234)

Economists have traditionally been engaged in analyzing the workings and implications of the market mechanism. Markets can undoubtedly be considered one of the most salient institutions that human beings have ever produced. However, recently it has been increasingly recognized that "institutions matter" for understanding the diverse economic performances of different economies, and when the phrase is cited, the reference is not always limited to markets. Indeed, in the last decade of the twentieth century we have witnessed various institution-relevant events and phenomena that have had, and in many cases will continue to have, significant impacts on the performances of the relevant economies. There were, for example, the demise of the communist states and the subsequent transformation of their economic systems, the emergence of the Silicon Valley phenomenon and e-commerce, the European currency unification and market integration, the Japanese and East Asian financial crises subsequent to their "miracle" phases, the persistent ethnic divides and the stagnation of African economies, the global integration of financial markets and recurrent currency crises, the re-examination of the role of international organizations with nation states as members, and the growing global, nongovernmental organizations. On the surface some of these may be thought of as purely market phenomena or matters of organizational design. However, if we try to understand the causes and implications of any of these events and phenomena at a deeper level, we are compelled to take their institutional aspects into consideration.

What are institutions? Can we identify them with statutory laws, informal norms, established organizations, contracts, people's mind-sets, or possibly combinations of some or all of these? A proper formulation of a concept, such as that of institutions, may depend on the purpose of the analysis. For example, consider the following question: If institutions matter to economic performance, why can't the best institutions from better-performing economies be learned and imitated by other economies? This was the major issue raised by D. North in a seminal book on institutions (North 1990). To deal with it, North conceptualized institutions as the rules of the game in a society. We were told that there are two types of game rules: formal ones (constitutional, property-rights rules, and contracts) and informal ones (norms and customs). Then, even if good formal rules are borrowed from without, tension may be created since indigenous, informal rules are inert and difficult to change. As a result a borrowed institution may be neither enforceable nor functional.

Consequently economists are becoming interested in the issue of enforceability. When do the rules of the game become enforceable? With the advent of an enforcer? But, how can the enforcer be motivated to enforce the rules of the game? In short, how is the enforcer enforced to do a prescribed job? A way out of this infinite chain of reasoning may be to show how the rules of the game are endogenously generated, and thus become self-enforcing through the strategic interactions of the agents, including the enforcer. A reasonable way of approaching institutions from this perspective is then to conceptualize an institution as an equilibrium outcome of a game. Thus we have recently seen the publication of some important works based on views of an institution as an equilibrium of a game, although most of them derive insights from historical cases (some representative works are referred to in the next section). Can we apply the same idea to the contemporary economy that appears to exist as a complex of many different institutions? Is this merely a bundle of more or less autonomous institutions, or does it exist as an internally coherent whole, that is, as an equilibrium phenomenon of some sort?

When we view institutions (and possibly their complexes) as equilibrium phenomena, this does not imply that institutions are rigidly frozen; they do change. The demise of the communist states and the subsequent transformation of the planning systems in Central and Eastern European economies is its eloquent manifestation. Then, how can one explain theoretically the emergence of an institution and/or an institutional change? In general, game-theoretic models can have multiple solutions (equilibria) and/or generate solutions highly dependent on the specification of models. Is it then that institutional emergence/change is explained merely as the selection of one equilibrium from the many that are equally possible and/or a transition from one equilibrium to another, given the fixed structure of the game? If so, is the selection/transition essentially technology—or market—induced, and does it eventually become locked in due to technological economies of scale? Alternatively, is institutional evolution programmed by "cultural genes"? Can change be engineered by political entrepreneurs or engendered by mutant entrepreneurs? Do cataclysmic political events have stochastic impacts on the selection of a new institution? Or, is there something else involved in the process of institutional change? In particular, how does the novelty often observed in the emergence of new institutions come about?

The basic research agenda of this book may be set forth as two problems: the *synchronic problem*, whereby the goal is to understand *the complexity and diversity of overall institutional arrangements across the economies as an instance of multiple equilibria of some kind*, and the *diachronic problem*, whereby the goal is to understand *the mechanism of institutional evolution/change in a framework consistent with an equilibrium view of institutions, but allowing for the possibility of the emergence of novelty.*

We will investigate the institutional diversity and the complexity of economies by looking into the nature of the interdependencies of institutions across economic, political, organizational, and social domains, as well as that of institutions linking those domains. In so doing, we will reconsider the framework of traditional economics and try to incorporate some important contributions to institutional issues in neighboring disciplines, such as sociology, political science, law, and the cognitive sciences. However, departing from the old institutional economics, we will analyze the sources and implications of institutional diversity within a unified, generic—game-theoretic—framework rather than merely compiling a rich institutional catalog or drawing an ad hoc taxonomy of institutions. Developing a unified conceptual and analytical framework and incorporating important contributions from different disciplines into it will help us gain a deeper theoretical understanding of the workings of the economic institutions.

However, we also emphasize game-theoretic analysis in the traditional sense cannot be complete by itself as a systemic study of institutions. The analysis of the interdependencies of institutions within a game-theoretic framework would indicate the possibility of *multiple,* suboptimal, Pareto-unrankable institutional arrangements. That is, institutional arrangements can be diverse across economies even if they are exposed to the same technological knowledge and are linked through the same markets. Thus we need to rely on comparative and historical information to understand why particular institutional arrangements has evolved in one economy but not in others. By this we imply that an institutional analysis must be also comparative and historical, and thus we have hope to provide the groundwork for *comparative institutional analysis* (CIA).[1]

In considering the diachronic process of institutional evolution, we will take an important departure from traditional game theory. Midway through the book (chapter 9) we will abandon the assumption that the players of a game have complete knowledge of the objective structure of the game they play. Instead, they are assumed to have individual, incomplete cognitive views regarding the structure of the game they play—what we call subjective game models. When actions taken by the players of the game based on their subjective game models become mutually consistent over periods (i.e., equilibrated), then their subjective game models can be confirmed by the observed reality jointly created by their action choices and reproduced as a guide for their further action choices. We will then conceptualize an institution as a salient, common component of the players' subjective game models—that is, as shared beliefs about the structure of the game that they actually play. When action choices derived from such models do not yield anticipated results for the players, and thus a state of general perceptual crisis is created, a search for new subjective models may be triggered and continue until new equilibrium is achieved. In effect, understanding the process of institutional change may be tantamount to understanding the ways in which the agents revise their beliefs in a coordinated manner. From this perspective we can analyze the roles of technological and other environmental changes, political programs and discourses, enactment of statutory laws, entrepreneurial experiments, cultural legacies and so forth, in the process of institutional change, but this will be done after we have dealt with the synchronic problem.

The composition of this introductory chapter is as follows: Section 1.1 provides an overview of the different conceptualizations of institutions that economists have proposed. Section 1.2 introduces our conceptualization of institutions based on an equilibrium view, subject to a precise formulation later (chapter 7). Section 1.3 introduces some basic notions such as the "game form" and the types of "domains" that will play important roles in this book and then presents the plan of the book.

1.1 Three Views of Institutions in Game-Theoretic Perspective

The statement that "institutions matter" does not make much sense unless we have a common understanding about what institutions are and how they are formed. Emile Durkheim, a pioneer of modern sociology, once defined the discipline of sociology as the "science of institutions" and that of economics as the "science of markets."[2] Leaving aside the old school of institutional economists, main stream economists of the past were indeed engrossed with market analysis.[3] Today we see that not only economics can make significant contributions to understanding the nature, origin, roles, and implications of institutions, but important economic phenomena and problems cannot be well understood without an analysis of nonmarket institutions. Recently an increasing number of economists have taken up the task of conceptualizing and analyzing institutions. As we will see, there are at least three different (yet interrelated) meanings that economists have attached to the word "institution." What we should be concerned with is obviously not a semantic clarification of the word as such, but a conceptualization that may be conducive to a better understanding of the workings of diverse economic systems.

In order to clarify the differences among the three meanings, or conceptualizations, of institutions that economists use, an analogy of the economic process with a game is apt. I have already indicated that the application of game theory is an indispensable component of comparative institutional analysis. The game-analytic apparatuses we will apply in this book to deal with the synchronic problem, namely those borrowed from the theory of evolutionary and repeated games, are relatively recent. However, the analogy of the economic process with a game can be dated back as far as Adam Smith, as the quotation in the beginning of this chapter shows. There the game is identified with a situation in which individual agents *strategically* interact with each other according to their own motivations, and this precisely corresponds to the situation with which modern game theorists are concerned. In the analogy of the economic process with a game, economists have regarded an institution as comparable to either players of a game, the rules of a game, or equilibrium strategies of the players in a game.

When people casually talk about institutions in daily conversation, they usually mean certain prominent organizational establishments. Some economists follow this convention, effectively identifying institutions as specific players of the game, such as "industry associations, technical societies, universities, courts, government agencies, legislatures, etc." (Nelson 1994:57). But there is a second view, as North argues, that institutions should be identified with the rules of the game as distinct from its players.[4] He opens his seminal book on institutions and institutional change with the following passage:

Institutions are the rules of the game in a society or, more formally, are the humanly devised constraints that shape human interaction. . . . In the jargon of the economist, institutions define and limit the set of choices of individuals. (North 1990:3–4)

Humanly devised constraints may be informal (e.g., social norms, conventions, and moral codes) or formal (i.e., consciously designed or articulated). Formal rules include political rules (constitutions, regulations), economic rules, and contracts. Economic rules define property rights, that is, the bundle of rights to use and dispose of an economic resource and to derive utility (income) from it. Contracts are (enforceable) agreements, embedded in property rights rules, regarding the use or exchange of goods. The formal rules of the economic game cannot be constructed (changed) by the players of the game themselves while they are playing. These rules are determined prior to playing the game. Since we are concerned with the origin of institutions, an immediate question arises: Who determines the economic rules? It is here that North draws a sharp distinction between the rules of the game and the players of the game (organizations and their political entrepreneurs) who can act as agents of institutional change, that is, as rule-makers. According to North, the existing rules of the game shape the incentives of the players as to how to transact and what to innovate, ultimately generating effective demands for new rules in response to changing relative prices. The new rules are then negotiated and determined in the "political market," that is, structured according to political rules. North claims, "[i]t is the polity that defines and enforces the property rights" (1995:23).[5]

A more technical formulation of the rules-of-the-game view is presented by Hurwicz (1993, 1996) who focuses on the issue of enforcement. In this approach the rules of a game are expressed by specifying who play the game, what actions players can choose ("a choice set") and what physical outcome corresponds to each profile of the players' choices ("an outcome function"). He calls such a triplet of specifications a "mechanism" or a "game form."[6] To illustrate, let us take the mechanism of price control whereby a seller is constrained by a ceiling set by the government on the sales price that can be charged. The constraint on his/her choice set is represented by a specific parameter value, which is, the ceiling price.[7] According to Hurwicz, other restrictions are needed as well for arriving at a proper definition of institutions. He considers that the rules need to be enforceable, or "implementable" in his terminology. Namely he requires that only a class of enforceable, human-made restrictions on actions qualifies as an institution. He formalizes the notion of enforceability in terms of *Nash equilibrium*. A profile of strategic choices by players is said to be a Nash equilibrium if no player has incentives to change his strategy when other players are expected to remain with the prescribed strategies. In order for a set of humanly devised restrictions on the game form to be enforceable, it must then contain a Nash equilibrium as players choose strategies freely from the sets of all technologically feasible actions.

Hurwicz's main concern is to inquire into the possibility of "designing" an institution that can implement a given social goal in a way that is compatible with the incentives of the players for a certain class of environment (technology, preferences, and resource endowments). A social goal (efficiency, equity, clean air and water, etc.) may be expressed in terms of a certain set of outcomes (consequences) to be attained for each economic environment. Suppose that a legislator designs a mechanism that implements the prescribed social goal. However, there is no guarantee that this mechanism is enforceable. For example, the legislator may expect that a price control can achieve the social goals of price stability and distributive equity, but there will always be sellers who find it appealing to sell in the black market at a price higher than the regulated ceiling price. Then price control is not self-enforceable, and thus not implementable.

If a mechanism that was designed with the purpose of achieving a prescribed social goal is not self-enforceable, then it needs to be supplemented by an enforcement mechanism. The game form must be altered by adding enforcers (the court, police, ombudsmen, etc.) with particular action sets (putting people in jail, etc.) and modifying the outcome function accordingly. But this creates a dilemma for the mechanism designer. To make the enforcement mechanism effective, appropriate incentives may need to be provided for the enforcers to perform their mission properly. Further the operation of the enforcement mechanism may require the use of resources that have to be diverted away from activities directly contributing to the prescribed social goal. As a result the achievement of the original social goal will need to be compromised.

In considering the incentives of enforcers, Hurwicz's idea of an institution actually comes close to the third, game equilibrium notion of institutions. One of earliest proponents of this third view is Schotter (1981).[8] More recently there have been two major developments in the game equilibrium view of an institution based on different equilibrium notions in the evolutionary game approach and the repeated game approach. Representative works of the former approach are by Sugden (1986, 1989), Aoki (1995), P. Young (1998), Okazaki and Okuno-Fujiwara (1998), and Bowles (2000).[9] In the evolutionary game approach, a convention of behavior establishes itself without third-party enforcement or conscious design. As a convention evolves, agents tend to develop particular traits (perceptions of the environment, preferences, skills, etc.) under the pressure of evolutionary selection. Thus a convention and associated individual traits may co-evolve. A convention may eventually be codified through the judicial process to reduce the costs of disequilibrium caused by mutation and mistakes. Also an articulation in words of conventionalized rules of conduct may help make clear a particular situation. However, Sugden argues, following the tradition of Hume, that it may be misleading to think of the law as a creation of the government imposed on its citizens. Rather, "the law may reflect codes of behavior that most individuals impose on themselves" (Sugden 1986:5).

An alternative game-theoretic approach to institutions is that developed by Greif (1989, 1994, 1997b, 1998b), Milgrom, North, and Weingast (1990), Greif, Milgrom, and Weingast (1994), and Calvert (1995), among others, who rely on sophisticated concepts of equilibrium, such as subgame perfect equilibrium, in repeated prisoner's dilemma games. The precise conceptualization of subgame perfect equilibrium will be given later in this book (chapter 7). However, it may be worth noting at this point that this and other related equilibrium concepts are useful in clarifying the role of expectations or beliefs shared by players of the game. A subgame perfect equilibrium prescribes a strategy for each player constituted as a comprehensive plan of action choices contingent on all possible future states of the game.[10] Any element of the comprehensive plan, that is, an action choice prescribed for a particular contingency, needs to be a Nash equilibrium when that contingency actually arises, and thus self-enforcing. As a result of applying subgame perfect strategies, some states may never be observed in the actual playing of the game. This is not because a path of play leading to such a state is excluded by exogenous constraints but because the strategic calculations of the players mutually deter them from choosing that path once the equilibrium "plan" are put into use. Since the portions of the equilibrium strategies that prescribe actions to be taken off the paths of play are not actually observed, they may be interpreted as representing the rational expectations or beliefs held by other players regarding what actions would be chosen by the relevant players once such paths are selected in the game.

The point may be illustrated by using the model of a merchant guild provided by Greif, Milgrom, and Weingast (1994). This game is played repeatedly between a group of merchants and the ruler of a city or trading center in the context of medieval trade. In order to expand trading opportunities, the trading center needs to be organized in ways that secure the person and property of the visiting merchants. The ruler of the city might pledge that visiting merchants would be provided with this security, but once trade is established, the ruler might be tempted to renege on the pledge. Suppose now that the merchants, who have organized themselves into a guild, adopt the following strategy: they trade in the city in a given period if and only if none of them has been cheated by its ruler. Otherwise, they organize a boycott (we leave aside the matter of the guild's ability to enforce compliance among its members). The ruler adopts the following strategy: he does not cheat unless a boycott is announced by the guild. Once a boycott is announced, the ruler cheats any trader who offers to trade. The authors proved that such a strategy profile constitute a (perfect) equilibrium. In the actual play of the game, cheating and boycotts may not be observed in normal circumstances. But this is not because they are a priori pre-cluded by the rules of the game, but because the ruler expects the guild to credibly boycott him if he cheats, so it does not benefit him to do so. The formation of the guild thus functions to force the ruler to credibly commit to his pledge and thereby to allow the city's trade expansion to proceed. In this example, the merchant guild (an organization) and its expected role of organizing a boycott in the event of cheating (the off-the-path-of-play portion of the equilibrium strategy) may be considered to provide a credible contract enforcement mechanism.

Based on this and other important works (1994, 1997b), Greif gives the following summary notion of an institution from an equilibrium perspective. Observe what this reveals the importance of beliefs and self-enforceability.

Given the technologically determined rules of the game, institutions—the non-technological constraints on human interactions—are composed of two interrelated elements: cultural beliefs (how individuals expect others to act in various contingencies) and organizations (the endo-genous human constructs that alter the rules of the game [relevant to the decision-makers]) and, whenever applicable, [they] have to be an equilibrium [and thus self-enforcing]. (Greif 1994:943)

Organizations, which are social entities such as the guild in the game above, are players of a game and subject to constraints implied by an established equilibrium of the game. Greif's conceptualization may be thus said to subsume the first, player-of-the-game view as well.

Regarding the origin of an institution, we have seen that the rule-of-the-game theorists tend to subscribe to the design view; namely rule-making is susceptible to conscious design by legislators, political entrepreneurs, or mechanism design economists. Among the equilibrium-of-the-game theorists, in the beginning there was no clear consensus on this issue. Those who took the evolutionary game approach clearly subscribed to the view of an institution as a "spontaneous order" (Menger 1883; Hayek 1973) or a self-organizing system. In contrast, the concept of subgame perfect equilibrium presumes that individual players are perfectly capable of deductive reasoning regarding a passible feedback mechanism between their own and others' choices. How is it that individuals will jointly select strategies that are mutually consistent and lead to the construction of an institution, especially where there are multiple equilibria possible? There is nothing that the notion of subgame perfect equilibrium can reveal about why a certain institution evolves in one place and another evolves elsewhere. Take the example above of medieval trade where the combination of no trade and cheating in each period (and thus the observation of only no trade) can be another subgame perfect equilibrium. It seems natural then to consider that even those who adopt the superrationality notions of equilibrium, such as subgame perfection, are doing so merely to show that a certain profile of strategies (actual plays and expectations) can become self-enforceable and sustainable, *once established.*

However, there remains one paradox that has to be resolved before we subscribe to the equilibrium view of institutions. If the role of an institution is understood as being to constrain the choices of the players in one or another way, how is such a constraint found and perceived as relevant by the players? By the emergence of an equilibrium? But, then, how does each individual player find and choose an appropriate equilibrium strategy of his own before knowing the equilibrium and thus without yet being constrained by it? In other words, how can consistency be induced in the players' beliefs regarding the emergent situation and in the actual situation created by the choices of the players based on these beliefs? This question may appear to be merely about the ordinary stability property of an equilibrium. However, we will see later in this book (chapter 7) that the problem is more fundamental and cannot be resolved so simply. This is why we propose a new definition of institutions essentially based on an equilibrium view but with a substantive qualification, as introduced in the next section.

1.2   Aspects of Institutions: Shared Beliefs, Summary Representations of Equilibrium, and Endogenous Rules of the Game

Our Conceptualization of Institutions

As already noted, which definition of an institution to adopt is not an issue of right or wrong; it depends on the purpose of the analysis. Since the main objective of this book is to understand the diversity of institutional arrangements as well as the nature of the process of institutional change, we now introduce a definition of institutions that will be useful and amenable to the analysis of these issues. Because it is hard to provide a brief definition and its full implications at the outset, we will tentatively characterize the institution as a *self-sustaining system of shared beliefs* about a salient way in which the game is repeatedly played. We can identify "a way by which the game is repeatedly played" as the rules of the game. However, by that we do not mean the rules exogenously given or conditioned by the polity, culture, or a meta-game, as the rules-of-the-game theorists do. We regard these rules as being endo-genously created through the strategic interactions of agents, held in the minds of agents, and thus self-sustaining—as the equilibrium-of-the-game theorists do. In order for beliefs to be shared by the agents in a self-sustaining manner and regarded by them as relevant to the consequences of their choices, they must have substantive bases. The content of the shared beliefs is a *summary representation (compressed information) of an equilibrium* of the game (out of the many that are theoretically possible). That is to say, a salient feature of an equilibrium may be tacitly recognized by the agents, or have corresponding symbolic representations outside the minds of agents and coordinate their beliefs.

By focusing on equilibrium "beliefs," we closely follow the conceptualization of an institution by Greif, as quoted above.[11] However, we keep the equilibrium notion behind our definition unspecified at this stage except that it is a Nash—that is, self-enforcing. Later, in chapter 7, we will propose a more precise, encompassing definition of institutions, inclusive of both the classical and evolutionary game approaches,[12] as well as some liberal modifications. Here we specifically refer to the "summary" or "information compression" nature of institutions. As is made clear subsequently, this specification will be useful for understanding the dynamic process of institutional change. In any case, from the proposed perspective, we are concerned throughout the book with what type of institutions can become viable under what conditions and how they relate to each other. Although it is yet premature to give a precise, generic formalization of this view, we will present here a basic underlying idea to motivate our study.

To begin, let us consider a game played by a fixed set of agents, each endowed with a set of technologically (and perceptually) feasible actions. For each combination of action choices by all the agents—referred to as an action profile—a specific payoff distribution among the agents is associated. Tentatively let us refer to the collection of the sets of feasible actions over the agents as the domain of the game and the rule (function) that specifies a payoff distribution for each action profile from the domain as an exogenous rule of the game. Given these characteristics of the game, each agent wants to maximize his/her payoff. However, his or her payoff cannot be solely determined by his/her action. The best action choice of each agent ought to be contingent on others' action choices, but how can agents infer others' action choices?

Suppose, for a moment, that a game is played repeatedly, out of which a stable outcome (an action profile) somehow evolves and each agent has come to have a reasonably good idea, based on his/her experience, about how the game is played in the domain. Namely agents may not be able to infer, or may not even need to infer, every detailed characteristic of the others' action-choice rules but come to perceive some salient features of private rules that relevant agents are believed to apply in making their action choices. Relying on such compressed information, each agent may also develop his/her own private rules—strategies—for making an action choice in response to an evolving state of the domain. Clearly, a complex feedback mechanism is operating here. All the agents form their own action-choice rules as their strategies in response to their subjective perceptions (beliefs) of others' action-choice rules even though in an incomplete and compressed form. Only when their compressed perceptions about others' action-choice rules become stabilized and reproduced, can their own action-choice rules also become stabilized and serve as useful guides for playing the game, and vice versa.

We may capture this consistency property evolving with respect to agents' beliefs and their strategic formation of action-choice rules by regarding them as being in (Nash) equilibrium. It is not beneficial for the agent to deviate from his/her own action-choice rule thus constructed, as long as their beliefs regarding other agents' action-choice rule are sustained. Institutions can then refer to that portion of agents' equilibrium beliefs common to (almost) all of them regarding how the game is actually played (how action-choice rules are applied by agents in the domain). Although they are equilibrium phenomena, they should be regarded neither as a result of perfect deductive reasoning in a one-shot game, nor a complete stasis to which no inductive reasoning needs to be applied by agents. They represent the substantive, self-sustaining expectations of the agents who have actually played the game repeatedly. As such, an institution is "the product of long term experiences of a society of boundedly rational and retrospective individuals" (Kreps 1990:183).

An equilibrium state is a socially constructed reality, and thus it is endogenous to the domain. It coordinates the beliefs of agents through its summary representations —tacit and symbolic. As an equilibrium phenomena, an institution cannot be ignored by any agent as far as others do not ignore and thus influence their strategic choices. Agents' strategic choices made on the basis of shared beliefs jointly reproduce the equilibrium state, which in turn reconfirms its summary representation. Thus the institution becomes self-sustaining and information compressed in it becomes taken for granted by the agents unless some events shaking the shared beliefs occur (see figure 1.1, where the dashed-line box represents an institution; we will momentarily ignore the dotted-line box). In this way, although endogenously created, an institution becomes objectified.[13] By relying on equilibrium analysis, we can understand this dual nature of institutions, endogenicity and objectivity, which may have been responsible for the somewhat confused bifurcation of endogenous versus exogenous rules-of-the-game views of institutions.[14]

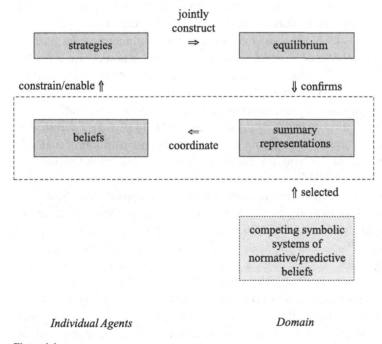

Figure 1.1
An institution as shared beliefs formed as summary representations of an equilibrium. An institution is represented by the broken-line box.

A critical feature of an equilibrium recognized as an institution may sometimes be represented in some explicit, codified and/or symbolic form, including statutory laws, agreements, social structures or organizations as systemic arrangements of differentiated roles, and so on. However, the point is that such a representation is an institution only if the agents mutually believe in it.[15] From this perspective, statutory law and regulations per se are not institutions if they are not necessarily observed. For example, even if the government prohibits the importation of some goods by a statutory law, but if people believe it effective to bribe customs officers to circumvent the law and make it a prevailing practice, then it seems appropriate to regard the practice rather than the ineffectual statutory law as an institution. On the other hand, certain practices, if not formalized, can be institutions as long as the agents believe in them as relevant representations of the internal state of the domain; they cease to be institutions when the agents' beliefs in them are critically shaken.

The equilibrium–summary-representation view of institutions helps clarify their dualistic constraining/enabling nature. The role of institutions is normally understood as a nontechnological constraint on the action choices of the agents by the exogenous rules-of-the-game theorists as well as the equilibrium-of-the-game theorists (recall the definitions by North and Greif discussed above). Indeed, an institution, by the very fact of its existence, controls agents' individual action-choice rules by coordinating their beliefs. These beliefs channel their actions in one direction against the many other directions that are theoretically possible (i.e., other equilibria). In this sense, controlling or constraining character is certainly inherent in institutionalization. However, an institution coordinates agents' beliefs only in summary and shared ways. In a world of incomplete and asymmetric information, an institution "enables" the bounded-rational agents to economize on the information processing needed for decision-making (see figure 1.1).[16]

Here, an analogy with the price mechanism familiar to economists may be useful. In the market mechanism, individuals do not need to know every detail of the internal state and external environments in which they make their choices, but only the relative prices (Hayek 1945). Leaving aside the problem of the enforcement of contracts and property rights, if there were a complete set of markets, relative prices could be formally regarded as "sufficient statistics" summarizing the data (preferences and technological possibilities of production) needed for the society to achieve the social optimum in the most efficient way. The dimensionality of relative prices does not exceed the number of goods traded minus one with one particular good serving as a numéraire (Koopmans 1957; Hurwicz 1960, 1973). Of course, in actuality markets are far from complete. Individual agents need alternative means to gain the useful information for making their choices. Various institutions other than markets then evolve in response to the failure of complete markets to exist (Arrow 1998). Thus individual agents are not only constrained but also informed by institutions. Just as markets transmit information regarding the economic environment (technologies, tastes and resource endowments) in the summary form of relative prices representing the marginal rates of substitution/transformation so do other institutions in alternative summary forms (chapter 6.2).[17] Also a summary representation of an equilibrium can be robust to the mildly changing environments of the domain, as well as the associated shift in equilibrium, because of its very nature of information compression.[18] Thus information compression embodied in an institution will make it possible for boundedly rational agents to efficiently collect and utilize the information necessary for their actions to be consistent with changing internal and external environments.

Five Reasons Why the Proposed Conceptualization Is Amenable to Our Analytical Purposes

A conceptualization of institutions is of course a matter of the theorist's taste and not a matter of right or wrong. However, in my view, there are at least the following five reasons why the shared-beliefs cum equilibrium–summary-representation view of institutions is useful for comparative institutional analysis. The first three points are applied to the institution-as-equilibrium-of-the-game view in general, while the last two, more or less specifically, to the institution-as-equilibrium–summary-representation view that emphasizes the cognitive aspect of institutions.[19]

Endogenous Treatment of Origins of Institutions and Enforcement   The institution-as-an-equilibrium approach in general can deal with the issues of the origins of an institution and its enforcement endogenously. As we have seen, if one subscribes to the exogenous rules-of-the-game view, then one must immediately face the issues of where and how the rules originated, as well as how they are enforced. An institutional origin may need to be found outside the domain of the economy in which the rules are applied: for example, in the polity domain or, theoretically, in the domain of a metagame in which rational agents collectively choose a rule from the set of many possible rules.[20] But how, then, are the rules of the game in the polity domain set? How are all the possible rules known to the players of the metagame, and how do they play the metagame? Where are the rules of the metagame determined? Thus a problem of infinite regression is bound to arise. Perhaps the right way to partially resolve this problem is to regard an institution as originating as a stable endogenous product of the game—in economic, social, or political exchange domains—while leaving the nontechnological rules of the game unspecified as much as possible at the outset.

One caveat is due, however. Although we wish to understand an institution arising in one domain as the "endogenous rules of a game" generated in that domain, we cannot build a model to make every possible institution simultaneously endogenous. In other words, what constitutes the "exogenous rules of the game"—namely the set of agents, the set of their action choices, the way in which each profile of agents' action choices is transformed into consequences—may not be completely described by technology, resource endowments, and the preferences of the agents alone. This is the point first addressed by Field (1979, 1981). To see the same point from a slightly different perspective, imagine hypothetically that the exogenous rules of some game are completely specified by technology. Even if it is possible to do so, however, there will be multiple equilibria in a repeated game situation, and as already pointed out, which equilibrium is chosen from among the many cannot be determined endogenously. We need to consult historical events and rules as well as rules prevailing in surrounding domains.[21] It may be that the particular subsets of actions that agents perceive as the sets of viable options are constrained by historical precedents, while the way in which the consequences of a certain profile of agents' actions are determined in one domain are affected by the institutional environments of the domain (i.e., endogenous rules of the game prevailing in surrounding domains). One can never have an institution-free world from which to start the analysis and completely eliminate appeals to exogenously given, humanly devised rule structures. Thus nobody can escape from the problem of infinite regression. However, we may seek to direct the infinite regression toward structures inherited from the historical past rather than the logical construct of the metagame.

A similar problem of infinite regression can arise with respect to enforcement in the exogenous rules-of-the-game approach. Leaving aside norms and conventions that are self-enforcing ("informal" rules in North's sense), if the rules of the game ("formal" rules) are to be enforced by an augmented player (enforcer), the question of the enforcer's motivation needs to be addressed. Who enforces the enforcer? That is, do we need yet another enforcer to monitor the rules of action prescribed for the original enforcer? As the preceding discussion regarding Hurwicz' contribution suggests, a solution to this problem is again to analyze a game that includes the enforcer as a player, and to see if the prescribed rules of action for the enforcer can become his/her equilibrium strategic choice and thus self-enforcing, given an equilibrium constellation of strategic choices by other agents, and vice versa. In this case, too, the presence of the enforcer as a player of the game at the outset is presumably given by history.

History Matters   Through the occurrence of multiple equilibria in specific models, the institution-as-an-equilibrium approach can shed light on the "humanly devised" (North 1990) nature of institutions rather than its ecologically, technologically, or culturally driven aspects. If there is only one equilibrium corresponding to the technological specification of the structure of the game, then that equilibrium is little more than a representation of the technological condition, and not an institution.[22] For example, often the evolution of community norms in East Asia is attributed to the climatic and ecological conditions there, which presumably make peasant family farming and collective use of the irrigation system more productive. However, Korea and Japan, which are characterized by similar ecological conditions, had subtly divergent institutional evolutionary paths in terms of village social structure and social norms. These sociological factors have had profound and long-lasting impacts on the subsequent institutional trajectories of both economies (chapters 2.2).

Usually, a multiplicity of equilibria is regarded as troublesome by game theorists, and they have spent many research efforts, without decisive success, in the so-called "refinement" of the equilibrium to enable them to identify only one equilibrium out of the many possible Nash equilibria. However, we consider that the multiplicity of equilibria of games should not be regarded as bothersome in comparative institutional analysis. On the one hand, by making institutions susceptible to equilibrium analysis, it can be made clear that institutions are humanly devised but can be neither arbitrarily designed nor discretionary implemented. On the other hand, once an institutional bifurcation occurs, even if two economies are exposed to the same technological and market environments afterwards, the subsequent overall institutional arrangements of the two economies may well differ, depending on their respective interim institutional trajectories. This phenomenon is known as the path dependence (David 1985). Thus equilibrium and historical analyses are mutually complementary and are both indispensable to comparative institutional analysis.

Given the impossibility of identifying every institutional phenomenon as an endogenous outcome at the same time, Greif (1998b) proposes the following an analytical procedure for dealing with historical information in the equilibrium-based approach to institutions: First, using historical and comparative information, sort out what technological and institutional factors can be treated as "exogenous" and what institutional factors are to be treated as "endogenous," that is, must be explained. Then, build a context-specific, game-theoretic model in which those exogenous factors define the exogenous rules of the game and solve for possible equilibria. Next, find out if some of these solutions are useful for understanding the nature of the institutional factors needing to be explained. Finally, examine what "historical" factors can be considered responsible for the selection of that particular equilibrium solution to determine the role of history.

Interlinkages and Interdependency of Institutions   The institution-as-an-equilibrium approach provides an analytically tractable conceptualization of the interdependencies of institutions operating within the economy. When the government drafts a statutory law for the purpose of introducing an "institution," its implementation may have unintended consequences in particular economic, political and social contexts. Take the example of a postcommunist economy where the government drafts a privatization law aimed at emulating markets for corporate control in an advanced economy. An outcome may be the widespread capture of corporate control by insiders, such as ex-industrial bureaucrats, directors of ex–state-owned enterprises, who amassed de facto control rights before the transition to a market economy.[23] This situation is somewhat analogous to the one in which a medicine tested in a laboratory has unpredicted side effects after it is administered to a human being because of the complexity of living organic systems. A major reason for such unintended outcomes is the absence of "fits" between the designed plan and the existing institutional environments that reflects a unique historical trajectory of institutional development. This suggests the possibility that only institutional arrangements that are mutually consistent and/or reinforcing may be viable and sustainable in an economy. Otherwise, an attempted institutional design may be highly unstable. It may not be accidental that co-determination in the corporate governance domain and social democratic corporatism in the polity domain co-evolved in Germany, while the main bank system, the lifetime employment system, and the close alliance between industrial associations and relevant administrative bureaus co-evolved in Japan, both in contrast to the so-called Anglo-American model (chapters 11 and 13).

We will consider institutional interdependencies as institutionalized linkages and institutional complementarities in part II. These intuitively appealing concepts are amenable to rigorous analysis when the equilibrium-oriented notion of institutions is applied. Specifically, we look at games in different domains of the economy, including organizational coordination, commodity trade, transactions of services of human and financial assets, political-transactions, and social-exchange. Then, in applying an analytical technique developed by Topkis (1978) and Milgrom and Roberts (1990), we analyze how an equilibrium constellation of strategic choices of agents in one domain can become strategically complementary to, or conditional on, the equilibrium choices of other agents in the same or other domain. In this way we can come to understand the conditional robustness of an overall institutional arrangement of the economy as well as the multiplicity of such arrangements.[24]

From this systemic point of view, both the usefulness and the limit of agency theory as a tool for comparative institutional analysis may be touched on. Agency theory casts the economic interaction of agents (in the generic sense) in a certain domain of the economy as a principal–agent relationship. Then it inquires into what type of self-enforceable (incentive compatible) arrangement can be established as a second-best response to environmental and incentive constraints when information asymmetry exists between the principal and the agent. However, the solution is usually responsive not only to the technological environment but also to the "institutional environments" hidden in parameters specifying the objective functions of the principal and agent, and the participation constraints describing the outside options of the agent. Thus caution should be taken in utilizing and interpreting the results of principal–agent models. These results may be valid only relative to an implicitly assumed institutional environment of the domain, and may not be exclusively technology-determined, second-best solutions applicable anywhere. A rough analogy may be drawn with the relationship between "partial" equilibrium analysis of individual choice behavior with prices as exogenous parameters, and "general" equilibrium analysis of market price determination in Walrasian economics. Agency theory provides a powerful partial equilibrium analysis of an institution in a particular domain of interaction between the principal and the agent (s), with institutional arrangements in other domains taken as given environments.[25] However, in order to really understand why a particular institution emerges in a domain of one economy but not in a similar domain of another economy, we need to make explicit the mechanism of interdependencies among institutions across domains in each economy.

Institutional Change through the Competition of Symbolic Systems of Beliefs   The equilibrium–summary-representation view of an institution suggests a new way to approach the mechanisms of institutional change. As was mentioned earlier, the information transmitted by an institution is never complete. But for the bounded-rational individual agents the compressed information may be adequate to make mutually viable choices under normal circumstances. They can still be guided by it in developing whatever skills or dispositions are in keeping with the endogenous rules of the game. However, when the pattern of choices becomes problematic because of environmental and internal changes, an "institutional crisis" in the cognitive sense may be triggered: the shared beliefs regarding the ways in which a game is played may begin to be questioned and the agents may be driven to reexamine their own choice rules based on new information not embodied in existing institutions.

A new institution will emerge only when agents' action-choice rules become mutually consistent in a new way and their summary representation induces convergent beliefs among them. But such a transition may not be just a move from one equilibrium to another for a given structure of the game. Rather, it may involve a novelty that cannot be characterized simply by a move from an equilibrium under given sets of action-choice rules of agents to another equilibrium under the same sets of action-choice rules (chapter 9). In the transition process, various choice rules involving new actions may be experimented with and put into competition by agents. How can the convergence of beliefs and the coordination of new choices be simultaneously induced in such a situation? As we will see later (chapter 7), the present state of economics has not been able to show that dual convergence, both in actual choices and beliefs, is possible through a reasonable mechanism of mutual interactions (i.e., actual choices are induced by beliefs and beliefs are formed by observations of actual choices), particularly when any novelty in action choices is involved.

But it can be through the guidance of a particular symbolic system of predictive/normative beliefs among the many competing ones presented in the transition process and recognized as "prominent" or "salient" that agents' new strategic action-choice rules are forced to coordinate (Schelling 1960). As agents' choices equilibrate, a guiding symbolic system becomes consistent with, and reconfirmed by, their experiences. It then serves as their summary representation of equilibrium incorporated into agents' stable beliefs, namely as an institution (as indicated by the line from the dotted box to the dashed box in figure 1.1). The point is that some symbolic system of predictive/normative beliefs precedes the evolution of a new equilibrium and then becomes accepted by all the agents in the relevant domain through their experiences. It could be "unsettled culture or ideologies—explicit, articulated, highly organized meaning systems—[that may] establish new styles or strategies of actions" (Swidler 1986:278), "an entrepreneur's vision that may trigger certain actions that eventually remove the limits of organizational capabilities and environmental constraints" (Fujimoto 1999:10), or even the political program of a subversive political party (e.g., "all factories to the workers! all the lands to poor peasants!"). In chapter 9 we will describe how bounded-rational, individual agents form their own "subjective models of the game" that they play, and discuss the mechanism of institutional change as a process of revision, refinement, and inducement of mutual consistency of such models incorporating a (common) representation system.

The Role of Statutory Laws and Public Policy Discourses   Whether the rules of the game constituting institutions are viewed as endogenous to the domain or whether they are exogenously set in the polity domain may have significant implications for interpreting the role of public policy. If one subscribes to the view that institutions are made of polity-determined rules and matter to the performance of an economy, the implications are that a badly performing economy can reform itself by government designing and implementing better rules, possibly emulating best practices elsewhere. If this is not realized, blame could then be placed on the government. However, there are two problems with this kind of argument. First is that the government itself is an organization of the people who have their own motivations and aspirations. It is an endogenous player of the game in the polity domain and the outcome of any policy-making should be understood as determined by the interactions of the strategic expectations among the players, the government, politicians, and private agents.[26] Blaming this on the incompetence of politicians may not pinpoint the real problem.

Second, as already noted, a policy may not yield the outcome intended by the government or politicians if it does not fit with existing institutions in other domains, an accumulated stock of competent agents, and so on. In this book we will treat statutory laws and regulations as exogenously set parameters for defining game forms (exogenous rules of the game), and examine what the outcomes will be of the strategic interactions of the agents under them.[27] Statutory laws or regulations may induce an institution to evolve, but they themselves are not institutions. Also an institutional outcome may be different from what a legislature or government initially intended. A careful and systematic study is called, including an investigation of how the initial "institutional" conditions, such as the legacies of old institutions and the prevailing informal rules (norms, social ethics, etc.), kinds and level of the existing stock of human competence, and so on, affect subsequent institutional change, how rule-setting in the polity interacts with the evolution of the endogenous rules of the games in other domains, and so on.[28]

A subtle issue is that endogenizing the government does not necessarily mean that the outcome of a game will be fully determined, leaving no scope for policy advise—a paradox referred to as the "determinancy paradox" (Bhagwati, Brecher, and Srinivasan 1984). In an "institutional crisis," individual agents may not have clear expectations about the state of the game, or even if they think they do, their beliefs may not necessarily be mutually consistent. Then there may be latitude for exogenous symbolic systems of predictive/normative beliefs to compete for the position of an attractor or a "focal point" (Schelling 1960) for the formation of coordinated beliefs. The system could well be a program or platform of competing political parties, professional political advice, an "elites' pact" (Weingast 1997), or the drafting and enactment of statutory law. Thus political discourses in and out of polity may have a certain imprint on subsequent institutional evolution.[29] No matter what the competing exogenous symbolic system may be, a crucial factor that will determine its impact is the "fits" with emergent practices in domains other than the polity.

1.3 Organization of the Book

Domains, Game Forms, and Institutions

We have introduced the basic conceptualization of institutions to be developed in this book. We plan to apply this concept and examine its implications for some important contemporary and historical institutional issues from a comparative perspective. In doing so, we will develop a unified framework for analyzing the interdependencies of institutions clustering in various economies. This analytical framework will incorporate contributions and insights from economics, as well as sociology, political science, law, and the cognitive sciences, wherever possible. Before we can develop such a framework, we first need to define the terms and concepts, such as domains and the game form, that will be used in our framework, and to specify some basic types of domains.

We will treat the domain of a game as a unit of analysis. The *domain* of the game is composed of a set of agents—either individuals or organizations—and sets of physically feasible actions open to each agent in successive periods.[30] A combination of actions chosen in one period by all the agents in the domain is termed an *action profile*. An action profile determines the distribution of the payoffs among the agents in the domain. We decompose the payoff functions—a rule assigning a payoff distribution for each action profile—into objective and subjective elements. Namely, given external environments and historically determined states of the domains at the beginning of a period, an action profile in that period first generates a consequence in the state space describing all possible physical states relevant to the welfare of the agents in the domain. The consequence of this period defines an initial state of the succeeding period. The function (rule) that assigns a physical consequence in the state space for each action profile and a historically given initial state is called the *consequence function*. Various environmental factors, such as technology and "institutions" prevailing in other, relevant domains, as well as statutory laws and policy determined in the polity domain, parametrically define the form of the consequence function. A domain and an associated consequence function specify a *game form*, which represents the *exogenous rules of the game*.

Each agent in the domain has a preference ordering over possible consequences for each period in the state space. The composite of the consequence function and the agent's preference function defines the payoff function of that agent in the ordinary sense of game theory. The reason we decompose this into the objective consequence function and the subjective preference function is to specify the notion of the exogenous rules of the game, as distinguished from endogenous rules of the game. Also in games that we will discuss in this book, we do not necessarily assume that the agents have knowledge about subjective preferences of other agents, and thus they may be guided in their action choices only by objective states (physical consequences) they can observe. If all the agents in a domain choose their private plans of action so as to maximize their current payoffs, or the present-value sum of their current and future payoffs, subject to their own expectations regarding others' strategic choices, the situation is characterized as a game and the agents may be interchangeably called the players. An action plan thus chosen by an agent is his/her *strategy*. A strategy may prescribe only one action or a comprehensive plan of actions contingent on the state of the domain (or past history of states).

We deal with six basic types of domains: commons, trade (economic exchange), organization, social exchange, polity domains, and generic organizational fields. We investigate what types of institution/convention can become viable within and across these domains. As mentioned in section 1.2, North excluded organizations from the category of institutions. This is because he is interested in understanding the role of organizations as agents of institutional change in the polity domain. However, this book will place relatively less emphasis on politically determined formal rules, or on the causality from the polity to the economic process. Admittedly the mutual feedback mechanisms between the outcomes of games in the polity domain and those in the economic-transaction domain are important, and we will place substantial emphasis on them and on organizational conventions of business enterprises and other private-order entities (e.g., financial intermediaries) as integral, endogenous elements of the overall institutional arrangements of the economy.

We distinguish the above-mentioned basic types of domains primarily according to the variability of the set of agents, and the nature of the choice sets across the agents. We try to do so only in terms of their technological properties in order to identify institutions that may endogenously evolve in each domain or across domains. However, in principle, it is impossible to start an analytical discourse on institutions in a purely institution-free, technology-only setting. Thus, in the following classification of the domains, some generic institutions, such as ownership, role-based expectations, or power distribution, are inevitably present or implicit, albeit in a primitive form.

Commons Domain   The set of agents in this type of domain is composed of those using common resources accessible by any one of them (and produced jointly by them). It is assumed to be technologically costly to exclude potential beneficiaries from obtaining benefits from the common resources, so the set of agents is assumed to be fixed. They may use common resources simultaneously or sequentially but not necessarily jointly.[31] We do not assume that the agents have a common objective or internalize a common value regulating the use of the common resources, but that they are strategic players interested in maximizing their individual payoffs subject to the expected choices of others. Since the presence of common resources is a defining characteristic of the domain, the action sets of the agents are essentially symmetric in that they all contain actions related to the production, maintenance and/or use of the common resources (e.g., contributing to the accumulation or depletion of the common resources, or using them at various intensity levels). Because of the fixity of the set of agents, individual action choices cause external economies or diseconomies throughout the domain (e.g., congestion in the use of common resources, free-riding in maintenance efforts, or benefiting others by producing common goods), but the agents may not be able to exit from the domain or to be excluded from it. An endogenous institution that may arise in this domain could be (customary) property-rights rules and group norms (chapter 2).

Trade (Economic Exchange) Domains   The domains of games of this type are composed of agents endowed with privately owned economic goods that they can trade at will. Although they are initially endowed with these goods in diverse patterns, their choice sets are qualitatively symmetric in including physically possible offers of various quantities of goods in exchange for specific quantities of other goods or money, acceptance/rejection of others' offers, and honoring/defaulting on agreed-upon terms of trade. One of the important characteristics of trade games is that all agents have an option of not trading. These domains may be more specifically differentiated into the financial transaction domain, labor transaction domain, supply domain, product market domain, and so on. Domains of this type may evolve, by itself or in conjunction with other types of domains, institutions dealing with problems arising from information asymmetries between trading agents that may otherwise lead to the breakdown of trade opportunities (chapter 3).

Organization Domains   In domains of games of this type, agents are able to produce goods (e.g., revenues) by their joint actions and distribute them among themselves. Although these joint actions may involve the use of some common resources (e.g., goodwill, accumulated information, and organizational infrastructure), domains of this type can be distinguished from the commons domain in two respects. First, it is optional for agents to participate in this type of game. In other words, if a game of this type is played repeatedly, agents have an option to exit, or an agent has an option to exclude others from the domain at the end of any period, and thus the set of agents is not fixed. Second, the sets of actions may be substantively differentiated across agents on the basis of the division of operational and cognitive labor (e.g., into managerial, engineering, and operational tasks), but there is a focal (centralized) agent—the management—whose role is to coordinate the choices of the agents in the domain.[32] Trade domains and organizational domains share a common characteristic in that participation is optional for agents. However, while coordination in trade games can be a achieved through a multitude of voluntary agreements between two traders, in organizational games systemic incentives need to be provided to all agents in order to induce their participation and properly coordinate their action choices (chapter 4).[33]

Organizational Field   We also consider a generic type of domain called the organizational field, which embeds individual organization domains. This is the relatively unstructured, primitive domain in which organizations are created by the matching of agents from the population of the domain. Depending on matched types of human assets that agents have invested for information processing, different types of organizational architectures may be generated. Agents may withdraw from this domain by choice, but they are assumed to be symmetric in their action choice sets. That is, they may choose types of human assets and decide whether or not to accept a particular matching, but no hierarchical assignment is specified prior to matching. This domain is conceived of as a theoretical construct, useful for understanding the logic involved in the co-evolution of a convention of organizational architecture and a type of human assets (chapter 5).

Polity (Political Economy) Domain   The set of agents in this domain contains a unique focal (centralized) agent—the government—endowed with a set of action choices asymmetric to those of the other agents who are called private agents. The latter can be citizens, interest groups, business associations and unions, economic classes, and so forth, depending on the context. The government's set of actions may include the unilateral extraction (transfer) of properties from private agents to itself or to other agents (e.g., taxes, subsidies, or fines), the compulsory mobilization of services of private agents (e.g., military and jury services), the organized infliction of physical violence on private agents (e.g., death penalty or arrest), and the monopolized supply of public services such as law enforcement. Private agents cannot escape from government action by choice, and thus the government has exclusive regulatory power. However, private agents may choose to support or not support (resist) the government. If government action invokes strong resistance from private agents, the consequence can be costly to the government (e.g., the loss of power), although resistance may be costly to the private agents as well. When a stable outcome is observed in a polity domain in which the focal agent is identified with a national government, we refer to its salient properties as a nation *state*. In other words, we distinguish the government as a player of the game and the state as a stable outcome of the game (chapter 6).[34]

Social Exchange Domain This domain plays an important complementarity role in understanding institutions, such as community norms, status differentiation, rank hierarchies within homogeneous teams or organizations, and so on.[35] In this domain noneconomic goods/bads (social symbols, languages) that would directly affect the payoffs of recipient agents, such as esteem, approval/disapproval, sympathy, accusation, benign neglect, and so on, are unilaterally delivered and/or traded with "unspecified obligations to reciprocate" (Blau, 1964/1988), and sometimes accompanied by gift-giving.[36] When exchanges are multilateral and diffusive among a fixed set of agents who are mutually identifiable, we call it a community. It can be the rural community, the community of traders, a professional community, and so on. These domains generate various types of social norms in conjunction with other types of domains (chapter 2).

Figure 1.2 provides a diagram of these six types of domains. The vertical dimension refers to the qualitative variation of the action sets across the agents in the domain; the horizontal distinguishes whether the agents have the option to exit, or to be excluded, from a game. The location of the six types should be evident from this characterization.

Since any classification of domain types cannot be made in purely technological terms, the domains presented above cannot be sharply delineated. If we take a particular set of agents who are strategically interacting with each other, classification

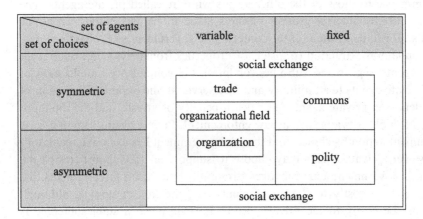

Figure 1.2
Six types of domains of games

may not neatly fall in with one of the types, but have multiple domain characteristics. Take the classification of a firm. A firm's most salient characteristics are organizational in incorporating a division of operational and cognitive labor. However, some contract-theory economists focus on the aspect of the firm as a "nexus of contracts" (Jensen and Meckling 1976): the aspect that can be understood as an institutional arrangement in the trade (economic exchange) domain. Generically, the evolution of a convention regulating the internal coordination of the firm may be captured as an outcome of an evolutionary game in the organizational field. The corporate firm also has a community aspect in which social exchanges take place among its members to form the corporate culture (e.g., "IBM man") and various suborganizational norms (e.g., shop-floor work norm). It has a modicum of the notion of a commons domain as well (e.g., in the use of intangible information assets). Finally, the firm is embedded in some governance structure that resembles an institution in the polity domain (corporate organ, workers cooperatives, kibbutz, partnerships, etc.). We cannot develop a theory of the firm taking into consideration all these characteristics at once from the beginning. In various parts of the book, we will focus on one aspect or another. However, our ultimate objective is to understand the logical structure in which the various facets of a business firm fit each other in alternative ways, depending on historical and environmental contexts.

Now let us reiterate the intuitive concept of institutions based on the shared-belief cum equilibrium–summary-representation perspective, subject to its formal and substantive refinement later in the book. Suppose that agents choose their action-choice plans strategically in a domain or across domains and that a stable outcome evolves in that domain or across those domains and is sustained over time. Then, provided that there is another equilibrium (or more generally, another sequence of equilibria), we identify an *institution* as follows:

An institution is a self-sustaining system of shared beliefs about how the game is played. Its substance is a compressed representation of the salient, invariant features of an equilibrium path, perceived by almost all the agents in the domain as relevant to their own strategic choices. As such it governs the strategic interactions of the agents in a self-enforcing manner and in turn is reproduced by their actual choices in a continually changing environment.

Five elements are present in this conceptualization: *endogenicity* (as implied by "self-sustaining," "self-enforcing," and "reproduced"), *information compression* (as implied by "a compressed representation"), *robustness* with respect to continual environmental change and minor deviance (as implied by "invariant features of an equilibrium path," "perceived by almost all the agents" and "reproduced ... in a continually changing environment"), *universality* of relevance (as implied by "shared beliefs", "govern the strategic interactions of the agents" and "perceived by all the agents"), and *multiplicity*. Depending on whether or not a domain is symmetric with respect to the action sets of agents, an institution can summarily represent distinct action-choice rules for different types, or identical rules for all the agents in the domain. In the polity domain, where the action sets are asymmetric across the agents, summary representations are comprised of expectations of distinct state-contingent action choices by the government and citizens/interest groups (recall the example of the merchant guild). By the same token, in the organizational domain, they can be comprised of distinct roles expected for agents occupying different positions (e.g., manager, foremen, workers) in the organization. On the other hand, in the commons and trade domains where the action sets are symmetric across the agents, they take the form of norms and self-enforcing contracts supported by certain shared beliefs about ways in which the game is repeatedly played.

The economy can be considered as constituted of myriad domains: commons, economic and social exchange, organization, and polity, some of which overlap, some of which are nested in others, and so on. For the same exogenous rules of the game (e.g., technology), multiple institutions are possible in each of these domains. Not only that, but institutions can evolve across different domains, linked by the coordinated strategic choices of agents. We refer to a synchronous set of institutions across constituent domains in the economy as an *overall institutional arrangement*. Needless to say, their structures can be very complex but not necessarily randomly figured. One purpose of this book is to discover the generic laws of regularities that prevail across different overall institutional arrangements.

The Plan of the Book

This book is composed of three parts. Part I takes up successively the six types of domains in primitive form and identifies the prototype institutions as stable multiple equilibria of games in each domain. This provides a foundation for the generic, game-theoretic framework constructed in part II for conceptualizing institutions, analyzing their interdependencies across domains and over time, and thereby understanding the mechanism of institutional change. Of course, we need to check if this framework is useful in order to understand the complexity and diversity of the institutional arrangements of the contemporary economies and their changes. This is done in part III.

Part I begins with chapter 2, which deals with the commons domain and the social exchange domain that embeds it. It derives the customary property-rights rules and a community norm as endogenous outcomes of the strategic interactions of the agents in those domains. Chapter 3 is concerned with trade (economic exchange) domains and derives various autonomous institutions that may govern and enhance trade and markets without the intervention of the government based on the rule of law. Chapter 4 focuses on the organization domain. It identifies the various organizational and quasi-organizational architectures of practical relevance, discusses their relative information efficiency, and examines their governance issues. Chapter 5 deals with organizational fields in which different organizational architectures can co-evolve as a convention with associated types of human assets (information-processing competence) and discuss ways in which gains from organizational diversity are exploited. Chapter 6, the end of part I, turns to the polity domain and identifies various types of states as stable equilibria of the political exchange game with the government as a player. Institutions identified and discussed in part I are referred to as *proto-institutions* because they are introduced one by one, in an inevitably primitive form and without an explicit analysis of the interdependencies among them. This part largely relies on the work of many authors, including myself, and provides an overview of the current state of analytical approaches. It is by no means intended to be a comprehensive survey, however.

Building on the foregoing preparatory, taxonomic analysis, part II is devoted to the construction of a generic analytical framework for institutional analysis. Illustrative examples and cases help provide the basic motive behind this unified framework within which the systemic nature of overall institutional arrangements of the economy, as well as their changes, can be analyzed. Chapter 7 takes a precise game-theoretic conceptualization of institutions as a self-sustaining system of shared beliefs cum summary representation of equilibria, and discusses the various roles of institutions. Chapter 8 provides systematic logic as to how the linkage of games across different domains can give rise to new forms of institutions, as well as the multiplicity of (suboptimal) institutional arrangements. The models of repeated games or evolutionary games applied in part I facilitate a rigorous analysis of individual institutions. However, because of the intended logical rigor, these models are also limited in their ability to capture the essential aspect of novelty, or innovation, in institutional change. Chapter 9 drops the assumption of objective fixation of the agents' action sets and introduces the concept of individual subjective game models through which agents subjectively view the structure of the games they play. By discussing how the agents cognitively revise their own subjective game models in response to external shocks or internal crises in a correlated manner, it attempts to describe a possible mechanism of institutional change. Chapter 10 turns to the objective mechanism of institutional change and discusses the diachronic interdependencies of institutions, leading to the path dependency of institutional change.

With a conceptual framework in place for analyzing the interrelationships among institutions across domains and over time, part III engages in comparative analyses of the practically relevant, and thus more complex, institutional arrangements of contemporary economies. Chapter 11 identifies several types of corporate governance institutions corresponding to different types of organizational architecture and examines their possible complementarities with institutions in other domains. Chapter 12 provides a new definition of relational financing and argues that despite the increasing globalization of financial markets, some types of relational financing based on the use of uncodified information may remain economically valuable. Chapter 13 deals with a case study to which the analytical and conceptual framework dealing with synchronic and diachronic institutional issues is systematically applied. It describes the mechanism of institutional emergence, coherence, and crisis with respect to a quintessential example of relational financing: the Japanese main bank system. Chapter 14 examines the Silicon Valley model and discusses under what conditions and in what sense this model can be an institutional innovation in the governance of technological product-system innovation. Chapter 15 concludes the book. It takes the analytical results developed along the way, and first identifies several important models of overall institutional arrangements and then present conjectures regarding why global, overall institutional arrangements will remain diverse despite increasing global integration of markets and the development of communications and information technology.

I PROTO-INSTITUTIONS: INTRODUCING BASIC TYPES

An economy is a complex arrangement of institutions. This arrangement is not only complex, it differs from one economy to the next. Although our primary interest in this book is to understand the reasons for, and possible benefits from, diverse institutional arrangements across economies and over time, it would not be wise for us to begin our inquiry by immediately confronting complex institutional arrangements in their entirety. We could easily get lost in the maze. In part I, therefore, we deal with what are considered generic forms of elementary institutions—*proto-institutions*. These are constructed in simple, thought-experiment settings in the expectation that they may reflect some rudimentary aspects of basic institutions (endogenous rules), such as ownership rules, social norms, self-enforcing contracts, third-party contract enforcement, conventions of organizational architecture and their governance, and states. Until the recent rise of interest in institutions among economists, these entities were taken as given in economic analysis in that they were supposed to be predetermined in extra-economic domains: legal, ecological, sociological, technological, or political. However, the development of game theory and other analytical tools has allowed economists to deal with questions about these entities such as: Why do they emerge in the economy and how are they sustained? What roles do they play? Why do they take diverse forms across economies with different performance characteristics?

The following chapters in part I illustrate such inquiries in an introductory manner. A number of parables will be narrated to illustrate the workings and self-enforceability of various proto-institutions in domains introduced in the introductory chapter. Also, when it is appropriate or helpful to understanding, we provide analytical taxonomy for basic types of proto-institutions in each domain and provide historical or contemporaneous illustrations for them. The narrative will generally evolve from institutions that are more primitive and limited in scope to those that are more elaborate and wide ranging, somewhat suggestive of their historical development. However, this does not necessarily mean that one institution is completely replaced by a later one in a historical process. Rather, the sequence of the narrative may also be regarded as reflecting aspects of overall institutional arrangements within contemporary economies: from more spontaneous and latent (e.g., customary property rights, norms, conventions) to more elaborate devices (contracts, organizational architecture, and states). Indeed, an overall institutional arrangement can be viewed as a complex, yet coherent, linkage of proto-institutions, whose structure will be the subject of study in the next part.

2 Customary Property Rights and Community Norms

Two men, who pull the oars of a boat, do it by an agreement or convention, tho' they have never given promises to each other. Nor is the rule concerning the stability of possession the less deriv'd from human conventions, that it arises gradually, and acquires force by a slow progression, and by our repeated experience of the inconveniences of transgressing it. On the contrary, this experience assures us still more, that the sense of interest has become common to all our fellows, and gives us a confidence of the future regularity of their conduct.
—David Hume, *Treatise of Human Nature* (1739 [1992]:490)

This chapter narrates two parables of quintessential proto-institutions: a customary property-rights rule and a community norm. As indicated in the introductory chapter, there cannot be any institution-free economic domain characterized by technological and ecological factors alone, but we try to construct these two parables in situations as primitive as possible in terms of social constructs. The purpose is not to suggest that these proto-institutions can emerge and govern the strategic interactions of the agents only in primitive situations, preceding the development of market economies. Rather, it is to clarify the basic logic involved in understanding why property rights and/or norms can serve as a fundamental social construct to regulate external diseconomies in a commons domain. In the parables, customary property rights are able to self-organize in the absence of a priori statutory law defining and enforcing legal rules of ownership; a norm does likewise without recourse to an exogenous cultural fixation albeit under specific social and political conditions. Though the parables may appear to be primitive or specific, the implications may be generic and profound: Effective property-rights laws can be derivatives of practices and conventions, and not vice versa, while norms can become social regulators in places where private ownership arrangements and markets fail even in a modern context. Besides, the first parable simulates the basic logic of evolutionary games, and the second introduces that of the equilibrium of a linked game and the related sociological concept of "embeddedness." These analytical and conceptual tools are taken up in varying contexts and with broadening scopes in subsequent chapters.

2.1 Customary Property Rights as a Self-organizing System

A Primitive Parable

One well-known view of the genesis of private property rights was given by Demsetz (1967). He argued that a primary function of private property rights is that of guiding the incentives of economic agents to achieve "a greater internalization of externalities." If a scarce resource is placed in the public domain, people will have an incentive to competitively exploit it to obtain private benefits, and may soon deplete its availability to a socially undesirable level. The establishment of a rule of private ownership of the resource, and the exclusion of non-owners from using (consuming) it, will facilitate rational calculation by the owner of the benefits and costs of using the resource. Further, if this ownership is transferrable to another agent who bids the highest price, then social wealth will be maximized. The ownership structure will eventually be rearranged in such a way that each resource is placed in the hands of the people who can derive the highest value from it. Thus the initial distribution of ownership structure does not matter from the viewpoint of efficiency. For the purpose of his theory, Demsetz was able to allow the determination of initial distribution to be "randomly determined" (1967:356). Preceding Demsetz, Coase (1960) had also argued that as far as the initial definition of property rights is legally determined, whatever it may be, social costs due to external diseconomies can be internalized through the bilateral negotiation of parties involved. The definition of property rights matters only from the distributional viewpoint, and not from the efficiency viewpoint.

It is true that once an initial distribution of private ownership rights is exogenously given, as in the case of the Arrow-Debreu model of general equilibrium, or that of Coase's model of social costs, mutually beneficial trading of rights voluntarily evolve from there. However, implicit in any institution of property rights is a stable resolution of conflicts of interest among individuals (families) in their command over scarce goods and resources. How can a stable arrangement of property rights emerges first of all among agents who are self-interested but whose rationality and information may be limited? Even where the rules of private ownership of goods are legally specified and the state is considered as an ultimate source of their enforcement, the government (the court) does not, and cannot, directly monitor every transfer of ownership to see if it is consistent with the rules. Yet in a stable society, property rights are largely honored by the people and disputes are often resolved without the direct recourse to the court. On the other hand, in other economies, property rights rules codified by the government are intentionally ignored and violated, even by the government officials themselves. This suggests that despite the conflict of interests there may exist some self-enforcing element underlying in sustained arrangements of property rights across individuals, which needs to be understood without initially invoking exogenous third-party definition and enforcement.

To show it is possible for self-interested, bounded-rational agents to self-organize a mutually beneficial proto-institution of property rights, let us look at a parable inspired by an ingenious bargaining model of Young (1992, 1998:ch. 8). Suppose that there is a field in which 100 rabbits can be caught in every season without depleting their capacity to reproduce. Two individuals inhabit this commons domain and both of them are interested in catching as many rabbits as possible for themselves. Imagine that individual A wishes to catch x in this season, while individual B wishes to catch y. Rabbits are indivisible, so x and y have to be integers. If $x + y \leq 100$, each person will catch rabbits in the desired quantities and those left, if any, will flee. If $x + y > 100$, neither person will derive positive satisfaction (all the rabbits will flee if too many are pursued at one time, catching too many will disrupt the ecological balance, or the two individuals engage in a unpleasant dispute over each other's aggressive behavior, etc.). Individuals A and B have utility functions $u(x : y)$ and $v(y : x)$ respectively, each of which is monotone increasing and concave in the first variable representing own catch, x or y, over the domain satisfying $x + y \leq 100$ with the normalization $u(0 : y) = v(0 : x) = 0$. To see better the externality effect, let us assume that the damages deprive both individuals of all the utility gains from any catch so that $u(x : y) = v(y : x) = 0$ whenever $x + y > 100$ and that the second parameters representing other's catch do not otherwise affect the utility levels.[1] The curvature of the utility functions (as measured by $-u''/u'$ and $-v''/v'$) represents the individual's attitude toward the risk of conflict. But this information is private; that is, neither individual knows the shape of the other's utility function.

Suppose that both individuals die after one season and their children, who have the same utility functions as their parents, play the same game in the next season. The games are repeated for many generations. Since neither individual in the current generation knows the utility function of his opponent, the strategies are devised based only on information available to the players from the past. In deciding on what amount to catch this year, each individual first collects information regarding what sizes of catch were made in the past by the ancestors of his opponent, whom he supposes to be of the same type as the contemporary opponent. However, each player does not precisely inherit his ancestors' information and collects the records of the (attempted) catches of his opponent's ancestors with imperfection. He is able to randomly collect information from $k(i)$ years out of the past m years. The ratio $I(i) = k(i)/m$ represents the amount of information collected by individual i ($i = A, B$). The capacity for information collection measured by this ratio is passed down from each generation to the next through time.

Using this information, each individual conjectures that a probability distribution of the catch his opponent is likely to attempt this year equals the frequency distribution of the catches in $k(i)$ samples. Against this estimate, each individual calculates the amount of catch that he should make this season to maximize the expected value of his own utility function (if there is more than one solution, then each solution may be chosen with equal probability). That is to say, individual A solves the following problem:

$$\max_{x} \sum_{0 \leq y \leq 100} \frac{n(y : A)}{k(A)} u(x : y),$$

where $n(y : A)$ is the count of (attempted) catch y in A's $k(A)$ record. The symmetric problem can be defined for individual B. After this calculation is completed, both individuals set out to the field and pursue the rabbits as planned (and they may engage in a dispute if their plans are not compatible).

Since the recollections of preceding events by the players are random, the sequence of pairs of (attempted) catches, $\{x_t, y_t\}_{t=1,2,3...}$ constitutes a stochastic process. Young showed that this stochastic process almost surely converges to a *convention* (evolutionary equilibrium) or *norm* from any initial state if the information-gathering capabilities of the players are imperfect and less than half.[2] A convention in this parable is a state in which a certain fixed division $(x^*, 100 - x^*)$ repeats itself for m years in succession. Since samples for the estimates of the probability of an opponent's catch are randomly drawn from the record of the previous m years, once a convention is established, it perpetuates if there are not any random shocks or mistakes by the agents. It becomes self-enforcing in that it becomes the best-response strategy for both agents to follow it, once it is established.

If they follow a convention, both players will not need to recalculate each year, in the absence of knowledge regarding the opponent's preferences, the size of catch they will make. They can attain collective efficiency by avoiding a costly conflict and the imposition of external diseconomies on each other. However, both parties could make mistakes in reading past records or experiment with how the other party and/or the nature responds to their catching smaller or larger amounts than is the convention. Suppose that mistakes or experiments by both individuals can occur with a small probability in each season and that, when they occur, the outcomes are afterward randomly sampled by succeeding generations for the formation of new probability estimates. The process will not then be stationary at a convention. It may still gravitate toward a former convention if mistakes occur only rarely. Occasionally, however, accumulated mistakes or experiments may push the process away from the convention. Therefore, over a long time, the process may be characterized by a succession of different conventions punctuated by occasional episodes of instability. In the very long run, there could emerge a convention that is infinitely more frequently observed than all others: the convention that is relatively most difficult to upset by mistakes or experiments once it is established. This particular convention is referred to as "generically stable" by Young. He showed that the generically stable convention is characterized by the unique division $(x^*, 100 - x^*)$ that maximizes a generalized Nash product function:

$$[u(x : y)]^{I(A)} \times [v(y : x)]^{I(B)}.$$

Then a larger share of catches goes to the player who is less risk-averse and has a higher level of information-gathering capacity measured by $I(.)$.[3]

Once a (generically stable) convention or a norm prevails, each player may come to regard a certain size of catch implied by the convention as his taken-for-granted right, while he may be compelled to regard the catch of the remaining number of rabbits by the other as her taken-for-granted right. The establishment of a convention in the parable may thus be identified with the emergence of a stable customary property-rights rule. The parable is simple, and readers may be skeptical about the generality of the modeling and its application: such as why players act only reactively to other's choices, why players give an equal weight to samples having lead to zero utility consequences in the past, why the agents do not experiment altruistically for own future generations, why repeatedly interacting generations of agents cannot guess more or less correctly the other party's risk preference and accordingly act more rationally,[4] or alternatively how can the bounded-rational agents perfectly foresees the consequence of collective over-hunting. Yet the outcome is suggestive. The customary property-rights rule is a self-organizing order that emerges out of interactions between self-interested, incompletely informed individual agents. Once established, it is *self-enforcing* in the Nash equilibrium sense: a state from which neither player will have any incentives to unilaterally deviate. Although the outcome is Nash, the players are not aware that Nash equilibrium will be played. They intend to behave rationally, but they cannot eliminate inferior strategies by a priori deductive reasoning to find a Nash equilibrium, as they do not have prior knowledge of the other's risk preference and information-processing capacity. They are neither aided by a neutral third party (like the Walrasian auctioneer) who mediates information regarding player's marginal preferences in the form of prices, nor a benevolent and omnipotent government who can calculate and enforce an efficient Nash equilibrium externally. Despite all these odds against them, they can spontaneously find a self-enforcing rule to their own advantage.

The Generic Roles of the Proto-Institution

From the parable built on the idea of Young, we have seen that a self-enforcing arrangement of customary property-rights can emerge in a situation where bounded-rational individuals compete for scarce resources. As already noted, the parable is by no means meant to be descriptive of any historical process of the formation of property rights. Property rights are considered to be one of the oldest institutions, to have come into existence in human society. But we have very little information about how this institution emerged, except for the conjecture that it was probably tools made and used by the same individuals that first came to be "owned," excluding their use by others. There must be many historical variations, however, in how various rights over resources (rights to catch, rights to cultivate, rights to dispose of or destroy, etc.) evolved and became arranged.[5] Surely, while the parable above is immensely distant from any historical experience, it can literally serve as a "parable." It suggests that the institution of customary property-rights rule, in the sense of stable expectation that as far as I observe other's rights the other will also honor my rights, emerged not as a result of rational, purposeful design by any individual or organization of individuals. It spontaneously evolved because the people learn from experience that following such a constraint can actually serve the ends that each pursues. If people fail to learn, an effective rule will not emerge, and the consequence is degradation and exhaustion of common resources, which could be interpreted as another possible equilibrium. The agents would then need to emigrate from the domain in search of new resources to be exploited, or else their collective survival would be threatened.

The parable clarifies, by its very simplicity, several roles of the proto-institution.

First, the proto-institution of customary property *reduces uncertainty* for the individual agents regarding the behavior of the others by coordinating their beliefs. This is useful for the agents, who have only limited information of others regarding their preferences (utility functions), knowledge, ability, and so forth. As the customary property-rights becomes established, players do not need to trouble themselves each year to find out the other's intentions and construct a subjective view of the choice environment from scratch.

Second, as the number of catch becomes habitual, the customary property rights become a part of the "backgrounds" (Searle 1998) for the agents to develop further related skills in ways consistent with their dispositions, preferences, and desires. They do not need to allocate their limited intellectual capacity for calculating how many catches to make every year to maximize their utility. Instead, they can use this scarce personal resource to develop skills and behavioral patterns, such as to hunt rabbits, cook rabbits, sew their skins into clothes, spare some meat for relatives as gifts. Thus, behaving consistently with the customary rights can greatly expand the range of ends agents can satisfactorily pursue.

Third, it serves to *coordinate the collective response* of the agents toward their environment without the explicit formulation of a collective goal. Specifically in this parable, it aids the self-interested players to avoid imposing on each other the external costs of overhunting (i.e., $x + y = 100$ at a convention). This is precisely the point emphasized by Demsetz (1967). Although the agents in our parable are not consciously acting according to the common objective of avoiding overhunting and/or maximizing the utility product, the establishment of a convention helps them internalize external diseconomies and maximize the utility product. However, it is important to note that this efficiency property holds because of the model's simplicity. In more complex institutions failure to coordinate agents' choices in an efficient manner can well arise. For example, as we will see later in chapter 5, in the organizational fields there can evolve multiple conventions and some conventions respond to certain technological environments with more efficient results than others though these conventions may not do better than others in some other technological environments. In any case, the point is that under a proto-institution bounded-rational, self-interested agents are unconsciously guided to produce a certain collective outcome that has corresponding impacts, efficient or inefficient, on their environment.

Finally, property rights *impute values* to the attributes of the individual agents. In the parable more rights are endowed to the agent who is less risk averse (i.e., more bold) and has a greater information-processing capacity. Although we treated these factors as exogenous parameters in the model, they can well be endogenous: the risk aversion of the individuals may be lessened as they accumulate wealth, and their information-processing capacity may also be improved by investment in learning as well as greater command over the resources needed for processing information. Therefore an institution could define an agent's incentives.[6] In the parable above the agents could become motivated to accumulate wealth and learning in order to obtain more command over resources. However, if the agents mutually collect too much information and react to it in a sensitive way but without being able to construct the precise knowledge regarding the other's utility functions, their behavior will become destabilized. Then self-organization of customary rights can become problematical.[7]

Two Kinds of Orders and Laws

Once a (generically stable) convention evolves, agents are disposed to behave in a certain manner but not otherwise. In other words, the agents will follow an implicit "rule of conduct," by which they jointly self-organize an order. This order may be considered as corresponding to what Menger (1883) called "spontaneous order" or what Hayek (1973) called "*cosmos*" in Greek, meaning "a right order in a state or a community." But such an order can still be subject to disturbances coming from the players' mistakes, the absence of clarity of the rule itself, intended deviation from the implicit rule, and so forth, causing various disequilibrium costs. To control such disequilibrium costs, the agents may find it (mutually) advantageous to make the implicit rules articulated, clarified, and enforced. For example, both agents in the parable above may agree on dividing the rabbit-hunting field into two parcels proportional to the respective sizes of catch implied by a customary rights, making it an explicit "rule" for each to hunt rabbits exclusively on the parcel allotted to him or her. Both individuals may agree to erect a fence that separates the two parcels. If one individual is negligent in maintaining the fence for which he/she is responsible and rabbits flee to his/her lot from the adjacent lot, the other individual may justly claim compensation. The players could settle this problem by a norm implying the division of the field.[8] If the dispute cannot be settled among the players themselves, they might ask for help from a third party. This third party does not need to be yet a court with enforcement power. It can be a mediator who refuses to take sides and encourages the parties to reach a mutual settlement. If this does not work, the third party could take the more active role of arbitrator who pronounces a resolution to the conflict, sometimes even designating one side as right and the other as wrong. But the role of the third party in this case may still be to restore the customary rights rather than to create and enforce a new order. While the third party lacks the power to enforce a judgment the pressures of neighbors and popular opinion could, bring compliance.[9] Law that is derived from the customary rights is referred to as *nomos*, or lawyer's law (common law), by Hayek.[10]

In contrast to a spontaneous order that self-organizes through the interactions of individuals, Hayek calls an intentionally designed order "an organization," or *taxis* in Greek, meaning a "made order." The government is one instance of *taxis*, and rules set by the government are referred to as a *thesis* or legislator's law (statutory law).[11] Two types of orders, spontaneous order and made order, as well as two corresponding types of rules, lawyers' and legislators' laws, may not necessarily be mutually exclusive, however (Hayek 1973:45). Even if some rules evolve spontaneously and are observed as custom by the people over time, the agents could learn to improve these rules as well as wish to represent them in clear and consistent way. A spontaneous order of customary property-rights rule may gradually be replaced by articulated legal codes enforced by the government (the courts), if not entirely. Designed ownership rules can become diverse and elaborated, including the assignment of ownership to made orders such as legal persons (corporations) and governments (state ownership). However, it is not the case that the legislature can create by the stroke of a pen whatever order they wish to have. The legislator's law must be able to create stable expectations among the agents in order for their intentions to be realized as an enforceable legal order. If a law is designed in a discretionary manner and an inconsistency is created in the expectations of agents, that law might be ignored at the least, or worse, give rise to adverse incentives among agents contrary to the original intention of the legislature. Basu put it as "[i]f a certain outcome is not an equilibrium of the economy, then it cannot be implemented through any law." (1997b:22)

2.2   Community Norms as a Self-enforcing Solution to the Commons Problem

In the parable of the previous section, if rabbits randomly traverse the field or require a large territory to reproduce, agents may find it difficult to draw a fixed line dividing the field into "privately owned" parcels. The bounded-rational agents may agree on keeping the field as undivided open commons and regulating the number of catches by customary rules implied by the convention.[12] But how can the customary rights be self-enforceable in the open commons? We observe that in some places in the world, and at some points of time in history, community control has evolved to regulate external economies arising in certain commons domains, like fishery grounds, grazing fields, irrigation systems, and forests. Rules of community control may be explicitly codified with a formal organization of enforcement, or they may be enforced by norms implicitly understood by members of the community with application on an ad hoc basis.[13] In this section we deal with community norms that autonomously arise in the community that is subject to a severe free-riding problem in the maintenance and use of commons.

From the perspective of comparative institutional analysis, there are many important issues to be discussed regarding community norms. In this section we focus on the basic nature of community norms: How do we conceptualize the community norm that regulates the community members' action choices toward the commons from whose use any member cannot be easily excluded technologically? Could these norms be treated as exogenous constraints on community members given by history, culture, or ecology, and thus robust to change in economic conditions, or should they be understood as endogenous, self-enforcing social constructs and thus to be reproduced through the strategic interactions of the agents?

The concept of (community) norms has been somewhat elusive to economists. Norms are often regarded as culturally determined or ecologically determined. We will construct a context-specific game-theoretic model in which the notion of a community norm is endogenously derived, and then we will examine conditions for its self-enforceability. We identify a community norm as a stable outcome of a game linking a commons (irrigation) domain and a community social exchange domain. To motivate the construction of a game-theoretic parable, we begin taking a short detour into the practices of a typical village in the eastern part of Japan during the Tokugawa period (seventeenth to midnineteenth centuries). Although this example is used because of its relatively clear implications, we argue that the structure of the derived game-theoretic parable has a close analogue to what the sociologist Granovetter (1985) conceptualized as "social embeddedness" and may have generic relevance for considering the role of informal rules in regulating the production and use of collective goods even in contemporary economies. In the appendix we will discuss the interactive roles of ecological (technological) condition and historical factors as determinant of community norm in the context of comparison between Tokugawa Japan and Yi Korea in seventeenth to nineteenth centuries.

A Historical Parable: The Irrigation System in the Village of Tokugawa Japan

The period from 1603 to 1867 is known as the Tokugawa period in Japan. It was characterized by remarkable domestic peace under the political hegemony of the Tokugawa *shogunate* (*Bakufu*) government in Edo (present-day Tokyo). The economic control power of the *shogunate* was limited, however. It controlled only its own territories for tax purposes, besides monopolizing the rights of minting coins and foreign trade with Western merchants through the port of Nagasaki. In parallel with the *Bakufu* government, two hundred eighty *daimyos* (lords) established their own *Han* governments, enjoying the exclusive rights of taxation in their territories and practicing proto-industrial policies promoting indigenous craft industries, often financed by bond issues to merchant houses and rice-trading houses in Osaka, the economic center. One important political-economy feature underlying this *Baku-Han* system, which has significant implications for the following discussion, is that all members of the *samurai* class were required to reside in Edo or in the castle towns of *Han* governments, so that a complete separation of political-military power from the agrarian community was realized.[14,15] The Tokugawa period is conventionally divided into two subperiods by economic historians: the first half extending from 1603 to the mideighteenth century and the second half over the remainder. The first period was characterized by the development of economic autonomy of the rural community, accompanied by growth of the population and farming lands, while the second was characterized by substantial permeation of market relationships into the rural community and the emergence of proto-industrialization there.

It is estimated, according to an authoritative economic demographic study, that between the years 1600 and 1721, the population grew from 8 or 10 million to 26 million, implying a 1.0 annual percentage growth.[16] This period is characterized as the period of great land reclamation for it realized a 40 percent increase in taxable farming lands. An expansion of such magnitude was largely achieved by the conversion of alluvial plains into rice paddy fields in the relatively underdeveloped eastern regions. Despite the remarkable expansion of arable farmlands, the rice production did not match the growth of the population, and the feasibility of productive reclamation became increasingly difficult as time passed. Therefore, around the end of the first subperiod, greater effort began to be directed toward improvements in irrigation, an increase in the use of commercial fertilizers (e.g., dried fish), and more intensive use of human labor.

With the development of the irrigation system, the dominant form of agricultural production shifted from dry field farming to wet farming. The production of rice requires timely planting of seedlings from beds to rice paddy fields, accompanied by an ample supply of water. Whereas in the western region of Japan irrigation drawn from reservoirs had been developed in earlier periods, rice farming in the eastern region was more dependent on new irrigation systems, often along (diverted) river flows, based on civil engineering techniques developed during the preceding Warrior period. However, because of the rapid water currents, control of the water supply required continual fine-tuning along the irrigation networks (often even across villages), depending on the conditions of weather and water supply, the growth stage of crops, and so forth. Further, the village cultivating system in the eastern region in the early period was characterized as the "scattered strip system" in which rice paddy fields possessed by individual peasant families for their own cultivation were scattered all over the village land and intermeshed. This system presumably evolved partly because of the incremental increase in farmland through the collective efforts of reclamation over many years. Another reason might have been the egalitarian distribution of advantageous access to the water supply and diversification of the natural risk associated with the location of paddy fields.

It is not yet a settled issue (among irrigation historians) when the arrangement of separate supplies of water to the scattered plots (paddy fields) of each family became a prevailing practice. Some irrigation specialists argue (convincingly to me) that it evolved at the latest in the second half of Tokugawa period (e.g., Nagata 1971:34–39). Other take the position that by the time of farmland re-zoning in Meiji, there was not necessarily a separate water intake point belonging to each paddy field, and irrigation at the time of seedling planting took the form of "across-paddy fields irrigation" (*tagoshi kansui*) over multiple family farms (Tamaki and Hatade 1974:234–35, Tamaki et al. 1984:20). This was a gravity irrigation system in which water drawn from a canal is successively supplied from one paddy field to the next by way of a natural slope. In any case, the development of individual farms constituted as integrated, closed sets of paddy fields was incomplete in the Edo period. Regardless of whether across-paddy fields irrigation was practiced beyond or limited to individual farmers, there must have been substantial needs for collective coordination and cooperative work among peasant families in the village community.

For example, the maintenance and productive use of the irrigation system required the hard work of removing dirt and weeds regularly from the water channel, cleaning drainage, keeping equipment in shape, preventing destruction of the system during floods, and actively participating in sometimes violent "water-disputes" (*mizuarasoi*) with neighboring villages located either upstream or downstream of the water supply system in times of scarcity, and so forth. Aggressive and egocentric claims over water rights needed to be restrained. Coordination in the timing of seedling planting, as well as drainage for preventing the excessive growth of stems in summer, needed to be made collectively. In the typhoon season just before harvest, flood control required the collective effort of village members on an ad hoc basis. An American authority on Japanese economic history, Thomas Smith, described the impact of this irrigation system on village life as follows: "A rice farmer never owned or controlled all of the essential means of production himself, and he could not individually make all of the critical decisions of farming. He might wish, for instance, to turn an unirrigated field into a paddy, but he would not be allowed to do so if this would impair the water supply of others." (Smith 1959:209)

How was the compliance of villagers in the collective control of construction, maintenance, and use of the irrigation system enforced? One consequence of the separation of military-political power from the rural community was the absence of an external enforcement mechanism. Once large-scale civil works encompassing multiple villages were completed under the initiative of *Baku-Han* governments, the construction, maintenance, and use of the local irrigation system was entrusted to the autonomous control of the village community. But a hidden implication of the technological-ecological characteristics of the irrigation system as described was that there was the potential hazard of free-riding among villagers in the collective work, as well as aggressive egocentric behavior exerting severe external diseconomies on others. However, once the peasant's farmland became integrated to the water supply system after construction, even if some family had shirked collective maintenance tasks or harmed others, it could have been difficult to technologically exclude it from using the water. However, despite technological nonexcludability, there was the credible threat of ostracizing the opportunistic family from participating in other spheres of the social, political, and economic life of the village: the practice known as *mura hachibu*, literally meaning 80 percent separation from the village. Other village families could refuse to cooperate with a shirker by denying him mutual aid when necessary (e.g., roofing thatching, helping with the sick) and excluding him from participation in social events such as ritualistic village parties and seasonal festivals—with the exception of fire extinguishing or funeral services. This threat was effective in eliciting a high degree of cooperative effort in constructing, maintaining and using the irrigation system without the intervention of an external enforcement mechanism.

A Community Norm as an Equilibrium of Linked Games

In the game-theoretic framework the situation we have described can be seen as a typical case in which linking two games and pooling incentive constraints helps lessen incentive constraints. Imagine that the village is composed of a number, say N, of homogeneous families playing a commons game called the irrigation game, and a community social exchange game simultaneously in each period over infinite periods of time (the continuity of the family (ie) may be a reasonable assumption when primogeniture is practiced, supplemented by the adoption of an heir by a family with no male child). In the domain of the irrigation game, families have an option to chose from the same strategy set {Cooperate, Shirk cooperation} in the collective tasks of construction, maintenance, and use of the irrigation system. Suppose that the effort cost to each family of cooperation per period in this game is C_i, and the benefit to each individual family from using the irrigation system per period is B_i when everybody cooperates, and $B_i - md_i$ when m families shirk. We assume that

$$C_i > d_i \quad \text{and} \quad C_i < Nd_i.$$

The first inequality implies that there is incentive for each individual to shirk, while the second shows that such shirking will impose external diseconomies on the community, resulting in net welfare loss. However, we assume that because of the technological nonexcludability of any family from use of the irrigation system, it is difficult to punish a shirker by excluding it from the future use of the irrigation system at a reasonable cost.

In the social exchange game each family can contribute to the production of social goods with some costs C_s, and enjoy the benefit from the consumption of social goods (perhaps in the form of tacit goods only measurable by utility unit). The utility from social goods, $B_s(n)$, is the nondecreasing function of the number of families, n, contributing to social goods. We assume that there exists $\hat{n} < N$ such that $B'_s(n) = 0$ for all n satisfying $\hat{n} \leq n < N$; that is, there exists a saturation point in the productivity of social goods. The community social exchange game is played repeatedly, and at the beginning of each stage game any family can be excluded from participating in the production and consumption of social goods by the other families. Imagine the path of full cooperation in the community social exchange game in which all N families cooperate without any exclusion. We want to see if there is any incentive for a family to deviate from this path when noncooperative social behavior is punishable by permanent ostracism from community social relationships. If this game is played separately from the irrigation game, the incentive compatibility condition for a family not to shirk cooperation is given by

$$C_s < \frac{\delta[B_s(N) - C_s]}{1 - \delta} \quad \text{or equivalently} \quad C_s < \delta B_s(N),$$

where δ is the time discount factor of the family. That is, the saving of the cost of effort by shirking (the left-hand side of the first inequality) should be less than the present-value sum of the sacrifice of future benefits arising from ostracism (the right-hand side). The right-hand side term of the first inequality may be identified as a village family's *social capital* to be lost by social ostracism.[17] We assume that this condition holds since δ is sufficiently large, meaning that the family is sufficiently patient. Let z denote slack, defined as $z = \delta B_s(N) - C_s$.

Now suppose that the irrigation game is played repeatedly by the same village families every spring, while the community social exchange game is played every autumn for an indefinite number of years. Village families can coordinate their strategies in both games contingent on the outcomes in the preceding games. Suppose that the families adopt the following state-contingent strategy combination: (1) Each family plays Shirk in the irrigation game and Do not participate in the community social exchange game if it has played Shirk in any previous irrigation game or it has been ostracized in the social exchange game. Otherwise, it cooperates in both the irrigation and social exchange games. (2) Families exclude any other family, and only that family, who has ever shirked in the irrigation game from enjoying the social goods in all future years. Suppose that the belief of each family is such that all other families have played, and will play in the future, the strategy combination prescribed above except in the case when they actually observe a deviation from that strategy.

To show the strategy combination as an equilibrium relying on a principle of dynamic programming, we only need to check if any one-time deviation from it is beneficial to any family. First, we note that if any family has ever shirked in the irrigation game before, cooperating in both games from then on will not improve its future payoffs. On the other hand, if a family has always cooperated in both games before, it does not pay to shirk in the irrigation game. The benefits of doing so are the saving of effort costs $C_i + C_s$ in each of the current and all future periods, while the costs are the sacrifice of benefits from cooperation $\delta B_s(N) + d_i$ in each of the current and all future periods. Therefore the incentive constraint for each individual family not to shirk is given by $C_i + C_s < \delta B_s(N) + d_i$, or

$$C_i < z + d_i.$$

It is clear that even if the incentive compatibility condition in the irrigation game ($C_i < d_i$) is not satisfied, but that of the community social exchange game is satisfied with a sufficiently large slack $(z > C_i - d_i)$, then this inequality can hold. Thus linking the two games relaxes the incentive constraints.[18]

To check if the second portion of the strategy combination is in equilibrium, note that there is no gain at all for other families to cooperate in the social exchange game with any family that had shirked in the irrigation game before, provided that the number of shirkers is less than $N - \hat{n}$. On the other hand, there is no gain from ostracizing any family who has never shirked, either, because doing so will invite retaliatory shirking from that family in the irrigation game. Therefore the threat of the conditional social ostracism is credible and cooperation among at least $\hat{n}$ families in the linked game can become an equilibrium outcome even if there is a strong incentive for free-riding in the stand-alone irrigation game. Thus cooperation in the irrigation game can become the norm of behavior at least among $\hat{n}$ families in the village community. The second part of the equilibrium strategy combination represents the collectively rational response of village families toward a family who has shirked cooperation in the irrigation game, once such shirking has occurred. Thus it may be interpreted as representing the rational belief that can be shared in a self-sustaining manner among village families regarding what would happen to them if they ever shirk. Such beliefs, once selected at the community level, can deter village families from actually shirking, and under normal circumstances only cooperative behavior among village families will be observed as a standard of behavior.[19] We refer to such a standard of cooperative behavior, supported by the shared beliefs of collective punishment of shirking as a *community norm*.

In repeated games there can be multiple equilibria. In the linked game above the repeated play of noncooperation among village families, or the permanent ostracism of a few families (less than $N - \hat{n}$), is another equilibrium outcome. Further we constructed the model in a specific way. For example, trading the ownerships of stripped paddy fields and associated water rights was not included in the set of feasible strategies of village families,[20] nor was the possible presence of a family that uses violence to punish the noncooperative behavior of other families recognized. Also we did not consider cases where village families are divided into subclasses, and specific social capital is produced for the members of each subgroup so that there is no unanimous interest in the village to punish a defaulting family by ostracism from the village as a whole (see the appendix to this chapter for such a case). By limiting our analysis to the context-specific model as formulated, we were able to identify conditions under which the community norm of cooperation in the commons domain could become self-enforcing, such as the homogeneity of members of the village community and the redundancy of community members in the production of social capital. The road to such structure was paved in Japan by a radical political event in the transition to the Tokugawa period. Toyotomi Hideyoshi, a champion of the preceding Warrior period, prohibited residents in rural villages from having any weapons. This was an attempt to prevent new *samurai* groups from emerging in defiance of the centralized authority he was about to establish. An unintended consequence of the success of this campaign—known as *katana-gari* (sword-hunting)—and the subsequent jurisdictional separation between towns and villages by the Tokugawa government, was the relative autonomy of villages from the direct control of the *samurai* class who were made to congregate in castle towns.

Its implication is that technological and ecological factors may not be the sole, albeit important, determinants in the selection of an equilibrium outcome of a particular type but that historical and social factors may also matter. Otherwise, norms (institutions) are nothing but a mechanical transformation of technological and ecological characteristics, and we are left with a technological-geographical determinant theory of institutional development. For example, peasant farming may fit better with the production of rice in monsoon Asia, which requires the continual delicate care of crops, while a large-scale plantation may not be efficient for the production of rice because of limits to hierarchical monitoring of hired laborers (Y. Hayami and Ohtsuka 1993:ch. 1). But even in regions where peasant farming is ecologically more favorable, a community norm facilitating the development of local public goods supporting it may not necessarily emerge in a straightforward way if there is no conducive initial political and/or social condition (see the appendix). We may draw an analogy with the equilibrium determination of price through the interactions of supply and demand factors. Namely, in the establishment of a norm, ecological and technological factors may determine which rules may be called for to achieve efficiency (demand factors), but social and historical conditions may constrain the supply of feasible rules.

Remarks on Embeddedness

Our main purpose in relating the case of the collective governance of local commons in the Tokugawa village was to make the structure and logic of the linked games transparent with a fairly clear example. Although the context was specific, the model has a sufficiently generic structure for us to draw two general implications from it: one about the nature of norms, and the other about the mechanism of regulating externalities (free riding, congestion) in the production, maintenance, and use of commons—the problem that can be referred to as the commons problem.

First, by using the idea of linked games, we have tried to show the circumstances that make community norms susceptible to economic analysis. In the pre-game-theory age, economists tended to regard norms as more or less irrelevant to economic analysis, or detrimental to the development of efficient markets (a notable exception was Arrow (1969, 1970). In sociology in the tradition of Durkheim and Parsons (1951) before the surge of various new schools in the 1960s and 1980s (e.g., phenomenological sociology of knowledge, social exchange theory, new institutionalism, rational choice theory), norms were primarily regarded as an a priori social entity that becomes internalized by individuals through the socialization process, and not something socially constructed and reconstructed through "everyday experiences" or "social exchange."[21] We have conceptualized a community norm as an endogenous outcome of linked games rather than seeing it as an exogenous constraint (rules of the game) given from outside the social system.[22] We have identified various conditions for a specific kind of community norm to evolve and become self-enforcing—such as the accumulation of social capital through social exchanges of a homogeneous community, unanimous interest in sanctioning deviants in the use of the commons, and political and historical conditions contributing to a community's homogeneity. Identifying these conditions helps clarify the role of norms in sustaining an economic order and provides some understanding of why other solutions, such as the integration of ownership to internalize externalities, might emerge elsewhere.

Potentially the conditions that make particular community norms viable could facilitate or deter the transition from a community-based economic order to a more market-oriented economy. For example, as extracommunity market relationships develop, the social life of village families becomes less coherent, and such forms of community sanction as ostracism become eroded. Community norms ingrained through practices of collective cooperation, reciprocity, and sharing become strained. Will they need to be replaced by entirely new market mores? Traditionally economists (e.g., Hicks 1969) and scholars in other social sciences such as economic anthropology (e.g., K. Polanyi 1944) have drawn a sharp line between the market economy and the pre-modern economy in entertaining this view. However, recently a revisionist view has emerged that contends that the rural community bound by cooperative norms has played a positive role in facilitating the gradual transition of pre-modern rural economies to market economies under certain circumstances. The complete destruction of rural communities is neither sufficient nor necessary for market development. Rather, under certain conditions the presence of community relationships may be complementary to, rather than a substitute for, market enhancement. To determine the conditions underlying such community roles, we need to understand the nature of institutions that can govern trade and other domains. We will reserve a discussion of this issue for chapter 10.1.[23]

Second, the logical structure of the linked game may suggest one generic way to cope with the commons problem. Self-interest in economic transactions need not necessarily imply that agents will be limited, willingly or not, to collect and utilize information available only in that domain. However, that is often the presumption made in the simplest public goods argument. According to such argument, private agents attempt to free-ride on the supply of collective goods, since they are not technologically excludable from the use of collective goods even if they do not bear the cost. As a consequence the possibility of efficient provision of collective goods is to be sought in the domain of governmental services. However, in that domain there is an equally troublesome problem of government failure. The government may not be responsive to the people's real needs because of its inability to collect necessary information, because of political bias, administrative inefficiency, or the difficulty in making social choice that is democratic, informationally efficient, and consistent at the same time. Is there any way out of this dilemma?

In making decisions concerning their own contributions to collective goods provision, agents may actually seek information from outside the relevant commons domain and be constrained in their choices by what that information implies. To illustrate, we take an interesting example described by D. Klein (1990) on the provision of turnpikes in early America. From the late eighteenth to early nineteenth century, the construction and maintenance of turnpikes in America was not managed by governments nor financed by taxes but commissioned to turnpike companies chartered by the states to issue stock. Turnpikes provided large external benefits to nearby farmers and businesses. However, subscriptions to stock in these companies as a means of paying for roads was not expected to be a profitable investment. It was costly to exclude "free-riders" from using turnpikes partly because of legal restrictions on toll collection. Thus people could have benefited directly and indirectly from the road without buying stock. Despite this free-riding problem, many citizens did subscribe to the stock. Why? Klein argues that they did so from a sense of social obligation sustained by "negative selective incentives." In particular, the largest subscribers were found in closed, homogeneous groups where the failure to cooperate would attract attention. Negative selective incentives became institutionalized as social pressure. This was exercised through morally obligatory participation in the town meeting where solicitation for stock subscriptions was made.

Formally this situation might be said to have a striking isomorphic relationship to our irrigation parable. Both cases involved credible threats of sanction, or "negative selective incentives," in the domain of community social exchange, and so regulated free-riding of community members in the commons (public goods) game. Only the social exchange domains in North American town communities would have been more internally diverse and the possible sanctions more subtle in manner, less austere in substance, and more permissive of deviance than those in the Tokugawa village. The logical structure is identical, however. Some strategies that are not an equilibrium (and thus not self-enforceable) in an isolated commons domain (here, cooperation in the irrigation domain or the turnpike provision domain) can become profitable strategies for agents, when that domain is "embedded" in a community social exchange domain. This situation recalls a notion of social embeddedness developed by the sociologist, Mark Granovetter, although he was primarily concerned with the embeddedness of trade or organizational domains within social networks of agents in the context of modern market economy.[24]

In a seminal paper on this subject, Granovetter (1985) criticized the oversocialized concept of the human in modern sociology as represented by Talcott Parsons, as well as the undersocialized concept of the human in neoclassical and transaction cost economics operating in the utilitarian tradition. He argued that systems of values and norms are not a once-and-for-all influence but an ongoing process, continuously needing to be constructed and reconstructed through interaction. In other words, values and norms may be perceived as exogenously received by individuals, though actually they are endogenously shaped by them, "in part for their own strategic reasons." (p. 57) On the other hand, he argues that agents in markets and organizations in the modern society generate trust and discourage malfeasance by being embedded in "concrete personal relations and structures (networks)." Granovetter does not commit to the view that the construction and reconstruction of norms can be exclusively explained by strategic motives but rather he emphasizes the need for examining the historical uniqueness behind the formation of a social network. However, the substance of his "social-embeddedness" theory arguably may be captured by the idea of linked games, joining the social exchange domain and economic transaction domains: be these commons, trade or organization.[25]

There are tremendous differences between the rural community in Tokugawa Japan, or the self-governing town in early America, and the social structure of contemporary society. Contemporary societies are becoming increasingly heterogeneous in citizens' wealth, educational and cultural backgrounds, and occupations. Citizens are mobile across communities. Thus it may appear at first sight that social relationships have lost regulatory power in the provision of public goods. Yet, there is growing awareness that nongovernmental organizations, voluntary associations, and professional communities play important roles in the provision of, and need for, public goods such as the natural environment, public safety, poverty and disaster relief, and technological innovation and transfer.

Today we can add to this list the phenomenon of open source software (OSS) for the internet, such as TCP/IP, Linux.[26] OSS is a public good par excellence in cyberspace because this is the basic infrastructure for internet communications, and it serves as well as the basis for further refinement programming. OSSs are distributed free with open source codes and are continually being improved through the participation of many programmers from all over the world via e-mail communications. As a result this software has become more stable and reliable than commercially licensed software protected by compiled object codes. Why do programmers actively participate in the improvement of OSS without direct pecuniary compensation?[27] Why not protect the intellectual property rights to codes legally since it is technologically feasible to do so? As legal protection would eminently retard the development of communication technology, participating programmers may be driven to improve on the software they themselves use, but they may also derive nonpecuniary rewards from their contribution to the collective good similar to that of academic scholars, particularly the recognition and esteem of their peers.

Another such example is considered by Saxenaian (1999). She examined the rise of the Hsinchu-Taipei region in Taiwan as a high-tech center, and found that a transnational community of U.S.-educated Taiwanese engineers—a community that spans borders and boasts as its key assets shared information, trust, and contact—contributed more to its success than government policy-makers or global corporations. This community has coordinated a decentralized process of reciprocal industrial upgrading between Silicon Valley and the Hsinchu region. They did so by transferring capital and skills, but also know-how between specialist producers in the two regions. Saxenaian claims that this case underscores the significance of a technical community for diffusing ideas.

The traditional economist's view was to regard the market and the government as substitutes with either of them in charge of public goods. There was no recognition of the role of intermediate associations in the highly developed market economy. However, partly from the rising ease of communications facilitating the formation of cross-border communities of various interests and partly due to the increasing cognizance of citizens' responsibility, such voluntary associations are becoming progressively active. An interesting point is that the primary importance of such voluntary organizations may not necessarily be limited to the direct provision of public goods but include the generation of unique intangible social capital for members (solidarity, social esteem, professional satisfaction, etc.) bound by common concerns, interests, and causes, so that civic norms and professional ethics conducive to the provision of public goods are allowed to evolve in a nongovernmental and diverse manner. Thus we may detect the relevance of social embeddedness in the commons domain even in the contemporary context. However, we must recognize that there is one important difference between the rural community discussed in this chapter and emergent voluntary associations and professional communities: this is a difference in the openness of membership. In the next chapter we deal with one way in which a community of interests could voluntarily and endogenously be formed in the atomistic trade domain.

Appendix: History versus Ecology as a Determinant of a Norm: The Case of Yi Korea

In section 2.2 we identified the conditions under which the community norm of cooperation in the commons domain could become self-enforcing, namely the generation of a substantial amount of social capital for all village families through their social association with the community. However, we also noted that there could be multiple equilibria and that the emergence of a community norm would not be the only possible response to the problem of the commons problem. We saw that particular historical and political events leading to the Tokugawa *Baku-Han* regime, that is, the "sword-hunting" and the eventual separation of the city and the rural community paved the way for the formation of a community norm regulating the commons problem. But, there is a school of thought that places emphasis on ecological, rather than historical, factors as a determinant of community norms. We referred to the Hayami's thesis that the ecological condition of monsoon Asia tends to induce peasant family farming and their cooperation in the use of collective goods. In this appendix we make a cursory, comparative historical observation on the evolution of rural community norms in Tokugawa Japan and in the later Chonson Dynasty in Korea to examine the interactive roles of history and ecological conditions.[28] Both were endowed with somewhat similar ecological conditions. In this regard Japan and Korea are like a paired control group in experimental psychology, selected to examine the possible impacts of social-historical factors on equilibrium selection.

The social and political structure of the village that prevailed in the seventeenth- and eighteenth-century Korean Peninsula was much more differentiated than that of contemporaneous Japan.[29] Basically there were three classes: the *yangban, nobi*, and the commoners. The *yangban* started to settle in the rural area between the fifteenth and seventeenth centuries. They were not a legally defined class but evolved as a social class, composed of families with lineage from an ancestor who passed the bureaucracy qualification examination à la Mandarin and had once served as a central bureaucrat for the dynasty (capital *yanban*). They lived in a local hamlet (*yangban* village) organized on a consanguineous basis. They legally possessed *nobi* (customarily translated as slaves), in some cases numbering as many as several hundred, who became objects of trade and inheritance among them. Some *nobi* lived outside the master's property, owned their own lands, and even other *nobi*. The number of people in the *nobi* class is considered to have increased to between 30 and 50 percent of the population during the fifteenth century, partly because a growing number of rural residents became landless due to the Manchu aggression in the north and Japanese piracy activities and Toyotomi's invasion in the south. The commoners possessed or leased small plots for their own cultivation but did not have *nobi* and had virtually all the burdens of taxation to the central government. These were estimated to be a majority of the local population in the sixteenth century, subject to rather discretionary tax collection as well as usury owed for grain loans that the magistrates forced on them.[30]

As rural settlements began to form in the fifteenth and sixteenth centuries, *yangban* became active in farmland development and the management of large-scale farming, relying on the labor services of *nobi* and poor commoners. However, the social barrier between the *yangban* and other classes had made it rather difficult for encompassing norms to spontaneously emerge and support the development of the local public goods as we observed in contemporaneous Japan. Their capacities to sanction others in a different social class are simply asymmetric. Complaints from *yangban* about embezzlement by *nobi* and their laziness are abundant in historical documents. But the threat of ostracism could not serve as a disciplinary device. Rather hard forced labor, as well as high rents, on *nobi* and small peasants often prompted their flight from their *yanban* lands. *Yangban* were legally allowed to harshly punish fleeing *nobi* in the event of their costly retrieval.

What then were the effects of such a differentiated social system on the institutional structure of the production domain of the village? Did the absence of common social capital across differentiated social classes make cooperative efforts in the production domain infeasible, and thus does the Hayami's thesis not hold on Koran Peninsula? In Korea dry farming was dominant until the fifteenth century. An influential book of farming instructions edited under the direction of King Sejong (1418–1450) advised against the use of wet farming because it was risky and vulnerable to rain shortages. It is also said that the rainy season on the Korean Peninsula comes later than in the Japan Islands, so wet farming is relatively ecologically unfit (Miyajima 1995). However, this problem could have been overcome by the development of irrigation systems. Indeed, the later history of Korea up to the present time indicates that their technological development contributed to the viability of more productive wet farming.

There were two major irrigation methods developed in the late Yi Dynasty: reservoirs and *pok* (Miyajima 1983). The construction and maintenance of reservoirs at the foot of mountain valleys to utilize the natural gravity to collect water required large-scale labor inputs, which had to rely on the mobilization of a labor force by the central government. Thus historical records of the rise and decline of reservoirs are found to coincide with the strength of local authority of the central government. In particular, reservoirs declined substantially in the nineteenth century when the bureaucratic initiatives considerably weakened (Miyajima et al. 1982). On the other hand, the *pok* was the method of diverting river flow to paddy fields through the construction of small dams to raise the water level, and so required the relatively smaller collective effort. Around the *yangban* village, clusters of the commoners (commoner's villages) gradually developed as satellites. In each village, there evolved cooperative associations or community compacts called village *kye* for various purposes, including pooling capital and lending it to members in rotation, keeping cultivating cows, and mutually helping in changing of roof hatches. Among them, one of the most important was the irrigation association. Thus, despite the initial differences in social status across villages, the community norm started to evolve and be institutionalized at least at the village level and then gradually beyond.

An interesting later development, in the late eighteenth and nineteenth centuries, was the upward mobility of commoners and *nobi* to the higher social status of local *yangban* or commoners. This was made possible by the "discovery" of family lineage records by commoners and even *nobi*, purchasing free status from the government, and bribery of local petty clerks. By the midnineteenth century the *yangban* proportion of the local population is estimated to have come close to a majority.[31] In parallel, high status *yangban* families became noncultivating landholders, abandoning the self-management of relatively large-scale farm lands. Lower status *yangban*, commoners, and *nobi* tended to become de facto peasants. In this way, in terms of cultivating units, the Korean farming system gradually adapted itself to the ecological conditions of rice production despite the persistence of an enormous disparity in legal land holding and capacity to extract rents. There is indirect evidence that community norms governing the local commons were evolving under the community compact. H. Miyajim et al. (1992) examined the development of the irrigation system in the 1930 promoted by the colonial government and found that the most effective system evolved in the area where the traditional irrigation associations had been active since the late Yi Dynasty, whereas the irrigation associations founded according to the legal stipulations of the colonial government and including new Japanese landlords had only a limited success.

Thus we have a rather intriguing picture. The traditional social and political factors seem initially to have deterred the joint evolution of extensive irrigation systems and community norms that governed them. Despite such barriers, the community of peasants gradually began to evolve in the cultivating economy toward the late Yi Dynasty as the Hayami's thesis indicates, although land ownership remained highly biased. Traditional emphasis is placed on the class conflicts in a manner reminiscent of Marx: rent exploitation by the central government and wealthy, upper-class *yangban*, and the consequential poverty of the lower class *yangban*, commoners, and *nobi*. The increasing revolt of peasants in the nineteenth century was interpreted as an expression of the latter's desperate revolt.[32] However, peasant insurrection in the nineteenth century was directed against officials and clerks and not the landlords, landowners, rich peasants, or private lenders (Palais 1975:67). Such circumstances are rather indicative of a mounting inconsistency of a political regime with evolving community norms latent in the development of the peasant cultivating economy. The frequent uprisings of peasants might likewise be regarded as the symptom of a widening gap between the aspirations of the peasant and the political constraints imposed on them rather than the spontaneous expression of their despair. This alternative hypothesis may be worthwhile exploring further.

3 The Private-Order Governance of Trade, Contracts, and Markets

It is in the ius gentium, *the law merchant, and the practices of the ports and fairs that we must chiefly seek the steps in the evolution of law which ultimately made an open society possible. Perhaps one might even say that the development of universal rules of conduct did not begin within the organized community of the tribe but rather with the first instance of silent barter when a savage placed some offerings at the boundary of the territory of his tribe in the expectation that a return gift would be made in a similar manner, thus beginning a new custom. At any rate, it was not through direction by rulers, but through the development of customs on which expectations of the individuals could be based, that general rules of conduct came to be accepted.*
—Friedrich A. Hayek, *Law, Legislation, and Liberty* (1973:82)

In this chapter we consider an important ramification of the establishment of private ownership rights: the voluntary exchange of private ownership over goods by individuals. If private ownership rights are established over a variety of goods sequentially, there is no guarantee that the resulting overall arrangements realize Pareto efficiency—the situation where individual utilities cannot be enhanced simultaneously by altering ownership rights arrangements in any way. Therefore incentives for individuals to exchange ownership rights over goods to their mutual advantage—simply referred to as "to trade"—would appear spontaneously. However, if opportunities for exchange were limited to individuals directly bartering their own goods for those of others within their own community, the gains from exchange realized would remain modest. Money and merchants emerge as intermediaries of trade and facilitate the expansion of exchange opportunities beyond the limit of a closed community, leading to what Hayek (1973) calls "the extended order of human cooperation." To achieve this state, however, some problems must be overcome. How do trading individuals (merchants and others) establish trust? Is a buyer's promise to pay on a certain date reliable? Will the money the buyer is about to hand over be accepted by others as means of future payment? Will a seller's promise to deliver certain goods at a certain date in a specified quantity be kept? How can the buyer be sure that the goods sold are not "lemons" (Akerlof 1970)? As Hicks once said:

Even the simplest exchange is a species of contract; each of the parties is abandoning rights over the things that he sells, in order to acquire rights over the things he buys. Now it will happen, very early on, that the things to be exchanged are not, or not all of them, physically present at the moment when the arrangement to exchange them is made. Thus the bargain has three constituents which soon become distinguishable; the making of the agreement, the delivery one way, and the delivery the other. As soon as this distinction is made, the agreement itself becomes no more than a promise to deliver. Trading is trading in promises; but it is futile to exchange in promises unless there is some reasonable assurance that the promises will be kept. (Hicks 1969:34)

In the separation of implementations of delivery from promises, a commodity exchange opportunity may be characterized as involving a typical one-shot Prisoner's

Trader 1 / Trader 2	Honest	Cheat
Honest	$\Gamma/2,\ \Gamma/2$	$-\beta,\ \hat{\alpha}$
Cheat	$\alpha,\ -\beta$	$-\gamma,\ -\gamma$

Figure 3.1
Payoff consequences of the trade game

Dilemma: two agents may each benefit from mutually honest trade. However, if either agent can unilaterally and solely cheat the other, there is an even greater gain for that agent at the expense of the other. If there were no device to control such dishonesty, then trade that could be potentially beneficial to both parties might not take place. Consider figure 3.1. The matrix represents payoff outcomes to two trading partners from a single exchange depending on the combination of strategies they adopt. H denotes playing honest and C denotes playing cheat. The first number in each entry indicates the payoff accruable to the row player (e.g., the buyer), and the second the payoff accruable to the column player (e.g., the seller). If they mutually play H, the net gains from honest exchange are Γ, which are equally divided between the trading partners. If both players play C, payoffs to both agents are negative $(-\gamma < 0)$. If either party unilaterally cheats the other, he/she can derive personal benefits measured by $a > \Gamma/2$ or $\hat{\alpha} > \Gamma/2$, while causing damage to the other party measured by $-\beta < -\gamma$ or $-\hat{\beta} < -\gamma$. In this situation there is a social loss measured by $\Gamma - (\alpha - \beta) > 0$ (respectively $\Gamma - (\hat{\alpha} - \hat{\beta}) > 0$). Each player has no-trade option that will yield zero payoffs to both players. Then, if either trader expects that the other will play C, he/she will opt for no trade. This is the unique Nash equilibrium when the game is played only once and in isolation.

The question now is: What mechanism is possible to constrain traders to choose H? In other words, how is it ensured that the promised exchange will be kept to the mutual advantage of traders in the process of exchange? In this chapter we discuss this mechanism, which is applicable to various trade domains and characterized by the payoff matrix above or some similar version, or by a bundling of such matrices across many potential traders. Those domains may include not only those in which the ownership rights over physical goods are tradable (via the intermediary of money) but also ones in which the promise to deliver a certain type of labor service may be traded for the promise to pay.

We refer to mechanisms that facilitate (honest) trade as the governance (mechanism) of trade or exchange. Considering that even the simplest exchange is a type of contract, the mechanism of governance of exchange can alternatively be referred to as "contract enforcement mechanism." Specifically, when a trade domain bundles togther many exchange opportunities among a large number of agents, each specified by a payoff matrix having the Prisoner's Dilemma characteristic noted above, a governance mechanism applied to such domain may be referred to as a "market governance mechanism."

In this and the sixth chapter we try to understand conditions under which a variety of governance mechanisms can become self-enforcing and sustain honest trade relationships among different agents with various characteristics. In other words, we examine under what conditions alternative governance mechanisms can generate stable expectations among traders so as to constrain their action choices to honest trading.[1] When the trade domain extends so that potential traders cannot identify ex ante their potential trading partners, a third party other than the direct trading partners may become necessary to govern such impersonal exchange. However, even in these cases we do not treat third parties as exogenous neutral parties in the sense that rules for action choices can be prescribed for them and automatically observed by them. Rather, we are concerned with whether rules for third party's action choices conducive to market enhancement can be voluntarily and credibly chosen. We need to examine how such rules can become incentive compatible for the relevant third party so that the prescribed governance mechanism becomes institutionalized as a stable outcome of the game with the third party as an augmented strategic player.

In this chapter we survey the private-order mechanisms of governance such as personal trust, traders' community norms, clientage and club norms, self-enforcing employment contracts, private third-party enforcement, and first-party enforcement (moral sentiments), relying on important works by various authors. Those readers familiar with this literature may skip the first part of this chapter and go immediately to section 3.5, where a substantive discussion examining comparative properties of, and interrelationships between, those governance mechanisms initiates. In the appendix we discuss the evolutionary argument as to how money as an intermediary of exchange of ownership rights over commodities can emerge and be sustained (we discuss another intermediary institution, merchants, in chapter 8.2). In this chapter we do not dwell on the state (the court) as a third-party contract-enforcement mechanism. The reason for this is that there can be different types of states performing correspondingly different roles of market governance, but to differentiate them, we need first to learn something about the role of organizations in markets. We will do this in next two chapters and then take up a variety of market governing roles of states in chapter 6.

Private-order mechanisms of trade and market governance may be thought of as having evolved prior to the emergence of the modern nation-state, and parables in this chapter are mostly drawn from such historical experiences. However, as we will show in the last section of this chapter, this does not imply that private-order governance mechanisms have entirely yielded their reasons for existence to the state nor that they have been subjugated to it. On the contrary, they continue to serve as sometimes complementary and sometimes substitute contract enforcement mechanisms of the state. Today, as trade domains propagate through globalized cyberspace, the ability of nation-states to function as a primary contract enforcement mechanism is beginning to be questioned. In lieu of the state enforcement mechanism, various private-order governance mechanisms are being experimented with in the trade domain in cyberspace, the so-called e-commerce domains. As the sharp reader will undoubtedly notice, many of these developing mechanisms resemble the mechanisms discussed in this chapter in terms of information structure and enforcement means. Thus, despite the simple nature of the historical parables introduced in this chapter, there is some inherent logic that connects them to contemporary situations.

3.1   Traders' Norms

Personal Trust and Traders' Community Norms

One well-known solution to the Prisoner's Dilemma is the so-called reputation mechanism. If say two traders, a buyer and a seller, meet repeatedly. The threat of terminating trade in the future by either partner in the event of the other's cheating may mutually deter cheating, provided that the future benefits from trade are not discounted too heavily (i.e., they are patient) and that the one-time gain from cheating is not too large. Now let us assume that the generic trade game as represented by figure 3.1 is repeated every week and that both players discount one unit of utility available after one week by the discount factor δ. Suppose that each party adopts the following contingent strategy: play H as long as the other party also plays H, and if the other party plays C this week, switch to no trade strategy forever.

Let us examine the effect of unilaterally deviating from this strategy for one week. Suppose that one trader plays C, while the other trader plays H. The current net gain for the former to play C is $\alpha - \Gamma/2$. The trader suffers from zero payoffs forever from the next period on because of the triggered punishment strategy of the other party, so the present-value sum of the costs of the deviation will be $\delta/(1 - \delta) \times \Gamma/2$. Therefore, if the discount rate δ is large enough and the one-time gain from cheating α is not too large relative to that from honest trading $\Gamma/2$ so that $\delta > (\alpha - \Gamma/2)/\alpha$, it will never be beneficial for the trader to play C. Thus the belief that cheating will invite costly punishment may deter agents from cheating. The mechanism for sustaining mutual honest trading by such beliefs may be referred to as mutual "personal trust."

The described strategy imposes a very high cost on the punishing agent, as well, even if strategy C is adopted by mistake by the trading partner: the cost is as high as that for the punished agent. Therefore let us consider an alternative strategy combination. Suppose that the trader who have played C once will be punished for the T consecutive weeks by the trade partner who adopts the C strategy as a punishment. If the former keeps playing H during this period, then he/she will be forgiven and mutually honest trading will resume after T weeks. If at any time during the punishment the punished ever plays C again, then the punishment phase is restarted. Suppose that one trading partner plays C in one week while the other plays H. Assuming that the other party sticks to the prescribed punishment strategy, then the cheater will not only lose gains from exchange $\Gamma/2$ but will also suffer from penalty cost β from the next period on for T periods. The present-value sum of the costs of the deviation is $\delta(1 - \delta^T)(\Gamma/2 + \beta)/(1 - \delta)$. If δ and T are large enough so that this sum is larger than the one-time benefit from deviation, $\alpha - \Gamma/2$, then it will never be beneficial for the trader to play C. On the other hand, it is necessary for T not to be so large that it is incentive compatible for the defector to accept the punishment by playing H while being retaliated against by his opponent. This condition is given by

$$-[\delta + \cdots + \delta^T]\beta + [\delta^{T+1} + \delta^{T+2} + \cdots]\frac{\Gamma}{2} > 0.$$

These two conditions are simultaneously satisfied for some positive T, if $\delta > (\alpha - \Gamma/2)/\alpha$ as before. On the other hand, if a trader plays strategy C, the best response of his/her trading partner will be to retaliate for T^* weeks, where T^* is the maximum T that satisfies the conditions above (assuming that only pure strategies are allowed). Then the belief that cheating will invite costly punishment for T^* weeks becomes credible, and it is possible to deter it from actually occurring.

Let us now imagine that a particular group of traders gathers to exchange goods at a local market that opens every week. Each trader is matched with another trader each week and all traders play the same trading game as specified in figure 3.1. If the same traders can meet every week repeatedly, then their personal trust will support mutual cooperation. However, suppose that traders randomly change their trading partners every week. Suppose that the traders play the honest strategy as long as their trading experiences have been satisfactory but that, if a cheating incident occurs in the market place, the news spreads very quickly and all traders stop going to the market forever (no-trade option). Then the incentives of each player are identical with those in the case of a permanent no-trade solution in the two-person repeated trading game. However, this solution is extreme in that any defection from honest trading by a single trader, even if by a mistake, will lead to the closure of the entire market domain and impose a very high cost on everyone.

Now, if cheaters can be correctly identified and made known to every trader in the market, then the limited punishment strategy described before can be selectively applied to a cheater (Kandori 1992: prop. 2; see also Okuno-Fujiwara and Postel-waithe 1995). That is, when the traders meet randomly, they will somehow identify whether the other party has cheated and thus refuse to trade honestly with that partner, forcing the partner to play *H*. However, if any other player cheats while a player is being punished, the latter will be forgiven and only the most recent cheater punished. This selective punishment requires more information about cheating (it is not sufficient to know that cheating has occurred) when the matching is random. The merit is in the lower cost imposed on honest traders in punishing cheaters, while cheaters are potentially exposed to the same degree of punishment as under the mechanism of personal trust. This abstract construct makes clear a generic informa-tion requirement for the market governing mechanism: if cheaters can be identified among the community of patient traders, repeated trading among themselves may generate and sustain beliefs that cheaters can be credibly punished. If honest trading is supported on the basis of such beliefs among the information-sharing community of traders, we may refer to it as the *traders' community norm*. Nevertheless, there will always be tension between the assumption of random matching (impersonal exchange) and that of perfect information dissemination. Is there any way to relieve this ten-sion in situations where no centralized, third-party information clearinghouse has emerged?

Clientage and Club Norms

For the innocent visitor, the bazaar appears to be a chaotic trade domain, warranting the assumption of random matching and lacking a centralized information dissemi-nating agent. How then can the temptation for dishonest trading by agents be con-trolled, if not perfectly? The sharp eye of economic anthropologist, Clifford Geertz, once recognized that in Morocco stable clientage ties between buyers and sellers, together with bargaining, constitute the most important elements of its institutional structure. He noted:

Clientalization is the tendency, marked in Sefrou, for repetitive purchasers of particular goods and services to establish continuing relationships with particular purveyors of them, rather than search widely through the market at each occasion of need. The apparent Brownian motion of randomly colliding bazaars conceals a resilient pattern of informal personal connections. (Geertz 1978:30)

Now we consider the evolutionary formation of personal trust in a trade domain where impersonal exchange (random matching) has initially prevailed. Although motivated by the trade example given above, the purpose here is not to reproduce the historical process of clientalization but to understand the basic logic involved in the ways in which norms evolve among endogenously formed groups of traders. This way the traders are better able to respond to system-level information deficiencies in a large trade domain.[2]

Let us assume that a stage game held every week in the bazaar is represented by an unstructured bundle of exchange opportunities as depicted in figure 3.1. The set of agents is composed of many traders who come from different localities and are randomly paired. They do not know the past history of their potential trading partners. They happen to meet at the bazaar and cannot be sure whether they can trust one another. However, we suppose that the matched traders could meet again in the future if they choose. In this sense the bazaar is not an anonymous marketplace.

If the matching continues to be random, the only possible Nash equilibrium would be no trade. Does this state represents the so-called evolutionarily stable strategy (ESS) in the sense of Maynard-Smith (1982)? Roughly speaking, the concept of ESS is intended to capture the intuition of an "uninvadable" state of the domain: if the domain is in an ESS, then an invasion of small mutants will eventually disappear under natural selection.[3] In the expectation of possible gains from long-term cooperation, some traders may wish to break the impasse of no-trade by exchanging words with certain other traders, indicating their intention to play H and to continue to play H if the relationship continues into the future. They try to convey their intention, as well as infer the intention of their trading partners, by using costless languages or signals, such as appearance, habits, accents, and names of mutual friends or relatives, whose meaning may not be obvious to the uninitiated others.[4] If words and/or types match, these traders may then be tempted to engage in trading. Robson (1990) refers to the matching thus made as the "secret handshake" by "mutants."[5] Then, can honest trading become gradually dominant, upsetting the no-trade equilibrium? The problem with this is that some traders could promise to cooperate in this way but then play C and never meet with the same partner in the future. Let us call them "parasites." Because of their existence, "cheap talk" with costless language cannot support honest trading. Eventually Nash equilibrium evolves in which every player defects from honest trading. Suppose then that there is a successive invasion of "mutants" who use a new language or signals that circumvent parasites and are engaged in secret handshakes among themselves. However, parasites corresponding to the new generation of mutants will soon emerge. This becomes a rat race, and thus there can be no Nash equilibrium such that every player cooperates. No-trade thus becomes ESS. (Robson 1990).

Imagine now that traders exchange gifts as they shake hands prior to trade, or sink some relationship-building costs in terms of time, such as make frequent visits or do favors) to demonstrate their good intentions (Carmichael and MacLeod 1998). The gift should be costly to the giver but not be of value for the receiver (e.g., in fancy wrapping paper) or be consumed quickly by the receiver. Otherwise, parasites could receive the gifts, then cheat, and recycle the gifts in deceiving their next trading partners—Carmichael and MacLeod refer to such players as "recycling parasites." Suppose that there are players who adopt the following strategy: if their messages, out of infinitely many possible messages, coincide with those signaled by a randomly matched trading partner, they exchange gifts or sink relational-building costs, play H with that partner, and, as long as the other party also plays H, stay matched until they die. Otherwise, they separate and seek new matches in the bazaar. Call those players who adopt this strategy "clienteles." In order for this strategy to be incentive compatible, the following two conditions need to be satisfied:

$$\frac{\Gamma/2}{1-\delta} - G > \frac{\alpha - G}{1-\delta}, \quad \frac{\Gamma/2}{1-\delta} > G,$$

where G is the cost of gift-giving or relationship-building. The first inequality says that the present-value gains from continued cooperation realized by one-time gift-giving/relationship-building this week are strictly greater than those from the parasite strategy, that is, renewed gift-giving/relationship-building every week and cheating. The second inequality says that the present-value gains from continued cooperation are greater than the cost of one-time gift-giving/relationship-building. Combining these two conditions, if it holds that

$$\frac{\Gamma/2}{1-\delta} > G > \frac{\alpha - \Gamma/2}{\delta},$$

a client relationship can be formed and sustained to the mutual advantage of traders.

Suppose that a small fraction of the trader population dies every year and is replaced. Most of the new generation simply mimics the strategies of their forebears, but a very small fraction experiments with randomly chosen strategies. For this kind of game, Carmichael and MacLeod showed that for the strategies of clientele with the same sized gift/cost satisfying the inequalities above, there exists a neutrally stable equilibrium characterized by the following two properties: (1) it is a Nash equilibrium, and (2) mutants can never realize a higher utility than that of the clientele, although new types of message may need to be continually created to circumvent parasites (strictly speaking, this equilibrium concept is formulated in terms of utility rather than strategy).[6] Specifically, neither of the following is strictly better off: a secret group of parasites who use a new message, exchange gifts, but defect against everyone else, nor that of agents who use a new message, do not exchange gifts, but cooperate among themselves. When an agent with the clientage strategy meets another with the same strategy, he/she leaves the matching market and stays with the other until one of them dies. Parasites remain in the market forever. The social cost of the gift exchange/relationship-building for enhancing an honest market transaction can be low if traders are sufficiently patient. If the discount factor is close to one, G can be very close to $\alpha - \Gamma/2$, which is far less than the gains from continued honest trade. Thus the creation of a clientele can be considered an efficient response by agents to information deficiencies of the bazaar.[7]

The mechanism above was formulated as emerging as quasi-permanent relationships between pairs of players who initially exchange the same signals and gifts (alternatively sink reputation-building costs).[8] However, just as personal trust (a bilateral reputation mechanism) can be replicated within a group of traders who know each other, it may be conjectured that such a mechanism can also be replicated by a group of players. For example, a group of traders in a population of many players could come to know each other by using the same language (signal) and sink initial "fees" to form a club or some relational association. The fees paid must be in a form that is useless for outsiders or not individually portable, for example, spent on ritualistic ceremonies, member certificates, or club monuments. The formation of a club then constitutes a separate subdomain of the initial market domain in which club-specific norms now regulate transaction relationships in a manner replicating the norm within the traders' community described in the previous section. Any violation of a behavioral standard (honest trading) is punished by termination of club membership. So the traders' community norms operate not only in domains where its membership is exogenously fixed, due to the technological nature of transactions or to geographical confines, but also in domains endogenously created by a particular group of agents who can identify each other as trustworthy, exclusive clientele. We may call such quasi-community norms operating in an endogenous group of agents the *club norms*.

One potential problem with the club norms as a market governance institution is the potential loss that may result from inertia. In the parable above, the technological environment of the exchange game (payoffs to traders) is assumed to be constant for indefinite periods of time. So it makes sense that trading partners who identify each other as honest trading partners maintain those relationships until they die. However, suppose that new merchants with new products arrive at the bazaars every week so that old relationships quickly lose their value. Yet "mistrust of strangers" may prevent established traders from exploiting the potential gains from such new opportunities. However, this is but one possibility. Under different conditions the norms prevailing in a closed community—whether rural or traders—will facilitate its transition to open market relationships. We will examine this possibility in chapter 8.2.

3.2 Cultural Beliefs and Self-enforcing Employment Contracts

As trading opportunities expand geographically, it may become necessary for merchants to hire agents to carry out their business on their behalf in remote locations. It may now be hard for the merchants to directly supervise and monitor the operational activities of their agents on a daily basis. So there arises the possibility of the agents acting dishonestly, for instance, embezzling the merchants' goods, acting opportunistically, or shirking in their obligations. Greif (1989, 1994) offers an interestingly original historical and comparative institutional analysis dealing with the one-sided Prisoner's Dilemma in the context of Mediterranean trade in the medieval world. He compares the different ways in which Genoese merchants from the Latin region and Maghribi merchants from Northern Africa would respond to the same agency problem. He does this to demonstrate the role of shared expectations (what he calls "cultural beliefs," for a reason we will see momentarily) in enforcing honest behavior of agents. These shared beliefs have implications for the historical trajectories of subsequent institutional evolutions.

At the core of his argument Greif utilizes a model of repeated merchant–agent games. The stage game begins with each merchant hiring an agent for some level of wage and ends with his deciding whether or not to fire the agent after observing the outcome of his performance. The strategy set of the agent while employed is composed simply of two choices, {Honesty or Cheating}. The merchant's objective is to control the agent's cheating and his strategy set is composed of setting a fixed wage rate w at the beginning of the stage game, deciding whether to rehire or fire the agent at the end of the stage game. If the merchant does not retain the agent, he must

Agent \ Merchant	Hire	Not to Hire
Honest	ω, $\Gamma-\omega$	0, 0
Cheat	α, $-\beta$	0, 0

Figure 3.2
Payoff structure of the merchant-agent game

decide whom to hire at the beginning of the next stage game. Suppose that the merchant can always fire the cheater, although he always pays the promised wage at the end of the period (so there is no cheating by the merchant).

It is assumed further that separation can occur not only when an agent has cheated but also with probability σ for some other exogenous reasons, such as the death or retirement of a merchant or the disruption of highly uncertain overseas commerce. The agent's gross benefit from cheating is α in the current period, while cheating inflicts a damage cost β on the merchant. The agent derives zero utility when unemployed. The payoff structure of this one-sided Prisoner's Dilemma employment contract game can now be represented as in figure 3.2. where the row player represents the agent and the column player represents the merchant. The merchant's strategy NH refers to nonhiring, while H refers to hiring.

This game differs from the original exchange game in that the payoff to the agent when both players play H is now to be endogenously determined by the merchant. Let us first consider which wage policy the merchant can choose to induce agents to be honest under the threat of firing cheaters. We refer to the wage level that satisfies this condition as the *efficiency wage*. Suppose, for a moment, that after separation, unemployed agents are rehired with the probability π_h if they have not cheated, and with probability π_c if they did cheat. By the optimal principle of dynamic programming, if it is not worthwhile for the agent to cheat once, it will never be worthwhile for the agent to cheat in any way. Therefore we only need to examine the condition under which it is not beneficial for the agent to cheat once, assuming that the cheating agent will never cheat after re-employment.

Denote by V^a the present value of the lifetime expected income of the currently employed agent who, whenever hired, is honest. Denote by V_i^u the present value of the expected lifetime income of the unemployed agent who has been honest but unemployed at the end of the previous period when $i = h$ and that of the unemployed agent who has cheated and unemployed at the end of the previous period when $i = c$. Then we have

$$V^a = w + \delta[(1 - \sigma)V^a + \sigma V_h^u],$$

$$V_i^u = \pi_i V^a + \delta(1 - \pi_i)V_i^u, \qquad i = h, c.$$

where δ is the discount factor. Cheating once gives the expected lifetime income $\alpha + \delta V_c^u$, and the agents will not cheat if this is smaller than V^a. This condition is satisfied if

$$w \geq \alpha[1 - \delta(1 - \pi_h)(1 - \sigma)]\frac{[1 - \delta(1 - \pi_c)]}{[1 - \delta(1 - \pi_h)]} \underset{\text{def}}{=} \omega$$

The wage rate ω thus defined can then be used by the merchants as an instrument to control agent cheating provided that it is smaller than the gross output Γ of the agent when he is honest. It is immediate from the condition above that the merchants' optimal strategy in choosing a wage is related to their probability assessment of π_i. In particular, the optimal wage ω is increasing in π_c. We have $\pi_c = \pi_h$ if the merchant expects others to employ agents from the pool of the unemployed indiscriminately regardless of their past conduct. Then the merchant needs to set the wage at $w = \alpha[1 - \delta(1 - \pi_h)(1 - \sigma)] \underset{\text{def}}{=} \omega_I$ to deter possible cheating by a hired agent. On the other hand, we have $\pi_c = 0$ if the merchant can expect that other merchants will employ only noncheaters. Then he can set wage at the level

$$w = \frac{(1 - \delta)}{[1 - \delta(1 - \pi_h)]}\omega_I \underset{\text{def}}{=} \omega_C.$$

Clearly, $\omega_I > \omega_C$.

Let us now distinguish two polar cases regarding the merchant's employment strategy: one in which the merchant adopts the strategy of not employing an agent who once cheated another merchant and offering wage ω_C to an employed agent; and another in which the merchant adopts the strategy of employing any unemployed agents indiscriminately and offers wage ω_I. The former strategy becomes feasible only when there is a dense information network among merchants and cheaters are easily identifiable, while the latter strategy can be pursued by any merchant without interacting with the others. Therefore Greif has called the former strategy the *collectivist strategy* and the latter the *individualist strategy*. The wage offered in each strategy type can prevent agents from cheating if the associated expectation is self-fulfilling. To see if it is self-fulfilling, we only need to examine whether each employment strategy is indeed the best response when cheating by an agent occurs. The merchants under the individualist strategy still employ anybody at the wage equal to ω_I. Therefore it is trivial that their strategy is sustainable. For the merchants under the collectivist strategy, it needs to be proved that not to hire the cheater and to hire only from the pool of honest unemployed agents is optimal. To see this, note that when merchants hire cheaters, they have to pay the higher wage ω_I to prevent future cheating. By a similar reasoning, it is not optimal for merchants not to fire an agent who has cheated. Thus the collectivist strategy also becomes self-enforcing. On the other hand, an agent's optimal strategy is to play H given the wage offered under either merchant strategy. Thus the collectivist strategy and the individualist strategy, together with the agents' strategy to play honest, constitute separate equilibria (sub-game perfect equilibria).

So far the model may appear to be a rather straightforward extension of efficiency wage models.[9] However, Greif's model is based on rich comparative information derived from a study of historical documents. In addition the implications of the model are tested in the light of the comparative historical information regarding subsequent institutional development. Under both the collectivist and the individu-alist equilibria, the equilibrium outcomes (on-the-path-of-play outcomes) are equally characterized by no cheating by the agents. However, these outcomes are generated by different self-enforcing expectations of the merchants, as well as of the agents, with respect to actions taken by others in the shirking contingency (off-the-path-of-play). Such expectations are called *cultural beliefs* by Greif. They are institutional constraints in that they can be multiple (therefore not technologically determined) and constrain the behavior of the economic agents through coordinating their beliefs. These constraints are cultural in that the cultural heritage of a society, together with the historical process through which various players interact, may have forced the convergence of expectations into one of multiple possibilities a natural "focal point." Greif regards the Maghribis (the Jewish traders who adopted the values of the Muslim society), who began trading in the Mediterranean early in the eleventh cen-tury, as having had collectivist cultural value, while the Genoese who began trading toward the end of that century had individualist cultural value. On the basis of his-torical documents, he indicates that the Maghribis had indeed developed dense in-formation networks among themselves and used collective punishments for improper behaviors in the light of their customs and tradition, while the Genoese were highly individualistic and lacked the ability of collective punishment and information sharing.

The collectivist and the individualist cultural beliefs have interesting implications for the subsequent trajectories of institutional development. Under collectivist cultural beliefs, the merchants can gain from mutually using each other as agents. Suppose that a merchant-cum-agent is dishonest in his capacity as the agent of another mer-chant. Then other merchants could coordinate collective punishment against that dishonest merchant by not punishing other merchant-cum-agents who cheat this merchant Then the merchant has to pay the higher wage ω_I to his own agent to control the latter's dishonest behavior so that his expected profit in each period will be $\Gamma - \omega_I$. Therefore, even if $\alpha + \delta V_c^u > V^a$ for some $w = \hat{\omega} < \omega_C$ so that the stand-alone incentive compatibility condition for an agent is not satisfied, for the same $\hat{\omega}$ it could hold that

$$\alpha + \delta V_c^u - \frac{\delta}{1-\delta}(\omega_I - \hat{\omega}) < V^a.$$

The last term on the left-hand side is the present-value sum of the extra amount the dishonest merchant has to pay to his own agent to deter her cheating as he cannot expect others' cooperation in punishing her in the event of cheating. If this inequality holds, then the merchant is deterred from cheating when he acts as an agent for another merchant The cost of being dishonest as an agent become extremely high for the Maghribi merchants. Therefore the agency fee for the merchant-cum-agent can be set lower than ω_C, and still dishonesty can be controlled.

The logic is similar to that of the previously discussed case in which the irrigation game and the community social exchange game are linked. Recall that the possibility of a strong collectively imposed penalty in the community/social exchange game can deter free-riding in the irrigation game, even if the incentive constraint in the irrigation game is not satisfied when it is played independently. In the current parable the merchant simultaneously plays the role of merchant-principal and that of merchant-agent in separate trade domains. Then, even if the agency fee is so low that a merchant is tempted to cheat another merchant in his capacity as an agent, doing so would invite costly penalties in other domains of games when he hires other merchants as agents. However, such linking is not possible under individualist cultural beliefs because the collective punishment of dishonest merchant-cum-agents is not feasible. Thus, under collectivist cultural beliefs, horizontal (reciprocal) merchant-cum-agent relationships would be induced, whereas under individualist cultural beliefs the vertical separation of a merchant class and an agent class might develop.

This difference has an important implication for the capability of the corresponding economic organizations to expand when exchange opportunities are broadened. The Genoese responded to such opportunities by extending their individualist strategy to create new merchant-agent relationships with non-Genoese. In that extent Greif regards the individualist equilibrium as integrative. In contrast, the Maghribis expanded their exchange activities only as far as other Maghribis became employable as agents because, as we have seen, doing so was cheaper. If they were to hire non-Maghribis to whom the collective punishment could not be applied, they would have to offer a higher wage than ω_C to prevent dishonesty. Therefore, even if there were better exchange opportunities, they might not have been regarded as profitable. Thus the collectivist equilibrium is segregative. While on a purely theoretical basis the individualist equilibrium may not necessarily be intrinsically more efficient, the collectivist society may be inferior in its capacity to exploit new exchange opportunities.

3.3 Private Third-Party Governance: The Law Merchant

One solution to controlling market exchanges between traders who do not meet again may be by the introduction of a third party who monitors cheating and disseminates information about cheating among the traders at some cost. This solution was discussed by Milgrom, North, and Weingast (1990) in the specific context of the law merchant in medieval trade. During the twelfth and the thirteenth century much of the trade between Northern and Southern Europe was conducted at the Champagne Fairs. At the fair merchants from different localities entered into contracts that required enforcement but did so without the benefit of legal enforcement. Merchants evolved their own commercial code, the *law merchant* (*lex mercatoria*), that governed commercial transactions and was administered by private judges drawn from the commercial ranks. Inspired by this historical information, the authors constructed a parable in which the introduction of such a third party can resolve the Prisoner's Dilemma in a market setting, at some cost, even when the pairs of traders do not meet more than once.

The new game is constructed by adding an agent who links the bundle of original trade games represented in figure 3.1 over time and embedding each of the trade games. This third agent, called the law merchant (LM), serves as a repository of information over time and an adjudicator of disputes between traders. One of the authors' theoretical innovations was to explicitly consider the incentives of the third agent in deriving an equilibrium outcome of the game. However, to avoid complications, we imagine first that the LM is a neutral agent that honestly performs its required functions. This way we can see how its information intermediation services can help the traders to avoid being trapped in a Prisoner's Dilemma. Subsequently we introduce the possibility of strategic behavior by the LM. So we will refer to the former game as the neutrally augmented game and to the latter as the strategically augmented game.

The neutrally augmented game is structured as follows: Two agents meet at the fair and play the exchange game described by figure 3.1. After learning the consequence of the game, either party may appeal to the LM at personal cost about the misconduct (playing of the C strategy) of the trading partner. The LM judges honestly. The

LM's judgment involves the ability to award damages to the cheated player. The defendant may pay the damages, or may refuse to pay at zero cost. The LM does not have the power to enforce payment by the defendant. It can only record unpaid judgments and make them available for future reference by other traders. Any future trader can check the records of the LM at cost Q to see if the other party has had any "unpaid judgments" in the past. The LM accepts appeals for judgement only from traders who have made such a query prior to playing the exchange game. The augmented stage game starts with the matching of two new agents and ends with LM's recording of unpaid judgements, if any. The sets of actions of traders is now composed of {Check record with the LM or not, Play honest or not, Appeal to the LM or not, Pay judgment or not} in the order of choice sequence. The augmented stage game is repeated indefinitely. However, no pair of players will ever meet twice.

Milgrom, North, and Weingast showed that the following strategic profile (rules for action choice) of the traders can ensure the average payoffs $\Gamma/2 - Q$ for the traders, provided that the discount factor δ is sufficiently close to one: Both agents check the records of the LM before playing the exchange game if they have no unpaid judgments against themselves. If they find any record of unpaid judgments for their trading partner, they do not exchange. Otherwise, both play Honest. If and only if one party cheats, the victim appeals to the LM. The LM awards damages J to the victim that are large enough to absorb the net gains from cheating $\alpha - \Gamma/2$. The defendant pays the judgment J if and only if he/she has no prior unpaid judgement. The authors showed that for certain parametric environments these strategy profiles constitute an equilibrium—sequential equilibrium—of the neutrally augmented repeated game under the beliefs of the traders that all other traders have played, and will play, the strategies prescribed above, except when they actually observe a deviation from that strategy themselves.[10]

Let us now drop the assumption of the neutrality of the LM and consider the possibility that the LM acts as a strategic player. There are several possible ways in which the LM might cheat. Consider a very simple case in which the LM may extort a bribe from a trader who has no unpaid judgments by threatening to falsely report to the other traders that he has. Now the LM's set of actions comprises {Ask for a bribe or not} at the beginning of the stage game. Consider the following addition to the strategy (rules of action choices) of the traders in the neutrally augmented game: whenever a bribe is solicited, the trader refuses to pay it and will not use the services of the LM for that year, if and only if the trader has never paid a bribe before. Otherwise, he pays a bribe B, if it is not greater than $\alpha - Q$, checks the LM's record of the trading partner, plays Cheat this year, and refuses to pay a judgment. As a strategy (rule for action choices) for the LM, suppose that the LM asks for a bribe B equal to $\alpha - Q$ from any agent who has ever paid a bribe even if he has no unpaid judgments. Otherwise the LM does not ask for any payment. Suppose that the LM acts contrary to the last rule. Then the trader refuses to pay and does not use the services of the LM that year, which costs the LM Q. On the other hand, if the LM does not ask for a bribe from any trader who has paid a bribe before, he will lose B. Neither case is profitable for the LM, so the prescribed strategy for the LM is incentive-compatible. Then the given strategy of the trader's belief that the LM acts justly becomes credible for them. We can see that the prescribed rules for trader's action choices are also incentive-compatible.[11]

Thus this parable suggests that under certain conditions a private third party can make the honest behavior of traders enforceable only by changing the information structure of the game. The information requirements of this mechanism are not very compelling. Traders do not need to know about any other traders except their immediate partners at the current year's fair. The LM keeps records regarding only those traders who have cheated and have not paid judgments. He does not need to have the power to enforce the payment of judgments by proven cheaters against their will. Rather, the payment of judgments is self-enforceable because knowledge of any trader's dishonest behavior will be credibly available to his future traders to his disadvantage.

However, note that the one-shot Nash equilibrium, namely no exchange, can be another equilibrium. If a credible third-party information-disseminating organization fails to evolve, then exchange opportunities among traders who are unfamiliar with each other may remain unexploited. A further complication arises when we allow for the possibility that the LM may receive bribes from a trader who has an unpaid judgment but wishes to have the record erased. Suppose that a trader gains from cheating in a large amount $\hat{\alpha} - \Gamma/2$ in each year, refuses to pay the judgment, but conceals the judgment by paying a bribe less than that amount in every year. Suppose that future traders who have been matched and cheated by this dishonest trader under the LM's misguided information stop making inquires to the LM from the next year on. Then the number of traders who do not use the LM's services increases in an arithmetic progression over time and the present value of the LM's future losses from bribe taking becomes equal to $\delta Q/(1 - \delta)^2$, even assuming that there is no communication among traders about LM's reputation. If this cost is smaller than $\hat{\alpha} - \Gamma/2$, it becomes incentive compatible for the trader and the LM to secretly negotiate on bribery. As a result the exchange domains linked by the LM's intermediary information services will gradually dwindle and the private third party mechanism may ultimately be undermined by a lack of sufficient revenue and reputation.

Historically we observe that the private-order institution of law merchants eventually yielded its reason of existence to a formal third-party mechanism based on legal codes implemented by the nation-state. Milgrom, North, and Weingast argue that as the nation-state came to have the coercive power to seize the property of individuals who refused to pay judgments or to put them in jail, the cost of punishing cheaters might have been saved. They also suggest that the cost of maintaining a third-party organization may have been substantially saved by replacing individual payments to the law merchants with a comprehensive state-run tax system. This is an efficiency-based argument. However, as the parable alludes above, it cannot be taken for granted that the nation-state will necessarily evolve as a credible mechanism for contract enforcement and, more broadly, as one for the protection of private property rights over goods in general—comprehensive rights over goods, including rights to utilize, derive returns from, and dispose them, as well as rights to control others' human assets who uses them in uncontractible events (residual rights of control to be introduced in next chapter). In particular, note that the state power to protect private property rights by force is double-edged, since it might endow the state apparatus with the power to transgress the private property rights as well (Weingast 1997). Indeed, the emergence of modern nation-states in the West was preceded by the struggles of the gentry, merchants, citizens, and others, against sovereigns to constrain the arbitrary power of the latter to tax, prey, and so on (e.g., see Rosenberg and Birdzell 1986:119–23, North and Weingast 1989; Olson 1997). Later, in chapter 6, we will use a game-theoretic model to show that the rule of law not only facilitates the development of the market exchange domain, when it exists, but also is more likely to evolve in tandem with the latter encompassing anonymous traders. However, this development may not necessarily be uniform everywhere. Different forms of state could arise as an equilibrium of the polity domain, sometimes deterring the development of the neutral legal system as a dominant market governance mechanism. However, the possible form of state may be related to ways in which organizations, interest groups, and markets evolve in the economy. Therefore we reserve a discussion of the role of state as a possible guarantor of private property rights until after chapter 5 which deals with organizational conventions.

3.4 Moral Codes

We have followed a quasi-historical logic by which customary property rights emerge and come to be enforced by multilateral reputation mechanisms (norms, implicit contracts) as well as by third-party mechanisms. This outer institutional development for protecting private ownership rights in the process of exchange can greatly facilitate and enhance the scope of market transactions. However, when the domain of exchange expands, mechanisms of norms and self-enforcing contracts may not be able to perfectly monitor and penalize all possible violations of private ownership rights at a reasonable cost. If we were to rely exclusively on legal enforcement by the government, on the other hand, this might entail an oppressive political atmosphere, and its administrative costs can become prohibitive. However, the parable in chapter 2 indicated that once the proto-institution of customary property rights is established, it becomes in the best self-interest of individuals to honor the rights of others, provided that they can reasonably expect other parties to do the same. Thus, while the proto-institution of customary property rights becomes externalized and articulated as a legal code on the one hand, it may also be internalized and crystalized within individual agents as a moral judgment, such as "thou shalt not steal another's property," which they are disposed to follow. Such a moral judgment need to be considered as neither being derived from an abstract super-natural axiom nor primarily imposed by an external authority, such as the schools or churches, but it can originally evolve from a custom. Reversing the possible order of causation between customs and moral judgments in an anti-Weberian manner is a distant echo of Aristotle, who noted that "moral goodness (*etike*) ... is the result of habit, from which it has actually got its name, being a slight modification of the word *ethos*" (book II.i:91). Arrow further interprets moral obligations as the "carrying out of [implicit] agreements" and that "internalized feelings of guilt and right are essentially unconscious equivalents of agreement that represent social decisions" (1967:79).

The Aristotelian view that a moral judgment is an outcome of a custom, and not vice versa, may be illustrated by the following simple example: suppose that a machine a worker operates breaks down on the shop floor, but a neighboring worker fails to help her to fix it after regular working hours. In this workplace the cooperation of workers, namely the exchange of help over time, has evolved as a custom. The neighboring worker may feel bad even if the time he quits the workplace is consistent with the formal work rule. However, if a machine breakdown happens in a workplace where the specialization of jobs is articulated in a collective agreement, "helping" may imply depriving a machinist of his property rights over the repair job. Therefore, having a cup of coffee while a sweating machinist is making the repair would be judged to be morally just by other workers and they would not need to feel any guilt.[12] Later in chapter 8.1 we will see that such different work customs or rules can indeed evolve as conventions (evolutionary outcomes) even for the same technology.

Self 1 / Self 2	Honest	Cheat
Honest	$\Gamma/2,\ \Gamma/2$	$-\beta,\ \hat{\alpha}-\hat{\mu}$
Cheat	$\alpha-\mu,\ -\beta$	$0,\ 0$

Figure 3.3
Payoff structure under the moral code

If property-rights rules are derived from and consistent with customs, they should generate associated moral judgments among individuals. Then violating the rules, whether customary or codified, should evoke autonomously negative moral sentiments and emotions, such as guilt, shame, or anxiety, within the agent's mind. This tendency may well be reinforced if the agent also has sufficient trust in others' disposition toward honesty. The situation might be such as to modify the original payoff structure as in figure 3.3, where the psychological cost of negative moral sentiment μ is large enough so that $\alpha - \mu < \Gamma/2$.[13] Agents experiencing this effect might refrain from violating rules even when they are not directly monitored by other agents or a third party. We call this first-party mechanism operating inside the self as an outcome of established customs the *moral code*. If there were no rule of property rights firmly grounded on custom, such moral code could not easily evolve. The instability is not the outcome of absence of a priori moral code, but likely the opposite case.

3.5   The Overall Arrangement of Market Governance

The Multiplicity of Trade Governance Institution

Table 3.1 summarizes various mechanisms of governance that are a stable outcome of the trade game of various types. The first column gives the mechanisms (we introduce the "digital enforcement" mechanism toward the end of this section). Entries in the second column refer to the agent(s)—traders themselves or augmented third-party players (organizations)—that act as the enforcer(s) of corresponding mechanisms. Entries in the third column refer to the salient features of the equilibrium strategy profile that coordinate traders' beliefs and thus constrain traders' choices under the corresponding mechanisms. They can be beliefs held by self-governing traders with respect to default contingencies (i.e., situations in which dishonest trading, breach of contract, and/or violation of private property rights takes place), information and sanctions expected to be provided by a third-party enforcer, or the expected

Table 3.1
Variety of trade governance mechanisms

Governance mechanism	Enforcement agent(s)	Endogenous rules of the game	Fitting domain characteristics
Personal trust	Trading partner (second party)	Termination of trade with dishonest trader	Repeated bilateral trade opportunities
Traders' norms	Traders' sharing communications network	Ostracization of dishonest traders from the community	Traders connected by communication networks
Clientage	Trading partner who has sunk relation-building costs	Termination of relationship against dishonest trader	Ex ante anonymity, ex post repeatable trade opportunities
Club norms	Traders who has sunk entry costs	Expulsion of dishonest trader from the "club"	Ex ante anonymity, ex post repeatable trade opportunities
Self-enforcing (employment) contracts	Traders in markets	Termination of contracts against dishonest traders and beliefs about its consequence	Actions and/or outcomes observable but unverifiable
Third-party information dissemination	Third parties (e.g., law merchants, escrow services, certified authorities, online auction sites)	Information dissemination regarding dishonest traders	Anonymous traders
Coercive enforcement by a third party	Third parties (e.g., political rulers, mafia)	Violent punishment of dishonest traders	Asymmetric distribution of coercive power; large gains from one-time dishonest trading
Moral codes	Self (first party)	Negative moral sentiments invoked by dishonest trading	Relatively homogeneous agents sharing customs
Rule of law	Courts	Rule-based punishment of dishonest trading	Anonymous traders, actions or outcomes verifiable, government monopoly of coercive power
Digital enforcement	Computer programs designed by trading agents	Delivery of goods only on the terms programmed to enforce	Trade of digital contents/services deliverable through cyberspace

moral sentiment inducing the trader's self-restraint against making the dishonest action choice. Finally, in order for a particular exchange governance mechanism to be effectively run at reasonable social cost—or more fundamentally, in order for a particular mechanism to emerge as a stable outcome of the game and thus be institutionalized—it is necessary that the domain of the exchange game satisfy certain properties in terms of, say, the range and characteristics of agents, the nature of information channels between them, their ability to meet again for trade, or the technological nature of their exchange and consequences. They are indicated in the last column and let us comment on some of them briefly.

The institution of the traders' community norms presupposes, for example, that the domain of the exchange game is restricted in such a way that agents can mutually communicate to identify agents who have committed dishonest trading. Their characteristics also need to be symmetric in that any one of them could be subjected to the same kind of punishment if he/she failed to meet the standard of trading behavior, and they are expected to (be able to) act in concert in implementing punishment of any dishonest members. In other words, none of them acts as a third party whose function is solely to verify and punish a defecting trader. Accordingly traders' community norms are likely to be institutionalized in domains where the number of trading agents is limited and relatively homogeneous in transaction characteristics, apart from the distinction between buyers and sellers. Ethnically homogeneous traders groups are one example.[14]

We saw that even if the domain of potential exchange becomes enlarged, a group of traders out of the potential many may form a relationship or an exclusive club at initial costs to regulate repeated trading among them through an endogenous formation of clientage or club norm. Even in advanced economies it is not hard to find such a mechanism. For example, in domains of supply of intermediate products specific to final products, the form of transactions can be either through a hierarchy, by relational contracting, or by spot transactions. When a need for transaction-specific investment is involved, the number of transacting agents may necessarily be limited ex post despite possible ex ante competition. Further, once investment in relation-specific assets is sunk by one partner, it becomes difficult for those assets to be diverted to alternative uses without a cost. Therefore conventional wisdom holds that the value of the assets can become the target of rent-seeking behavior by the other party. This is the so-called holdup problem: if this risk is anticipated by the investing partner, it will become optimal for her to reduce the level of relation-specific investment below the socially efficient level. It is claimed therefore that a solution to this problem needs to be the integration of property rights over the specific assets involved, that is, the hierarchical control of investment by either transacting party (Klein, Crawford, and Alchain, 1978; Hart 1995). However, in many such domains (e.g., the Japanese automobile industry, the Italian garment industry, the German machinery industry), supply transactions are often regulated by relational contracting rather than by integration (hierarchical control). As we will see in the next chapter, there can be an informational reason for nonintegration to be potentially more efficient. Yet there must be an exchange governance mechanism in which relational contracting is mutually honored and not spoiled by the opportunistic behavior of either party. Club norms (informal norms among customary traders or within corporate groups such as *keiretsu*) seem to be one answer. In this view, mutual investment in intangible relationship-building efforts may be taken as an initial gift exchange, whose value is not portable outside the orbit of the club, rather than as a possible target of opportunistic rent-seeking behavior.

The mechanism of club norms to control dishonest trading behavior is possible only in a domain where trading agents can meet frequently after the initial meeting, if they choose, to benefit from repeated transactions. If the domain of the exchange game is extended to cover many potential traders who may not meet with each other frequently because of the nature of the transaction (e.g., ordinary people do not normally buy a house frequently), or they are mobile, or for some other reason, then traders who have breached contracts and/or violated another trader's property rights in the past may not be easily identifiable by potential trading partners through their communications network. Then the no-trade option can become an equilibrium strategy without an alternative market governance institution. One solution is to add agents (an organization) to the original exchange game who are specialized in collecting and disseminating information about the violation of property rights among traders. Law merchants are one example of such mechanisms of historical importance. Various credit reference bureaus are devices of more contemporary vintage, endowed with a similar information structure.[15]

Another interesting example of private third-party mechanisms is escrow services in the United States that intermediate transactions be conducted fairly. The escrow agent acts as a clearinghouse, completing the transactions after all the necessary elements of the transactions are assembled. For example, in terms of simple real estate transaction, by channeling the deed and the money through an escrow agent, the buyer is assured that s/he is getting a valid deed and the seller is guaranteed that s/he will receive the money agreed upon.[16] In order for this mechanism to be effective, the third party—the escrow agent—must be neutral so that the transaction can be completed in a fair manner. Although laws specify the duties of escrow agent to protect both parties from attempts of fraud by the other, this is in part self-regulating: an escrow agent needs to have a solid reputation, or else the parties will not conduct business with him. Indeed, escrow has emerged spontaneously prior to laws.[17]

Recent analogues to the law merchant can be found in trade (e-commerce) domains in cyberspace (Hadfield 2000). For example, eBay.com, founded in 1995, is the world's largest, online, auction Web site.[18] eBay.com maintains a record of trading experiences (positive and negative) by buyers regarding sales agents and their numerical indexes, that are available to anyone who transacts through eBay.com. It also announces records of buyers' past assessments. Thus one can find a fair amount of information on the reliability of an otherwise anonymous trading partner. Certification authorities (CAs), such as VeriSign, that provide a "public key" infrastructure for encryption is another example. This infrastructure allows information such as orders, delivery sites, and credit card numbers, necessary for e-trade involving anonymous traders, to be encoded and decoded, as well as its source to be verified by a recipient. An online agent who wishes to be identified can obtain a digital certificate maintained on CA's secure server, while a recipient can contact the CA to confirm the identity of a certified sender by clicking the seal of the CA posted on the latter's site. These steps can be done almost instantaneously in cyberspace. A certification authority monitors the agent's proper use of the infrastructure and revokes a certificate in the event of misuse (ostracization). Auctioneers and CAs are private agents, and their incentives to be neutral and honest are provided by their own reputation concerns, supplemented by their submission to auditing agents.

In bilateral or multilateral reputation mechanisms, dishonest traders are punishable only by a no-trade action choice by potential trading partners who have been informed of their misconduct. However, if the one-time gain from dishonest trading is very large relative to the benefits of honest trading ($\alpha - \Gamma/2$ is large) and/or the time discount factor of potential cheaters is small (δ is small), such spontaneous punishment may not be strong enough to deter them from cheating. In such cases the only deterrence is the expectation that severe and immediate punishment is imposed on dishonest traders. Even in bilateral or multilateral relationships, dishonest trading may sometimes be retaliated against by the victim's use of physical violence. However, such voluntary punishment may impose a high cost on the victim as well. Therefore in the domain of trade where opportunistic gains by short-sighted traders are high, a demand for physical retaliation services may emerge for the violation of private property rights. The political rulers who amassed the physical capacity for violence during the transition to enhanced market economies gradually emerged as (near-) monopolistic suppliers of such services in exchange for taxation rights (Olson 1993). Monopoly could have been an efficient solution given the possible economies of scale in the exercise of physical violence. But there were, and still are, privately organized, competing services as well, where the enforcement power of rulers, or that of the government in the modern context, is weak. For example, in a fascinating sociological study, Gambetta (1993) characterized the Sicilian mafia as "a specific economic enterprise, an industry which produces, promotes, and sells private protection" (1993:1). As such, "[i]t is an equilibrium: no one has an immediate interest to behave differently and fight it even if one sees its drawbacks." (ibid.:8).

As already noted, if a political ruler, sovereign or government, is strong enough to enforce private property rights using its effective monopoly on physical violence, however, it may also be strong enough to prey on private property owners through discretionary punishment as well as taxation. This is what Weingast (1997) calls "the fundamental political dilemma of an economic system." Constraining the political ruler or the government to follow well-defined rules for action choices with the threat of punishing their violation by the withdrawal of political support can be one equilibrium solution among many that are logically possible in the polity domain (chapter 6). If such an outcome emerges, one of important derivative mechanisms can be the settlement of contractual disputes by an independent judiciary branch of the government, namely the courts based on codified legal rules and verifiable facts. But the requirement of contract violation verification at the court implies a limit to the applicability of legal rules as a market governance institution. There will be many trade domains in which the violation of contracts cannot be easily verified with hard evidence or in which the specification of contracts for all possible contingencies is not possible in advance. Thus, even in the most advanced market economies, the governance of market exchanges is not limited to the system of legal rules. It needs to be supplemented by many other institutions of private-order governance.

We have seen that self-enforcing contracts can be such a mechanism. Especially in the domain of employment transactions, contracts may implicitly imply rewards for relation-specific efforts that are not verifiable (bonuses, promotions, etc.). Firing or quitting as a means of sanctioning a contractual breach of the other party can be privately costly, however, to the party who performs it. Also, even if implicit contracts are expected to be self-enforcing, there can be always mistakes, random experiments, and mutations. In order to cope with these problems various complementary private dispute settlement mechanisms have evolved to protect legitimate property rights to jobs, as well as management prerogatives against the abuse of such rights.[19] These include organizational grievance and penal procedures, work councils at the factory level, and collective bargaining apparatuses. The labor arbitration board is an example of a quasi-legal third-party mechanism for settling industrial-relations disputes over job control rights specified in private collective agreements or simply by workplace customs. In relying more on customs or on trying to find a "good" practice rather than trying to prove and punish misconduct on either side, private arbitration may be less costly to use in dispute settlement in terms of time and effort, and may help preserve a nonconfrontational atmosphere conducive to productivity enhancement in the workplace, even though it lacks the power of legal enforcement. In the domain of labor transactions, the court can thus be the last resort for dispute settlement. Private third-party mechanisms are normally invoked first in this domain, and thus their existence facilitates and complements the bilateral governance of implicit contracts.

Another example of cases where a definition of property rights is difficult to articulate, and thus their violation is costly to judge or verify in a formal judicial procedure, may be found in the domain of trade and use of intellectual property rights. New designs emerging in the communication and information industry often become obsolete so fast that the protection of rights to them and their efficient use may be hard to achieve through the conventional patent system or the formal judicial system. To find private property-rights agreements that can be mutually beneficial and incentive-compatible demands a state of art services from specialists in the intellectual property rights law as well as those versed with professional knowledge (e.g., engineering) in products involved.[20]

Finally, even social norms à la chapter 2 may be invoked to supplement, or substitute for, the rule of law in situations where the corresponding requirements are satisfied by relevant domains. In a book based on field work on the settlement of neighborhood disputes in Shasta County, California, Ellickson reported that ranchers settle most of their disputes (e.g., over border fence financing or damage caused by highway collisions involving stray livestock) without any recourse to, and sometimes even inconsistently with, the legal system (e.g., the damage costs of a collision may be shared between the parties involved rather than being borne by the driver of the vehicle as California law dictates). He claims that "neighbors achieve (a) cooperative outcome ... by developing and enforcing adaptive norms of neighborliness that trump formal legal entitlements" (1991:4). From this viewpoint, he criticizes the "legal centrism" of the so-called Coase theorem on social costs. According to his interpretation of the theorem, Coase took the legally defined entitlements as initial starting points for dispute settlement and "failed to note that in some contexts initial rights might arise from norms generated through decentralized social processes rather than from law" (1991:138–39). Ranchers have spontaneously developed standards for conflict resolution, supported by the expectation of punishment of violators by victims ranging from circulating gossip in the community to violent "self-help" (e.g., shooting of stray livestock).

Summarizing the argument so far, we may assert the following:

CLAIM 3.1   Even in advanced market economies, private property rights and contracts are not solely enforced by the formal system of legal rules. They may be governed by a complex of institutional arrangements, private and public, formal and informal, that simultaneously operate.

We may refer to the entire complex of mechanisms operating in the economy as the overall (institutional) arrangements of market governance.

Complementarities and Substitutabilities of Market Governance Institutions

We have just stressed that diverse characteristics of different trade domains can be a reason for the complexity of overall arrangements for market governance. But it should not be taken as implying that technological factors are the sole, albeit important, determinants of the configuration of the overall arrangements. Even if the underlying technological conditions of trade domains are the same, there could be the possibility for diverse arrangements to evolve across economies. How and why such diversity could arise may not be fully accountable at this stage of logical development, but a basic direction for further discussion may be indicated here.

The fact that diverse trade governance mechanisms coexist in one economy may be regarded as the segmentation of the entire domain of market exchanges into subdomains, in each of which a different strategy profile establishes itself as a stable equilibrium rule for action choices by the agents within it. In each subdomain individual agents are ex ante endowed with various action possibilities. For example, the ranchers in Shasta County can have a choice, if they wish, between employing a lawyer to sue a damage-inflicting neighbor, on the one hand, or settling damage compensation through private negotiation, on the other. Likewise a manufacturer can procure either standard parts from one of multiple independent suppliers through an auction web site, or modular subsystems from a few selected suppliers on a continual basis on line. However, the actual strategic choices of individual agents are affected by those made by their neighbors or business partners. Thus, suing could be rather an outlier choice for the ranchers, although, if the same rancher moves to a city, he may find it difficult to rely on private violence or spreading rumor to retaliate transgressing partners. By the same token Kranton (1996) finds that the division of an economy between monetary market exchange and reciprocal exchange—personalized exchange between people who know each other well with the passage of time between quid and quo—depends on the relative numbers of agents initially involved in two modes: "if many people in the economy engage in reciprocal exchange, the market is thin, and it is hard to locate trading partners in the market. Market exchange yields lower levels of utility. On the other hand, if many people engage in market exchange, the market is thick, and . . . it is difficult to enforce a long term exchange agreement" (1996:831).

If relational contracting is established as a custom in a certain supply transaction domain in a technologically advanced economy, it would become difficult for firms making all-purpose standard parts to make a profitable entry into the domain, even if they could be profitable in another domain where legal contract enforcement is in place or transaction protocol is standardized through a business-to-business (b2b) e-commerce service provider. We will conceptualize such choice interdependencies among agents in one domain as strategic complementaries (chapters 5 and 8). Namely, even though substitutable action choices are available to individual agents, their actual choices may be affected by the prevailing strategy profiles in the domains in which they are active.

A more subtle case can be that of mixed strategy equilibrium. For example, it is conventionally thought that the Japanese bring disputes to court less frequently than others. This tendency is casually attributed to the Japanese cultural trait of exhibiting relatively stronger reservations about open disputes in public, preferring a private compromise. However, some disputes actually do make it to court. In examining these data, Ramseyer (1990) found that the terms of out-of-court settlements for damages from traffic accidents were statistically on a par with those awarded by the courts in Japan (also see Ramseyer and Nakazato 1998). The private settlement of auto accident damages may be facilitated by the predictability of court decisions, while the prevailing custom of private settlement can save on the costs of frequent litigation. Thus private settlement and ligation are substitutes at the individual level, but their mixture (mixed strategy profile) could become an equilibrium at the social level. Litigation alone, or out-of-court settlement alone, may not be viable as an equilibrium.

The possibility of strategic complementarity suggests the possibility of multiple equilibria, that is, the viability of different governance mechanisms existing in each subdomain. How then does a particular governance mechanism become dominate in one domain from among many that are logically possible or prevalent in similar domains in other economies? Casual historical observations suggest that the more extensive the extent of trade becomes, the more likely it is that the trade domain will be governed by traders' community norms rather than personal trust, by club norms and self-enforcing contracting rather the traders' community norms, and by the rule of law rather than the protection/transgression of private property rights by discretionary political power holders. Indeed, various trade governance mechanisms can be substitutes, rather than complementary, with respect to a particular trade domain. If more than one substitute mechanisms are competing in some domain, and each requires a large setup cost, the situation may not be stable. For example, in an economy where the government and the mafia are competing in the provision of services of private property-rights protection, citizens may be subjected to dual costs, taxes and extortion, but also provided with inadequate protection by either of them because of their excessive competition or collusion. In economies where trade domains develop, we usually observe that the government suppress, if not completely, private violence.

We also observe that middlemen or third parties of various types have successively evolved in history to mediate trade across thereto separated trade domains. Then, a new governance mechanism may emerge to replace old ones operating in old domains. For example, we have seen that the law merchant as an information intermediary evolved to replace traders' community norms operating within closed traders' communities. Thus the history of trade governance may be interpreted as the process of successive equilibrium selection in each trade domain or in newly bundled domains in response to changing internal and external conditions. As a more effective governance mechanism is established, its consequences will be characterized by more, mutually beneficial trade rather than no trade (another Nash equilibrium) or frequent disruption by dishonest behavior. Thus it appears that the more market-enhancing a governance mechanism is, the more likely it is to survive and cover a wider range of trade domains.

However, if one takes a look at the relationships among various market governance mechanisms in one economy at any particular point in time, their relationships may be complementary in the following sense: the effectiveness (or the presence) of one exchange (property rights) governance mechanism can be reinforced, either directly or indirectly, by the presence (institutionalization) of a particular mechanism in the same or embedding domain. This kind of relationship between institutionalized mechanisms may be referred to as institutional complementarity, related to but conceptually distinct from afore-mentioned strategic complementarity leading to a particular governance mechanism in a single domain (a more formal treatment of these concepts will be elaborated in chapter 8). Some illustrative, elementary examples may be cited. For example, the monitoring and enforcement costs of the rule of law in a particular trade domain may be saved if moral codes inducing the unconscious enforcement of contracts are widely shared. Conversely, the unjust and unfair management of the legal system may corrupt the moral sentiments of individuals and weaken their self-restraint against dishonest trading and violation of private property rights. Thus market-supporting moral codes (first-party mechanism) and a just system of the rule of law (formal third-party mechanism) can be complementary. If they do not co-evolve, then a likely outcome could be the reliance of the agents on private violence for the protection of private property rights.

As another example, suppose that a manufacturer and a supplier consider the possibility of relational contracting in which the former is supposed to supply technological knowledge to the latter, while the latter makes investments in matching human assets. If the Walrasian discipline prevails in the labor transaction domain, however, the workers or engineers of the supplier firm who have acquired technological knowledge from the manufacturer may then quit the firm to realize higher values elsewhere without bearing the cost of investment in learning in portable knowledge. Thus, in the absence of bilateral commitment in the labor transaction domain, relational contracting may not evolve easily in the supply transaction domain. In such case the manufacturer may attempt to integrate the supplier, which would imply placing the domain of supply trade under a different governance mechanism (i.e., organizational governance), or relying on legally enforceable spot-transaction contracts for the supply of standardized parts. This is an instance of institutional complementarity between the labor transaction domain and supply transaction domain. We will observe later a similar, but more complicated case of institutional complementarity between the domain of financial transactions and the domain of labor transactions (chapter 10).

Just as strategic complementarity implies the possibility of multiple equilibria in one particular domain, institutional complementarities across domains may imply the possibility of multiple overall institutional arrangements of market governance that are not reducible to technological differences. Each of those arrangements may form a coherent whole, because a component mechanism may not be easily replaceable with another type in piecemeal manner in the presence of mutually reinforcing complementarity. Thus we tentatively submit the following claim:

CLAIM 3.2   One source of the diversity in overall institutional arrangements in market governance is mutually supportive, complementary relationships among constituent governance mechanisms. The presence of complementarity implies that the configuration of overall arrangements can be internally coherent and robust.

If there are multiple arrangements that are internally coherent, how does one of them get selected over all others in an economy? An obvious point is that "history matters." For example, we often observe that in economies where market exchange domains gradually evolved out of traditional rural communities, club norms tend to emerge on a relatively larger scale as a mechanism governing market exchanges. This development may not necessarily be straightforward (chapter 10.1), but a possible reason for it could be that agents having common rural roots may be able to find a common "language" and communicate with relatively more ease in identifying possible clientele partners even in an enhanced market environment. On the other hand, in economies inhabited by citizens of different ethnic backgrounds, impersonal third-party mechanisms, private and public, seem to be invoked more frequently to enforce contracts, settle disputes, and establish themselves as a core market governance institution. Such differences may have wide-ranging impacts on the respective overall institutional arrangements through the net of complementarity/substitute relationships among governance mechanisms.

The government could have a certain influence, through the design of statutory laws and regulations, on the dynamic trajectory of overall institutional arrangements. The presence of an effective, formal third-party mechanism could expand the horizon of the trade domain by generating stable beliefs among potential traders in the enforceability of contracts and the safety of private property rights. But at the same time the government could be greatly limited in its ability to impose its own design of governance arrangements if they are inconsistent with the spontaneous order evolving in the trade domain. As suggested above, the effectiveness of the formal third-party mechanisms may lie primarily in their complementary support of private-order mechanisms but less so in entirely replacing them. Thus the role of the government in market governance may be viewed as endogenously determined by its overall arrangements rather than an autonomous determinant of it.[21]

The complementary nature of the government in the historical evolution of an overall arrangement may be illustrated by the development of escrow services in the United States. Escrow services initially evolved without direct government involvement. Cheated parties in real estate transactions could go before the courts for redress. However, the costs of doing so could be so high compared to the damages, that the cheated party might regard that redress through the court system was not an easy option. Escrow services spontaneously emerged as a device to cope with this problem, and initially none of escrow action was regulated or controlled by the government. In 1947, the California Legislature passed the Escrow Act with the consent of most of the companies handling escrows, "while there were no specific complaints directly against the companies generally" (Home 1952:242). Thus the act complemented the creditworthiness of the escrow companies to fulfill their particular role as a private third-party mechanism for transaction facilitation, while ensuring that the escrow agents would remain neutral and not fraudulent. There has been no parallel development of a private-order third-party mechanism in real estate transactions in Japan, although property rights in real estate become legally enforceable only when registered with the government registry office. Registration applications are often carried out by an agent of the buyer, a mortgage-financing bank, or a real estate agent. The underdevelopment of the private third-party mechanism in Japan can be attributable to the relative underdevelopment of competitive real estate markets, and vice versa.[22]

The Governance of Trade in Cyberspace

Despite the presence of a variety of overall institutional arrangements for market governance and the role of the government within them, one may suspect that the global integration of trade domains will eventually lead to their convergence to a unique mode of overall arrangement. More specifically, one could wonder whether or not the expansion of the anonymous trade domain will give rise to the universal preeminence of a formal third-party mechanism. However, the recent emergence of e-commerce appears to indicate a limit of the formal third-party mechanism.

As the domain of e-commerce expands beyond national boundaries, the question of which national law ought to be applied to a judgment on a possible breach of contract becomes problematical when there is inconsistency among them. For example, while the so-called moral rights in intellectual products are inalienable and sovereign under the French law, American, computer-made contracts require that those rights be waived when agents submit or upload digital contents to a contracting partner online (Radin 2000). One may hope that such inconsistency problems will eventually be resolved by the harmonization of laws across nations, as certainly they should.[23] Conflicting national laws and customs and uncertainty over territorial jurisdiction would make some of e-commercial potential unmaterialized.

However, there is always the question whether the international provision of substantive rules for e-commerce will be able to keep pace with the progress of technology applied to the e-commerce domain. At the formative stage of e-commerce, various experiments in the private domain may need to precede to it and be evolutionarily selected. Indeed, various private or quasi-public, third-party mechanisms have emerged in this domain. As indicated, there are information-mediating services such as auction web sites and certificate authorities that issue certification icons to creditworthy traders in cyberspace. Because the speed of communications among anonymous potential traders can be so fast in cyberspace, information on any misconduct by third parties or trading agents may be propagated quickly. This possibility may make private-order, third-party mechanisms effective on an unprecedented scale.[24] Also unique to e-commerce are technology-based "digital enforcement mechanisms" (Radin 2000), such as the digital rights management. They are programmed, for example, to prevent the delivery of a piece of digital content until payment is received, or to erase the content from the licensee's computer if unauthorized copying is attempted. Under these mechanisms, breach of contract does not occur but is technologically prevented. Further, as suggested in the end of chapter 2, even norms embedded in professional communities may play a role in defining and enforcing property rights in cyberspace. The open source "movement" promoted by the Free Software Foundation obliges each licensee of the Linux operating system to make public any improvements it applies to the source code. Because of its narrowing effect on copyright, the license is known as "copyleft."

As some of private-order practices becomes widely accepted, they may become de facto standards worldwide or may be even enacted into law (or they may not). Because of such possibilities there are incentives for industries to work out global e-commerce mechanisms by themselves in the concurrent absence of harmonization of national laws, especially those defining fundamental private rights and rules governing the private organizations supplying contract-enforcement infrastaructures. The emergent situation is somewhat reminiscent of the one prevailing prior to the emergence of nation states when many private-order mechanisms were experimented and competed.

Will history repeats itself? Namely will a stable, uniform, overall market governance arrangement eventually emerge, this time globally? The global integration of trade domains through digital communications and the evolutionary selection of workable governance mechanisms, complemented by efforts for the harmonization of law in the international polity domain, will undoubtedly have convergent effects on institutional arrangements for market governance on a global scale. However, later in part III, I will argue that intensified competition based on digitalized information may, because of its very nature of universal accessibility, enhance the economic values of tacit, uncodifiable knowledge, available only onsite or among the community of relevant agents (professionals, specialists), and that the best use of it may require the effective functioning of fitting (localized) mechanisms. However, the ability of a locality or a community of professionals to develop such a mechanism may be conditioned by the historical path, as well as the overall institutional arrangements beyond trade domains, in which they have been embedded. Thus the possibility that the complexity and diversity of overall arrangements for market governance will persist well into the digital age does not seem to be dismissed.

Appendix 3.1 Money as an Evolutive Convention

If two individuals need to exploit possible gains from exchange only through direct barter transaction, their opportunity for being able to do so would be greatly limited by the problem of Jevon's "double coincidence of wants" (1875)—the problem that, when two agents randomly meet, an agent not only has to have what the other want but also has to want what the other has. If money appears as an intermediary of exchange, such opportunity may be greatly enhanced. But why do the people accept money? Rather, in an economy where money has fully developed, the people come to face the constraint that "[m]oney buys goods and goods buy money; but goods do not buy goods" (Clower 1967).

There have been two main streams of thought on the circularity of money: the commodity theory of money and the fiat theory of money. The former regards that the money serves as a medium of exchange because of its own intrinsic value as a commodity. As well known, this view was systemized and integrated into a coherent theory of market exchange by great classical economists such as Adam Smith and David Ricardo, and adapted by Karl Marx to a labor theory of value. For them, the people accept money because of the intrinsic use value of materials of money (gold, silver) or the labor value embodied in it. In contrast, the fiat theory of money asserts that money does not need to have its own intrinsic value but that its circularity originates in the conscious design of an exogenous authority outside the exchange process, such as an agreement in the community, a decree of the ruler, a social contract among citizens in the natural state, or a legislation of the state.

There has been, however, another important view of money which regards money as a convention. According to this view, each of us accepts money because everybody else has done so in the past and is expected to do so in the future (Iwai 1993). Monetary exchange evolves and is sustained as an equilibrium in the exchange game based on, and continually confirming, such expectation. Once such expectation is shaken, the convention would frail and barter exchange would replace it. According to Aristotle, "[b]y a convention demand has come to be represented by money. Money (*nomisma*) exists not by nature but by custom (*nomos*), and it is our power to change its value or render it useless" (*Ethics* [1955]:184). Hume argued that property right "arises gradually, and acquires force by a slow progression, and by our repeated experience of the inconveniences of transgressing it." And "in like manner do gold and silver become the common measures of exchange, and are esteem'd sufficient payment for what is of a hundred times their value" (Hume 1739[1992]:490). The emergence of an international currency, such as dollar, that is not convertible any more, and that of electronic money which circulates in cyberspace, seem to suggest us to take this evolutionary view seriously.

Although not explicitly evolutionary, an interesting model that accounts for the nature of money as a convention is presented by Kiyotaki and Wright (1991).[25] They built a model in which money does not either provide direct utility, aid production, nor be a convertible claim to some other commodity. There is *no* external constraint to enforce the circularity of money and barter transactions are allowable. There is no difference in transaction costs between barter exchange and monetary exchange. Thus they exclude most factors employed by various theories of money to explain its raison d'être. Still they were able to show that money can function as money because the people follow the convention of monetary exchange.

In their model the double coincidence problem is formulated as follows: There is a continuum of agents who have diverse tastes and a continuum of differentiated goods. Each of the agents and each of the commodities are expressed by a point around a circle. For each agent there corresponds a commodity of ideal type, represented by the same point on the circle, from which he or she can derive the highest utility. According as the commodity which s/he is endowed with at random intervals or obtain through exchange becomes distant from the point representing the ideal one, his/her utility declines. Suppose that agents in the market are randomly matched in a pair over time at some fixed arrival rate. An exchange occurs, either using or not using the money, if and only if matched agents agree to do so. The agent chooses a strategy (a complete plan of choices) for determining whether to exchange with or without money in order to maximize the expected discounted utility from consumption net of transaction costs. Strategy will be conditional on beliefs on probabilities of exchange opportunity involving or not involving money. Outcome of this "monetary market exchange game" at each moment of time is described by the distribution of the population among traders with commodity and those with money. A rational expectation equilibrium of this game is defined as a sustainable symmetric strategy for all agents for which expectations are self-fulfilled and the distribution of the population becomes stationary.

Kiyotaki and Wright found that for any fixed supply of money sufficiently small relative to the size of the agents there is a monetary economy equilibrium in which the probability of money being accepted becomes one and money is universally accepted. However, monetary exchange is sustained only because the agents believe that others would always be willing to exchange commodity for money. Such beliefs are formed from their past experiences, and kept confirmed in equilibrium. If the quantity of monetary exceeds a certain size, no agent will accept money and barter transactions will prevail. The convention of monetary exchange collapse. It is suggestive that the sustainability of the monetary exchange convention and its coordinating role in resolving the double coincidence problem hinge on the stable control of the quantity of the money.

Their model does not explain how money emerges and came to be accepted by traders. Historical studies of money showed that at a primitive stage of commodity exchange often materials—such as heavy stones that were hard to carry and almost useless in themselves—were used as money, suggesting its conventional nature. It is true that in the medieval era when commodity exchange evolved to occur at a larger scale, money was often coins minted with precious metal and engraved with ruler's sign or seal. The engraving was the indication that they would be accepted as a means of tax payments, which reinforced the expectation that it would be generally accepted. Thus the circularity of money may not be taken as unilaterally imposed by the ruler, but bilaterally agreed upon between the ruler and its taxpayers-cum-traders. Also the last observation in the previous paragraph suggests that the government can destroy the circularity of money by violating its commitment to an upper limit on the quantity of money, with the result of threatening its own tax basis. In these senses, the money and the state co-evolve. It is not that the money circulates because of the authority of the government.

4 Organizational Architecture and Governance

[T]he term organization *refers to the complex pattern of communications and other relations in a group of human beings. This pattern provides to each member of the group much of the information, assumptions, goals, and attitudes that enter into his decisions, and provides him also with a set of stable and comprehensible expectations as to what the other members of the group are doing and how they will react to what he says and does. The sociologists call this pattern a "role system"; to most of us it is more familiarly known as an "organization."*
—Herbert A. Simon, *Administrative Behavior* (1957:xvi)

Opportunities for commodity exchange between potential sellers and buyers were enhanced by the emergence of merchants. Although the merchants may have had several economic functions,[1] their goal was undoubtedly simply to buy goods and sell them for higher prices and thereby to profit. Likewise the origin of the factory system might have been diverse, but there is no doubt that the primary motive of its first organizers was analogous to the "capitalist" pursuit of the merchants: they sought to "buy" labor services and other factors of production and "sell" their output for higher prices and thereby to profit. This historical development had a profound impact on economists' conceptualizations of the firm. The ability of the firm to transform the inputs into the output is recognized only in the form of a technological black box (the production function), so the firm in this view is nothing but an intermediary agent in the market-exchange domain. However, as we already hinted in chapter 1.4, the firm has various aspects having other domain characteristics.

This chapter tries to focus on aspects of the modern firm in the market economy that may not be simply subsumed under employment contracts, that is, the attribute of organization as an information system distinguished from the price mechanism and its governance. In market exchange domains, agents coordinate their activities leading to the reallocation of privately owned goods primarily through the medium of prices. In organizational domains, agents coordinate their activities through a much more rich media of communication. Consequently organizational architecture, viewed as a coordination mechanism or an information system, becomes complex and diverse. The primary task of this and the next chapters is to ask how organizational architecture can be different, why different types of organizational architecture evolve, how they can be governed, and what their implications are.

The questions asked in this chapter closely relate to one of the most celebrated questions in modern economics, first raised and answered by Coase: "Why does the firm emerge in the market economy?" Coase's answer was: There are "costs of using the price mechanism" which may be reduced or eliminated by entrepreneurial coordination. Specifically he points to two kinds of costs: the cost of "discovering what the relevant prices are" (Coase 1937:390), and the cost that may be saved by making "a long-term contract for the supply of some articles or services" (ibid.:391) instead of short-term successive contracts. In the last three decades or so, economists have been elaborating on Coase's basic insight and debating over the question of what the most important parameter is for determining transaction cost-saving by the firm. However, the focus of the debate seems to have been directed toward the implications and ramifications of the "long-term" nature of contracts leading to the formation of the firm: the aspect of the firm as an agent in the market exchange domain.[2] Instead, our primary focus in this and the next chapters is on the aspect of the firm that realizes the first type of cost-saving, namely organizational coordination substituting for market coordination.

Individuals are limited in their scope of attention, in their ability to monitor the environment and calculate optimal decision choices, as well as in their range of activity (Simon 1982). Organizations may thus be considered a device to partially overcome these individual limits by "division of cognitive labor" (Williamson 1999). Organizations can divide managerial, developmental, engineering, production and marketing tasks among organizational participants of different types and accordingly expand the scope of information processing regarding production environments. Organizations can utilize dispersed information more effectively—"the knowledge of particular time and circumstances available to men on the spot," according to Hayek's well-known expression (1945). They can do so by developing appropriate organizational rules and procedures, routines, and norms regulating communication and decision-making.[3] However, the sum of individuals with bounded rationality cannot create an entity having perfect rationality and competence. The implication is that even leaving aside incentive problems, there will be no organization that can perfectly process and utilize information regarding its continually changing environment (marketing and technological) to realize the first-best outcome. Thus there can be diverse ways of organizing information collection, transmission, utilization (decision-making), and accumulation among organizational participants to coordinate their actions; their relative informational efficiency may vary, depending on the nature of organizational environments. This possibility calls for a comparative study of the firm viewed as a non-price-mediated coordination mechanisms.[4]

Economists, including Coase (1937) and Williamson (1975, 1985), conceptualize the basic nature of a mechanism of organizational coordination as a hierarchy. Although accurate as a generic characterization, this encompassing conceptualization may miss some structural differences across firms that are relevant and have significant implications for comparative institutional analysis. Within the general framework of a hierarchy, different kinds of information can flow vertically, upward and downward, as well as horizontally, within individual firms. Organizational architecture viewed as an information system can become diverse and complex, conditioned by various factors including the state of information and communications technology, available types of human assets (as information-processing mental programs), modes used for codifying economically valuable information, structures of information-connectedness among task units, and so forth. Further, similar factors may facilitate the emergence of various types of quasi-organizational coordination across firms or within a group of firms in the trade domain, distinct from the Walrasian price mechanism. Therefore the first task of this chapter is to develop an analytical taxonomy of organizational and quasi-organizational architecture that is meaningful for, and will facilitate, a comparative institutional analysis. We also identify a few basic environmental conditions that may have impacts on comparative informational efficiency of different types of organizational architecture.

In making comparison of organizational architecture, we first assume that organizations are "teams" in the sense of Marschak and Radner (1972), composed of members having a common objective function. It amounts to not taking explicitly the game aspects of the organization into consideration. However, as the quote from H. Simon at the beginning of this chapter indicates, organizational architecture may not be viable unless stable expectations among the organizational participants are sustained, letting them rely on each other's decision choices on a relational basis. In other words, organizational architecture needs to become institutionalized (recall our conceptualization of an institution as a system of shared beliefs). An inquiry in that direction requires the explicit introduction of human elements into discussion. The last section of this chapter takes up this task.

The previous chapter dealt with mechanisms of governance in the trade domain. Personal and market exchanges can become mutually beneficial only when various governance structures sustain stable expectations among traders that enable them to rely on relational or impersonal exchange. By the same token, organizational activities can be coordinated for an organizational purpose only when some governance structure can generate and sustain stable expectations among organizational participants that constrain the misuse of human assets (shirking, embezzlement, negligence, noncooperation, sabotage, recklessness, etc.). Just as our discussion of market governance started with the case of primitive, two-party personal exchange domains, our discussion of organizational governance in this chapter also starts with primitive, two-party organizational domains without (financial) market interfaces. The purpose of this exercise is to identify governance issues unique to respective organizational architectural structures and associated human asset types. Specifically, we will examine how some basic types of organizational architecture can raise distinct governance issues, calling for respective solutions that may not be resolved entirely in a closed manner. However, we will be able to develop more complete arguments directed toward their solutions in part III only after preparing more conceptual and analytical tools to deal with market-organization linkages.

4.1   Organizational Building Blocks: Hierarchical Decomposition, Information Assimilation, and Encapsulation[5]

Any organizational architecture fundamentally exhibits a hierarchical structure in the way in which interrelated activities are modularized into disparate task units, and are arranged in a "tree structure" in terms of superordinate and subordinate relationships. In order to contribute to an organizational objective, the levels of activities, as well as the attributes and quantities of products, of the constituent task units need to be adjusted in a coordinated manner. Also the constituent task units may be competing in the use of scarce organizational assets (human, physical and financial). One of the important tasks of the management is to allocate scarce organizational resources among constituent task units knit into a complex web of technological and informational relationships and provide a framework for their organizational coordination. In this sense any organization is engaged in central planning.

However, with an ex ante plan alone the organization cannot compete effectively in competitive markets and under changing technology. It needs to continually adjust the activity of each task unit to changing environments in order to remain competitive (e.g., if demands for a product model are higher than expected, their production, and accordingly that of the modular parts, needs to be accelerated; if an unexpected breakthrough in technology is announced elsewhere, the resource allocation to an ongoing, in-house, development project may need to be reassessed; if a machine on the assembly line breaks down, it should be immediately decided whether or not to stop the entire line). However, information processing regarding the evolving market, technological, and operational environments of an organizational domain cannot be completely centralized in an effective manner, as the experiences of centralized planned economies amply indicate. Indeed, many corporate firms of the present day face much more complex information-processing requirements than most of the old centralized economies. Nor can information processing be decomposed simply in a way that is congruent to the division of operational tasks. Some economically valuable information may be better utilized immediately at the site where it becomes available. Some information may be better shared among different task units to attain superior organizational coordination, while other information may be better processed in parallel and utilized independently so that task units will not simultaneously commit the same fatal mistake. Or, even if the sharing of information among task units is potentially economically valuable, there may be a significant disparity in their information-processing capacities, making joint information processing potentially costly. Alternatively, if the uncertainty of the environment is very great, duplicated information processing by multiple task units may become potentially valuable for leaving future options open. Thus, within a general framework of hierarchy, there can be a complex division of information-processing activity (cognitive labor) together with the division of operating tasks.

Information processing can be aided by the development of information and communication technology (e.g., computers, networks, sensors), and this is increasingly happening. However, the elements of human assets, namely "programs—skills, if you prefer—that in the past have been frozen into the design of machines but largely stored in minds of men" (Simon 1982:107), remain essential within any organization. The capacities of such programs, or information-processing capacities in short, are not unlimited, however. Also there may be a trade-off between the benefits from information processing and the costs arising from diverting an agent's attention away from production operations (actions) as such, although there may be some complementarity between the two kinds of activities (e.g., learning by doing). Further, agents may differ in the types of information-processing capacities they possess. "At any given moment an individual is a bundle of abilities and accumulated information. He may easily find it cheaper to open certain information channels rather than others in ways connected with these abilities and their knowledge" (Arrow 1974:41). Thus there can be variety in the modes of division of information processing across organizations that may be conditioned by the technological characteristics of internalized tasks, by their external environments, and by the nature of organizational human assets available internally and/or externally. We refer to the distribution of information-processing activities across organizational subunits ("the division of cognitive labor") within an organization as *organizational architecture*. Associated with it is the division of operational tasks, but we focus on the information-systemic aspect of the organization.

The primary task of this section is, as already stated, to identify several important types of organizational (and quasi-organizational) architecture of recent vintage and discuss their fits with emergent technological and market environments. We may envision organizational architecture as a set of vertical information connectedness between the superordinate and its subordinates and horizontal information connectedness among subordinated task units. We first note that there can be only three generic modes of information-connectedness in either vertical or horizontal relationships. Then we construct types of organizational architecture of practical relevance using these generic modes as building blocks.

Suppose that there are only two elementary task units, denoted by T_1 and T_2, in a generic (sub-)organization domain. At this stage, they should be taken as abstract entities, although it does not do any harm to imagine them either as the management unit and the operational unit, the R&D unit and the manufacturing unit, two work-shops, two work teams, or two individual tasks for illustrative purposes. Suppose that the two units can jointly produce a certain amount of organizational payoff, using common (and separate) resources. The payoff depends on the configuration of the decision choices of the task units, x_1 and x_2, as well as on the state of environments, represented by a vector of stochastic parameters. Suppose that the choice variables, x_1 and x_2, are aligned (continuously or discretely) on one-dimensional domains. Each choice variable represents the intensity of activity, the level of an output, or the specification of attributes of output design (e.g., analogue vs. digital attribute in device design).

Let us imagine that before the activities leading to the production of organizational payoff begin, the organization has prior estimates of the distribution of the environmental parameters, possibly formed from experiences in the past and/or formal knowledge. From this prior knowledge the optimal decision choice for each task that would maximize the expected payoff is derived and made known to the relevant task units as a plan, a manual, etc. This ex ante "optimal" decision choice without any further knowledge about environments may be referred to as a plan or a standard, depending on context.

After the production begins, particular parametric values of environments are realized. Then, if the organization can monitor the emergent states of environmental parameters and adjust its choice variables accordingly instead of implementing the plan as it is, the organizational payoff may be enhanced. However, the monitoring of environments by any task unit cannot be perfect because of its limited ability to process the environmental information. The question then is how to distribute the tasks of information processing between the two task units within the organization and what ex post choice rules should be applied to observation(s) at their level. This design problem provides a basis for the design of overall organizational architecture. There are three important factors to be taken into consideration in this basic design problem:

• The emergent values of environmental parameters will affect the (marginal) contributions of decision choices of the task units to the organizational payoff in different ways and the planned choices need to be adjusted accordingly. Suppose that the environment can be decomposed into three segments, each represented by E_s, E_1, and E_2. The states of E_s and E_1 affect the productivity condition at T_1, and the states of

E_s and E_2 affect that at T_2. We refer to E_s as the systemic segment of the environment, and E_1 and E_2 as idiosyncratic segments. We assume that any posterior information regarding the idiosyncratic segments is Hayekian in the following sense: they can be observed only by the relevant task units, and observed values of environmental parameters cannot be transmitted ex post from the observing unit to the other with precision within the time period in which planned decisions may be revised. Namely they are "the knowledge of the particular circumstances of time and place," only available to men and women on the spot (Hayek 1945:521).

· The overall payoff may also depend on the configuration of decision choices of both task units so that their choices need to be coordinated. For example, when the outputs of one task unit are used as inputs of the other, a cost from excess inventory holdings or inventory shortages may be incurred if the activity levels of both units are not adjusted in the same direction (technological complementarity); if the decision choices of both units are adjusted in the same direction, the use of organizational resources may be congested (technological externalities); the design attributes of outputs of both tasks may need to be compatible to form a consistent product-system (attribute complementarity), or alternatively, may be better differentiated to meet diverse outside demands or to keep future options open (attribute substitutes). When complementarity relationships (technological and attribute) dominate substitute/externality relationships in the Edgeworth sense (i.e., the marginal payoff of an increase in one decision variable could be enhanced by a simultaneous increase in the other decision variable), we say that the two tasks are *complementary*. Otherwise, they are said to be *competitive* (or substitutes, depending on context).[6]

· How much decision variables should be adjusted ex post in response to an observed environmental change depends on the *precision* of the observation.[7] If the precision is low, overreacting to the observed environmental change may have an adverse impact on organizational payoffs. The precision of an observation may depend on the information-processing capacity of the observing unit (or units), the information-processing technology available to it, as well as its effort intensity in information-processing activity. Also we assume that there is a fixed cost involved for each task unit to switch its observation between different segments of environments.

Since idiosyncratic segments of environments can be observed only by relevant task units, there are the following three—and only these three—*generic modes* of information connectedness among the two task units, depending on how the information-processing task regarding the systemic segment of environments is distributed among the two task units. For the moment we leave unspecified the action choice rule for each task unit to apply when transforming ex post information into its own decision choice.

1. *Hierarchical decomposition (HD)*. The systemic environmental parameter is observed only by T_1. T_1 adjusts the level of its own choice variable x_1 according to its own environmental estimates including that regarding its own idiosyncratic environmental parameter. T_2 is informed of the decision (or T_1's observation of the systemic environment parameter) with some communication errors (e.g., communication noise, reception errors), and adjusts its own choice variable.

2. *Information assimilation (IA)*. The systemic segment of environments is monitored by both task units. Suppose further that their observations are correlated so that they form an *assimilated* cognitive representation (posterior distribution) of the systemic segment of environments (in the analysis below we assume for simplicity that their observations are perfectly correlated so that their posterior distributions are the same). They can do this in two ways. Both units extract the same codified data from a common digital information network open to the environment, or alternatively, they pool a set of (uncodified) samples they generated separately from the environment and collectively construct a joint posterior estimate of its subjective distribution from those samples. We refer to the former as *network-induced* information sharing and the latter as *contextual* information sharing in the sense that information sharing is accomplished in the context of specific units connection.

3. *Information encapsulation (IE)*. Both systemic and idiosyncratic segments of environment are observed independently by both task units. Thus their observation errors are assumed to be uncorrelated so that their cognitive representations (posterior distribution) of the environment are differentiated. We refer to this generic mode as the information encapsulation mode because the outcome of information processing by each unit is "hidden" from the others. There is a degenerate case of this mode in which both task units process only respective idiosyncratic-environmental parameters and the systemic-environmental parameter is not observed by either of them.

Figure 4.1 shows these three modes. Since they are only generic, real organizations are thought to nest these generic modes, vertically as well as horizontally, in diverse ways. However, before delving into such complexities and identifying and relating types of nested architecture to real world organizations, it is useful to examine the basic informational-efficiency properties of these generic information modes.

As mentioned above, the precision of observations by the task units depends partially on the effort levels of their information-processing activities (or the effort levels

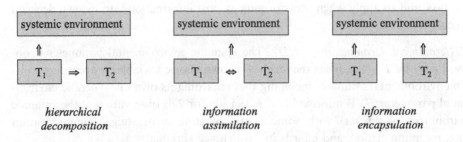

hierarchical   *information*   *information*
decomposition   *assimilation*   *encapsulation*

Figure 4.1
Three generic modes of information connectedness between task units, by way of ⇑ environment monitoring (information processing), ⇒ information flow (command), ⇔ information sharing. The observations of idiosyncratic segments of environments by relevant units are not shown because they are identical for all three modes.

in their investment in information-processing capacities). The question of how this level is determined is an incentive (governance) issue of organizational architecture, which must be dealt with by each information mode in its own distinct way. We will deal with this issue in section 4.3. In the remaining part of this section, we will set this issue aside and assume that the precision of observations is solely determined by given levels of information-processing capacities of task units and the information-processing technology available to them. Now, as mentioned above, suppose that in each mode the respective observations are transformed into decision choices, or to put it differently, revisions of the standard choices, according to a rule specified ex ante for each task unit. We call this rule the decision rule. If there exists a set of ex ante decision rules for mode M under which the organizational payoff is expected to be greater for some classes of environments than when under mode N with any set of decision rules, then we say that mode M is *informationally more efficient* than mode N for this class of environments. These rules may be designed analytically, found accidentally, or simply have evolved from practice; at this stage we are not concerned with how they came about. It is sufficient to note that organizations with better rules will be more likely to survive competition so that the outcome of the competition would be as if organizations design the "second-best" decision rules, given the bounded rationality of the units in information processing.

The following propositions provide benchmarks for three-way comparisons of the information efficiency of the generic modes under the second-best choice rules.[8]

PROPOSITION 4.1 (Cremer) Suppose that the precision of information processing is identical for two task units across the three modes. If these tasks are competitive, the information-encapsulation mode is informationally more efficient than the information-assimilation mode. If they are complementary, the opposite is true.[9]

Intuitively, if two tasks are complementary, it is always desirable to adjust the choice variables of both units in a coordinated manner (i.e., in the same direction) in response to changing environments to maximize payoffs (minimize the cost arising from coordination failure). This objective can be better achieved by assimilating the information utilized for decision choices by both agents. If the opposite is true, it is better to hide the information utilized by each unit so that a correlated adjustment of choice variables can be avoided. Otherwise, the risk of over- or underutilization of internal resources due to the inevitable imprecision of environmental observations would be amplified. The same reasoning can be applied to the comparison of the information encapsulation and hierarchical decomposition modes. In the hierarchical mode, information about the environment is assimilated because of the exclusive information processing and its dissemination by T_1, albeit subjected to communication noise and perception errors of the recipient unit in the process of hierarchical communications.

PROPOSITION 4.2   If two tasks are complementary, the hierarchical-decomposition mode is informationally more efficient than the information-encapsulation mode, provided that the communication costs between the two units in that mode are not too large.

For a comparison of the information-assimilation mode and the hierarchical-decomposition mode, we need to introduce a possible difference in the distribution of the information-processing capacity across two task units in each mode. Suppose that the collective information-processing capacity in the (tacit) information-assimilation mode is the average of both units' individual capacities.[10] Face-to-face communications and consensus-building in tacit information assimilation require time and effort. It is intuitive that two-way communications and joint posterior estimates among units of unequal capacities are more costly relative to exclusive information processing and its dissemination by the unit of higher capacity, if the hierarchical communication cost from T_1 to T_2 is not too large. Thus we may claim the following.

PROPOSITION 4.3   If there is a sufficient disparity of information-processing capacity among two task units, the hierarchical-decomposition mode is informationally more efficient than the (contextual) information-assimilation mode, provided that hierarchical communication in the former is sufficiently precise. On the other hand, if there is a significant degree of similarity in the information-processing capacity of two units, and their communications costs in pooling sample observations and constructing a common perception about the environment are relatively low, the opposite is the case.

The following proposition essentially deals with the comparative merits of the network-induced information-assimilation mode and should be intuitively clear:

PROPOSITION 4.4 Whenever the use of digital communications technology can reduce the disparity of information-processing capacity across task units, the relative informational efficiency of the hierarchical-decomposition mode vis-à-vis the network-induced information-assimilation mode diminishes when two tasks are complementary.

So far we have not taken into consideration the possible fixed cost involved in the switching of an observation by a task unit between the systemic and idiosyncratic segments of environments. Such costs may be due to the required training, dispersion of attention, setup of the monitoring apparatus and stage, and so forth. In this situation, if the variability of either systemic or idiosyncratic-environmental parameters is small relative to that of the other, it may be informationally more efficient for both or either task unit to specialize in monitoring that particular segment of the environment. When the variability of the systemic-environmental parameter (measured by its prior variance) is large (alternatively, small) relative to those of idiosyncratic-environmental parameters, we say the environments that the task units face are statistically correlated. Then, the following proposition holds. It is intuitively clear, but it has interesting implications in a subsequent comparative analysis.

PROPOSITION 4.5 If the statistical correlation between the environments of the constituent task units is very high, the hierarchical decomposition becomes informationally most efficient, provided that their tasks are complementary. On the other hand, if the statistical correlation is very low, the information-encapsulation mode (in which only the idiosyncratic-environmental parameters are processed) is informationally most efficient regardless of complementarity/substitute relationships among the tasks.

The results are summarized in figure 4.2. Thus, when information processing regarding the systemic and idiosyncratic segments of environments are equally important for constituent task units that are mutually complementary, the information-assimilation mode is expected to be informationally more efficient than the other modes. But this mode needs to be supported by the development of communication technology or the relative homogeneity of the information-processing capacity between task units. The information-encapsulation mode is expected to be informa-

statistical correlation	low		high
tasks			
complementary	information encapsulation	information assimilation	hierarchical decomposition
substitute	information encapsulation		

Figure 4.2
Distribution of the informationally most efficient mode

tionally more efficient when the environments of task units are statistically independent or their decision variables are substitutes. The hierarchical decomposition is expected to be informationally more efficient when the environments of mutually complementary task units are highly correlated and there is a significant disparity in information-processing competence between the task units. These comparative results provide only basic benchmarks.

4.2 Types of Organizational Architecture

First, imagine that task unit T_2 in the organization can be further decomposed into two subunits, T_{2a} and T_{2b}. We may now envision that T_1 refers to the superordinate of the organization, performing the managerial tasks, and that the T_2's are its subordinates performing operational tasks. We then can differentiate the basic information architecture of the organization by the ways in which the two generic modes are combined: one representing the vertical mode of information-connectedness between T_1 and the T_2's and the other representing the horizontal mode between T_{2a} and T_{2b}. The former deals with information processing of the systemic segment of the environment relevant to the productivity of both T_1 and the T_2's, while the latter that of the subsystem segment relevant to the productivity at the T_2's level only. We assume that the idiosyncratic segments of the environment that may affect T_1, T_{2a}, or T_{2b} independently, can be processed only by relevant units.

Denote the hierarchical-decomposition mode by HD, the information-assimilation mode by IA, and the information-encapsulation mode by IE. Since the the primary task of the superordinate in any organization architecture is coordination based on the knowledge of the systemic environment (recall the basic conceptualization of the organizational domain in chapter 1), we expect that the vertical relationships are either *HD* or *IA* but not *IE*. Otherwise, disorganization will occur. As for the horizontal relationships, either *IA* or *IE* can be observed. *HD* induces only vertical relationships, resulting in a three-tiered hierarchy. Thus, as long as we confine our attention to two-tiered architecture, we get only four possible prototypes: *HD–IE*, *HD–IA*, *IA–IA*, and *IA–IE*, where the first item in each of the following prototypes refers to the vertical relationship and the second to the horizontal relationship. We further distinguish two types of information-assimilation mode: *network-induced* and *contextual*, denoted by *IA(n)* and *IA(c)*, respectively. The former refers to information sharing through the formal intraorganizational network of communications that carry digitalized information, while the latter refer to information sharing involving face-to-face communications as an important, if not exclusive, means. Also there may be cases in which a vertical or horizontal relationship is characterized as a mixture of two information-connectedness modes, one primary and the other subsidiary (We denote this mixture of two modes by indicating a primary mode followed by a subsidiary mode in "[.].")

Then we identify the following types of organizational (and quasi-organizational) architecture. When we discuss a practical example for each architecture, it may be envisioned that a firm, or a group of firms, nests the relevant architecture in a multi-layered hierarchy with an unspecified span (number of subordinates) of control. However, it is to be kept in mind that the following taxonomy is made only in reference to the information-systemic characteristic of organizations, abstracted from other important dimensions, such as governance, market-conditioned contracts, and organizational cultures. We discuss their relationships in section 4.3 and later in part III.

HD–IE: (Decision-Integrated) Functional Hierarchies [FH]

In this architecture, T_1 exclusively monitors the systemic environment and adapts its choice variable accordingly. T_1 sends its decision as a common message to each subordinate, who receives it with independently distributed noise. The T_2's observe the subsystem environment common to their level independently of each other, as well as the respective idiosyncratic segments of the environment.[11] Thus observations and decision choices are entirely encapsulated within cach task unit at the T_2-level, while decisions at the T_1-level perform the sole coordinating role. We refer to this bifurcated hierarchical decomposition mode as a (decision-integrated) *functional hierarchy* because each unit performs a specialized function, whether it is a coordination task by T_1 or specific operating tasks by the T_2's. The functional hierarchy is the architecture that underlies most economic modeling of the internal organization of the firm.[12] Since there is no direct, horizontal information-connectedness among the T_2's, this system works better if complementarities between the operating tasks at the T_2-level are not strong and the variance of subsystem segments of information is smaller in comparison to those of idiosyncratic segments (i.e., the environments of subordinates are not statistically correlated). The former requirement can be achieved, for example, when both operating tasks are modularized so that they can be executed without close continual coordination. The latter requirement may be satisfied by the design of the work organization in which each operating task is made engineering-autonomous from the other. If their tasks are technologically interrelated through input-output relationships, the cross-task impacts of common stochastic factors may be mitigated by holding a sufficient inventory stock of intermediate products.[13]

A quintessential historical example of functional hierarchies can be found in the so-called American system of manufacture that developed in the U.S. machinery industry in the early to midnineteenth century. At the Crystal Palace Exhibition of 1851 in London, American manufacturers, particularly firearm manufacturers, amazed British spectators by their ability to mass-produce firearms and repair them with precision and speed, using the method of assembling interchangeable standard parts. By then British master gun-makers had typically possessed neither factories nor workshops and arranged to acquire components from specialized handicraftsmen who worked at home or in a more sizable workshop establishment (Rosenberg 1969:34). The British House of Commons sent the Committee on the Machinery of the United States to study the sources of the emergence of the United States as a world economic power, and its report made in 1875 summarized its findings as a distinct American system of manufacture.[14] In this system the owner of the firm controlled a two-tier functional hierarchy, in which each job specialized in the production of interchangeable parts with the support of special purpose machines. By decomposing a product system into standardized modular parts, attribute-complementarities between tasks were dealt with by the adjustments of inventory, while individual workers were concentrated within their specialized tasks. The focus of the system was more on the smooth coordination of production tasks rather than direct hierarchical monitoring of individual workers. Workers at each task were easily replaceable by others properly trained for it. The American system of mass production, or the Fordist model, that developed later in the 1920s inherited the essential information-architectural characteristic of the American system of manufacture and is thus considered its direct descendant. When product systems became more complex, as in automobiles, the degree of specialization in operational tasks needed to be made ever finer. To coordinate an increasingly larger number of specialized tasks, they were arranged into subgroups according to the degree of statistical correlation of their subsystem technological environments. For each subgroup in which subsystem environments were common, there was an intermediate superordinate specialized in information processing for that segment of the environment to coordinate the tasks in that subgroup. Intermediate superordinates were then controlled by a higher-ranked superordinate who processed information regarding the wider systemic environment of relevance. Thus multilayer hierarchies ensued, but their essential information-architectural characteristics remained as nested HD–IE modes.

It is well known, and therefore further elaboration is not necessary here, that as the size of firms became large, an organizational innovation called the M-form organization (Chandler 1977; Williamson 1975) emerged to replace the functionally based, unitary organizational form (U-form). In the M-form organization, the corporate headquarters controlled multidivisions through financial means, while each division internalized its own functional hierarchy, keeping information necessary for divisional operational decisions encapsulated from each other. In this way the cost of hierarchical communications that could multiply with increasing numbers of layers was avoided.[15]

$HD–IA(n)$: Network-Integrated Functional Hierarchies

As the ability of supplying a variety of products in response to emerging competitive market conditions becomes a crucial factor determining the competitiveness of the firm, the number and kinds of products multiply. Then economies of scale realized by (decision-integrated) functional hierarchies start to diminish and the costs of inventory holding can become high. Also, in the absence of horizontal communications, impacts of continually changing technological and market environments can reduce the information efficiency of decision-integrated functional hierarchies. Specifically, in the presence of a strong complementarity and high statistical correlation of environments at the T_2-level, the information sharing among task units at that level becomes indispensable for coordinating their decision choices. The development of communications and information-processing technology can respond to these problems. On one hand, T_1 can design and provide a formal, organization-specific, communications network for the task units at the T_2-level to have access to common information jointly relevant to them (proposition 4.4). On the other hand, by grouping together statistically correlated tasks and relegating them to a single unit, it can remove an intermediate coordinating unit that is specialized in making subsystem environment information assimilated among separate units. Such broadening of the range of tasks by a single unit at the T_2-level can be facilitated by the use of information-processing technology, such as computers or robots. As a result the span of control of functional hierarchies (the number of subordinates that a superordinate supervises) can become large and its depth (the number of levels) can be cut short.

For example, IBM running more than forty research centers and a global network of sales and manufacturing bases worldwide developed the Development and Production Record System (DPPS) and the Corporate Central File (CCF) in the 1970s for intraorganizational information sharing. Through CCF, engineers had reference code numbers assigned to the parts they had developed so that those parts would become identifiable and usable anywhere in the world within the corporation at any time, using up-to-date design specifications. When engineers wanted to check if suitable parts were available for their pilot products, they accessed DPPS, specified their requirements for size, function, material, cost, and so on, and conducted a search. Thus an R&D lab in Europe that was developing a new product system could communicate with a manufacturing site with specific expertise in South America for contracting a supply of specific parts. By keeping the basic feature of functional hierarchies in a more elaborate way, network-integrated functional hierarchies were able to respond to environmental change (technological and market) more quickly. However, the kinds of information shared at the T_2-level were subjected to the prior design of the information system and the direction of R&D was constrained by the standardized information available in-house.

HD–IA(c): Hierarchical-Controlled Teams

In this architecture the vertical relationship between the T_1 and the T_2's is regulated by the hierarchical-decomposition mode, but at the T_2-level there is information assimilation among constituent units regarding their common subsystem environment. A primitive example would be the truck loading team given by the seminal Alchian-Demsetz paper (1972). The task of the team can be directed by the boss, but the members of the team need to coordinate their actions spontaneously in the work process to accomplish the planned target. Informationally homomorphic architecture can be found in an organization producing a highly sophisticated, one-time product through the coordination of specialized talents under the direction of a superordinate taking eminent leadership. Such architecture is somewhat analogous to a sports team in which players' actions are coordinated on a continual, ad hoc basis within the strategic framework set by the head coach. Examples of organizational architecture of this kind can be found in teams engaged in creative team work, such as in film-making, sophisticated application of software design, or developmental design work for highly sophisticated products.[16] This architectural type is effective if the attribute or technological complementarities among component tasks are high in order to generate an impeccable product, even though each task may require highly specialized operating skills. Further, as their subsystem technological environments can involve a new, nonrepeatable situation each time, information assimilation remains more or less tacit.

$HD[IA(c)]-IA(c)$: Horizontal Hierarchies [HH]

In this architecture the T_1 and T_2's tacitly assimilate their information regarding the systematic environment to a significant extent within a general hierarchical framework (management-subordinates division). At the T_2-level, operational task units are engaged in contextual information sharing regarding their common subsystem environments. We call this architecture a *horizontal hierarchy* in the sense that bidirectional information flows extend to the vertical relationship. Accordingly, decision choices (strategic decisions) at the T_1-level involve an element of consensus or joint decision-making.

As is fairly well known, intensive information assimilation—vertical and horizontal—throughout the organization, characterizes one essential aspect of the stylized Japanese firms.[17] Management decisions are often made after communication and negotiations with relevant constituent units, a practice referred to as "root-wrapping." An often-cited practice exemplifying a high degree of horizontal information-connectedness is the so-called *kanban* system, which facilitates the "just-in-time" delivery of modular parts from the supply to the user units through their direct communications without the intermediary of an inventory-control office.[18] The practice of job rotation on the shop floor (in the case of blue-collar workers), as well as across offices (in the case of white-collar workers), helps the workers become familiar with various facets of the work process and thus nurtures their collective ability of problem-solving in emergent local irregularities, such as machine breakdowns and defective product parts.

This type of information architecture is able to coordinate tasks that are strongly attribute-complementary as well as statistically correlated (as in automobile assembly or the steel manufacturing process). Also it is relatively more conducive to continual process innovation through information interactions across R&D, manufacturing, and marketing tasks than product-design innovation that involves conceptual breakthroughs (Aoki and Rosenberg 1989; Aoki 1990). However, the information load in this kind of architecture can become heavy as an organization expands. This is one reason why Japanese manufacturing firms tend to rely more on outside suppliers by spinning off some tasks to them, which leads to the architecture discussed below.

Also, as communication technology develops, the comparative advantage of this architecture in the presence of strong complementarities may decline relatively vis-à-vis the network-integrated functional hierarchies.

$HD[IA]–IE[IA]$: Participatory Hierarchies

This is the architecture characterized by cross-border information sharing within the general framework of a functional hierarchy (task specialization). As suggested by proposition 4.3, if the information-processing capacity of the T_2-level is relatively high, then it is informationally more efficient to feed their observations regarding the systemic segment of the environment into decision-making at the T_1-level. Also, the increasing degree of complementarity among operational task units at the T_2-level necessitates horizontal information sharing. Thus we may call functional hierarchies supplemented by a sizable degree of vertical and horizontal information assimilation *participatory hierarchies*.

Conventional wisdom holds that the stylized German firm—G-firm—is a sharp contrast to the stylized Japanese firm—J-firm—in terms of work organization. In the former the workers specialize in particular tasks based on occupational qualification certificates portable across firms, whereas in the latter the workers are engaged in intrafirm job rotations so that the range of their skills tends to be broad and firm-specific. However, as Koike (1988, 1994) emphasizes, the role of rotation and teamwork at the Japanese factory was never intended to make workers' skills homogeneous but rather to enhance their problem-solving capabilities—collective and individual—by facilitating their deeper understanding of the nature of the work processes they are engaged in. By the same token, an authoritative analysis based on the detailed field work of German firms compared to French firms revealed that the Germans certified as skilled workers were actually capable of filling a large number of posts in one firm. It also points out that "since not only production foremen but also many technicians, engineers, and managers began their careers with training as skilled workers, this system of socialization establishes a broad professional community and tends to facilitate communication and cooperation among employees occupying different positions in a firm's hierarchy" (Maurice et al. 1986:93). Further, in response to competitive challenges from Japanese firms, the number of occupational categories in Germany has been substantially reduced in recent years, and in practice the overlapping of occupational demarcations have been enhanced at the workplace to facilitate horizontal coordination and communications among workers within different occupational categories. A sharp academic observer summarizes the situation in this way:

By the late 1980s qualification architecture and work organization in Germany were moving away from Taylorism fast in a direction prefigured by the earlier German deviations from the Taylorisit basic model: ... achievement of flexibility through skill overlaps and horizontal and vertical integration of skill profiles; reintegration of conception and execution above all by expanding the content of occupations, and only on this basis by introducing "group work"; and reduction of managerial supervision and organizational pressure by assignment of broader responsibilities to more broadly trained workers.   (Streeck 1996:161)

One cannot fail to be struck by the similarity of the argument advanced some time ago by Koike on the Japanese work model. Also vertical communications between management and the workers have been formalized in the German factory through the machinery of consultative work councils. Thus, in terms of information architecture, the German firm can be characterized as having aspects of both horizontal and functional hierarchies, entailing some modicum of similarity between the Japanese and German firms than was conventionally thought.[19] A difference between the two is that information assimilation in German firms is achieved using a higher degree of codified messages exchanged through formal organizational apparatuses such as the work councils, while the Japanese firms rely more on the exchange of tacit knowledge through organizational conventions. Another difference between the two can be found in the area of corporate governance. Later, in chapter 11, we discuss why this difference has co-evolved.

Let us move to quasi-organizational information architecture among a cluster of firms that is connected by more dense information exchanges than under the neo-classical price mechanism. There can be many varieties, and below we only touch on three types that we will refer to, or take up for detailed analysis, later in the book.

$HD[IA(c)]$–IE: Suppliers Keiretsu

In this architecture T_1 and each unit at the T_2-level share information regarding the systemic segment of the environment to a certain degree within a general framework of a functional hierarchy. Between units at the T_2-level, information is basically encapsulated. The Japanese suppliers *keiretsu* in the automobile industry provides a rough analogue of this architecture.[20] In this interpretation, T_1 corresponds to the core final-assembly firm, such as Toyota, and task units at the T_2-level to firms supplying various relation-specific modular parts to T_1 through multiple-vendor relational contracting. T_1 plays a leading role in processing systemic information such as that leading to the development of new models. Coupling the core firm with each of the T_2-level firms is relational, which indicates substantial information sharing between them, ranging from the formation of joint development teams to the use of the *kanban* system across them to cope with a high degree of technological and attribute complementarities between their tasks. However, also note that this quasi-organizational architecture serves as a way of avoiding the heavy information overload of an integrated horizontal hierarchy by spinning off various subsets of tasks outside the core firm. The design specification of parts is entrusted to T_2-level firms and thus is encapsulated from T_1.[21] Suppliers at the T_2-level are either competitors in supplying the same relation-specific modular parts or belong to separate niche markets (a lower statistical correlation of their environments). So there is no substantial information assimilation across the T_2-level except during extraordinary emergencies and exchanges of general market and engineering information. Firms at the T_2-level may further decompose their modular products into component parts and subcontract their productions to still other firms, say at the T_3-level, and so on. Therefore the relational suppliers *keiretsu* can involve hierarchical nesting of $HD[IA(c)]$–IE modes.

$HD[IA(c)]$–$IA(c)$: Italian Industrial Districts

Let us envision a case where T_1 (a firm) is still in the position of coordinating the tasks (firms) at the T_2-level, but there is also some information sharing between them as well as between task units at the T_2-level. It then has an architecture similar to a horizontal hierarchy as discussed above, but task units at both the T_1- and T_2-levels are now autonomous firms rather than internal units of a firm. Therefore coupling between a firm at the T_1-level and those at the T_2-level may be more ad hoc, although the practice of information sharing tends to make it relational. A quintessential example of this type is found in relational networks of firms in the so-called industrial districts in Italy (*distretti industriali italiani*), clustering in a particular locality such as Prato (wool), Como (silk), Carpi (knit apparel), and Biella (wool).[22] In this interpretation, T_1 is identified with the core firm specializing in information processing regarding fashion trends, product design, coordination of work processes, and marketing of products, while the T_2's are small subcontracting firms, each specializing in a specific stage of the work process leading to final products. For example, in the silk print industry in Como, the role of T_1 is born by mutually competitive firms called converters, and the T_2's are composed of small firms specializing in design, spinning and weaving, dying, screen manufacturing, printing, and finishing.[23]

There is a high degree of attribute-complementarity between design and manufacturing skills in the fashion industry where high quality and a short product cycle are the norm. Sophisticated design requires the right materials and appropriate processing, as well as high-level manufacturing skills that may not easily be formalized into manuals (e.g., the finishing process in Como). Thus contextual information sharing between the core firm and contracting firms may enhance the ability of the former to innovate in design, while the latter may benefit from information regarding fashion trends to develop potentially useful skills and knowledge. Horizontally as well, tasks performed by individual small firms need to be coordinated flexibly and quickly in both quantity and variety in response to volatile seasonal fashion (highly correlated market environments), while constrained by a high degree of technological- and attribute-complementarities (e.g., there are close preparatory communications between screen manufacturers and printers in Como prior to a final decision on design). Continual communications across firms, on and off the job, facilitate coordinated work scheduling in response to emergent demands, while continual contacts among firms in the same task category facilitate reciprocal work sharing over seasons in response to the seasonally changing patterns of excess/shortage of individual production capacities across them. Also the clustering of firms in a particular locality helps them upgrade manufacturing skills through mutual learning and emulation, as well as coordinate innovation efforts across different tasks that can be highly attribute-complementary (e.g., a new dying technique may require a corresponding upgrade in fabric).

$IA–IE$: Third-Party Information Mediation—Silicon Valley Clustering

This is the quasi-organizational architecture in which task units (T_2's) encapsulating operational information assimilate a modicum of systemic information through a third-party intermediary (T_1). A not-so-obvious but important example of this architecture is found in the information-connectedness among startup entrepreneurial firms clustering in Silicon Valley. There are two, mutually related, but subtly distinct, conditions for making architecture truly innovative. First, almost all firms in this cluster compete in innovation with some others in a particular niche market. The technological environments that these firms face are therefore the same (highly statistically correlated) and their innovation efforts are highly substitutable. As a result their information processing needs to be encapsulated, both from the viewpoint of individual competing firms and from the systemic information-efficiency point of view (proposition 4.1). Next, unlike older integrated firms such as IBM which develop their new concepts for possible technological systems (e.g., IBM360) ex ante in a centralized manner, these firms are engaged in innovation efforts in a decentralized manner. New technological systems, such as computers or the internet, can be evolutionarily formed ex post by combining modular products, such as CPU, LC monitors, software, or routers, generated by successful individual firms from different niche markets. This change in the innovative process is made possible because information processing (innovative efforts) in different niche markets is as independent and self-contained as possible.[24] The innovation, in turn, is facilitated by the development of the information-processing competence of the entrepreneurs, as well as by supporting technology that allows the information processing of statistically correlated development environments to be encapsulated in an integrated manner within a single firm (proposition 4.5). This is the second informational condition for making the Silicon Valley architecture workable.

Then, in order for an evolutionary selection of modular, component products to form an innovative technological system, only common standards for interfaces, as well as a common protocol for data transmission, among them, needs to be provided. Such standard-setting may come from leading established firms in respective niche markets or standard-setting industrial associations. Or, they may evolve de facto through competition, since they are difficult to set a priori in highly uncertain technological environments. Venture capitalists play a further important role in mediating systemic information among competing firms regarding evolving standards and the end-product system. Their information-mediating role is relatively less imposing in comparison to that of the manager in the functional hierarchy and more detached in comparison to that in the horizontal hierarchy, although they also play a unique governance role in this system (see section 4.3 and chapter 14).

In her book based on detailed field work, Saxenian (1994) raised an intriguing question as to why the two important clusters of the high-tech information industry, Silicon Valley and Route 128 in the greater Boston area, exhibited different performances after a business setback in the mid-1980's in response to a serious challenge from Japanese competitors. Silicon Valley recovered from that challenge with strengthened vigor, whose major driving force was the thrust of less integrated, market-focused, new firms. On the other hand, Route 128 remained stagnated longer, Saxenian argued, possibly because relatively integrated, hierarchical firms were dominant in that region and they were not informationally connected to each other. Our information-architectural characterization of the Silicon Valley model seems to be in accord with her observation.

Quasi-organizational architecture is composed of multiple firms. The role of T_1 may be performed by a single firm, as in the Japanese supplier *keiretsu*, or by multiple firms like the converters in the Italian industrial districts and the venture capitalists in Silicon Valley clustering. Accordingly there is a difference in the degree of T_1's information controllability across them. Also note that the second item in each characterization denotes horizontal relationships *among* firms (T_2's) but not organizational architecture *within* them. They themselves have their own internal organizational architecture. In the case of the Japanese supplier *keiretsu* and the Italian industrial districts, each of the subcontracting suppliers internalize horizontal hier-

systemic information / local information	hierarchical		strongly assimilative		weakly assimilative
encapsulated	functional hierarchy				Silicon Valley clustering
assimilated (network-induced)	network integrated f-hierarchy				
	h-controlled teams	particpatory hierarchy		Japanese *keiretsu*	
(contextual)			horizontal hierarchy		Italian industrial district

Figure 4.3
Types of organizational and quasi-organizational architecture

archies (or hierarchical-controlled teams led by a skilled craftsman in some Italian firms). On the other hand, the organizational architecture characterizing start up firms clustering in Silicon Valley can be diverse. Their internal architectural types can be closer to either horizontal/particpatory hierarchies or "star-led" (hierarchically controlled) teams, but not as much to functional hierarchies, at least initially (Baron et al. 1996; Hannan et al. 1996).[25]

Figure 4.3 shows the taxonomy we have so far developed. Notice that the degree of centralization of systemic information (information relevant to the entire organizational domain) in the various architectural structures ranges from centralized processing in the hierarchical decomposition mode in the extreme left, to the "strong" information assimilation mode in the middle in the sense that systemic information is assimilated with the T_1 unit (the management of the firm) as a focal point, and finally to the "weak" information assimilation mode in the extreme right in the sense that systemic information is assimilated across multiple organizations by the intermediary of multiple T_1 units (e.g., venture capitalists and converters). The vertical location represents the degree of information encapsulation/assimilation between the horizontal task units within the respective types of architecture. The formal information assimilation mode through the digital network is located between the two. The location of each entry should be obvious from the discussions above.

4.3   Governance of Organizational Architecture: A Preliminary Discussion

In section 4.1 we identified the three generic modes of information-connectedness among organizational units and examined various conditions under which each mode could be informationally more efficient than the other on the assumption that information-processing precision of constituent units is the same. We have hinted, however, that the precision of information processing may be dependent on the incentives of agents in charge of information-processing tasks. However, a particular type of organizational architecture may entail respective incentive problems inherent to it and thus unique governance problems. In this section we deal with the three generic modes of information-connectedness and see how each may raise distinct governance issues calling for corresponding solutions. On the basis of this pre-liminary discussion, we will come back to a more comprehensive treatment of orga-nizational governance in part III after making more analytical and conceptual preparations.

We first note that each generic mode embraces the deployment of particular types of assets, human or physical, as well as tangible or intangible. In the next chapter we will develop an elaborate discussion regarding a distinction of types of human assets attuned to the hierarchical-decomposition and information-assimilation modes. Here we tentatively identify them respectively as individuated and context-oriented human assets (see figure 4.4). Roughly speaking, in the hierarchical decomposition, human assets need to be individually attuned to functionally decomposed information-processing tasks, while in the information-assimilation mode, the orientation of human assets needs to be directed toward the organizational context of information sharing. In this section we will first see that what is vital for the governance of the hierarchical-decomposition mode is the issue of which owner of individuated human assets controls the use of the physical assets involved. This discussion relies on con-

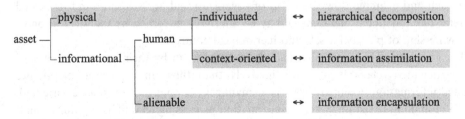

Figure 4.4
Types of organizational architecture and associated assets

tributions of the property rights theorists, such as Grossman and Hart (1986), Hart and Moore (1990), and Hart (1995). Then we will discuss how in the information-assimilation mode free-riding in teamwork in the sense of Alchian and Demsetz (1972) presents a unique incentive problem that cannot be resolved by a closed, internal ownership arrangement of physical assets.

Following Brynjolfsson (1994), human assets, both individuated and context-oriented, may be treated together as "inalienable information assets" in that information-processing skills are embodied in human beings and cannot be separated from them. In contrast, nonphysical, nonhuman information assets, such as software programs, digital contents, and inventions, may be characterized as "alienable information assets." This is because, once produced, their property rights can be separated from their producers and traded. However, it may be difficult for the producer (inventor) to establish property rights over half-processed information assets in the process of production (research and development), yet access to them may be economically valuable to others as well. Because of this public goods property, information-processing activities leading to the production of alienable information assets (i.e., inventive activities) may be hidden (encapsulated) from each other. Later in this section we will deal with a system of agents (organizations), each engaged in encapsulated-information processing that leads to the production of alienable information assets. In this system the uses of information assets, human and alienable, play a crucial role, but not physical assets. Therefore their governance as well calls for an approach that cannot be reduced to a prior ownership arrangement for physical assets.

The Integration of Hierarchical Decomposition Mode and Asset Ownership: The Hart-Moore Firm

We start out with the hierarchical-decomposition mode. We will interpret its essential features in terms of the Grossman-Hart-Moore framework of the property-rights approach and examine how this form of organizational architecture (and its nested systems like functional hierarchies) may be internally governed by the integration of the ownership of physical assets and hierarchical control.

The contents of hierarchically decomposed tasks can by their nature be specified and articulated relatively more distinctively than those in horizontal hierarchies (nested-information assimilation). The manager is engaged in market-oriented, decision-making based on systemic information processing as well as organizational-coordinating tasks, while each worker is engaged in a distinct operational task. The human assets (skills) necessary for the performance of each task are individuated.

The nature of each worker's task can then be described in contracts with the "firm," and remuneration can be specified depending on the human assets the worker possesses. Yet the articulation of job descriptions is bound to be incomplete because of the bounded rationality of the contracting partners who are unable to enumerate all possible future contingencies. This contractual incompleteness means that there must be an arrangement for what Hart calls the "residual rights" of control pertaining to the use of assets (in this case human assets) in noncontractible contingencies. According to Coase (1937) and Simon (1951), the residual rights of control over the use of human assets in hierarchies belong to the employer within a general bound set by employment contracts. However, why are the workers willing to accept the employer's authority (residual rights of control)? Also the actual performance of each worker's task may require the use of a certain skill that can be acquired only through training and learning on the job. The level of effort in training also may not be contractually specifiable, and thus not court-enforceable. Our interpretation of Hart and Moore's argument is that the integration of the ownership and thus residual rights of control of physical assets with hierarchical coordination is essential in the following sense: it provides the owner-cum-manager with not only his/her incentives to accumulate his/her own task-relevant skill but also the ability to indirectly control and motivate the workers who need the physical assets in order to be productive.

In order to take a look at the basic logic developed by Hart and Moore, suppose that there are only two agents who are matched to form a hierarchical organization. One of them (T_1) processes systemic information about the environment surrounding the organization and tells the other agent (T_2) what to do, while T_2 processes only the idiosyncratic information needed to do the job. Let us call the former the manager and the latter the worker. The organization can last for one period composed of two stages, provided that both parties agree to work together. Suppose that both manager and worker invest in their respective human assets (e.g., managerial information-processing capacity and training in operating a machine, respectively) in the first stage, which is costly in terms of effort. In the second stage, these human assets are used by each party, together with physical assets, to generate quasi-rents to be divided between both agents. Denoting the levels of investment in human assets by the manager and the worker by e_m and e_w respectively, let the total value of revenues made possible by their cooperation be $V(e_m, e_w)$, and let the outside-option values of the human assets of the manager and the worker without the cooperation of the other be $\bar{v}_m(e_m)$ and $\bar{v}_w(e_w)$ respectively. As will be specified shortly, the outside-option values, $\bar{v}_m(e_m)$ and $\bar{v}_w(e_w)$, may be parametrically dependent on the ownership structure of physical assets. But, for the moment, we leave the ownership structure of physical assets unspecified and the relevant parameters suppressed. It is assumed that $V(e_m, e_w) - (\bar{v}_m(e_m) + \bar{v}_w(e_w)) > 0$, and that $\partial V(e_m, e_w)/\partial e_m - \bar{v}'_m(e_m) > 0$ and $\partial V(e_m, e_w)/\partial e_w - \bar{v}'_w(e_w) > 0$. That is, the average and marginal quasi-rents are positive with respect to investments in human assets by the manager and the worker. So both assets are firm-specific in the average and marginal sense. Let $c_m(e_m)$ and $c_w(e_w)$ be the costs of the effort investments by the manager and worker respectively, with increasing marginal costs so that $c'_m(e_m) > 0$ and $c'_w(e_w) > 0$, as well as $c''_m(e_m) > 0$ and $c''_w(e_w) > 0$.

Suppose that the levels of investment are mutually observable at the end of the first stage, but not court-verifiable, so they are not contractible at the beginning of the first stage. After first-stage investment but before the second stage, the manager and the worker bargain over a contract regarding the division of the quasi-rents realizable at the end of the second stage. Assume that they split the quasi-rents from cooperation fifty-fifty. Given equal bargaining power, the manager will get $\frac{1}{2}[V(e_m, e_w) - (\bar{v}_m(e_m) + \bar{v}_w(e_w))] + \bar{v}_m(e_m)$, and the worker will get $\frac{1}{2}[V(e_m, e_w) - (\bar{v}_m(e_m) + \bar{v}_w(e_w))] + \bar{v}_w(e_w)$. This means that each gets half of the quasi-rents plus the outside-option value of his/her own human assets. Anticipating this bargaining outcome, each agent determines the level of his investment in the first stage in such a way that the private marginal return from his own investment is equal to its marginal cost. Since the former equals half of the marginal return, this Nash equilibrium condition is represented as

$$\frac{1}{2}\left[\frac{\partial V(e_m, e_w)}{\partial e_m} + \bar{v}'_m(e_m)\right] = c'_m(e_m),$$

$$\frac{1}{2}\left[\frac{\partial V(e_m, e_w)}{\partial e_w} + \bar{v}'_w(e_w)\right] = c'_w(e_w).$$

However, efficiency requires that the full marginal return be equated to the marginal cost for each agent. Since each party can hold up half of his opponent's human asset values, underinvestments will result. Hart and Moore therefore seek the second-best solution. It is at this point that the ownership structure of physical assets needs to be made explicit.

Suppose that in the second stage the manager and the worker can use their respective accumulated human assets productively with only the help of the respective physical assets (offices, information networks, files, etc., for the manager, and a machine and tools for the worker), denoted by a_m and a_w. Let us assume that if they agree on a contract for the division of quasi-rents, they are to use the human as well as physical assets in the most efficient way. Thus, second-stage moral hazard problems are assumed away for now. However, if both parties fail to reach a contractual agreement at the end of the first stage, the outside-option values of their respective human assets may depend on the ownership structure of the physical assets. Then ownership structure becomes an important determinant of both parties' bargaining positions at the end of the first stage. What ownership structure is the most efficiency enhancing in the context of the hierarchical-decomposition mode? Hart and Moore examined the implications of alternative ownership structures in the context of various technological environments. Of these, the case most relevant to the present context is the following.

Suppose that for each level of e_w, the outside-option value of the worker's specific human assets $\bar{v}_w(e_w)$ is not affected by the structure of ownership of physical assets in the absence of the manager's specific human assets, while the outside-option value of the manager's human assets $\bar{v}_m(e_m)$ is greater for each level of e_m, if the manager owns both a_m and a_w than otherwise. Namely the manager's human assets are "essential" in the Hart-Moore sense, while those of the worker are not.[26] This corresponds to the situation where the manager's systemic information-processing task is indispensable to the productive use of physical assets in the hierarchical-decomposition mode, so the worker cannot enhance his productivity without it, even if he owns the entire set of physical assets. On the other hand, the manager can enhance her outside-option value if she owns the physical assets and retain the residual rights of control over them vis-à-vis an untrained alternative worker. In this case it is clear from the Nash equilibrium condition above that the second-best solution is for the manager to acquire the ownership of the entire set of physical assets. In this way, the manager is more motivated to accumulate the indispensable human assets of her own.[27] Thus it holds that:

PROPOSITION 4.6 (Hart-Moore)   For controlling functional hierarchies in which the manager's systemic-information processing is essential in the Hart-Moore sense, it is optimal for the manager to own the entire set of physical assets.[28]

Let us now relax the assumption that the manager's human assets are essential, and allow the marginal outside-option values of both the worker's and manager's human assets, $\bar{v}'_m(e_m)$ and $\bar{v}'_w(e_w)$, for each level of e_w and e_m, to vary depending on the ownership structure. Suppose first that the marginal outside-option values of both human assets are enhanced when both partners possess the residual rights of control over the respective physical assets that they themselves use but are unaffected by the ownership of the physical assets used by other parties. This is the case where physical assets are "independent" in the Hart-Moore sense. Then it is clear from the Nash equilibrium condition above that in order not to dilute the worker's incentives, the manager should not own the physical assets used by the worker. In this case the worker ought to become an independent contractor (e.g., subcontractors in Italian industrial districts discussed in section 4.2). Now, if the physical assets are complements in the sense that the marginal values of both worker's and manager's human assets increase more when the residual rights of control over both physical assets are retained by either manager or worker, but if this effect is stronger with the manager, it becomes a more efficient arrangement for the manager to own both physical assets. If the relevant portion of the physical assets (e.g., machines or tools) are owned by the worker, the manager's incentive to invest in human assets will be reduced because the worker could hold up a portion of their value ex post by threatening to walk away with their assets if an agreement cannot be reached. Under the manager's ownership the worker's incentives are reduced too, but the overall efficiency impact is less.[29] Likewise, by owning complementary physical assets, the manager can threaten to deny the worker access to the physical assets without a contractual agreement and thus a share in the organizational quasi-rents. To make this option irrational for the manager to implement, however, the worker then ought to invest in specific human assets in the first stage. "A firm's non-human assets, then, simply represent the glue that keeps the firm together, whatever this may be." (Hart 1995:57)

The arrangement in which the hierarchical decomposition of organizational-information processing is combined with centralized ownership of physical assets by the manager is referred to as the *Hart-Moore firm*, which captures an essential feature of the classic proprietor's firm. Later, in chapter 11, we will see how this essential feature can be modified, when the owner-cum-manager of the organization does not have enough financial assets to own the entire set of physical assets so that the proprietor's firm needs to be transformed into a corporation with many shareholders.

The Limit of Insider Control of the Information-Assimilation Mode

In discussing the emergence of the Hart-Moore firm, we assumed that the levels of investment in human assets by the manager and the worker were not contractible ex ante (before the first stage begins), but were observable ex post (after the first stage). So the second-stage contract could be written on the basis of mutually observable investment levels. This was possible because the organization-specific human assets were decomposed into the individuated assets, one accumulated by the manager and the other accumulated by the worker. Further there was a fundamental asymmetry in the importance of the human assets possessed by the manager and by the worker. These two assumptions are reasonable first-step approximations to the basic nature of the hierarchical-decomposition mode and its nested structure, functional hierarchies. However, they may not be equally good approximations for another generic mode of organizational coordination: the information-assimilation mode and its nested structure, horizontal hierarchies.

The defining characteristic of this type of organizational architecture is that the participating agents share information and interact in decision-making, vertically and horizontally, to such a great extent that the organizational returns may not be clearly decomposable into their individual contributions. Then, without a proper governance structure there can be incentives for agents to free-ride on each other's efforts in accumulating and using human assets. This moral hazard problem of free-riding is different in nature, and thus in its solution, from the holdup problem in the hierarchical-decomposition mode. Further, even if a whole set of physical assets is in place, if the manager and the worker are separated from each other, their human assets may be valued less because of their "connectedness." In the Hart-Moore sense, this is equivalent to saying that both parties' human assets are essential in that their outside-option values in isolation are fixed, regardless of the ownership of physical assets involved. This is admittedly an extreme assumption, but as a first approximation it captures the basic nature of the information-assimilation mode. The centralization of ownership of physical assets may not be a good solution to the governance problem for this type of organizational architecture. Can there then be an alternative internal governance structure? Does making every participant an equal claimant over the organizational quasi-rents (with the joint ownership of physical assets) solve the problem?

We assume that agents' efforts in making investments in the improvement of context-oriented human assets are not separately observable. Economists have dubbed production organizations in which individual (investment) effort levels are not observable *teams* and have proposed a few solutions to the moral hazard problem inherent to teams. The contractual approach to it was first pioneered by Alchian and Demsetz (1972), who argued that the essential function of the firm lies in the hierarchical monitoring of free-riding among team members. The monitor would be motivated to monitor if he or she is entitled to realize the full benefits of monitoring. In other words, the team nature of the organization calls for control and monitoring by a third party. They argued that this third party can be identified with the owner of the firm, who has access to quasi-rents. However, it is vital to their argument to assume that the third party has a perfect ability, if properly motivated, to observe the individual actions of team members. This perfect-observability assumption, however, is not consistent with the original concept of teams.

Holmstrom (1982) was the first to dispense with the perfect-observability assumption. He showed that if a third party (the principal) can observe only the joint outcome of team members and if he or she can exercise the threat of a severe collective penalty against an underperforming team, then an approximate first-best solution can be obtained. He regards the essential function of the third party as being able to "break the budget of teams," rather than to monitor the individual actions of team members. However, if this budget-breaking punishment is to be administered by a third party who can derive utility from penalties, she may be better off if she lets the team fail to achieve its goal. Therefore, as Eswaran and Kotwal (1984) pointed out, there may be a risk of clandestine collusion between the third party and a single team member, so that the latter shirks in order to cause the entire team to fail and they share the penalty between them. It is rather hard to imagine an institution of organizational governance in which the principal monitor benefits from the failure of the team. Also, the team members must bear large penalties even when the team fails due to an uncontrollable stochastic event. Further, if there is a wealth constraint for the team members, the scheme may not be implementable.

However, there is an element in Holmstrom's model that may be potentially useful as a device to resolve the free-riding problem in teams in a second-best manner. This is the possibility of imposing large external penalties indiscriminately on the members of badly performing teams. Let us assume there is a team composed of two identical members, indexed by w and m. The output of the team is determined as a joint outcome of the levels of their human asset investments and of the state of the environment, which the members cannot control. Denote the value of team output by V, and let $F(V : e_m, e_w)$ be the cumulative probability-distribution function of V, conditional on a vector of investment effort levels e_m and e_w undertaken by the members. We assume that the total value is observable ex post, but that individual members' investment levels are not. It is assumed, however, that the observed value of V serves as a fairly good indicator of the levels of members' investments as a whole, in that greater investments reduce the probability of output in the lower tail while increasing it in the higher tail.[30]

Suppose that each member receives an equal share of output value, $\frac{1}{2}V$, while incurring the cost of investment effort, $c(e_i)$. Then, analogous to the Hart-Moore case in the previous subsection, the agent chooses e_i to satisfy the net income-maximizing condition: $\frac{1}{2}\partial E[V(e_m, e_w)]/\partial e_i = c'(e_i)$ where $E[V(e_m, e_w)]$ denotes the expected value of team output. The first-best condition calls for $\partial E[V(e_m, e_w)]/\partial e_i = c'(e_i)$. Thus an undersupply of investment effort (free-riding) ensues. Suppose, however, that when the team's output value falls below a critical level, $\underline{b}$ say, a penalty J is somehow imposed externally on each team member. Then the individual member's problem of choosing the optimal e_i is transformed into

$$\max_{e_i}\left\{\tfrac{1}{2}E[V(e_m, e_w)] - F(\underline{b} : e_m, e_w)J - c(e_i)\right\}.$$

The solution to this problem is given by the following Nash condition:

$$\frac{1}{2}\frac{\partial E[V(e_m, e_w)]}{\partial e_m} - F_m(\underline{b} : e_m, e_w)J = c'(e_m),$$

$$\frac{1}{2}\frac{\partial E[V(e_m, e_w)]}{\partial e_w} - F_w(\underline{b} : e_m, e_w)J = c'(e_w).$$

where $F_i(\underline{b} : e_m, e_w) = \partial F(\underline{b} : e_m, e_w)/\partial e_i < 0$ $(i = m, w)$ for sufficiently low $\underline{b}$. That is, extra investment effort by each agent would reduce the probability of the total output value falling below the critical level $\underline{b}$. The marginal private benefits of extra investment in human assets by each member are comprised of two elements: a 50 percent share in the marginal output value *plus* the marginal reduction in expected penalty due to the decreased probability of a bad collective performance. Then, in equating the marginal private benefit with the marginal private cost of investment, each team member would be motivated to invest more than if he or she were subjected only to the internal incentive mechanism of equal sharing. The question then is whether it is somehow possible not to provide incentives for a third-party monitor to gain from the failure of the team as in the Holmstrom scheme. In chapter 11 we will formulate a third-party mechanism, called relational-contingent governance, that can answer this question in the context of particular institutional environments. Particularly, we will discuss how this type of governance becomes more effective if the information-assimilation mode (or its nested structure, horizontal hierarchy) is established as a convention in the economy.

Governance of the Information-Encapsulation Mode by Tournament

We have argued that the Silicon Valley clustering of entrepreneurial firms can be characterized as an instance of the information-encapsulation mode where the venture capitalist plays a limited role of information mediation. Actually the venture capitalist plays a unique governance role as well. The entrepreneurial firms in Silicon Valley have one feature that makes them distinct from the Hart-Moore firm. Most of them are financially constrained at the outset and externally financed by venture capitalists to whom they relinquish control rights (Hellmann 1998). Thus physical assets do not constitute a major "glue" for these firms.[31] What else then motivates these entrepreneurs? Suppose that they are given stock options by the venture capitalist. However, their value materializes only when they win a competition in product development with other firms in the same niche markets. Otherwise, they may be weeded out before the completion of the development process. Thus the essential nature of the overall governance mechanism operating over the cluster of entrepreneurial firms can be characterized as a kind of tournament.

The unique properties of this competitive process will be analyzed in chapter 14, but the basic logic of its incentive effects on the entrepreneurs' development efforts can simply be summarized as follows. First, consider a domain in which a financier invests in only one wealth-constrained entrepreneurial firm engaged in R&D. The outcome of the R&D is highly uncertain, but its expected outcome value depends on the level of the firm's effort. However, the effort level is not observable by the financier, so it is not contractible. Suppose that the financier and the entrepreneurial firm agree on a fifty-fifty outcome-sharing contract. Let $E[V(e)]$ and $c(e)$ be the expected outcome value of R&D and its private cost to the firm respectively, both depending on the level of the firm's effort e. Then the entrepreneurial firm will choose effort level e that equates the private marginal benefit of extra effort with its private cost: $\frac{1}{2}E[V'(e)] = c'(e)$. Since social efficiency requires that the social marginal benefit of extra effort is equal to its marginal cost: $E[V'(e)] = c'(e)$, an undersupply of R&D effort ensues.

Suppose that a third party—the venture capitalist—bundles two such domains where both firms, indexed by $i = 1, 2$, are engaged in the *same* R&D. The venture capitalist, who can observe the outcomes of R&D of both firms (but not the interim effort expenditure of entrepreneurs), runs a tournament between them. She compares the R&D outcomes between both firms and provides the winner, who has achieved a better outcome, with a 50 percent share of its market value as in the single domain, but gives none to the loser. The financier's cost of investment is duplicated. Also, because only one R&D outcome is to be adopted ex post, the R&D effort of the loser becomes a deadweight loss. However, externalities are created by the intermediated bundling by the venture capitalist, which may induce higher R&D efforts by the entrepreneurial firms. To see this, denote the levels of the firms' investment efforts by e_1 and e_2 and the probability function of their winning a tournament by $F(e_1, e_2)$ and $1 - F(e_1, e_2)$ respectively, where $F(e_1, e_2) = 1 - F(e_1, e_2) = \frac{1}{2}$ when $e_1 = e_2$. Then each firm tries to maximize $\frac{1}{2}F(e_1, e_2)E[V(e_1)] - c(e_1)$ or $\frac{1}{2}(1 - F(e_1, e_2))E[V(e_2)] - c(e_2)$. Since the two firms are identical, the maximization requires the following Nash condition to hold:

$$\frac{1}{2}\left\{ F(e, e)\frac{dE[V(e)]}{de_i} + \frac{\partial F(e, e)}{\partial e_i}E[V(e)] \right\} = c'(e), \qquad i = 1, 2.$$

That is, the marginal private benefits of extra efforts in R&D by an entrepreneurial firm (the left-hand side of the equation) are now composed of half of the following two factors: the probability of winning a tournament (half in equilibrium) times the expected marginal value of the winner's R&D outcome, plus the marginal improvement in the probability of winning a tournament times the total expected value of the winner's R&D outcome. In comparison to the Nash condition in the single domain, the first factor is reduced by half due to the uncertainty of realizing the value of a R&D outcome in a tournament, but the additional incentives are through the externalities of bundling. The net effect depends on the magnitude of $E[V(e)]$ relative to that of $dE[V(e)]/de_i$. That is, if the expected value of a successful outcome is very high relative to its marginal expected value, each firm will expend a higher R&D effort in the tournament than in the case where only one firm is in the development process. A possible increase in the expected success–outcome value may compensate for the costs of duplicated finance for the financiers, as well as provide rent opportunities for the venture capitalist.

We have discussed basic governance issues unique to each of three generic modes of information connectedness. However, it is clear that the discussions are not entirely closed yet. Although we have seen that the integration of hierarchical control and the ownership of physical assets à la Hart and Moore is a solution to the governance problem for the hierarchical-decomposition mode, if the manager of the hierarchical-decomposition mode is capital-constrained, the closed classic solution leading to the proprietor firm is not tenable. We have seen that the closed internal governance of the information-assimilation mode would be inherently inefficient and a third-party intervention contingent on the poor performance of the insider team is called for. We have not yet been able to discuss incentives for a third party that would be able to intervene. Likewise we have hinted that governance by tournament may be an effective external control of encapsulated R&D information processing, but incentives for a venture capitalist–like third party to administer the tournament have not been fully discussed yet except for referring to possible rent opportunities. These unresolved problems likewise call for inquiries into the question of "who governs the governor" in each type of organizational architecture. We plan to discuss this issue in part III in the context of where firm organizations are embedded in complementary institutional arrangements in financial transaction and other domains. In this context organizational governance problems will be transformed into "corporate governance" problems.

5 The Co-evolution of Organizational Conventions and Human Asset Types

One might ask, as one does frequently in the theory of the firm, why all firms do not have the same codes, so that training in the code is transferable? In the first place, in this combinatorial situation, there may easily be many optimal codes, all equally good, but to be useful in a firm it is important to know the right code. The situation here is very much that of the games of coordination which have been stressed so much by Schelling. If it is valuable for two people to meet without being able to communicate with each other during their trips, the meeting place must be agreed on before hand. It may not matter much where the meeting is to be. But a person who learned one meeting-place is not much use to an organization which has selected another.
—Kenneth J. Arrow, *The Limits of Organization* (1974:56)

In the last chapter we identified different types of organizational and quasi-organizational architecture. But, if there is a variety in organizational and quasi-organizational architecture, how is a selection of architectural structure is made from the many possibilities? Do firms adopt the best architecture only in response to evolving technological and market conditions? Recent theories of the firm seem to imply that an answer to this question could be, or at least ought to be, affirmative.[1] Technical details leading to these predictions need not concern us now, but the logical implications of technological determinism common to all of them do: organizational architecture ought to converge among firms in the same human facing similar technological and market parameters. However, we often observe firms with different architectural and governance characteristics, as well as different degrees of integration, in the same industry across regions and economies. Why could this be the case?

There are undoubtedly elements of rational design in any particular organizational architecture, but there may also be an element of convention due to the "bounded rationality" of agents and accordingly of firms. Once organizational conventions develop, there can be a tension between structural inertia and competitive pressure from the changing environment. Entrepreneurs try to experiment with new organizational design or emulate an organizational practice that evolved elsewhere with perceived superiority. However, the usual outcome of such experiments and emulations, even if they occur in a critical mass, is neither a dramatic switch from one convention to another, nor a "chaotic" cohabitation of widely divergent organizational architecture. Rather, they are likely to result in a "modification," or a "ramification" of conventional organizational architecture that may significantly alter some characteristics of the existing conventions, yet retain other basic features. Alternatively, the emergence of new practices may occur as a clustering of new firms on the periphery of traditional industrial centers, as in Silicon Valley.[2] Thus, as we observed in the previous chapter, references are often made to national or regional forms of organization, such as Silicon Valley firms, the American system of manufacture and the Fordist mode of production, the German participatory firms, the

Japanese *keiretsu*, and Italian industrial districts. Some argue that interregional/ international differences in organizational architecture and implied organizational competence may explain the patterns of regional/national advantage in industry and trade.[3]

However, unlike the naturally endowed resources that constitute the source of Ricardian comparative advantage, the organization is a human contrivance. As such, shouldn't it be ultimately transplantable (mobile) across national economies? Or, even if the bounded-rational entrepreneur cannot implement the optimal design of organizational architecture, will competitive selection eventually weed out inefficient organizational architecture that do not fit the technological imperatives of each industry? Therefore, as Alchian (1950) and M. Friedman (1953) argued some time ago, won't the competitive outcome look as if the optimal design is implemented? Especially, doesn't the growth of transnational firms and globalization of financial markets finally pave the way for the convergence of organizational architecture across economies toward industrial technological imperatives? These are the questions that we plan to deal with throughout the rest of this book, and this chapter begins our journey. For that purpose we envision a relatively unstructured domain of the game, the organizational field, in which organizational architecture of firms may be simultaneously chosen.[4] We will construct a model of an evolutionary game played on this domain that is too simple to be testable yet that may be of heuristic value for considering the questions above.

We will first elaborate the point cursorily dealt with in the last section of the previous chapter that different types of organizational architecture require correspondingly different types of information-processing capacity—more conventionally, human assets or skills—from participating individual agents. In that chapter we compared the informational efficiency of three generic organizational modes under the assumption that the levels of the information-processing capacities of agents are quantitatively comparable.[5] However, not only do the information-processing capacities of individual agents quantitatively differ, but there may be important qualitative differences as well. If so, since individual capacity for information processing is generically limited, the individual needs to invest in a particular type and sink cost. When agents make this strategic human investment choice, their decisions may be conditioned by a prevailing organizational practice. On the other hand, when entrepreneurs make a strategic choice of organizational architectural design, their choices may be conditioned by available skill types. We will capture such reciprocal relationship as strategic complementarity in the domain of organizational field, analyze the possible co-evolution of a convention in organizational architecture and human assets types, using a simple evolutionary game model.[6] Contrary to the

Alchian-Friedman conjecture, we will observe that a suboptimal convention of organizational architecture can evolve in a closed organizational field under evolutionary selection pressure.

However, as hinted above, the increasing ease of geographical mobility of human assets, interpenetration of firms of different regional/national origins into others' traditional territories, availability of more precise information regarding better organizational practices elsewhere, and the like, may contribute to the viability of mutation within suboptimal conventions having evolved in closed organizational fields. Will the integration or interactions of organizational fields then eventually weed out inefficient forms of organizational architecture in each industry and evolve an efficient configuration of organizational architecture across them? In other words, will it contribute to the realization of gains from organizational diversity in the sense that the most efficient form of organizational architecture prevails in each industry, depending on characteristics of goods and technology involved? In order to examine this issue, we analyze consequences of various types of interactions of organizational fields having evolved different conventions and examine its implications.

In the end of the chapter, we will comment on practical relevance, as well as a limit, of the evolutionary game approach that we will have employed. We will provide our answer for finding a way out of this limit in chapter 9.

5.1 Types of Mental Programs: Individuated versus Context-Oriented Human Assets

As we saw in chapter 4, any activity within an organization, including the most primitive physical work, has an aspect of information processing. It implies that when engaged in an organizational activity, the agent runs his/her own mental program—or cognitive mechanism—in order to recognize and interpret the state of relevant environments, predict the consequences of various alternative actions on the state (including other agents' reactions), and make an action choice from among them to solve relevant problems. Such programs are composed of a bundle of "rules," usually in the form of if–then. For example, a doctor in a hospital may interpret a patient's situation and try to solve a problem by mobilizing stored rules, such as "if the X-ray film shows this image and the stethoscope examination detects that sonic pattern, then the patient suffers from bronchitis," "if he has this medical record, it is highly probable that he will have an allergic reaction to this medicine," and "if there is such a risk, then it should not be given to him," and so forth. Such rules are accumulated, revised over time, organized in the mind of the agent in a certain way, and "triggered" by a perceived situation (Holland et al. 1986). Thus three rules—interpretive, predictive, and decision—have aspects of capital-human assets. To simplify the discussion, for now let us regard the mental program of the agent as composed simply of two kinds of rules: *cognitive rules* that are used by him or her to form interpretative representations of the relevant situations from cognitive inputs (digital data, written reports, icons, conversations, observed gestures, and expressions, etc.), and *decision rules* that are used to make a choices from a set of feasible actions based on the interpretative representation of the situation.[7] Note that "decision rules" here refer to components of the individual, internal mental program, and not to organizational or administrative rules/procedures by which the collective decision-making process is arranged—although both are undoubtedly in constitutive relationships with each other.[8] We are concerned here with internal organizing principles for these rules, only to an extent necessary for a basic classification of the mental programs relevant to our discussion.

In the previous chapter we considered the obvious fact that the execution of an individual task in an organization involves information processing regarding the respective idiosyncratic environment. In that sense any organization embraces the division of information-processing labor. However, what makes the firm an *organization* is the presence of a common segment of environment whose state is simultaneously relevant to multiple constituent task units. Without it the division of information-processing labor can be performed just as well without organizational cooperation. It is precisely the ways in which that part of the environment is informationally processed that differentiates one type of organizational architecture from all others. We have observed that in this regard functional and horizontal hierarchies stand diametrically opposed.

In functional hierarchies, the environment relevant to an organizational domain is completely decomposed in a disjointed manner for the specialized division of information processing. Thus the division of information-processing labor is complete. In terms of an individual mental program, this implies that the sole inputs to cognitive rules (the "if ..." part of the rules) mobilized for interpreting relevant environmental situations are messages that each agent processes directly from those segments of the environment, while the inputs to decision rules are his own interpretative representations of relevant situations, together with messages transmitted to him or her from other designated agents in the form of formalized codes, such as commands, briefings, reports, and e-mail messages. In this sense mental programs are run separately by agents in different task units. The agent may polish, add, and reorganize his/her own store of cognitive and decision rules based on his/her own experiences and learning. If the agent faces the same (or a similar) task, the accumulated store may remain valuable in any functional hierarchy. A mental program embodying the

types of cognitive rules and associated decision rules effective in functional hierarchies can thus easily be portable from one functional hierarchy to another, as long
as the tasks the agent faces are designed similarly across functional hierarchies in
terms of the range and object of information processing required. Thus, we may
characterize this type of mental program as *individuated* (separated) and refer to the
capacities and skills of individual agents to effectively run them as *individuated human
assets.*

The situation is different with respect to mental programs that operate in a horizontal hierarchy (nested information assimilation). In this type of organizational
architecture, the information-processing labors of the agents are not entirely decomposed in a nonoverlapping manner. Regarding the segment of the environment
common to them, the agents in a horizontal hierarchy process information in such a
way as to assimilate their interpretations about it and to construct a common basis
for decision-making. At the basic biological level, agents individually perceive various
messages from the environment just like their counterparts running individuated
mental programs do. But, in order to arrive at an assimilated cognitive interpretation
and to form a common basis for decision-making, the agents need to utilize, not only
their own individually processed messages from the relevant environment but also
messages—tacit and explicit—from the relevant others regarding their cognition of
the same environment; that is, one needs to take into account how the relevant others
perceive and interpret the common environment. Borrowing an expression from
M. Polanyi (1958), we might as well say that the agents must "indwell" with each
other in a common environmental situation.

This is an entirely different type of information sharing from the one we observe in
a network-integrated, functional hierarchy in which agents draw the same digitalized
information from a formal communication network as input to organizationally
designed decision rules. To arrive at an assimilated interpretation as a basis for
decision-making, the agents may possibly discard individually idiosyncratic elements
of cognitive inputs as organizationally irrelevant. Thus cognitive rules and the
associated decision rules used by individual agents may involve more dialectic, rather
than analytical, reasoning.[9] In this way some potentially valuable information
may be sacrificed, but as we have seen, it may serve the organizational goal better
when technological and/or attribute complementarities between tasks are high, the
information-processing capacities of agents are relatively equal, and the environments of task units are highly correlated and fairly stable.[10]

The type of mental program operating in a horizontal hierarchy is thus made
qualitatively distinct from the individuated ones in that it incorporates the mechanism of cognitive and evaluative assimilation as an essential element. As such, the

mental programs of this type within an organization are mutually connected. Thus we may characterize this type of mental program as *context-oriented,* and the capacities or skills of agents to effectively run them as *context-oriented human assets.* The essential characteristic of this type of mental program would not by itself preclude its portability across organizations. The required skill for running the mechanism of interpretative and evaluative assimilation, once acquired, can remain valuable if it is put to work with others of the same type. However, the effectiveness of context-oriented human assets may be enhanced by their continued connectedness. In that sense context-oriented human assets may be more organization-specific than individuated human assets.

So far we have implicitly assumed that appropriate types of human assets are available for both functional and horizontal hierarchies. But this premise can now be questioned. If environmental parameters change, a type of organizational architecture that has enjoyed an efficiency advantage may lose its position to another type. But, can the new architectural structure then quickly replace the original one? If this replacement requires a basic shift in the types of required human assets from context-oriented to individuated, or the reverse, the transition may not be automatic. As defined, the actual mental programs of any individual at any point in time are composed of a bundle of cognitive and decision rules. These rules may be revised, refined, and incrementally restructured over time by individual learning, both formal and on the job, and the organizational experiences of the agent. In this sense, any mental program may be simultaneously individuated, context-oriented, and path-dependent in varying combinations. However, a meta-rule for organizing these rules determining whether or not the mechanism of assimilated cognition is incorporated as an essential element of the mental program may not be so flexibly altered once formed.

Then the situation is seen where agents face the following choices prior to entry into any organization: whether to invest in an individuated human asset useful in a specialized task across organizations, or to invest in a relatively more general, communications and problem-solving skill, expecting that it will be molded into a more context-specific skill after being matched with a particular organization. However, an actual individual choice of which type of mental program to develop is greatly affected, consciously or unconsciously, by the societal institutions of education and training, the cultural meanings attached to an appropriate self, and, more economically, which type of organizational architecture is dominant in the organizational fields to which agents expect to have access. We note that recent works in cultural psychology on this topic are theoretically consistent with, and empirically supportive of, our categorization of individuated as opposed to context-oriented.[11] Scholars in that discipline argue that while a cultural view may be transformed into either of the attributes of the self, the latter supports and reproduces the prevalent pattern of individual psychology. Thus psychological processes and a cultural system are mutually constitutive.

Similarly we submit that a type of human asset (mental program) and a type of organizational architecture may be mutually constitutive and co-evolve. While the formation of individual mental programs useful in an organization may be affected by the dominant organizational architecture, the design of organizational architecture by the entrepreneurs may also depend on the distribution of available human asset types in the population. Thus there is an important complementarity between their choices in the domain of the organizational-field. If individuals or entrepreneurs (organizers of firms) deviate from the dominant pattern of types, they may face a higher risk of mismatching with a wrong type of organizational architecture or pool of human assets. Thus, even if one type of information architecture has a better fit than others with the technological environments of certain industries, it is not certain whether that architectural structure will dominate everywhere in those industries. If the distribution of types of human assets in the population is highly skewed toward one fitting a particular type of organizational architecture, that type may persist as a convention in the organization field, even if technologically suboptimal. An organizational convention can thus be viewed as a coordination device by which the choice of investment strategy (human assets formation) by agents is aligned in one way or another in the organizational field, thus helping them avoid the risk of costly mismatching. We formalize this intuition in terms of an evolutionary game in the next section.

5.2   The Evolutionary Dynamics of Organizational Conventions[12]

Imagine an organizational field consisting of a large number of population of agents in which a firm is organized by the matching of two agents. Each agent invests for his/ her lifetime either in individuated human assets or in context-oriented human assets. Agents die or quit work and are replaced by their children at a certain rate. If two agents who have invested in individuated human assets are matched to form a firm, its organizational architecture will be a functional hierarchy (functional specialization), whereas if two agents who have invested in the context-oriented type are matched, it will be a horizontal hierarchy.[13] Suppose further that there are two types of industries, B and D. Functional hierarchies have an informational efficiency advantage in industry B, whereas horizontal hierarchies have an informational efficiency advantage in industry D.[14] If a mismatching of two different types of human assets occurs, that organization will be the least efficient in both industries. This assumption can be represented by two matrices, one for each industry, showing the costs of unit-production contingent on the matching of human assets types. Denote the human assets types by I (individuated) and C (context-oriented), and the unit output cost of the industry B (alternatively D) by b_{jk} (alternatively d_{jk}), when the matching of human assets types j and k $(= I$ or $C)$ occur. We have

$$B = \begin{bmatrix} b_{II} & b_{IC} \\ b_{CI} & b_{CC} \end{bmatrix} \quad \text{and} \quad D = \begin{bmatrix} d_{II} & d_{IC} \\ d_{CI} & d_{CC} \end{bmatrix}$$

where $b_{II} < b_{CC} < b_{IC} = b_{CI}$ and $d_{CC} < d_{II} < d_{IC} = d_{CI}$. Agents work in one of the two industries, $i = B$ or D. Let us denote the distribution of the population over human assets-types and industries at a particular moment in time as $\mathbf{m} = (m_{CB}, m_{CD}, m_{IB}, m_{ID})$, where m_{ki} represents the proportion of the population that chooses industry i with a type of human asset k so that $m_{CB} + m_{CD} + m_{IB} + m_{ID} = 1$. A firm can produce two units of output at any moment with a specified unit-cost contingent on the mode of matching, namely on the type of organizational architecture. The revenue of the firm, net of production cost, is equally shared between the two agents forming the firm.

Regarding matching technology, assume that the agents equipped with individuated human assets are mobile between the two industries at any moment in time. The agents with context-oriented human assets sink some cost in a particular industrial-organizational context. Those agents who are invested in context-oriented human assets are not as easily mobile across industries (organizations). Because of their relative immobility, agents with human assets of that type select matching partners more carefully. Let us assume that the probability of agents equipped with context-oriented human assets being matched with the same type in industry i is given by

$$\pi_{Ci} = \left[\frac{m_{Ci}}{m_{Ci} + m_{Ii}} \right]^{\gamma}, \qquad i = B, D$$

where $0 < \gamma \le 1$. If $\gamma = 1$, the matching is random, and if it is less than one, the matching is positively assortative. Then, as γ decreases, the probability of proper matching increases. We will see shortly how the perfect mobility of an individuated type can be formulated.

All agents in the organizational field have identical consumption tastes and spend their incomes on the product of the B and D industries in the proportions β and Δ, where $\beta + \Delta = 1$. Recalling that each firm is producing two units of the product, the total outputs of industries B and D are $m_{CB} + m_{IB}$ and $m_{CD} + m_{ID}$ respectively. Prices of products B and D are then given by the unit-elasticity inverse demand function

$$p_B = \frac{\beta}{m_{CB} + m_{IB}}, \quad p_D = \frac{\Delta}{m_{CD} + m_{ID}}$$

respectively.

The expected payoffs of agents possessing context-oriented human assets and working in industries $j = B, D$ is then given by

$$u_{CB} = \frac{\beta}{m_{CB} + m_{IB}} - \pi_{CB} b_{CC} - (1 - \pi_{CB}) b_{CI},$$

$$u_{CD} = \frac{\Delta}{m_{CD} + m_{ID}} - \pi_{CD} d_{CC} - (1 - \pi_{CD}) d_{CI}.$$

For example, an agent who enters the B-industry has the probability, π_{CB}, of being matched with an agent of the same type, and consequently bearing the cost b_{CC}, while having the probability $1 - \pi_{CB}$ of being mismatched with an agent of the different type of human assets and consequently bearing the larger cost, b_{CI}. He receives an equal share of the net revenue with his partner, whoever she may be.

Likewise the expected payoffs of agents with individuated human assets working in industries B and D are given by

$$u_{IB} = \frac{\beta}{m_{CB} + m_{IB}} - \pi_{IB} b_{II} - (1 - \pi_{IB}) b_{IC},$$

$$u_{ID} = \frac{\Delta}{m_{CD} + m_{ID}} - \pi_{ID} d_{II} - (1 - \pi_{ID}) d_{IC},$$

where $\pi_{IJ}(j = B, D)$ is the probability of agents with individuated human assets being matched with others of the same type of human assets in industry i. These probabilities can be determined by the labor market clearing conditions:

$$(1 - \pi_{Ci}) m_{Ci} = (1 - \pi_{Ii}) m_{Ii}, \quad i = B, D.$$

That is, even if agents miss a correct matching, they are matched with an agent of the different type, so there is no unemployment. The agents with individuated human assets do not select the same type of human assets in an assortative manner, but they are more flexible in choosing the industry because their functional specialization is useful in either industry. We can assume that they instantaneously choose the industry in which they expect to earn a higher income. So the agents with the individuated human asset type are allocated between the two industries in such a way as to equalize their expected incomes.

With this, we have completed the specification of the state of the organizational field at any moment in time characterized by the truncated distribution of population $m = (m_{CB}, m_{CD}, m_{IB} + m_{ID})$. The next task is to describe a dynamic process of the organizational field domain over time, along which the distribution of the population evolves, and inquire into the nature of the equilibria of such a process. Though we will not explicitly model the dynamics, a brief description of a process that might underlie such a model may be stated as follows.

At each moment in time a fraction of the population is replaced by a new generation of individuals, most of whom mimic the strategies of their parents. A small fraction of them, however, choose their strategies to mimic the existing strategy with the highest expected return (we will consider later the possibility that an even smaller fraction experiments with random choice). As a result only the most successful type will increase its relative share in the population. Such dynamics is called the *best-response evolutionary dynamics*. An *equilibrium* of these dynamics is any population distribution $\mathbf{m}^* = (m_{CB}^*, m_{CD}^*, m_{IB}^*, m_{ID}^*)$ at which the distribution of population across human asset types and industries becomes stationary. An equilibrium is said to be an *evolutionary equilibrium* if it is locally asymptotically stable (D. Friedman 1993). That is, all states near an evolutionary equilibrium will eventually converge toward it.[15]

There are nine equilibria for the best-response evolutionary dynamics, all of which are Nash equilibria. They are shown diagrammatically in figure 5.1 which depicts the distribution of the equilibria in the three-dimensional simplex representing $m = (m_{CB}, m_{CD}, m_{IB} + m_{ID})$ and their dynamic properties. Among them, *P, I, C,* and *L* are evolutionary equilibiria (*IP, IL, CP,* and *CL* are saddle points and *W* is a source).

Of the nine equilibria, the *P-equilibrium* is the unique Pareto-optimal equilibrium in which an optimal diversity of types of organizational architecture (the most efficient matching) is realized across both industries: that is, functional hierarchies in *B*-industry and horizontal hierarchies in *D*-industry. In the *I-equilibrium* and *C-equilibrium* all agents adopt a uniform choice strategy regarding human assets type, either individuated or context-oriented, regardless of industry, and thus functional hierarchies or horizontal hierarchies prevail as sole organizational architectural type. Once these two equilibria are established historically, it would be difficult to upset them despite their suboptimality, because the deviation of a small group of agents from the corresponding equilibrium strategy would be heavily penalized by the larger risk of mismatching. The adoption of the prevailing human asset type would then

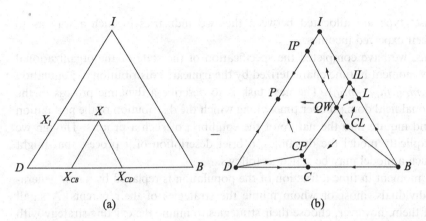

Figure 5.1
Evolutionary equilibria in the organizational field: Simplex representation. The triangles are two-dimensional simplexes, a device for showing the distribution of three-dimensional variables in two dimensions. Each side represents the size of the population normalized to one. Let us tentatively assume that the population distribution of the economy is represented by point X in (a). From this point, draw a straight line parallel to each side of the triangle. When this is done, segment DX_I represents the proportion, $m_I = m_{IB} + m_{ID}$, of agents with individuated human assets in the economy, segment BX_{CD} the proportion, m_{CD}, of the population with context-oriented human assets working in the D-industry, and segment DX_{CB} the proportion, m_{CB}, of the population with context-oriented human assets working in the B-industry, respectively. Because individuated human assets are mobile instantaneously between industries, there is no need to show explicitly their distribution between industries.

In (b) this device is used to show the location of each equilibria of the evolutionary dynamics. The I-equilibrium, where the entire population specializes in individuated human assets, is represented by point I. The C-equilibrium, where the entire population specializes in context-oriented human assets, is represented by point C in the middle of the bottom side of the triangle. The P-equilibrium can be represented by a point located in the middle of side DI, at which segment DP represents the proportion of the population equipped with individuated human assets working in the B-industry and segment IP represents that with context-oriented human assets working in the D-industry. The L-equilibrium is a pathological equilibrium in which the least efficient matching is sustained in both industries. The areas containing points I, C, P, and L, indicated by arrows pointing to them, are called the basins of attraction for their respective equilibria. That is, when historical initial conditions lie within one of these areas, evolutionary game dynamics eventually converges toward the corresponding equilibrium. Even if these equilibria have been temporarily disturbed by the invasion of a small group of mutants, they will be restored as long as the disturbance remains within one of these areas. QW is a quasi-Walrasian equilibrium where all economic agents equipped with either individuated or context-oriented human assets can expect equal payoffs in both industries, but it is an unstable equilibrium that is referred to as the source in dynamic terms. The others, IP, CP, CL, and IL are unstable equilibria called saddle points.

become a *convention*, and as a result functional or horizontal hierarchies would be established as organizational conventions regardless of industries. Since neither of these organizational conventions has an absolute advantage but only a relative one, different organizational fields internalizing different organizational conventions may enjoy advantages only in particular industries. The *L-equilibrium* is a pathological equilibrium in which less efficient matching prevails in both industries by historical accident.

5.3   The Interactions of Organizational Fields and Gains from Diversity

The preceding model indicates that the Pareto-efficient industrial structure involves a diversity of organizational architecture, contingent on the technological and market parameters of each industry, whereas an organizational field in which some type of organizational convention prevails cannot achieve the same level of efficiency. The efficiency gains from the diversity of organizational architecture are referred to below as the *gains from organizational diversity*. The model so far has not predicted which evolutionary equilibria are likely to emerge, except that the outcome depends solely on the initial condition. As already suggested, however, any economy (national or local) tends to be more or less characterized by the relative uniformity of organizational architecture, although it may be preceded by a period of cohabitation of diverse organizational experiments.

Suppose that at an initial stage of the market economy a more primitive organizational mode, say classical hierarchical decomposition, prevailed, in which operational tasks were served by a simple skill type under commands of the proprietor-entrepreneur. Imagine that multiple organizational experiments subsequently emerged, which relied on the information-processing capacity of the workers at the operational task level. These can be functional hierarchies based on individuated, task-specific human assets, or team-oriented horizontal hierarchies based on context-oriented human assets. In any case suppose that both of them are more efficient than classical hierarchies in both industries, as they can make better use of ex post information evolving at the operational level. But suppose that both of them has an absolute productivity advantage vis-à-vis the other in only one industry, as specified in the cost matrix introduced in the beginning of the last section, provided that corresponding human assets type were available.

In the beginning, there might be competition among the new organizational experiments, but suppose that either one gains a momentum due to relatively abundant supply of the fitting human asset type. Then, even if the other one were potentially more efficient in some industry, evolutionary pressure might make the sustainability of the latter increasingly harder. Because of the fear of the higher risk of mismatching, it becomes ever less advantageous for the new generations to invest in the type of human assets tailored to the less dominant organizational architecture (this is an instance of strategic complementarity). Thus the presence of evolutionary pressure suggests that organizational diversity in the sense of cohabitation of diverse organizational architecture in a single organizational field cannot be taken for granted. However, the possibility of multiple equilibria also suggests that the evolution of different organizational conventions across different fields (e.g., national economies and localities) may occur. Given such a possibility of cross-field organizational diversity, let us now consider several avenues for exploiting the gains from diversity through interactions or integration of two organizational fields that have evolved different conventions.[16]

Free Trade

First, let us consider if the gains from an organizational diversity can be exploited by free trade between two organizational fields, *FH* (referring to an organizational field realizing the convention of functional hierarchy) and *HH* (referring to an organizational field realizing the convention of horizontal hierarchy), that have historically developed two different organizational conventions. Assume that the tastes of the populations of the two organizational fields are identical. We assume that the organizational convention of each field persists after market integration because of a barrier to free mobility of agents across the borders of two organizational fields. There are two possible classes of trade equilibrium, depending on the relative size of the two organizational fields.

First, suppose that one of the two organizational fields (e.g., *HH*) is very small, but has developed an organizational convention (e.g., *HH*-convention) that has gained a productivity edge in a particular niche industry (e.g., *D*). Then this organizational field will be specialized in that advantageous industry at free-trade equilibrium. However, the supply capacity of the organizational field is so small that a part of the population of the relatively larger organizational field (e.g., *FH*) is also engaged in that industry to meet demands despite the productivity gap. The equilibrium price levels remain the same as the ones that prevailed when the larger organizational field remained closed so the disadvantageous industry in that field still can survive to meet global demand after opening to free trade. Therefore there is no gain from free trade for the larger field, but for the smaller field there are gains in the form of quasi-rents from the organizational innovation in its specialized industry.

Next, suppose that the size of the two organizational fields are relatively equal, but they are heterogeneous in organizational convention. Then both fields can engage in mutually beneficial free trade by specializing in respectively advantageous industries. As organizational conventions persist in both organizational fields as an equilibrium, the aggregate gains from free trade do not match those available from the optimal organizational diversity (P-equilibrium), however, except for the unlikely case where the relative population size of the two organizational fields (thus the supply ratio of the two goods) happens to be equal to the ratio of aggregate demands for the two goods.

PROPOSITION 5.1   The gains from free trade are greater for a smaller organizational field that has developed an organizational advantage in some industry. However, the quasi-rent from the organizational advantage will decline as the relative size of the organizational field becomes larger. The global aggregate gains from free trade will not reach the optimal level except by chance.

The Integration of Human Assets Market

Suppose that the two organizational fields, *HH* and *FH*, that have previously hindered the free mobility of agents remove the barrier. Then agents from both fields are now matched according to the model in the previous section. The following proposition is intuitive:

PROPOSITION 5.2   For any technological and demand conditions, the integration of two organizational fields that have developed different conventions will lead to the Pareto-efficient organizational diversity, provided that neither field is too large nor too small vis-à-vis the other organizational field. Otherwise, the convention of the smaller field will disappear after integration even if it has an absolute advantage in an industry, unless assortative matching develops among agents with context-oriented human assets (i.e., γ becomes sufficiently small).

This proposition may be interpreted as a kind of path-dependent property of evolutionary dynamics: once an organizational convention has been formed in a closed organizational field of a certain size and acquired a certain scale, it is able to exist, even if the initial condition that facilitated its emergence disappears. On the other hand, even a potentially efficient organizational innovation may become extinct by "premature" integration with a larger field, if that innovation has arisen in a relatively small field.

Organizational Experiments and Foreign Direct Investment

The possibility of trade and labor mobility may be limited for various technological and politicoeconomic reasons (transportation costs, intrinsic immobility of certain goods and services, trade barriers, etc.). However, the source of possible gains from diversity in our model is organizational architecture which is a human contrivance. Human asset types, either context-oriented or individuated, are not to be considered as genetically or culturally fixed. They are objects of human investment decisions. This consideration might lead one to wonder if the gains from organizational diversity are not realizable through choices of agents.

Even though it is not situationally rational for agents not to conform to an established convention in their organizational field, they may experiment in unconventional human asset type, for example, by investing in individuated human assets when the horizontal hierarchy is a convention, or alternatively, investing in context-oriented human assets when the functional hierarchy is a convention. These random experiments are analogous to mutations in biological evolution, independent of the natural selection of the fittest. Social mutations may occur, for example, when a small proportion of the population is replaced by a new generation that is not bound by a traditional convention, a number of agents who are exposed, educated, and trained in a foreign convention return to the home country, or when a foreign firm makes a direct investment and consciously selects workers fitting their organizational architecture (positive assortative matching). What would be the long-run outcome of evolutionary selection when such mutations occur? Is it still difficult to upset an existing convention? To explore this issue theoretically in the context of a closed organizational field, let us introduce the notion of the cost of transition by experiments from one convention and reach the Pareto-efficient diversity as the minimum proportion of the current population who must mutate.

First, as a benchmark consider the situation where cost coefficient matrices and demand parameters are symmetric, so there is no intrinsic advantage for either industries, B or D.[17] Further assume that agents with context-oriented human assets are randomly matched ($\gamma = 1$). Then the following proposition holds:

PROPOSITION 5.3   Suppose that technological and demand conditions are symmetric for both industries and that agents possessing context-oriented human assets are randomly matched. Then the cost of transition by experiments from the convention of functional hierarchies (I-equilibrium) to the efficient organizational diversity (P-equilibrium) is smaller than that from the convention of horizontal hierarchies (C-equilibrium).

The relative advantage of the FH field in embracing diversity derives from the flexible mobility of the individuated human assets type across industries. They can more easily move out of the relatively disadvantageous industry, D, in the face of emergent experiments that may have a potential advantage there. However, under the HH

convention, the agents who invested in context-oriented human assets specific to industry B cannot easily move out form that industry despite emergent, potentially more productive experiments there. Thus the HH convention is more susceptible to inertia.

The assumption of random matching by the agents with context-oriented human assets is not realistic, however, and is meaningful only as a benchmark. It is then interesting to examine how this relative difficulty of the HH field for embracing the organizational diversity can be overcome by introducing the possibility of assortative matching, as well as asymmetry in demand and technological parameters. This question is answered by the following proposition:

PROPOSITION 5.4 (1) The more severe the relative inefficiency of horizontal hierarchies in the B-industry vis-à-vis mutant functional hierarchies, (2) the smaller the relative demands for the product of the inefficient B industry, (3) the higher the degree of assortative matching of agents with context-oriented human assets, and (4) the wider the productivity differential between the two industries under the prevailing horizontal hierarchies, the lower will be the cost of transition by experiments from the HH convention to the optimal diversity.[18]

These results are consistent with the often observed stylized facts that organizational conventions are rather robust in a relatively efficient economy, but organizational learning sometimes proceeds at a faster pace and generates a new type of organizational architecture, when a large productivity gap with a foreign economy is perceived. Also, if the degree of positive assortative matching is higher so that agents with context-oriented human assets tend to congregate more, the less evolutionary pressure will be exercised on individuated mutants because of the reduced risk of mismatching. Then the mutant organizational architecture becomes more viable and the cost of transition is lowered. This is analytically intuitive, but a conventional argument does not seem to necessarily run in this vein.

"Organizational Design" Based on Foresight

Best-response evolutionary dynamics are characterized by two elements of bounded rationality: (1) myopic choice of human assets type and industry by the agents, without any foresight but rather based on simple imitation of the best practice in the organizational field, and (2) inertia, which makes complete, instantaneous, optimal adjustment impossible. These two bounded-rationality factors were responsible for the path-dependent selection of a nonoptimal equilibrium (the emergence of an organizational convention). The preceding paragraph indicates that mutations may play a role in helping the economy to overcome historical determinism. However, the barrier to realizing the gains from organizational diversity by means of mutations could remain formidable. Therefore one may wonder if adding some element of "rationality" may help the economy to realize the efficient choice of an organizational arrangement. Let us therefore ask the following question: If a small number of agents are successively able to form foresight regarding the potential future value of an unconventional organizational architecture, choose a strategy accordingly, and adhere to it over time, will the efficient organizational diversity self-organize itself?

It is difficult to present a convincing formulation of expectations that carries a certain bounded-rationality feature. Therefore let us make the following compromise: a certain proportion of the population, a group of entrepreneurs, say, randomly selected at each moment in time, form perfect foresight and base their strategic choices on that expectation, while others are attached to current strategies with inertia. We can assume that the relative size of the entrepreneurs at each moment in time is proportional to the conceived magnitude of disequilibrium. This means that the greater the discrepancy of the potential asset values between the two human assets types, the more agents are compelled to make a choice by forming expectations.

In order to make the analysis tractable, let us assume that the agents choosing the C-strategy are always engaged in the technologically advantageous D-industry. Thus the strategy set of the agents is reduced to the strategy choice of I versus C. The agents choosing the I strategy can be mobile between the B and D industry at any moment in time as before.[19] Let Q_C represent the implicit asset value of the context-oriented human assets over that of the individuated human assets. Thus it can have either sign. Given the rate of future discount, ρ, the arbitrage condition requires that

$$\frac{dQ_C}{dt} + \Delta u_C(t) \leq \rho Q_C(t), \qquad \text{with equality if } m_{CD} > 0.$$

where Δu_C is the difference of the payoff level between the agent with the context-oriented human assets over that with the individuated human asset. In other words, the implicit net asset value is determined at the level at which the sum of expected net capital gain and the current net income from possessing the asset are equal to the interest income available from investing the same value of wealth in riskless assets.

Suppose that at each moment in time a group of agents can perceive correctly the difference in implicit asset values between the two human assets types, Q_C, and base their investment decisions on that expectation. Specifically we assume that

$$\frac{dm_{CD}}{dt} = \lambda Q_C(t),$$

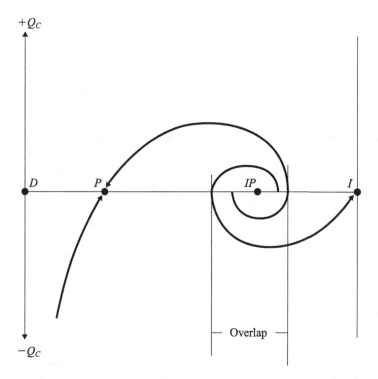

Figure 5.2
Bifurcation of evolutionary path when the initial point is far from equilibria. The vertical axis measures the asset value of the context-oriented human minus that of the individuated human assets, Q_C, and the horizontal segment represents side DI of the simplex in figure 5.1. From the left corner (alternatively, the right corner) the proportion of the population invested in individuated human assets is $m_{IB} + m_{ID}$ (respectively, context-oriented human assets m_{CB}). When the initial distribution of the population lies in the overlap region, the evolutionary dynamics may converge either to P or I depending on the entrepreneurial expectation on the level of Q_C.

where λ represents the level of the entrepreneurial spirit in the economy. The formula implies that the higher the disequilibrium state measured by the absolute value of Q_C is, the greater the relative size of the entrepreneur group.

The two differential equations given above define Krugman-Matsuyama-type equilibrium dynamic paths.[20] See figure 5.2 for the equilibrium paths of this dynamic in which an entrepreneur's expectation can become self-fulfilling. The vertical axis measures the level of Q_C and the horizontal segment from the left corner (alternatively, the right corner) measures the proportion of the population invested in individuated human assets $m_{IB} + m_{ID}$ (respectively, context-oriented human assets m_{CB}). The phase diagram indicates the following:

PROPOSITION 5.5   If the discount rate ρ is lower and the level of entrepreneurial spirit λ is higher relative to the cost of mismatching,[21] then the dynamic equilibrium path cannot be uniquely determined by the initial position alone when it starts far from the convention and optimal diversity. Depending on the initial expectations of entrepreneurs, equilibrium path can self-organize to either the optimal diversity or a less efficient convention.

If the said condition is satisfied, entrepreneurial foresight matters, but the direction of their activity is not clear. In figure 5.2 on the segment between equilibrium I and P, there is a band of positive length including IP such that if the initial position is located within it, the dynamic path can go to either I or P. In other words, far from equilibria I and P, the dynamic path bifurcates. It either converges to the efficient diversity or leads to the formation of a subefficient homogeneous convention. Which way the economy evolves may depend on some historically unique factors affecting entrepreneur's expectations that the economic model above is unable to capture. If entrepreneurs form the expectation that the future return to investment in context-oriented human assets is high (low) and behave accordingly, then that expectation may become self-fulfilling and the relatively efficient organizational diversity (respectively, the relatively inefficient F-convention) may evolve. In any case this proposition suggests that chaos far from equilibria may destroy rigid historical determinism. However, it also implies that the introduction of elements of rational expectations will not necessarily guarantee the convergence of dynamics to the efficient arrangements of organizational architecture in the economy.

5.4   The Relevance and Limits of the Evolutionary Game Model

One primary objective of this chapter has been to see how different organizational conventions can arise in different economies/localities and become a source of relative industrial advantage/disadvantage, even if potential technologies and tastes were the same everywhere. The reason for the evolution of multiple, suboptimal organizational conventions is not increasing returns as focused on recently in economics, but complementarity among the strategic choices of agents. If a large proportion of the population is adopting a certain strategy, it becomes the best response for agents to adopt the same strategy. The apparent difference from the contract theory of the organization which prescribes/predicts a (second) best response of the principal to exogenous parameters arises from the fact that the principal–agent theory treats outside options open to the principal and agents as exogenously given, while in evolutionary models, alternatives open to each agent are determined endogenously as a result of the strategic interplay of agents.

The model presented in this chapter is extremely simple: there are only two human asset types and two types of organizational architecture. Technological and market conditions are parametrically fixed. Although the setting of the model thus remains at an extremely abstract level, it attempts to capture some fundamental factors that underlie the observed diversity of organizational architecture across economies and the co-evolution of a diversity of human asset types. More specifically, we submit that if one compares two (possibly polar) cases of organizational evolution in North America and Japan, one cannot fail to notice the striking relevance of the distinction made in this chapter (and later) between functional and horizontal hierarchies, as well as individuated and context-oriented human assets types.

Think of some notable examples of innovation in the area of work organization that were initiated and institutionalized in North America: such as the afore-mentioned American manufacturing system developed in the last century in New England machinery industry (Rosenberg 1963; Pine 1993); the Taylorist scientific management movement (whose innovative nature has often been misunderstood; see Wredge and Greenwood 1991); and the subsequent development of management hierarchies, bureaucratization of personnel administration (Jacoby 1985; Baron et al. 1986) and associated job controlled unionism in the 1930s and 1940s. All these examples have a common characteristic in either having introduced or institutional-ized a new method of combining individuated human assets at progressive degrees of maturity—human assets that became embodied in individual workers, engineers, and managers through professional and vocational training, even though some elements of organizational contextuality cannot be entirely ignored. The organizational inno-vation that underlies Silicon Valley may appear to be a radical departure from tra-ditional functional hierarchies in which bureaucratic control of highly segmented jobs is the norm. However, an excellent description and analysis of Baldwin and Clark (2000) shows that it may be also considered as an unintended evolutionary outcome from the centralized control over modular tasks as represented by the design of the IBM360. We will analyze later in chapters 10.2 and 14 in what respects the Silicon Valley model differs from, as well as conforms with in some respects, the traditional functional hierarchies and why it evolved in a periphery of industrial America.

If we turn to historically known examples of organizational practices and innova-tions that affected the evolutionary path of organizational practices in Japan, a striking contrast to the American path is immediately discernable. For example, think of the design of the seniority and bonus payment system by advanced factories at the beginning of the twentieth century as means of restraining excessive quits of skilled workers; collective, ad hoc problem-solving self-organized by the workers on the shop floor in response to the scarcity of tools and materials during the Second

World War; the transformation of the American-born, engineer-led quality-control system into shop-floor level work-group practices; the evolution of the *kanban* system in the 1950s which partially emulated an inventory restocking method used by American supermarket firms.[22] In contrast to the American case, reliance on information channels shared by workers within the context of a particular organization is a distinct attribute, even though more recent innovations seem to increasingly accommodate elements of the workers' individuated information-processing skills. For example, the now famous *kanban* system could not have been implemented without the ability of individual workers to cope with emergent events on the spot, such as breakdown of machines, or spotting defective parts. But even these capabilities were backed up by the workers' information networking channels (e.g., mutual help in teams, the sharing of engineering and production knowledge through job rotation and cross-functional meetings, company-specific training programs). It is worth noting that when the idea of the *kanban* system was brought back to America in the 1980s as a lesson from the so-called Japanese management style, it was transformed into something different, yet consistent with the American path—the lean production method (Warmack et al. 1990) which would reduce inventories and hierarchical layers of production-control by flexible matching (outsourcing) with specialized suppliers.

The brief observations in the last two paragraphs indicate the limits of applying the results of a "stationary" evolutionary model for interpreting real phenomena. By "stationary" we specifically refer to the assumption that the strategic choice set of each agent is exogenously given and fixed. Therefore, in our theoretical model, "innovation" in one economy can occur only in the form of a shift from one equilibrium to the one characterized by diversity. Competition among economies often induces an attempt to emulate an organizational convention prevailing in a foreign economy which may be perceived to be a superior practice. However, as just mentioned above regarding the evolution of the *kanban* system and its recycling into North America, learning from a foreign practice may not result in a simple transplant or a hybrid but in the enrichment or adaptation of indigenous organizational practice. Also entrepreneurial experiments that eventually lead to the rise of a new type of organizational architecture may actually be a new type of bundling of existing skills, as in the case of Silicon Valley firms. Both possibilities alter and enlarge the agents' sets of strategy choices.

Thus actual organizational evolutionary processes involving innovation cannot be characterized as a mere shift from one convention (e.g., *C*- or *I*-equilibrium in figure 5.3) based on one type of human assets merely to a diversity mixing the two (e.g., *P*-equilibrium). One conjecture is that the organizational evolutionary process can be characterized by successive equilibria, at each of which one type of human asset is sequentially enriched by learning and intentional design. In this regard the following comment made by the pioneer of the evolutionary game theory in biology, Maynard-Smith, is highly suggestive: "Whenever an optimisation or game-theoretic analysis is performed, an essential feature of the analysis is *a specification of the set of possible phenotypes* from among which the optimum is to be found. This specification is identical to a description of developmental constraints" (1982:5; italics added). In other words, the analysis of optimization (i.e., evolutionary selection) can explain the phenomena of multiple organizational conventions once developmental constraints (i.e., possible types of human assets) are given, but cannot explain how developmental constraints themselves are determined. In order to understand the mechanism of organizational change, we need to go beyond the scope of stationary evolutionary modeling as presented in this chapter. A preliminary attempt toward such direction will be attempted in chapter 9.

6 States as Stable Equilibria in the Polity Domain

In all governments there is a perpetual internecine struggle, open or secret, between Authority and Liberty, and neither of them can ever absolutely prevail in contest. A great sacrifice of liberty must necessarily be made in every government, yet even the authority which confines liberty can never and perhaps ought never in any constitution to become quite entire and uncontrollable. The sultan is master of the life and fortune of any individual, but will not be permitted to impose new taxes on his subjects: a French monarch can impose taxes at pleasure, but would find it dangerous to attempt the lives and fortunes of individuals.
—David Hume, *Essays, Moral, Political, and Literary* (1741:116)

In chapter 3 we showed that as market exchanges expand, the nation-state tends to emerge as a primary, albeit not exclusive, third-party mechanism for protecting property rights and enforcing contracts. Private agents can reciprocally discipline private third-party agents, such as the law merchants, escrow companies, and auction web sites, by choosing not to use their services in the event of misconduct. But the unitary national government is characterized by exclusive, compulsory coverage within its geographical territory. There is no way for private agents residing there to exit from the domain unless by emigration, and other governments may not have any obligation to accept fleeing agents. Further, private third-party agents lack lawful enforcement power, whereas the national government possesses a monopoly in the lawful use of force with which to enforce its own judgments and impose taxes on private agents.

Although economists have tended to regard the role of the government in defining and enforcing property rights as exogenous to a market system, it cannot be thus taken for granted that the power of the government is always used to enhance markets. This is what Weingast called the "fundamental political dilemma of an economic system":

A government strong enough to protect property rights and enforce contracts is also strong enough to confiscate the wealth of its citizens. Thriving markets require not only the appropriate system of property rights and a law of contracts, but a secure political foundation that limits the ability of the state to confiscate wealth. Far from obvious, however, are the circumstances that produce a political system that plays one role instead of the other. (1995:1)

In this chapter we begin by identifying three prototype states in the polity domain that may or may not resolve the dilemma. Then we proceed to derive evolutionary ramifications of these prototype models and examine their implications for the security of private property rights and the development of markets.

In deriving prototype models of states and their ramifications, this chapter makes a clear distinction between the government as an organization, and thus as a player of the game in the polity domain, on the one hand, and a state as a stable order of relationships between the government and private agents, on the other. The word *state* derives from the Latin *stare* (to stand), and more specifically *status* (a standing or condition). *Status* applies to something that is established, recognized as fixed or permanent in a particular position, as do its derivative English words, static and stable.[1] As such the state may be thought of as being amenable to "equilibrium" analysis, yielding possibly many varieties. We conceptualize states as stable multiple equilibria of a generic political exchange game in the polity domain by which a government and the private agents settle on a certain order between them. Thus a state is not merely a government organization or the rules that it makes (which could be broken or ignored) but an order that the government itself is subject to. It may comprise stable collective beliefs held by private agents, as well as by the government, regarding the possible outcomes of their (deviant) behavior, so they may sustain a predictable pattern of behavior. In this sense, the state may be said to have an aspect of endogenous normative order. As will become subsequently clear, conceptualizing the state as an equilibrium phenomenon helps us understand the nature of the relationships between the state and other institutions in the economic domain, and thus the nature of the political economy in a comparative perspective.

Section 6.1 identifies three prototype modes of the state as stable outcomes of the same generic game constructed à la Weingast (1993, 1995, 1997).[2] These are the democratic, predatory, and collusive states. As we will show, the democratic state in its most generic form may be considered, if it exists at all, as the least intrusive in the spontaneous order of property rights. However, the emergence of such a state may not be automatic and taken for granted. In some circumstances the collusive state, the state in which the government (presidential office, permanent bureaucracy, dictator, ruling party, etc., depending on context) colludes with particular private agents (interest groups) for its advantage may appear as a stationary or cyclic state. Even in a large part of the twentieth century, the aspect of the collusive state was sustained in many economies, among these Stalinist communist states, destabilizing or deterring the development of markets and the economy in the long run. But there have also been various evolving states, depending on the political context, that could remedy or safeguard themselves against the asymmetric, predatory nature of the collusive state. In section 6.2 we discuss some ramifications of those forms: market-preserving federalist states, liberal democratic states, social compact corporatist states, (rural-inclusive) developmental states, and bureau-pluralistic state. Their viability may be interdependent on institutional arrangements in domains other than the polity, which we will address in parts II and III. The task of this chapter is more or less limited to identifying the different states derived from generic forms. In explicitly recognizing a government as a strategic player that may pursue its own objective but be constrained by strategic interactions with private agents, we depart from the neoclassical economist's view of the government as a benevolent welfare maximizer or a potentially omnipotent social engineer, as well as from the ultralibertarian view of the government as inherently infringing on individual rights.[3]

6.1 Three Prototypes of the State

Let us consider a simple game situation with the government and private agents as players. The private agents need the protection of their property rights in order to engage in economic activities. The government can provide this protection at some cost by its monopoly in the use of force. These costs may be charged to the private agents through taxation. Further the government may potentially have the power (and motivation) to transgress the property rights of some, or all, of the private agents by charging higher taxes, confiscating wealth, issuing too much currency (inflation tax), and so on, unless it is effectively restrained from doing so. However, it may be the case that any private agent alone is not able to cope with the potentially abusive power of the government. Under what conditions, and how, can the limited use of power by the government to protect private property rights become self-enforcing? The answer cannot be simply a written law, for rules can be changed or ignored by the government as well as private agents. It must be in the self-interest of the government, as well as the private agent, to honor and protect private property rights.

In considering this issue, let us imagine the following simple political exchange game à la Weingast (1993, 1997) played by the government (a generic expression for sovereign, an organization composed of legislature, executive offices and a judiciary body, autonomous administrative bureaucracy, ruling party, etc.,) and two private agents, A and B (generic expressions for citizens, voters, interest groups, etc.).[4] In the second half of this chapter we will attach more specific attributes to the government and private agents to distinguish practical forms of states. Suppose for now that an arrangement for economic property rights has been set up and that if the government limits its role to only securing those rights, it can do so at minimum cost $2t$ financed by private agents. Then the private agents can each enjoy utility Γ, while bearing the tax cost t each owes to the government. When such a state is realized, it may be referred to as the "minimalist state" following Nozick (1974), or the "nightwatchman state" (Adam Smith 1776). Suppose, however, that the government can derive benefits for itself (empire building, wealth accumulation and consumption by government officials, redundant bureaucrats, etc.) by transgressing the limits of the

the nontransgressed the transgressed	resist	submit
resist	2t−C, Γ−c, Γ−c	2t+α, Γ−α−c−Δ, Γ−Δ
submit		2t+α, Γ−α−Δ, Γ−Δ

Figure 6.1
Payoff matrix of political exchange game

minimalist state. Suppose that it tries to capture additional α units of benefits from either agent, say A, by a tax increase, a confiscation of some property, and the like. To counter such a transgression of private property by the government, both agents can either resist or submit.

The outcome of the game in the event of a government transgression is represented by the payoff matrix in figure 6.1, where rows (respectively, columns) indicate the strategies of transgressed agent A (respectively, nontransgressed B) and the first, second, and third entry of each cell represent the payoffs to the government and the private agents, A and B respectively. It costs each private agent c to resist the government, regardless of whether he cooperates or not in their resistance. If private agent B cooperates with private agent A in resistance against the government, the government's attempt to violate A's property rights is doomed to fail, costing it a large sum C (e.g., loss of power). On the other hand, if B does not cooperate with A, the sole resistance of A is not effective and the government succeeds in capturing α units of benefits from him. Suppose, for a moment, that the predatory behavior of the government threatens the security of private property rights and thus reduces the efficiency of the private sector, creating the additional deadweight loss 2Δ, which is borne by A and B equally. If A does not resist, it can save on conflict cost c, although the same inefficiency cost Δ is imposed on each private agent by government transgression.

Suppose that this game is played only once and that it is not possible for the private agents to arrange an enforceable side payment ex ante. If $\Delta - c \leq 0$, that is, the cost for agent B to cooperate with A in resisting the government transgression is greater than the deadweight efficiency loss from the transgression, the best strategy of B is not to cooperate and secure $\Gamma - \Delta$. Anticipating such a strategy, the best strategy of A is also to submit to the government transgression to avoid the conflict cost c. Thus the private agents fail to coordinate their resistance, and the combination of {Transgress, Submit, Submit} is a static Nash equilibrium outcome of the one-shot game.

Suppose now that the game is played repeatedly. Since a static Nash can also be an equilibrium of a repeated game, the following *predatory state* may become self-enforcing: either A or B always becomes a prey of the transgressing government, but both submit for fear of conflict costs, thus incurring the social cost 2Δ per period.

Suppose next that $\Delta - c > 0$; that is, the deadweight loss caused by the transgression of the government is comparatively greater than the cost for agent B to cooperate with agent A in resisting government transgression. In this case it may become in B's interest to cooperate with A. But, if $\Delta - c < \alpha$, the government can be better off making a side payment (bribe) to B in the amount s, satisfying $\Delta - c \leq s < \alpha$. Then B loses the incentive to cooperate with A, and it is not worthwhile for A to resist either. Thus the combination of {Transgress and bribe, Submit, Accept side payment and submit} can become a static Nash equilibrium outcome of the one-shot game, with pay offs $(2t + \alpha - s, \Gamma - \alpha - \Delta, \Gamma - \Delta + s)$. When such an outcome is sustained in a repeated game, we may refer to it as a *collusive state*. In the collusive state, the government and private agent B collude in transgressing the property rights of A to their mutual advantage, while perpetuating social costs 2Δ per period.

In both of the preceding cases, private agents A and B fail to coordinate in resisting government transgression and suffer from the deprivation of property rights as well as deadweight efficiency losses. What can make coordinated resistance to government transgression by private agents self-enforcing? Imagine the situation in which the government cannot identify agents A or B in any stage game and can only randomly aim at transgressing the private property rights of either agent with an equal probability. We will discuss what kinds of conditions would warrant such an assumption momentarily. For now we limit our attention to the implications of the anonymous relationship between the government and the private agents. We suppose that the payoff structure of the stage game when the government transgresses the property rights of B is symmetrical to the matrix above. Consider the following strategy profiles: (1) the government always transgresses either agent randomly, if and only if A and/or B has not resisted its transgression in the past. Otherwise, it honors the private property rights of both agents. (2) When the government transgresses, private agents submit if and only if either of them has done so in the past. Otherwise, they always coordinate resistance against the government's transgression. Suppose further that all the players believe that the other players have played these strategies and will continue to play them, unless they themselves observe a deviation from them. It is immediate, then, that there is no incentive for the government to defect from honoring private property rights in any stage game, if and only if the threat of cooperative resistance is credible. Therefore we need to check if it is in the interest of any private agent to cooperate in resistance if the other party's property rights are transgressed.

Consider a deviation from the private agent's strategy to resist government transgression on the other agent's rights. The present-value sum of future losses from not resisting is $\delta(\alpha + 2\Delta)/2(1 - \delta)$, since the government will keep transgressing against either party with probability $\frac{1}{2}$ in future periods, while the current net cost of coordinated resistance is $c - \Delta$. If the private agents fear the costs of random transgressions by the government in the future relatively more than the current cost of coordinated resistance, the threat of coordinated resistance can become credible. After rearrangement, this condition can be seen to hold if $\delta > 2(c - \Delta)/(2c + \alpha)$ for $\Delta - c \leq 0$ and for any positive δ if $0 < \Delta - c$. Then it becomes in the government's self-interest to limit itself to protecting and honoring private property rights. We may refer to this outcome as the *democratic state*. In this state the commitment of the government to limited power is credible, since the prevailing belief is that any predatory action by the government is punished by the withdrawal of the support of private agents, both the direct victims of government transgression as well as the nonvictims, regardless of their political preferences in other respects (Weingast 1993, 1997). Thus, if $\Delta - c \leq \alpha$, there can be multiple (subgame perfect) equilibria, and the democratic state, as well as the predatory and collusive states, can become self-enforcing once either of them is established. However, these different states can have different implications for the security of private property rights and thus for the enhancement of markets. We will also see momentarily that conversely, the mode and extent of market development may have implications for the selection of equilibrium among the possible states.

In the parable above, in order for democratic control of the government by private agents to become incentive compatible for them and thus self-enforcing, it is essential that all private agents expect to equally face a high degree of uncertainty regarding whom the government will prey upon. If it is known that the government always targets particular agents (interest groups) for predatory action, other agents may be induced to stay mute or collude with the government. It is the fear of being subjected himself to the government's random predatory action that can motivate each agent to participate in resistance against any predatory action by the government. What kind of situation can we imagine in which private agents would reasonably have this kind of fear? In other words, what kind of situation can we imagine in which the government cannot identify a certain type of agent as a specific target for predatory action, and others as coalition partners or passive bystanders?

Returning to the realm of the parable, a hypothetical situation that may warrant the described presumption is one in which the private agents in the polity domain are symmetric to the government. Suppose, for example, that the private agents in the polity domain are dominated by more or less undifferentiated market traders in terms of wealth position, although differentiated in their preferences and relative composition of initial holdings, so that the government lacks ex ante information to discriminate among them for profitable transgressing opportunities (we need to visualize here that there are numerous private agents rather than only two as in the generic model above). It appears appropriate to describe this situation as one in which the private agents are anonymous to the government. But since economists use the word "anonymous markets" in a specific sense,[5] we avoid that expression and describe it as the polity domain being dominated by "symmetric" traders. Needless to say, it is a purely theoretical construct, without a real counterpart. However, by examining the logical consequence of such a presumption, we gain some insight into an aspect of states evolving in places where homogeneous members of some class are exclusive participants in the polity (as in the Glorious Revolution in the seventeenth-century England or the Republic of Venezia), or where the middle class establishes political hegemony in a representation system (as in nineteenth-century England; see below).

If the government is uninformed ex ante as to who can be most profitably and effectively targeted as a possible prey, it can select a possible victim only randomly rather than systematically, if it wishes to prey at all. One may note a modicum of logical tension between this presumption of uninformed government, on the one hand, and that of the government as an enforcer of property rights, on the other. How can the uninformed government identify and credibly punish those who violate the rules of property rights and contracts? Let us suppose that although traders themselves as well may not be able to identify their opponents in the process of trade bargaining, they can identify trading partners who have committed theft, fraud, extortion, payment default, and so on, after an initial agreement is reached, and bring the offenders to the government (court). If the government is susceptible to bribery by offenders or makes arbitrary judgments, then honest traders who are ex ante unrecognized to the government become in effect subject to direct or indirect transgressions by the government. In order to prevent the government from making arbitrary judgments, it then becomes in the traders' general interests to constrain the government to make judgments only on the basis of a rigorous application of the rules of law to verifiable facts regarding an offence. An instance of violation of the rules of law by the government can alert all the private agents that the same ill-fate may befall them in the future. It will become in the mutual interest of the private agents (traders) to coordinate resistance against arbitrary predation, or violation of the rules of law, by the government and replace it through the withdrawal of support. Then the use of force by the government could be limited to cases in which the violation of private property rights is ex post verifiable and punishable on the basis of ex ante rules.

It is important to note, however, that it is not the articulation of law alone that makes the rule of law workable, but the presence of general beliefs that the violation of law by the government will be punished by the coordinated resistance of the private agents. Such beliefs become credible because of the symmetry of traders in markets and the absence of ex ante knowledge regarding the characteristics of traders on the side of the government. Paradoxically, the limit of government control to the rule-based, ex post intervention could thus be the outcome of its ex ante ignorance. In other words, the lack of government's information about the identity of individual traders can become a commitment device for the government to abstain from random extortion.

Markets in which traders appear to be symmetric to the government may be considered as roughly correspondent to competitive ones in which no traders exercise monopolistic/monopsonic market power. Otherwise, the government may be induced either to collude with monopolists/monopsonists or to exploit them. Thus the reasoning above may be roughly paraphrased as that competitive markets can be a source of the democratic state in which the government follows the rule of law. Reciprocally, the third-party governance mechanism implemented by the rule of law under the democratic state can enhance the domain of market exchange. That is, a greater number of agents will be actively engaged in market exchange because of credible beliefs in government's willingness and ability to indiscriminately protect private property rights and enforce contract (chapter 3). Thus we may claim the following purely theoretical proposition:

CLAIM 6.1   One source of a democratic state in which the government follows the rule of law may be competitive markets in which no traders exercise monopolistic or monopsonic power. Conversely, the third-party governance mechanism based on the rule of law can enhance the domain of market exchange. Thus the rules of law and the symmetric markets can co-evolve.

The rule of law is thus not simply an exogenous prerequisite for the functioning of competitive markets as "legal centrism" (Ellickson 1991) might imply. Rather, there may be a feedback mechanism operating from competitive markets to the rule of law as well.

An alternative situation in which the target of future predatory action by the government becomes highly uncertain may arise when the constituent population is divided into two (interest) groups, each clustering around common interests in defining and defending property rights, and in which sizes are relatively equal and demarcation is fluid. A small number of constituent members may randomly drift from one group to another or a new generation with uncertain interests may continually arrive, swinging a majority between the two groups in an unpredictable manner. Further assume that the government (the legislature) is regularly elected through popular vote and that two parties, each in a coalition with a separate group competes for winning a majority. Suppose that there are some random elements at each election that may sway the voting of a small number of randomly selected voters, and that can be decisive in the outcome of the election. Therefore the currently ruling party may possibly lose power in the next election. There can be two outcomes in such a situation.

One outcome can be that each newly elected representative government modifies the preceding property rights arrangement in favor of a winning faction of the population through transfer payments, tax changes, and other means, thus creating cyclic collusive states. However, if the voters are sufficiently patient and risk averse, and if the costs of political cycles of property-rights rearrangements are perceived to be very high because of damage done to the incentives of both groups in supplying their resources, then another equilibrium outcome may arise. Voters may prefer the stable sustenance of a property-rights arrangement by limiting the ability of the government to prey or modify the existing property-rights arrangement. Then an agreement can be reached (by the two parties) to limit the power of the government that is enforced by the credible threat of coordinated resistance of the voting citizens against a defecting ruling party. Thus a democratic state may ensue. The representative system would then serve as a device for placing an appropriate limit on the ability of the government to transgress private property rights. However, which of the equilibria emerge—the cyclic collusive states or democratic state—cannot be theoretically predicted and is dependent on historical context.

There can be still another situation in which the government may be constrained against predatory behavior. So far we have assumed that there is no possibility of a self-enforcing contract between the private parties by which a transgressee makes a side payment to the other party contingent on the latter's cooperation of resistance. If the private agents are numerous and not organized into any particular interest groups, such a contract will not be negotiable and agreed upon ex ante. Even in the case in which such a contract is made ex ante, there is no guarantee that the transgressee would not renege after successful coordinated resistance. For example, after the transgressing government is overthrown by the cooperative resistance between agents A and B, transgressed A may collude with a new government (or form a government) against nontransgressed B.

Dropping the assumption of symmetry, imagine a situation, without asking momentarily how it could be possible, where an ex ante contract on the ex post contingent side payment as described above is somehow negotiable between the two parties. Suppose further that they adopt the following strategy. When the government transgresses, private agents submit if and only if either of them has done so in the past or either party has ever defaulted on the promised side payment. Otherwise,

they always coordinate resistance against government transgression, and after successful resistance the transgressee makes side payment σ to the other party such that
$\alpha \geq \sigma \geq \Delta$. Then it is in the interest of the government to honor the property rights of
both agents unless either of them has failed to resist its transgression in the past. The
problem is how such a side-payment contract between the private agents can be
agreed upon and become self-enforcing. Obviously it cannot be the government that
arranges and enforces such private contract. It needs to be self-organizing and self-
enforcing in the private sector. Assume that private agents A and B are the peak
organizations of two interest groups, say business and labor, rather than symmetric
market participants. Imagine that their political powers are almost comparable in
terms of potential ability to forge a collusive state with the government. Then the
same reasoning, leading to the democratic state under the assumption of symmetric
agents or a (two-party) representative system, can be applied to this situation. Both
peak organizations would prefer to have a private contract between them than to
have cyclic collusive states because of the fear of unpredictable victimization by a
collusive state and the associated efficiency losses. The contract is self-enforceable
because defaulting on it would be punished by the withdrawal of cooperation in the
future by the other party. The equilibrium outcome is the same as would emerge in
the democratic state under the condition of symmetric agents or a (two-party) representation system, but the underlying mechanism is different. The constraint imposed
on the government not to transgress is the private (implicit) contract, rather than the
lack of information on the side of government, so we call this type of democratic
state the *social-compact democratic state*.

6.2   Various Forms of the Democratic and Collusive States

In the previous section we derived three generic forms of states within a framework of
a simple political exchange game in the polity domain and suggested a few situations
under which the emergence of the democratic state might be facilitated. But the discussion remained at an extremely abstract level. Ways in which the government
transgressed the property rights of private agents were largely unspecified. The condition of symmetric traders is not likely to be met literally under any historical conditions. The consequence of a fluid population composition around a two-party
system can be highly context specific. It has not been discussed either how a social
compact could emerge. In some situations a form of collusive state may evolve,
affecting the distributive pattern of property rights in a particular way. The collusive
nature of a state, or a particular way in which the government transgresses private

property rights, may eventually create political instability and/or economic ineffi-ciency. In response, the government may be subsequently made decentralized or modified in a significant way through the strategic interactions of private agents and a government, generating a new form of state.

In this section we abandon the symmetry assumption by taking into account the differentiated characteristics of private agents, and we examine their implications. The private agents may be identified, for example, with specific interest groups or classes representing common interests as suppliers in particular factors or product markets (e.g., landed gentry, workers, capitalists, the middle class, peasants), orga-nizations in particular product markets (firms, business associations, labor unions, etc.). These characteristics are taken as parameters. Their values are assumed to be set in economic transaction domains. A more explicit analysis of interactions between the political exchange and economic transaction domains will be made in later chapters. Although the level of abstraction in this section remains high, the derived models of states are of greater relevance to the actual forms of states in the real world than those in the previous section, while retaining the basic structural characteristics of a prototype.

Liberal Democratic versus Social-Compact Corporatist States

An analysis of the Glorious Revolution (1688–89) in England by North and Weingast (1989) illuminates the nature of the parliamentary monarchy as a stable outcome in a particular historical context where the polity domain was limited to only the king and parties representing the different interests of the gentry class. By the late sixteenth century there were two political parties under the rule of the Stuarts: Whigs, who were more focused on commercial activities and thus favored lower and stable duties, and Tories, who favored lower and stable taxes on land. In colluding with the more conservative Tories, the king attempted to transgress the political, and thus eco-nomic, interests of the Whigs. However, after successfully raiding the interests of the Whigs, James II, the last of the Stuart kings, turned to prey on the Tories. This time, the Whigs and Tories coordinated their resistance, forcing the king to flee. In bring-ing in a new king, both parties made it explicit in the Declaration of Rights that future transgressions on either party would not be tolerated. In this new institutional device, both parties did not need to agree on political ideals. In fact they remained divided on political issues. They only needed to agree that they would coordinate their withdrawal of support for the king if he violated certain codes of behavior. The effective limiting of the king's powers did not require another organized authority. By agreeing only upon what they should do if the behavior of the king did not meet certain expectations, they were able to ensure that their political and economic rights would be secure. Once such a constitutional change was set in place, the king became limited in his ability to regulate the economy.

As has been said, this stable outcome emerged within the limited domain of polity between the king and the property class. A century later Adam Smith remarked in 1776: "Civil government, so far as it is instituted for the security of property, is in reality instituted for the defense of the rich against the poor, or of those who have some property against those who have none at all" (Wealth of Nations: 715). However, by the midnineteenth century industrial development and urbanization gave a rise to middle classes of various types and the extension of suffrage to this class led to the eventual establishment of their political hegemony. The middle classes were obviously concerned with the protection of their property rights. Because of the diversity and size of their property ownership they were active, yet relatively "symmetric," participants in expanding markets, while they were not so divisive as to allow the traditional gentry class to sustain political power, possibly in collusion with some subgroups of them. Thus the middle classes provided a broader, and therefore more stable, basis for the democratic control of the government.[6] The democratic control of the government and increasingly unregulated markets developed in tandem.

The passage of Second Reform Act of 1867 enfranchised a great majority of the urban working class. One of the most crucial issues to determine the nature of state in response to the development of market economies in nineteenth- to twentieth-century Europe was the question of how to accommodate the aspiration of growing, propertyless working class for economic and political rights. The solution that evolved in England in the late nineteenth century was to subject their political quests to the representation system. Given the established political hegemony of the middle classes, such a choice might have been also an effective way for the working class to assert their rights in the polity domain, while the middle classes had little to fear or lose by it. Thus there evolved political alliance (collusion) between the liberal wing of the middle classes and labor unions—what the late political scientist Luebbert (1991) dubbed the "Lib-Labism."

Nevertheless, the defense of economic rights by the workers was left to decentralized bargaining with employers, and labor unions were thus essentially made to submit to market discipline. We may refer to this democratic outcome in the polity domain that evolved in tandem with unregulated labor markets as the *liberal democratic state*. In this state the government was controlled by the representation system whose outcome was largely influenced by the middle classes, while the government did not intervene in market exchange processes. Occasionally harsh labor disputes broke out, like the General Strike of 1926, but the state was able to continue to contain and submit labor unions to market discipline. The Lib-Lab coalition was broken in the 1930s and the middle classes came to forge a consolidated coalition among themselves against the rising unions' aspirations for advancing their economic interests through political process (e.g., nationalization of industries). It was not until after the war, however, that a great majority of the workers voted for the Labor Party and such program was began to be implemented.

In contrast, in late-nineteenth-century Germany, the middle classes were more divided than in England because of pre-industrial structures of regional segmentation, the separation of the city and the country, the religious cleavage between the Protestants and Catholics, and so forth.[7] Thus the authoritarian regime of Prussia was able to sustain itself by maneuvering elusive collusions with various constituencies. The liberal hegemony of unified middle classes had not been established by the time the workers emerged as an important political and economic class. Lib-Labism was not therefore a feasible equilibrium solution. The working class chose the alternative route of aligning themselves with the social democratic party. Bismarck, an uncompromising enemy of organized socialism, introduced a compulsory public health insurance system as a way to co-opt the workers. However, its decentralized self-administration with parity representation of workers and employers had the unintended effect of initiating a long subsequent process of subsuming labor into the political-economic process.[8]

Labor inclusion process received another impetus during the First World War when the government restricted the mobility of workers and negotiated their mandatory assignment to the armaments industry in exchange for the establishment of work councils. The Weimar Republic legalized the work councils. However, the polity domain defined by the Weimar Constitution failed to generate a stable outcome because of the failure of any effective political coalition to form among divisive classes—business, workers, proprietary peasantry, urban middle classes—and the absence of a party able to commit and control the government. The rise of the Nazi party filled the vacuum, and it meant a serious setback to the process of democratic inclusion of labor. However, "[a]s the economic policy of the Nazi leadership was dominated by the preparations for the war, the regime attempted to learn from the experiences of the 1914–1918 war economy in a path-dependent process, and in a sense, among the legacies of the Nazi era is also an unintended strengthening of some of those path-dependent patterns that had become visible in the First World War" (Lehmbruch 1999:38). Under the Nazi state, autonomous labor organizations were suppressed. Instead, labor was re-organized into the *Deutsche Arbeitsfront* (DAF), an organization of the masses under the control of the Nazi party. Business associations were transformed into state-controlled industrial associations with compulsory membership and functional monopolies.

The end of the Second World War meant, of course, a sharp departure from the central elements of the Nazi state, but the legacies of inclusive business and labor organizations continued. The *Deutscher Gewerkschaftsbund* (German Confederation of Labor Unions) was reorganized, encompassing the traditionally divided socialist, Christian, and liberal organizations but sustaining industry-based organizations. Both government's coercive suppression of, and exclusive collusion with, the working class was clearly not a viable solution in the polity domain. Lehmbruch succinctly summarized the nature of the emergent state in postwar Germany as follows:

[t]he political position of organized labour was considerably bolstered by the sympathies of the occupation authorities (notably in the British zone), and this in turn led business leaders to seek support of the unions in their defence against the dismantling of plants, as well as against eventual threats to their property rights. This was particularly true for heavy industry in the Ruhr region which in the Weimar Republic had been most strongly anti-labor, and this signified a decisive change of climate. For its part, labor leadership deliberately opted for co-operation with organized business as it had already done in 1918, and this time both sides of industry strongly concurred in rejecting any state intervention in industrial relations. (Lehmbruch 1999:44)

This description is reminiscent of the theoretical construct of the social-compact democratic state derived at the end of the previous section in which organized labor and businesses commit themselves to a social compact in restraining government intervention. The forms of state thus emergent in Germany, as well as in Scandinavian countries prior to the end of the war, are referred to as the *corporatist state*.[9] In this state the top organizations of business and labor in each industry autonomously bargain for and secure the property rights and job rights of the respective owners of factors of production that they are representing. They restrain intra-market competition and negotiate collective terms of exchange and other employment conditions. These top organizations are mutually interested in reaching an agreement, and the outcome of bargaining becomes self-enforcing because expectations are held by both parties that a failure to reach an agreement, or any default on an agreement, will result in a depreciation of the values of their own property rights, either through the postponed enjoyment of payoffs or from credible retaliation by other parties.

  On the other hand, the government recedes to the position of enabling industrial associations and trade unions to attain the status of quasi-state organs by allowing bargaining outcomes legally binding to all competitors in relevant markets. Streeck (1997) refers to this type of state decentralization as a *enabling state*. Transgression by the government into the self-governing process is held in check by the democratic control of the government by various property-rights owners, inclusive of the workers (human assets owners), exercised through the representative voting process and implicit social compacts among them. But this democratic state is distinct from the liberal democratic state in that labor unions are not subjected to decentralized market discipline but are enabled to act like a quasi-state organization. Besides the provision of the enabling framework, the government limits its own function to relatively neutral policy domains that are not appropriate as a collective bargaining issues, such as diplomacy, monetary policy, and antimonopoly regulations. In addition, as we will see in chapter 11, the corporatist state plays an important role as a complement to a particular form of corporate governance structure—codetermination.

Market-Preserving Federalism

Besides taxation, the government may affect the overall property-rights arrangement in the economy through various regulations, such as industrial relations laws, corporate chartering, farm products subsidies, and social securities provisions. It may favor the interests of particular groups, such as employers or workers, big or small businesses, farmers or consumers, and pensioners or health-service industry. Also a subtle way that the government can transfer the wealth possessed by private agents is to create a large amount of money to reduce the value of currencies. How can interest groups of various types protect their interests against the government or the collusion of other interest groups with the government? How can the "soft budget" tendency of the government to create excess money be credibly controlled? Even if some interest groups resist the regulations of the government that are disadvantageous to them, it may not be guaranteed that they themselves will not collude with a future government to promote regulations in their interests. Also the resistance against an inflationary monetary supply may be hard to coordinate, because it may be caused by the government's effort to simultaneously please all interest groups.

One possible organizational device to control the government's soft-budget-constraint tendency, as well as the adverse implications of a possibly collusive state, is a federalist arrangement of government. If the organizational structure of the government is unitary, then, as indicated in the introductory remarks of this chapter, private agents cannot escape the impact of action taken by the government. Also the government can control monetary quantity in its territorial domain in order to meet budgetary demands. However, the potentially abusive power of the government can be constrained by decentralization—the federalist state being one form of it. The federalist form of government nests a hierarchy of governments, with local levels being autonomous in a certain class of regulatory choices in their own geographical jurisdictions of political authority, while the federal government is specialized in the provision of public goods on the national scale, such as military defense, diplomacy to defend the Westphalian sovereignty of the federal states, and regulations concerning interstate trade and the environment.

The so-called "first-generation federalist theory" (Qian and Weingast 1997), as represented by Tiebout (1956) and Oates (1972), claims that if private agents can be mobile across the jurisdictions of different local governments, then they can strategically choose a jurisdictional domain in which a preferred regulatory choice is taken by its government. Then, if a government tries to regulate in disfavor of a certain interest group, members of that group can flee from the jurisdictional domain of the government and relocate themselves in another jurisdictional domain where their preferred regulatory choice, if any, is implemented. Some argue that it is indeed unlikely that a similar pattern of collusion could arise in all localities under the federalist system. However, mobility may not be equally easy for all interest groups (e.g., the mobility of workers may be much more restricted than capital movement). Thus one cannot exclude the possibility that a similar pattern of collusion could appear in all localities as a stable outcome of competition among local governments to attract more mobile factors of production.

"The second-generation theory" (Qian and Weingast 1997) instead emphasizes the aspect of federalist arrangement as a commitment device for the hard-budgeting of governments. Of particular relevance to this theory is a subset of federalism called "market-preserving federalism" (McKinnon 1997; Weingast 1995; Montinola, Qian, and Weingast 1995). A federalist state is market preserving if it satisfies the following three conditions: First, lower-level governments have primary regulatory responsibility over the economies of their jurisdictions so that the homogeneity of regulations across lower-level jurisdictions is avoided. Second, interjurisdictional mobility of goods and factors is secured. Third, and most important, the lower governments face a hard budget constraint; that is, they have neither the capacity to print money nor access to unlimited credit, but retain fiscal sovereignty within their respective territorial domains. This last condition is not met if the federal government bails out a lower-level government whenever the latter faces fiscal problems. Under market-preserving federalism there will be competition among constituent local governments in public-policy choices over taxes, provision of local public goods, regulations affecting the interests of various groups, and so forth. However, they are subject to hard-budget discipline not to compete with each other in the expectation of being bailed out by the federal government. If they are to run budget deficits at all, they have to compete with private agents in financial markets.

When does the commitment of the federal government not to bail out become credible and not subjected to renegotiation ex post? One commitment device is a lack of ability by the federal government to control a sufficient amount of revenue through taxation. If at the initial stage of designing a federal system significant authority for collecting taxes is allocated to local governments, then any attempt by the federal government to broaden its tax base may be met by concerted resistance of local governments. It is important that decisions on the monetary supply be placed under a neutral, unitary, monetary authority in order to impose effective fiscal discipline on local governments. If local governments were financed by the seigniorage that they gain by issuing currency, they would be tempted to run budget deficits to finance risky and ambitious projects or to please their constituent interest groups without being subjected to financial market discipline.

The best-known example of the federal system is, needless to say, the one that emerged in North America after the independence of the thirteen states following colonial rule by England.[10] The issue of monetary control was contentious at the time of the founding and remained so even long after that, however. In the beginning the United States was not ready to turn over monetary control to a monolithic central government agency. "[The] fear of centralized power was one source of the American resistance to the establishment of a central bank" (Mishkin 1995:437).[11] Instead, the First Bank of the United States (1791–1811), as well as the Second Bank of the United States (1816–1836), featured a central bank system that shared control with the states. After the renewal of the Second Bank was vetoed in 1832 by President Jackson, who believed that it breached its constitutional limits, state banks become the sole providers of paper currency, known as "wildcat currency." However, the federal government needed a way to finance the Civil War. The Banking Act of 1863 was passed to serve this fiscal need by establishing a national system of banks and issuing a national currency. Thus the dual system emerged.[12]

Yet this dual system did not operate smoothly. There were financial panics in 1893 and 1907. Since there were two sets of regulators in the banking system, there was a race to the bottom for banking regulations, which might have been beneficial to the bankers but did not result in economic stability. The bank panics sparked a renewed debate over a central bank. In 1913 Congress responded by creating the Federal Reserve System—a collection of twelve regional banks. However, the lack of coordination among them marred the monetary policy in the first twenty years of the Fed. Eichengreen examines cases and reaches the conclusion that "in the early years of the Federal Reserve System, authority was much more decentralized and disputed than is suggested by many histories of the U.S. central bank. Decentralization created problems not anticipated by the framers of the Federal Reserve Act" (Eichengreen 1992:21). In fact he regards the first two decades of the Federal Reserve as a period of trial and error before an effective centralization of authority could be established.

Congress acted during the Great Depression to produce the last major reform of the Federal Reserve System and strengthen the power of the central part of the system, making the Board of Governors the head of monetary policy.

Two newly emergent systems of fiscal federalism can be found in the European Union and China. In the former, national governments of member countries become like the local governments of a federal system. The power of the EU bureaucrats has become rather limited after the abandonment of their long-standing attempt to harmonize regulations related to industrial relations, corporate governance, and the like, among member countries. Thus national governments retain a large degree of regulatory discretion and fiscal sovereignty. On the other hand, they are subjected to increasingly competitive pressure from within and beyond the Union over attracting or retaining productive resources, such as capital, managerial, and entrepreneurial resources. Meanwhile, the supply of unitary money, the Euro, began to be controlled by the European Central Bank (ECB). Thus the fundamental framework for a federalist system—the centralization of monetary control and decentralization of fiscal sovereignty and regulations—is now implemented. Whether or not market-preserving fiscal federalism will be institutionalized as a stable outcome under these rules will be crucially dependent on the autonomy of the ECB in supplying money. The outcome has yet to be seen, but it is noteworthy that the anticipation of loss of control over the monetary supply has already exerted a significant degree of hard-budget discipline on member countries like Italy and Spain, which were traditionally known to be soft.

"Federalism, Chinese style" (Montinola, Qian, and Weingast 1995; Jin, Qian, and Weingast 1999), is emerging as a result of the spontaneous devolution of centralized power. Since the central government did not have its own tax collection machinery until 1994 and had to rely on provincial and other local governments for tax collection on contractual basis, the latter have been enjoying a substantial degree of fiscal autonomy despite occasional attempts by the central government to tighten control. De facto federalism evolved as a consequence. One of the initial problems associated with this spontaneous decentralization was the ability of provincial governments to obtain credits from provincial branches of the central bank by colluding with their local officers. This loophole for the soft budget constraint was closed by the enactment of the 1995 People's Bank Act, which prohibits the central bank from making direct loans to local governments. This policy may be considered one of the important factors responsible for the containment of inflation in the second half of the 1990s in China.[13] Although it is yet to be seen how the central government will react to the fiscal problems of local governments, the ever-increasing shortage of fiscal funds at the central level tends to diminish the expectations of local government to receive financial aid. Later in chapter 8.2 we will discuss how such spontaneous ordering of fiscal federalism can function as a credible institutional device for hardening the budget of state-owned enterprises.[14]

There are large differences between the emergent systems of the EU and China: the former is being formed through the designed integration of democratic states, whereas the latter by the spontaneous decentralization of a nonrepresentative state dominated by communist bureaucrats in a coalition with the working class as a weak partner. Further the interprovincial mobility of financial and human resources is severely regulated in China, while in European countries those resources are much more mobile and social norms are much diverse because of different paths of institutional evolution observed among them. Yet there is a modicum of commonality as well in the fiscal autonomy of lower-level governments (national governments in the EU and provincial and other local governments in China). Whether or not their systems evolve to institutionalize market-preserving federalist states will crucially depend on, among other things, the ability of their banking systems to be autonomous enough to prevent both central and local governments from softening budget constraints for political expediency.

The Developmental State

Social democratic corporatism evolved in European and Latin American economies as a stable outcome in the domain of the polity game as a mechanism for accommodating the challenge of the working class.[15] However, in East and Southeast Asia where workers did not establish themselves as a dominant class distinct from the landholding peasantry, an alternative form of state evolved in the second half of the twentieth century in response to the growing awareness of development needs by relatively autonomous governments whose primary objective was to preserve and enhance national sovereignty in particular international contexts.[16] We will conceptualize some essential aspects of it as the developmental state and try to clarify its analytically tractable characteristics as a stable outcome of game in the domain of polity of specific characteristic.

In the parable related in the previous section, the payoff structure was assumed to be symmetric for private agents. In particular, it was assumed that the government's transgression on the property rights of any private agent beyond the limit of the minimalist state would impose equal efficiency losses on both private agents. We now modify this assumption and examine its implications. Let us take the minimalist state as a benchmark and consider the following possibility of transfers mediated by the government: at the beginning of each period, the government imposes taxes on private agent A—say, the agricultural sector—in the amount of τ in excess of the minimalist state charge (by direct taxation, inflation, or through the price control on government-procurement farm products), causing an efficiency loss Δ to A and administrative and political conflict cost $c(\tau)$ to itself, where $c(.)$ is assumed to be a monotone-increasing convex function with $c(0) = c'(0) = 0$. Suppose that a transfer payment s is made by the government to private agent B—the (industrial) business sector—at the beginning of each period. This transfer payment can be used as capital to produce output $s^\alpha e$ $(0 < \alpha < 1)$ at the end of the period, if combined with effort e of agent B which costs e^β to it $(1 < \beta)$, or consumed. The government tries to tax agent B's output.

Suppose that there cannot be ex ante commitment on the side of the government regarding the amount of tax on B. Instead, the government tries to squeeze as much output from B as possible, but it can obtain only a fixed proportion T of the output at the end of the period, either because of incomplete monitoring capacity and bargaining power or some other transaction cost reasons. Denoting the discount factor by δ, the profile of present-value sums of net payoffs from this one-shot mechanism is $\{\tau - c(\tau) + \delta T s^\alpha e - s, -\tau - \Delta, \delta(1 - T)s^\alpha e - e^\beta\}$ in the order of the government, A and B. Then agent B will choose the effort level that will maximize his gain; that is, $e(s)$ for which $e(s) = [\delta(1 - T)s^\alpha/\beta]^{1/(\beta-1)}$. For any combination of relative bargaining power and monitoring capacity represented by T, the government can maximize its payoffs net of political conflict cost with agent A by choosing $\tau = \tau^*$ and $s = s^*$ such that $\tau^* = s^* = c'^{-1}(1)$. We refer to the strategy of the government composed of (τ^*, s^*) as the static Nash strategy. The collusive state under this strategy is not necessarily efficiency-enhancing despite agent B's growth opportunity as the wealth extraction from agent A causes political conflict cost $c(s^*)$ and efficiency loss Δ. Further, potentially productive activity by agent B cannot be fully mobilized because the government can hold up agent B, extracting ex post the share T of the output. In this situation agent B's effort supply will be below the first-best level. Thus the collusive state under the static Nash strategy may fail to exploit developmental opportunity.

Let us see if the holdup problem associated with the static Nash strategy of the government can be resolved in the repeated game framework, even if the level of effort is not court verifiable and so not contractible. Suppose that the government is expected to stay in power forever and announces the following contingent subsidy policy: it will supply subsidy s^* to agent (sector) B and tax at the end of period. However, the renewal of the subsidy in the following period is conditional on the tax payment $Ts^{*\alpha}e^o$ by B, where e^o is the first-best effort level satisfying the condition: $\delta s^\alpha = \beta[e^o]^{\beta-1}$. Then, if

$$\frac{1}{1-\delta}[\delta(1 - T)s^{*\alpha}e^o - (e^o)^\beta] > \delta(1 - T)s^{*\alpha}e(s^*) - e(s^*)^\beta,$$

namely if the expected gains from continued subsidies net of first-best effort costs for indefinite future periods (represented by the left-hand side of inequality) is greater than one-time net gains from shirking (right-hand side), it would become an equilibrium response for agent B to continue to exercise the first best effort e^o indefinitely. However, the question remains as to how the government's commitment to such a contingent subsidy policy could be credible. Even if agent B's effort is below the first-best level, is it not that the government will be induced to continue the subsidy if agent B renegotiates and promises to deliver a positive tax equal to the static Nash equilibrium rate from then on? If agent B is not replaceable, the government may be induced to abandon the announced policy and make a compromise ex post. The threat of exercising the contingent subsidy policy is not thus made credible to begin with and the equilibrium outcome of the game will be the static Nash.

However, following Murdock (1996), imagine that agent B is actually the business sector composed of multiple industrialists, incumbent and potential, while agent A is the agricultural" sector composed of landholding peasants. For simplicity's sake, suppose that the government selects two of the supposedly most productive—or most trustworthy—industrialists for subsidization. Suppose further that these two industrialists cannot coordinate their strategies vis-à-vis the government. Then the government can adopt the following contingent subsidy strategy: if both industrialists pay taxes corresponding to the first-best output, the government will continue to subsidize them. If one industrialist defects, meaning fails to pay a tax corresponding to the first-best output, the government will terminate the subsidy to that industrialist and replace him with another industrialist. This replacement may cost the government K because of the low potential productivity of a substitute firm, its need to learn, political adjustment, or some other reason. If both industrialists defect at the same time, the government will play the static Nash strategy in all future periods. As we have seen, as long as the maximal punishment strategy of subsidy termination is credible, it is the best response for an industrialist to produce the first-best output if he has been selected for a subsidy and has never defected. Therefore we only need to check the incentive compatibility of the described government strategy.

Let us denote the present-value sum of government tax revenues from the first-best output under the contingent subsidy policy by T_{cont} and that under the static Nash strategy by T_{Nash}. Suppose that one industrialist defects. In applying the maximal punishment strategy, the government will benefit $2T_{\text{cont}}$ per future period because the new and retained old industrialist both produce the first-best output in the future. Otherwise, it will get only $2T_{\text{Nash}}$ per future period because without punishment both industrialists will defect in the future. Therefore, if $2(T_{\text{cont}} - T_{\text{Nash}}) > K$, the threat of the maximal punishment strategy becomes credible, even though it may not be credible in a game where $T_{\text{cont}} - T_{\text{Nash}} < K$ or incumbent industrialists are able to collude against the government. Another important condition for the contingent subsidy strategy to work is that the discount factor of sector B must be high enough so that the previous inequality holds. If industrialists in sector B regard the government as short-lived, they may think it more profitable to grab the subsidy now and shirk.

When resource extraction from the agriculture sector and its government-mediated contingent transfer to selected industrialist elicit high industrial growth performance, we call such an equilibrium the *(market-enhancing) developmental state*. In conventional usage, the term "developmental state" refers to a government that aims toward maximizing an economy's growth by directly "governing markets" (Ward 1990). But here the emphasis is on the government altering the incentives of industrialists through the provision of *contingent rents*, $\delta(1 - T)s^{*\alpha}e^o - e^{o\beta}$ contingent on $e = e^o$, in each future period to selected firms (Murdock 1996; Aoki et al. 1997). These rents are not provided to industrialists, either in a discretionary manner or according to a prefixed schedule. They are provided contingent on the performance of industrialists. This is similar to a characteristic of the patent system, which does not ensure (innovation) rents to inventors but makes them only contingent on the successful commercialization of an innovation.

We have pointed out two important conditions for the evolution of a developmental state that may be worth reiterating. First, the beliefs prevails among industrialists that the government administering a contingent subsidy policy is long-lived. Second, there is sufficient competition among industrialists, and possible collusion among them in shirking can be effectively restrained. The preceding characterization of the developmental state may be thought of as capturing some important aspects of the role of governments in an East Asian phase now referred to as the "Asian Miracle" (Aoki et al. 1997). In these Asian economies governments were perceived to be long-lived or run by career bureaucrats who survive beyond changes in political leaders, whether elected or dictatorial. In my view it is the perception or belief, held by those in the business sector, of a continuity of government policy stance that has made the contingent subsidy approach effective, rather than merely the authoritarian nature of political leadership or collusion between the government and individual industrialists. Wherever a contingent subsidy policy was successful, we find that the government-promoted competition among individual industrialists (e.g., Korea at the time of President Park's rule).

The developmental state may be considered as derivative of the collusive state in that the government policy is in favor of enhancing growth of the B (business) sector based on resource extraction from the A (agricultural) sector. Although particular groups of industrialists may be selected for subsidy and other favorable treatment, a developmental state will generate industrial growth if the selection is made according to competitive performance criteria. When this criteria is not observed either because of parochial collusion with specific industrialists, incompetence or nepotism of the government, or the moral hazard behavior of the industrialists, the developmental state will be doomed to degenerate into an inefficient collusive state the degenerate developmental state (e.g., a so-called crony capitalism). Also the criteria may become hard to implement/enforce once subsidized firms become too large to be easily replaced by the government. In this sense the legacy of developmentalism may be thought to harbor its own seeds of self-destruction.

Any underdeveloped economy needs to start its industrial accumulation by extracting resources from the traditional agricultural sector except in the unlikely case that its investment is fully financed by the rest of the world (even in this case, foreign debts should be redeemed by future savings so that net flow is zero in the long run). Such a sectoral transfer would continue until the urban industrial sector has grown enough to be able to finance its own investment. According to a recent study by Juro Teranishi (1997) in the period of 1960 to 1984, there was little difference between Latin American and Subsaharan African economies, on the one hand, and East Asian economies (Korea, Malaysia, Philippines, Thailand), on the other, in that a substantial transfer of resources from the rural sector took place in the form of direct and indirect taxes or overvaluation of the home currency.[17] However, in sustaining this extraction, the government faced the risk of political conflict with farmers and peasants. The government might try to ease this conflict by transferring back a portion of the developmental returns to the rural sector as ex post compensation for the initial resource extraction. In the manner in which such a compensating transfer is made, however, there is a remarkable contrast between the two economies.[18] In Latin America and Africa (urban-based) governments have compensated certain groups within the rural sector—landed elites in the case of Latin America and politically influential ethnic groups in the case of Africa—through the supply of private goods (subsidies for machinery, fertilizer, etc.).

In contrast, East Asian governments delivered rural expenditures mostly in the form of collective infrastructures such as irrigation and transportation infrastructure. The rural areas of East Asia are populated by many small, independent peasants. Thus the governments could deliver value to these interests by providing public goods. Combined with the gradual emigration of the younger generation into the industrial sector, a consequence of such policy measures was a steady and universal increase in the income level of small-scale farming in the rural sector, although it lagged behind in the level of industrial development. The rising income level of the rural sector then expanded markets for industrial products. By selling products in domestic markets and receiving feedbacks of users' reactions to product quality, and so forth, industrialists could accumulate in turn industrial production skills (learning by using) and develop a capacity to compete in foreign markets. This is the virtuous cycle of *rural–inclusive developmentalism.*[19]

However, such a virtuous cycle may not be sustained as a stable outcome forever if resource extraction from the agricultural sector becomes more difficult politically or economically. Government-industry collusion has to then rely more on external resources (capital inflow) to sustain its development, unless it becomes capable of generating internal funds for development. Then the viability of a developmental state becomes vulnerable to external shocks affecting capital supplies. When the credibility of governmental discipline becomes doubtful and/or the perception that the economy is expanding too fast beyond its capability begins to spread in the international capital market, the external supply of developmental resources may be withdrawn, making the sustenance of the value of domestic currency difficult. This was indeed what happened to some developmental states in East Asia in the late 1990s (see chapter 12 for more on this).

Microcorporatism and the Bureau-Pluralistic State

Earlier in this chapter we saw that the dominance of symmetric traders in the polity domain could theoretically enhance the possibility of the democratic state based on the rule of law. Alternatively, if the workers as the owner of marketable human assets try to defend and assert their economic rights through their own organizations (industrial unions and a labor party), the quest may eventually result in the evolution of national corporatism. However, in chapter 5 we saw that there can be an alternative to the development of competitive markets for mobile human assets: the evolution of an organizational convention—horizontal hierarchies—based on workers' context-oriented human assets. The holders of context-oriented human assets are not as mobile across firms as those with functionally specialized, individuated human assets (chapter 5). Instead of organizing themselves into industrial unions according to their marketable skills, the holders of these human assets may find that their economic rights and interests are more effectively protected through the employing firm. On the side where the legal "owners" of firms supply the financial corporate assets, there may be reciprocal interests in sharing organizational returns with those organization-specific human asset holders.

Thus the convention of horizontal hierarchies can give rise to the formation of segmented coalitions (organizations) between the holders of financial corporate assets and firm-specific human assets.[20] One of the primary roles expected of management in each of these coalitional organizations is to strike a balance of interests between the two constituent bodies of the coalition in managerial decision-making and internal income distribution (e.g., wage-setting, dividend payout, and internal retention of earnings). It amounts to finding a self-enforcing bargaining equilibrium and making it a focal point of the game in the respective organization domain. We call such an organizational outcome *microcorporatism* in contrast to national corporatism (Aoki 1984, 1988). The workers become the members (stakeholders) of the firm in contrast to their counterparts in national corporatism who become "industrial citizens" (Marshall 1964; Streeck 1996).

Another important role of management in microcorporatism is to represent and promote the interests of its stakeholders (job security, value gains in corporate assets, tax reduction, and subsidy receipts) vis-à-vis the government and other interest groups, whenever possible. However, firms in the same product markets are mutually substitutable, so their bargaining power, vis-à-vis other interest groups, is weaker when they act individually. Therefore they may be induced to form and rely on an industrial association in the polity domain with an all-inclusive firm membership to represent their common, industry-specific interests. However, note that unlike their counterparts in national corporatist states, the industrial associations thus formed are not aimed at bargaining vis-à-vis the industrial unions in respective industry on behalf of the owners' interests. They are rather a suprastructure of microcorporatism practiced at member firms, and one of their primary functions is to secure the jobs of employees in the industry, with government assistance if necessary. Therefore, when there is a heritage of the permanent bureaucracy—the bureaucracy administered by lifetime, professional bureaucrats—in the government organization as in Japan, mutual incentives will develop for the industrial associations and the corresponding bureaus to form respective coalitions in the polity domain. By mediating and formulating emergent public policy demands of jurisdictional interests into the administrative process, the bureau can enhance its reason for existence. This may often involve competition, rivalry, and bargaining among bureaus within the administrative bureaucracy.

This type of segmented collusion among industrial interests, politicians, and bureaus evolved in Japan in the 1950s: the outcome often described as an "iron triangle." As such, it may be considered a variant of the developmental state. However, in the context of the constitutional rule of a democratic representation system of the government, such exclusive collusion could not be stable for long. Disadvantageous groups and organizations comprised of producers of less productive industries (e.g., farmers cooperatives, local chambers of commerce inclusive of small shop owners, local contractor's organizations, and pensioner's organizations) also aspired to assert their interests in the polity domain. To gain broader political supports, politicians were eager to expand their domain of influence through which they could channel and promote their constituents' interests into the administrative process. Relevant bureaus served as the ports of entry for ever-inclusive sectorial interests to be mediated into the administrative process.[21]

We call this sectorial interest group representations via multiple coalitions between administrative bureaus (ministries), jurisdictional interest groups and associated politicians, combined with intergroup interest mediation through the political-administrative process, the *bureau-pluralism*. Bureau-pluralism is not a state defined and prescribed by a formal constitutional rule, but an equilibrium outcome sustained and reproduced through hierarchically structured, ongoing practices of bargaining in the polity domain within the constitutional framework of a democratic representation system. At the lower tier, there are continual communications and negotiation between a bureau, on the one hand, and an industrial association or sectorial interest-group organization, on the other. At the upper tier, there is multilateral negotiation among bureaus (ministries), mediated by a ruling party and a coordinating bureau (the bureau empowered to make government budgetary allocation is particularly important).[22] The bureaus are thus located at nodal points of the two-tier social bargaining. This structure makes the bureaus Janus-faced (Aoki 1988): in the upper tier, interministerial bargaining, bureaus are constrained by the demands of their own jurisdictional interests. In the lower tier, bargaining vis-à-vis jurisdictional organizations, bureaus are constrained by the availability of budgets and other administrative resources that they can mobilize through interbureau competition, as well as the objective of their own organizational survival.

It is essential to note, however, that the Japanese bureau-pluralistic state is embedded in the representative system of the government (the legislative body and the cabinet). Although the career members of the permanent bureaucracy cannot be replaced immediately by voters, politicians are under the control of the representation system, and thus the bureaucracy is ultimately under its indirect control as well. Also the bureaucracy is subjected to public control in that any policy or bureaucratic behavior perceived to be against the "public interest" may weaken its legitimacy and affect its survival.[23] Nevertheless, as long as interest mediation through the administrative process keeps yielding a stable social outcome, the representative system will play only a secondary role as a direct check and balance mechanism in the state (the long-lasted, one-party rule in Japan was a symptom). Only when some internal conflict that is unresolvable through the conventional administrative process becomes apparent, a significant shift in the balance of power, or public sentiment expressed in the representative process, will emerge, and the political weights placed on bureau-pluralistic interest mediation will become substantially altered to restore stability.[24] Under what conditions such unrest occurs, and how it becomes resolved, can be highly context-specific. We will discuss this issue in a recent Japanese context in chapter 13.

Bureau-pluralism can be seen as one mechanism for rearranging and sustaining the property-rights order through bargaining (consensus-making) in the polity domain. In this regard it shares a modicum of commonality with national corporatism vis-à-vis the representative liberal democratic state. In the liberal democratic state property-rights arrangements are basically subjected to market discipline, even though market-determined outcomes are modified by taxes and subsidies, while the workings of markets are often regulated according to interest group pressure. In national corporatism, the government delegates the task of finding a bargaining solution to peak organizations representing opposite sides of labor markets. In bureaupluralism social bargaining which supplements product-market competitions is mediated through the administrative process. As stated, what underlies at the heart of this mechanism are industrial and other sectorial associations organized on the principle of inclusive membership and consensus-based collective action in respective markets. Thus sectorial-interest aggregation by these organizations tends to be egalitarian and often vetoed by the least advantaged.[25] Further, at the level of interbureau bargaining, possible failure of an agreement implies the status quo, so vested interests are well protected. When politicians intervene the administrative interest arbitration process, they tend to place more weight on demands by those interest groups that are less productive and accordingly coherent and aggressive in seeking political support in exchange for votes (e.g., farmers cooperatives, contractors, various financial industrial associations). Thus the outcome of social bargaining under the bureau-pluralistic state can be both market restraining and "egalitarian" at the same time.

Figure 6.2 graphically summarizes the arguments in this chapter. The horizontal dimension distinguishes the extent and mode of inclusiveness in the private agents' control over the government. In the extreme right, only private property owners are included in the polity domain, and in the extreme left, they are excluded. In between, the interests of property owners are represented as well as those of workers. The middle domain is further subdivided into two classes depending on whether the representation of workers' interests is subjected to market discipline or expressed through organizations such as industrial unions, national labor organizations, or employing firms via an industrial association.

The vertical dimension distinguishes the mechanisms involved: the rule of law, corporatist rule-making enabled by the government, and collusive/coalitional states.

Domain / Mechanisms	Private property owners excluded	Labor represented by an organization	Labor subjected to market discipline	Exclusively private property owners
rule of law			liberal democracy two-party democracy	Glorious Revolution
rule-making delegated to associations		social-compact corporatism		
collusive (representative)		bureau pluralism		
			cyclic collusion	developmentalism
(nonrepresentative)	communism			

Figure 6.2
Types of states

Collusive/coalitional states are further distinguished, depending on whether they are embedded in a representation system or not, as well as the extent of inclusiveness of collusion (coalitions). From the information perspective, the ordering from the top to the bottom roughly corresponds to the degree of universality/particularity, or the formality/ad hoc-ness, of the code (language) used in communications between the government and private agents. The liberal democratic state that relies on the rule of law applies in principle the same codes (laws) to all private agents and is thus placed at the top. In the two-party representative democratic state, government policy may be influenced by interest groups in coalition with the ruling party to some extent and may be less universalisitic than under the rule of law. In national corporatism, the peak organizations in respective markets strike formal agreements applicable to relevant domains, which supplement laws applicable in the economywide domain. Bureau-pluralism mediates pluralistic interests through ad hoc bargaining, and thus relies on more interest-specific codes (e.g., a ministry's so-called informal administrative guidance in Japan).[25] However, as it becomes more mature, bureau-pluralism also tends to rely more on formal rules than specific discretion. An example of the cyclic collusive state is the cyclic alternation between the populist national corporatism based on union organizations and military dictatorship in alliance with the property owners, as observed in some Latin American countries up to the 1970s. Their rule was more or less discretionary. The communist state may be considered as a collusive state in which dominant party bureaucrats weakly collude with the working class by assuring their job and other social security benefits, while seeking rents for themselves by denying private ownership of production assets to everyone else. The predatory state that utters discretionary commands to any agent on an ad hoc basis is placed outside the box.

Theoretically the liberal democratic state based on the rule of law, if viable, may be the most accommodating to the development of global markets. For example, traders who enter domestic markets from outside the jurisdictional domain can expect to be treated indiscriminately by the government. Thus the regulatory range is open-ended. However, nonliberal states may face various dilemmas when the economic domains under their jurisdictions become open to outsiders. Even the two-party representative democratic state may exhibit a protectionist tendency toward the outside in favor of the domestic interests of particular businesses, labor unions, or their alliances. We have already hinted that the virtuous cycle of rural–inclusive developmentalism can harbor the seeds of a crisis when the government begins to rely more on external resources (capital imports) for development. Corporatist interest mediation restrains domestic market competition. However, as financial, human, and organizational resources become more readily mobile across national borders, the outcome of national bargaining may become more easily overridden by resource outflow. Some people argue therefore that the framework of the social-compact corporatist state may be encroached by the increasing cross-border mobility of resources. Also the protection of vested interests by the bureau-pluralist may deter industrial restructuring that can exploit new economic opportunities made possible by the global integration of markets. Competitive firms may not need the protection of the bureau-pluralist, and may try to drift away from it but be forced to bear a substantial portion of the redistribution costs of the equalizing bureau-pluralist state. Thus competitive firms show an increasingly ambivalent attitude toward bureau-pluralism while less productive sectors seek its protection more.

We need to examine the dilemmas inherent in these forms of states in new international environments and see whether they need a drastic redefinition, possibly in the direction of a liberal democratic state. This issue is highly intriguing and intricate, and an answer to the question is not so trivial as was commonly thought. Its examination requires more analytical preparation, particularly the analysis of the mechanism of institutional change, as well as the interdependencies between the state, on the one hand, and various institutional arrangements in the private sector, on the other. Therefore we reserve discussions of this issue to the concluding chapter.

II A GAME-THEORETIC FRAMEWORK FOR INSTITUTIONAL ANALYSIS

In part I we showed how various proto-institutions can emerge as stable products of the strategic interactions of agents in primitive domains. As such, there can be several varieties rather than only one ideal type for each of them. However, this does not imply either that there ought to be separate logics and different languages for explaining the emergence and sustenance of different institutions nor that institutions can be easily constructed, deconstructed, and reconstructed at agents' will. In this part we try to build a unified analytical and conceptual framework for understanding the emergence, sustenance, and changes of institutions.

We begin by precisely defining the shared-beliefs cum equilibrium–summary-representation view of the institution proposed in chapter 1. Based on this conception of an institution, we analyze how institutions are linked across domains and over time and how they link different domains of the economy into an integrative whole. We illustrate the discussion with many interesting examples drawn from the literature, as well as introduce contemporary institutional issues to be further discussed in the next part.

The game-theoretic approach can sharpen the conceptualization of institutions because of its analytical rigor and clarity. However, this property can become a liability in looking at the diachronic structure of institutional change. If agents know a priori the entire set of all possible choices and act accordingly, or if they can eventually explore all the relevant possibilities with the aid of accidents and chance, then they will eventually be able to find the best overall institutional arrangement as time passes. Only new technology, preference change, and other exogenous environments will modify the overall institutional arrangement. Although this is close to the ideal view of the world with which economists are familiar, it appears to be a rather mechanical one. Isn't there also a room for innovation and novelty, as well as degeneration, in institutional evolution? In this part we present the argument that agents hold subjective, compressed views regarding the structure of the game they play—the subjective game models—and revise them in interactive and innovative ways when they face large external shocks and/or cognitive crises that the internal dynamics of the objective game endogenously generate. We then analyze mechanisms through which individual experiments, decentralized subjective revision of beliefs, and policy designs may or may not generate a systemic change in agents' beliefs, that is, institutional change. The process of institutional evolution can thus be characterized as a "punctuated equilibrium," featuring both path dependence and novelty, as well as both endurance and juncture points.

7 A Game-Theoretic Concept of Institutions

Let the physical basis of a social economy be given,—or, to take a broader view of the matter, of a society. According to all tradition and experience human beings have a characteristic way of adjusting themselves to such a background. This consists of not setting up one rigid system of apportionment, i.e., of imputation, but rather a variety of alternatives, which will probably all express some general principles but nevertheless differ among themselves in many particular respects. This system of imputations describes the "established order of society" or "accepted standard of behavior."
—John von Neumann and Oskar Morgenstern, *Theory of Games and Economic Behavior* (1945:41)

Let us begin by recalling the shared-beliefs cum equilibrium–summary-representation view of institutions tentatively proposed in chapter 1:

An institution is a self-sustaining system of shared beliefs about how the game is played. Its substance is a compressed representation of the salient, invariant features of an equilibrium path, perceived by almost all the agents in the domain as relevant to their own strategic choices. As such, it governs the strategic interactions of agents in a self-enforcing manner, and in turn reproduced by their actual choices in a continually changing environment.

Recall also the five characteristics of institutions that are implicit in this conceptualization: *endogenicity*, *information compression* or *summary representation*, *robustness* or *durability* with respect to continual environmental changes and agents' minor deviance from the implied rules, *universality* of relevance to all agents in a domain, and *multiplicity*. This chapter provides a formal definition of institutions implying all these characteristics and discusses their bearings on the roles of institutions. The attractiveness of the formal definition to be developed is not just conceptual, however. As we will see in the following chapters, it renders an understanding of the nature of synchronic and diachronic interrelationships among institutions that is analytically tractable.

In order to prepare for the formalization of the shared-beliefs cum equilibrium–summary-representation view and its applications, section 7.1 introduces notations and a generic framework for describing the "objective" structure of strategic interactions among agents in the repeated game and discusses the complementary nature of the two approaches of the game theory—the classical and evolutionary approaches—in developing an appropriate concept of equilibrium. This section may be skipped except for the introductory subsection by those readers who are familiar with the game theory without losing a thread of argument. Section 7.2 forms the core of the chapter. It gives a formal game-theoretic definition of institutions from the shared-beliefs cum equilibrium–summary-representation perspective and illustrates it with examples drawn from chapters in part I. Section 7.3 discusses the interactive, feed-back relationships among institutions (endogenous variable), on the one hand, and the exogenous rules of the game of the domain, on the other, which also serves as an introduction to the themes of the remaining chapters of this part.

7.1   Exogenous Rules of the Game and Endogenous Action-Choice Rules

A Generic Game Form

Let us deal with a *domain* of the economy as a unit of analysis. The domain consists of the set of a finite number of agents (players)—individuals and organizations—and the sets of all technologically feasible actions, one for each agent. Time consists of an infinite sequence of periods, each denoted by t, within each of which agents choose and implement actions. We can assume here that the characteristics of the domain will be stationary over all periods. The combination of actions by all agents in one period is called an action profile, and an actually realized action profile is the (inter-nal) state of the domain. The data given to the domain are the set of technologically feasible physical consequences of action profiles and relevant to agents' welfare, and a technological relationship that assigns a consequence for each technologically fea-sible action profile.

Let us introduce the following notations:

$\mathcal{N} = \{1, 2, \ldots, n\}$ = set of agents,

$\mathcal{A}_i = \{a_i\}$ = set of all technologically feasible actions of agent i ($i \in \mathcal{N}$),

$\mathcal{A} = \times_i \mathcal{A}_i = \{a\} = \{a_1, \ldots, a_i, \ldots, a_n\}$ = set of all technologically feasible action profiles,

$\Omega = \{\omega\}$ = set of physically possible, observable consequences,

$\phi : \mathcal{A} \to \Omega$ = consequence function that assigns $\omega = \phi(a)$ in Ω for each a in $\mathcal{A}$.

Let us call triplet $\ll \mathcal{N}, \mathcal{A}, \phi \gg$, composed of the set of agents, the sets of all technologically feasible actions for each agent, and the consequence function, the *game form*.[1] It is important to note that the action sets of agents include all techno-logically feasible actions and do not exclude any actions that may be constrained by human devices. Actual choices of actions by agents may not necessarily be observable by others, but their consequences are. The consequence function defines the *exoge-nous rules* of the game. Its shape depends on a set of parameters representing the state of the environment surrounding the domain. The parameters may relate to the state of technology, the initial endowments of resources, or the (equilibrium) states of other domains of the economy (institutional environments) than the one under consideration. For now, we assume that the environment of the domain is stationary over time. In particular, in order to keep the conception of the institution focused, we reserve the explicit treatment of an institutional environment until the next chapter. So for now we will proceed as if the exogenous rules of the game are completely technologically determined.

Let us assume that each agent chooses an action in each period according to a private *action-choice rule*, $s_i : \Omega \rightarrow \mathcal{A}_i$ $(i \in \mathcal{N})$ such that

$$a_i(t + 1) = s_i(\omega(t)) \qquad \text{for all } i.$$

That is, agents choose an action in each period in response to the observable consequence of the action profile in the preceding period.[2] For the moment we will treat the content of this rule as a black box. As we will see below, it may be interpreted as implicitly incorporating an agent's adaptation of expectation about others' action choices through the observations of consequences, and/or representing an agent's comprehensive path-contingent action plan that was deduced by a priori reasoning from the environmental data. We discuss these specific cases in the following two subsections.

Action rules and the consequence function then defines the transition of the internal state of the domain from one period to the next:

$$\boldsymbol{a}(t + 1) = \boldsymbol{s}(\phi(\boldsymbol{a}(t)) = F(\boldsymbol{a}(t)) \qquad \text{for all } t,$$

where $F : \mathcal{A} \rightarrow \mathcal{A}$ is the *transition function*. When the internal state is stabilized as $\boldsymbol{a}(t) = \boldsymbol{a}(t + 1) = \boldsymbol{a}(t + 2) = \cdots = \boldsymbol{a}^*$ with $\boldsymbol{a}^* = F(\boldsymbol{a}^*)$, we say that the internal state of the domain is in a steady-state equilibrium and refer to $\boldsymbol{a}^*$ as a steady state.[3] How can the domain be equilibrated? It obviously depends on the nature of the action-choice rules of individual agents, which we have not yet specified.

We assume that the agents intend to maximize their payoffs (over periods) from their action choices, even if they are bounded in their abilities to do so. We assume that each agent has the payoff (utility) flow function u_i defined on the consequence space and a constant discount factor δ (depending on context, the discount factor may be zero, meaning that the agent is completely myopic). Each agent needs to form an expectation about the others' action-choice rules in order to predict the consequences of his or her own action choices in the current period and possibly future periods as well. Given an expectation, the agent is able to strategically choose the subjectively best action for each period or the best action-choice rule once and for all.

The structure of the game relevant to any individual agent in the domain can then be represented by the 2×2 tableau shown in figure 7.1. The left column represents

	parametric data (exogenous rules of the game)	endogenous variables
internal to agent (micro)	(A) sets of feasible actions	(S) strategic choice of an action (plan)
external constraints (macro)	(CO) consequence function	(E) expectation of others' strategic choices

Figure 7.1
COASE box representation of the generic structure of the game

the data, or exogenously determined rules of the game, to an agent, while the right represents his or her variables. The first row refers to the microdimension internal to the individual agent as the choice subject, and the second to that macrodimension external to him/her. The *CO* cell records the impacts of environments on the consequences of agents' action profile as represented by the consequence function. The *A* cell registers the set of action choices by an agent. The *S* cell represents the strategic choice of an action (plan) by the agent conditioned by his/her expectation of others' strategic choice recorded in the *E* cell. Thus the tableau is referred to as the *COASE box* hereafter. This box representation will serve as an aid throughout part II in clarifying the structure of argument, which may sometimes become quite intricate.

Taking this generic setting, we next consider two contrasting mechanisms by which a steady-state equilibrium of the domain may be derived.

Subgame Perfect Equilibrium and Credible Beliefs[4]

Suppose first that the agent's discount factor is zero, so his or her action choice is completely myopic within the time horizon and limited only to the current period. Following a convention, denote the action profile deleting the action of agent i by $\mathscr{A}_{-i}$, and let $a_{-i} \in \mathscr{A}_{-i}$ be agent i's expectation regarding others' action choices $(i \in \mathscr{N})$. Suppose that agents' expectations about others' action choices in one period are consistent with actual choices and that the choice of each agent in that period is the best response to his or her expectation. By this we mean that there exists $a^N \in \mathscr{A}$ such that

$$\alpha_{-i} = a^N_{-i},$$

$$a^N_i \in \underset{a_i \in \mathscr{A}_i}{\operatorname{argmax}} \, u_i(\phi(a_i, \alpha_{-i})) \qquad \text{for all } i.$$

Then we say that the action profile a^N is a *static Nash equilibrium*. As we have already often seen in part I, a sequence of such static Nash equilibria, $a(t) = a(t+1) = a(t+2) = \cdots = a^N$, constitutes an equilibrium of the internal state (equilibrium outcome) of the domain. But this is not necessarily a "good" equilibrium. For example, in the model of the irrigation game in chapter 2.2, the sequence of {Shirk, Shirk, Shirk, ...} by every agent is such an equilibrium state.

Suppose, instead, that every agent is foresighted and so discounts future payoffs at positive discount factor δ. Then agents need to take into account the impact of their current action choices on future payoffs through others' reactions and coordinate their own action choices over time periods. Suppose that every agent makes a comprehensive plan of future action choices contingent on the evolving state. For simplicity let us assume that $\Omega = \mathcal{A}$ and $\omega(t) = a(t)$, meaning that the consequence of the game in each period is completely described by the action profile in that period. Further assume that the agent chooses a rule for action choices in all future periods once and for all contingent on the outcome of the game in the previous period. Thus the action-choice rule by each agent is given by the functional form $s_i(.) : \mathcal{A} \to \mathcal{A}_i$, rather than by a particular action choice in a particular period. Then the transition function $F(.)$ is simply given by the profile of agents' action-choice rules, $s(.) = \{s_1(.), \ldots, s_i(.), \ldots, s_n(.)\}$. When the internal state of the domain in period t is $a(t)$, the game evolving from that period on with that state as the initial position is called a subgame. The internal state of the subgame at time $\tau > t$ evolving according to the profile of agents' action-choice rules s is denoted by $s(\tau : a(t))$.

Let $\sigma_{-i}(.) : \mathcal{A} \to \mathcal{A}_{-i}$ be agent i's expectation of other agents' action-choice rules. Suppose that the expectation of each agent about others' action-choice rules are consistent with their actual choices, and that the choice of each agent is the best response to its expectation for all subgames starting from any $t \geq 0$, whatever the state $a(t)$ is at that point (its history up to that point). So there exists $s^P(.)$ such that

$$\sigma_{-i}(\tau : a(t)) = s^P_{-i}(\tau : a(t)),$$

$$s^P_i(.) \in \underset{s_i(.)}{\operatorname{argmax}} \sum_{\tau > t} \delta^{\tau - t} u_i(s_i(\tau : a(t)), \sigma_{-i}(\tau : a(t)))$$

for all $a(t) \in \Omega$, $t \geq 0$, and i.

Then we say that the action-choice rule profile $s^P(.)$ is a *subgame perfect equilibrium*. In this situation it is not beneficial for any agent to unilaterally deviate from the specified strategy at any moment of time, whatever the history up to that point may be, and thus the chosen *action-choice rules become self-enforcing*.[5]

The equilibrium just specified prescribe the action to be taken by each agent for all possible future states, even for states when the prescribed strategic plan implemented by every agent at any moment of time is never realized. As a result a particular steady-state equilibrium trajectory, say $a(t) = a(t+1) = \cdots = a(t+n) = a^P = s^P(a^P)$, may be observed. For example, in the community irrigation exchange game of chapter 2.2, the state constituting choices {Work, Cooperate} by all agents may be sequentially observed year after year as the steady-state outcome of subgame perfect equilibrium. The trajectory of states realized when the equilibrium strategy is followed by every player may be referred to as the path of play and the unobservable states as the off-the-path-of-play states. The component of an agent's equilibrium strategy corresponding to the off the-path-of-play states may be interpreted as the rational *beliefs* of the agents about how the other agent would act were those states to occur—say by an accident, mistake, or experiment. The rule takes the "if ..., then" form, such as "if any family shirks cleaning the irrigation channels, that family will be ostracized by other families." As we saw in chapters 1.2 (the guilds), 2.2 (the irrigation game), 4.2 cultural beliefs, and 6.1 (the democratic state), such beliefs constrain the actual observable history to a certain sequence of internal states while the beliefs are self-sustained.

Applying the concept of subgame perfect equilibrium amounts to eliminating all Nash equilibria that may contain an incredible threat, that is, a plan of action choices which an agent announces he will take at a certain contingency but that are not incentive compatible for that agent to actually implement when that contingency occurs. For example, in the polity game of chapter 6.1, the business organization may announce its commitment to the social compact in that if the government transgresses the rights of the union, it will coordinate with the union and resist the government. However, when that event actually happens and the business organization believes that the situation will continue forever, it may find the breach of compact beneficial.

Although the concept of subgame perfect can considerably reduce the number of Nash equilibria of repeated games, there could still remain a large number of equilibria (the folk theorem). For this reason some theorists maintain that the subgame perfect equilibrium notion lacks predictive power and so is disappointing. However, I hope that readers who have followed the discussion in part I will concur with the assessment of Osborne and Rubinstein, that "the main contribution of the theory is the discovery of interesting stable social norms (strategies) that support mutually desirable payoff profiles, and not simply the demonstration that equilibria *exist* that generate such profiles." (1994:134).

The structure of a repeated game generating subgame perfect equilibrium may be visualized as depicted by the COASE box in figure 7.2. The one serious question

	parametric data	endogenous variables
internal to the agent (micro)	(A) complete knowledge of feasible (future) actions	(S) comprehensive strategic plan of contingent future action choices
external constraints (macro)	(CO) complete knowledge of the consequence function	(E) common beliefs regarding others' actions on and off the path of play

Figure 7.2
COASE box representation of subgame perfect equilibrium

that cannot be resolved endogenously in this framework is how common beliefs can be constructed among the agents. However, games that are relevant to the study of institutions must be those played repeatedly by the same agents, even if there are turnovers of agents over time. So we provide a steady-state interpretation of the equilibrium: "Each participant knows the equilibrium and tests the optimality of his behavior given this knowledge, which he has acquired from his long experience" (ibid.:5).

Evolutionary Equilibria and Mutations[6]

In deriving the concept of subgame perfect equilibrium, it is assumed the agents are perfectly competent in forming expectations about others' action choices for off-the-path-of-play states and rational in making a contingent action choice with respect to those expectations. In contrast, the evolutionary game approach introduces elements of agents' bounded rationality explicitly and focuses on experience-based inductive reasoning of the agents. Examples were provided by the model of customary property rights in chapter 2.1 (in which the number of players was two) and that of conventions in organizational architecture in chapter 5. In the latter model the set of agents was represented by a continuum, so, strictly speaking, the present framework does not apply. However, let us loosely assume that it is an approximation of a finitely very large number and use it as an illustrative example.

In that model the action sets of agents are assumed to be identical and games are played repeatedly over periods from indefinite past. In each period the agents know which action choice yielded the highest average payoffs as the consequence of action profile in the preceding period. The average payoffs in this instance represents a sort of "fitness" of the corresponding action choice. With such limited, marginal information about the consequence function, and static expectations that other agents on

	parametric data	endogenous variables
internal to the agent (micro)	(A) fixed sets of actions	(S) inertial imitation plus mutation
external constraint (macro)	(CO) knowledge of "fitness" of strategies constructed from observations	(E) inferences from limited memory (static expectation)

Figure 7.3
COASE box representation of the evolutionary game

average follow the same choice as in the preceding period, the agents make bounded-rational action choices to try to maximize the immediate payoffs (i.e., $\delta = 0$) by imitating the action choice whose fitness appears to be the highest with some inertia. Thus the choice rule formulated as (5.1) represents adaptive behavior of the agents rather than a plan of future action derived by deductive reasoning. Any novel action choices that cannot be captured by such bounded-rationality supposition are regarded as random events—mutations, mistakes, or random experiments. From this example we draw the generic structure of the evolutionary game for individual agents as in figure 7.3.

For evolutionary models like the one in chapter 5, we can re-formulate the transition function as follows: suppose that all the agents are symmetric in having the identical set of actions $\mathscr{A}$ and identical payoff function specified below. Let $\hat{a}(t) : \mathscr{A} \to [0, 1]$ denote the distribution of the agents' action choices at time t over the set of actions. The transition process is reformulated as

$$\hat{a}(t + 1) = F(\hat{a}(t)) = \hat{a}(t) + f(\hat{a}(t)) \qquad \text{for all } t$$

with restrictions to ensure that the number of agents never get negative for any action and their sum is always one.[7] We say that the transition process is compatible with evolutionary selection when the following is always true: for any two action choices the one that was observed to yield a higher (alternatively lower) average payoff (fitness) in the last period is adopted (respectively, abandoned) by a larger number of agents in this period so that the corresponding component value of f is higher (respectively, lower). Formally

$$f_j(\hat{a}(t)) > f_k(\hat{a}(t)) \quad \text{if and only if}$$

$$u(\phi(a_j(t - 1), \hat{a}(t - 1))) > u(\phi(a_k(t - 1), \hat{a}(t - 1))),$$

where $u(\phi(a_i(t-1), \hat{a}(t-1)))$, $i = j$, k, represents the payoff of the agent who adopted action a_i in period $t-1$ when the distribution of agents in that period is represented by $\hat{a}(t-1)$. It is analogous to the fact that a (biological) type with higher (alternatively lower) fitness grows (respectively, decays) relatively faster.

There are two important equilibrium concepts in this evolutionary transition process. The simplest one is the asymptotically stable dynamic equilibrium, $\hat{a}^E$, such that $\lim_{t \to \infty} \hat{a}(t) = \hat{a}^E$ for any initial position, $\hat{a}(0)$, in the neighborhood of $\hat{a}^E$. This equilibrium may also be called *evolutionary equilibrium* (D. Friedman 1991). It is an action (in which case $\hat{a}^E$ is a point mass) or a distribution of actions to which the distribution of the agents tends to converge as time passes, if the initial distribution is located nearby. Such equilibrium is hard to upset once it is established, because it has a higher peak in the neighborhood landscape, so to speak, than in other states. An evolutionary equilibrium as defined is always a Nash equilibrium.[8] The choice rule at an equilibrium pinpoints one particular action choice (or a mixed strategy choice) rather than represents a comprehensive contingent action-choice plan as in the subgame perfect equilibrium. However, as shown in chapter 5, it is also the cost imposed on deriants that drives agents to follow the equilibrium action. The dynamic process on the organizational field analyzed in chapter 5 is compatible with evolutionary selection. Of the nine Nash equilibria of that model, the P-, H-, F-, and L-equilibria are evolutionary equilibria.

The dynamic process of customary rights formation chapter 2.1 is also compatible with evolutionary selection, when the definition above is properly modified for the case of a finite history memory. However, any division of 100 rabbits among the two agents can be a limit point for some initial history, so the dynamic process may be called *quasi-stable*, but there is no evolutionary equilibrium in the sense defined above. However, we have seen that the introduction of randomness in choice made it possible for an alternative type of equilibrium to evolve in that model. Let any individual action choice in the agents' action profile compatible with evolutionary selection perturbed to any other action choice with a very small probability ε at the end of each period. Then the state of a game at period t can be described by a probability distribution of the agents, $\hat{a}(\tau : \varepsilon)$ on $\mathscr{A}$. Suppose that this probability distribution always converges in long run to a particular probability distribution, $\hat{a}^S$, regardless of past history, when the rate of perturbation becomes very small. Formally, $\lim_{\varepsilon \to 0} \lim_{t \to \infty} \hat{a}(t : \varepsilon) = \hat{a}^S$ for any $\hat{a}(0)$. Then we identify the limit distribution as *stochastically stable* (Foster and Young 1990). This is the distribution that we can expect to observe when the evolutionary dynamic system with mutation runs for an infinitely long time. If we reformulate the dynamic process of chapter 5 as a game with a finite number of the agents making a choice at a discrete time with a small probability of mutation, we can conjecture that the only stochastically stable evolutionary equilibrium will be the efficient equilibrium P characterized by organizational diversity.[9]

The conventional idea is that the most efficient strategy will dominate in the long run because other strategies will be weeded out by competition (Alchian 1950; M. Friedman 1953), so the message of the analytical insight of evolutionary game theory just referred to above is somewhat ironical. It is the stochastic event—such as a mistake or an unexplained mutation occurring in a critical mass at some point of time, and not pure competitive selection alone—that assures the efficiency of an evolutionary equilibrium.[10] The reason for this is the existence of multiple evolutionary equilibria under the condition of bounded rationality. There must be some external impact to wipe out the "not-so-good" memories in order for bounded rational agents to be able to locate a good equilibrium. In my view, however, the result that the stochastic evolutionary process will lead the system to the most efficient strategy cannot be taken literally as an approximation of real world processes. Rather it provides a theoretical frame of reference by which factors deterring, or facilitating, the transition of the economy from a subefficient state to the efficient state can be identified (as we tried to do in chapter 5.2). We may consider that in a treatise of institutions, the multiplicity of equilibria, when reduced to a set of several "reasonable" ones, is not necessarily a demerit for a model, for the diversity of institutional arrangements is undoubtedly an important characteristic of history and of the contemporary world. Indeed, like Sugden (1986), we made multiplicity an essential element of the proposed definition of institutions.

The Complementarity of the Classical and Evolutionary Game Approaches

So far the classical and evolutionary game approaches appear in opposition to each other in terms of the world view. The classical approach assumes that agents are superrational in information collection, expectation formation, consequence inference, and choice of an action rule. Yet it remains mute on how the achievement of common expectations can be justifiable. On the other hand, agents visualized in evolutionary theory are far more limited in rationality. They are driven by inertia and simple imitation, limited by experience-based beliefs on others' actions, while possible convergence to an efficient outcome relies on unexplained stochastic events. Despite such differences and limits, both approaches may not be entirely incompatible. Each can be a useful tool for comparative institutional analysis depending on the nature of the institution that a model wants to explain.

Loosely speaking, equilibrium conceptualized under the rational, classical approach (e.g., subgame perfection) may be understood as an outcome of learning. Although an approach along this line of thought is not yet firmly founded, in the process of learning the occurrence of random events such as mistakes and experiments may be inevitable. Indeed, theoretically, a sort of impossibility theorem has been submitted to indicate that bounded-rational learning alone without any random elements may not converge either in observable state or beliefs about others' action choices (Foster and Young 1998).[11] On the other hand, as the evolutionary approach tries to capture, inertia, imitation, imperfect inference, as well as random elements (e.g., mistakes), undoubtedly characterize aspects of human behavior. But it also seems true that economic agents intend to be as much rational as possible in interpreting history and/or exercising deductive reasoning. For example, the occurrence of a critical mass of mutations, which plays such a prominent role in determining the stochastic stability of evolutionary dynamics, may be thought of as the outcome of calculated experiments among foresighted entrepreneurs learning from better practice elsewhere (see chapter 5.2).

Thus the evolutionary and classical approaches focus on different, but essentially inseparable, dimensions of the game that the agents play: the mimetic, inductive, bounded-rational dimensions, on one hand, and the calculative, deductive, rational dimensions, on the other. However, generally speaking, the evolutionary game approach is more suitable for analyzing the self-enforceability of institutions in forms of conventions and customs. In these institutions the basis for compliance with implied rules is provided by their "taken-for-grantedness" nature to the agents who have evolved individual traits (values, preferences, competence, etc.) fitting with them.[12] Mechanisms of such co-evolution can be better analyzed with evolutionary models constructed on the presumption of relatively unstructured domain characteristics. The customary property rights discussed in chapter 2.1 evolve among agents possessed of only limited information processing capacities. Conventions of organizational architecture discussed in chapter 5 evolve in the primitive organizational field where other institutional arrangements are unspecified.

On the other hand, the classical game approach may be seen as more suitable for analyzing the self-enforceability of institutions, such as norms, contracts, and various governance structures. These institutions entail more explicit mechanisms of enforcement, involving coercive sanctions or normative expectations. Compliance with the rules implied by these institutions is then based more on the rational beliefs of the self-interested agents about the possible consequences of default behavior. Such beliefs are more explicitly dealt with by classical repeated game models constructed on the presumption of relatively well-structured domain characteristics. For example, the community-embedded norm discussed in chapter 2.2 was seen as sustainable in the domain characterized by the homogeneity of the agents inhabiting it. The various trade governance mechanisms are more or less specific to particular trading structures, as discussed in chapter 3.5. The different states discussed in chapter 6 also presupposed the presence of a government, as well as certain social structures specifying the characteristics of constituent private agents. In such relatively well-structured domains, agents may develop, or will develop relatively easily, the capacity to infer possible strategic-choice rules that other agents apply.

Besides that, the evolutionary and classical game approaches may be complementary with respect to domains that they can be applied; in some cases they may even imply the same solutions (institutions) in the same domains. Namely an evolutionary equilibrium may be identical to the internal state (observable outcome) of a subgame perfect equilibrium, although the agents' beliefs regarding the possible reactions of others for off-the-path-of-play contingencies are not made explicit as in the subgame perfect equilibrium strategy. There are indeed a few important analytical results suggesting the identity of both equilibria.[13] For example, the generically stable equilibrium of the customary property-rights game à la Young (chapter 2.1) is surprisingly identical to the subgame perfect equilibrium of the bargaining game in which two rational agents alternatively make offers and counter-offers regarding the division of goods (rabbits) until they come to an agreement, while the value of the goods depreciates (rabbits run away) at a certain rate until an agreement is reached (Rubinstein 1982). However, in the latter approach, it is assumed that both agents somehow know each others' payoff functions (utility functions). Presumably they must construct such knowledge from past experiences and observations, along with occasional mistakes and experiments. The identity of the solutions in both approaches suggests that the aspects of human behavior focused on by each are both essential and not inconsistent.

Thus, given the stage of the incomplete development of game theory, the two approaches may be considered complementary rather than mutually exclusive to each other in focusing on different, yet inseparable, aspects of human inferences: deductive reasoning versus inductive, observation-based learning; as well as regarding the origin of institutions: designed versus evolutive. In my view, a potentially more serious limit common to both approaches as tools for institutional analysis may lie, as already suggested at the end of chapter 5, in the presumption of the fixedness of the agents' sets of choices. How can the agents know all the possibilities of their actions? Don't they explore a new action possibility in response to an unprecedented observation? A difficulty of this presumption becomes apparent, however, only when we explicitly deal with issues of institutional change. For now we may assume that the agent commands a fixed set of actions constructed from past experiences. As we have somehow reconciled the classical and evolutionary approaches under this presumption, let us now move on to conceptualize institutions based on the general notion of Nash equilibrium without refining it further.

7.2 The Institution as a Summary Representation of an Equilibrium Path

Recall the five properties that are relevant for the conceptualization of institutions. First, institutions are *endogenously* created in the domain rather than exogenously given from the outside. Second, in making their own choices, individual agents cannot form, and need not form, expectations regarding every detail of action-choice rules that other individual agents employ. Rather, agents are largely guided and/or constrained in their action choices by institutions as the conveyers of compressed information regarding how the game is actually played by agents in the domain. In other words, we attribute to institutions the role that *summarily represents* some salient features of the internal working of the domain and thereby reduces agents' uncertainty regarding others' action-choice rules. Third, a property associated in common with various notions of an "institution" is its *durability* or *robustness*. That is, it is robust with respect to the continually changing environment, although this property may be subjected to a test when environmental changes go beyond a certain threshold point, the (accumulated) consequences of internal dynamics in the domain endogenously create a crisis state or an impasse, or more likely the both are combined. Thus an institution should not simply be identified with a particular (equilibrium) state of the subeconomy under consideration at a particular moment of time. It should be identified with something invariant within a certain bound of environmental and internal changes. Also a concept of institution ought to capture its robustness to minor mistakes, experiments, and deviance of the agents from institution's implied rules. Fourth, an institution is universally relevant to all the agents in the domain, providing with them a *common* understanding, or *shared* cognition, about ways in which the game is played in that domain, although they may attach different meanings or interpretations to it. If the way in which the game is played is regarded by some agents as relevant in making action choices, but ignored as irrelevant by the others, it should not be recognized as an institution (although it may be within the former group of agents). Fifth, institutions are humanly made orders. As such an institution is not a natural order which is uniquely determined by the technological and ecological environment of the domain of the economy under consideration. There should be *multiple* ways of institutions being established under the same technological and ecological environment. Thus we seek a concept of an institution, derived from, and related to, the notion of multiple equilibria.

First, suppose that for a stationary environment there exists an equilibrium strategy profile, $s^* = (s_1^*, \ldots, s_i^*, \ldots, s_n^*) \in \mathscr{S} = \times_i \mathscr{S}_i$, where $\mathscr{S}_i$ denotes the set of action-choice rules (strategies) of agent i ($i \in \mathscr{N}$). Suppose that there is associated with this equilibrium a function $\Sigma_i^*(.)$ for each i that maps $\mathscr{S}$ into a space of the smallest dimensionality such that

whenever $\Sigma_i^*(s) = \Sigma_i^*(s^*)$ *for* $s \in \times_i \mathscr{S}_i,$

$$s_i^*(\phi(s)) = s_i^*(\phi(s^*)).$$

This function defines a partition of the strategic profile set as follows: There exists a subset $\mathscr{S}_{-i}(s^*)$ of $\mathscr{S}_{-i}$ that contains s_{-i}^* such that if $s_{-i} \in \mathscr{S}_{-I}(s^*)$, then $s_i = s_i^*$. The value $\Sigma_i^*(s^*)$ summarizes information regarding the equilibrium profile, s^*, to an extent sufficient for agent i to make the corresponding equilibrium action choice of his/her own, s_i^*. That is, if the agent receives the same information as this in other (nonequilibrium) states, the agent will still make the same choice, s_i^*, regardless of the other details of those states. In other words, the details of the equilibrium not included in this information set are redundant or irrelevant to the agent. We call $\mathscr{S}_{-i}(s^*)$ agent i's information set at s^* and $\Sigma_i^*(s^*)$ its summary representation.

At this point an analogy with the price vector as an information medium may be suggestive, although this analogy will not be carried through up to the end of our conceptualization of an institution. In the primitive trade domain, agents are engaged in bargaining, while mutually processing specific information regarding offers and rejections/acceptances by particular trading partners. As the scope of trading expands so that the trade domain evolves into a more anonymous, competitive market exchange domain, uniform exchange ratios (prices) can emerge as an outcome of an equilibrium strategy profile and the agents can rely on that compressed information for their transaction choices.[14] Then the agent does not need to bother with identifying who offers the desired goods with what technology, who else demands the same goods, and so forth. The competitive price vector of the dimensionality equal to the number of commodities becomes a summary representation of other agents' strategic choices for every agent, enabling him or her to economize on information-processing while constraining his or her choice by defining his/her budget-constrained choice set.[15] However, prices will change accordingly as the environment (technology, tastes of agents) changes and does not satisfy the robustness requirement. So the price vector itself cannot be the institution that we are trying to define. Furthermore the agents need to have some beliefs regarding the enforceability of contracts in order to be active in the market exchange domain.

In order to capture the robustness property of institutions, we now explicitly introduce the variability of the environment. Let $\mathscr{E} = \{e\}$ be the set of environmental parameters and $\hat{\mathscr{E}}$ be its connected subset on which a continuous equilibrium mapping, $s^*(e)$, to the set of strategy profiles exists. Roughly speaking, this continuity assumption implies that, as far as the environment is (mildly) changing within the range covered by $\hat{\mathscr{E}}$, "qualitative" characteristics of equilibria evolving over the period remain invariant. Suppose, albeit somewhat loosely, that there is a common characteristic $-\Sigma_i^*$ of $\Sigma_i^*(s^*(e))$ on $\hat{\mathscr{E}}$, such that

Σ_i^* is implied by $\Sigma_i^*(s^*(e))$ for any $e \in \hat{\mathscr{E}}$.

That is, Σ_i^* is the summary representation of the internal state of the domain which agent i perceives when the environment remains on $\hat{\mathscr{E}}$. If we continue to employ an example from the market exchange domain, Σ_i^* may be thought of as representing an agent's general beliefs such as "money can buy goods in markets and the goods bought will be delivered as promised," and "if I retain good credit records, I can buy things anywhere, even through the Internet, with a credit card," and so forth, with the exact levels of prices unspecified. In order to make a strategic choice in a market place, however, the agent needs to find the actual prices prevailing in the market as the environment evolves. On the other hand, outside the information set that induces an agent's participation in markets, such statements as "a mafia is employed to enforce contracts," and "supplies can be obtained only through barter exchanges with a particular business partner with whom we have sustained a relationship over time," and so forth, may hold.

Finally, suppose that one can find a common element of private summary representations Σ^* over all agents in the domain such that

Σ^* is implied by $\ll s_i^*(e), \Sigma_i^* \gg$ for any $e \in \hat{\mathscr{E}}$ and   for all $i \in \mathscr{N}$

where $\ll s_i^*(e), \Sigma_i^* \gg$ is a pair of agent's actual choices and his/her summary representation of the equilibrium path. Σ^* captures the common perception held by all agents about how the game is played and sustained by the actual plays of the agents when the environment varies within $\hat{\mathscr{E}}$.

It is now clear that the information represented by Σ^* satisfies the conditions of endogenicity (because it is derived from equilibria), summary representation, durability, and commonality. Finally, assume that there exist different paths of equilibrium strategy profiles, $\{s^{**}(e)\}$, $\{s^{***}(e)\}$, ..., on the same subset of environments and derive respective, shared, invariant, summary representations, Σ^{**}, Σ^{***}, ... If they are mutually distinct, the multiplicity requirement also holds. Then we may

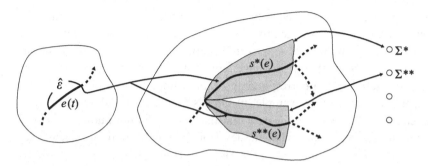

Figure 7.4
Institutions as summary representations of equilibrium paths. From left to right, the set of environments $\mathscr{E}$, the set of strategy profiles, $\mathscr{I}$, and the set of institutions are depicted. Environment-dependent equilibrium paths $s^*(e)$ and $s^{**}(e)$ are summarily represented by Σ^* and Σ^{**} respectively when the environment remains on $\hat{\mathscr{E}}$.

identify those representations as *institutions* (see figure 7.4). For example, if either of the two sets of statements quoted hold univesally across all agents along an equilibrium path, then it may be considered as constitutive of an aspect of the "credit-based market institution," or the "low-trust, barter-exchange institution," respectively.

When the environment varies on $\hat{\mathscr{E}}$, each agent takes the same compressed information represented by Σ^* (or Σ^{**}, Σ^{***},...) as given. The beliefs of the agents are partially coordinated by it. In order to make an actual strategic action choice when the environmental state is $e \in \hat{\mathscr{E}}$, each agent additionally processes the *residual private information* $I_i^*(s^*(e))$ not included in it but relevant to him or her, $I_i^*(s^*(e)) = \Sigma_i^*(s^*(e)) \sim \Sigma^*$. Then the equilibrium path $\{s^*(e)\}$ will continue to be generated, which in turn reaffirms the information compression Σ^* and accordingly reproduces the institution (recall figure 1.1). Thus the institution becomes self-sustaining on $\hat{\mathscr{E}}$. Although the institution is socially constructed as an equilibrium phenomenon, it becomes objectified to the agents in the domain as if it were independent of, and beyond the control of, individual agents.

The role of an institution as a representation of a salient, invariant feature of the equilibrium path in a compressed form may also resolve the paradox referred to in chapter 1.2 and the theoretical difficulty referred to earlier in this chapter: How can each individual player find and choose an equilibrium strategy before the equilibrium is established and thus the equilibrium choices of other agents are known? Individual agents do not need to know the details of the equilibrium choices of other agents beforehand but do need a summary representation plus a modicum of private information. Note that summary representation, Σ^*, coordinates agents' expectations and helps them find the corresponding equilibrium strategy profile, $\{s^*(e)\}$, but that the summary representation does not need to be necessarily derived from the equilibrium path, because the former represents coarser information than the evolving equilibria. This suggests the possibility that a summary representation can emerge even before the game can precisely locate a corresponding equilibrium, and even precedes it and guides the agents to find it. For example, in Greif's model of the Maghreb traders discussed in chapter 3.2, it may be the case that the traders did not know, and could not fully know in the beginning, what the level of the equilibrium efficiency wage would be. However, the belief implied by the Maghreb culture that cheaters would be ostracized from the (merchant) community might have been enough to guide them to eventually find equilibrium contracts by processing more detailed local information with that belief as a common informational background. We will discuss the intuition above and its implications in chapter 9.

Some examples of Σ^* representing shared beliefs may be drawn from part I. Some of these take the form of the if–then rule representing possible mechanisms of enforcement, while others prescribe a particular normative role expected for an agent type in a domain (here an if–then condition specifying possible sanctions against the default of the normative expectation may be implicit).

· *Customary property rights*. One does not capture rabbits on another's parcel of land (chapter 2).

· *Community norm*. Any family not cooperative in the maintenance and use of the village irrigation system would be ostracized from community interactions (chapter 2).

· *Employment contract*. Workers who do not make a required effort will be fired and have a difficult time finding employment elsewhere (chapter 3).

· *Money*. Money buys goods, goods buy money, but goods do not buy other goods (chapter 3).

· *Organizational conventions*. The foreman promotes team work, or he coordinates tasks of subordinates by issuing commands (chapter 5).

· *States*. A sovereign who raises taxes rate without the consent of a council will find his position imperiled, or any bank in danger of bankruptcy will be bailed out by the government (chapter 6).

The compressed information needs to be known, shared, and believed by all agents in a domain for it to become an institution. However, the information does not need to have the same meaning for all agents. For example, take the above-mentioned labor contract institution. The employer may feel it as legitimate to discipline unproductive and unreliable workers, but the workers may regard this as the part of a collusive plot by the capitalist to make them work harder. The variety of meanings attached to an established institution by agents in different roles may be identified as ideologies. Despite interpretative differences, however, the substance of information has an impact on every agent's choice.

7.3   Feedback Loops of Institutionalization

The previous section conceptualizes an institution as a compressed, commonly perceived representation of ways in which a game is played. As such it facilitates the generation and sustenance of equilibrium in a domain of the economy. Accordingly we may refer to the making of a convergent beliefs that generates, and at the same time is reinforced by, a (moving) equilibrium as *institutionalization*. The present section tries to understand the implications of institutionalization by considering various feedback mechanisms operating in tandem within the domain and at its interfaces with environment.

As we have seen, an institution may evolve as spontaneous order (*cosmos* in the terminology of Hayek), such as customs and conventions, as well as the rules (*nomos*) derived from them, such as norms, self-enforcing contracts, common laws, and moral codes. We may classify this type of institutionalization *autonomous* in that institutionalization autonomously unfolds and an institution self-organizes within the given exogenous rules of the game. Alternatively, institutionalization may occur as a result of a designed change in the game form. Adding an artificial agent (an organization) endowed with a unique set of action choices (e.g., legal punishment) and having its own preference ordering over consequences is an example of change in the game form. Another example is a change in legislative law (what Hayek refers to as *thesis*, or set law). In the first case, the set of agents who strategically play the game is augmented, while in the second, the consequence function is altered to incorporate information stipulated in legislative change (e.g., if I smuggle drugs and am caught *and* if the enforcer follows the set law, then I will be jailed). We may categorize the type of institutionalization evolving out of designed change in the game form as *induced*. The governance of impersonal trade at the Champagne Fair implemented by the introduction of the law merchant is one example (chapter 3.3). However, as has been frequently noted, merely introducing a third party or writing a statutory law is not sufficient to achieve an intended internal state (outcome). The expected strategic choice of the enforcer, as well as those of other agents, matter. Even if a statutory law regulating drug traffic is enacted, if the enforcing officers customarily take bribes from the smugglers, then the institution of corruption is induced. The important distinction here is that an institution must be sustained as an equilibrium outcome of the game, while a set law (*thesis*) should be regarded as a parameter of the exogenous rules of the game (a consequence function) that induces the equilibrium, intended or unintended.[16]

We have introduced the distinction between autonomous and induced institutionalization primarily to make the point clear that the introduction of a set law alone should not be thought of as institutionalization.[17] In practice, however, the distinction between the two may be hard to draw. Rather, there may not even be a purely autonomous institution, since it is not possible to conceive of a game situation where all the exogenous rules are entirely technological to the agents in the domain (Field 1979, 1981). Even conventions and norms may evolve within domains that are more or less structured by set laws. Conversely, in order to make an interpretation of endogenous, informal rules (common law) precise in a particular context and consistent across different cases, or to improve on their performance in changing environments, they may become formally codified and consciously redefined. Also, even where a policy design by a political entrepreneur or a legislative law appears to have created a focal point for inducing convergent beliefs among agents, there might have been some preceding practices anticipating a new institution. For example, we saw that there was a rather long history of corporatist experiences in Germany despite of the disastrous interim experience of the destabilizing Nazi state that preceded the formal design of the national corporatist state (Lehmbruch 1999).

Once the endogenous rules of the game, autonomous or induced, are created and sustained, they may become a basis for further institutionalization through their formalization, as well as through interactions with the design of new statutory laws and evolving environments. The process can keep going, ad infinitum, in a spiral fashion. We will deal with this spiral process of institutional change in chapters 9 and 10.[18] To do so will require a substantial expansion and modification of the conceptual framework introduced in this chapter. As an initial, preliminary step toward it, however, let us now re-employ the COASE box and try to identify the implications (feedback impacts) of institutionalization for the various elements of a game as represented by the four cells of the box.

First, let us note that an equilibriating process in the game implies the mutually reinforcing, simultaneous stabilization of the endogenous variables of the game, that is, the strategic choices by the agents, S, and their expectations (beliefs) regarding others' choices, E. Agents' beliefs are coordinated through institutionalization. As was pointed out in chapter 1.3, this has dual implications for the strategic choices of the agents. On the one hand, it helps individual agents to economize on information

	An institution does.......	
	through feedback to data	through internal feedback loops
on micro (individual) dimension	(A) imputes values to accumulated abilities of the agent, and thereby defines incentives for further capacity development;	(S) enables the individual agent to economize on information-processing, while constraining agent's strategic choice by the implied endogenous rules of the game;
	⇐	⇓ micro-macro loop ⇑ macro-micro loop
on macro (collective) dimension	(CO) impacts on technological and institutional environments.	(⇒) ⇓ ⇑
		(E) coordinates agents' beliefs by generating and reproducing compressed representations of salient features of equilibrium.

Figure 7.5
COASE box representation of institutionalization and feedback mechanisms

processing by making a subjectively rational action choice consistent with the internal state and external environments. On the other hand, it imposes "humanly devised constraints" (North) on the choice process of the individual agent by channeling his/her action choices in one direction against the many others (other equilibria) that are theoretically possible. This is the dual, enabling (information–cost saving) and controlling, nature of the "macro-to-micro loop" from the E-cell to the S-cell of the mechanism of institutionalization. Conversely, there is a "micro-to-macro loop" from the S-cell to the E-cell. By acting consistently with the endogenous rules of the game implied by an institution, the agents as a collectivity reproduce and reaffirm the institution (see figure 7.5).

In parallel to micro–macro reciprocal loops, there are other types of feedback loops: from the endogenous equilibrating process to exogenous parameters (from the right- to the left-hand column of the COASE box) and the reverse. As institutionalization occurs in a domain of the economy, it regulates the distributional consequences of the game within it. For example, the establishment of customary property rights, as discussed in chapter 2.1, ascribes a greater number of caught rabbits to an agent who excels in information-processing and risk-taking capacity. Various forms of state discussed in chapter 6 have respective distributional impacts.

For example, the corporatist and bureaupluralist state may institutionalize higher levels of safety nets through social or bureaucracy-mediated bargaining, whereas the liberal democratic state may entail wider income inequality among agents according to the distribution of their marketable capabilities. We can think of the action sets of individual agents, exhibited in the A-cell of the original COASE box, as representing their individual capabilities. Then the distributional consequence of institutionalization imputes a particular pattern of value to agents' capabilities. So, "different institutional rules will produce different incentives for tacit knowledge." (North 1990:81). The rules may reinforce the further development of certain types of capacities while depreciating the value of others. Thus, agents in the rabbit-hunting parable may be motivated to accumulate information-processing capacity. On the other hand, as Platteau and Hayami observed in a provocative essay (1998), a certain norm may have adverse incentives on skill development. According to them, when a family in a sub-Saharan African village has exceptionally good harvests or catches for a few years in a row, other families regard it as a magical act of witchcraft and deprive the surplus from that family in a solemn religious ritual. They interpret this practice as one form of the norm of the "sharing of consequences" among farmers under a severe ecological condition. If the fruits of hard labor or ingenious entrepreneurial activities are expected to be taken away by other families, no one will have the incentive to develop skills to enhance productive or entrepreneurial capacities.

If we consider a feedback loop from institutionalization to the development of capability and competence by individual agents, it becomes clear that it is not quite appropriate to regard the action set of an agent as exogenously fixed as we have done so far. However, at this moment we can make the following compromise: suppose that the "true" action set of an agent includes infinitely many (all physically conceivable) actions. Out of this complete set of an infinite dimensionality, individual agents normally activate only a small subset, spanned by the finite dimensions of action choices, as a repertoire for strategic choice at any point in time, and add new dimensions only gradually because of their limited capacity for cognition, evaluation, and calculation. Institutionalization of a particular type warrants such limited attention. But in response to some external shocks, or as a cumulative consequence of capacity development, agents may be induced from time to time to search for new action possibilities that may lie in hitherto-inactivated dimensions. If this search activity changes agents' (subjective) game forms drastically, the sustenance of an old institution may become problematic. This is an instance of unstable feedback from the left to the right columns of the COASE box. We will discuss such dynamics in chapter 9.

The final feedback loop of institutionalization focuses on the *CO*-cell of the COASE box incorporating the environmental condition of the domain. As noted, we have included as elements of the environment wide-ranging parameters, such as technological, ecological, institutional (in other domains), and international, although explicit consideration of the last two is at this moment reserved for later chapters. The evolving internal state of a domain is nothing but a collective choice induced by an institution, and as such it has an impact on the environment. While the evolution of customary property rights, as discussed in chapter 2, may restrain congestion in the use of natural resources, the assignment of legal property rights in rain forests to "customary users" might induce practices that would have an environmentally devastating impact, such as continual logging by professional loggers to enhance customary rights" (Binswanger 1991). For another example, a certain convention in organizational architecture may be conducive to the faster development of innovative technology but also have the tendency to destroy traditional craft skills, while another form of organizational convention may be inertial in the use of technology. These are impacts of institutionalization on technological environments. But the outcome of institutionalization also constitutes environments to other domains of the economy, influencing the parametric shape of consequence functions there, and vice versa. We will discuss such institutional interdependencies across different domains of the economy in the next chapter. The possibility of destabilizing feedback from technological and other environmental factors that may trigger the process of institutional change will be discussed in chapter 9.

8 The Synchronic Structure of Institutional Linkage

In any group of men of more than the smallest size, collaboration will always rest both on spontaneous order as well as on deliberate organization.... That the two kinds of order will regularly coexist in every society of any degree of complexity does not mean, however, that we can combine them in any manner we like. What in fact we find in all free societies is that, although groups of men will join in organizations for the achievement of some particular ends, the co-ordination of the activities of all these separate organizations, as well as of the separate individuals, is brought about by the forces making for a spontaneous order. The family, the farm, the plant, the firm, the corporation, and the various associations, and all the public institutions including government, are organizations which in turn are integrated into a more comprehensive spontaneous order.
—Friedrich A. von Hayek, *Law, Legislation, and Liberty* (1973:46)

So far, except for chapter 2.2, we have only dealt with a single domain of the economy at a time, whether the commons, trade, organizations, organizational field, or polity. What was happening in other domains of the economy was subsumed, together with technology and ecology, as environmental factors, and possible interrelationships across domains were not explicitly analyzed except for occasional verbal discussions (e.g., chapter 6). It is now necessary to explicitly consider how games in different domains are linked synchronically (i.e., contemporaneously) as well as diachronically (i.e., over time). The previous chapter conceptualized the institution as a robust, summary representation of a stable equilibrium path that is collectively perceived by the agents and governs their strategic interactions in a particular domain of the economy. One of the great advantages of this equilibrium-based approach to institutions is that it becomes analytically tractable to deal endogenously with types of institutions that may emerge across different domains as well as possible interlinkages among institutions. For example, recall the model of the Tokugawa village in chapter 2.2. There the emergence of a community norm was explained as an endogenous outcome of a game linking the social exchange domain and the commons domain rather than by invoking the exogenous notion of culture. Also, as hinted in the discussion of possible relationships between types of market institutions and types of states in chapter 6, fits among institutions may be understood in terms of general-equilibrium-like feedback among the strategies of individual agents across different domains of the economy. Then an economy as a whole may be viewed as a robust and coherent overall cluster of mutually interdependent institutions.

This chapter identifies two classes of linkage of games—institutionalized linkage and institutional complementarity—and discusses their implications. The first refers to a situation in which agents strategically coordinate their choices across domains of the same or different types (as in the model of chapter 2.2), and as a consequence an institution emerges that is not feasible when agents are confined to making separate choices in isolated domains. Through this type of linkage some kind of externalities may be created and the gains from them may be accruable to all or some of the agents involved in the linkage as rents, which will contribute to the sustenance of the linkage. Types and ranges of the agents who are instrumental in creating the linkage and derive rents therefrom can be diverse. They may be the members of a community, that of an endogenously formed club, a single agent, a third party, market participants, or a combination of these, and the resulting institutions can accordingly be diverse although the logic involved is the same (sections 8.1–8.2).

The second class deals with an interlinkage among institutions that may arise in a situation where agents may not strategically coordinate their choices across different domains because of a limited scope of choices, limited perception, or for other reasons, but their choices are parametrically affected by prevailing rules of action choices (institutions) in other domains. As a consequence there may arise interdependencies of institutions across domains, which we will conceptualize as institutional complementarities (section 8.3).

One caveat is due at the outset. Understanding institutionalized linkages and complementarities as equilibrium phenomena does not imply that they are necessarily efficient. For example, the emergence of an institutionalized linkage may provide new rent opportunities for some (linking) agents but make the others worse off. Thus an institutional innovation realized through a new institutional linkage is not necessarily a Pareto-improving move. Further, rents derived from an existing institutionalized linkage can be incentives for some agents to resist a reconfiguration of linkages that are made possible by technological innovation or knowledge enhancement but would dissipate the current rents. We will also show that Pareto-suboptimal, overall institutional arrangements can exhibit robustness because of complementary relationships among constituent institutions, even if there are attempts to remedy inefficiency in a piecemeal manner. In chapter 10 we will examine the implications of institutionalized linkages and complementarities to gain an understanding of the mechanism of institutional evolution. They tend to make existing institutional arrangements robust vis-à-vis changes in external and internal domain characteristics, but they may also, in certain roles, set institutional evolution in a direction distinct from the many others that are logically possible. In order to understand all of these, however, we must first understand the logic of synchronic linkage of institutions. This is our task in this chapter.

8.1 Social Embeddedness

In this and next sections, we deal with the situation where agents can strategically coordinate their choices across domains of different types—the case of linked games. In doing so, agents may effectively enrich their viable choices, and thus enable a new institution that is not feasible without such linkage to emerge. We categorize the strategic linkage of domains giving a rise to, and in turn sustained by, institutions as *institutionalized linkages*. In this section we take up one particular class of this category: the social embeddedness in which the social-exchange domain "embeds" another type of domain and enables some strategy profile to be sustained in the latter that would not be otherwise viable. In the next section we take up various other types. This distinction does not lie so much in the logical structure of linked games as in their socioeconomic implications.

We saw in chapter 2.2 that even if the cooperative standard of behavior in a commons game, such as in the irrigation game and turnpike provision game, does not appear self-enforceable in isolation because of the technological difficulty of excluding free-riders, a cooperative standard may become enforceable when the same agents are engaged at the same time in a social exchange game that can produce a sufficiently large amount of social capital for them. The social capital refers to the present-value sum of future benefits, including intangible goods such as status, social approval, and emotional stability, that individual agents expect to derive from cooperative association with the community in the social exchange game. In order to derive returns from it, individuals must invest in it and maintain it through social exchange.[1] The fear of denial of access to social capital by other community members makes it incentive-compatible for each member to observe the cooperative standard, while members' concerns with the disruptive impact of deviant behavior in the commons game make it in their common interests to impose social sanctions on the deviant in the social exchange domain. The analyzed linkage was between a commons domain and a social exchange domain. But the same idea can be extended to a linkage between another type of domain, such as trade, organization, and even polity, on one hand, and a social exchange domain, on the other.[2] As mentioned in chapter 2.3, although not explicitly formulated in game form, what sociologist Granovetter deals with in his seminal paper, subtitled "The Problem of Embeddedness" (1985), may be considered to be such a situation. Thus we call this type of linkage *social embeddedness*.

Example 8.1 Stratified Distribution of Social Capital (Platteau and Seki) In chapter 2.2 the domain characteristics of the linked irrigation and social exchange games were assumed to be symmetrical with respect to the agents. In particular, the amount of social capital each agent obtained from following the community norm was assumed to be identical. It is considered that the relative homogeneity of the members of the community is in general an essential prerequisite for the community norm to operate for the ease of peer monitoring, the effectiveness of incentive provision for a uniform choice standard, as well as the equalization of outside-option values.[3]

However, in some cases the agents in a commons domain may be differentiated by ability and other endowments in the provision of commons goods. Then an institutional arrangement may require the dictum, to be applied to the effect, that "each contributes according to his ability, all equally enjoy common goods." How can such a norm become self-enforceable?

Comparative fieldwork in contemporary Japanese fishery communities by Platteau and Seki (2001) offers an interesting perspective on this issue. They found variations among the fishermen's groups they studied: the most productive group was characterized by various cooperative norms and practices, such as the active sharing of expertise and current information regarding the best fishing location, well-developed collective control over access to fishing space, collective retrieval and repair of lost net, and synchronization of fishing hours and the number of hauls. This group also practiced the equal sharing of net incomes among fishing units. On the other hand, among other groups work coordination was limited and the sharing of knowledge minimal, and there was no or limited pooling in incomes and input costs. The authors collected evidence to show that the former group intended to, and indeed did, enhance aggregate profits through the reduction of congestion costs and risk of net damage, better exploitation of the gains from specialization, as well as monopolistic control of sales price for fish. However, the cooperative norms regarding effort expenditure and knowledge sharing, combined with the income and material input cost pooling, may imply that the more able fishermen were, the less favored they were materialistically in comparison to their counterparts in other, less cooperative groups. Why were the able people willing to comply with the egalitarian-cum-cooperative arrangements instead of defecting from it like their counterparts in another group did some years ago to dissolve the cooperative group?

The authors submitted interviews supporting the idea that the fishermen were able to gain higher status and esteem within the cooperative group by making best efforts in contributing to collective incomes. In terms of economic jargon, the opportunity costs of cooperation incurred by the more able fishermen is compensated for by a greater amount of social capital allotment to them. We will see presently the prevailing isomorphic structure as it is more formally institutionalized in the Japanese workshop.[4] The Platteau and Seki study suggests that despite differentiated characteristics of agents in the commons game (fishery game), there can be multiple equilibria: socially embedded cooperative fishing with income pooling, and competitive fishing based on individuated skill.[5]

Example 8.2   Two Kinds of Work Place Norms (Burawoy)   In chapter 5 we noted two types of organizational architecture that could evolve as conventions: one based on individuated specialized skills and the other on context-oriented skills incorporating information sharing. It may be thought that a piece rate system is a good incentive device for utilizing specialized skills efficiently, as far as workers could be assigned to a well-defined single task,[6] while a more egalitarian payment scheme fits the second type better so as not to encourage egocentric competition. However, the piece rate could instigate a "rat race" (Akerlof 1976) among the workers, triggering price cuts and creating a Prisoner's Dilemma type of situation. On the other hand, the egalitarian scheme applied to the second type of organization could discourage the efforts of the most able one, with the whole work group trapped in a low productivity equilibrium. In either case, however, the way social capital is used and distributed among workers within the workshop could lessen these problems to some extent.

An interesting example of how small work group norms counteract the adverse effects of competition among themselves is provided by Burawoy (1979) who gives a rich ethnographical description based on his own work experiences. He showed how the workers themselves developed rules in reaction to the incentive scheme of piece rates in a machinery factory near Chicago. At this factory, the piece rate was defined by the machine the workers ran more or less autonomously. The operators were paid basic earnings plus a price times the excess of the production rate over 100 percent, with rates established on an individual basis, varying with the job, machine, experience, and so on. In their scheme the workers aimed at achieving—"making out" in their slang—a certain individual target rate. Some were satisfied with 125 percent, while other would aim at a higher rate. But there was a ceiling (e.g., 140 percent) imposed and well recognized by all participants. If someone tried to achieve more than the ceiling, he would be ostracized (although some might not mind being ostracized), while anyone who could not attain 100 percent was scorned and "few but the greenest would condescend to engage [him] in conversation." (1979:64)

Burawoy argues that "making out" cannot be understood simply in terms of achieving greater earnings; its rewards included relieving boredom and obtaining social relations and psychological rewards, while it restrained overcompetition. The culture of "making out" is generated by the workers themselves, but once established it is experienced as a set of externally imposed relationships. He interprets this situation from the Marxian perspective as that, by playing games according to the rules, the workers provided "consent" to capitalist exploitation of surplus value.

In contrast, in the typical Japanese workshop, informal cooperation is the norm, ranging from the voluntary teaching of green workers by veteran workers and the sharing of knacks for doing things not found in manuals, to mutual help in solving problems, such as machine breakdown, defective supplies, tool repair, and the like. It is important to note that the assiduous workers in such activities are generating a substantial degree of externalities. Although there are elements of reciprocity, disparity among workers in a workshop team in ability to provide externalities is inevitable. Are they fully compensated by wage differentials reflecting such disparity? The workers at the Japanese factory have been traditionally paid according to ranks unrelated to job classification, and wage differentials across ranks are rather compressed. Further, promotion along the rank hierarchy is not a tournament type such that only the winner can catch all prizes associated with the highest rank. The general expectation is that everybody will sooner or later reach the highest rank in their lifetime (this is the crux of the so-called seniority wage), but differentiated by the speed of promotion (the high flyer may be promoted to a foreman with which a different rank hierarchy may be associated). Differentials in the speed of rank promotion, say whether promotion to the fourth rank in ten can be achieved by age 35 or not, is of great concern to the workers.[7] It seems doubtful, however, that lifetime income differentials associated with relatively faster promotion awarded to more able and helpful workers are sufficient to compensate for the complete value of the externalities they are generating, because wage differentials across ranks are compressed and the speed of promotion is in general only gradual. Yet it is apparent that more able workers obtain nonpecuniary satisfaction from the recognition that faster promotion symbolizes, while other workers have high esteem, and sometimes jealousy as well, for those workers. Usually the individual contributions of workers to collective productivity, as well as to other's capacity development, are well recognized within the work group on the shop floor and room for managerial discretion on promotion is severely limited.

In the factory where Burawoy worked and studied, the established norm may have reduced the rat race among the workers, but at the same time it impeded the development of cooperation and participation in work-process improvement among workers. On the other hand, while the Japanese practice may have facilitated the development of such an efficiency-enhancing practice, it appears that social pressure on the shop floor permeated the lives of the individual workers. Striking a balance between the individualist and cooperative approaches might appear to be ideal. However, it is intuitive that each of the norms discussed above is generated by, and in turn supports, a respective organizational architecture of the shop floor: a functional hierarchy based on the clear decomposition of jobs and a horizontal hierarchy based on information- and experience-sharing, respectively. Thus it is far from obvious how such a seemingly ideal combination can be feasible without a fundamental modification in traditional organizational architecture as well.

8.2 Linked Games and Institutionalized Linkages

In social embeddedness the agents simultaneously belonging to the social exchange and another linked domain. They may be the members of an irrigation community, a fishery community, or a work group in the modern factory. In this subsection we consider other types of institutionalized linkage: (1) linkage of games by contracts between the same agents (linked contracts), (2) bundling of (identical) domains by a single agent internal to all the domains to be linked (integrative bundling), (3) bundling of (identical) domains by a third party not belonging to any of the original domains (intermediated bundling), and (4) bundling of (identical) domains by market participants. The linkage of games may change information or/and incentive structures of games and thus make some strategic choices of agents credible that would not have been otherwise.

Contractual Linkage

We first consider the case where more than one game is linked by a coordinated design of contracts by an agent. In this way the agent may change the incentive structure of a contracting partner, creating rents opportunities for him or herself (and possibly for the contracting partner as well). The following example and related ideas have been extensively discussed in development economics.

Example 8.3   Linked Transactions in a Rural Development Context (Bardhan, and Braverman and Stiglitz)   Imagine the rural village in the developing economy where the set of agents is composed of a wealthy landholder, poor landless laborers, and outside money lenders. Suppose that the laborers supply labor services to the landholders under a sharecropping arrangement as a convention or by a contract. Under the sharecropping arrangement, only a share of the marginal labor product accrues to the laborer. Therefore, if the laborer enters into a sharecropping arrangement in an isolated labor exchange domain and maximizes its utility surplus by equating marginal contractual income with marginal labor disutility cost, an undersupply of efforts ensues.[8] Further it may be the case that the landlord has a limited monitoring capability, so the laborer can embezzle seeds/crops, and so forth. On the other hand, suppose that the laborer does not have any means to survive in the spring before farming starts, so he needs to borrow either from the landholder for whom he works or from a money lender at a competitive rate. Suppose that the landlord offers consumption credit, repayable by crops in the autumn and thereby links a credit transaction domain and a labor exchange domain.

Suppose that the landholder uses the following strategy: lend money to the laborer at a rate lower than the rate the outside money lender offers. If the laborer defaults on the repayment because his income in the autumn falls short of the debt repayment plus subsistence level consumption, then the landlord will require him to provide extremely unpleasant extra labor services. We assume that this bonded labor service clause is enforceable. The laborer's strategy is to borrow money to a certain amount in the spring and work harder between spring and autumn to avoid default. The linkage of the two domains induces a higher effort from the laborer. Because of such externalities, the landlord induces the laborer to borrow more at an interest rate below the market rate. Bardhan and Rudra (1978) reported that West Bengal landlords indeed offered such loans, sometimes even interest-free consumption loans. As a result of more effort by the laborer than under an isolated sharecropping arrangement, the utility possibility frontier will expand outward, regardless of whether the market environment for a sharecropping arrangement is competitive, monopolistic, or bilateral-monopolistic (Braverman and Stiglitz 1982). However, its distributional consequence may depend on the market structure. Both the landlord and laborer may be better off, or the landlord may capture total gains from externalities (e.g., in competitive or monopolistic environments).

There is a relatively rich literature on linked contracts in the development context, for example, labor supply, future crop delivery, and putting-out contracting, on the one hand, and credit, land leasing, and consumption goods supply, and the like, on the other.[9] In general, the linked contracts can be efficiency-enhancing and is not necessarily an inefficient response to a particular institutional environment (e.g., the landlord's power, legal restriction on usurious interest rates). The specification of linkage above assumed a sharecropping arrangement, but the efficiency enhancing or preserving result can hold, for example, for stepwise linear wage contracting as well (i.e., a lower wage rate up to a certain amount of crops and the competitive wage rate thereafter).[10] However, the distributional consequence of linkage is unambiguous. As before, both landlords and laborers could be better off, or the landholders could obtain total efficiency gains, depending on various sociopolitical and environmental factors.

Integrative Bundling

This is the class of linkage in which domains of the same type are bundled by an agent internal to the domains. By coordinating his or her strategy across the domains, the linking agent may make a commitment to some strategic choice credible (e.g., punishment of a contracting partner contingent on a certain outcome), which is not self-enforcing in isolated domains and can thereby elicit desired choices from the other agents.[11]

Example 8.4 The Factory as a Bundle of Employment Contracts (Murdock)
Suppose that an employment game is played repeatedly between an employer and a worker in an one-sided Prisoner's Dilemma situation just like the game between a merchant and his agent in the Greif's model in chapter 3.2. In that model, the merchant was able to adopt the efficiency wage discipline vis-à-vis his agent in order to control her shirking. As no cost was incurred for the merchant to replace an agent, the merchant's threat to fire a shirking agent was credible. We now consider the situation in which the employer has a maximal punishment strategy against the worker's shirking, say the termination of an employment contract, that could induce cooperation from the worker. However, it is costly for the employer to adopt this strategy, as the transaction cost of doing so, T, say the cost of replacing a worker, is greater than the difference between the continuation value V_{coop} of cooperative outcome characterized by the strategic profile {Efficiency wage, High effort} and the continuation value V_{Nash} of a noncooperative static Nash outcome characterized by the strategic profile {No firing–low wage, Shirking}. Therefore the threat of exercising this maximal strategy by the employer is not credible, and the equilibrium outcome of the game is the static Nash.

Now suppose that two such games are bundled by a single employer but that the two workers cannot coordinate their strategies. Then the employer can adopt the following strategy: if neither worker shirks, he will hire both workers at the efficiency wage level. If one worker ever shirks, the employer will exercise the maximal punishment strategy and replace him or her by another worker with cost T. If both workers shirk at the same time, the employer will play the static Nash strategy in both games in all future periods. Now let us see if it is profitable for the employer to deviate from this strategy. Suppose that one worker shirks. By applying the maximal punishment strategy the employer will benefit $2V_{coop} - T$, since the new and retained old worker will both cooperate in the future. Otherwise, he will gain $2V_{Nash}$, because without punishment both workers will shirk in the future. Therefore, if $V_{coop} - V_{Nash} > \frac{1}{2}T$, then the threat of the maximal punishment strategy becomes credible in the bundled game, although it is not in a single game (Murdoch 1996).

Thus, despite the absence of employer's credible commitment to the maximal punishment strategy in each game in isolation, bundling will make the cooperative outcome possible, although noncooperative static Nash equilibrium can remain as another possibility. The implication is that the divide-and-rule policy of the classical factory system in which workers' communications were restrained was to make efficiency wage discipline more effective than independent employment or putting-out contracting. Of course, the described characteristic is only one possible aspect of the factory system, and there are other important aspects such as gains from the coordination of production activities among workers. Also, needless to say, the divide-and-rule strategy of the employer can be made ineffective by the countervailing coordination of bargaining strategies among the workers through the formation of a union.[12]

Example 8.5 The Multi-vendor Subcontracting System In example 8.4 above, let us substitute a core manufacturer for the employer and a supplier for the worker. The implication is that a multi-vendor system, as observed in the supplier relationships in the Japanese automobile industry, may be understood as a device to control the holdup problem between the manufacturer and the supplier that was discussed by B. R. Klein, Crawford, and Alchian (1978) in their often quoted paper.[13] Their solution to this problem was the hierarchical control of suppliers through integration, but it is not the only possible institutional response (as we showed in chapter 4.1, integration is not informationally efficient relative to the subcontracting system in the automobile industry when appropriate incentives are provided). In fact a recent historical study of company documents by Freeland (2000) indicates that the holdup problem may not be resolved even after integration. Fisher Brothers (the pre-acquisition owners of Fisher Body) held up the GM headquarters by withdrawing the supply of their expertise (human assets) even after giving up property rights of physical assets. They were able to derive a favorable stock option plan from GM after the integration by threatening to leave GM. In contrast, by keeping multiple supplies outside in repeated transactions, Japanese manufacturers seem to have controlled any potentially adverse impact of a supplier's bargaining power with the credible threat of contract termination.

Intuitively it may be thought that a similar logic can be applied in explaining some other forms of bundling of business activities, such as the so-called multi-divisional form (*M*-form) of organizational architecture, conglomerates, and diversified business groups. We will discuss this idea in conjunction with other aspects of those forms in example 8.10 below.

Intermediated Bundling

Unlike the integral bundling of domains by an agent—an integrator—who is an original player in those domains, this type of bundling involves intermediation by a third party. The incentives for the third-party to link games are rents made possible by the creation of externalities in the form of new information otherwise unavailable to the original agents (examples 8.6 and 8.7) or a change in the incentive structure of the original agents (example 8.8).[14]

Example 8.6 The Law Merchant (Milgrom, North, and Weingast) Chapter 3.3 provided an example of intermediated linkage. Honest trading in anonymous trade games became self-enforcing when multiple anonymous games were bundled over time by the intermediation of a third party—the law merchant. The law merchant changed the information structure of the agents by strategically transmitting information regarding the record of unpaid judgments by any agent.

Example 8.7 The Merchants as Information Intermediaries (Che) Suppose that there are a group of farmers and a group of consumers. Each farmer produces a unit product of a crop. The quality of the product is uneven. The probability of a farmer's product being of good quality is q and of being bad quality, $1 - q$. Each consumer can visit only one farmer. Consumers cannot precisely assess the quality of the product before purchase. However, they can form a conjecture about the quality of the product by inspection before purchase. The better the real quality of a product, the higher the consumer's assessment. In negotiating the purchase price, the consumers do not have any bargaining power, so they can only refuse to buy if the price offered is not agreeable. Obviously the higher the consumer's postinspection belief about the quality of the product, the higher will be the price they are willing to pay. Let us call the trade game between a farmer and a consumer the direct trade game, in which the producer's set of choices is composed of a range of selling prices and that of the consumer is {Buy, Not buy}.

Suppose now that merchants (middlemen) appear between the group of farmers and that of consumers. They buy products from two farmers for the price that the consumers would pay. However, they are capable of judging the real quality of products. Also, if they find a farmer's product to be of poor quality, they can go to other farmer(s) and find product of good quality at some private cost, if they choose to do so. Suppose that such activity is socially beneficial (i.e., consumer surplus net of the merchants' search cost is positive), but it is not privately profitable for the merchants to do so if the consumer's beliefs remain the same. Also there is no a priori reason for the consumers to believe that the merchants' expertise is not used for their own advantage.

Now assume that each merchant can intermediate two direct trading games and coordinate his choices between them. The merchants will then have two strategic decisions to make: when they find the product of one farmer to be of poor quality, whether or not they should go elsewhere and find a product of good quality at a cost, and when they find the products of both farmers that they initially contact unsatisfactory, whether or not they should go to other farmers, and, if so, how many units of product, one or two, of good quality they should find. If they search for two good units, the search cost will be doubled. In any case the merchants will have two units of product, either good or bad, from two farmers on display. Suppose that each consumer is randomly allotted to one particular unit of product of a merchant but he or she can refuse to buy for the price offered after examining *both* products that the merchant displays.

Che (1997, 1999) proved that the following strategy profile is the only stable equilibrium, provided that the probability q of an product being of good quality is sufficiently high: the merchants incur the additional cost of searching for one unit of good quality if and only if the product of only one farmer that they initially contact is of bad quality; and the consumers pay higher prices than in the direct trading game if and only if they receive signals that both units on display at their merchants' shop are of good quality. Given the merchant's strategy, the units on display at a merchant shop's are either both of good quality or both of bad quality The probability of a product offered to a consumer being of good quality is now $2q - q^2$ and higher than q (the probability of both products being initially of good quality was q^2, and that of one product being initially good and one product being initially bad was $2q(1 - q)$, in which case the merchant must search for a product of good quality). Although the consumers still receive imperfect signals from pre-purchase browsing, the chance that they will form favorable postexamination beliefs is altered upward. The consumers who have limited monitoring capacity are better informed. Intermediated bundling can thus creates externalities. The merchants who have products of good quality in stock can charge a higher sales price than the price that the consumers were originally willing to pay directly to the farmers and still have a chance of the higher price being accepted. In other words, the merchants capture the values of externalities. Therefore they will be better off even after incurring search costs. Those who stock only products of bad quality must sell them at a lower price. However, the probability of products of bad quality being sold in markets is now reduced from $(1 - q)$ to $(1 - q)^2$ and the consumer surplus from products of bad quality also increases because of a lower purchase price.

In the model above, substitute "entrepreneur" for "farmer," "investor" for "consumer," and "financial intermediary" for "merchant." Then it explains one aspect of the role of financial intermediaries: to reduce an investor's uncertainty regarding the riskiness of investment projects proposed by entrepreneurs through their superior monitoring capability. In his original model (1997), Che interprets the role of the township and village government in China as that of a de facto corporate head-quarters that aligns the qualities of investment projects of township and village enterprises in a consistent manner so that the uncertainty of outside buyers and investors is reduced.

Example 8.8   Venture Capitalist Bundling of R&D Financing   Suppose that invest-ors who do not have the capacity to monitor R&D activity finance a single entre-preneur for a development project. Suppose that the contract between them is such that a certain share of the value of the completed R&D project will accrue to the entrepreneur. Then a moral hazard problem could arise where the entrepreneur does not expend sufficient R&D effort and wastes funds because he cannot obtain the full value of his effort. Suppose, alternatively, that the venture capitalist raises twice as many funds from investors and finances two entrepreneurs engaged in the same R&D project—namely the venture capitalist bundles two R&D financing domains. The venture capitalist runs a tournament and promises the entrepreneurs to provide the same share of the value of a successful project as in direct financing to a winning entrepreneur but none to a loser (e.g., only a successful entrepreneur can go to the IPO (initial public offering) market). It was shown in chapter 4.3 that if the total value of a successful project is expected to be very high, even though each entrepre-neur has only a 50 percent chance of winning, a higher R&D effort will be elicited from both entrepreneurs. This in turn enhances the expected value of the successful project. Under certain conditions these external effects can become large enough to compensate for the cost of duplication of R&D, and as a result rents may accrue to the venture capitalist (chapter 14.2).

Market-Mediated Linkage

In example 8.6 the intermediating role of the law merchant is to affect the incentives of the traders indirectly by changing their information structure. However, the law merchant does not have the power to enforce punishment on cheaters. The formal third-party enforcement mechanism of the courts further strengthens the incentives of the agents to trade honestly in this regard. The development of markets made pos-sible in this way enhances the linkage of various domains, such as organization domains. By being exposed to market competition under which strategies vis-à-vis markets and within the organization need to be coordinated, the managers and workers of the firm can be disciplined to make efficient action choices. Example 8.9 applies a somewhat similar logic to the linkage of political-economic domains, each composed of (local) government and state-owned enterprises. Example 8.10 discusses the roles

government SEO	hands off	bail out
make effort	γ, π	
shirk	0, 0	Γ, β

Figure 8.1
Consequence structure of the political economy domain

of business groups (bundling of diversified business firms), when the market-mediated linkages have not been well-developed because of the lack of an effective third-party enforcement and information-disseminating mechanism.

Example 8.9 Market-Linked Federalism (Qian and Roland) Suppose that a single domain of a simple political economy game repeatedly played by the government and the representative state-owned enterprise (SOE). There is also a private sector in the domain, whose investment returns are dependent on the level of government investment in social infrastructure. The structure of strategic interactions between the government and the SOE is represented by the consequence (not payoff) matrix in figure 8.1. In this matrix, rows indicate the strategic choices of the SOE management/workers and columns indicate the strategic choices of the government. The first entry of each cell represents the nonverifiable (nontaxable) private benefits net of effort to the SOE management/workers, and the second represents the verifiable return that can be fully taxed by government. We assume that $\Gamma > \gamma$ and $\gamma + \pi > \Gamma - \beta > 0$. The government can obtain positive tax revenue π only when the SOE management/workers exercise effort. However, the strategy choice of the SOE management/workers is not verifiable in the court, so it is not contractible.

Suppose that the SOE management/workers move first and the government follows. If the SOE management/workers choose to shirk, the SOE makes a loss $-\beta$ on the books. At that time the government has to choose whether to bail out the troubled SOE by diverting fiscal resources β from investment in the social infrastructure, assuming that the total budget of the government is fixed. The private benefit to the SOE management/workers, inclusive of the saving of effort cost, is highest at Γ if they are bailed out. They get zero return if liquidated. Suppose that the government is benevolent or politically motivated in that it regards the suffering of the laid-off SOE management/workers from the closure of the SOE, meaning $-\Gamma$, as a social loss or amounting to the own cost of loss of political support. Then it will bail out the troubled SOE, provided that the bail-out benefit Γ is greater than its opportunity cost β in the form of reduced private sector productivity caused by the short supply of the social infrastructure. Knowing this ex ante, the SOE management/workers will then shirk and enjoy an easy life (large positive payoff Γ). Thus the {Shirk, Bail out} combination becomes an equilibrium yielding low aggregate benefits, $\Gamma - \beta$, which may be referred to as the *soft-budget* equilibrium.

Now suppose that multiple domains of the political economy game are bundled by a third party, the federal government. The federal government is interested in the maximization of aggregate social returns across domains. Suppose that the federal government deregulates the flow of private investment so that private investment is freely mobile across the domains. Now each government in a single jurisdictional domain needs to compete for the supply of private investment to maximize domain's products. To attract investment, local governments can invest in complementary infrastructure (roads, airports, etc.) that would improve its marginal productivity. Additional investment by the government would attract external resources to its jurisdictional domain from another domain, even with the total amount of private investment in the economy as a whole fixed. The marginal local benefits of investment in infrastructure, rather than bail-out, then include the marginal benefit, say ρ, derived from the induced inflow of investment from other domains, in addition to the marginal productivity β of increased infrastructure. Because of these externalities, marginal benefits of infrastructure, $\beta + \rho$, are now opportunity costs of the bailing-out of the SOE by a government. If this opportunity cost exceeds the bail-out benefit Γ, then the local government will spend the amount β of its fiscal resources on infrastructure rather than bailing out the troubled SOE. The commitment of governments to harden the budget vis-à-vis the troubled SOEs thus becomes credible, and the management/workers become compelled to make an effort. Then the strategic profile of {Effort, Hands off}, yielding higher aggregate benefits, $\gamma + \pi$, becomes an equilibrium, which may be referred to as the *hard-budget equilibrium*.

The bundling of the political economy domains as described above is a simple example of market-preserving federalism as discussed in chapter 6.2.[15] It can serve as a coordinating device for achieving high equilibrium in a situation where the effort levels of the SOE's management/workers are not verifiable. Competition among governments in the linked game can harden budgets for the SOE and discipline its management/workers. The social gains from budget hardening are efficiency gains from disciplining the SEO, $\gamma + \pi - \Gamma$.

In the example above, the amounts of investment in the social infrastructure by local governments are assumed to be fixed except for their possible diversion to bail-out expenditures. However, local governments may actually compete with each other in the amount of investment in infrastructure in the presence of externalities created by federalist bundling. While containing a soft-budget constrain tendency, federalist bundling may thus lead to socially excessive investments.

Example 8.10 Diversified Business Groups (Khanna, Palepu, and Rivkin) In relatively less advanced market economies (referred to somewhat loosely as "emergent markets"), we often find the formation of business groups organized across diverse markets. *Zaibatsu* in pre-war Japan, *chaebol* in Korea, *grupos* in Latain America, and business houses in India are notable examples. They can be formed as a group of firms bundled centrally by a closely held holding company (as in the pre-war *Zaibatsu*), a business holding company (as in *chaebol*), through cross-holdings by member firms with a core firm (India, Chile), and so forth. Also they are often connected through family ties or the other social relationships of owners, directors, and managers of member firms.

What are the functions of these diversified business groups? One conventional view based on information and transaction-cost economics is to regard them as substitutes for capital markets.[16] When financial intermediaries specializing in market monitoring and information dissemination are underdeveloped, problems arising from the information asymmetry between investors and borrowers need to be responded to by an alternative (organizational) approach. Thus a holding company may emerge to fund and finance member firms at its own risk, monitor their management, and discipline them in case of management failure. In advanced financial economies these functions are specialized and dispersed among various organizations, such as investment banks, commercial banks, venture capital funds, market analysts, accounting firms, fund managers, bankruptcy courts, reorganization specialists, takeover raiders, and financial journalists. Besides acting as a substitute for missing capital market institutions, diversified business groups may also internalize managerial labor markets in the absence of competitive external markets and accreditation organizations such as business schools. For example, the pre-war *zaibatsu* and *chaebol* centralized the recruitment and assignment of managers (Okazaki 2000).

Further, if a third-party, contract-enforcement mechanism based on the rule of law has not been developed, alternative mechanisms for governing trade must exist for the enhancement of markets. These can be the self-enforcing club norms among member firms with mutual stockholdings as initial gift-exchanges or membership fees (chapter 3.1), integrative bundling of business firms by a holding company as a mechanism of credible commitment to punishment of failed management (example 8.5), the internalization of third-party contract intermediation in the form of a member trading company (example 8.7), or a combination of some of these. If the role of business groups is indeed to substitute for market-governing institutions, then it can be expected that the more diversified the group is, the more profitable it will be, up to the point where the technological and other diseconomies of scale set in. For this reason Khanna and Palepu (1997, 1999a) argue that focused strategies and the breakup of business groups may be a misplaced policy recommendation for emerging markets.

Another class of economic interpretations of the business groups in emerging markets focuses on the monopoly power of business groups, often formed in collusion with the government and capable of capturing policy-induced rents. There are two variations in this class of interpretations regarding their developmental implications. One is to regard the rents as generated by unproductive rent-seeking behavior of the business groups in collusion with the corrupt government (Krueger 1973; Bhagwati 1982). This well-received view roughly corresponds to the model of the "degenerate developmental state" we discussed in chapter 6.1. However, the "market-enhancing developmental state" model can be another possibility. Its logical structure is the same as in example 8.4. If the provision of policy-induced rents by the government is conditional on the developmental performance (e.g., export performance) of a business group, and if the threat of the government to terminate a subsidy and other favoritism for a business group in the event of its poor performance is credible, government-induced monopoly arrangements may not necessarily be deterrents to economic development. If so, the phenomena of government-business collusion, and the first view of the business group as a substitute for formal and intermediating market-governing institutions, may not necessarily be mutually exclusive.

There is also a sociological interpretation of the business group that emphasizes the aspect of social relations, such as familial and school ties, and ethnic networks among firm owners and managers (Granovetter 1994; Hamilton 1995; Khanna and Rivkin 1999b). But if such social relationships embed economic transactions among member firms of the business group in a way reminiscent of the models of chapter 2.2 and example 8.1, they can serve as an effective contract enforcement mechanism. Also the family "name" of a business group may serve as a repository of reputation (Kreps 1990; Tadelis 1999) in product markets, as well as in accessing foreign technology. Then the sociological focus on family ties and other social relationships as the defining factors of the business group may not necessarily be inconsistent with the first view. Economic ties through cross-stockholding or a holding company, on one hand, and social ties based on the mutual holding of social capital, on the other, can be complementary for the sustenance and profitability of business groups.[17]

Which view mostly likely explains the role of business groups in the less mature market economy, as well as whether business groups create or destroy values, is an open issue. Various empirical results suggest that "the normative debate concerning business groups is unlikely to be resolved simply in favor of either the 'groups as paragons' school, where groups are primarily a response to market imperfections ..., or the 'groups as parasites' school, where groups are primarily devices for rent-seeking behavior" (Ghemawat and Khanna 1998). With the United States as a benchmark, Khanna and Rivkin (1999a) did crosscountry empirical studies on business groups in thirteen emerging economies. They find no correlation between measures of group profit performance and several measures of government-related distortions in the economy, so this casts doubt on the conventional view of groups as rent-seeking devices. They conclude that groups can exist for different reasons and perform different functions, contingent on a broader, overall or institutional context. For example, as indicated above, the impact of government or business groups depends on the nature of the state evolving in the polity domain, while social embeddedness may sustain either low or high multiple equilibria (more on this later in chapter 10.1).

Khanna and Palepu (1999b, 2000a, b) conducted more in-depth studies on business groups in India and Chile where better data are available. They showed that the diversified business groups became more profitable only when their scope exceeded some threshold point. Therefore, if unproductive rent-seeking behavior is not a primary source of the profits (crosscountry, survey-based index compilations suggest there is very little corruption in Chile), the economies of scope of business groups may stem from their various, value-enhancing, trade-governing roles indicated above. They also constructed indexes for labor and capital market intermediation by Chilean and Indian business groups and showed that the business groups expanded these roles in response to deregulation of (primary resource) markets and other liberalization measures.

However, as markets further expand, competencies useful for formal or intermediating governance mechanisms may gradually accumulate. Then substituting more open external mechanisms for information intermediation and contract enforcement for internal, private mechanisms may become potentially less costly, and accordingly the transition to a looser bundling of business firms becomes potentially more conducive to further market development. Although how such transitions can be realized is far from obvious, the *zaibatsu* dissolution in the postwar Japanese reform provides a dramatic example of such a transition initiated by a political shock. The centralized holding company was legally banned during the reform. In response, ex-member firms started to restructure groups based on the cross-stockholding among them.[18] The role of the group as a trade-governing mechanism declined over time (symbolized by the decline of the intermediating role of trading companies in member-firm transactions). The governance role of the pure holding company was replaced by the mechanisms in which a member bank intervened in the corporate governance of other member firms, conditional only on their financial distress—the so-called contingent governance mechanism (chapters 11.3 and 13). However, as we will see in the next two chapters, a political shock alone is not either a sufficient nor necessary condition for an institutional change.

8.3 Institutional Complementarity

Let us now turn to a situation in which agents do not strategically coordinate their choices across different domains of games, yet their choices are parametrically affected by the prevailing choices in other domains. So far we have treated the exogenous rules of the game, specifically the consequence function of a domain, as being determined technologically, and possibly by historically precedented social constructs such as law (chapter 8.3). Now, however, we explicitly allow for the possibility that the consequence function, and thus the payoffs of the agents in one domain, may be affected by the institutions prevailing in other domains. Obviously the agents cannot strategically coordinate their choices across different domains, if they do not participate in them simultaneously. But, even if they do participate, when they make an individual choice in each domain, they may perceive the prevailing institutions in other domains as objectified and thus exogenous parameters because of their bounded rationality in perception and choice.

An institution prevailing in one domain constitutes an *institutional environment* for agents in other domains, as far as those agents perceive it as exogenously given and beyond their control. However, just as in the Walrasian economy where agents subjectively make choices in response to price parameters, but actually generate feedbacks to price formation, strategic choices made by individual agents in one domain with an institution in another domain as an environmental parameter may influence the strategic choices of the agents in the latter domain and thus its institutions; and vice versa. There can indeed be synchronic interdependencies among institutions emerging as equilibrium outcomes in each game domain. We explore this possibility below whereby one type of institution rather than another becomes viable in one domain when a fitting institution is present in another domain, and vice versa. We call this interdependence institutional complementarity. The presence of complementarity implies that a viable overall institutional arrangement, across different domains, constitutes a coherent whole and individual institutions therein may not easily be altered or designed in isolation. As we will see shortly, this implies that viable institutional arrangements may not necessarily be Pareto efficient but still be robust with respect to isolated experiments to overcome the inefficiency in each domain.

To see this and other important implications of institutional complementarity, we need to build a rigorous definition of this concept in accordance with our equilibrium-oriented conception of institutions. Let us try to do this with respect to a simple model, relying on the theory of supermodular games developed by Topiks (1978, 1998) and Milgrom and Roberts (1990).[19] First, suppose that there are two domains, $\mathscr{D}$ and $\mathscr{G}$, with sets of agents, $\mathscr{M}$ and $\mathscr{N}$ (e.g., the polity domain and the organizational field), that do not directly interact. Nevertheless, an institution implemented in one domain will parametrically affect the consequences of the other game by changing its institutional environment. For simplicity we assume that the technological and natural environment is constant. Suppose that the agents in domain $\mathscr{D}$ face the choice of a rule from either Σ^* or Σ^{**}, while agents in domain $\mathscr{G}$ face the choice of a rule from either Λ^* or Λ^{**}. For a moment, let us assume that all agents in each domain have an identical payoff function $u_i = u(i \in \mathscr{M})$ or $v_j = v(j \in \mathscr{N})$ defined on binary choice sets of their own, either $\{\Sigma^*; \Sigma^{**}\}$ or $\{\Lambda^*; \Lambda^{**}\}$, with another set as the set of parameters. Let us say that an (endogenous) "rule" is institutionalized in a domain when it is implemented as an equilibrium choice of the agents in the relevant domains.

Suppose that the following conditions hold:

$$u(\Sigma^*; \Lambda^*) - u(\Sigma^{**}; \Lambda^*) \geq u(\Sigma^*; \Lambda^{**}) - u(\Sigma^{**}; \Lambda^{**})$$

$$v(\Lambda^{**}; \Sigma^{**}) - v(\Lambda^*; \Sigma^{**}) \geq v(\Lambda^{**}; \Sigma^*) - v(\Lambda^*; \Sigma^*)$$

for all i and j. They are the so-called supermodular (complementarity) conditions. The first inequality implies that the "incremental" benefit for the agents in $\mathscr{D}$ from choosing Σ^* rather than Σ^{**} increases as their institutional environment in $\mathscr{G}$ is Λ^* rather than Λ^{**}, and the second inequality implies that the "incremental" benefit for the agents in $\mathscr{G}$ from choosing Λ^{**} rather than Λ^* increases if their institutional environment in $\mathscr{D}$ is Σ^{**} rather than Σ^*. Note that these conditions are concerned with the property of incremental payoffs with respect to a change in a parameter value. They do not exclude the possibility that the level of payoff of one rule is strictly higher than that of the other for the agents of one or both domain(s) regardless of the choice of rule in the other domain. In such a case the preferred rule(s) will be implemented autonomously in the relevant domain, while the agents in the other domain will choose the rule that maximizes their payoffs in response to their institutional environment. Then the equilibrium of the system comprised of $\mathscr{D}$ and $\mathscr{G}$—and thus the institutional arrangement across them—is uniquely determined by preference (technology). But, if neither rule dominates the other in either domain in the sense described above, the agents in both domains need to take into account which rule is institutionalized in the other domain. Under the supermodularity condition there can be then two pure Nash equilibria (institutional arrangements) for the system comprised of $\mathscr{D}$ and $\mathscr{G}$, namely $(\Sigma^*; \Lambda^*)$ and $(\Sigma^{**}; \Lambda^{**})$.[20] When such multiple equilibria are possible, we say that Σ^* and Λ^*, as well as Σ^{**} and Λ^{**}, *institutionally complement* each other.

If institutional complementarity exists, it may be the case that possible overall institutional arrangement are not mutually Pareto comparable, or that one of them could be even Pareto suboptimal to the other.[21] Suppose that $(\Sigma^{**}; \Lambda^{**})$ is a Pareto-superior institutional arrangement in which $u(\Sigma^{**}; \Lambda^{**}) > u(\Sigma^*; \Lambda^*)$ and $v(\Lambda^{**}; \Sigma^{**}) > v(\Lambda^*; \Sigma^*)$. However, if for some historical reason Σ^* or Λ^* is chosen in either of the domains and becomes an institutional environment for the other domain, the agents in the other domain may correspondingly react by choosing Λ^* or Σ^*. Thus the Pareto-suboptimal institutional arrangement will result. This is an instance of coordination failure in the presence of indivisibility. There also exists the case where $u(\Sigma^{**}; \Lambda^{**}) > u(\Sigma^*; \Lambda^*)$ but $v(\Lambda^*; \Sigma^*) > v(\Lambda^{**}; \Sigma^{**})$. This is the case where the two viable institutional arrangements cannot be Pareto ranked.

We have dealt with a simple case where there can be only one strategic choice for the agents to make in each domain and there are only two domains, each inhabited by homogeneous agents. However, the reasoning can be extended to more general cases. Suppose, for example, that domain $\mathscr{D}$ contains three types of agents, $i = 1, 2, 3$, where each has a choice set $\{\sigma_i^*, \sigma_i^{**}\}$ and a payoff function $u_i(\sigma_i : \sigma_j, \sigma_k, \Lambda)$, $j, k \neq i$. Institution Σ^* (alternatively, Σ^{**}) establishs itself if $\sigma_i = \sigma_i^*$ (respectively, $\sigma_i = \sigma_i^{**}$) for all $i = 1, 2, 3$. Agents may have different preferences regarding institutional arrangements, that is, some agents may be better off under $\{\Sigma^*; \Lambda^*\}$, while the others may be better off under $\{\Sigma^{**}; \Lambda^{**}\}$ although their actual choice behavior may be affected by other's choice in the domain as well as the institution prevailing in the other domain. In particular, suppose that they are assimilative in the limited sense that their payoff functions are all supermodular; that is, if any of σ_j, σ_k, and Λ shifts from $\sigma_j^{**}, \sigma_k^{**}, \Lambda^{**}$ to $\sigma_j^*, \sigma_k^*, \Lambda^*$, payoff differential $u_i(\sigma_i^* : \sigma_j, \sigma_k, \Lambda) - u_i(\sigma_i^{**} : \sigma_j, \sigma_k, \Lambda)$ becomes greater for all i and $j, k \neq i$. Put differently, incremental gain (which can be negative) in strategy switching from σ_i^{**} *to* σ_i^* improves if it is complemented by a similar shift by any other agent or an institutional change from Λ^{**} to Λ^{**} in the other domain. Then, depending on whether $\Lambda = \Lambda^*$ or Λ^{**} in domain $\mathscr{G}$, either Σ^* or Σ^{**} will establish itself as a corresponding institution in domain $\mathscr{D}$, even though some agents may be better off in another institutional arrangement.

We have assumed that the two domains are inhabited by different agents. However, we may also apply the foregoing result to the case where the same agents play the games in both domains, with their payoff functions given by a separable function $u + v$. If each agent is small relative to the whole population so that the impact of individual choice is perceived to be negligible, then agents do not coordinate their choices in both domains but rather make a choice in one domain by taking an institution in another domain as given and unchangeable.[22] Therefore we may claim the following:

PROPOSITION 8.1 When there are institutional complementarities across different domains, Pareto-suboptimal overall institutional arrangement may become viable. Also there can be multiple overall institutional arrangements that are not mutually Pareto rankable.

We hinted in chapter 6 that there can be mutual interdependencies between forms of state in the polity domain and institutional forms prevailing in market exchange or organization domains. We conjectured there that the development of markets giving rise to the middle class and the liberal democratic control of the state may be mutually reinforcing, while the social-compact control of the government may emerge as an equilibrium outcome when the workers' collective ability to control labor supply is strong. On the other hand, we saw that the evolution of an organizational convention based on context-oriented human assets may complement the evolution of the bureau-pluralist state; the bureau-pluralist state reinforces that convention by deterring the development of competitive labor markets across organizations through mutually exclusive jurisdictional regulations. These relationships are intuitive. But we established the notion of institutional complementarity in order to prove and derive the subtle implications of such a relationship, which allows us to engage it in formal analysis. We will provide such an analysis of the possible institutional complementarities among the corporate governance, organizational architecture, financial transaction, and polity domains in part III.

We have seen that equilibrium institutional arrangements across domains can well be suboptimal in the presence of institutional complementarities. The synchronic structure of overall institutional arrangement can therefore be multiple and diverse. In order for a Pareto-suboptimal institutional arrangement to change, do complementary institutions need to be changed simultaneously (the Big Bang approach), or will a change in one institution in one domain trigger a chain reaction in other institutions through the very complementarity relationship (the sequential approach)? Institutionalized linkages, such as social embeddedness, integrative and intermediated bundling, may also provide the property of robustness and inertia to existing institutions. Although the emergence of a new type of linkage may imply the enhancement of viable choices and thus an institutional innovation, its establishment may eventually deter the emergence of still another potential linkage, since the unbundling of the established linkage may encroach rents enjoyed by some agents. Then the economy may be trapped in a stagnate state or, far worse, may decline. We now turn to the conceptual and analytical framework for analyzing and understanding such dynamic possibilities.

9 Subjective Game Models and the Mechanism of Institutional Change

People play "silly" games because they are not quite so smart as we typically assume in our analysis. The rules of the game ... are all akin to equilibrium expectations; the product of long-term experience by a society of boundedly rational and retrospective individuals.... [T]he inertia we see in institutions mirrors the inertia we see in equilibrium expectations, and the ways of groping for more efficient institutions—gradual evolution of institutions, the adaptation of institutions to sudden drastic changes in the environment, more conscious and purposeful breaking-out of well-worn equilibrium patterns and (perhaps) plunging into a period of disequilibrium, and everything between these—mirror similar sorts of changes to equilibrium expectations.
—David M. Kreps, *Game Theory and Economic Modelling* (1990:182–83)

The theme of this and the next chapter is the dynamic mechanism of institutional evolution. This involves two questions: one relatively easy and the other, notoriously hard. The first is the question of why institutions tend to be robust and enduring in face of some environmental changes in spite of possible suboptimal arrangements. The basic elements of an answer have been provided in the last two chapters, and we begin this chapter by succinctly summarizing these points (section 9.1). In the literature, technological economies of scale (setup costs) and network externalities are often cited as major reasons for the robustness of institutions or persistent patterns of doing (e.g., David 1985; Romer 1986; Arthur 1989). Instead we emphasize factors inherent to institutions conceptualized as shared-beliefs-cum-equilibrium-summary-representation. The second question is why and how institutions can nevertheless change. This question has hardly been satisfactorily dealt with in economics or in the other social sciences, and our exposition will be necessarily preliminary and experimental. By our definition of institutions, an institutional change may be identified with a situation where agents' beliefs on the ways a game is played are altered in critical mass. This should be distinguished from mere changes in statutory laws and marginal changes in agents' strategic choices in response to mildly changing environments according to chosen rules. Therefore, to deal with the second issue, in this chapter we focus first on the mechanism of systematic changes in cognition and learning, as well as that in strategic choices made by individual agents and their interactions. Essentially we will be dealing with the cognitive (subjective) aspect of the mechanism of institutional change. In the next chapter we will discuss the objective aspects of the mechanism of institutional evolution: how the diachronic linkage of institutions may affect the nature and course of their evolution.

Orthodox game theory, classical and evolutionary, defines its analytical framework in such a way as to regard the sets of choices by the agents fixed a priori. For both approaches there can be multiple equilibria. Then an institution, viewed as an equilibrium phenomenon, can be seen merely as a shift from one equilibrium to another.

What brings about change? In Nash equilibrium no rational agent will find it beneficial to change his or her strategy unilaterally. But one might argue that if agents' sets of all possible actions are objectively known and fixed, some rational agents could perceive the possibility of a "better equilibrium," either through deductive reasoning or by learning from best practices elsewhere, and thus become engaged in activity that makes its choice a focal point. Often such a rational role is expected from the government. However, the government itself is an agent, with its own incentives and limits in cognition and reasoning, as well as limited ability of persuasion and limited impacts. It is not clear at all that the government is able to, or even be willing to, lead the coordination necessary for a move from one equilibrium to another.[1] More important, the mechanism of institutional change seems to often involve a novelty or change in the agents' set of possible actions from which their strategy can be constructed.

In this chapter we develop a conceptual framework for understanding the dynamic mechanisms of institutional change that is consistent with and extends the synchronic conceptualization of institutions given in chapter 7. We visualize institutional change as a process by which the agents discover a new way of doing things in response to their own crises of shared beliefs caused by environmental shock, an internal crisis of the domain, or more likely, their combination. Through the agents' strategic interactions a new kind of equilibrium and its compressed representation become self-organized. In developing this framework, we depart from the usual game-theoretic presumption that the agents have complete (or incomplete) knowledge of the objective structure of the game. Instead, we believe that they have subjective views of the structure of the game they play in the form of what we call subjective game models. Particularly, we submit that individual agents subjectively activate only small subsets of technologically feasible actions and/or their combinations as "repertories" (Dosi and Marengo 1994) of choice at any one time. Then the process of institutional change may be conceived of as one in which the agents are induced to re-assess and substantially revise their subjective game models, and thus possibly introduce a new repertoire of action choices. The reassessment and reconstruction of subjective models by the agents is not done in a random, mutually independent way. To generate a new shared system of beliefs—a new institution—this needs to eventually take on a mutually consistent form. What mechanism obviates their random re-constructions but generates eventual consistency among them? When this issue is discussed, we will see that the shared-beliefs-cum-summary-representation of the equilibrium view of an institution becomes highly relevant, for it is by this means that the synchronic and diachronic approaches to institutions can be synthesized.

9.1   Why Are Overall Institutional Arrangements Enduring?

Why do institutions tend to be robust to normal environmental change? Answers suggested by the treatment so far can be summarized as follows.[2]

First, if an institution is nothing more than a statutory law, then it may be easily changed by legislation or government decree. But let us recall that we conceptualized institutions as a shared system of beliefs about how the game is being repeatedly played and that it can be formed through the strategic interactions of individual agents. As a shared mind-set, institutions are stable and durable if environmental change is not drastic. A mere change in a statutory law is not an institutional change unless it simultaneously and systematically alters the perceptions of individual agents as regards how the pattern of their strategic interaction is formed and accordingly induces a qualitative change in their actual strategic choices in critical mass. In general, once institutionalization is achieved, marginal, random drifts of individual perceptions and associated strategic choices will have only negligible effects on the generally held beliefs of agents, because of the anonymity of individual agents and/or by the working of the law of large numbers. Further, as discussed in chapter 7, institutions not only transmit information to individual agents but also do so in specific compressed forms. In other words, one may say that an institution has its own "codes of communication" (Arrow 1974). The rules implied by particular market governance institutions, organizational conventions, and community norms may be explicitly or tacitly well understood only by agents in the relevant domain. Even if there are experimental or innovative choices of individual agents, they may not be transmitted to the great majority of the agents, or even if they are, their meanings may not be immediately understood to alter their beliefs and action-choice rules.

Second, the feedback mechanism between institutionalization and competence development of the agents, as mentioned in chapter 7.3, reinforces the durability of institutions. As said, an institution imputes values generated in the domain to agents' physical and human assets in an institution-specific manner. In response the agents adapt their efforts to accumulate assets and develop competence in the direction to enhance their values, which in turn supports the expanded reproduction of the institutions. For example, the competitive labor market institution rewards agents possessing individuated functional skills that are valuable across competing organizations. The efforts of agents to develop highly rewarded skills facilitate the expansion of organizations following an organization-architectural convention relying on such skills. As discussed in the previous chapter, Buroway interprets that the workers at the factory he observed provide "consent to the capitalist exploitation of surplus value" by developing individuated skills and traits that fit the workshop culture of "making-out." Within the liberal democratic state in which disputes over property rights and contracts are settled relatively more often through litigations, there are higher demands for educational services to train legal specialists. A third party who mediates a particular pattern of bundling of economic activities can acquire rents derived from created externalities (chapter 8.2) and use them to perpetuate that pattern of bundling, whereas those agents attempting a new pattern of bundling may not have the resources to finance the setup costs for doing so. In general, competition among the agents to develop institution-relevant skills and traits thus contributes to the accumulation of human assets instrumental for the reproduction of the institution.

Third, an institution also imputes political power to agents in a manner that is conducive to the status quo. Those agents that benefit relatively more from an existing institution may be endowed with resources and competence to perpetuate it, while the potential beneficiary of an alternative, potential institution may lack resources to realize it. For example, when the control of a representative system over the bureau-pluralistic state is weak, the bureaus are expected to, and subjectively seek to, play the role of elitist protectors of respective jurisdictional interests in the administrative process. With selective recruitment and bureaucratic competition, the exclusive ethos of the bureaus can be reproduced. In a collusive state, government officials can actively cultivate support from the collusive groups by side payments, and vice versa, but the victimized class may lack political and economic resources necessary for staging effective resistance. Some agents who perceive themselves to be at disadvantage in their political power and social roles may be discontent with an existing order. But under normal circumstances they may not be the ones who can afford, or are ready, to bear the costs necessary for new institution-building. These costs may include those of organizing effective political movements advocating a new system of normative beliefs in the polity domain, as well as experimenting with a new organizational form embryonic of a new institution, or various disequilibrium costs to be incurred during the transition, and so forth.

Fourth, various interlinkage of institutions as we saw in the previous chapter may make it difficult to change institutions in a piecemeal manner. The existing literature of institutions emphasizes that once an institution is set up, it will become durable, either because of increasing returns to scale (setup costs) or network externalities. However, these phenomena should not be viewed in purely technological terms but as endogenously emanating from the inherent nature of overall institutional arrangements. The various linkages of games discussed in chapter 8 are sustained by externalities they create by themselves. As the game form of the social-exchange domain is likely to change only slowly, it may embed various domains in a steady manner. The linked contracts across trade domains may make a new entry difficult. For example, the landlord who possess loanable funds can fend off competition from other financiers by linking cheaper credits and sharecropping contracts (chapter 8.2). A new type of intermediated bundling of domains may be possible only when an old type of integrative bundling is unbundled (an example is provided in the next chapter). But agents who have vested interests in the latter might resist and try to block institutional innovation in the Schumpeterian sense of "new combinations." Also complementary institutions are mutually supportive, even if they are suboptimal arrangements (chapter 8.3). Institutional complementarity is an instance of non-convexity (economies of scale): there may be many ways of arranging institutional configurations across domains, but their mixture (convex combinations) may not be viable. The situation is analogous to a jigsaw puzzle: it is difficult to replace one piece (an institution) without affecting the integrity of the whole picture (an overall institutional arrangement). However, these points do not by any means imply that a system is frozen. Rather, as we will see presently, institutional complementarity has significant implications for ways in which a systematic change can take place too. If a change occurs in a key domain of the economy and triggers a change in another related domain through the very complementary relationships, the momentum for new institutionalization may be created. To be sure, different systems may have different modes of institutionalized linkages, some being more tightly knit than others. Such differences may also have implications for the adaptability of overall institutional arrangements of different economies to the same environmental shock, whether technological or international.

9.2   Subjective Game Models and General Cognitive Equilibrium

Despite the various causes of institutional robustness described in the previous section, institutional change does occur. What is the mechanism for change? According to the equilibrium-of-the-game view of institutions, an institutional change may be identified with a shift from one equilibrium (sequence) to another equilibrium (sequence) associated with a systematic, qualitative change in the action-choice rules of agents as well as their common cognitive representations (beliefs) about them. At first, it may appear that there are two ways of realizing such a change of equilibrium in parallel to the dichotomy of institutions made in chapter 7.3: autonomous and induced. For one, it may be thought of as occurring as a spontaneous ordering out of the *decentralized experiments* of agents trying new strategies from the given sets of action choices. Alternatively, equilibrium change may be thought of as being introduced by the *collective design* of a law and/or a new type of agent—an organization

—equipped with a fundamentally different set of action choices from the ones possessed by incumbent agents.

However, we have repeatedly argued that the introduction of a law per se and an associated new regulatory agency is nothing more than a change in the data—exogenous rules of the game—in the game form that the agents perceive. We will discuss below how such a change in law or policy may affect the process of institutional change by providing a focal point for agents who are forming a new shared system of beliefs as well as altering individual strategies. However, in understanding the impacts of a designed change, we need to trace the process backward as well as forward. On one hand, we may ask: How can a statutory law be introduced or changed? How do agents come to (collectively) recognize the need for a new (regulatory) organization? On the other hand, we may ask: How does a new law and organization affect the beliefs of agents and accordingly their strategic choices? Do they always generate intended consequences?

These questions help us see that notwithstanding an apparent difference between spontaneous and induced institutional change (and that between autonomous and induced institutions), there is a common condition involved in bringing about a change by either route. The critical mass of agents needs to begin, even if gradually, to modify their cognitive representations about the internal state of the domain, as well as about the impacts of changing external environments, in a consistent manner so that they will generate a new equilibrium (sequence). If we think in this way, the distinction between the two mechanisms of institutional change become blurred. Even if there is a deliberate, collective choice of a new law and the introduction of a new agent (e.g., a regulatory agency) to enforce it, the accumulation of decentralized private experiments or a substantial agreement in policy-making through political discourse may precede this. On the other hand, a change in the game form (e.g., policy change) needs to actually induce a new equilibrium, intended or unintended, by facilitating the convergence of expectations among all the agents in a relevant domain.

But how do agents perceive benefits from a change in their own strategic choices and generate a new system of shared beliefs? Does change happen merely by chance (mutation)? If so, how can one expect that chance events will occur in a critical mass at once? Alternatively, should the adoption of new strategies by individual agents be regarded only as a rational response to an environmental change or preference change? If so, is institutional change uniquely and steadfastly conditioned by the course of environmental change? How does preference change occur? Or, even if the credibility of agents' common beliefs begins to be questioned, and thus the stability of an institution is shaken, will an institutional change evolve through a trial-and-error process of cognitive reconstruction of individual beliefs? As a conceptual frame for dealing with these and other issues of institutional change, we now modify the classical and evolutionary approaches in one important respect and introduce the concept of subjective game models.

Recall that, in the basic (objective) game structure as displayed in the COASE box in figure 7.1, the entry in cell A was the set of all technologically feasible action choices of an agent, while the entry in cell CO summarized relationships between technologically feasible action profiles and technologically feasible consequences, given various environmental conditions. Subsequently we incorporated the possibility that the consequence of the game may be affected by the equilibrium strategy profiles, and thus institutions in other domains (chapter 8.3). In any case, we assumed that given the exogenous rules of the game, as represented in the left column of the COASE box, and given an expectation (belief) about other agents' choices, as represented in cell E, individual agents make the best strategic choice S perceived by them. As an action-choice profile becomes stablized, its substantive part becomes crystalized as institutions (i.e., as shared beliefs).

Now let us modify these presumptions and suppose that individual agents cannot have a complete knowledge of the technologically determined rules of the game, nor can they make perfect inferences about other agents' strategic choices or environmental states. Instead, we assume that at any point of time each agent is assumed to have a limited, subjective perception of the structure of game that he/she plays, constructed from the past experiences and to revise it in response to drastic environmental change and internal crisis. We call the agent's subjective cognition of the structure of the game the agent's *subjective game model*[3] and visualize it in terms of the modified COASE box as follows. (Our intention is to define it on a generic level rather than on the basis of specific equilibrium concept, so we deal directly with agents' sets of strategic choices rather than construct them from agents' sets of action choices.)

Suppose a period of time in which the environment of a domain (e.g., technology, institutions outside the domain, statutory laws) is stable. This environment can vary within a limited range, but for simplicity we assume that it is represented by a single vector, **e**. Under this condition, suppose that the following four conditions hold:

· (A) Over a period of time, the agent may have only a limited repertoire of strategic choices from infinitely many technologically feasible choices. Technically the objective set of all "technologically feasible" strategic choices of an agent $\mathscr{S}_i (i \in \mathscr{N})$ may be represented in a space of infinite dimension, but only a finite-dimensional subset is activated for possible strategic choice. We may call this subset the *activated subset* of strategic choices and represent it by $\mathscr{S}_i$ (technically it is a hyperplane of the entire set of technologically feasible strategic choices).

· (E) Agents shares a system of common beliefs Σ^*—an institution—about the endogenous rules of the game. Besides, each agent forms private residual information $I_i(s)$ about the internal state of the domain, when the actual play (strategic choice profile) of the game is $s \in \times_i \mathscr{S}_i$.[4]

· (CO) Given perceived institution Σ^*, each agent has the subjective consequence function of the form $\phi_i(., I_i(.) : \Sigma^*, e)$, according to which physical consequence $\phi_i(s_i, I_i(s) : \Sigma^*, e)$ of his own choice $s_i \in \mathscr{S}_i$ is inferred, depending on his/her private residual information $I_i(s)$.[5] Implicit in the functional form is also an agent's view or interpretation about the environment of the domain e, such as the state of technology, statutory laws, and institutions outside the domain. We refer to the functional form as the *subjective inference rule*.

· (S) The agent chooses a strategy from his/her activated subset of strategy choices $\mathscr{S}_i$ that, given an institution, private information about the internal state of the domain and inference regarding the environment impacts, is predicted to maximize his/her own utility (payoffs). Namely the agent chooses s_i^* in $\mathscr{S}_i$ that maximizes $u_i(\phi_i(s_i, I_i(s) : \Sigma^*, e))$, where $u(.)$ is the payoff predictor. We call this operation the *best-response choice rule*.

The foregoing specifications may be summarized by the modified COASE box shown in figure 9.1. The agent's subjective expectations regarding others' choices in the E cell of the original COASE box is now partially replaced by institutions (the I cell) common to all the agents and thus perceived as the objectified reality by any single agent. This cognitive belief is incorporated into his/her inference about the consequences of his/her strategy choices. Accordingly, the I cell is made stretched to the region of parametric data (i.e., the left-hand side column) of the COASE box, although it is generated and reconfirmed endogenously in the domain.

	parametric data	endogenous variable
internal to the agent (micro)	(A) activated subsets of choices	(S) best-response choice rule
external to the agent (macro)	(CO) inference rules	(E) private beliefs
	(I) institutions (shared beliefs)	

Figure 9.1
COASE box representation of the subjective game model of an individual agent

When the agent repeatedly uses the same set of rules for inferences, payoff prediction, and strategy choices, together with the same phenomenological perception of institutions, we say that the subjective game model is reproduced (or in *cognitive-equilibrium*) at the individual level.[6] Note that the subjective game model thus defined roughly correspond to the notion of "mental models" in the induction theory of Holland et al. (1986). They conceive of mental models as "models of the problem space" that cognitive systems construct, and then "mentally 'run' or manipulated to produce expectations about the environment." (ibid.:12). But, following the pioneering work of Denzau and North (1994), our conceptual framework emphasizes the interactions of such models with those of other agents so that the subjective game models of individual agents incorporate institutions that are constructed and perceived by all the agents.[7]

In chapter 7 an institution Σ^* was regarded as being generated and self-enforcing as a joint product—a summary representation—of the strategic choices of agents who play an objective game. We can extend this notion to the present case where the agents play their respective subjective games simultaneously. Let us assume that the following "fixed point" property holds at the level of the domain:

$$s_i^* = \operatorname*{argmax}_{s_i \in \mathscr{S}_i} u_i(\phi_i(s_i, I_i(s^*) : \Sigma^*, e)) \qquad \text{for all } i \in \mathscr{N}.$$

This is a Nash equilibrium condition. It represents the situation in which all agents perceive the institution Σ^* as a relevant constraint and act accordingly, and as a result the equilibrium strategy profile s^* and its summary representation Σ^* become consistent with each other and are sustained. When this condition holds, we say that subjective game models are in *general cognitive equilibrium* so that institution Σ^* is reproduced.[8] The reproducibility of the institution may not necessarily require the rigid reproduction of all the individual subjective game models. As discussed in chapter 7, the agents might marginally and/or parametrically change their sets of rules for personal inference, payoff prediction, and (action) choice, or randomly experiment, but the preceding general equilibrium condition via information compression by Σ^* could still hold.

9.3   The Mechanism of Institutional Change: The Cognitive Aspect

When an existing set of rules does not produce satisfactory results relative to an agent's aspirations, the agents may start questioning the relevancy as well as usefulness of their own subjective game models. They may try to substantially revise/refine the set of rules that they have used. In particular, they may search for and experiment on new strategic choices (rules) involving the expansion of the repertory of action choices, namely that of the dimensionality of the activated subset of choices. But when such a gap between aspiration and achievement occurs in a critical mass, the situation may be called a *general cognitive disequilibrium*. This could happen when there is a drastic environmental change, along with cumulative dynamic outcomes affecting the objective structure of the game. We may think of the following events as environmental triggering conditions:

• New technological innovation occurs so that new action choices become feasible (hitherto inactivated dimensions of the choice sets can be invoked).

• Closed domains come into contact with expansive external market exchange domains.

• External shocks, such as the defeat of war, perceived productivity and innovation gaps with foreign competitors, or prolonged depression, compel agents to perceive a need for change in legal and organizational framework, improvement in productivity or other performance characteristics.[9]

• A large-scale institutional change occurs in a neighboring domain (including international domains) where strong institutional complementarity exists.

As internal cumulative impacts, we may think of the following:

• Cumulative consequences of repeated games under certain rules, exogenous and endogenous, have generated a change in the distribution of assets, power, and expected roles among agents, so the implementability or enforceability of those rules has started to become problematical.

• A substantial number of mutant action choices and associated competence that may be neutral, or slightly suboptimal, to the existing institutional arrangement have accumulated internally.[10]

External shocks alone may not be sufficient to trigger institutional change. Without the accumulation of the seeds for change, agents may adapt their subjective game models only marginally in response to external shocks without changing the substantive character of their action choice and other rules. In the worst case, absent any possibility of mutation, the economy will fail to generate effective adaptative strategies even when it is exposed to a large external shock (we will consider an example below in 10.1). However, as the model in chapter 5 shows, when the performance characteristics of the domain are relatively satisfying and no significant gap between aspiration and achievement is perceived by the agents, entrepreneurial mutation will have limited impact (proposition 5.4). It is rather a general sense of large disequilibrium in the subjective game models, caused by the combined effects of endogenous and external factors as described above, that triggers synchronized searches among agents for a redefinition of their respective subjective game models. Any mutation (deviance) that is neutral or not profitable under the stable external environment and internal state may then be expected to yield higher payoffs, provided that similar choices or complementary new choices will occur in the same or complementary domains. There may also appear agents that start to re-examine the effectiveness of their own activated choice sets and "discover" novel actions or a new Schumpeterian bundling of domains, enriching the repertoire of strategic choices. Successful mutant choices or new choices will likely be emulated by other agents. The problem-solving incentives to search, learn, and emulate generated by the macro crisis are highly context-specific, and the feedback process can trigger further search, learning, and emulation. Thus the triggering conditions and feedback mechanisms can obviate random search and experiment.

As simultaneously implementation of new choices begins, the existing institution will cease to provide a useful guide for individual choices. It will be incapable of providing an effective summary representation of newly emergent choice profiles and thus cannot be helpful in informing agents' expectations. This is what is meant by an *institutional crisis*. The taken-for-grantedness of the old institution are called into question. Agents need to be confronted with larger amounts of information regarding the internal state of the domain than they did when the institution was intact. In particular, they have to process more information and form expectations regarding emergent patterns of choices by others that may be relevant to their payoffs. In this connection agents need to revise their rules for inference, payoff prediction, and action choice. In the end, all agents need to reconstruct their subjective game models.

Now the problem-solving search under an institutional crisis may involve various kinds of information that may anticipate the emergent rules of the game. For example, agents may try to emulate practices that they see operating effectively in other domains (including those in foreign economies). In polity domains there may be a few alternative "discourses" (Lehmbruch 1999)—a set of cognitive and normative ideas—that compete with each other for hegemony and that may help in designing new policy. A political leader or entrepreneur may try to signal a desired direction of change by a symbolic action (e.g., Deng Xiao Peng's visit to a free economic zone in Shengzheng in 1992, signaling the liberalization of markets in the centrally control economy). Even the sensational public disclosure of some untoward behavior that was tolerated under the normal state may have a decisive impact on agents' perception of what is or is not a proper choice of action. So a few *systems of predictive and normative beliefs* should emerge[11] and compete with each other. Competition among these beliefs characterizes the transitional process. Which competing system becomes a focal point where the expectations among agents converge, and thus a candidate for a new institution, will depend on how learning, emulation, adaptation, and inertia interact across economic, political, and social exchange domains and become stabilized. In next chapter we will discuss some of the basic interactive mechanisms that influence the direction of institutional change and provide some cases.

A new model of subjective game becomes cognitively equilibrated for each agent when (1) the system of predictive and normative beliefs that has guided the learning of (dominant) agents becomes perceived to be consistent with emergent internal state of the domain, (2) the application of new inference rules for predicting consequences of action choices does not yield a big surprise for almost all the agents, and (3) the choice from a new activated subset of choices generates a satisfactory payoff. The transition process will come to rest when the continually revised subjective game models of agents become consistent with each other and simultaneously equilibrated in the sense defined above. The system of beliefs that become mutually consistent, and thus shared, will then become self-enforcing and established as a new institution. The transitional juncture of the process of institutional evolution comes to an end and another spell of relative stability over periods is initiated. Figure 9.2 summarizes

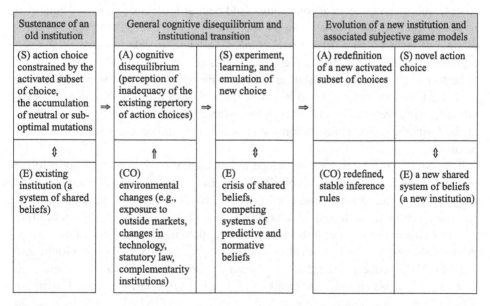

Figure 9.2
COASE box representation of the mechanism of institutional change

the mechanism of institutional evolution in terms of the modified COASE box. From the left it deals with the choice of endogenous variables in the "old" subjective game model, the initiation of search for their revision in response to environmental change and cognitive disequilibrium, the possible impacts of competing, symbolic systems of predictive and normative beliefs, and finally the emergence of a new institution and an associated new subjective game model.

An important question is how long a period of transition take. Since we are still working within the diachronic framework ordered by logical time rather than real historical time, we cannot answer this question simply in terms of long or short. Also it is unrealistic to presume that there is a clearcut separation between the transition period defined above and the period during which institutions become stabilized. An institution may emerge only gradually after the general cognitive disequilibrium arises and continue to evolve until it becomes ruptured by the next round of turbulence. Further complications arise if we consider changes in the overall institutional arrangement in the economy rather than a change in an institution in a rather limited domain. Institutions in some domains may change at a faster speed, while those in other domains may have much more inertia (chapter 10.1). Thus, depending on which domain is our focal point, the process of institutional transition may appear short or long, as well as radical or gradual.

However, one hypothetical conjecture could be that the transition period can often be further divided into two subperiods: the relatively short, turbulent period of institutional crisis in which a drastic environmental change (or internal crisis) triggers a cognitive disequilibrium among the critical mass of the agents, and various new, or hitherto mutant, choices are "started" as experiments on a greater scale, on the one hand; and the subsequent period in which these choices are placed under the "evolutionary pressure of selection." The latter subperiod may eventually become intermeshed with the period of institutional stability as some choices become evolutionarily dominant.

If we focus our attention on the subperiod of institutional crisis, we may perceive that the process of institutional evolution is punctuated by occasional juncture points. On the other hand, if we extend our horizon to cover the second subperiod of evolutionary selection, institutional change may appear gradual. If this conjecture applies to many instances of institutional change, then institutional evolution may be more analogous to the biological evolutionary process that biologists Gould and Eldredge (1977) conceptualized as *punctuated equilibria* instead of a steady, gradual, Darwinian process (possibly in terms of a vulgar interpretation of the Darwinian theory).[12] An evolutionary process characterized by punctuated equilibria is one in which long periods of stasis are broken by short (in geologic time) episodes of rapid speciation. Although biological metaphors and analogies are not perfect, nevertheless, these concepts are suggestive to some degree. Once a particular system of choices/selections (phenotypes or choice repertoire) is placed under evolutionary pressure, the fittest may eventually be selected. However, a change in the system itself is more likely to be initiated by a large external shock rather than something continual and gradual.

The reconstruction of subjective game models during and subsequent to the time of institutional crisis imposes constraints on future possibilities (path dependence). However, it is not certain whether the transition to the subsequently emergent institution was the only possible trajectory from the initial state of disequilibrium. How the subjective game models come to an general cognitive equilibrium may depend on the complex process of interactions between environments (e.g., technology) and (accidental) clustering of complementary choices across various domains, as well as intentional designs, emulation, learning, and experiments of individual agents.[13] Thus institutional evolution may be characterized by path-dependence and novelty, as well as by critical junctures and evolutionary selection (equilibrium).[14]

10 The Diachronic Linkages of Institutions

Human Society is viewed as a system of molecules, which, in space and in time, possess certain properties, are subject to certain ties, subsist in certain relationships. The reasonings (derivations), theories, beliefs that are current in the mass of such molecules are taken as manifestation of the [psychic] state of that mass and are studied as facts on a par with the other facts that society presents to view. We look for uniformities among them, and try to get back to the facts in which they in turn originate.... We are concerned to discover in just what relations, in time and in space, derivations and beliefs stand towards each other and towards all other facts.
—Vilfredo Pareto, *The Mind and Society*. (1916:1919)

The theme of this chapter is the diachronic linkage of institutions. In the previous chapter we discussed the mechanism of institutional evolution from the angle of agents' subjective games. We suggested that during the period of institutional transition (at the time of equilibrium "punctuation") various experiments in agents' choices take place in response to external shocks and internal crises, and that they compete as viable alternatives to worn-out strategies. But viable rules for action choices, and thus institutions as their summary representations, are not selected in an entirely random way, even though they are, to some extent, influenced by chance events. They are selected primarily through the dynamic interactions of the strategic choices of agents across different domains. There can be diachronic (temporal) linkages of institutions, parallel to their synchronic (cross-sectional) linkages. In this chapter we turn to the objective aspect of institutional evolution. We identify three diachronic mechanisms behind a strategic innovation that induces an institutional change, or alternatively deters an institutional change with the consequence of a system crisis or performance stagnation. As is easily seen, each is a dynamic counterpart of a class of synchronic linkage mechanisms discussed in chapter 8.

The first diachronic mechanism may be termed overlapping social embeddedness. In chapter 8 we saw that an institution can be created by the social exchange domain embedding other private transaction domains and call the class of institutions arising in such relationships as social embeddedness. Data characteristics of constituent domains (represented by the left-hand column of the COASE box), including policy and legal parameters, the accumulated level of institution-specific competence and assets, and so forth, can change over time. However, the speed of change will differ significantly depending on domain type. Characteristics of the social-exchange domain change more slowly, while new private transaction domains will emerge frequently with new types of organizational agents, replacing old transaction domains for technological, demographic, and other reasons. Thus the pattern of overlapping embeddedness will vary from time to time. Sometimes the isomorphic structure of social embeddedness will recur with some modifications, while under other conditions social embeddedness will facilitate or deter institutional evolution. The possibility of overlapping embeddedness suggests that in the long run institutional evolution has a highly path-dependent nature.

The second class of diachronic mechanisms we will consider is the reconfiguration and/or reshuffling of linkage of games other than social embeddedness. There can be two subclasses to this mechanism. One, as economic activities expand spatially over time, the hitherto geographically separated domains of trades may begin to be integrated, allowing agents from these domains to strategically interact. As a result extant institutions in the respective domains will disappear, persist despite the strategic interactions of agents, or become transformed as new organizations emerge to mediate or govern them. Second, an institutional innovation may emerge as a new type of domain bundling facilitated by an organization or an intermediary, possibly entailing the unbundling of an existing type. On the other hand, institutional stagnation may occur if worn-out bundling persists and blocks the emergence of new bundling. Indeed, according to Schumpeter (1934, 1947), innovation can be conceptualized as a new way of combining things based on the "creative destruction" of older combinations.

Third, there is an important mechanism of diachronic institutional complementarity. A newly activated choice, or a mutant choice, is not always viable as a stand-alone choice. However, if a complementary institution already exists in another domain, or a parametric change in that direction is initiated there, mutual reinforcement occurring between the two may create momentum for new institutional building. Through this mechanism, exogenous changes in the parameters of the game form in one domain, say systemic policy reform, can propagate and amplify their effects, which in the end leads to the emergence of a new overall institutional arrangement. However, in order not to be trapped in a policy-deterministic view of institutional change, this possibility needs to be subjected to a careful analysis. Also, as we will see in later examples, a consequence of diachronic complementarity may not necessarily be the same as that which a policy designer originally intended.

In this chapter we formalize each of the mechanisms noted above, derive analytical implications, if any, and provide illustrative examples, some of which anticipate more substantial analytical treatments in part III. These diachronic mechanisms operate simultaneously or in sequence, and their natures and effects are sometimes hard to distinguish from each other. However, they merit a separate treatment as a first step toward an analytical understanding of the complex process of institutional evolution.

10.1   Overlapping Social Embeddedness

At the start of chapter 8 we dealt with the synchronic linkage of domains across which agents can coordinate their strategies and examined its implications for the synchronic structure of institutional arrangements. We saw that institutions that are not possible when both domains are separated can become viable. Particularly, we focused on the mechanism of social embeddedness in which investments in social capital in the social exchange domain deter noncooperative action choices in the commons, trade, and organization domains. As already implied, the basic nature of social capital in the social exchange domain may remain relatively robust over time, which roughly corresponds to what is normally referred to as a cultural pattern (but we do not take it as exogenously given and fixed). In contrast, the game forms of economic transaction domains may change at relatively faster speed.[1] The competence, capacities, dispositions, and other traits of agents relevant to economic activities accumulate or depreciate through learning and demographic change. Their information structure relevant to economic transactions and the range of their economic activities are also refined and expanded by the development of communications and transportation technology. Production technology, legal rules, and the like, that parameterize the consequence functions on economic transaction domains also change. Thus the data characteristics of economic transaction domains may be transformed, depreciated, or even created at a relatively fast speed. Then, what will happen to any linkages of these economic transaction domains with the social-exchange domain? Existing social embeddedness may deter or facilitate the transition to a new institutional arrangement, or it may be evoked in a different context or be entirely replaced by a new type of embeddedness, depending on context. Let us discuss each type in turn with some illustrative examples.

Types of Overlapping Embeddedness and Their Path-Dependence Implications

Community Embeddedness That Deters a Community's Adaptation to Environmental Shock   Suppose that the closed-community exchange domain $\mathscr{D}_s$ embeds an economic transaction domain $\mathscr{D}_t$ and that a community-embedded norm regulates the action choices of the agents in the latter. Let the latter domain face a new environment, such as a new technology or new external market opportunities. Then community embeddedness may deter the transition to a new institutional arrangement that can exploit such opportunities. For example, in a rural African village community, the younger generation provides foodstuffs to the elder generation in exchange for the latter's advice on farming based on tacit knowledge about ecological, meteorological, and other environments. The social security mechanism is embedded in a social structure in which higher social esteem is paid to the elder generation. However, the latter is also conducive to blocking the introduction of more "efficient" farming methods based on the applications of mechanization that depreciate the productive value of the elder's knowledge (Baker 1997). Similar examples abound and need not be enumerated. The example related next captures a generic tendency despite its extreme nature. Closed-community embeddedness that does not allow room for the internal accumulation of mutant competence is fragile and self-destructive when it becomes exposed to large external systemic shock.

Example 10.1   The Self-destruction of the "Theater State" (Geertz)   Recall from chapter 8.1 the two examples of stratified social embeddedness whereby the Japanese fishermen's village and the Japanese factory shop floor exhibit an isomorphic social-embeddedness structure. The differentiated distribution of social capital, in terms of achievement of social status, esteem, or self-satisfaction, releases possible social and psychological tensions that may arise from the strenuous effort to cooperate in the economic transaction domain, as well as the inevitable unequal assignment of benefit or (effort) costs among members with different capabilities. If the norms of cooperation supported by status differentiation ubiquitously govern economic transaction domains across an economy, then, projecting and symbolizing the generic structure on a larger scale helps ease tensions and reinforces the effectiveness of social differentiation. In other words, if the generic social-exchange game is played symbolically in a way that is isomorphic to the equilibria in parallel micro, social-exchange games, the generic structure becomes subconsciously reproduced in the minds of agents, helping mold their internal ethical life. This result may contribute to the reinforcement of the equilibria in the economic transaction domains. Geertz (1980) relates a famous ethnological study of the political institution of nineteenth-century Bali, and his theoretical comments can be interpreted from this perspective.[2]

Bali's political social system in the nineteenth century was basically composed of two parts: *negara*, meaning "state," "town," or "palace," at one extreme, and *desa*, meaning "village" and "world," at the other. The former was a confederation of noble houses with the king at the apex, whose status was hierarchically differentiated on the basis of descent lineage but also intricately knit by patronage and treaties. However, *negara* was not directly involved in the allocation of public goods or enforcement of property rights. The allocation of water rights, essential for rice production, was handled by the irrigation community organized along the irrigation system, while the provision of other public goods, such as civil-dispute settlement and local public safety, were in the domain of the village community. The "body of citizenry" appointed leaders in the village and irrigation communities, but they were more like agents of the body than rulers. "And it was a sovereign body in all hamlet affairs, punishing any incorrigible resistance to its authority, no matter how apparently trivial, by ostracism. Small wonder that the Balinese still say that to leave the *krama* (meaning "member") is to lie down and die." (ibid.:49) Note that this norm is very close to the community-embeddedness norm discussed in chapter 2.2.[3]

Noble houses were not directly involved in the economic and social affairs of the *desa* except in leasing their scattered lands to individual farmers and collecting rents from them just like other landholders who lease. From these communities, however, the noble houses drew men and resources to stage very elaborate ceremonies (e.g., funerals) to demonstrate high status in the political order. The king was represented as the central focal point of the status differentiating order, which was seen as a reflection of a more encompassing cosmic order. Elaborate ceremonies and rituals were staged with priests presiding and members of the *desa* as spectators and participants. They were arranged as a systemic representation of symbols which Geertz interprets as being homeomorphic relationships to social institutional forms. In both, elements were subtly arranged in a sinking order with an exemplary focal point. Thus he characterized the polity of Bali as the "theater state," meaning that ceremonial ritualism was "not merely the drapery of political order, but its substance" (ibid.:32). The state symbolically represented the generic organizing principle of community relationships within the *negara* and *desa*, as well as the relationships between them, all characterized as stratified coalitions of agents rather than domination-subordination relationships. In this way the state represented a generic normative order and thus aided the integration of social orders governing micro commons domains across hamlets and irrigation communities, partly autonomous and partly knit with each other. Geertz expressed the essence of the institutionalized linkage as "[t]he state created the village as the village created the state." (ibid.:46)

Such mutual reinforcement must have brought a solid, static stability to the institutional life of the Balinese people, as long as they were insulated from external turbulence. However, when the state became exposed to an extraordinary external shock, the stability collapsed largely by its own logic. Facing the aggression of Dutch imperialists, the last King of Bali and the court staged a dramatic finale to the theater state. They paraded unarmed into "the reluctant fire of the by now throughly bewildered Dutch troops" (ibid.:11) and perished. There was no room left for them to modify their closed state, open only to the spiritual universe, and squarely face the new reality of the aggression of Western imperialists.

Community Embeddedness That Facilitates Adaptation to a New Outside Opportunity
In contrast to the preceding case, there may be a situation where social embeddedness

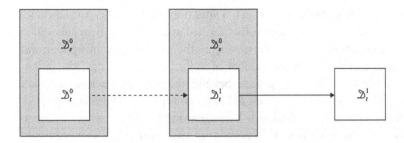

Figure 10.1
Transitional embeddedness. $\mathcal{D}_s$ represents the social exchange domain and $\mathcal{D}_t$ represents economic transaction domains. Superscripts refer to time sequence 0 and 1.

linking a community and a closed economic transaction domain may facilitate the
latter to adapt itself to a new environment, such as a new contact with external
markets, new technology, institutional change in outside complementarity domains,
and so forth. Sometimes it leads to the emergence of a new institution in an expanded
economic transaction domain and/or its emancipation from the embedding commu-
nity norm. To illustrate, let $\mathcal{D}_s^0$ denote the domain of social exchange and $\mathcal{D}_t^0$ and $\mathcal{D}_t^1$
be the domains of economic transactions with different game-form characteristics,
whose sets of agents are partially overlapped with that of $\mathcal{D}_s^0$. Suppose that $\mathcal{D}_s^0$
embeds $\mathcal{D}_t^0$ in the beginning. Suppose further that subsequently $\mathcal{D}_t^0$ incorporates new
action-choice opportunities for the agents and transforms itself into $\mathcal{D}_t^1$. Then $\mathcal{D}_s^0$
may embed $\mathcal{D}_t^1$ in a manner isomorphic to the old, but $\mathcal{D}_t^1$ may eventually become
emancipated from $\mathcal{D}_s^0$ by generating a new institution that autonomously governs
transactions in that domain (see figure 10.1). This institution will differ from the one
that would prevail if domain $\mathcal{D}_t^1$ stood alone from the beginning, or was linked to a
different social-exchange domain than $\mathcal{D}_s^0$. In the next example the embedding of $\mathcal{D}_t^1$
by $\mathcal{D}_s^0$ appears as a transitional process, but this transition is essential for the nature
of the (autonomous) institution that will eventually evolve in $\mathcal{D}_t^1$. Thus the historical
path of institutionalized linkages can leave its imprint on the nature of succeeding
institutions even after the linkage structure changes.

Example 10.2 Community-Induced Transition to Open Market Relationships   In
chapter 2.2 we saw that a community norm can regulate free-riding in intracommunity coordination in the use of commons. The institutional constraint that
deterred free-riding was the shared belief of the denial of access to social capital by a
defector. This mechanism presupposed the relative homogeneity of families in the
village community, which might entail the relative homogeneity of the kinds of pro-

duction activities they are engaged in. In such a situation opportunities for mutually beneficial, intracommunity trade may be rather limited and thus may be regulated by personal trust or a community norm. However, as the productivity of agricultural crops gradually rises through the improvement of indigenous technology, the potential for surplus products and working time beyond the subsistence level and tax obligations can gradually expand in the closed rural community. In order to exploit the gains from such potential, the relatively homogeneous rural community needs to open up trade with outside parties. However, does the existence of a community norm to regulate deviant behavior not hinder the development of individualistic mores conducive to market relationships? The following parable is constructed as a sequel to one in chapter 2.2, and meant to capture some aspects of the stylized historical reality of the Tokugawa village. It may indicate that the presence of a norm in the rural community may not necessarily be a deterrent to its transition to market development.

Suppose that there is a community of merchants who reside in a castle town remote from a certain village. These merchants have developed a traders' community norm to regulate commerce among themselves. They are interested in expanding the range of profitable commercial activities into rural communities, but naturally they cannot expect their reputation to be automatically extended into those communities. Suppose that a city merchant visits the village community and tries to deal with individual village families. He would soon discover that this it is not an easy undertaking. Village families are hesitant to deal with the outsider individually, out of fear of being cheated or abused by the stranger as well as being treated as deviants by fellow village members. From the merchant's viewpoint, the village members cannot be differentiated in the beginning, and he senses that it would be extremely time-consuming to build up personal trust with any of the suspicious farmers. However, being a shrewd merchant, he quickly detect the structure of the village and he pays a visit to the village headman and gives a gift, indicating his willingness to open exchange with the village. The village headman returns the courtesy, and an agreement is reached between them (recall the gift exchange model in chapter 3.1). The merchant agent promises to come regularly, bringing goods such as a new type of fertilizer (e.g., dried sardines) and cloth, which will be made available to village families. In return, he wants some yields of crops (e.g., surplus paddy rice, rape seeds, or cotton) or hand-processed products (e.g., yarn, indigo balls, papers). The village headman offers to act as a representative of the village families and collect all the goods they can offer. He assures the quality of the goods or crops are of a high standard.[4]

This agreement is effective in opening up trade between the outside merchant and village families. Since village families offer more or less same goods, they are mutually substitutes as trading partners to the merchant. Therefore, if the merchant were able to trade with them individually, he could prey on some families and then switch to other families to gain from further cheating. However, he is compelled to believe that if he behaves opportunistically, he will be excluded from any further trading with anybody in the village and lose the value of his initial gift. This belief is based on the presumed ability of a village community to punish any member of the community who defects from boycotting trade with a dishonest merchant. On the other hand, the merchant could threaten to terminate trade if any commodity is not exchanged honestly and to tell his story to fellow merchants back in the city. If the future value of trading is assessed by the village members as better than a no-exchange option, even if individual temptations to cheat vis-à-vis the merchant are high, peer pressure will persuade them not to jeopardize future trading opportunities. For example, if any family delivers defective products to the headman's garden, the defector could easily be spotted by other village members and accused in a manner reminiscent of the community norm. Thus the vesting of social capital with village families provides a foundation for them to initiate exchange with outside merchants and enforces honest trading on both sides as an viable starting point.[5]

Community cohesion among villages begins to erode as productivity differentials in cash crops or craft production widen and their products become gradually specialized. The option values from outside exchange increases for entrepreneurial village families, while social slack from the community social-exchange game declines for them. By then, the outside merchant also becomes more knowledgeable about the traits and capabilities of some families in the village. The outside merchant and families in the village now initiate individual contracting, particularly putting-out contracting for the supply of craft products such as textile yarn and fabrics. Further, as will be seen shortly in example 10.3, more successful entrepreneurial families will start organizing subcontracting relationships with less entrepreneurial families. In this way trade relationships first induced by the presence of a community norm start to destroy the relative homogeneity of the village community, thus encroaching upon the social basis of the community norm. The community norm, based on the symmetric ability of community members to punish a possible deviant in the social-exchange game, then must be superseded by personal trust and/or traders' community norms based on their ability to identify and punish an individual deviant in the exchange domain. But information networks necessary for sustaining such mechanisms would have already been prepared within the community prior to, and in the transition to, such relationships.[6]

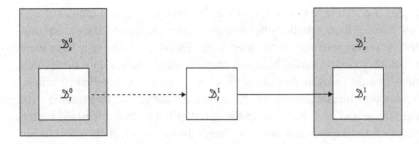

Figure 10.2
Transplanted embeddedness. $\mathscr{D}_s$ represents the social exchange domain and $\mathscr{D}_t$ represents economic transaction domains. Superscripts refer to time sequence 0 and 1.

Transfer of Social Capital across Different Transaction Domains Suppose that $\mathscr{D}_s^0$ embeds $\mathscr{D}_t^0$ in the beginning. Subsequently $\mathscr{D}_t^1$ emerges outside $\mathscr{D}_t^0$, but with the partial immigration of agents from $\mathscr{D}_t^0$ to $\mathscr{D}_t^1$. Suppose that an autonomous governance mechanism is devised and experimented with on $\mathscr{D}_t^1$, but it never gets firmly institutionalized or it malfunctions after its initial implementation. Meanwhile the agents in $\mathscr{D}_t^1$ form a new social exchange domain $\mathscr{D}_s^1$ through their continued participation in $\mathscr{D}_t^1$. In response to the shock or crisis, a mechanism to regulate agents' choices in $\mathscr{D}_t^1$ may eventually evolve in a manner somewhat isomorphic to the embedding of $\mathscr{D}_t^0$ by $\mathscr{D}_s^0$ (see figure 10.2). Since the set of agents of $\mathscr{D}_s^0$ and those of $\mathscr{D}_s^1$ are not identical, albeit partially overlapped, it may not be precisely the transfer of the old community norm. However, the partial overlapping of agents between the two may make the isomorphic embedding a natural focal point. The following two examples illustrate it.

Example 10.3   The Clustering of New Small Firms in the Italian Industrial Districts
The Italian industrial districts inhabited by small enterprises in the garment industry, and referred to in chapter 4.2, emerged after highly integrated textile companies failed to survive because of high wages and labor disputes in the 1960s, and finally the highly protective Workers' Statute adopted in 1970. Skilled workers released from large companies were encouraged to establish their own enterprises, often by purchasing equipment from large companies that were closing (Barca et al. 1999). The types of transactions and coordination that quickly developed among these firms, such as the reciprocity of subcontracting and sharing of productivity-enhancing knowledge, would not have been feasible without mutual trust as an essential governance mechanism. They became possible because the transaction domain was embedded in a preexisting social-exchange domain in which the new owners of those small firms had invested a significant amount of social capital as the members of the

civic community and/or labor organizations which confronted the old integrated companies.

The important role of "social capital" in Italy is also pointed out by Putnam (1993) in the context of democratic management of the civic society. However, his concept of "social capital" substantially differs from the one employed in this book (also see Coleman 1990). Putnam's social capital comes into being not through individual intentional action but is "inherited" with its origins hidden in the mist of the past. The existing stock cannot be individually owned, but can be "cultivated" through the collective practice of "gardening." There may be returns from it, but they come as by-products. On the other hand, we conceive of social capital as individually to be invested, albeit in a specific context of social exchange, in order to derive returns.

Example 10.4   The Quasi-replication of a Community Norm in an Industrial Context
A claim often made is that the group norm as observed on the shop floor or in the internal business organization of the Japanese firm is a replication of the community norm from the pre-market economy.[7] But the mechanism of this transplant remains unexplained. As we have seen, the ability of community norms to control severe free-riding in the production domain was due to the presence of an embedding social-exchange domain that can potentially generate a large amount of social surplus for community members. It would be difficult for such a condition to immediately prevail in the transition from a pre-modern economy to an industrial economy. It would be more likely for the coherence of the social-exchange domain to be eroded by the immigration of the rural population to the urban industrial center. It is also not self-evident how an alternative social-exchange domain with a functional equivalence can be reconstructed in the context of the modern factory.[8]

In Japan around the turn of the century, emergent industrial factories relied on contractors for the recruitment of groups of workers from the rural sector. This practice reflected the competition from the rural-based putting-out system (see example 10.6) and indicated that the residue of social capital held by peasants constrained their mobility to the urban industrial sector in mass. Skilled industrial workers remained scarce and were able to reap premium wages by responding to competition among employers in recruiting. There was no need to fear exclusion from the yet unformed social capital at the workplace. Around the time of the First World War advanced government-run armories and shipbuilding yards started to introduce seniority wages and bonuses as devices to retain workers in whom training costs were invested. But these experiments were mostly limited to those organizations in the beginning. It is symbolic to note that a major demand of militant workers at privately owned factories in the Keihin (Tokyo-Yokohama) industrial district in the late 1920s was to be recognized as "an equal member of the company" together with white-collar workers rather than to assert their class interests like contemporary European workers (Gordon 1985). Yet the management, which kept a social distance from the workers, often relied on the police to constrain labor discontent.

Labor immigration from the rural to the modern industrial sector started to rise, both through supply push and demand pull, in the 1930s when the rural economy suffered from a prolonged depression and the government started to intervene in every aspect of the economy to accelerate heavy industrialization. In the 1940s when the war economy deteriorated, the mobilization of the work force into the industrial sector, in quantity as well as incentivewise, became one of key policy agendas the government faced. Further the emergent problems on the shop floor, such as machine breakdowns, material and labor shortages, and widespread absenteeism of the workers, needed to be dealt with by ad hoc collective adaptation on site. However, the shortage of skilled workers was severe, and despite wage control over new hires their mobility remained high.[9]

As a way to cope with these problems, the wartime government tried to mobilize "social pressure" on the workers through the formation of an enterprise branch of the Industrial Patriotic Society. This organization encompassed blue-collar as well as white-collar workers, and tried to reduce long-standing status differentiations among them. In the midst of scarcity and the need to support the families of drafted workers, the enterprise branch of the Society evolved to partially function as a mutual aid organization. It also became increasingly difficult for the workers to voluntarily quit war production factories because of the intensified monitoring by the government to curb mobility. "Noncollaborators" in production were threatened with exclusion from mutual aid benefits (e.g., the distribution of rationed products like food and cloth) or punished morally and physically (labeled as a "nonpatriot," victimized in military drills, etc). This is somewhat reminiscent of the social ostracism in the Tokugawa village. However, the workers at this time were coerced into participating in the punishment of noncollaborators out of fear that they themselves might be punished as noncompliants by the military representative in the establishment. It is closer to what may be referred to as the "government-led, quasi-community control" of the production domain, made possible by linkage with a predatory state rather than an autonomous community.

An unexpected twist of history is, however, that despite the ordeal of military repression, the unprecedented mass mobilization of the population to the industrial sector and military organizations during the war ushered in a new organizational era. Partly embedded in quasi-community control and partly due to the traditional high esteem placed on craft skills, the practice of collective problem-solving started to spontaneously evolve on the shop floor. The exercise of a foreman's authority not based on knowledge and skills was perceived to be illegitimate, while workers who were gifted in craft-type skills enhanced their standing by taking problem-solving initiatives. A fundamental change in the social structure on the shop floor thus began to take place under the shock of the war economy. The postwar demise of the military state made the sustenance of government-led quasi-community control impossible. Instead, in the first two years of the postwar period, the all-inclusive unionization of workers at the grassroots factory level proceeded at a rapid rate, often under the political leadership of the same workers who had taken initiative in problem-solving on the shop floor during the war. In some factories they took over control from a management in disarray in order to protect their jobs.

In retrospect, the period of the 1930s and 1940s can be regarded as one of transition to a situation in which shop floor life became the focus of the workers' social exchange. When the turmoil of that period subsided, the management of the J-firm (an acronym for the stylized Japanese firms during the 1950 to 1990 period), promoted from the ranks of employees in hierarchies found it imperative to elicit cooperation from the quasi-community of workers on the shop floor. However, the emergence of the quasi-community social-exchange domain on the shop floor per se need not be efficiency enhancing from an overall organizational perspective. The workers may socialize on the job with less attention to productive efficiency. A group norm that deters management intervention on the shop floor could also emerge. To illustrate, when Toyota tried to introduce a multiple-machine manning method on the shop floor in the early 1950s, it met with the collective resistance of manually skilled workers, because they feared that more work effort would be required on their part. Efficiency-enhancing group norms on the shop floor (e.g., the reciprocity of help, peer monitoring of the work pace) will emerge and serve the overall organizational arrangement only when there is present an effective organizationwide governance mechanism (discussed in chapter 11 and 12). Otherwise, the shop floor group will be trapped in a low-effort collusive equilibrium, often entailing serious organizational inefficiency.

The Displacement and Reconstruction of Social Capital

At the start of this section, we mentioned the possibility of social capital serving as an intermediary for a traditional economic transaction domain to adapt to the newly emergent environmental condition. However, this may not be the only possibility. Example 10.2 suggested that the closed nature of a community is crucial condition for the existing social capital to be mobilized for an intermediary role. If a relevant change in the environment of the economic transaction domain involves opportunities for the community members to separate from the community (e.g., the enhanced outside [labor] market opportunity), social capital will disband. In order for a new institutional arrangement to evolve, a new kind of social capital must be constructed. So we have the possibility that an institutional trajectory can take a different direction from the one observed in example 10.2.

Example 10.5   Institutional Bifurcation between English and Japanese Farming in the Seventeenth and Eighteenth Centuries (Allen)   We saw in chapter 2.2 and in example 10.2 that the substantive constituent members of the Tokugawa village were the so-called *hon-hyakusyo* (literally meaning the "real farmers") who were homogeneous, quasi-proprietorial peasants. They were behind the agricultural productivity increases throughout the Tokugawa period, collectively governing the commons through the mutual accumulation of social capital, on one hand, and exercising individual initiative in the improvement of farming methods and other proto-industrial activities, on the other. In this regard they are somewhat analogous to the independent yeomen in pre-enclosure England who cultivated in the common fields. The common fields in the pre-enclosure England were not open access resources in a fishery sense as is often misunderstood, but they were a group of fragmented, scattered plots whose use (in terms of crop rotation, pasturing, etc.) was commonly regulated: an arrangement that recalls the scattered paddy fields in the Tokugawa village integrated by the common use of an irrigation system despite wide difference between them in conditions of farming and kind of crops (see chapter 2.2). The yeomen likewise achieved a remarkable productivity increase.

One difference between the *hon-hyakusho* and the yeomen that has potentially significant implications for the subsequent bifurcated institutional development may be noted, however. The former had rather secure quasi-proprietorial rights over their cultivating lands, administratively granted by the *Baku-Han* governments for tax collection purposes. Therefore their social capital was primarily used for controlling mutual behavior vis-à-vis local commons and outside market opportunities. In contrast, the yeomen were in formal contractual relationships with their lords, who lived in manorial houses and held their own demesne on the manor.[10] The common field village fostered solidarity among the tenants, but their social capital was often mobilized for acting in concert to protect their interests vis-à-vis the lord.

The function of the enclosure for the landlord was to consolidate the numerous rights of use of common fields and commons through re-contracting and negotiation, and then let them on short-term leases to large-scale farmers hiring landless laborers.[11] The traditional explanation for the second wave of enclosures in the eighteenth century has been that the open and common field arrangements were inefficient because of the usual "tragedy of the commons" problem (overgrazing, undersupply of effort for sustaining collective goods such as drainage, etc.), which also led to the failure to exploit economies of scale and the collective choice problem in which the least entrepreneurial farmer could block innovation in the use of open fields and crops. But recent studies—micro, macro, and comparative—show that many of the productivity gains, in terms of yields per acre or output per worker, were already achieved by the seventeenth century when the yeomen still occupied the land, while the difference between open and enclosed yields in the eighteenth century was often small, if not nonexistent (Allen 1992, 1999, 2001). Recent scholarly works also show that there is not much evidence for the tragedy of the commons problem, either. Many villages were found to be aware of the commons problem and set limits on grazing.[12]

If productivity gains were substantially achieved and the commons governance problem was reasonably well handled by the community of landholding peasants both in England and in Japan, why then did the enclosure occur in England but not in Japan (or elsewhere, including advanced continental European economies)? As the conventional interpretation indicates, advanced industrialization, urbanization, and consequential labor market development led to the decline of the yeomen community in England. However, the more subtle question is: In what way did these environmental changes make possible a decisive break in the institutional structure of farming? One explanation that has been advanced from the institutional perspective is that by R. Allen (2001). Allen attributes the relatively stronger legal power of the landlords in England, the rapid development of urban labor market, to the erosion of the social cohesion supporting the community of yeomen.

When land yields steadily increased in the seventeenth century, the yeomen on long contractual leases were in a good position to capture entrepreneurial rents because of their continual innovative efforts. As the productivity gains (total factor productivity) started to taper off, so did the entrepreneurial rents. Nevertheless, an increasing demand for farm products, because of rapid urbanization, kept the prices of agricultural products rising, and thus the portion of Ricardian rents accruable to landholding per se was also increased. Recapturing the Ricardian rents from the yeoman doubtlessly became a big interest to landlords. To do so, however, the landlords did not bargain for short-term leases with every individual yeoman but rather negotiated selective bids with farmers who could compete in the savings of hired labor and material inputs (e.g., animal). So economies-of-scale in the use of labor might be viewed as one factor. However, there is some evidence that output per worker in England had ceased to increase in the mid-eighteenth century after it caught up with, and slightly exceeded, the advanced levels of the Netherlands and Belgium where family farming prevailed (Allen 1998). Therefore there must have been also a nontechnological, historical factor unique to England.

So now we have the possibility that the social cohesion of the yeomen community made the recapturing of Ricardian rents through individual recontracting relatively costly for the landlords. The consolidation of open fields was first attempted through private contracting, such as refusing contract renewal following the death of yeomen or the expiration of a beneficial contract term. However, the enclosure of common fields originally required the unanimous agreement of the many small landholders in each common field that was to be enclosed. In such a situation any landholder had an incentive to hold out for extracting side payments. Or, relatively homogeneous landholders could have had unanimous interests in keeping their social capital and shares in Ricardian rents intact. Therefore, equipped with traditional manorial power as well as political influence over local parliaments, the landlords began to rely on parliamentary resolutions as a device to cope with this coordination problem. As a parliamentary enclosure still required a majority of the votes of the farmers involved, however, the transition to large-scale farming was not smooth where the cohesion of the community of small landholders was strong.[13]

When the enclosure was successful, the landlords tended to rent their lands to farmers on short-term leases. Leases were renewed repeatedly in most cases. When rent was to be raised, this was done by a bureaucratic procedure such as having the estate reevaluated by a hired surveyor. Allen argues that in this way tenants had incentives to improve on productivity and identify their fortunes with the estate rather than with their fellow villagers. However, landlords gained as tenants felt a long-term attachment to the estate. As Allen points out, the terms of tenancy, and the associated norms of behavior in expectation of proper treatment, were forms of "social capital."

Thus the social norms prevailing among the yeomens' community was gradually replaced with a new form of social exchange between the landlords and the farmers. This transition was possible without self-destructive political and social instability, perhaps because of the ability of the developing urban labor market and political institutions to absorb the population migrating from the rural sector, facilitate the reconstruction of social capital among the urban working class, and accommodate their political aspirations into the emergent liberal democratic state in the polity (chapter 6.2). This interpretation is in striking reversal to the long-held influential view of Marx who argued that it is the enclosure that swept the way toward capitalist development by releasing the reserved army of the proletariat for the industrial capitalists.

10.2   The Reconfiguration of Bundling

In this section we consider the mechanisms of institutional change caused by the new linkage of domains other than social-exchange types. We first consider cases where two domains that developed different or similar institutions in isolation come to be in contact, and examine the consequences for postintegration institutional arrangements. Second, we consider the possibility whereby a new type of bundling replaces an old type of bundling in business organization domains, which may be identified as a Schumpeterian institutional innovation.

Institutional Consequences of Economic Integration

An integration of two domains may occur, for example, as a result of the geographical expansion of trade and organizational activities. The pre-integration game-form characteristics (sets of agents, their choice sets, and consequence functions) could have substantially differed across domains because of differences in historical path, regulations, types and levels of agents' accumulated competence, the nature of the transactions involved, and so on. For simplicity we consider two domains $\mathscr{D}_1$ and $\mathscr{D}_2$ that have respectively generated governing institutions Σ^* and Σ^{**} of the same or different types in isolation. One possible institutional consequence of their integration is the emergence of a new institution Λ^* generated by, and supporting, a new type of strategic choice across the linked domain $\mathscr{D}_1 \cup \mathscr{D}_2$. Given the multiplicity of possible institutions, the nature of the new institution Λ^* may not be solely determined by the technological structure of the linked domains. The selection of the new institution Λ^* from the many that are logically possible may be conditioned by the preexistence of either or both of the old institutions Σ^* and Σ^{**}. The historical examples 10.6 and 10.7 that follow illustrate the case.

Another possibility is the persistence of an old institution, Σ^*, Σ^{**}, or both, after the integration of domains with different game-form characteristics. Their initial evolutions may have been partially conditioned by the pre-integration game-form characteristics of their respective domains (e.g., regulations). After the integration the game-form characteristics of linked domains may be substantially altered (e.g., some regulations may not be tenable, agents possessing different types of competence may become mobile across the domains). Yet there may be cases where original institutions persist, even though both or either of them would not have been viable if the postintegration game-form characteristics of the linked domains had existed from the beginning. Thus the historical path of institutionalized linkage can leave its imprint on the nature of succeeding institutions even after the exogenous rules of the game have changed. This is an instance of path dependence par excellence. We hint at such a possibility below in example 10.8 and subject it to analytical justification later in chapter 12. An additional example can be found in proposition 5.2 of chapter 5: the emergence of organizational diversity after the integration of organizational fields in which different conventions in organizational architecture prevailed.

Example 10.6 A New Institution Intermediating the Urban-Rural Nexus—The Putting-out Contract System and the Rural Industry in Japan (Tanimoto) As we suggested in example 10.2, the rural communities of Tokugawa Japan accumulated the capacity to supply nonfarming, commercial products by the mideighteenth century. However, outside the rural communities commercial networks developed with specialized merchants guilds in Edo (Tokyo) and Osaka as nuclei. When the linkage of these two types of domains, rural communities and national trade domains, was limited to the trading of more or less standard products, such as lighting oil, rice, processed foods, and cotton yarn, the intermediation was primarily performed by specialized wholesalers in local cities and their brokers in rural communities. Now, around the late nineteenth century the interlinkage of the two evolved into a new intermediating institution—putting-out contracting in fabric manufacturing. Despite the parallel development of the factory system it remained as a major constituent of the Japanese textile industry until as late as the mid-1920s.[14] The large factory system was more concentrated in the spinning of cotton yarn and production of standard fabrics, while smaller-scale factories and producers under putting-out contracts were more specialized in differentiated fabric manufacturing. The organizers of the putting out system were indigenous merchants (*zaichi shonin*) residing within the neighborhoods of villages where actual production took place. Many of these merchants were originally entrepreneurial farmers and accumulated commercial experience first as brokers. The contractors were mostly peasant families who kept farming as their major production activity. The integration of farming and domestic manufacturing within individual peasant families was a major feature of the Japanese system, distinct from the proto-industrialization observed in eighteenth-century Flanders where grain-producing farming and rural-based industry became bifurcated into separately managed activities (Mendels 1972).

It is claimed that in the West the putting-out system was replaced by the factory system because of the transaction costs involved in the collection of outputs of geographically scattered contractors, particularly embezzlement of materials by them. However, a recent study by Tanimoto suggests that in Japan the indigenous merchants played a unique coordinating role between product market demands and the peasants' rational choices. On one hand, they were connected to the newly emergent wholesalers in cities that had grown outside the old guild system of the Tokugawa order, taking advantage of expanding domestic markets for textile products. From this network they obtained information regarding seasonal demands and user-specific requirements for product differentiation because of wide climatic differences across regions and over seasons. On the supply side, they faced peasant families who allocated efforts among various farming and nonfarming activities as an integrative decision-making unit. Depending on seasonal and emergent needs arising from farming, the time and effort allocatable to contracting work could not be spread evenly throughout the year or matched easily with seasonal demands for their products. The putting-out contacts needed to be packaged in such a way that requirements from both ends were coordinated. Geographical proximity to the producers also made it possible for the indigenous merchants to closely monitor the progress of the work process and enforce contracts. This coordinating role of the indigenous merchant could create unique economic rents that might not have been immediately possible in the modern factory system.[15]

The decline of the putting-out system in the 1920s is usually attributed to a technological reason: the introduction of efficient machinery, such as the power loom, by the modern factory system. However, theoretical analysis indicates that the increase in the uncertainty of farming income (measured by the variance of farming income per amount of time) could also be responsible for the comparative advantage of the factory-wage employment system over the putting-out system.[16] Indeed, the late 1920s was the time when the economic conditions surrounding the peasantry became highly uncertain because of the government policy to expand food imports from colonial economies. Even after the decline of putting-out contracting, many small-scale factories thrust in rural areas employed surplus farm labor, which constituted one important feature of the Japanese industrial economy until the beginning of the era of high growth in the 1960s. This historical experience suggests that the putting-out system was not a route merely facilitating the transition from the pre-modern peasant economy to the modern factory system. It organized peasants' surplus time without releasing them entirely from farming and transforming them into industrial workers who were mobile in competitive labor markets. By so doing, the putting-out system constituted an alternative that, although destined to lose its comparative advantage to the factory system, shaped the ways in which the industrial system was to evolve in Japan.[17]

Example 10.7 A Transitory Institution Based on Pre-integration Institutions— The Community Responsibility System (Greif) Suppose that several communities of traders develop intracommunity contract enforcement mechanisms within their respective domains that can identify and punish dishonest members. Say the traders from these communities become mutually active beyond their own domains, setting up trading facilities within the territories of other communities. In the absence of a formal intercommunity contract enforcement mechanism, how could trade and credit between traders from different communities be expanded? Greif (2001) submits that during the late medieval commercial revolution of Europe (the eleventh to thirteenth centuries) the so-called "community responsibility system" evolved in response to such a challenge, and he analyzed its implications. This was an institutional device to regulate dishonest actions in the intercommunity trade domain, relying on the existing intracommunity enforcement mechanisms. These enforcement mechanisms could be formal or informal, but let us refer to them generically as the "courts."

Suppose that a trader from one community, say $\mathscr{A}$, cheated his trading partner in the latter's territorial domain, say $\mathscr{B}$. Then the cheated merchant appeals to the court in community B. If the court verifies the cheating, it seizes the properties of any or all members of community $\mathscr{A}$ present in the territorial domain of community B and holds them as pledges. The court in community $\mathscr{B}$ then demands compensation from the court in community $\mathscr{A}$. Upon the presentation of an evidence by the former, the latter compensates for the damage done, by recovering it from the cheater if identifiable or by any other means available. The court in community $\mathscr{A}$ then awards the compensation to the plaintiff. Thus the community is held responsible for dishonest trading by any of its own members in otherwise impersonal trade across the communities. Greif showed that the prescribed procedure can be sustained as an equilibrium outcome, if each community's court maximizes the sum of payoffs of its living community members derived from intercommunity trade. Conversely, it is in the interests of the community to establish such a court (or any mechanism that replicates the prescribed procedure) if the prescribed procedure is expected.

However, the community responsibility system harbors its own seeds of destruction. If traders can credibly expect compensation for cheating by impersonal foreign traders, they may shirk proper ex ante monitoring (due diligence) of trustworthiness of contracts that they are about to enter. As trade expands under the community responsibility system and traders' communities grow in size, it may also become increasingly difficult for communities to identify actual contract violators and punish them. Thus the running costs of the system increase because of the development of trade that it generates. Greif argues that such internal development was indeed the driving force behind the demise of the community responsibility system in the late thirteenth century, leading to the establishment of alternative contract enforcement institutions, particularly those based on a legal system administered by nation states. Thus the community responsibility system served as a transitional governance mechanism in the process of bundling separate domains of traders' communities. Through its semi-impersonal nature of the mechanism, operative on information regarding trade partners only up to a community affiliation, this mechanism became an important route to the evolution of a comprehensive legal mechanism regulating impersonal trade in increasingly integrative, but internally heterogeneous trade domains.

Example 10.8 Path-Dependent Persistence of an Old Institution—Relational Financing in Global Financial Markets Relational financing is a type of financing in which there is a credible commitment on the side of the financier to make additional financing available to the present borrower in the event of uncontractible contingencies, such as the financial distress of the borrower (we will discuss this concept more fully in chapter 12). Such a commitment becomes credible only if it is believed to be profitable for the financier to follow such a strategy. For example, the borrower may be willing to pay a premium in exchange for maintaining a credit line. However, the borrower will not enter into such relationship with a financier (e.g., a bank), if the cost of arm's-length financing is cheap enough in comparison to the insurance benefit provided by relational financing. There is thus a trade-off. Therefore, in a financial transaction domain where the capability of borrowers to raise funds through bond markets is restrained by regulation, relational financing may relatively more easily emerge. Suppose that it has been the case, but eventually the domain has become linked with global competitive capital markets so that these policies become untenable. Is the established institution of relational financing no longer viable? The answer is not straightforward. In chapter 12 we will see that under some conditions relational financing may remain viable, although the financier needs to cultivate a new type of information-processing competence in the new environment.

The Schumpeterian Process of Unbundling and Re-bundling

Let us now shift our attention to another, albeit related, class of linked game: bundling of domains by organizations or third-party intermediaries. As suggested in chapter 8.2, bundling will arise where rents are accruable to the bundling agent, either through new information or the externalities he or she creates. However, in the dynamic context a new type of bundling is possible when an old established type disintegrates from an internal crisis, or more likely, when a new type encroaches or destroys the rents accruable to the old type. Thus the institutionalization of a new bundling arrangement is not necessarily smooth. It requires a vigorous thrust of Schumpeterian entrepreneurship in a "creative destruction of old combinations." (1934, 1947)

Example 10.9 Evolutionary Ex post Bundling of Development Activities (A&D)
The clustering of small entrepreneurial startup firms in Silicon Valley and other high-technology centers has a common characteristic from the perspective of the current topic. It has emerged as a result of the unbundling of business activities integrated within the organizational architecture of the traditional integrated firm.[18] In the traditional integrated firm, business activities such as design, manufacturing, and marketing were bundled under the same corporate headquarters roof.[19] Design activities themselves were modularized and organized in a hierarchical manner, starting from the central conceptual design of an integrated product system at the highest level, to an analytical design, to detailed designs of modular parts, to a manufacturing process design, to manufacturing of a pilot product, and finally to its improvement. In contrast, Silicon Valley startup firms have tended to be specialized in modular product design, although they sometimes include the production of pilot products targeted for particular niche markets. Other activities, such as large-scale manufacturing and marketing, are considered to be outside their immediate scope of business.

As already pointed out (chapter 4.2), these entrepreneurial startup firms compete with each other in specific niche markets for the innovative design of modular products. The winner in each market is likely to be acquired by leading firms in markets of broader range (e.g., Cisco Systems, Lucent Technologies, Intel, and Microsoft) that aim at forming an innovative product-system. Thus, from the viewpoint of product-system innovation, the system integration of component technologies is evolutionarily realized by the ex post bundling of selected modular products developed by entrepreneurial firms, in contrast to the ex ante bundling of comprehensive design activities within the framework of centralized planning of a single integrated firm (e.g., the development of IBM 360). Clearly, the former type of bundling, referred to as A&D (acquisition and development), in contrast to the traditional intraorganizational R&D (research and development), is more flexible in keeping alternative options open until the uncertainty involved in viable system-design is reduced. The cost of running this Schumpeterian process is the duplication of development efforts by multiple competing entrepreneurial firms before selection. We will analyze later the technological and institutional conditions under which the benefits from this Schumpeterian process can more than compensate for the social costs, as well as the unique intermediating role of the venture capital in that process (chapter 14).

Example 10.10 The Dilemma of the J-firm in the Digital Age A crucial factor that has made the Silicon Valley clustering viable is the development of the information technology and an accumulation of human competence, which made the encapsulation of information-processing for the design of modular products feasible at the level of individual entrepreneurial firms (chapter 4.2). In contrast, the same technological development has undermined the relative competitiveness of the organization architecture that the J-firms—stylized Japanese firms—developed in the 1970s and 1980s. The J-firm has been operating on the principle of intense contextual information sharing and interpretative assimilation among the internal task units: the organizational architectural type conceptualized as horizontal hierarchy in chapter 4.2. The task units are tightly bundled through centralized personnel administration that recruits, rotates, assigns, and promotes the employees across various task units from an overall organizational perspective. This practice has proved not only to facilitate contextual information sharing but also to provide an incentive framework for team work based on the internal rank-differentiation of the lifetime employees (chapter 8.1, example 8.2). Thus the horizontal hierarchy and the centralized personnel administration have been institutionally complements for making the J-firm a coherent organizational entity.[20]

In the development of information technology, however, the comparative advantage of contextual information sharing vis-à-vis network-induced information sharing has been greatly eroded, if not entirely (chapter 4.1). Organizational coordination based on the interpretative assimilation of (tacit) knowledge among organizational participants loses its competitive efficiency as the amount of information circulated and shared through networks across organizations becomes large (proposition 4.4). It also lacks flexibility in product-system design in comparison to the emergent Schumpeterian process mentioned in the previous example.

Because of the context-oriented nature of human assets that the Japanese workers and managers have invested in, as well as the limited acceptance of their native language, the comparative advantage of the J-firm may not be restored easily by merely emulating the grand-scale network-integrated functional hierarchies that Anglo-American firms have been developing globally. Further, the above-mentioned institutional complementarity implies that the organizational architecture of the J-firm may not be easily altered without a simultaneous change in the traditional personnel administration. The problems facing the J-firm need to be resolved in a path-dependent manner. In particular, the J-firm is faced with the challenge of redesigning its organizational architecture in such a way that task units are more loosely bundled, while encapsulating contextual information sharing and interpretive assimilation, whenever useful, within each of them.[21] As we saw in chapter 4.1, contextual information sharing does not entirely lose its relative informational efficiency if it is limited to a sphere of the organizational domain within which activities are mutually complementary and their work environments are statistically correlated. In chapter 14.1 we will compare the merits of Silicon Valley clustering with the J-firm type of organizational architecture in terms of information efficiency in new product-system design.

10.3 Diachronic Institutional Complementarity

In this section we consider dynamic interactions among complementary domains. We are interested in the effect of a parametric change on the game forms of complementary domains, such as policy reform, enactment of a new statutory law, organizational design, accumulation of competence of certain types of human assets, or technological innovation, that is, any parametric change that may mediate and induce (alternatively deter) the emergence of a new institution or affect the overall institutional arrangements.

The Momentum Theorem

As in the simplest case of chapter 8.3, let us assume that there are two domains $\mathscr{D}$ and $\mathscr{G}$ with the sets of agents having identical payoff prediction rules (utility functions), u and v, and only two possible choices over rules *cum* institutions, denoted by $(\Sigma^*; \Sigma^{**})$ and $(\Lambda^*; \Lambda^{**})$, respectively.[22] We likewise assume that the supermodular condition (chapter 8)—that is, Σ^* and Λ^*, as well as Σ^{**} and Λ^{**}—are institutionally complementary. In addition we have parameters θ and η characterizing the (subjective) game forms of the agents in $\mathscr{D}$ and $\mathscr{G}$ that affect their payoff predictions (via consequence function). These parameters could represent agents' perceptions of the technological environment, types and levels of the human assets they possess, statutory laws, regulations, government policy orientation that affect the consequence of the games, and so forth. These parameters are treated here as *institution-relevant* in the following sense. They are ordered along the real line $\mathfrak{R}$, or take binary values, say 1 or 0 (this ordering assignment may be just used to distinguish two types, e.g., individuated and context-oriented mental programs, and does not necessarily have any inherent ranking implication). Each payoff prediction rule has increasing differences in its own variable and its relevant parameter in that

$u(\Sigma^* : \Lambda, \theta) - u(\Sigma^{**} : \Lambda, \theta)$ *is increasing in θ for any fixed value of Λ, and*
$v(\Lambda^* : \Sigma, \eta) - v(\Lambda^{**} : \Sigma, \eta)$ *is increasing in η for any fixed value of Σ.*

These specifications imply that θ and η are ordered in such a way that their higher values make their relative fit with Σ^* enhanced vis-à-vis Σ^{**} and with Λ^* vis-à-vis Λ^{**}, respectively. Therefore we may refer to an increase (decrease) in the value of θ or η as a parametric change complementary to Σ^* or Λ^* (respectively, Σ^{**} or Λ^{**}). Finally, we assume that the values of Σ and Λ are chosen by the agents in $\mathscr{D}$ and $\mathscr{G}$ in each period $t = 1, 2, \ldots$, so as to maximize the respective payoffs, u and v, with the variable set in the other domain regarded as given.

Denoting the values of the variables and parameters at time t by postscript (t), we specify ways in which parameter values can shift from the initial point of time on according to the dynamic system:

$$\theta(t+1) = F(\theta(t), \eta(t), \Sigma(t), \Lambda(t)),$$

$$\eta(t+1) = G(\theta(t), \eta(t), \Sigma(t), \Lambda(t)),$$

where F and G are nondecreasing functions in all the parameters and variables. This implies that there is no reversal in parametric impacts on endogenous variables (no reversal of policy, continual accumulation of institution-relevant competence, etc.). Also, by the nondecreasing assumption with respect to endogenous variables, the parameter values will not receive a negative feedback, but possibly a positive one, from endogenous variables (e.g., no policy adversarial to the prevailing institution is adopted, the competence level of human assets (mental programs) that fits the existing institution accumulates through learning by doing).

With this setup, let us examine the possible effects of institutional complementarity on the mechanism of institutional evolution. First, let us consider the case in which at time $t = 0$ institution Λ^* exists in $\mathscr{G}$, while $u(\Sigma^* : \Lambda^*, \theta(0)) < u(\Sigma^{**} : \Lambda^*, \theta(0))$ in domain $\mathscr{D}$. That is, despite the presence of Λ^* in $\mathscr{G}$, a complementary institution Σ^* has not been established in $\mathscr{D}$ because the value of institutionally relevant parameter θ is low (e.g., the accumulated level of competence supportive of Σ^* is not sufficient, or the regulatory environment is not favorable). However, let us suppose that $\theta(1) > \theta(0)$ and $\eta(1) > \eta(0)$; that is, there are initial improvements in institution-relevant parameters complementary to Σ^* and Λ^*. Then, by successive applications of the increasing property of G and F, we derive that $\theta(t+1) \geq \theta(t)$ and $\eta(t+1) \geq \eta(t)$ for all $t > 1$. Therefore the relative disadvantage of Σ^* vis-à-vis Σ^{**} may be (successively) narrowed by the increasing differences of the payoff function u in θ. If the stronger condition of institutional complementarity holds so that not only the difference $u(\Sigma^* : \Lambda^*, \theta(t)) - u(\Sigma^{**} : \Lambda^*, \theta(t))$ is nondecreasing over time but also it becomes strictly positive for sufficiently large $\theta(t)$, the institution Σ^* can eventually emerge in $\mathscr{D}$, even if it could not do so if institution Λ^* did not exist at the outset in $\mathscr{G}$. Thus we claim the following variant of the momentum theorem from Milgrom, Qian, and Roberts (1991).

PROPOSITION 10.1 (Milgrom, Qian, and Roberts) Even if the initial level of institution-relevant parameters is too low to make institution Σ^* viable in an isolated domain, the presence of complementary institution Λ^* can amplify the impact of an initial improvement in the value of the institution-relevant parameter complementary to Σ^*. If cumulative complementary effects are strong enough, the institutionalization of Σ^* may eventually be induced.

Next we take the case where institutions Σ^{**} and Λ^{**} have prevailed in the past up to time $t = S$. At time $t = S$, an external technological shock, or policy change, occurs that enhances the parameter values complementary to Σ^* and Λ^*. By the assumption of increasing F and G, we then have $\theta(t+1) \geq \theta(t)$ and $\eta(t+1) \geq \eta(t)$ for all $t > S + 1$. Suppose that for some sufficiently large $\eta(t)$ that can be achieved with the dynamic process, we have the stronger version of increasing differences, $v(\Lambda^* : \Sigma^{**}, \eta(t)) - v(\Lambda^{**} : \Sigma^{**}, \eta(t)) > 0$. Then, there will be a time $T > S + 1$ when switching from Λ^{**} to Λ^* occurs. By applying the same logic that we have used in proving proposition 10.1, Σ may also eventually shift from Σ^{**} to Σ^*. In paraphrasing the result we arrive at the following variant of the momentum theorem:

PROPOSITION 10.2   Suppose that institutions Σ^{**} and Λ^{**} have prevailed up to a certain point in time, when a policy change and/or initial accumulation of competence complementary to alternative institutions Σ^* and Λ^* occurs in each domain. While an institutional change may not immediately occur in either domain, if the change/accumulation is sustained, its cumulative, complementary impacts may lead to the emergence of a new overall arrangement of mutually complementary institutions (Σ^*, Λ^*).

The preceding propositions indicate that the presence of a complementary institution and/or complementary changes in the values of institution-relevant parameters can trigger the emergence of a new institution in a domain or a change in overall institutional arrangements across domains. However, the impact is not automatic; it hinges on the strength of complementarity relationships among institution-relevant parameters and corresponding endogenous choice variables, and among endogenous choice variables across domains. The subtlety of the process is that the emergence of an institution, or a change in overall institutional arrangements, in response to changes in institution-relevant parametric values, may only be latent at the outset but eventually be realized by their mutually reinforcing, cumulative impacts.

The Role of Policy in Institutional Change

The Possibility of an Unintended Institutional Outcome as a Consequence of Policy Change and Organizational Design of the Government   By the momentum theorem, we can derive a few interesting implications about the role of government policy and organizational design in institutional change. First, suppose that an overt policy objective is to move agents' choices in a certain direction. However, through cumulative, mutually reinforcing interactions of agents' strategic choices across complementary domains, an unintended overall institutional change can evolve. One example, which we will consider more fully in chapter 13, is the Japanese main bank system and the associated institutional arrangements that evolved in the 1950s. Its emergence may appear to have been initially affected by policies and organizational designs set by the military government before and during World War II (credit control through banks, restraint of stockholders' control in corporate governance domains, etc.). The intention of the government was to strengthen control over the economy conducive to the enhancement of war-related production. This purpose was not to be fulfilled. The main bank system nevertheless evolved because the vectors of policy and organizational design were continued in an institution-relevant manner during the postwar democratic reforms and subsequent periods (e.g., the removal of capitalist control in corporate governance through *zaibatsu* resolution). More fundamentally, the main bank system emerged and was sustained because there were strong complementarities between emergent organizational practices (horizontal hierarchies as conceptualized in chapter 4.2), on the one hand, and relational financing and the associated corporate governance structure, on the other. However, the outcome was far from what the military government initially intended.

Policy Failure to Produce an Intended Outcome due to the Absence of Relevant Human Assets Even though a policy change may be thought to be conducive to the development of an alternative institution in a particular domain, if complementary human assets are absent, the intended outcome may not result. This is the case with the failure of Russia to develop a market-oriented corporate governance structure, as we illustrate in example 10.11 below.

Conflicting Movements of Institution-Relevant Parameters and the Role of the Government The momentum theorem dealt with cases where institution-relevant parameters moved together in a complementary. However, at the macro level, the direction of movement of institution-relevant parameters may not necessarily be complementary. Say that a Schumpeterian innovative reconfiguration of economic activities spontaneously emerges. Associated competence starts to accumulate in a certain private economic-transaction domain, but the emergent pattern of bundling is not complementary with the existing patterns of bundling in other private economic-transaction domains. This could happen for example, if an emergent organizational architecture needs financing different from the established type or if it undermines the established community norms in an rural sector. Suppose that the external environment of the economy is changing in such a way that rents accruable to the existing patterns of bundling (old financial institutions, the rural community, etc.) could diminish in the development of the new pattern of bundling. So, interest groups associated with the old patterns of bundling become engaged in rent-seeking behavior in the polity. If the existing state is not liberal in the sense defined in chapter 6, the government will respond to the established interest group pressures by mobilizing its regulatory power or enacting statute law in their favor. Such policy will have an adverse effect on the efficient deployment and further accumulation of competence relevant to the new pattern of bundling.

Now, if the government does not collude with the interest groups but becomes engaged in a policy of gradually phasing out old patterns, a slow transition may take place. Rural-based developmentalism provides a good example (see chapter 6.2). Although policy alone does not generate an intended institution in the private domain, the direction and speed of transition from the old to the new is partially dependent on the nature of the institutionalized state. As we saw in the previous chapter, ideological "discourses," as well as competition among systems of predictive and normative beliefs advocated by various interest groups and professional advisors for hegemony in political re-orientation, can have noticeable effects on nascent institutions. Conversely, through the interactions of agents across private economic domains and the polity domain, the nature of the state as an equilibrium in the polity domain may be modified in the process.

Example 10.11   The Evolution of the "Virtual Economy" in Russia (Gaddy and Ickes, OECD)   An essential ingredient of the communist state in the USSR was a hierarchical bundling of (economic) organization domains by the planning apparatus. The state-owned enterprises (SOEs) were first bundled into the relevant industrial ministries, numbering almost 100 at their peak in the late Brezhnev era, and then the industrial ministries were bundled into Gosplan (the State Planning Commission).[23] Party bureaucrats moved through common internal labor markets as ministerial officials and directors of the SOEs. These internal markets served as the cement of a collusive state in which the Communist Party bureaucrats were a dominant collusive partner with the workers, to the exclusion of legally protected private property rights. The position of the SOE directors was pivotal in this coalition. Once assigned, the SOE directors had to deal with idiosyncratic uncertainty at the level of SOEs, such as chronic shortages of material inputs. In their subsidiary role as the heads of the workers' collective, they chose actions in a dense network of formal and informal relations with their workers. By partially representing the interests of their workers, the SOE directors were able to effectively demand more materials or social benefits from the planning apparatus.[24] Thus, toward the end of the communist state, there was a tendency toward a certain autonomy of the directors in coalition with their workers vis-à-vis other bureaucrats.[25]

This hierarchical bundling of organizational domains by the planning apparatus was undone by the demise of the communist state, and the privatization of SOEs in the nonenergy sector was implemented by the so-called voucher privatization of 1993, in which the directors and the workers were given priority in obtaining a majority of the marketable shares of their firms.[26] An overt hope of the privatization authority and their foreign advisors from the international finance organizations and academics was that the privatization scheme would eventually lead to the formation of markets for corporate control. However, the actual outcome was an unintended one. Immediately after the implementation of the scheme (1994), I submitted that:

We cannot ignore the path-dependent nature of the transition process. The legacies of socialism, and the increased autonomy of managers of state owned enterprises in the last phase of the communist regime, or the strong political power of the workers as in Poland, seem to have left strong constraints on the privatization process of the succeeding transitional economies and the nature of the evolving corporate control structure. In many transitional economies the phenomena of insider control are becoming evident. By this we mean *de facto* or *de jure* capture of controlling rights [in the ex SOEs] by the managers and the strong representation of their interests in corporate strategic decision making, often in collusion with the workers. There is no external agent with the decisive power to dismiss the managers of inefficient enterprises. (Aoki 1995b:xii)

The postcommunist reforms changed the legal ownership structure in the organizational domains from state to private ownership. However, under communist rule these domains had been embedded in a collusive state in which de facto ownership was ambiguously shared by the state bureaucrats, SOE directors, and, to a lesser degree, by the workers whose job rights were secured by the chronic labor shortage. In the turmoil of the transition process, this coalition structure was reshuffled at the level of individual enterprises, yet the dominant corporate governance structure that evolved was managerial or "insider" control, inheriting the above-mentioned, latent structure of organizational governance from the final days of the communist state.[27] This development indicates that the mere introduction of corporate law and legal private ownership was not enough for the emergence of market-oriented corporate governance. In order for markets for corporate control to be institutionalized, complementary competencies in investment banking, security analysis and rating, fund management and market arbitrage, corporate reorganization, securities market regulation and monitoring, as well as legal enforcement of contracts and private property rights, need to initially exist or to be cultivated in the domain of financial transactions. Russia apparently lacked these capabilities initially and has been unable to accumulate them yet.

Under these circumstances the formal unbundling of organizational domains from the polity domain did not lead to the subsequent emergence of market relationships among privatized firms and a noninterventionist liberal state in the polity domain. Instead, diachronic complementarities operating between those domains gave rise to new overall institutional arrangements that have become referred to as a "virtual economy."[28] As increasing demonetization in industrial transactions and budgetary operations became prevalent, involving a rapid increase in arrears and the use of various money surrogates, such as commodities (barter), offsets between delivery of goods and writing-off of debts as well as between tax and budgetary fulfillment, and various bills of exchange issued by large reputable enterprises.[29]

One impetus for this development was the organizational framework of de facto quasi-federalism in which the formal expenditure obligations of regional and other local administrations are largely derived from ambitious federal laws and regulations, but the regional and local administrations exercise de facto authority in their implementation primarily through informal means that circumvent laws and regulations (OECD 2000; Litwack 2001). Under this framework, collusion between the subnational government and its constituent firms, on the one hand, and the failure to restructure inefficient firms, on the other, become mutually reinforcing equilibria. Suppose that in the organizational domains privatized firms have two alternative strategies: to restructure or to become "virtual" (Gaddy and Ickes 1999), that is, not to restructure and continue the practice of insider control relying on "relational capital" vested with other firms and (local) government officials. Restructuring may contribute to overall industrial efficiency through the development of market relationships among firms, although there are social and private costs involved in doing so in terms of layoffs of redundant workers, closure of inefficient firms, and so forth.

Suppose that regional/local administrations also have two strategies: liberal (not to intervene in private domains except for rule-based contract enforcement, tax collection and expenditures) and collusive (described in more detail shortly). Suppose that as in example 8.10 of market-linked federalism, regional/local administrations derive positive payoffs from employment stability in their jurisdictional domains. Also regional/local administrations try to keep as much tax revenue as possible by themselves. Thus they may allow firms to pay taxes in commodities to avoid the use of bank accounts that may be seized by the federal tax authorities or the courts. They may also offset taxes against their own expenditure obligations dictated with federal mandates, even if this causes significant transaction costs. These measures facilitate the reallocation of revenue from the federal to regional or local budgets. Further, nonrestructuring firms may pay the monopoly suppliers of natural resources and power in the form of commodities or other money surrogates at inflated values.[30] This amounts to an income transfer from resource-rich natural monopolies to non-restructuring firms without adversely affecting the balance sheets of the former. In exchange, regional/local administrations may compensate natural monopolies by means of profitable export licensing, provision of transportation infrastructure, political influence, voting their shares with managers, and so forth. (Gaddy and Ickes 1998). The goods handed over as payment may be exchanged and delivered to final consumers, often through specialized professional intermediaries (OECD 2000:86, 103). The presence of such intermediary organizations also facilitates noncash payments between firms to evade tax, legitimate wage, and other arrears.[31]

Given such an environment, the relative advantage of the strategy of not restructuring may be enhanced for all firms, potentially efficient ones and inefficient ones alike (Ericson and Ickes 1999). Thus the widespread development of barter-exchange and de-monetization of the economy may not be simply a result of "disorganization" (Blanchard and Kremer 1999) of supply chains caused by the removal of the planning apparatus. Rather, the virtual economy may be understood as an institutional response (i.e., an equilibrium response) to the legacies of communism (poor market-governance competence, de facto insider control, declining power of the central government, etc.), combined with postcommunist changes in "institution-relevant" parameters (privatization, legal fiscal federalism, the regulation of natural monopolies, etc.). Otherwise, it is hard to explain why these collusive arrangements started to increase only after 1995, but not immediately after the removal of the planning apparatus.

Thus insider control in the organizational domains, nonmonetization in the goods- and services-transaction domains,[32] and a collusive federalist state (with collusion between subnational governments and natural monopolies as senior partners and the insiders of nonrestructuring firms as junior partners) in the polity domain may cohere and constitute a fairly robust institutional arrangement, rather than a transitory state en route to the liberal market-economy arrangements (Gaddy and Ickes 1999; Ericson and Ickes 1999; Litwack 2001). One possibility could be that the costly, informal arrangement of the use of various monetary surrogates will be gradually replaced by the organizational development of diversified business groups and group-specific intermediaries such as trading firms (see example 8.10 on diversified business groups). However, their efficiency may remain problematical, particularly if this tendency is led by the dominant natural monopolies and their political allies who derive rents by depreciating the value of natural resources at an unsustainable rate.

III AN ANALYSIS OF INSTITUTIONAL DIVERSITY

In part II we constructed a generic framework for analyzing institutional linkages and changes with illustrative examples drawn from various domains of different economies—contemporary and historical, as well as developing, transitional, and developed. In this part we focus primarily on the domains of corporate and financial transactions of developed market economies and apply our framework to them. We try to understand how and why different corporate governance institutions have emerged and been sustained in these economies, how institutional complementarities manifest themselves with respect to those institutions, how policy and technological change have affected their evolution, and whether differences in institutional arrangements across advanced market economies will disappear as a result of the globalization of markets and the development of communications and information technology. The concluding chapter deals with the last issue as a way of succinctly summarizing the book.

The basic reason why institutions evolve, after all, is because of the bounded rationality of individual agents. Institutions convey useful information in compressed forms that can guide agents' choices under the constraints of information asymmetry and incompleteness. However, a subtle implication of this is that information will not be made completely transparent and transmittable in codified forms through the workings of institutions, no matter how much these codes are perfected. Actually some economically valuable information may not be readily codifiable, and some institutions may emerge to make better use of such knowledge. This is not the case only for underdeveloped economies, as is often misunderstood, but also true for most advanced market economies. This is the most important reason why diverse institutional arrangements will continue to evolve. The parable of Silicon Valley to follow has implications that extend far beyond it and should clarify the point.

11 Comparative Corporate Governance

The paradox of the hired manager, which has caused endless confusion in the analysis of profit, arises from the failure to recognize the fundamental fact that in organized activity the crucial decision is the selection of men to make decisions, that any other sort of decision-making or exercise of judgement is automatically reduced to a routine function. All of which follows from the very nature of large-scale control, based on the replacement of knowledge of things by knowledge of men.
—Frank Knight *Risk, Uncertainty and Profit* (1921:297)

This chapter is concerned with corporate governance mechanisms. What is corporate governance? What does it do? How does it work? In approaching these issues, there have traditionally been two opposing perspectives: the shareholder-value versus stakeholder-society perspectives. The former perspective may be considered as originating in the neoclassical view of the profit-maximizing firm. Recently it has been put in more blunt terms by Shleifer and Vishny: "corporate governance deals with the ways in which suppliers of finance to corporations assure themselves of getting a return on their investment" (1997:737). These ways may include the design of an appropriate private incentive contract for the managers as the agents of shareholders, as well as legal provisions that afford appropriate rights to the shareholders while imposing on the board of directors fiduciary duties to the shareholders in their direction of the manager. The shareholder perspective is often considered as rationalized by the notion that the corporate firm is the property of the shareholders, while the agents supplying other resources, such as human assets and intermediate goods, can safeguard their interests through legally enforceable contracts.

An early forceful argument for the stakeholder-society perspective was pronounced by Dodd (1932) who argued in rebuttal to the shareholder-value position of Berle (1931) that the directors of a corporation must become trustees (if they are not already) not merely for shareholders but also for other constituents of the corporation, such as employees, customers, and particularly the entire community.[1] Corporate firms are thought to emerge because in the course of their relationships they can jointly generate benefits—quasi-rents—that are not feasible only through pure market transactions. There must then be rules to regulate the division of these quasi-rents. Also the actions taken by the investors and managers of a corporate firm may exert external economies on other stakeholders. From this perspective Tirole proposed a definition of corporate governance as "the design of institutions that induce or force management to internalize the welfare of stakeholders" (2001:4).[2]

It is often claimed that in practice, the difference between the two perspectives is not substantial. If, against the interests of the shareholders, the firm does not realize a profit, then the firm will not be able to survive, so stakeholders' interests will be hurt as well. Therefore, it is argued, both perspectives may lead to similar legal and contractual recommendations regarding the regulation of managers' actions. Others find a problem of the stakeholder-society perspective in not being able to find a clear-cut rule for the manager to follow in the interests of multiple stakeholders. For example, Tirole (2001) points out the difficulty of designing focused incentives for managers, as well as an undivided control structure from the stakeholders-society perspective, although he cautions us that this claim does not necessarily vindicate a hardline position on shareholder value. Some others go on to argue from the shareholder-value perspective that the stakeholders-society perspective is the disguised defense of the manager's self-interest independent of investors' interests.

Below we consider corporate governance somewhat differently from the usual normative approach, whether of the shareholder or stakeholder perspectives, in three respects.

First, our approach is *comparative*, both theoretically and empirically, rather than normative (design-oriented). That is, rather than attempt to design the most desirable (legal) structure of control and managerial incentive contracts, we try to understand why there can be a diversity of corporate governance mechanisms, although we admit that in the long run, less effective governance mechanisms may be weeded out through competition among firms in product markets.

Second, we adopt a *game-theoretic approach* in identifying alternative mechanisms of governance. Namely we view the corporate organizational domain (the domain linking the organization and financial transaction domains) as composed of three basic types of players (together with other subsidiary players depending on the context) who interact strategically: the investors who supply financial assets, the workers who invest in organization-specific human assets, and the manager who is entrusted with directing the use of these financial and human assets in uncontractible events, but who may have interests of his or her own (e.g., income, career concerns, perks, and survival). This situation is somewhat analogous to that of the polity domain composed of the government and private actors, as discussed in chapter 6, in that there is a focal player—the manager. Following initial financial decisions by the investors, a profile of manager's and worker's actions yields a certain organizational outcome (quasi-rents) within a certain period of time. The outcome may be distributed among the players according to contracts, legal rules, managerial discretion, customs, and so on, depending on the context. In response to these distributive consequences, the workers and the investors may strategically revise their subsequent action choices as well as chose a sanction on the manager, if necessary. In anticipation of their possible strategic responses, the manager may adapt its strategy choice in directing the use of the financial and human assets entrusted to the organization.

Following the basic framework we developed in part II, we identify corporate governance institutions as self-enforcing mechanisms that govern such strategic interactions among the players. Namely a corporate governance mechanism is *a set of self-enforceable rules (formal or informal) that regulates the contingent action choices of the stakeholders (investors, workers, and managers) in the corporate organization domain.* In particular, the crux of such a mechanism is managers' beliefs regarding possible strategic reactions of other agents in default contingencies—such as failure to realize satisfactory organizational quasi-rents—that may constrain and discipline his or her action choice ex ante. There can be multiple such mechanisms just as there are multiple states in the polity domain.

Third, in discussing the self-enforceability of governance mechanism, we particularly attend to possible *institutionalized linkages* between the organization domain and the financial transaction domain, as well as institutional constraints exercised from such complementary domains as labor transaction and polity domains (*institutional complementarity*). As was already shown in chapter 4.3, different types of organizational architecture present governance issues that can be responded to only with particular linkages to financial transaction domains. Also codified rules of corporate governance, that is, the legal rights afforded to various agents (particularly shareholders and employees) and the associated legal procedures, define the exogenous rules of the game in the corporate organization domain, and as such they may affect the beliefs and incentives of the agents and thereby corporate performance (La Porta et al. 1998). However, legal rules that are not consistent with equilibria in complementary domains may not yield the outcome intended by the legislature on the corporate organization domain. For example, the Japanese Commercial Code provides minority shareholders with one of the strongest rights at stockholders' meeting.[3] However, its governance mechanism is normally not considered to be stockholder controlled. On the other hand, we will see that some sustainable legal rules for corporate governance may be understood as the codification of an equilibrium arrangement in response to certain institutional environments (e.g., codetermination in Germany).

The discussion of this chapter succeeds the preliminary discussion made in chapter 4.3. There we identified basic governance issues posed by the generic modes of organizational architecture without explicit consideration of the financial domain. In this and following chapters we consider ways in which those issues may or may not be resolved by some forms of institutionalized linkage between the organization and financial domains respectively. We begin with the governance of functional hierarchies (nested hierarchical decomposition) when the manager is financially constrained. Section 11.1 discusses the ways in which the governance of the management-controlled, hierarchical, organizational architecture à la Hart-Moore is modified when the manager needs to rely on debt or equity financing. Section 11.2 analyzes the ways in which codetermination (the sharing of control rights between the investors and workers) evolves as a complementary governance institution, as well as how functional hierarchies are transformed into participatory hierarchies, when the corporatist wage regulation prevails in the labor-transaction domain. Section 11.3 turns to the governance of horizontal hierarchies relying on context-oriented human assets. It first derives relational-contingent governance as the second-best governance mechanism for this type of organization architecture. It then goes on to examine possible moral hazard problems that may arise when this kind of mechanism is to be implemented in the world of incomplete contracts.

11.1 Governance of the Functional Hierarchy

In chapter 4.3 we dealt with the organization domain structured as a hierarchical decomposition mode in isolation. In this and the next section, we will look at its linkage with the financial domain and identify several forms of governance mechanisms as equilibria of this linkage under various conditions, including the amount of the entrepreneur's equity, the type of the state in the polity domain as an institutional environments, and so on. As we do this, we will specify the structure of the game by extending a model of Tirole (2001) and making explicit the presence of the worker as a player in the organization domain.

The organization domain is assumed to be structured as a functional hierarchy simply composed of the risk-neutral manager and the (representative) worker, while the manager coordinates his strategy vis-à-vis the investors in the financial domain together with that vis-à-vis the worker. Depending on contracts in the financial domain as specified below, the manager can either be identified as an entrepreneur or as an employed manager, while the investors can be either creditors or shareholders. The manager has a one-period project that requires investment I at the beginning. Initially he may or may not have sufficient equity. If not, he must raise funds in the financial domain at the beginning of the period (the financing stage) by borrowing or relinquishing his control rights to the investors. As in chapter 4.3 the production period is divided into two stages, which we will refer from now as the first and second moral hazard stages for a reason to be made clear momentarily. In the first moral hazard stage the manager and the worker invest in specific human assets, and in the second moral hazard stage they engage in implementation of the project, using physical as well as their respective human assets.

The project generates some verifiable revenue at the end of the period (the outcome stage). It may be a success, yielding positive income $R > 0$, or a failure, yielding zero income $R = 0$. The probability of success depends on the effort levels of the manager and the worker. For simplicity we assume that the manager and the worker make simple binary choices, "high" or "low," regarding respective effort levels. We write the probability of success of the project as $p(e_m, e_w)$, where $e_m = H_m$ (high) if the manager makes high effort in both moral hazard stages or L_m (low) otherwise, and similarly $e_w = H_w$ (high) if the worker makes high effort in both moral hazard stages and L_w (low) otherwise. We assume the following conditions:

$$p(H_m, H_w) > p(H_m, L_w) > p(L_m, H_w) = p(L_m, L_w).$$

Namely cooperative efforts by both parties throughout the production period maximize the probability of success. The last equality may be rationalized by the "essentiality" of the manager's effort in hierarchical decomposition (recall the condition provided in chapter 4.3). That is, without high effort by the manager in both moral hazard stages, high effort by the worker alone cannot enhance the probability of success.

We assume that in making high effort, the manager and the worker incur private cost (or sacrifice private benefits) $\frac{1}{2}c_m$ and $\frac{1}{2}c_w$ respectively per moral hazard stage. Both parties do not discount the future within the period. We assume that $p(H_m, H_w)R - c_m - c_w - I > 0$ but $p(L_m, L_w)R - I < 0$. That is, the expected organizational quasi-rents are positive when both parties' effort levels are high, but they are negative if they are expected to be low. We also assume that $[p(H_m, H_w) - p(H_m, L_w)]R - c_w \geq 0$, so the marginal expected net value of worker's effort is positive. We now distinguish three governance mechanisms: owner control disciplined by debt contract, shareholder governance and markets for corporate control, and codetermination (next section), depending on the way in which the organization domain is linked to the financial or polity domain and on how management decisions are controlled.

Owner Control (the Hart-Moore Firm) with the Debt Contract Discipline

First, as a benchmark case, assume that the manager has sufficient equity of his own for financing the project, implying that he can own all physical assets used in the implementation of the project. Namely the manager is an entrepreneur (owner-manager) of the Hart-Moore firm. On the other hand, the workers do not have any physical assets, and they can expect only a fixed outside option value which is normalized at zero. Motivated by the discussion of chapter 4.3, let us assume that the entrepreneur decides at the end of the first moral hazard stage whether or not to renew the worker's employment, contingent on the worker's observed effort in the first moral hazard stage. If the worker is observed not to have made high effort in accumulating firm-specific human assets, the entrepreneur terminates the employment contract with zero (rent) payment and employs an alternative worker, in which case the probability of success is equal to $p(.,L_w)$. Otherwise, the entrepreneur offers the worker renewed employment. To be productive, the worker needs the entrepreneur's hierarchical direction and the use of the physical assets that the entrepreneur owns, while the entrepreneur needs the worker's cooperation for a higher probability of success of the project. Therefore it is in their mutual interest for them to make high efforts in the first moral hazard stage and renew the employment contract before the second moral hazard stage, provided that both agents are credibly believed to make efforts in the second moral hazard stage.

We assume that the intermediate contract specifies payment ω (a share in the quasi-rents) to the worker such that $p(H_m, H_w)R - c_m - I > \omega \geq c_w$.[5] This contract may be thought of as either a formal fixed wage contract or an implicit agreement in which the payment is conditional on second-stage high effort by the worker. If the worker is re-employed for the second moral hazard stage, the worker makes high effort, while the entrepreneur keeps his contractual promise of payment, whether formal or implicit. Although a repeated game setting is not explicit, we may regard it as implicit here so that the worker is subjected to efficiency wage discipline, and the entrepreneur's commitment to rent-sharing is self-enforcing because of his reputation concern.[4] In any case, as the sole residual claimant after the post–first-stage contract, the entrepreneur is also motivated to make high controlling effort in the second moral hazard stage. His income at the outcome stage is $R - \omega$ in case of success and $-\omega$ otherwise (we assume that the entrepreneur's initial equity is greater than $I + \omega$). This provides a benchmark case.

Now suppose that the entrepreneur of the Hart-Moore firm is cash-constrained at the beginning of the period and tries to borrow the deficient funds, say $B = I + \omega - A$, from investors in the financial domain, where A is the entrepreneur's equity. Suppose that the effort levels of the entrepreneur and worker in the first moral-hazard stage yield a noise-free signal (e.g., short-term profit) at the end of that stage and that the investors renew the debt contract then, if and only if they receive the good signal (high-effort signal). Otherwise, they liquidate the firm, recovering the salvage value of assets $L < B$.[6] The threat of liquidation provides incentives for the entrepreneur and the worker to make high efforts in the first moral hazard stage.

However, as a portion of the revenue from success at the outcome stage goes to the investors, the entrepreneur's incentive in the second moral hazard stages becomes diluted. In order to continue to finance the project, the debt holders must ensure that their expected income would not fall short of their outlay B. Assuming that the entrepreneur's net income is $M - \omega$ in success and $-\omega$ in failure, the entrepreneur makes high effort in the second moral hazard stage, if $[p(H_m, H_w) - p(L_m, L_w)]M \geq \frac{1}{2}c_m$, or equivalently $M \geq \frac{1}{2}c_m/[p(H_m, H_w) - p(L_m, L_w)]$. Then the investors can receive $R - M$ in case of success and zero in case of failure. Therefore, if and only if

$$p(H_m, H_w)\left[R - \frac{\frac{1}{2}c_m}{p(H_m, H_w) - p(L_m, L_w)}\right] \geq B.$$

the investors are willing to renew the debt contract B with the entrepreneur (Tirole 2001). For given technology, this inequality can be satisfied for sufficiently low values of B. That is, the entrepreneur is more likely to be financed when he has more equity, which reduces the amount of borrowing needed, B. Assuming that competition in the financial domain makes the debt-contract holders just break even in equilibrium, the condition above holds with equality, and entrepreneurial expected net income becomes $p(H_m, H_w)[R - B] - \omega$.

Without a short-term debt contract with the threat of liquidation, by applying the same logic as above, we see that the investor is willing to agree on a two-stage long-term contract in the competitive credit market only up to the amount:

$$B^* = p(H_m, H_w)\left[R - \frac{c_m}{p(H_m, H_w) - p(L_m, L_w)}\right],$$

which is less than B. Thus, by subjecting himself to the bankruptcy discipline, a more cash-constrained entrepreneur is able to raise more funds in the financial domain. The time line of the game above is shown in figure 11.1.

Financing stage	1st moral-hazard stage	Interim contract renewal	2nd moral-hazard stage	Outcome stage
Project costs I. The entrepreneur has insufficient equity; borrows from investors	Choice of effort levels in specific human assets by the entrepreneur and the worker	Liquidation if signal (1st stage profit) is bad; otherwise, employment and debt contracts renewed	Choice of effort levels (probability of success of project) by the entrepreneur and the worker	Verifiable revenue: R with probability p. Distribution of R according to the interim contracts.

Figure 11.1
Time line for the entrepreneurial control with debt contract discipline

Shareholder Governance and Markets for Corporate Control

Suppose now that the inequalities above do not hold. This is the situation where the entrepreneur does not have sufficient own equity, so that the investors in the financial domain regard a debt contract as too risky. In this situation the entrepreneur needs to relinquish his control rights to the investors in order to induce them to supply the funds necessary for the implementation of the project. Then the investors become the shareholders of the firm, while making the manager their agent. For simplicity, we assume that the manager does not own any equity, so the whole of the projects' financing is to be provided by the investors. Let us assume for a moment that $p(L_m, L_w)R - I < 0$. Then, in order for shareholding to be worthwhile for the investors, they have to ensure that both manager and worker will make high efforts. Suppose first that the initial shareholders are expected to remain as stable shareholders over two stages. Suppose further that the short side of the financial market is the supply side, while the short sides of the managerial and labor markets are the demand sides. Then the shareholders only need to make the manager break even in equilibrium and reward the worker with c_m for high effort (the Walrasian discipline). Suppose that the manager is given an outcome-contingent incentive contract by which he receives M in case of success and zero in case of failure. For the manager to be motivated to make high effort, M must be set so that $[p(H_m, H_w) - p(L_m, L_w)]M = c_m$. If such an incentive contract is given, it becomes in the interest of the manager to induce the worker to make high effort also. He can set the payment per stage to the worker at $\frac{1}{2}c_w$. The shareholders claim the residual in the event of success of the project, so their share value before the first moral hazard stage ends becomes

$$V = p(H_m, H_w)\left[R - \frac{c_m}{p(H_m, H_w) - p(L_m, L_w)}\right] - c_w$$

Next, consider the possibility that a novel action becomes known in the middle of the first moral hazard stage. This interim action raises the possibility of success uniformly by $\tau > 0$ regardless of the effort combination of the manager and worker in any stages, while causing the private cost $\gamma > 0$ to the worker in the second moral hazard stage (Tirole 2001). For example, the worker may be laid off. If the worker is not compensated for this cost, he may then retaliate by becoming noncooperative in the second stage, once the novel action is implemented. As a result he may receive zero wage (no rent). However, assume that $[p(H_m, L_w) + \tau]R - I - \frac{1}{2}c_w > 0$, so the net present value of the project now becomes positive even with the noncooperation of the worker. Anticipating the worker's reaction, the incentive compatibility condition for the manager is now given by $[p(H_m, L_w) + \tau - p(L_m, L_w) - \tau]M^* = c_m,$

where M^* is the output-contingent managerial compensation. As $p(H_m, H_w) > p(H_m, L_w)$, it must hold that $M^* > M$. That is, because of the noncooperation of the worker, the manager must be provided with more incentives to make high effort. The expected shareholder value following the new action becomes

$$V^* = [p(H_m, L_w) + \tau]\left[R - \frac{c_m}{p(H_m, L_w) - p(L_m, L_w)}\right].$$

Therefore, if the gains from the new action in the shareholders' returns at the outcome stage (i.e., the incremental net returns due to the increased probability of success τ and the saving of the wage premium in the second moral hazard stage) becomes larger than the required manager's incentives plus the expected loss of efficiency due to the worker's noncooperation, then it holds that $V^* > V$. Note that this condition can hold even if $\gamma > \tau R$ so that the revenue-enhancing action may reduce the total welfare including the worker's (Tirole 2001).

If $V^* > V$, then we can imagine the possibility of the following mechanism: the initial shareholder hires the manager with an incentive contract characterized by M, and the manager in turn commits to the worker with a payment (or implicit benefit) c_w. The worker invests in a relation-specific effort in the first moral hazard stage. Then an equity price of V prevails in the financial domain. In the middle of the first moral hazard stage, another group of investors foresees the possibility of enhancing value with the new action (e.g., by restructuring). They take over the firm by purchasing the control rights from the original shareholders at V and then install new management with the incentive contract characterized by M^*. The new management implements the action, while inflicting the private cost γ on the worker in the second moral hazard stage. The worker responds to this "breach of trust" (Shleifer and Summers 1988) with a low effort. Yet shareholder value can be increased even if the total welfare declines. If $\gamma < \tau R$ so that the new action is welfare enhancing, the new shareholder may agree to compensate the worker for the private cost and entice him to make a high effort in the second moral hazard stage. In this case the market for corporate control functions as an efficiency-enhancing mechanism. See figure 11.2 for the time line of the game.

11.2 Codetermination in the Participatory Hierarchy

In the previous section it was shown that following the acquisition of an individuated firm-specific human asset, the worker in the organization of the functional hierarchy type can obtain a wage contract specifying an income above his or her market-

Financing stage	1st moral-hazard stage	Take-over and restructuring	2nd moral-hazard stage	Outcome stage
Initial shareholders finances project costs I.	Choice of effort levels in specific human assets by the incumbent manager and the worker	New shareholders install a new manager who takes action enhancing probability of success	Choice of effort level by the new manager. The worker becomes either cooperative or non-cooperative	Verifiable revenue: R with probability p+τ. Distribution of R according to contracts.

Figure 11.2
Time line for the shareholder control

determined outside option value. Thus the worker is made subjected to the efficiency-wage discipline in his/her use of the acquired human asset at the second moral hazard stage. For this labor-market institution the control of the firm by the owner of physical assets à la Hart-Moore, or its extension by the market for corporate control, is likely to be an equilibrium. Let us consider an alternative situation in which firms of the functional hierarchy type are situated in an institutional environment of social-compact corporatism which regulates economywide wage setting for standardized occupations (chapter 6.2). Then the employer's ability is constrained in inducing the worker to acquire and use a firm-specific asset with the promise of a contingent firm-specific payment. Symmetrically, the worker may not be able to credibly threaten to quit the job for a better-paying job. How can the worker be motivated to acquire and use a firm-specific human asset in such a situation?

Let us first assume an embryonic situation, as in chapter 4.3, in which the employer is an owner-manager of a firm unconstrained by its own equity capital. Also let us leave unspecified for a while the nature of the external market domain. Suppose that the game is repeatedly played between the owner and the worker over indefinite periods. The owner makes a choice between the following reciprocating strategy Σ^* and the Hart-Moore exchange strategy Σ^{**} in each period before the first moral hazard stage begins and sticks to it throughout the period, while the worker likewise makes a choice between the following reciprocating strategy Λ^* and the Hart-Moore exchange strategy Λ^{**} in each period before the first moral hazard stage begins and sticks to it during the period.

• With Σ^* the owner allows the worker to participate in the "residual rights of control" (Grossman and Hart) provided that the worker has always cooperated (made effort) in past periods, and otherwise keeps the residual rights of control and does not make any payment beyond what is determined in the external labor transaction domain. With Σ^{**} the owner does not allow the worker to share the residual rights of control, but promises to pay wage premium c_w conditional on the worker's effort.

$\cdot$ With Λ^* the worker makes a reciprocating effort provided that the owner has always partially relinquished residual rights of control to the worker in past periods, and otherwise shirks. With Λ^{**} the worker makes an effort in response to the owner's promise of a wage premium, and otherwise shirks.

Let us assume that the worker can reduce his or her effort cost by participating in the residual rights of control, possibly because of improvements in working conditions, participation in workplace design, more autonomous control of his/her work, and so forth. This implies that the participation of the worker in the residual rights of control transforms the organizational architecture from a functional hierarchy to a participatory hierarchy introduced in chapter 4.2. On the other hand, there is some reduction in the owner's utility in the event of partial relinquishment of residual rights of control. The owner may not be able to implement the work plan, and so forth, that she likes the best. The mismatching of strategies, (Σ^*, Λ^{**}) or (Σ^{**}, Λ^*), always ends up with the no-effort choice by the worker and no rights-sharing choice by the owner as actual outcomes. However, there will be two Pareto-superior Nash equilibria over periods: the reciprocating equilibrium (Σ^*, Λ^*) and the Hart-Moore exchange equilibrium $(\Sigma^{**}, \Lambda^{**})$ leading to the formation of the Hart-Moore firm. We cannot make a definite Pareto-ranking between the two equilibria as the owner experiences disutility from the partial relinquishing of residual rights of control.

The determination of the basic wage has been implicit so far. Now let us consider the two cases: in one case the basic wage rate is competitively determined in the external competitive markets, and in the other it is regulated by corporatist national bargaining (chapter 6.2). In the former case, the owner is free to choose the level of the wage premium, while in the latter, the owner is constrained to set it at zero. Clearly, the relative advantage of the reciprocating strategy (alternatively, the Hart-Moore exchange strategy) is enhanced for each player if corporatist regulation (respectively the unregulated external market) prevails in the labor-exchange-cum-polity domain. Thus the corporatist state is seen to be institutionally complementary to the particpatory hierarchy, whereas the liberal state that does not intervene the determination of the employment condition is seen to be institutionally complementarity to the Hart-Moore firm (functional hierarchy).[7]

Now, as in the previous section, suppose that the owner of the rights-sharing firm is cash-constrained and needs to be financed externally. The owner of the firm unambiguously prefers debt-financing, as he does not need to relinquish the remaining control rights to the investors unless he declares bankruptcy. The worker also prefers a debt contract because his or her interest may be more congruent with the debt-contract holder than the shareholders for the following reason: The worker's nonwage benefits may be relatively flat with respect to the level of the firm's revenue, and the return curve of the debt contract is also concave (increasing with the firm's return in the lower tail and flat beyond the value of credit).[8] Therefore the worker and the debt-contract holder may find a mutual interest in restraining excessive risk-taking by the owner (manager) of the firm. For this reason the debt-contract holder can partially rely on the worker's monitoring through the sharing of control rights and so be willing to relax the financial constraint of the owner of the firm in the form of a long-term contract more than vis-à-vis the Hart-Moore firm. Thus we have

PROPOSITION 11.1 The corporatist wage-regulation in the polity-labor transaction domain is institutionally complementary to the participatory hierarchy in which the residual rights of control over uncontractible issues are shared between the employer and the worker. When control rights are shared with the worker, more external financing will be made in the form of long-term debt contracts.

When the equity of the original owner of the firm is still too small relative to the required capital, it becomes inevitable that the individual equity-ownership of the firm by its manager-cum-owner need to be abandoned. However, in this case the governance structure cannot be the same as the shareholder governance discussed in the previous section because the worker participates in the residual rights of control. Suppose that both the worker and investors (shareholders and creditors) are able to cast a veto vote vis-à-vis a management action that they prefer less than the status quo, or deny the reappointment of the manager for the next round of the game, depriving him of an opportunity to obtain an employment continuation value. Thus the workers and investors can exercise separate control rights over the management. We call this governance mechanism *codetermination*.[9] Then any unilateral new action that would hurt the worker as described in the previous section could be blocked by a worker's veto and by the manager's career concerns. On the other hand, assume that although the investors supply full financing, they have little useful information for facilitating the smooth operation of the participatory hierarchy within the firm, and thus are passive in formulating a business plan. The possibility of new interim actions (restructuring) after initial financing can be perceived only by the manager who has invested in firm-specific human assets in the first moral hazard stage. However, the investors can threaten to withdraw financing at the interim stage and the workers can be uncooperative in the second moral hazard stage if they choose.

The conditions above imply a three-person bargaining situation (see figure 11.3). For simplicity, let us assume that in the absence of cooperation from the remaining

Financing stage	1st moral-hazard stage	Interim codetermination	2nd moral-hazard stage	Outcome stage
Investors finance project costs I.	Choice of effort levels in specific human assets by the manager and the worker	Manager implements success-enhancing new action conditional on every party's agreements.	Cooperative choice of effort levels by the manager and the worker	Verifiable revenue: R with probability p+τ. Distribution of R according to corporatist regulation and contracts.

Figure 11.3
Time line for codetermination

third party, no two-person subcoalition can produce positive net quasi-rents nor can any single party in isolation, so $p(e_m, e_w) = 0$ unless $e_m = H_m$, $e_w = H_w$ and $B > 0$, where B is the total amount of financing supplied by the investors (either equity or credit). Then the three parties will agree to implement a new interim action if and only if it is welfare-improving for every party concerned, where the benefits that accrue to the worker are in a form other than the explicit regulated wage (this corresponds to the case where $\gamma < 0$). However, some stock-value-enhancing policies may not be implemented if they hurt the worker or the manager. Summarizing, the following comparative proposition holds:

PROPOSITION 11.2   There may be a management plan that can be chosen under stockholder governance but not under codetermination, if it is expected to have a welfare-reducing impact on the worker and incite retaliatory uncooperative effort by the workers. The two governance mechanisms are not necessarily Pareto-rankable.

11.3   The Relational-Contingent Governance of the Horizontal Hierarchy

In the two preceding sections we considered governance mechanisms for the organizational architecture of the functional hierarchy and participatory hierarchy types. In this section we turn to a governance mechanism for the organizational architecture of the horizontal hierarchy type (nested information assimilation mode). In comparison to the former, the nature of this governance mechanism is not necessarily well understood in the theoretical literature of corporate governance, so the following treatise is somewhat more elaborate than the one in the previous sections. Tirole (2001) cautiously commented that the stakeholder-society perspective has so far not been provided with a good theoretical rationale, as it is difficult to theoretically design multiple-task incentives for the manager or an effective arrangement for the division of control rights among stakeholders. The governance mechanism designed in this section does not provide an arrangement for "divided" control, but for control rights "shifting" between stakeholders—specifically between the insiders (the mangers and workers) and a designated agent of the investors—contingent on the outcome of the stage game in a repeated game context. Thus we call the governance mechanism the relational-contingent governance. We first derive this mechanism theoretically as a second best solution to the free-riding problem inherent to organizational architecture of the horizontal hierarchy type. Then we discuss various institutionalization of this mechanism in the context of incomplete contracts.

The Parable of Relational-Contingent Governance

In chapter 4.3 we indicated that the free-riding problem inherent to organizations of the information-assimilation mode cannot be resolved by the ex ante allocation of ownership of physical assets. Instead, we suggested that the problem may be resolved in a second-best manner by the threat of external penalties for bad collective performance. In this subsection we try to develop this idea. We start out with the following simple structure of linkage between the organization and financial domains.

1. The organization domain is structured as a H-firm (horizontal hierarchy) composed of N homogeneous members, called the *insiders*. Production can take place with the aid of a fixed amount of financial assets in each of a sequence of time periods. The value of output of the H-firm in each period, V, is the joint outcome of the insider's effort levels, $e = (e_1, \ldots, e_i, \ldots, e_N)$, in that period and the current state of technological environments. The effort level of each insider is not observable. It is assumed, however, that the observed value of V serves as a fairly good indicator of the level of insiders' efforts as a whole in that greater members' efforts reduce the probability of output value in the lower tail while increasing that in the higher tail.[10]

2. Each insider has an identical per-period utility function of the type $u^W(w, e_i) = w - c(e_i)$ for $w \geq w_{min}$, where w is the level of current income and w_{min} is the minimum income required by the insiders to survive. The firm has specific collective human assets that would be destroyed if the firm were terminated (i.e., insider's human assets are context-oriented). In the event of termination of the H-firm, each insider is expected to suffer a reduction of income by amount J, indefinitely over every future period.

3. There are two types of outsiders to the H-firm: passive *investors*, who provide a fixed amount of financial assets when they can expect to obtain a certain level of returns per period, ρ. They cannot, however, observe even the aggregate output value of the H-firm ex post, but can observe only the court-verifiable event of the termina-

tion of the H-firm. They entrust the enforcement of financial contracts to a particular *relational monitor* (*R-monitor*) who can observe the aggregate output value of the H-firm at the end of each period and then exercise control rights over the H-firm according to a contract agreed with the H-firm at the beginning of the period. The R-monitor requires a certain expected level of income per period for this service, say M, payable from the current output of the H-firm.

The characterization of the H-firm 1 may be regarded as an abstraction of the nature of a firm whose organizational architecture is structured as the (nested) information-assimilation mode. The distinction between the manager and the workers is not explicitly taken into consideration (see chapter 4.3 for a rationalization). As the output value of the H-firm is observable by the R-monitor and the insiders of the H-firm, the R-monitor's payment schedule, s^{RM}, may be made contingent on the H-firm's output value, V. Her expected value, M, may be determined by her bargaining power relative to the insiders, which is parametrically given to the model. In particular, the possibility that her ex post pay may become negative for some values of V is not excluded. As for the passive investors, their payment schedule, $s^I(V)$, should be made contingent only on a simpler event that they can observe—namely whether the H-firm terminates or continues at the end of each period—as long as the expected rate specified ex ante satisfies the exogenously given rate of returns, ρ. An identical schedule of payments for each insider, $w(V)$, needs to be specified in a manner compatible with the contracts with the outsiders. Also, because of the wealth constraint, regardless of realized value of V, the minimum income, w_{min} needs to be guaranteed for the insiders. Thus we have the overall budget constraint for a nexus of contracts:

$$y = s^I(V) + s^{RM}(V) + Nw(V) \quad \text{and} \quad w(V) \geq w_{min} \qquad \text{for all } V. \qquad \text{(BC)}$$

Suppose that each period is divided into three stages: the contract stage at the beginning of the period, the moral hazard stage in the middle of the period, in which production takes place and free-riding by each insider may become a possibility, and the outcome stage at the end of the period, at which time the level of the H-firm's output value is observed by the R-monitor and the insiders. As the effort levels of insiders are not observable ad interim and contracts cannot be revised accordingly, the two moral hazard stages in the preceding sections are collapsed into a single one here and the contract can be written only in its beginning. These three stages are characterized next.

The Contract Stage In this stage contracts are agreed on among the insiders, investors, and the R-monitor, and financing is provided by the investors to the H-firm

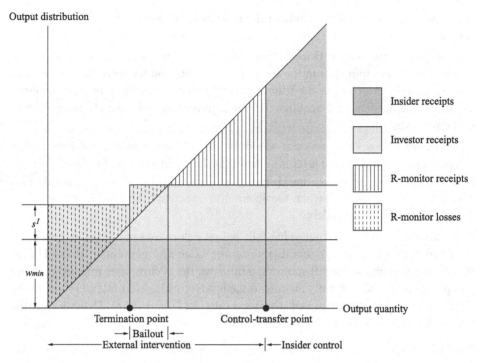

Figure 11.4
Contingent governance structure

accordingly. Imagine that a nexus of contracts of the following form—a *H-nexus of contracts*—is agreed upon in a manner that satisfies the above-mentioned overall budget constraint

• *H-nexus of contracts.* This divides the entire range of the H-firm's possible output value into the following four regions in the order of the highest to the lowest, and specifies control rights to be exercised either by the insiders or the R-monitor at the outcome stage, contingent on the region in which the output value is observed at that time (see figure 11.4).

• *Insider-control region.* When the output value level is higher than a certain level, say $\bar{b}$, called the control-transfer point, a fixed rate of returns higher than the expected rate of investor's returns $(s^I(V) = \bar{s}^I > \rho)$ is paid to the investors. The R-monitor is compensated only as an investor, provided she supplies a portion of the financing. Otherwise, she does not receive anything from the H-firm. The residual output value is equally shared among the insiders. The H-firm continues to the next period.

• *R-monitor-control region.* Once output value falls below the control-transfer point, control rights to output shift to the R-monitor. The R-monitor pays the same rate of return to the investors as in the insider-control region, pays the minimum required income to the insiders, and acquires the nonnegative residual. The H-firm continues to the next period.

• *Bailing-out region.* The payment schedules are the same as the previous region except that the output value level is so low that the residual borne by the R-monitor becomes negative. However, the H-firm is still sustained to the next period. This corresponds to the case in which the R-monitor "rescues" the H-firm comprised of the wealth constrained insiders.

• *Termination region.* If output value falls below a threshold point, say $\underline{b}$, called the termination point, control rights to the output value and continuity of the H-firm shift to the R-monitor. The R-monitor terminates the H-firm after making contractual payments of the minimum income to the insiders and a fixed rate of return to the investors lower than the expected investor's rate $(s^I(V) = \underline{s}^I < \rho)$. Deficits after the termination are to be borne by the R-monitor.

The Moral Hazard Stage   In this stage the insiders engage in production by expending mutually unobservable efforts. They choose individual effort levels so as to maximize the present value of their expected current and future flows of utility. In so doing, they have to take into account the possibility of output value falling below the termination point due to a lack of sufficient efforts and thus the possibility of suffering a reduction in their incomes from the next period on. They choose the level of effort so as to equate the marginal benefit of additional effort with its marginal cost. As shown in chapter 4.3, the former is comprised of two factors: the marginal increase in expected current income and the marginal reduction in the flow value of future penalties due to termination of the H-firm. That is, increased efforts will reduce the probability of termination.[11]

The Outcome Stage   In this stage the joint outcome of the insiders' efforts and the state of the environments becomes observable by the insiders and the R-monitor. The specifications of the H-nexus of contracts are executed accordingly. However, there may arise a potential problem of enforceability. Imagine a situation where the observed output value of the H-firm falls short of the termination point, $\underline{b}$. As the termination of the H-firm imposes on the insiders the deadweight loss, $[\delta/(1-\delta)]NJ$ (δ is the time discount factor), in the value of contextual human assets, which are not enjoyable by any outsider, there may arise a possibility of renegotiation between them and the R-monitor to prevent such an event from occurring. We can assume that renegotiation does not involve the investors because they are numerous and cannot effectively organize themselves. However, the insiders may try to bribe the R-monitor not to terminate the H-firm by offering her an amount not greater than the deadweight loss. There must be some safeguard against such a possibility, to keep the R-monitor committed to honest output monitoring and to taking the disciplinary action whenever appropriate. Such a mechanism may be provided if the R-monitor is better off by terminating the H-firm whenever it is appropriate to do so rather than receiving a bribe from the insiders and letting them survive. This can be made possible by a stepwise schedule of payments to the investors, depending on whether or not the final output value is in the termination region or in the other higher regions. Suppose that a contract can be written, and legally enforceable in such a way that in the event of termination the, R-monitor pays a lower rate to passive outside investors by an amount equal to the H-firm's deadweight losses of continuation values (in equivalent flow terms). Then it is not profitable for the insiders to bribe the R-monitor ex post not to terminate the H-firm and the threat of termination becomes credible. However, this creates another moral hazard problem on the side of the R-monitor by providing her with incentives to terminate, rather than bail out, the H-firm, when output value is in the lower range of the bail-out region. We will later see how this problem may be resolved in a certain institutional environment.

The H-nexus of contracts defines a basic mechanism of governance regarding both the disposition of the H-firm's output and its' continuation at the end of each period. Since control rights shift between the insiders and the R-monitor in a punctuated manner contingent on the value of the H-firm's output, we may call this mechanism *relational-contingent governance*. In the insider-control region, the insiders become the residual claimants, as in the case of an insider-controlled firm. However, if such a status were to extend over the entire range of output value, the moral hazard inherent to H-firms would become unavoidable. Further, if the value of output is very low, it may not be sufficient to guarantee the minimum required income of the insiders. For these two reasons, if the value of output falls below the control-transfer point, the residual claimant status shifts to the R-monitor à la Aghion and Bolton (1992). If the value of output falls even further to below the termination point, the H-firm is terminated and its members have to accept inferior outside options. This efficiency-wage-like discipline can provide incentives for the insiders not to shirk. Thus, in organization domains where H-nexus of contracts are implemented, we do not frequently observe the event of termination as an outcome. On the other hand, the insiders are at least guaranteed their minimum income over the entire range of output value.

It can be shown that there exist $\underline{b}$ and $\bar{b}$ with $\underline{b} < \bar{b}$ that make the corresponding H-nexus of contracts the second-best governance mechanism for the H-firm in the following sense: the value of the organizational quasi-rents—net of insiders' effort costs, expected penalties, and exogenously determined expected payments to the investors and R-monitor—is maximized subject to the individual choices of effort level by the insiders being incentive compatible and the overall budget constraint being satisfied.[12]

LEMMA 11.1   There exists a pair of the control-transfer point and the termination point under which a H-nexus of contracts provides the second-best governance mechanism for the H-firm.

The idea of breaking the budget of the H-firm ex post by a third party is essentially inherited from Holmström (1982). There are, however, a number of differences between the two schemes that have important implications for their implementation. Holmström's scheme can approximate the first-best solution, while the mechanism of relational-contingent governance can achieve only the second-best outcome (i.e., the first-best among incentive compatible nexus of contracts). Now Holmström's model achieves its objective by the threat of transferring very large amounts from the insiders to a third party in the event of output value falling below a critical level. In contrast, in our model budget-breaking by the R-monitor occurs in the form of income insurance for the wealth-constrained insiders in the bailing-out and termination regions. The penalty in our model that mitigates the disincentive effect of the insurance takes the form of a deadweight loss of employment continuation value because of the termination of the potentially productive H-firm, and thus is not enjoyable by the R-monitor. Therefore the R-monitor cannot expect higher returns ex ante by colluding with an insider in the hope of collecting penalties. Lower effort supply by the insiders would only increase the probability of output value being in the bailing-out or termination regions, and thus hurt the R-monitor herself. Further, even if the potential penalty takes the form of a deadweight loss, the insiders of a failing H-firm cannot effectively renegotiate with the R-monitor to prevent costly termination.

When the termination point, $\underline{b}$, is raised (lowered), then we say that the R-monitor hardens (softens) the ex post budget constraint of the insiders, since this implies that the range of bailing-out is made shrunk from below (expanded downward). The mechanism of relational-contingent governance exhibits the following comparative static property:[13]

LEMMA 11.2   The lowering of the outside option values for the insiders makes the hardening of their ex post budget constraint by the R-monitor the second-best arrangement. These two factors together strengthen the effectiveness of the relational-contingent governance of the horizontal hierarchy, inducing the insiders to make higher efforts and thus easing the free-riding problem inherent to this type of organizational architecture.

The outside option value may be taken as a parameter by the insiders of an individual H-firm, but its lowering may be regarded as a (general equilibrium) outcome of the convention of horizontal hierarchies in organizational architecture. Namely, if all firms are structured as H-firms relying on the context-oriented skills of their members and individuals' skills are thus geared toward a particular firm, they cannot freely move between firms without suffering a loss in their employment continuation value.[14] Thus the effectiveness of the relational-contingent governance is enhanced when horizontal hierarchies are established as a convention in the organizational field. Conversely, lemma 11.1 suggests that horizontal hierarchies are run more efficiently when the relational-contingent governance are institutionalized (i.e., implied transfers of control rights contingent on organizational performance are generally expected). Thus they are mutually reinforcing.

PROPOSITION 11.3   The convention of horizontal hierarchies in the organizational field and the relational-contingent governance in the corporate governance domains are institutionally complementary.

As just said, the imperfection of the midcareer job market enhances the efficiency of horizontal hierarchy via the relational-contingent governance. Conversely, the midcareer job markets become less competitive as horizontal hierarchies evolve as a convention. Therefore they are also mutually reinforcing.

COROLLARY 11.1   Imperfect midcareer job markets and horizontal hierarchies are institutionally complementary.

The Dilemma of the Relational Monitor's Double-Edged Commitment

What enables the relational monitor to credibly commit to her governance roles, specifically to taking the ex post costly action in the bailing-out region on the one hand, and terminating a very badly performing firm on the other? If a breach of the relational monitor's contractual obligations in the mechanism of relational-contingent governance were court-verifiable, their enforcement could ultimately be entrusted to the courts. Indeed, her contractual obligation to the passive investors may be made court-enforceable, since it is specified in such a way as to be contingent only on the court-verifiable event of H-firm termination (liquidation). However, whether the state of value of the H-firm is above, or below the second-best termination point—namely whether the financially distressed firm should be bailed out or terminated according to the H-nexus contracts—would be hard for a neutral, third party (the court) to judge and/or verify. Given the complexity of the admixture of insiders' action choices and unforeseeable environmental events, the termination point is clearly not even be contractually specifiable ex ante. Notwithstanding this practical difficulty of precisely implementing the second-best contracts, we say that the relational-contingent governance is institutionalized in that economy when the expectation is widely held among agents in the corporate governance domains of the economy that firms with very bad performance outcomes will be punished by their termination, but those with mildly poor performance outcomes may be bailed out by ex ante specified relational parties.

We suggested earlier that the lower repayment to the passive investors in the event of termination may mitigate the incentives for the relational monitor to soften the insiders' budget constraint through ex post renegotiation. We also pointed out that the same device may, however, provide adverse incentives for the relational monitor to terminate the H-firm even when the firm should be bailed out. To counteract these incentives, there must be some intrinsic values—rents—available for the relational monitor by credibly committing to a bailing-out operation whenever it is appropriate to do so. Leaving these rents unspecified for the moment, we must consider one important dilemma inherent in the mechanism of relational-contingent governance: the double-edged commitment problems arising from the practical difficulty of writing and enforcing explicit second-best H-nexus contracts.

On one hand, if rents are not sufficiently high, the relational monitor may be motivated to terminate firms that should be bailed out. That is, valuable organization-specific assets may be destroyed even when mildly poor performance occurs due to uncontrollable stochastic events but not due to the actions of insiders. This tendency for the monitoring agent to lack the commitment to rescue may be referred to as the short-termism syndrome. On the other, if the rents made possible by bailing-out are too high, the monitoring agent may be motivated to bail out a firm that should not be bailed out. If such expectation prevails, then the mechanism of relational-contingent governance fails to provide proper incentives ex ante for the insiders of horizontal hierarchies to make sufficient effort. This tendency, interpreted as a lack of commitment on the side of the relational monitor to punish badly performing firms, is referred to by economists as the soft-budget constraint syndrome (Kornai 1980, 1992; Dewatripont and Maskin 1995). As in statistical inference, short-termism syndrome could also be referred to as an error of type I in the sense that what should be accepted is rejected, while the soft budget constraint syndrome might represent an error of type II in the sense that what should be rejected is accepted.

Which syndrome or error prevails in a particular economy where a relational-contingent governance mechanism is institutionalized depends on the relative magnitudes of those costs and rents facing relational monitors. As mentioned, explicit contracts of relational-contingent governance are hard to write because of the complexity of the contractual environment. Further the rents from bailing-out may not be determinable in individual organization domains but may be specified and generated only in a broader institutional context in which they are embedded. Then one cannot in actuality assume that costs and rents are arranged in such a way that the second-best solution can be implemented with precision in each organization domain. It is reasonable to expect that one or another of the syndromes will prevail. Yet, in environments where rents and costs remain fairly stable, if not balanced in a second-best way, the behavior of relational monitors may become predictable, and firms of the horizontal hierarchy type may accordingly be disciplined while being able to accumulate and preserve organization-specific assets in a more or less steady fashion. However, when there is an environmental change that drastically transforms the parameter values defining the costs and rents of bailing-out, expectations cannot be clearly formed regarding the monitoring agents' actions and this impinges on their relational-contingent governance role.

Institutional Forms of Relational-Contingent Governance

Our discussion so far has remained at an abstract level. In particular, we have been silent about who relational monitors can be and what their incentives to bail out financially depressed firms are. There are several institutional possibilities of contingent governance relationships: (1) between firms and banks, (2) between subsidiary corporations and their holding/management company, (3) between entrepreneurial start-up firms and venture capital funds, (4) between state-owned enterprises and the government, or (5) between banks and a government regulatory agency. Let us briefly touch on each of them.

Bank-Based Contingent Governance   Financially sound firms are able to rely on internal cash flow or bond markets for financing investment. When their financial states or reputations are insufficient to warrant market financing, such firms will rely on bank credits and yield some rents to the banks if their business performances are acceptable. They may further expect additional financing from the same banks when they face mild financial distress or have an urgent need for the infusion of funds in noncontractible contingencies, although the controlling power of the banks would accordingly be strengthened. If a firm's financial state worsens even further, the banks may refuse to provide additional financing, triggering a court-led bankruptcy procedure. There can be various sources of bank rents that may sustain such a *bank-based* relational-contingent governance institution: information rents, monopoly rents, reputation rents, and policy-induced rents. In the next chapter we discuss the nature of these rents and see under what conditions they may become conducive to the institutionalization of relational-contingent governance.[15]

It is worth noting here that while shareholder-controlled governance is applicable only to publicly held corporate firms, bank-based relational-contingent governance may at least theoretically be compatible with diverse ownership structures of firms. These may include worker-controlled firms, workers' cooperatives, closely held limited liability companies, and partnerships. Unless their financial state is excellent, firms of these types rely on funds from banks for their operations and investments. An inability to repay these debts will automatically trigger the bank's intervention. It is not immediately clear how the banking system can cope with the double-edged commitment problems vis-à-vis these firms. But, as we have demonstrated, at least in theory the mechanism of bank-based relational-contingent governance can serves as an effective governance device for any ownership structure, provided that human assets are context-oriented.

There is some empirical evidence (e.g., Petersen and Rajan 1995; Gande et al. 1997) that relationships between small American firms and their commercial banks resemble relational-contingent governance (see next chapter for this). The Japanese main bank system institutionalized the relational-contingent governance mechanism in the postwar period between 1950 and mid-1970. The nonfinancial firms whose internal organization depended on the context-oriented human assets of their permanent employees was disciplined by the fear of bank control in the event of serious financial distress, though they expected that they would be assisted by their main banks in the event of liquidity needs including mild financial distress (Aoki, Patrick, and Sheard 1994; Hoshi, Kashyap and Sharfstein 1990; Sheard 1994). The investments of these firms were mostly financed by bank loans from multiple banks, but each of them was monitored by a particular relational bank called its main bank. A general expectation was that the financial distress of any borrowing firm was to be covered by its main bank at its own cost. As long as firms remained going concerns, other banks were assured of repayments of their initial loans. That is, they showed the essential characteristic of the outside investor in the model of the H-nexus of contracts in that the monitoring of firms was delegated to their main banks.[16] Although this system worked as an effective governance mechanism in the environmental contexts of the 1960s and 1970s, it began to exhibit misfits with evolving institutional, technological, and international environments in the 1980s, culminating in the bank crisis and the vacuum in corporate governance in the 1990s. As we will see later (chapter 13), the shared belief that "the government will take care of the banks' bad debt problems" systematically promoted the banks' excessive soft-budgeting syndrome, and many firms that should have been restructured or liquidated were kept viable.

Organizational-Based Contingent Governance A parent company (alternatively management partners, e.g., LBO associations or a holding company) may allow the management of well-run subsidiary companies to be relatively autonomous, while providing the management with equity incentives and other private benefits derived from informal control rights. It can, however, closely monitor the cash flow of each subsidiary company by selecting for it a highly leveraged financial structure. When any of the subsidiary companies is not run efficiently, the problem can then be detected quickly, and the parent company can intervene at an early stage to reorganize and work out the problem. Jensen (1989) called such an arrangement the "privatization of bankruptcy."[17] In this case the rents accruing to the parent company from bailing out may include the potential future values created by reorganization and/or the saving of the costs of liquidation due to short-termism. We classify this variety of relational-contingent governance as *organization-based*.

Venture Capital Governance Venture capital financing-cum-governance is characterized as staged financing. The financing starts as seed financing of an entrepreneurial project and ends with its IPO (initial public offering) or acquisition by an established firm. During this period the venture capitalist and entrepreneurial firms maintain close relationships, where different rights, such as cash-flow rights, voting rights, board representation rights, and liquidation rights, are bundled in various ways contingent on the development performance of the entrepreneurial firm. Based on an analysis of 200 samples of venture capital financing, Kaplan and Strömberg (2000) found that when a company performs poorly, the venture capitalists take full control. As company performance improves, the entrepreneur retains/obtains more control rights. When a company performs very well, the venture capitalists still control cash-flow rights but will relinquish most their liquidation rights. This observation appears to match exactly the theoretical structure of relational-contingent governance, with the venture capitalist corresponding to the relation monitor. This is not surprising if we consider that the entrepreneurial firm often involves team work: the development of new technology and its commercialization crucially depends on the collective efforts of the closely knit members of the entrepreneurial firms, so their individual contributions may not be evident. In chapter 14 we will analyze aspects of venture capital governance, particularly the implications of a specific form of termination rights accrued to the venture capitalist.[18]

Soft-Budget Constraint Syndrome of the Government   Let us consider relationships most typically found between the government (government-controlled banks) and state-owned firms in mixed or transition economies. Then the rents accruing to the government from bailing-out financially distressed firms may be considered political rents made possible by social stability and political support derived from job security of the workers (Kornai 1980; Shleifer and Vishny 1994). Recently Che (2000) has proposed an interesting model that recalls this view. He argues that the soft-budget constraint, in the sense that it allows loss-making firms to be financed, may contribute to macro stability, by which sufficient labor demands may be created. Suppose that there are incentives for the suppliers of human assets to upgrade their quality and competence only when there is sufficient demand. On the other hand, some loss-making firms have incentives to restructure themselves when they find human assets of good quality. Thus generating enough demands for human assets can create externalities. The centralization of financing by the government can internalize these external economies through increased repayments of debts made possible by macro stability. However, small banks cannot do this, and they tend to remain subjected to to the short-termism syndrom. An interesting question there is: Why does the government not make direct subsidies to the human assets holders rather than soften budget constraints of loss-making firms? One consideration is that firms can monitor the quality of human assets better than the government. Firms behave like "middlemen" by making use of their screening capacity in order to make profits (or reduce losses).[19]

Government and Bank Relationships   Although the banks may play the role of relational monitors in the bank-based mechanism of relational-contingent governance, banks themselves are also firms that need to be governed (Dewatripont and Tirole 1995). When banks internalize information assets that are relation-specific to client borrowers but are not embodied in their employees in a decomposable way, an incentive problem similar to that inherent to the organization of the information-assimilation mode may arise in banks. For example, each individual bank officer may free-ride on the bank's reputation and not exercise due diligence and appropriate *ad interim* monitoring of borrowers, thus exposing their banks to excessive risks. On the one hand, the liquidation of a bank and the destruction of its nontransferable, intangible information assets may create significant diseconomies by causing a credit crunch for its healthy borrowers, since other banks may not easily step into the breach.[20] Thus the government regulatory agency may be forced to assume a role analogous to the relational monitor vis-à-vis troubled banks by infusing public funds, coordinating the organization of a rescue package by other financial institutions, and so forth. However, the implementation of such a bailing-out operation, particularly by the use of public funds, can be politically unpopular, often preventing a quick action by the government when necessary. On the other hand, if the expectation prevails that the government will not ignore the trouble of banks that are "too big to fail," this may induce moral hazard behavior on the side of banks. Thus, in this case too, the double-edged commitment problem of the relational-contingent governance manifests itself. Particularly, if the bank's soft-budgeting syndrome is systematically unresolved, the problem will result in a banking crisis from cumulative bed debts.

A major focus of the corporate governance literature has been on the ways in which a manager's action can be aligned with the interests of investors through legal provisions, incentive contract design, and the like. This approach presupposes the presence of well-functioning financial markets, or regards development in that direction as being the most desirable from the efficiency point of view. In contrast, one of the main objectives of this chapter has been to place the role of investors in corporate governance in a relative perspective. In order to make the point clear, we begin this chapter by recalling the preliminary discussion in chapter 4.3. By focusing on the organization domain without explicit consideration of its interface with the financial domain, that discussion indicated that there can be distinct governance problems, and associated solutions to them, for different types of organizational architecture.

Earlier in this chapter we introduced the linkages between the organization domain and the financial transaction domain, and between the polity and labor transaction domain when appropriate, and examined how the agents coordinate their strategic choices across these domains. We identified types of corporate governance institutions as distinct equilibrium patterns of agents' choices in the linked games. As we saw in part II, an overall equilibrium pattern, once established, would then be perceived by individual agents as a set of external constraints and become self-enforcing. Thus we defined a corporate governance institution as a set of self-enforcing constraints on the choices of the agents active in the organization domains and those linked to them: specifically, the investors, managers, and workers.

From the comparative perspective that we have adopted, a corporate governance institution is not shaped by financial markets alone. We have demonstrated this is not from an a priori normative perspective of a stakeholder society but is a result of an equilibrium analysis of linkage and complementarities existing between the organization domains and other related domains of the economy. We also suggested that there may be some circumstances in which stockholder governance is not efficient or effective. We saw that shareholder control may sometimes implement an action that reduces overall welfare and is ineffective in controlling and/or preserving context-oriented human assets.

The institutionalization of a corporate governance mechanism may be affected by the type of state prevailing in the polity domain (through institutional complementarity). In chapter 6 we characterized one essential feature of the liberal democratic state as being the subjection of the working-classes' economic demands to unregulated market discipline. This form of state is clearly complementary to owner's control, as well as stockholders' governance, which rely on the Walrasian or efficiency wage discipline to control the workers' holdup threat in hierarchical context (section 11.2). Conversely, autonomous competition in labor markets reinforces the liberal democratic state (proposition 6.1). On the other hand, as demonstrated in section 11.2, the corporatist framework of labor market regulation is complementary to the sharing of residual rights of control between the worker and the owner. We will observe in the next chapter how one type of institutionalization of the relational-contingent governance, the main bank system, was made feasible by the generation of bank rents conditional on the bank's fulfillment of implicit obligations in the relational contract.

12 Types of Relational Financing and the Value of Tacit Knowledge

The declared aim of modern science is to establish a strictly detached, objective knowledge. Any falling short of this ideal is accepted only as a temporary imperfection, which we must aim at eliminating. But suppose that tacit thought forms an indispensable part of all knowledge, then the ideal of eliminating all personal elements of knowledge would, in effect, aim at the destruction of knowledge. The ideal of exact science would turn out to be fundamentally misleading and possibly a source of devastating fallacies.
—Michael Polanyi, *The Tacit Dimension* (1966:20)

In chapter 11 we mentioned that relational-contingent governance, which has fits with the organizational architecture of the horizontal hierarchy type, may be institutionalized with banks as relational monitors. However, the banking crisis in Japan in the 1990s, as well as the currency and banking crises of other East Asian economies (Korea, Thailand, Indonesia, and Malaysia), were widely perceived as casting doubt on the viability of relational banking in the increasingly integrative and competitive financial markets. For example, analyzing the cause and nature of the East Asian crisis, Rajan and Zingales (1998) submit that relation-based financial systems work well only in places where contracts are poorly enforced and capital scarce. The relation-based financial systems ensure a return to the financier by granting him some form of power over the firm borrowing his money, but they suppress the price system and can thus greatly misallocate capital. Therefore, while there may be some short-term benefits for the crisis-inflicted East Asian economies in reverting to the relationship-based financial system, the authors argue, in the long-run they will be held back unless they have transparent disclosure, legal contract enforcement, and competition of the arm's-length type.

While agreeing with the need for more transparent, rule-based prudential regulations on banks whenever possible, we will see that there are various types of relational financing as mechanisms of information-processing cum monitoring and that one cannot dismiss relational financing in general as intrinsically inferior to, and/or needing to be replaced by, arm's-length financing. We will present a new conceptualization of relational financing, that is general enough to cover its various types, and then will examine the associated bases of knowledge and sources of economic rents for the viability of each, as well as its potential implications for economic performance. In chapters 3 and 4, we saw that trade and organization domains can be governed in a number of ways depending on their information, structural, or architectural natures. We will try and accomplish in this chapter something in the same spirit. Financial transaction domains may be governed in different ways depending on the kind of knowledge held by the financier dealing with the information asymmetry and incompleteness inherent to external financing.

We will adhere to an important premise that the economic knowledge necessary for doing new things (investment, innovation efforts, etc.), and generated by such novel efforts, often remains tacit at least in the beginning rather than codified. We refer to *codifiable* knowledge as knowledge that can be formalized in such forms as accounting numbers, written and verbal reports, and court-verifiable documents, as well as that which is gained through the analysis of their contents. This type of information on the performances and obligations of corporate firms and their financial states is increasingly available for global market arbitration. The standardization of accounting methods and the disclosure of corporate data from every corner of the global economy will certainly enhance the information efficiency of integrated global financial markets. However, the type of information that can be digitalized, and thus circulated in the open network and/or corporate information networks, is not limitless. Profit opportunities from arbitration based on universally accessible digitalized information may also be limited over time. Paradoxically, some types of *tacit* (personal) knowledge, as well as codifiable but still uncodified knowledge of the financier —we will distinguish between them below—may be potentially value-enhancing despite, or rather because of, the ever increasing circularity of digital information. *Tacit* knowledge is defined as knowledge that cannot be obtained by a mere sum of codified (digitalized) information. It can be generated through intimate "indwelling" (K. Polanyi 1966:17) within a relevant local domain, or as personal knowledge through particular experiences and/or due to inherently personal qualities and competence; therefore it cannot become immediately available in open markets.[1]

Let us mention a few examples of this paradoxical situation. The first example is drawn from a most advanced domain of financing, venture capital, to indicate that our claim is not of a development-stage-specific nature. The reason why venture capitalists tend to cluster together with entrepreneurial start-up firms in a particular locality, such as in Silicon Valley, is that in this way they can gain information necessary for selecting promising innovation projects through stage financing. Of course knowledge at the initial stage of venture capital financing is tacit and hardly articulated. The unique feature of the Silicon Valley model does not lie solely in the ability of venture capitalists to supply risk capital per se. It lies more in their ability to select evolutionarily, instead of by ex ante design, promising projects that may constitute innovative technological product systems, while rejecting financing and refinancing to technologically and commercially unpromising ones at as early a stage as possible. Knowledge and judgment based on experience, together with highly specialized technical expertise, are thus necessary for venture capital financing and governance. Their involvement in start-up firms ends when they are acquired by other established firms or offered to the public. Thus the information-processing function of the venture capitalist may be regarded as that of eventually transforming the initially tacit, unarticulated knowledge (uncertain innovation possibilities) into codified forms (buyout or acquisition contracts, prospectuses and other documents for public offerings, etc.). About half of the venture capital funds in 1996 were supplied by mutual funds, banks, and insurance companies. Since these financial firms operate primarily on digitalized information, and thus lack such experience and expertise, they need to delegate the monitoring and governance of entrepreneurial start-up firms to the venture capitalists (chapter 14).

Second, the prospect of financing for new, as well as incumbent, firms in developing and transition economies can be highly uncertain and may require the exercise of a judgment based on less standardized, unquantifiable knowledge, such as on the quality, trait, personality, and reliability of entrepreneurs and managers who seek financing, as well as the accumulation of organizational competence placed at their disposal. In the absence of developed, third-party enforcement mechanisms, contract enforcement may also need to be complemented by a reputation mechanism (personal trust) based on past conduct of entrepreneurs. A major reason why international financiers lent short to indigenous banks prior to the East Asian currency crisis was precisely because the former lacked accessibility to such local information and insured themselves by securing the flexible withdrawal of funds. However, the mismanagement of the interfaces between domestic and international money markets (foreign markets), as well as the absence of a proper governance mechanism over indigenous banks, eventually led to a currency and bank crisis of the capital-importing economy (discussed later in more detail). Blaming ex post the lack of information transparency on the borrowing countries as a sole cause of the crisis does not seem very constructive, however. The problem of the lack of information processing competence existed symmetrically on both sides of international markets.

Finally, empirical studies by Petersen and Rajan (1994), Gande et al. (1997), among others, found that there were benefits to relational financing between banks and small- and medium-sized firms, even in the United States prior to a firm's entry into the securities markets. Firms that rely on relational banking with a limited number of banks may yield monopolistic information rents to these banks, while insuring themselves for possible refinancing needs in uncontractible events (e.g., temporary financial distress). In this way they are able to mature faster than firms without relational banking and reach the stage of raising funds through securities markets based on the supply of codified information at a cheaper cost. The situation is similar to venture capital financing. It indicates that even if information about these firms ultimately becomes codifiable and transmittable through the market, until then relational banks can monopolize tacit/uncodified knowledge about them and eventually derive rents therefrom (Yasuda 2001).

Obviously it is not insightful to lump together different types of relational financing in different contexts and submit a case in favor of the relational-financing system in general. We need to carefully sort out how and under what conditions a type of relational financing may become conducive to a better use of economical uncodified knowledge, while others may not. To make an attempt in that direction, section 12.1 begins with a new, generic conceptualization of relational financing. It distinguishes among the different types of knowledge utilized by the financier. Section 12.2 is concerned with various types of economic rents afforded to relational financiers as their incentives. This amounts to examining relationships between the information structural aspect and governance aspect of relational financing. This section also examines how increasing competition in financial markets, in particular, in the development of international bond markets, affects relational financiers' rents and, accordingly, their viability.

12.1 A Generic Definition of Relational Financing and Its Knowledge-Based Taxonomy

We begin with the following new conceptualization of relational financing

Relational financing is a type of financing in which the original financier is expected to provide additional financing in a class of court-unverifiable future states in the expectation of their obtaining rents in the more distant future (Aoki and Dinç 2000).

We refer to types of financing that are not relational as *arm's-length* financing. In this definition expectations (beliefs) play important roles in a two-tier structure: first at the time of initial financing as a borrower's expectation of future contingent financing, and then as the financier's expectation of future rents at the time of refinancing. If the first-tier expectation holds, entrepreneurs or small proprietors are able to initiate development projects or expansion investments that are impossible within the constraint of their own funds or by arm's-length financing alone. Or, a firm may undertake investment in firm-specific assets (human and nonhuman) in the expectation of refinancing in the event of mild financial distress. However, these expectations need to be grounded. This is the financier's commitment problem, as initially discussed by Mayer (1988) and Hellwig (1991). This point was raised in the previous chapter specifically with respect to the relational-contingent governance mechanism. The financier's reputation concerns, his informational advantage, his market power in the future financing of the borrower, the threat of a regulatory punishment or the promise of political and economic rewards from the government, and so forth, may induce the financier to keep his commitment. If any of these is expected, then, by backward induction, the borrowers may expect a corresponding type of contingent refinancing by the financier. Therefore, in order to predict the viability and economic consequences of a relational financing institution, it is critical to understand how incentives are created so that the financier will make additional financing available in particular contingencies. When beliefs are held among financiers and borrowers in a financial transaction domain in such a way that relational financing become self-enforcing, we say that relational financing is institutionalized in that domain.

From the definitions of codified knowledge and relational financing given above, it is clear that some kind of uncodified knowledge on the side of the financier is involved. If a financial transaction can be made based solely on the codified knowledge of the financier about the borrowers, then contractual terms can be articulated ex ante in a court-verifiable manner and enforced ex post as such. Such contracts may be transacted in markets ad interim. Thus the financial contract based on codified knowledge becomes an arm's-length type. However, if a financial contract is drawn and expected to be enforced on the basis of some kind of tacit or uncodified knowledge of the financier, then it is bound to have a characteristic of relational financing. However, the ways in which uncodified knowledge is utilized have different implications. In fact the types of relational financing can be differentiated, depending on the kinds of knowledge exercised by the financier at various stages of financial decisions. For the purpose of making economically meaningful taxonomy, we therefore begin by distinguishing three stages of monitoring and the types of knowledge used therein. By monitoring, we refer to the financier's information processing regarding a borrower's plan, activity, and financial state.

We refer to the exercise of the financier's knowledge at the stage of initial financing as ex ante monitoring. This is considered as primarily dealing with possible adverse selection problems, that is, the information asymmetry existing between the financier and the borrower before actual financing regarding the riskiness of a proposed investment project, the borrower's competence, and so forth. If this kind of monitoring is based primarily on the analysis of codified information, it corresponds to what is referred to in practice as due diligence. However, the scope of ex ante monitoring may not be limited to the adverse-selection problem. There may be situations in which the possible value of a proposed project is more uncertain for a borrower. For example, the value of individual projects may depend on a parallel presence of mutually complementary projects. In this kind of situation, a financier who can bundle the financing of complementary projects will have a greater informational advantage than individual borrowers, yet his or her knowledge may not be made completely codified (digitalized) because of the absence of markets that can assess the synergy effects of those interdependent projects.

Corresponding to our definition of relational financing, let us next focus on the use of knowledge by the financier in making a judgment on whether a court-unverifiable state which calls for refinancing has actually occurred and, if so, how the refinancing is to be done. Evidently this requires the deployment of uncodified knowledge (otherwise, refinancing could have been made in an arm's-length fashion). We call this stage of information processing ex post monitoring. We refer to information processing by the relational financier in between as ad interim monitoring. It contributes to the accumulation of the financier's knowledge regarding the borrower and his/her ongoing projects, tacit or potentially codifable. Then relational financing may be also characterized as the integrative bundling of the three stages of monitoring and the complementary use of knowledge across them. In contract, if we conceptualize ex post monitoring within the framework of arm's-length financing as the execution of a term of court-enforceable contracts then the arm's-length financing may be characterized as the type of financing in which three stages of monitoring are dispersed among different agents, depending on specialized, codified knowledge (e.g., ex ante monitoring may be carried by investment banks who underwrites new bond issues, ad interim monitoring by security analysts who rate marketed securities, and ex post monitoring by the bankruptcy court, reorganization specialists).

Next, let us proceed to the classification of knowledge used by financiers in financial transaction domains. For that purpose, we use the taxonomic framework represented by figure 12.1. The vertical dimension refers to whether knowledge might or might not in principle be presentable or storable in codified forms, such as accounting numbers, court-enforceable contracts, prospectuses for potential investors, or borrower's credit records. On the other hand, the horizontal dimension refers to the degree in which

	manifest	latent
codifiable	arm's-length, VC at IPO stage	relational contingent monitor: ex post, "crony" financing; ex ante, ex post
tacit	relational: ex ante VC: interim/ex post	[VC: ex ante]

Figure 12.1
Types of knowledge and financing

knowledge appears manifest or latent. The latter case may occur either because knowledge is in principle codifiable but making it explicitly codified and shared in a domain is privately costly (relative to its benefit) to a financier (as in the northeast cell), or because doing so is intrinsically hard (as in the southeast cell). The latter case arises when knowledge generated and used is highly tacit, and a personal judgment based on intuition, immediate apprehension, and so forth, is involved. This taxonomic framework is borrowed from an insightful work by Cowan, David, and Foray (2000) but departs from theirs in the use of "tacitness," which is much closer to the one originally developed by M. Polanyi (1958, 1966), and in differentiating between tacit knowledge and codifiable but uncodified knowledge (the northeast cell).[2]

Using this taxonomic framework, let us identify the information-structural characteristics of representative types of relational financing. Consider first venture capital (VC) financing. Its ex ante monitoring is characterized as a "tacit-latent" case when a highly uncertain, innovative project is the object of possible financing. Namely, when the venture capitalist or the so-called angel initially chooses start-up firms for initial funding (seed financing), the potential values of the proposed innovation projects might be highly uncertain, so their financial decisions may be based on personal and intuitive judgment on the personal quality of the entrepreneurs as well as the nature of the projects.[3] Refinancing in the court-unverifiable state corresponds to the successive stage financing contingent on the progress of developmental projects pursued by the entrepreneur. Thus knowledge accumulated through and used in, succeeding financing stages would become progressively articulated, although it would remain largely tacit. Only when a successful entrepreneurial firm is offered to the public or is about to be acquired by an established firm, can a deal be made primarily on the basis of codified knowledge, such as prospectuses for public offering or disclosure schedules attached to buyout (acquisition) contracts. Thus venture capitalist "staged financing" (Sahlman 1990) follows first from the eastsouth corner in a westward course and then a northern course to the northwest corner.

Next, consider a financier engaged in the relational-contingent governance of a firm. Refinancing by a bank to a client firm when the latter is in temporary need for additional financing may sometimes be explicitly codified, as in the case of credit-line contracting. But if a relational-contingent governance contract with a bank is written in an implicit manner, knowledge accumulated up to, and used during, ex post monitoring (e.g., bailing-out of a financially distressed firm) may remain uncodified (at least to outsiders), even though it may in principle be codifiable. One potential merit of this could be that the potential financial problems of a firm can be discovered by the bank at an earlier stage, and thus a costly bankruptcy may be avoided (Sheard

1994; Aoki et al. 1994). On the other hand, to control the possible soft budget constraint tendency of relational banks, an expectation must be held that they themselves will not be compensated by a third party (e.g., the government) for its adverse consequences. However, if this expectation does not hold (e.g., "crony capitalism"), allowing the relational bank to hold information in an uncodified manner can induce their moral hazard behavior (e.g., an excess soft budget constraint tendency, shirking of ex ante and ad interim monitoring of borrowers). The conventional argument against relational banking and the associated argument for the need for "transparency" of information involve such cases (e.g., Rajan and Zingales, 1998).

However, there are cases where knowledge may not be entirely codifiable. As said, in the development stage or transitional phase of the economy as well, markets may not be mature enough to yield a prospect for the profitability and riskiness of a proposed project in the form of objective knowledge (e.g., market analysis, engineering feasibility analysis) as much as that of tacit knowledge regarding the personal ability, quality, and integrity of individual entrepreneurs and/or the organizational competence of firms that pursued the proposed projects. Also the ex ante monitoring of small firms prior to their entries into financial markets in advanced economies may involve tacit knowledge. This kind of knowledge may be manifest to a competent financier who can closely observe a borrower, but it may not be easily available to others. Therefore, just as the venture capitalist, when needs for refinancing occur, the initial financier may be in a better position to promptly judge what and how to accomplish this. This is when tacit knowledge can be potentially valuable. However, whether or not such knowledge can be properly used to yield real economic values depends on the incentives provided to relational financiers, to which we now turn to.

12.2 The Institutional Viability of Relational Financing

Types of Relational Financier's Rents[4]

Let us now turn to the various sources of relational financier's rents that can serve as incentives. As already indicated, these rents are closely related by the ways in which relational financing is governed and institutionalized in a financial transaction domain. They can be roughly grouped into the following four classes: (1) The *monopoly rents* that a financier can extract from the firm that he refinances through his advantageous position vis-à-vis other financiers, (2) the *policy-induced rent* that a financier can extract through some kind of government intervention in the domain in exchange for its implicit obligation to relational financing, (3) the *reputation rent* that a financier can extract by building a reputation for commitment to relational contingent governance, and (4) the *information rents* that a relational financier can gain from the firm through the production of economically valuable knowledge that is not immediately available to others. As we will see shortly, these groups are not always clearly distinguishable, though we conceptualize them separately for discussion purposes.

Market Power and Monopoly Rents If the financier has market power, he can expect to earn a positive net return from financing. This may allow him to smooth financing costs over time, which in turn may provide him with incentives to undertake financing in less favorable situations and receive compensation in the long run.

In this category of relational financing, there can be different subtypes, depending on the development stage of the economy. The simplest example is the one in which the financier owns the firm. In other cases banks may collude not to interfere in each other's business territories. This collusive behavior will be reinforced by the government that restricts entry into the banking sector. In these cases banks may have uncodified knowledge about firms that is not available to outsiders, but there is no guarantee that such knowledge is utilized for sound ex ante monitoring (i.e., for new investment decisions) as well as for ex post monitoring (i.e., for refinancing decisions). For example, the bank's market power may sometimes lead to the bailing out of financially distressed firms that have undertaken inefficient projects ex ante but are profitable to bail out ex post—"the soft budget constraint problem" à la Dewatripont and Maskin (1995).

Relational financing can also be created when a firm owns a bank (or nonbank), or a holding company owns both bank and firms. In this case rents expected by refinancing accrue to the owner firm or the holding company. Some economists reserve the word "relational financing" (or more crudely "crony capitalism") only for the mechanism in which banks are captured by politically influential industrial and commercial interests and serve as instruments for collecting household savings, as well as drawing in government funds and channeling them to the controlling interests. In this mechanism the banks' autonomous monitoring roles will be compromised and the soft budget-constraint syndrome can become uncontrollable. Thus there ought to be little controversy over the regulatory need for restricting lending by banks (or nonbanks) to controlling interests.

Even though collusive behavior by banks is restrained and government intervention is minimal, the bank's informational advantage over outside lenders may endogenously provide it with market power. After the initial financing is offered, the financier often gains access to information about the firm that other financiers do not have. This informational advantage gives him rent opportunities, in which the nature of the rents is somewhat difficult to distinguish from the fourth category to discussed below. The possibility of these rents may induce him to monitor the firm to obtain better information (e.g., von Thadden 1995), and allow him to provide financing to the firm even in situations in which other (outside) financiers are not willing to lend.

The Japanese main banks had monopolistic ties with client firms through mutual stock holdings in their heyday (1950–1975) and enjoyed an important informational advantage through the semiexclusive management of the latter's payment settlement accounts and directorate holdings. Through these channels, the main bank was able to observe the financial state of a client firm as if it could open the latter's books at any time. Thus it was able to find the potential financial problems of client firms at an earlier stage and intervene their management, à la relational-contingent governance mechanism. Similarly it is observed that lending relationships between American banks and small firms help alleviate the liquidity constraints of the firms. This effect is stronger, the smaller is the number of banks with which the firm maintains a relationship, and the higher is the number of additional financial services it obtains from the same bank (see Petersen and Rajan 1994; Berger and Udell 1995). Information monopolies in these cases may not always be beneficial to the borrower, however. The possibility of losing the project's surplus to the relational financier may negatively affect the firm's ex ante incentives to invest (Sharpe 1990; Rajan 1992).

By assuming that a bank's market power decreases as the number of banks increases, Petersen and Rajan (1995) show that intertemporal smoothing by banks becomes more difficult as the number of banks increases. Since decreasing market power means a decreasing share of the project's surplus for the bank, banks are less willing to take actions for which they can be compensated only by sharing the future surplus with other financiers. The authors supply empirical evidence on bank lending to small firms in the United States that supports this theoretical result. When the principal incentive of the relational financier is rents from its inherent informational advantages, however, an increase in competition may not necessarily have a strong adverse effect on relational financing. Rajan (1992) shows that such rents depend on the number of financiers from whom a firm chooses to borrow, not on the number of outside financiers that an inside financier faces after they establish a relationship with a borrower. Hence, by limiting the number of financiers at the initial financing stage, a firm may sustain a relational financing arrangement even if the financiers face increasing competition ex ante. On the other hand, by increasing the number of relational financiers, a firm can mitigate the financier's ability to control the firm and extract higher rents.[5]

Policy-Induced Rents and Pseudorents   As suggested above, the government can create bank rents by restraining competition among banks in the lending markets.

However, even if competitive lending prevails, the government may still be able to create bank rents by intervening on the liability side of banks. We discuss such possibilities for two cases: one in the economy with an insulated domestic banking sector and the other in the economy open to international lending markets.

Financial Restraint and Policy-Induced Contingent Rents   Hellmann, Murdock, and Stiglitz (1997, 1998) introduced the concept of policy-induced contingent rents, largely inspired by the East Asian development experiences in its Miracle phase. They argued that the government can regulate the deposit rate to be at a level lower than the Walrasian rate. If this policy is combined with stable macroeconomic policy, the real rate can be maintained at a positive level. They call this government intervention "financial restraint," as distinct from "financial repression." In the latter, the real deposit rate becomes negative due to a high inflation rate, and transfer of wealth occurs from the household sector to the government. The rent created through such a mechanism will become the target of unproductive rent-seeking behavior by interest groups. In contrast, they argue, financial restraint only creates "rent opportunities" for the banking sector, whose realization is contingent on the competitive efforts of individual banks to mobilize deposits. An analogy can be drawn with the patent system, which can create "rent opportunities" for would-be inventors but allows their realization to be contingent only on a successful invention and its commercialization.

They argue that the realization of policy-induced contingent rents can provide "franchise value" for licensed banks, whose productive uses may include the expansion of bank branches to capture more deposits. If the saving propensity of the household sector is inelastic to the interest rate, and if in response to the bank's efforts households hold more of their assets in the form of deposits rather than in unproductive forms (cash in a bedroom chest, gold, etc.), financial deepening will occur and the welfare loss from price distortion may be minimized. In Japan the capture of policy-induced contingent rents by individual banks in the heyday of the main bank system was conditional on their compliance with government policy, since the monetary authority controlled branch licensing as an effective instrument with which to punish noncompliant banks (Aoki et al. 1994). It is clear that government preferences included lending to growing firms, as well as the rescue of financially distressed firms by their main banks, to avoid social and economic instability. However, note that the government did not intervene directly in the financing decisions of banks.

The mechanism of financial restraint is seen to be isomorphic to the mechanism of the market-enhancing, developmental state formulated in chapter 6.2 if we substitute the depositors and the banks for the agricultural sector and the industrialists in that model respectively. The two mechanisms are identical in that the government transfers financial resources from one group (through deposit-rate regulation in the present context) and distributes them to the members of the other groups according to the latter's growth-enhancing performance (the deposit collection and relational-contingent governance of client firms in the present context). The depositors are partially compensated ex post by the security of deposits. On the other hand, since the banks were able to derive policy-induced contingent rents, they may have required a lower rate of returns from firms (also under the implicit pressure of the government) than under unregulated financial markets. This has an effort-enhancing effect on firms through the mechanism of relational-contingent governance, because a greater share of profits remain with firms.[6] Thus we may claim,

PROPOSITION 12.1   The developmental state is institutionally complementary to the *bank-based* relational-contingent governance.

Policies to control the deposit rate directly or indirectly become difficult to maintain with the global integration of financial markets. Once regulation of the deposit rate is removed, the source of policy-induced, contingent rents disappears.

Unhedged International Borrowing and Government Loan Guarantee   The possibility of international borrowing and the implicit government guarantee of bank borrowing may create the (unfounded) expectation of rents among banks under the condition of misalignment of the foreign exchange rate. The "overborrowing syndrome" (McKinnon and Pill 1999) of the East Asian economies (Korea, Thailand, Malaysia, and Indonesia) that resulted in their currency crises in 1997 was the result of such an expectation.[7]

Imagine an economy with a domestic deposit rate i that is higher than the deposit rate of the same maturity in U.S. dollars, i^*. If there are no barriers to international financial flows and no domestic deposit rate control, competitive market arbitrages will lead the nominal interest-rate differential to be equal to the forward exchange-rate premium f, so that $i = i^* + f$. If this condition holds in markets (otherwise, market arbitragers can make unbounded profits without any risk) the position of any individual bank accepting dollar deposits and hedging in the forward market will be equivalent to borrowing in domestic currency. Therefore, if banks are required to hedge all their foreign exchange borrowing in the forward market, there would be no incentives for them to "overborrow" from international markets.

Suppose, however, that there is an expectation among banks that bank deposits are implicitly guaranteed by the government. This expectation alone would induce the moral hazard behavior of banks that underestimate downside bankruptcy risks.

Suppose further that the regulatory agency does not impose the 100 percent hedging requirement on domestic banks. The interest rate spread, $i - i^*$, is then explained as the risk premium formed through the interactive estimates by market makers on foreign exchange risk. But this spread may provide incentives for some banks to ignore the risk of bankruptcy and currency devaluation. "Therefore, moral hazard could lead banks to take unhedged foreign exchange positions, borrowing foreign currency to on-lend to domestic residents at much higher interest rates in domestic currency, while implicitly transferring most of the currency risk incurred onto the government through the deposit insurance scheme" (McKinnon and Pill, ibid.). The expectation of the 100 percent deposit guarantee itself may be further backed by the expectation of a bail-out by international organizations such as the IMF and foreign governments in the event of a currency crisis. Competitive pressures in domestic credit markets would force even traditionally prudent banks to pursue the riskier unhedged strategy, which creates a domestic boom.

The boom in investment increases demands for nontradable input such as labor. The government may try to keep the exchange rate fixed to cope with increasing inflationary pressure on consumption goods. However, an eventual arrival of a downside productivity shock is inevitable. Accordingly, as some episodes of bankruptcy trigger the sentiment in international markets that the boom is almost over, foreign lenders start to call in loans and a downward adjustment in the foreign exchange rate becomes unavoidable. Speculative attacks around this time may amplify the magnitude of foreign exchange adjustment. The banks suffer not only from huge capital losses due to their unhedged foreign exchange exposure but also from the defaults of their domestic borrowers. The banks are forced to squeeze lending and the credit crunch even lets healthy projects collapse.

A consensus that was quickly forged within the international financial circle immediately after the crisis was to pinpoint the sources of the crisis in the misalignment of foreign exchange rates and nontransparent banking practices in borrowing economies. The associated policy reform prescriptions were the adoption of a flexible exchange rate regime, greater supervision and transparency in local financial markets, and stricter enforcement of contracts. Relational banking was thought to be the essential glue of opaque, inefficient, unfair "crony capitalism," and the superiority of the Anglo-American, arm's-length, financial system was triumphantly declared by some.

However, resorting to a flexible exchange rate regime is not a cure-all medicine. The choice of a foreign exchange regime should be judged by its ability to limit a bank's incentive for overborrowing, since an exchange rate regime cannot obviate the need for the prudential regulation of domestic banks against undue risk-taking.[8] The crucial question remains as to how the development of a sound financial system less prone to moral hazard banking behavior can be facilitated in economies during intermediate financial development. The need for well-articulated prudential regulations on banking, such as on substantial capital reserve requirements, may be less controversial as a general principle.[9] However, the processing of tacit knowledge unique to maturity transformation services in those economies may remain an essential ingredient, if not an exclusive one, of a transition system. Thus an attempt to make a wholesale transition to an arm's-length financial system once-and-for-all may be too simple-minded.

Since it is difficult to enforce a sufficient hedging requirement on banks in these economies, some measures to control the flows of short-term capital into these economies may be warranted to insulate domestic banks from volatile short-term capital movement and provide them with the time to develop the skills conducive to risk management and maturity transformation at the international interface. For example, the imposition of a fixed-term, unremunerated reserve requirement was successfully imposed in Chile in 1991 on all foreign inflows that did not increase the stock of physical capital, and its practice has been extensively studied. Such capital controls can be counterbalanced by allowing competition from a limited number of foreign banks in domestic markets, which contributes to the transfer of skills and the technology of banking, as well as infusing them with indigenous customs and local tacit knowledge.[10]

Insurance Premiums and Reputation Rents   One of the incentives commonly found in enforcing a financier's commitments to repeated transactions is his concern for reputation. If the future returns to a financier are conditional on his maintaining a good reputation, this may induce him to take costly actions in court-unverifiable states to protect its reputation (Sharpe 1990; Boot et al. 1993; Aoki 1994; Dinç 1997a). For example, a bank can be induced to keep its commitment to provide rescue credits to a distressed borrower if failing to do so would tarnish its reputation and cause it to lose profitable future loan opportunities. In fact these future financing opportunities need not be limited to the same borrower, but may be entertained by other borrowers. The bank only needs to bundle lending with a bailing-out commitment over periods.

Following Dinç (2000), let us consider a game in a financial transaction domain in which the players are risk-neutral firms, each having a two-period project, and banks. Each firm's project requires one unit of a bank loan at date 0 (we consider the possibility of bond financing later) and returns are obtained at date 2. In order to focus on the bank's commitment problem, we do not explicitly consider whether or not firms live beyond date 2. At date 1, the project can be observed to be at one of three states: success, distress, or failure, with respective probabilities p_S, p_D and

$1 - p_S - p_D$. If the state is success, the project is known to yield a cash flow Π_s to the firm. In failure, returns are zero. In distress the returns are the same as for failure unless the firm is financed by the bank at date 1 with one more unit of a rescue loan. If bailed out, cash returns are Π_D at date 2. In addition, non-transferable returns N_D accrue to the insiders of the firm. It is assumed that the bailing-out operation is not profitable for the bank even if it is able to capture all the cash returns Π_D (i.e., $\Pi_D < 1$), although it is socially efficient (i.e., $\Pi_D + N_D > 1$). Let the net rescue cost be $C_D = 1 - \Pi_D > 0$. Assume that the project is ex ante profitable at date 0 (i.e., $p_S \Pi_S - p_D C_D > 1$).

Suppose for a moment that according as the uncertainty about the project's state is revealed at date 1, it is publicly observable but not court-unverifiable, so enforceable loan contracts cannot be written contingent on this state. Then, if this game is played only once between a firm and a bank, there cannot be any equilibrium in which the bank bails out the firm in distress at date 1. Let us assume instead that the banks live forever and engage in repeated lending to the same or different firms. Let us consider the following strategy profiles for banks and firms: if a bank does not bail out a firm in distress, it loses its reputation, and no future firm will take a loan with the promise of bail-out from such a bank. If any firm borrows from such a bank, then the bank will not bail out the firm if it is in distress. Banks with no reputation can earn the rate ρ from riskless lending. Suppose, however, that banks with good reputations can lend to firms, with the promise of a rescue in the event of distress, in exchange for a premium return R^G in the event of the project's success. For the moment the rate R^G is taken as given. In order for a bank with a good reputation to be able to commit to rescue, it is necessary that a one-time deviation is not profitable. This condition is given by

$$\frac{\delta}{1-\delta}[p_S R^G - p_D C_D] - C_D \geq \frac{\delta}{1-\delta}\rho$$

where the left-hand side represents the present value of future returns from sustaining a reputation net of the current rescue costs and the right-hand side represents the present value of future returns if the reputation is lost. Firms prefer to borrow from banks with a good reputation, as long as the competitive rate without commitment ρ is greater than $p_S R^G - p_D N_D$. Deviant banks have no incentive to rescue, because once they have shirked no firm will borrow from them for a rate greater than ρ. The inequality above is rewritten as

$$\delta \geq \frac{C_D}{(p_S R^G - \rho) + (1 - p_D)C_D} \tag{RF}$$

The right-hand side defines the minimum discount factor that can make a bank's commitment to bailing out self-enforceable. This factor declines with the reputation rent defined as $p_S R^G - p_D C_D - \rho$.

We have so far treated the premium rate R^G as given. Dinç (2000) derived the rate R^G as a function of the number of competing banks that are capable of screening the creditworthiness of projects and deduced the following important implication.[11] When the number of banks is less than the minimum number, the banks only make loans without commitment because they can extract high monopoly rents from firms in this case. On the other hand, if the number of banks is very large, the right-hand side of the inequality above approaches one, implying that it becomes increasingly difficult to sustain the reputation mechanism. Thus, given a discount factor of less than one, a relational financing institution is only feasible when the number of competing banks with a commitment to rescue is neither too large nor too small (see also Aoki 1994). From the view point of the firm, $p_s R^G - p_D N_D - \rho$ may be interpreted as an insurance premium for bailing out the relational financier in the event of financial distress. Thus collecting reputation rents as insurance premiums paid by firms may be a way to resolve the downside commitment problem of the relational monitor-cum-financier discussed in the previous chapter: the short-termism syndrome.

So far we have assumed that the interim state is publicly observable, although not court-verifiable. Instead, consider the case where the state can be observed by the initial lending bank only and that knowledge can remain as its tacit knowledge. The effectiveness of a reputation mechanism may be undermined by information asymmetries. For example, if other firms cannot observe whether a firm's distress is only temporary or liquidation is a better option, the bank's concern to keep its reputation may lead to the bailing out of firms that are no longer economically viable, causing the soft budget constraint syndrome. Particularly, when such banking behavior is systematically supported by the general belief that the government will exogenously guarantee banks' rents by some means, the banks will fail to effectively perform the function of a relational monitor in the contingent governance.

At first sight it may appear that declining reputation rents due to increasing competition from bond markets will necessarily diminish the viability of a relational banking institution. However, Dinç (2000) showed that there are cases in which an increase in competition may actually enhance the effectiveness of the reputation mechanism relative to arm's-length-financing. This can be seen by examining the derived (RF) inequality above where the minimum discount factor that can make a rescue operation by banks self-enforceable declines with $p_s R^G - \rho$. Even though increasing competition from the bond markets may decrease a bank's return from relational financing R^G, it may decrease its "outside option" even more—the return ρ from the arm's-length loans to which the bank will have to retreat if it does not maintain a good reputation. In particular, because bonds are a closer substitute for arm's-length loans than for loans with a relational commitment to bail out, the disincentive impacts of new competition from bond markets on relational banking may not be as large as those on arm's-length banking. In fact there can be an equilibrium in which "mild" competition from bond markets will enhance the value of relational banking relative to arm's-length banking. However, there can be multiple equilibria. Depending on the technological parameter values, even the feasibility of relational banking could completely disappear because of competition from bond markets.[12]

Summarizing, we have

PROPOSITION 12.2 (Dinç)   The relational-contingent governance mechanisms in the organizational domains may be institutionalized by being embedded in the bundling of relational financing by neither a too large nor too small number of banks in the financial transaction domain. The moderate competition from the bond market may not necessarily make the relational banking institution unsustainanble.

Information Rents   As we have discussed above the financier often gains access to information about the borrowing firm that other financiers do not have after the initial financing is made. Thus it is sometimes difficult to distinguish the monopoly rents and the information rents that are returns to the knowledge stock of the financier. However, there are situations in which economic values are created by the unique tacit knowledge of the financier at the ex ante stage of monitoring (i.e., at the initial financing stage) as well. We can think of at least two such situations. In the first, economic values are initially created by the "entrepreneurial" ability of a financier to intuitively grasp the possibility of a new economic opportunity.[13] For example, even though the separate projects proposed by different firms or entrepreneurs happen to be technologically complementary and potentially constitute a new product-system, this prospect may not be fully appreciated to any one of them. A financier who has a broad systemic perspective may be able to form better assessments and more realistic expectations that may not be completely represented in a codified form. For example, when there are technological complementarities, there can be multiple equilibria. A well-informed financier may have some notion of the future trajectory to one of those equilibria, but still be unable to define it precisely, because there is no future market simulating it. Earlier we saw that venture capital financing starts in this way. At first sight, venture capital financing may appear as in merely risk-taking financing. However, the venture capitalist at the formative stage was unique in his or her intuitive ability to foresee new technological opportunities—an ability somewhat analogous to that of intuitively grasping the direction of a new scientific discovery. As noted already, the potential value created by the entrepreneurial financier may ultimately be realized only if his or her tacit knowledge is eventually codified and transmitted to financial markets. But if there were no financing based on initial tacit knowledge, such a value would not have been possible in first place.

Another type of tacit knowledge that is useful at the ex ante monitoring stage is what a financier has learned regarding the competence of an entrepreneur or a relatively unknown firm through his or her interaction with the latter in some context. Such knowledge can be highly complementary to codified information, as represented in a project proposal, but the knowledge itself may not be effectively transmittable in a codified form. A financier who has this kind of personal knowledge can initiate financing and reap economic rents afterward by maintaining an interactive relationship with the initial borrower until he or she is ready for market financing.

In these cases, economic returns to financiers who have the tacit knowledge may take the form of capital gains from initial and subsequent investment financing, underwriting fees from security issues at later stage, new lending opportunities that initial financing created through spillover effects, and so on. Although rents are generated by the information assets of financiers, the rents ought to be differentiated from the returns to the abilities of investment banks, hedge funds, fund mangers, and the like, that process and analyze digitalized information transmittable through cyberspace. These abilities are becoming highly relevant to returns to individual portfolio investment in the age of the digital revolution. However, apart from the economic values derived from better risk management, the information processing of digitalized knowledge cannot generate economic values of its own. As the efficient market hypothesis implies, this could become paradoxically even more true as more information becomes digitalized and available to everyone. The fetish of "transparency," that is, the ideal of eliminating all personal elements of economic knowledge, is thus "fundamentally misleading" in the finance domain, as Polanyi said regarding scientific knowledge.

We have discussed various sources of rents to financiers who engage in relational financing. However, an actual institution of relational financing need not be reliant on a single source. In other words, these rents need not be mutually exclusive. The possibility that the sources of the rents acquired by a relational financier may be manifold suggests that a relational financing institution can change, adapting the composition of rents in response to the changing environment in a path-dependent manner. On the other hand, when it fails to do so, its viability may become frail.

The Path-Dependency of the Institutional Responses to the Global Integration of Financial Markets

Let us compare the situation where lending with a bailing-out commitment prevails as the relational banking institution with the situation where the opposite is the case; that is, the static Nash equilibrium prevails as the arm's-length banking institution. If the parameter values of the game satisfy the feasibility condition for relational banking as represented by the (RF) in equality above, both the arm's-length and the relational banking institutions can be (separate) equilibria and thus be self-enforcing. We have not yet discussed the selection of equilibria. Following Dinç (1996), we consider this problem by distinguishing two types of banks that differ in their ad interim monitoring capabilities: informed banks (I-banks) and uninformed banks (U-banks). The I-banks can monitor the true state of a project at date 1 at some cost, while U-banks cannot differentiate between the states of distress and failure or does not make effort to do so. A bank's type is private information, but there is a common prior belief that the probability of a bank being of type U is η_0. Before their types are revealed, both types of banks may promise to rescue so that they can charge a higher rate. As a bank's type is not initially observable by firms, so the rate a bank can initially request depends on the borrower's beliefs about the bank's type.

Over time U-banks, which do not engage in monitoring, incur liquidation ex post with higher frequencies, and this is observable by the public. Therefore the less frequently a bank liquidates troubled firms, the higher the posterior probability that it is of the I-type. Then firms may be willing to borrow from that bank, even with a higher premium rate, in the expectation of being rescued in the event of distress. Therefore, if the prior probability of a bank being of the I-type exceeds a certain threshold point, that bank has an incentive to build a reputation and engage in relational banking with a bailing-out commitment. However, the premium rate the I-bank can demand from firms may decline due to competition from the bond markets. As discussed above, developed bond markets may even inhibit the feasibility of relational banking altogether.

Suppose then that in one economy, say the R-economy, bond issues by firms were regulated so that a relational banking institution has evolved, while in the other economy, say the A-economy, bond markets are fully developed so that arm's-length financing prevails. Now suppose that the financial markets of the two economies are integrated in a big bang manner, so that firms in the R-economy can now issue bonds. All the technological conditions are the same for both economies after integration except for the reputation of banks, namely the history of financial institutions. In the R-economy a certain number of I-banks have revealed their types, while in the A-economy none have done so. What will happen to the relational banking institution in the R-economy after the shock of integration?

If the values of technological parameters are such that lending with a bailing-out commitment is not possible with the presence of a bond market, then relational banking will disappear. However, if the reason why relational banking had not evolved in the A-economy was that reputation-building costs are too high in the presence of developed bond markets—meaning that the interest rate that I-banks could charge in the reputation-building process was not high enough relative to bailing-out costs—then the story will be different, because I-banks that have revealed their type in the R-economy have already sunk these costs and thus may be able to survive. "Building" a reputation is more costly than "maintaining" one. Hence, even if new financiers do not have incentives to build a reputation after integration, those financiers who have already built their reputations may have incentives to continue relational banking. Dinç (1996) formalizes this idea and proved the following:

PROPOSITION 12.3 (Dinç) Suppose that relational banking has already emerged in the R-economy without developed bond markets, but not in the A-economy which has developed bond markets. After a big-bang financial integration of the two economies, one of the following two cases may be possible:

Case 1 (Convergence). If relational banking is not feasible with developed bond markets, the relational banking institution of the R-economy disappears after integration.

Case 2 (Path dependence). If reputation-building costs for relational financing were low enough in the absence of developed bond markets, relationship banking may continue to survive in the R-economy after integration. But borrowers start raising funds by issuing bonds as well and the profit of banks decrease.

This result has important implications for the evolution of financial institutions. It indicates that if two economies start with different regulations on banking entry and bond issues, and if these regulations remain in place long enough, not only will the type of financial institution be different in each economy initially, but these differences will survive deregulation. The path-dependency of the second case suggests that restrictions on competition in the bond market may be necessary for the emergence of relational banking, but these restrictions need not remain in place once relational banking is institutionalized (return to proposition 5.2 in chapter 5 for a similar result). However, this argument does not deny the possibility that the number of viable relational financiers becomes smaller under increasing competition through merger or exits. Nor does it preclude the possibility that relational financiers need to shift the source of reliable rents.

As already noted, reliance on policy-induced contingent rents and monopoly rents can become increasingly untenable under competition. However, if relational financiers have unique capability to process tacit knowledge about borrowers and their projects, they will maintain their stakes in the expectations of realizing information rents in the future (capital gains, premiums on underwriting fees, insurance premiums, etc.). Such relationships with relational financiers allow young firms to initiate marketable securities issues earlier than they otherwise could. By these and possibly other information reasons, competition does not necessarily wipe out relational banking. Relational financiers may fail to remain viable, however, if they rely on types of rents that are not sustainable under competition. In the next chapter we will examine a case where a once-reputable relational financing institution encounters a crisis in failing to adapt its knowledge base in a changing environment.

13 Institutional Complementarities, Co-emergence, and Crisis: The Case of the Japanese Main Bank System

[I]t is likely that the dilemma of bureaupluralism will persist for some time to come. It might be that the LDP-bureaucracy alliance will retain its role as quasi agent of benefit recipients, backward groups, and those in a declining economic sector, while limiting itself gradually to a laissez-faire policy-making role in the jurisdiction where private entrepreneurial initiatives are active. Ultimately, however, such a move would not resolve the dilemma. Whether the tension created by the dilemma will give rise to stagnant, inactive conservatism that could pose a threat to efficiency, fairness, political stability, and international harmony, or whether the Japanese polity will continue maneuvering to meet political exigencies and eventualy arrive at some kind of solution that is consistent and harmonious with pluralism and the future international environment remains to be seen.
—Masahiko Aoki, *Information, Incentives and Bargaining in the Japanese Economy* (1988:297)

In part II we proposed an equilibrium-based conceptualization of institutions and provided a theoretical framework for analyzing synchronic, as well as diachronic, interdependencies of institutions in the economy. In the preceding two chapters, using that framework, we identify the multiple institutions that may arise on the domains of corporate governance and finance through synchronic complementarities. In this chapter we turn to a case study of diachronic institutional complementarities surrounding a particular financing institution and try to narrate a parable of its emergence, sustenance, and crisis. The institution we address ourselves to is an important example of relational financing: the Japanese main bank system.

The Japanese main bank system provides an interesting case of institutional evolution in many respects. First of all, almost all people in Japan had some rough idea about what the main bank meant and what their roles were. However, there was no statutory law nor explicit contract that defined or articulated the contents of the system and obligations of the agents involved. In that sense the main bank may be considered a quintessential example of institutions conceptualized as a self-sustaining system of shared beliefs. In section 13.1 we make explicit what those beliefs were. Although the Japanese main bank system as an objective mechanism of financing started to lose its vigor in the mid-1970s and exhibit various symptoms of unfitness with evolving international and technological environments since then, its crisis did not manifest itself until the 1990s and its demise as a system of shared beliefs until the end of that decade.

Second, the main bank system provides an interesting case for the emergence of an institution. In chapter 10.3 we submitted that even though the object of an implemented policy is to create a certain institution in a certain domain, if there is no accumulation of competence supporting the policy objective in the relevant domains and/or if complementary institutions do not exist nor co-emerge, the intention of the government cannot be fulfilled. We illustrated this proposition with the recent attempt in Russia to create a market-oriented corporate governance. The outcome was rather the unintended emergence of the so-called virtual economy (example 10.9). Similarly we may conjecture that even though the object of an implemented policy is to create a certain institution in a certain domain, if a new type of competence (human assets) started to accumulate in a complementary domain, interactions between the domains may eventually lead to the spontaneous co-evolution of institutional arrangements that was not intended. The main bank system provides a splendid example of this. Many scholars submitted that the main bank system originated in the policy of the wartime government. The direct intention of the government was unambiguously to strengthen its centralized control of the economy. That intention failed with the Japanese defeat in the war. But why, after postwar democratic reforms, did the main bank system emerge from the ashes of a corrupt organizational design introduced by the wartime government? Here we need to examine the intricate workings of spontaneous diachronic complementaries between the financing and political-economy domains, on one hand, and private organization domains, on the other. We do this in section 13.2 by piecing together some of the analytical results that we have obtained so far with respect to those domains in isolation (chapters 4, 6, 10, 11, and 12) and casting them in a dynamic context.

Third, the examination of the later main bank system reveals a robustness of institutional arrangement. It is an exemplary case where the success of an institutional arrangement in promoting economic development breeds the seed of its internal inconsistency, and changing technological and international environments aggravate the problem, yet the institution persists because of the mind-set of the people. As we conjectured in chapter 9, in order for a process of earnest institutional change to be triggered, a large crisis of shared beliefs must be perceived by the people. In popular discourses, sources of the persistent dismal state of the Japanese economy in the 1990s has been attributed to government's mistakes in macroeconomic policy, over-regulations of powerful bureaucrats, incompetence of political leadership, and the like. Section 13.3 contends that the situation was not that simple. In Japan the situation rather signifies a more fundamental need for the re-alignment of extant institutional arrangements. It may be regarded that at the turn of the twenty-first century, this need has come to be widely perceived by the public. However, it by no means implies that the direction of change is clear and agreed. The transition process characterized by evolutionary selection from many competing agenda is still under way, and we do not yet know how long it will continue and what its final outcome will look like. As we will see below, there are reasons why this process is slow and gradual.

13.1   The Main Bank System as a System of Shared Beliefs

To attempt to unravel the institutional dynamics of the Japanese main bank system, we need a logical benchmark. We seek it in a model of synchronic institutional arrangements in financial transactions and its complementary domains that reflect the stylized facts prevailing in the heyday of the main bank system—the period between the mid-1950s and the mid-1970s.[1] This model is presented below and shows the analytical results obtained so far. As such it captures a set of stable beliefs collectively held by the agents in those domains under a certain class of environments and thus govern their strategic interactions therein in a self-enforcing manner. It is essentially a logical construct rather than a faithful description of realities. But equipped with an internally coherent model of synchronic structure of the main bank system, we have a solid reference point by which we examine such diachronic issues as: How did the Japanese main bank system emerge in observed historical circumstances; what role did policy have in that process; why did the main bank constitute an essential element of the overall institutional arrangements during the time of high growth; and how did it endogenously generate the seeds of its own destruction under changing international and technological environments?

The main bank system as an institution across organizational, financial transaction, and polity domains may be considered as constituted of the following three arrangements and associated beliefs:

• *Relational-contingent governance.* A single major bank, known as a main bank, acted as a sole relational-financier cum relational-monitor of the contingent governance vis-à-vis each nonfinancial firm. Nonfinancial firms following the convention of horizontal hierarchy were disciplined by the fear of bank control in the event of serious financial distress, but were able to expect refinancing by their main banks in the event of their mild financial distress.

• *Financial keiretsu bundling.* Each bank bundled exclusive main bank relationships with multiple client firms over time along a financial *keiretsu* in which both sides were bound by cross-stockholding.[2] Unless they were in a favorable financial position to obtain occasional regulatory approval for bond issues, nonfinancial firms had their investments mostly financed by loan contracts from multiple banks and other financial institutions (thus loan relationships are not exclusive). Generally, the main bank was expected to be solely responsible for contingent governance (thus the governance relationship is exclusive). This implies that co-financing banks reciprocally delegated monitoring of borrowed firms to their main banks. The general expectation was that the financial distress of any borrowing firm ought to be handled by its main bank at its own cost. On the other hand, main banks were able to expect reputation and monopoly rents through *keiretsu* bundling (proposition 12.2).

• *Bureau-pluralist governance of banks.* The administrative bureau in charge of the banking sector (the banking bureau of the Ministry of Finance, MOF) assured banks of contingent rents through financial restraint and limiting the availability of bond issues by nonfinancial firms (proposition 12.1), although the bureau did not directly intervene in the loan decisions of banks. The ownerships of banks were widely dispersed, so there was no effective stockholder control. Instead, the banking bureau was expected to play the role of quasi-relational monitor vis-à-vis banks in the following sense: the MOF was expected to arrange nonliquidation solutions for troubled banks, for example, by an acquisition of such banks by financially healthier, larger banks in exchange for preferential regulatory treatments of the latter such as in branch licensing. This mechanism of bank governance was referred to in Japan as the "convoy system," as the government was believed to be committed to insure deposits at even financially weak banks with the aid of large banks. One important feature of the bureau-pluralist framework was the jurisdictional separation of the securities and banking industries under the two corresponding bureaus within the MOF. The banks were barred from securities underwriting businesses, while securities houses were able to free-ride on banks' monitoring competence and enjoy handsome underwriting fees and brokerage commissions.

Note that apart from the jurisdictional separation of financial supervision between the banking and securities bureaus introduced in 1967 and associated regulations concerning bond issues, none of the above characteristics were explicitly written in either a law or private contracts. They were basically collectively shared beliefs held by the agents that were endogenously formed and sustained through their strategic interactions.

In the early period of the main bank institution, the borrowing firms endeavored to improve on imported technology. They did so, relying on feedback from the manufacturing and marketing experiences to engineering redesign, as well as by the development of cross-functional coordination of organizational learning. Such organizational orientation toward horizontal hierarchies required the long-term association of employees with a firm, and thus the so-called permanent employment was practiced even at the level of blue-collar workers (chapter 5.1). The resulting labor market imperfection made the threat of bank control (and possible liquidation) in the event of poor corporate performance an effective external discipline for the firms, while the accumulated organizational assets could be safeguarded from temporary shock by the expectation of main bank's refinancing (proposition 11.3).

The mechanism of reciprocally delegated monitoring disciplined main banks to monitor their client firms, since the cost of bailing-out of failed firms in their financial *keiretsu* needed to be exclusively born by them. Also the political-economic framework of the bureau-pluralist state dominated by industrial interests was conducive to directing the large supply of household savings to the industrial sector as growth funds (proposition 12.1). Thus the bank rents that contributed to the evolution and sustenance of the Japanese main bank system could be considered to have comprised an admixture of policy-induced contingent rents extracted from household savers; of monopoly rents made possible by entry regulation, bond issue repression, and financial *keiretsu*; reputation rents yielded by corporate clients in exchange for the bank's unique insurance role in relational-contingent governance; and in some cases information rents derived from tacit knowledge held by entrepreneurial bankers about their client firms and small emergent firms that eventually grew to world-class firms.[3]

13.2   Institutional Emergence: Unintended Fits

We observed that horizontal hierarchies, relational-contingent governance, the main bank's relational financing, and the bureau-pluralist state were linked through complementary relationships in the postwar period and thus formed a coherent institutional arrangement (propositions 11.3 and 12.1). How then did the main bank system come into existence? Was it formed by a conscious public policy design of the government? Or, was it induced by the technological and international environment that the Japanese economy then faced? Alternatively, was it a spontaneous, endogenous outcome of an evolutionary process? Did some exogenous events effect its emergence? Policies, environmental factors, spontaneous elements, and historical chance all play a part but no single one was strong enough to induce the emergence of the system. However, we submit below that the diachronic dynamics leading to the evolution of the main bank system were consistent more with the theoretical prediction of the momentum theorem discussed in chapter 10.3. If changes in institution-relevant parameters, such as regulatory policies, organizational design, and accumulation of a particular human assets and competence occur in consistent (albeit unintended) ways in complementary domains, a dynamic process for institutional change may be set in motion. But above all it would have to be *complementarities* among endogenous variables (agents' strategies) that would provide the momentum for the emergence of a new institutional arrangement. Let us examine this historically.

One could characterize overall government-policy stances toward capital markets in the 1920s as basically laissez faire except for the persistent BOJs refinancing of banks' bad loans that originated in the aftermath of the great 1923 Tokyo earthquake.[4] Until 1927 banking law reform anyone could open a bank if the then lax minimum capital requirements were satisfied. In fact before 1927 a large number of banks existed: some 2,001 in 1920 and 1,283 in 1927. The structure of the banking sector was also then heterogeneous. There were five large *zaibatsu* banks,[5] which held 24 percent of the total bank deposits in 1925, and some well-run commercial banks with solid regional business bases. Then there were banks that collected deposits with higher interest premiums and were closely connected to a particular group of industrial and commercial firms, often with the same directors sitting on the boards of both sides. As is usually the case in exclusive relational banking, many banks were exposed to excessive idiosyncratic risks. Somewhat surprisingly, relatively large *zaibatsu* banks did not play such a prominent role in financing related firms in the 1920s. The major sources of external financing to major corporate firms were through securities markets (corporate bond and new equity issues) rather than bank loans.[6]

The moral hazard of banks under the soft-budget constraints of the BOJs refinancing and crony relational banking culminated in the financial crisis of 1927, triggering 42 cases of bank failure. It had a profound impact on policy-makers. The 1927 Banking Act raised the minimum capital requirement of banks and did not allow a single bank to meet the requirement by capitalization, thereby forcing the merger of small banks. Also the gold embargo was lifted in 1929 and the mechanism of gold standard payment settlement was expected to exercise high-powered market discipline on weak segments of the economy. These two policy measures put severe deflationary pressure on the economy into motion.[7] The number of commercial banks was reduced to 625 by 1932 through acquisition and closures, which caused widespread credit crunches. The policy stance was reversed by Finance Minister Takahashi in 1932 who designed a policy mix that anticipated the Keynesian policy (expansionary fiscal expenditures, depreciation of the exchange rate through the re-embargo of gold, and a low-interest rate policy through BOJ financing of the budget deficit).[8] This policy change was successful in reversing the economic slow-down more quickly than in any other industrial economies hit by the Great Depression. However, at this point government interventions in the economy were still limited to demand stimulus to which the industrial sector responded by activating market mechanisms. In 1934 corporate bond issues surpassed the pre-Depression peak, and labor mobility between large firms, as well as from large firms to smaller ones, became noticeable again, reflecting the shortage of skilled labor.[9] Thus, as far as the industrial domain was concerned, the evolving path might not have looked so different at this point from the one that the United States had pursued before and after the Depression.

However, the industrial domain in Japan was embedded in traditional sectors, and it was in the latter that institutional misfits of the growing impact of the competitive market mechanism became apparent.[10] The 1929 to 1931 depression did not seem so severe in terms of GDP growth rate, but the rates of deflation were not even, hitting particularly hard the agricultural and traditional rural industrial sectors.[11] Anti-market, anti-business rhetoric captured the sentiments of intellectuals as well as lower-ranking military officers who had roots in the rural area. *Zaibatsu* tried to respond to this institutional crisis by making their governance of business groups more open and transparent (e.g., offering the stock of member firms to markets, the professionalization of the management structure). However, the tactful military bureaucrats were successful in usurping the government by 1937.[12] They successively introduced the anti-market, anti-capitalist policy measures to strengthen their bureaucratic control over the economy and mobilized resources to enhance war-related production. The Planning Agency was created to direct the production of military equipment as well as regulate the supply of resources and the funds necessary for its implementation. Industrial Control Associations (*Sangyo Tosei Kai*) were created as intermediaries between the Planning Agency and firms on industrial basis for information collection and plan dissemination.[13]

Policy measures particularly relevant to the evolution of the main bank system were the promotion of bank consortia for long-term investment loans initiated in the 1930s and the introduction of the designated banking system in 1944. Major banks first responded to the government's promotion of a loan consortium by carrying out the reform of their internal organizations to set up an independent section of credit analysis.[14] By the first phase of the war, the banks still had discretion on individual loans. However, in the last phase of the war, for each company receiving military procurement orders (munitions companies), a single bank was designated by the government and funds were supplied to the company through that bank. The firms were made to hold their deposit and loan accounts with their designated bank—a prototype of the payment settlements account aspect of the main bank relationship. Before the war, major banks carefully avoided overcommitment to particular firms. However, wartime loans, which turned into bad loans after the war, became an "unintended tie" between banks and companies. At the end of the war, the designated banking system applied to 2,240 firms, of which 1,582 were assigned to one of the five major *zaibatsu* banks. Also, through coerced mergers and acquisitions, the number of banks was reduced to 65 by the end of the war. In parallel, the government introduced measures to restrict the role of stockholders in corporate governance. The 1943

Military Procurement Company Law required each military procurement company to appoint a production manager with the approval of the government, who was supposed to have exclusive rights to represent the company and override the control of stockholder's meetings. Further the payment of dividends was restrained and the stock market was closed in 1944.

Policy parameters were set to restrain the competitive capital-market control of corporate governance, as well as the allocation of resources through market-driven incentives. Some authors, like Noguchi (1995, 1998), argue therefore that the present-day Japanese institutional arrangements are essentially nothing but the artifacts of those policies to be characterized as the "1940 regime." As Okazaki (1993) documented and analyzed, however, even setting aside the obvious reason of the destruction of production equipment and the diminishing supplies of energy and other natural resources,[15] the planned war economy was doomed to fail because there were no market incentives for the managers. How then could such a regime support the subsequent high growth that occurred in the postwar period? If we conceptualize the main bank system as one of shared beliefs as summarized in the previous section, the mechanism of governance that the military government tried to articulate was far from sustaining such beliefs. All economic agents, including bankers, production managers, and workers, were aware that the intention of the military government was to control resource allocation for the purpose of war production. The sustenance of individual corporate firms and banks per se was not the immediate purpose of the government and their incentives was to be compromised and constrained by the discretionary intervention of the government.

However, there was one subtle but significant parallel development in the labor transaction and organization domains. Starting in 1938, the military government also intervened in the labor market and introduced a successive policy measure to restrain the interfirm mobility of workers and engineers.[16] In order to enhance the training of the workers, factories of more than a certain size were required to organize intrafirm training programs for their workers. Further, as war-production planning became hard to implement toward the end of the war because of the shortage of workers and undersupplies of equipment, material, and resources, ad hoc problem solving at the site became indispensable. Classical hierarchies that would not allow the delegation of decision-making to lower levels of workers were modified. This applied not only to the relationships between an industrial control association and factories but also to that between the managements of factories and work sites. In chapter 10.1 (example 10.4) we saw that the need for ad hoc problem-solving at the grassroots level of the factory led to spontaneous team work. This collaborative effort could be considered an embryonic form of the later horizontal hierarchy. But, just as the main bank system had not yet evolved as an institution in the financial transaction domain, neither had horizontal hierarchies in the organization domain, at least in a clear form.

After the defeat in the Pacific war and under the governance of the Supreme Commander of Allied Powers (SCAP), the ideological context of the policy stance underwent a radical transformation from the authoritarian promotion of devotion to a national cause to one of democratic principle. However, in many important domains, particularly in those relevant to the formation of subsequent economic institutions, the vector of policy parameters essentially remained headed in the same direction (see figure 12.2). The *zaibatsu* conglomerates were dissolved and holding companies were made illegal for the purpose of democratizing stock ownership along the idea of the New Dealers in SCAP, but the effect was the sweeping dismantling of *zaibatsu* governance, which the military government had originally sought in a much more modest form. The stock market remained closed in the 1945 to 1949 period when massive stock transfers took place from *zaibatsu* families, holding companies, and major member firms to the government as part of the *zaibatsu* dissolution process. The government owned an estimated 40 percent of the total stock outstanding in 1947, prior to its subsequent sale to individuals. Priority in purchasing government-owned stock was given first to a firm's workers, then to residents of localities in which plants were located.[17] When the stock market opened in 1949, nearly 70 percent of the stock was owned by individuals. The democratization of stockholding appeared to have been achieved, but it turned out to be a decisive blow to stockholder control of corporate governance. The management that replaced the purged wartime management emerged as a critical player in the corporate organization domain.[18] They gradually crafted cross-stockholding among firms with old *zaibatsu* connections, yet the result was not a revival of *zaibatsu* control but a clever means of insulating themselves from takeover threats, eventually leading to the establishment of micro-corporatism (chapter 6.2).

In the domain of financial transactions in the summer of 1946, the Japanese government repudiated its guarantee of bank credits to munitions companies, as well as government debts and insurance obligations to munitions companies in order to control rising inflation.[19] Banks and firms hit by the government's actions were made to separate balance sheets into old and new accounts. Debts and paid-in capital were placed into old accounts, and entries into new accounts were limited only to those assets deemed absolutely necessary for current operations (inventories, cash, etc.). The amounts of these assets were then recorded as accounts payable to the old account. "The idea behind the operation was to clean up bad loans (alternatively debts) [in old accounts] without interfering with ongoing ... business" (Hoshi 1995:305). The two accounts were to merge after reorganization, as they indeed did so after several years

of joint effort between firms and their former designated banks. Hoshi (1995) described this process in detail and pointed out that the close relationships and information
sharing that developed between them were instrumental to the evolution of the main
bank relationship.

In the political economy domain of government-business relationships, industrial
control associations were abolished. However, these associations were staffed by
government officials and personnel dispatched by major companies, and their experiences in working together provided the basis for the postwar government-business
interactions through consultative industrial councils. The primary function of these
councils became information assimilation about investment environments rather
than plan-making as such. Also the industrial associations were created as quasi-
administrative organizations, and they evolved as a catalyst of the emergent bureau-
pluralist state (chapter 6.2).

At this point we need to re-emphasize the distinction between policy and organizational parameters defining the exogenous rules of the game, on one hand, and
institutions endogenously generated as equilibria under those rules, on the other (see
figure 13.1). We have seen that there were a set of parameters during and immediately after the war period that were particularly relevant to the emergence of the
main bank system and the embedding bureau-pluralist state. They were instrumental
in enhancing the *relative* attractiveness of strategies of private agents that, if taken
together, would generate those institutions. However, these parameters did not
immediately translate into an *absolute* advantage of those strategies. As we observed
in chapter 10.3, there had to have been an endogenous, self-sustaining mechanism
for inducing the emergence of those institutions, beyond the initial impetus of the
institution-relevant organizational and policy parameters. This was provided by diachronic complementarities between the relational financing strategies in the financial
transaction domain and the strategies conducive to the convention of horizontal
hierarchies in the organizational field.

Let us recall an important theoretical insight gained in section 12.2, that efficient
relational financing may not evolve if the number of the banks is too large or too
small (proposition 12.2). As we have seen, the number of banks was drastically
reduced from 1920 to 1945, first by the government's concern over the stability of the
financial system and later by the government's move to strengthen the controllability
of funds allocation. However, the reduction in the number of the banks itself does not
automatically guarantee banks active role as the relational-financier-cum-monitor
in relational-contingent governance. There must be demands for that role from the
firm's side as well. The joint problem-solving between munitions companies and
former designated banks in the postwar period prepared the ground for the building

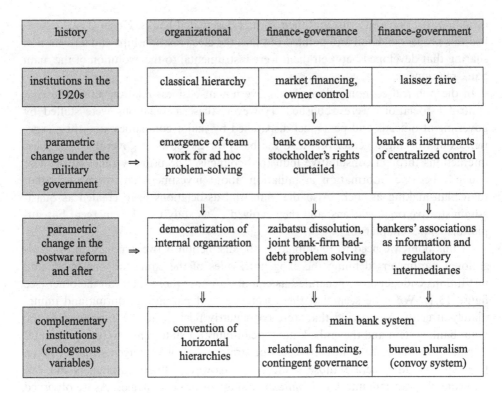

history	organizational	finance-governance	finance-government
institutions in the 1920s	classical hierarchy	market financing, owner control	laissez faire
	⇓	⇓	⇓
parametric change under the military government ⇒	emergence of team work for ad hoc problem-solving	bank consortium, stockholder's rights curtailed	banks as instruments of centralized control
	⇓	⇓	⇓
parametric change in the postwar reform and after ⇒	democratization of internal organization	zaibatsu dissolution, joint bank-firm bad-debt problem solving	bankers' associations as information and regulatory intermediaries
	⇓	⇓	⇓
complementary institutions (endogenous variables)	convention of horizontal hierarchies	main bank system	
		relational financing, contingent governance	bureau pluralism (convoy system)

Figure 13.1
Structure of unintended fits

of mutual trust, but it was essentially complementarity between horizontal hierarchies and the relational-contingent governance system that gave rise to the main bank system as a coherent institutional arrangement (proposition 11.3).

The "1940s regime" view claims that the prevailing institutional arrangements were created by the government as substitutes for markets and therefore were an aberration from the laissez faire norm that had previously existed. A public policy implication of this view is to revert to the laissez faire "market fundamentalism." In contrast, we submit that the sweeping organizational changes introduced by the military government in the sphere of finance, corporate governance, and government-business relationships were indeed intended as substitutes for markets but that the aim failed. The reason that they appear to have long-lasting impacts is that they, and subsequent policy changes in the postwar period, paradoxically set in motion the mechanism of diachronic complementarities with the emergent convention of horizontal hierarchy. Although the eventual outcome of the mechanism was not the one intended originally by the government, it came nonetheless to constitute a coherent system. Because of its coherence, the system cannot easily be reversed to a laissez faire system nor gradually modified in piecemeal fashion. However, as it started to become less fit with the emerging configuration of technological and market environments, the institutional inertia led to an internal crisis. We now turn to this phase of the Japanese main bank system.

13.3 Endogenous Inertia, Misfits with Changing Environments, and a Crisis of Shared Belief

During the two decades of the high-growth period between the mid-1950s and mid-1970s, the main bank system functioned well as a mechanism of intermediating personal savings into industrial capital accumulation through relational and long-term bank lending. It successfully resolved the problem of maturity transformation inherent to the developing economy. Also the main banks performed, or at least were believed to perform, the relational-contingent governance role. Although the system may have been biased toward a soft-budget constraint syndrome under the convoy system, when the government (the MOF and the BOJ) bailed out financially distressed banks and other financial firms, they punished failed management by replacing it with their own people or other trusted bankers. In parallel, when banks bailed out financially distressed firms, they punished failed management by replacing it with their own people. This prospect has provided credible discipline on the management of financial firms as well as nonfinancial firms. As a result nonfinancial firms try to become as free from reliance on bank loans as possible.

However, the success of the system bred the seeds of its self-destruction. As better-run firms developed the ability to generate more funds internally under the discipline of the contingent governance, the bargaining power between them and main banks latently began to tilt in favor of the former. A crucial divide that made this change overt arrived in the mid-1970s. In 1974 the Japanese economy contracted for the first time in the postwar period and industrial firms started to adapt to it by restructuring assets and reducing debt burdens. Better firms took the opportunity to reduce the compensating balance with main banks (demand deposit accounts that had been required to hold under a low interest rate in compensation for borrowing at a higher rate as a bond of the main bank relationship). At the same time the government withdrew its direct control over deposit rates and the major pillar of financial restraint was removed. A dramatic reduction of bank rents was triggered by these two events.[20]

On the other hand, massive government bond issues to finance budget deficits caused by increasing social security and other expenditures began in 1975. In order to market national debt issues, the MOF relied on a consortium of financial institutions, including banks. This would eventually make it necessary for the MOF to deregulate secondary markets for national bonds. As an inevitable result of market forces, it became increasing harder for the regulatory authority to prevent banks from engaged in capital markets ever more actively. In 1980 the Foreign Exchange and Trade Control Act was revised to allow designated banks (*tamegin*) to engage in foreign exchange brokerage without restriction. Better-run firms then became able to issue bonds at a cheaper capital cost in the Euro-market to circumvent domestic regulations of bond issues via their main banks and securities houses. Their main banks tried to keep relationships with them through securities subsidiaries abroad and offered underwriting and foreign exchange related services in lieu of traditional domestic lending. Thus the deregulation in the interface of domestic and international financial markets made the bureau-pluralistic jurisdictional separation between banking and securities industries less tenable.

Indeed, in the middle of 1980s some discussion was initiated within the MOF and its consultative committee about possible options for removing the jurisdictional wall (e.g., the deregulation of universal banking, financial holding companies, and bank subsidiaries in the securities business). However, this initiative was promptly aborted by the lobbying of the securities industry and possibly by long-term credit banks that had enjoyed privileged positions in securities markets with the exclusive rights to issue bank debentures. Three bureaus of the MOF (Banking, Securities, and International Finance) issued instead an agreement that disallowed bank subsidiaries abroad to be a lead manager of a bond underwriting consortium for Japanese firms. This could be regarded as a quintessential instance of the bureau-pluralist state at work. It further suggests that bargaining power between the MOF and the financial industries within the framework of bureau-pluralism was tilted in favor of the latter. The MOF was beginning to lose power to implement policies that might fit more with changing environments but were opposed by private jurisdictional interests. As we will see, however, bureau-pluralistic inertia only aggravated the emergent chasm between the main bank system and the increasingly globalizing market environment. Before we can discuss this, we need to consider the impact of another fundamental change in the environment of the main bank system: the coming of the information-communications-technology (ICT) revolution.

The development of ICT had two interrelated effects on the institutional arrangements in the global financial domain. On one hand, the increasing availability of digital information on the financial state of corporate firms made various market-oriented financial expertise, such as that embodied in investment banks, different funds, market arbitrageurs, and security analysis services, more valuable. On the other hand, the same factor enhanced the potential value of economic knowledge that cannot be digitalized immediately. In response to these changing environments, investment banking grew in the United States and overtook commercial banking in terms of profits in the 1980s. Venture capital funds evolved to establish a niche in financial markets using unique expertise to judge potential new technological systems.

It was desirable for the Japanese banks (and other financial firms) as well to reconfigure the portfolios of their financing-cum-monitoring activities instead of exclusively sticking to traditional bundling of ex ante, ad interim, and ex post monitoring through main bank lending. Banks ought to have shifted rent sources to specific knowledge and information-processing expertise in order to maintain productive relationships with better-run firms (section 12.2). However, the bureau-pluralist regulatory framework, as well as the institutional arrangements surrounding the main bank system, prevented banks and other financial firms (e.g., securities houses) from nurturing market-related financial expertise. Nonfinancial firms internalizing horizontal hierarchies were not ready to be engaged in corporate restructuring through mergers, acquisition, and asset sales (see example 10.10 in chapter 10.2), so there was no domestic demand for investment-banking services. The regulatory framework might appear, on the surface, similar to the separation of the securities business and commercial banking as stipulated in the Glass-Steagall Act in the United States. However, in the United States, banks were able to appeal to the courts: the Supreme Court decision in the mid-1980s allowed banks to by-pass the regulatory restrictions by means of financial holding companies. In contrast, in Japan the legal prohibitions of the holding company made it impossible for banks and other financial firms to flexibly reconfigure their business domains, while they were severely constrained in new product development by the regulatory authority. Going to the court was not considered as a viable option for the banks protected by the framework of bureau-pluralist state. Finally, but as important, the bankers' association and other financial industrial associations (securities, trust bankers' and insurance) as bureau-pluralist intermediaries induced information assimilation among member firms and fastered herd behavior among them rather than competing in entrepreneurial reconfiguration of focused businesses.

As better-run firms drifted away from the banks' orbit, where they were barred from securities-related services and devoid of expertise attuned to emergent technology, banks rushed to engage in real estate lending with high risk and high returns. Their new clients were wealthy individuals (some of them were simply gamblers) and small firms.[21] In lieu of spending high monitoring costs, banks now regarded high risks hedged by the expected rising values of real estate held as loan securities, while implicitly transferring the risk to the government through the convoy system. A conventional view holds that the great asset inflation in the late 1980s was created by the excess supply of liquidities by the monetary authority, fearful of the deflationary impact of yen appreciation after the Plaza agreement in 1985. However, the wholesale and retail price indexes did not increase during the same period and only asset prices became inflated; the increased liquidity supply was accommodating the demands created by the banks' herd behavior in speculative real estate and stock dealing lending (Yoshitomi 1998). Although some nonfinancial firms were also involved in asset-value speculation through the inducement of banks, healthier firms became more independent from the banks, releasing themselves from the discipline of contingent governance (Miyajima and Arikawa 2000). As a result the financial and nonfinancial sectors became somewhat disjunct, creating vacuum in the governance structure (Jensen 1989). So, more than anything else, the great bubble of the late 1980s can be considered the symptom of institutional misfits with the competitive market environment.

The eventual bursting of the bubble in the early 1990s ushered in a decade of bad debt problems and undercapitalization of banks. The initial crisis erupted in a segment of the financial sector, housing loan corporations (*jusen*), which were nonbank institutions owned and financed by banks and other financial firms that had been engaged in high risk–high return lending during the period of asset inflation. They were forced to liquidate, with the infusion of public funds to repay their liabilities. The largest beneficiary of this resolution was the financial arm of the powerful agricultural lobby which had lent heavily to *jusen*. The amount of public funds used in this resolution was relatively small in comparison to the amount of funds that had to be made subsequently available for bailing out banks, but it was enormously unpopular politically. That made the MOF and politicians extremely cautious about an early decisive intervention in the banking crisis. The convoy system was thus driven at bay. Confidence in the main bank system was further undermined by the successive disclosures of scandals, both in the MOF and banks, which made a collusive solution between them behind the scenes increasingly difficult. Rather, the MOF had to confront the problem of organizational legitimacy and survivability on its own. The separation of the regulatory and supervisory functions from the MOF was being placed on the political agenda.[22] The MOF started to keep some distance away from banks and securities companies whose reputation was tarnished.

The MOF announced the so-called financial Big-Bang in 1996 that would successively remove various traditional regulations of the financial industry within five years time, such as walls between various finance activities, restriction of foreign exchange brokerage to licensed banks, entry regulations, unlimited deposit guarantees, and regulated brokerage fees and insurance premiums.[23] This policy change might not have been possible if financial firms had not had jepordized their reputations by internal scandals, misconduct, and mismanagement. However, the most dramatic, final demise of the main bank system as an institution (i.e., as a system of shared beliefs) came with the end of the convoy system: the bankruptcy of a major city bank, the license cancellation for one of four major securities houses in the fall of 1997 and their subsequent liquidation, and the disclosure of the insolvencies of two long-term credit banks. These events were unavoidable because of the assault of massive stock sales of these firms, and the MOF was no longer in the position to bail these firms out. The bank failures triggered a tremendous crisis of confidence in the financial institution, propagating widespread external diseconomies of the credit crunch. It damaged the balance sheets of firms, particularly small and medium-sized firms, and caused macroeconomic instability, reversing the 1996 signs of recovery. It was widely felt that drastic action was needed to resolve the banking crisis. After rather complicated international and domestic political hagglings, legislative measures were finally worked out with plans for the temporary nationalization of insolvent banks and the infusion of massive public funds before more bank failures could occur.[24]

This brief overview of the recent history of the main bank system indicates that the banking crisis and the prolonged stagnation of the Japanese economy in the 1990s was not simply created by a mistake of macroeconomic policy, unilateral regulatory power of the bureaucracy, or moral hazard and incompetence of the finance industry alone. It was created, above all, by the misfit of the overall institutional arrangements surrounding the main bank system with the changing environment—particularly the globalizing financial markets and the ICT revolution. However, since the main bank system had evolved as a coherent system, it was hard to change it in a piecemeal way in the early 1980s when the economy seemed to be doing so well and powerful private interest groups were in ascendance vis-à-vis the bureaucracy. In an economy like Japan where various institutions intimately complement, and/or tightly linked with, each other, it was necessary for a general cognitive disequilibrium to occur before the agents could search for ways to adapt themselves to the changing environment. Only then were the MOF and politicians able to distance themselves from the private interest groups and break the inertia of the bureau-pluralistic frame of protection, even if partially and not thoroughly.

Three latent properties of the bureau-pluralist state became evident in the process. First, the connectedness between the bureaus and jurisdictional interests is not an invariant, natural order dictated by a cultural norm nor an inviolable bureaucratic power, but a collusive outcome of calculated strategic moves by both sides (chapter 6.2). When either party is confronted with issues of its own survival and legitimacy, an old collusive agreement may be broken, even if only temporarily, until a new strategic equilibrium is generated.

Second, the dismantling of the traditional regulatory and organizational framework was decided on by the MOF rather unexpectedly and abruptly at the point when their reputation was at its lowest. MOF conduct and policy were under the severe scrutiny of "public opinion," with the sensational disclosure of their scandals —misconduct that had almost been taken for granted until the end of the bubble—as a symptom. Failure to respond to a crisis in the "public interest" could have been costly to politicians as well. Toya (2000) argues that such situation indicates that bureau-pluralistic interest mediation is increasingly embedded in electorate politics and thus constrained more by public opinion.

Third, by the same token the bureau-pluralistic state is embedded ever more closely in the increasingly competitive, globalizing (financial) markets. Regulatory measures to protect domestic interest groups against this environment can thus only amount to inconsistencies and backfire. The MOF was not able to perform the traditional governance role expected under the convoy system and had to accept, willingly or unwillingly, the force of market discipline in responding to the crisis. It is not still clear how this situation will affect the interests of the state in the near future. On one hand, in industries that are competitive on a global scale (e.g., export industries) or that are difficult to insulate from international competition, corresponding bureaus may increasingly accustom themselves to hands-off, market-oriented administration to preserve their legitimacy and raison d'être. On the other hand, there are less productive sectors that seek bureau-pluralist protection via the backing of elected politicians. Further, what the outcome will be in the long term of the soft-budgeting tendency of the banking sector supported by the bureau-pluralistic protection of government—with the critical accumulation of bad debts—remains problematic. Clearly, these dual tendencies are showing that they are neither compatible nor sustainable. The cost of bureau-pluralistic administration is being incurred by the competitive sector and future generations, and this will hurt in the long term the competitiveness of the economy (on this dilemma, see Aoki 1988: ch. 7, 1995/2000: ch. 7). Whether the result will be long-term political-economy stagnation or some constraints on the bureau-pluralistic protection of less productive, traditional interest groups, perhaps with an end to the soft-budgeting tendency of the public and financial sectors, will largely depend on the collective voice of taxpayers in the political domain.

14 Institutional Innovation of the Silicon Valley Model in the Product System Development

[L]earning machines must act according to some norm of good performance. In the case of game-playing machines, where permissible moves are arbitrarily established in advance, and the object of the game is to win by a series of permissible rules according to a strict convention that determines winning or losing, this norm creates no problem. However, there are many activities that we should like to improve by learning processes in which the success of the activity is itself to be judged by a criterion involving human beings, and in which the problem of the reduction of the criterion to formal rules is far from easy.
—Norbert Wiener, *God and Golem, Inc* (1964:76–77)

The subject of this chapter is the Silicon Valley model as a new coordination-cum-governance mechanism of technological product system development. So far in this book we have touched on various aspects of the so-called Silicon Valley phenomenon as illustrations of the development of our argument concerning institutions and their mutual linkages: the aspects of information-systemic architecture (chapter 4.2) and complementary governance structure (chapter 4.3); synchronic bundling of R&D financing (chapter 8.2) and diachronic Schumpeterian re-bundling of innovation activities (chapter 10.2); and venture capital financing as a type of relational financing (chapter 12.1). Although dealing with different aspects, the thrust of the arguments has been the same: in order to understand the truly innovative nature of the Silicon Valley phenomenon and its implications beyond Silicon Valley, it is not enough to formulate it as either a principal–agency relationship between a single individual entrepreneur and a venture capitalist, or as a de-integrated property rights arrangement.[1] It is necessary to grasp the phenomenon as an emergent system composed of a cluster of entrepreneurial firms, on one hand, and various intermediaries, such as venture capitalists, leading firms in relevant niche markets and other professional service providers, on the other. In other words, it is necessary to have a broader perspective that deals with the overall Silicon Valley phenomenon as a unit of analysis and capture them as a coherent system. Only by doing so, we can understand them as an institutional innovation in the domain of technological product system development.

As described in the appendix to this chapter, the venture capitalist usually retains a control block of shares in entrepreneurial firms and exercises a broad range of governance roles with them. It is certainly not the case that residual rights of control over physical assets are firmly integrated within the hands of entrepreneurs if they are cash-constrained at the outset. However, this does not imply that the entrepreneurs of product-development firms play a less autonomous role in information processing. Indeed, they are more autonomous in the production of knowledge in some technology areas than the traditional research and development laboratories of established firms. Nevertheless, as Saxenian (1994) documented, there is a substantial degree of

information sharing across those entrepreneurial firms mediated by venture capitalists and others. How can these ostensibly contradictory characteristics coexist? How
can we understand their unique contributions to the process of technological product
system innovation? What incentive impact does the apparently strong governance
role of the venture capitalist have? Is there anything that the Silicon Valley model can
do that cannot be duplicated in either a single firm or in arm's-length market relationships? Is the Silicon Valley model applicable elsewhere and in industries other
than the high-technology industry? Are there any specific social costs and wastes,
together with social benefits, associated with this model?

In order to consider these issues, this chapter puts together conceptual and analytical pieces we have constructed so far and tries to build a coherent, theoretical
construct that is referred to as the Silicon Valley model. Its construction is motivated
by observations of the stylized Silicon Valley phenomena as summarized in the
appendix to this chapter. But stylized facts are changing fast, so any model cannot
capture every aspect of their dynamic trajectories all at once. Further, while some
changes do possibly reflect the endogenous evolution of a new institution, some others
are merely generated by business cyclic factors. Therefore, in building the model, we
will limit our focus to some generic, systemic features of the Silicon Valley phenomena
that we regard as essential and unique for considering the above-mentioned issues.

The plan of the chapter is as follows. The first section deals with the information-
systemic architecture of the Silicon Valley model. The entrepreneurial firms in Silicon
Valley compete in innovation in selective niche markets and thus their activities are
fundamentally substitutes. Therefore their information processing activities need to
be encapsulated from each other in order to surpass competitors (chapter 4.1).
However different from older established integrated firms, such as IBM which conceived ex ante of a concept for a possible new technological product system in a
centralized manner, these firms are engaged in innovation efforts in particular niche
markets in a decentralized way. A new technological product system therefore
is evolutionarily formed by selecting and combining ex post mutually compatible
module products by successful firms. The first section examines technological and
organizational conditions under which this type of information-systemic architecture
can generate technological product system innovation more effectively than traditional corporate R&D organizations, albeit with associated social costs of duplicated
innovation efforts and financing. This focus on ex post flexibility in the design of a
new technological product system differs in emphasis from the conventional one in
the technology literature on increasing returns (Arthur 1989; Romer 1986), and
accordingly will have different public policy implications.

The second section then proceeds to the analysis of the governance role of the venture-capitalist complementary to this type of information-systemic architecture. We characterized the mechanism of venture capital governance as a tournament game played among initially funded firms for the subsequent staged financing necessary for the completion of projects (chapter 4.3). We will examine the conditions under which the associated threat of termination of financial support by the venture capitalist is seen to provide greater incentives for the entrepreneurs than under arm's-length financing. We will see, among other factors, that the entrepreneur's confidence in the venture capitalist's ability to judge the outcome of tournament precisely and fairly plays an essential role in eliciting their innovation efforts. This suggests that the provision of incentives for the venture capitalists is also an essential ingredient of the Silicon Valley model. The third section turns to this aspect of the Silicon Valley model and discusses the importance of the role of venture capitalists' reputations and subnorms in capital markets in eliciting their monitoring and governance efforts. Also this last section discusses some broader institutional ramifications of the Silicon Valley model, such as the endogenous formation of the entrepreneurial risk-taking tendency, complementary between mobile engineers' markets and venture capitalist governance. The appendix provides stylized factual backgrounds for modeling. Those readers who are relatively unfamiliar with venture capital contracting and related facts are advised to read it first.

14.1 The Information-Systemic Architecture of the Silicon Valley Model

Comparative R&D Architectures

To begin an inquiry into the overall Silicon Valley phenomenon as a system, we first focus on its information-systemic architecture. In doing so, we apply and extend the comparative organizational framework prepared in chapter 4.1 to the product-system innovation domain and see under what technological and organizational conditions the Silicon Valley clustering mediated by venture capitalists may, or may not, be superior to the traditional, corporate in-house R&D organizations.

Imagine that an innovative technological product system can be generated by a new combination of modular component products (element technologies). For example, a laptop computer as a technological product system consists of component elements as a LC monitor, MPU, image-processing LSI, hard disk drive, OS, audio and communication devices, and the like. In order to develop such a product system, modular component products must be designed in such a way that they fit with each

Organization / Environment		(E$_s$) Systemic-industrial environment	(E$_e$) Systemic-engineering environment	(E$_i$) Task-specific engineering environment	Fitting engineering environment
model	characteristic				
Waterfall model (functional hierarchy)	Hierarchical ex ante design of product system	development director's conceptual design	middle manager's analytic design	detailed design by functional units	high systemic uncertainty, disparity in information processing competence
Star model		development director's integrative design		Supplementary design by subordinates	
Interactive R&D organization (horizontal hierarchy)	Interactive design improvement	information assimilation led by "heavy weight" development manager	information-sharing among task units	modular product design by task units	high attribute and technological complementarities
SV model	Evolutionary product system constitution	VC's mediation of information assimilation, ex post selection of module products	information encapsulation by entrepreneurs across and within niche markets		weak complementarity, relative independence of modular design problems

Figure 14.1
Comparative information-systemic architecture of R&D organizations

other to form a coherent, high-performing, market-competitive, technological system. Suppose, for simplicity, that a generic R&D organization is constituted simply of the development management, denoted as M, and two task units, denoted as T_i ($i = a, b$). The management may be engaged in the planning and systemic design of a technological product system innovation, involving such choices as system attributes, component composition, and the allocation of R&D funds between task units. The task units are engaged in the design of modular products, each of which is to constitute a component of an integral technological system.

The organizational environments are segmented like the first row of figure 14.1. Namely there is a systemic segment, E_s, that simultaneously affects the organizational returns to an entire technological product system, such as emergent industrial standards and availability of R&D funds. We assume that information regarding this segment is primarily processed by the management. Next, there are the segments of the environment that affect the organizational returns to the designs of new modular products by the T_i's, say engineering environments, which can be further divided into three subsets: E_e, common to both task units, and E_a and E_b, idiosyncratic to respective units. The processing of information regarding the common segment is necessary for resolving engineering problems underlying the designs of both modular products (reduction of problems that may occur at the interfaces of modular products, reduction of poor performance characteristics that may arise as synergy effects of operating the modular products, etc.). The information regarding an idiosyncratic segment of the engineering environment is relevant only to the design of a respective modular product. Thus the environments of the development of a product system innovation constitute a hierarchical order. However, although the processing of the idiosyncratic environment at the lowest level needs to be performed at the relevant task unit, the common segment of the engineering environment (and to some extent the industrial systemic environment as well) may be processed, and associated decisions may be made, by M and/or the T_i's in various ways to be specified momentarily. We refer to the processing of information regarding engineering environments as "development," and the actions taken based on development as "design."

Analogous to the taxonomy of three generic modes of information connectedness in the organizational architecture developed in chapter 4.1, let us identify the following three types of information-systemic architecture in the technological product-system-innovation domain.

The Waterfall Model and the Star Model   This model corresponds to the functional hierarchy (the nested hierarchical-decomposition mode) introduced in chapter 4.2. Say that M is the research director of an integrated firm and that the T_i's are its internal design-task units. Between them we now insert an intermediate product development manager, IM. M analyzes the systemic environment, E_s, conceives of a conceptual design for a potential technological product system innovation, and then communicates its decisions to IM. IM performs an analytical design that determines the division of design-tasks among the subordinate units within the budget and other systemic constraints imposed by M by analyzing the systemic-engineering environment, E_e. Then he hands over his decisions to T_a and T_b. The design-task units then resolve detail design problems that arise in their respective task-specific engineering environments, E_i $(i = a, b)$. This organization reflects the essential aspects of the R&D organization of traditional, large, hierarchical firms, sometimes referred to as the waterfall model (Klein and Rosenberg 1986).

Another analogue of this model can be found in what Hannan et al. (1996) called the "star model": a class of internal coordination mechanisms that they find among some entrepreneurial firms in Silicon Valley, in which wide-ranging systemic design ("the larger strategic directions shaping the work") is entrusted to a star. He is instrumental in analyzing the highly uncertain systemic segments of the environment and after the completion of the analytical design, detailed designs may be reduced to relatively routine tasks. This model is adopted where there is a large amount of systemic uncertainty involved in developing a technological product system that requires distinguished competence to resolve (proposition 4.3). This is often a characteristic of academic research groups in fields such as biotech.

Interactive R&D Organization   This model corresponds to the horizontal hierarchy (nested information-assimilation mode) introduced in chapter 4.2. In this type of organization, M is the project manager and the T_i's are the design-task units. There is information sharing among them all regarding the systemic environment, E_s. The two design-task units collaborate on development affected by the systemic engineering environment, E_e, while coping individually with technical and engineering problems arising in their own segments of the engineering environment, E_i $(i = a, b)$. Each design-task unit thus has wide-ranging information about environments, partially shared and partially individuated, on which their respective decision choice (modular product design) is based. This system corresponds to what S. Klein conceptualized as a chain-link model (Klein and Rosenberg 1986; Aoki and Rosenberg 1989). In this model information assimilation is realized through the feedback of information from the lower level to the higher level, as well as through information sharing and joint development efforts across design-task units on the same level, as multiple cross linkages. This model is innovation-productive (informationally efficient) when there are high technological and attribute complementarities between modular component products while resolving design problems at each design-task unit requires specific expertises (propositions 4.2 and 4.4).

This model is akin to the coordination aspect of what Hannan et al. called the "peer and cultural control model, where the employees have extensive control over the means by which work gets done but little control over strategic directions, projects to be pursued, etc." (1996:512–13) They found that some of the emergent Silicon Valley entrepreneurial firms internalize such a model. We also find that a mode of development teams in the automobile industry shares features with this architectural type. Clark and Fujimoto identified the most competitive type of development team in this industry as the one led by the "heavy weight product development manager— a combination of a strong project coordinator and a strong concept leader" (Clark and Fujimoto 1991; see also Fujimoto 1999:ch. 6). In this model the product development manager leads a development team encompassing work groups drawn from various functional units in development, as well as manufacturing and marketing representatives. The manager exercises strong leadership in the entire process of developing a new product, starting from the conceptual design, based on the perception of potential future markets, to various downstream stages, such as analytical design, detailed design, manufacturing process design, as well as feedback for design improvement from manufacturing and marketing experiences to upstream design stages. Needless to say, modular components of an automobile as a technological product system are characterized by high attribute complementarities. For example, making a vehicle compact, less noisy, energy-efficient, and resistant to wide-ranging temperature variation, requires mutual fitness and finely coordinated designs of modular parts, as well as specific engineering expertise in resolving problems within each design task.

Silicon Valley Model   This model is a variant of the IA–IE combinatorial architecture introduced in chapter 4.2. In this system there is a modicum of information assimilation regarding the systemic environment between M and the T_i's, somewhat like in an interactive R&D organization. However, there are two additional characteristics to this system: on one hand, design tasks are modularized from each other in that there is less statistical correlation between their engineering environments—that is, engineering problems facing both design tasks can be resolved independently as each of them is constituted of an integrative design problem rather than mutually interrelated; on the other, each design task is simultaneously performed by multiple units in competition and the final technological product system is formed by selecting the best combination of one development outcome from each of the design tasks ex post (after the completion of development effort). The first characteristic renders encapsulated information processing of the engineering environment by individual design tasks informationally more efficient (proposition 4.5). The second characteristic entails that information processing of the engineering environment is encapsulated by individual design units *within* the same design task because they compete in development outcomes (proposition 4.1). Despite of these two characteristics there must be a modicum of information assimilation among all design units so that their modular products are compatible to an integrative technological system. The role of M in this system is to mediate such information assimilation and select the best combination of modular products from both design tasks ad interim (after development efforts by design-task units started, but before they are completed) and/or ex post (after they are completed).

We submit that this model captures in an embryonic form the information-systemic architecture of the Silicon Valley model. In this interpretation, multiple units at the T_i level are independent entrepreneurial firms. Instead of creating mutually competitive, stand-alone products of their own, they are specialized in the design of modules in the evolving technological product system. This way they are able to carve out niche markets and gain a better bargaining position vis-à-vis larger firms that try to acquire new technologies. The standardization of interfaces across modular products and protocols of communications among them may be a product partly of architecture defined by dominant firms (e.g., Intel, Cisco Systems, and Microsoft) and partly of industry standard-setting organizations (e.g., Semiconductor Equipment and Materials International [SEMI] and the Internet Engineering Task Force [IETF]). Firms like Sun with Jini and Java, as well as cooperative ventures like Linux, also compete to define new standards for emerging markets. Thus standards are evolutionarily formed and modified through the interactions of firms, large and small as well as established and new. The venture capitalists help in mediating the information necessary for the evolution of industrial standards across these agents.

The selection of competing products in each niche market is done in a stepwise fashion. At the time of start-up the venture capitalist commits only a fraction of the capital needed for the ultimate development of a project, with the expectation that additional financing will be made stepwise, contingent on the smooth course of the project that may not be contractible—a process that Salman (1990) called "staged" capital commitment. There are thus many business failures among entrepreneurial start-up firms. If the project is successful, relational financing terminates either with an initial public offering (IPO) or buyout (acquisitions) by other firms. These firms themselves often used to be entrepreneurial firms that have been successful in assuming leadership in setting standards in their niche markets. They want to acquire successful start-up firms, either to kill off potential sources of challenge to their set standards, or to further strengthen their market positions by bundling complementary products to form a more comprehensive technological product system. In comparison to the R&D organizations of previous types, they can shorten the period of technological product system innovation by substituting the so-called A&D (acquisition and development) for self-closed, in-house R&D. For further discussions of stylized facts about the Silicon Valley phenomenon that substantiate the present modeling, see the appendix.

We may summarize the above classification of R&D organizations in the technological product-system innovation domain and their relative performance characteristics in figure 14.1. In sum, the waterfall model or the star model would be the most productive arrangement (in the sense of information efficiency as defined in chapter 4.1) when the conceptual design of the product system itself is highly uncertain and/or there is a significant disparity of development competence among organizational participants. On the other hand, if relatively independent, integrative design problems need to be resolved at the level of modular product design, the Silicon Valley model can be more productive in innovation. Interactive R&D organization is expected to perform better in the industry where attribute complementary between modular products are high, and when both systemic and idiosyncratic segments of the engineering environment need to be analyzed with equal weight. Thus no model can perform absolutely best in all industries regardless of industrial and engineering conditions involved. In the following subsection we amplify further some organizational and institutional conditions that would make the Silicon Valley model innovative.

Information Encapsulation and Evolutionary Constitution of Product Systems

Implications of Standard Setting We have indicated that there are two distinct properties characterizing the Silicon Valley model: the relative independence of processing of engineering environments across design tasks and the competition among multiple units in designing any single modular component product. Let us take up the first characteristic and examine its implications, leaving consideration of the second one for the next subsection. In other words, we assume for a while that there is only one unit (entrepreneurial firm) for each design task in the Silicon Valley model—call this the quasi–Silicon Valley model. In this model information processing leading to the development and design of a modular component product is encapsulated. But, even if the engineering environments to be processed by design units (firms) in respective product design are mutually independent in terms of information (e.g., the development of software and hardware requires different development efforts), the advantage of this model may be reduced, or even the feasibility of this model may become problematical, if there is large attribute complementarity between their modular products in constituting a consistent system. That is, even if the design contents of component products are modularized, their interfaces or communications protocols need to be standardized and made compatible.[2]

Interface standards can be set centrally and ex ante (in the sense "before research and development") by a dominating firm, or in some cases even by the government. But such a centralized and ex ante approach may not yield a good outcome when there is a high degree of ex ante uncertainty involved in product-system design as well as module-product design. In this case, emergent information in the process of development effort needs to be better utilized. One possible informational advantage of an interactive R&D organization vis-à-vis the waterfall model may be its flexibility in fine-tuning interfaces in response to emergent information. However, in the interactive R&D organization ad interim adaptation to emergent information is not in general limited to interface designs but often involves simultaneous changes in the contents of product designs by both design-task units. Thus the information load in these types of organizations can become high, and accordingly desirable ad interim adjustment may take time and involve extra efforts.

In contrast, in the quasi–Silicon Valley model, the information assimilation role of the VC is limited to mediate the systemic-engineering information among the T_i's (entrepreneurial firms) regarding interface standards endogenously generated through their development processes, by standard-setting organizations, or by established firms. Then individual task units (entrepreneurial firms) can adapt to emergent standards without their design of product contents being affected.

LEMMA 14.1   Accordingly as the designs of modular products by individual entrepreneurial firms are made self-contained and less complementary, the innovative capacity of the Silicon Valley model is enhanced. VC's information mediation can create such situation endogenously by mediating interface-standard setting and thus becomes complementary to independent development efforts by individual entrepreneurial firms.

The Evolutionary Nature of the Innovation Process under the Silicon Valley Model

The comparison of informational efficiency among alternative organizations above is based on the assumption that the stochastic distribution of parameters characterizing technological and other environments are ex ante known and unchanged during the period of product development and design (chapter 4.1). However, such an assumption may not be tenable as the complexity of technological environments becomes ever greater. The arrival of new discoveries and innovation may unexpectedly change the horizon of the landscapes of technological environments. The inevitable bounded rationality of agents may compel their perception of the distribution of stochastic events to be revised now and then beyond Bayesian learning, because they can never have a complete description of possible states of nature ex ante. Does the Silicon Valley model have unique characteristic in coping with such uncertain, increasingly complex, technological environments?

Consider an innovation process of a large-scale, complex, technological product system. Suppose that it can be hierarchically decomposed into several distinct steps, such as basic conceptualization, system analysis, module design, process design, pilot manufacturing, and testing. Some steps may be further decomposed into sub-task units. In such a hierarchical decomposition, once a system concept is centrally conceived and a system design is drawn accordingly, even if some revision to the system is perceived as necessary afterward because of the occurrence of unanticipated events at a later stage, it will be too costly to redo the whole process from the beginning.

Then the design will have to be only partially revised on an ad hoc basis at a later stage, sometimes losing the internal coherence and consistency initially intended. If a new generation of the technological product system is to be designed, the whole process must be renewed, which takes time and resources.

The interactive R&D organization can possibly cope better with emergent un-expected events by using frequent feedback mechanisms between different stages of product development, as well as collaboration in problem solving between task units engaged in interrelated design tasks at the same level. In this type of organization the technological product system can be continually improved, or accumulated learning from unexpected events at all development stages can be utilized for the design of a new generation of the system. However, once communications channels are set up between different developmental stages and task units, it becomes difficult to change the basic organizational architecture of development in a radical way, such as replac-ing a group of tasks. Accordingly innovation in the technological product system tends to be incremental.

Even in functional and horizontal hierarchies, the detailed design of components of a large, complex, technological product system can be modularized. However, in the former the modular structure is designed centrally and fixed once and for all. In the latter information needs to be exchanged among task units in order to keep their product compatibility fine-tuned in response to emergent events so that the informa-tion-connected among task units need to be tight and their modular component products cannot easily be coupled with products of other organizations.

However, if there are competing design units in each design-task unit as in the Silicon Valley model, the development of a large, complex, technological product system can be evolutionary. It can evolve without a centralized design or a fixed structure. In order to understand this, it is very important to recognize that in the Silicon Valley model not only does each entrepreneurial firm develop modular com-ponent products, but *its information-processing activity (analysis, development, and design) is also modular (i.e., encapsulated) across tasks units.* As a result of this dual modularization in information processing and product, the complexity of the internal workings and informational content of modular products will be hidden from each other, and a relatively weak information linkage (the standardization of interfaces) will be provided to the rest of possible systems. This has two interrelated implications.

First, information encapsulation insulates each entrepreneurial design from outside interventions by protecting its design effort from relying on the details of how the content of other modular products might change over time. Thus autonomous and continual improvement of modular products by each entrepreneurial project becomes possible without hurting the integrity of existing systems. Further, because of the presence of multiple competing units (entrepreneurial firms) in the design of same modular component products, an innovative technological product system may evolve without a priori centralized design but by continual reconfiguration of modular products. The system design can be free from the forces suppressing a radical departure from existing patterns of bundling modules. It may rapidly evolve from a relatively simple prototype system into an ever more complex system by flexibly re-bundling improved modular products from different entrepreneurial firms. An often invoked analogy to this ex post flexibility is Lego building blocks with their interlocking-cylinder faces. The number of objects that can be built with Legos is limited only by one's imagination (Pine 1993). There are, of course, transaction costs involved in the process of evolutionary selection under the Silicon Valley model. In particular, there is the cost involved in attaining ex post flexibility in the form of the duplication of development efforts and the resource expenditures supporting them. In the next section we analyze how the governance aspect of the Silicon Valley model tries to strike a balance between benefits and costs in a unique way.

The Parallel Paradigm Development in Software Technology

The observation in the preceding paragraphs has an interesting parallel in the paradigmatic development in computer software technology. Initially large-scale software development followed the so-called waterfall paradigm in which a solution to computing tasks is first analyzed and then tasks of design, coding, testing, and maintenance are hierarchically organized in discrete steps. Only the completion of one task leads to the next step, just as water falls from a higher level to a lower level. Needless to say, this paradigm is isomorphic to the model of hierarchical R&D organization.[3]

However, as computer hardware technology developed with enormous enhancement of computing capability and accessibility, requirements for software development became more demanding and complex. The iterative programming paradigm characterized by feedback mechanisms from downstream stages to upstream stages was a natural response to improving the development process and making it faster. For example, the accumulated stock of subroutine programs helped shorten the time needed for the design of an improved program version. Or, problems frequently encountered in the maintenance stage might suggest a new approach in the design stage, and so forth. This iterative paradigm can be regarded as somewhat analogous to the model of the interactive R&D organization in that information sharing across different tasks plays an essential role. However, the basic subdivision structure of the development cycle remained intact and, once the actual programming has begun beyond the stage of analysis, this structure does not allow any radical modifications. As computing tasks got even more complex and rapidly changing because of the fast development of the business, scientific, and hardware environments, the interactive method began to feel burdensome. As iterative improvements on old programming accumulated, it became increasingly difficult to predict the impacts that further local improvement would have on the workings of the whole program. It also takes time to reach an agreement about a basic system design of new programming that will not exhibit serious problems afterward.

In order to cope with the need for rapid programming development, a less centralized way of developing programming evolved, first among practitioners, and then gradually becoming established as a new paradigm known as "object-oriented" programming. In this paradigm the design of programming for a complex computing task utilizes classes of reusable software "packets" referred to as objects. Objects encapsulate a collection of related data elements and a set of procedures (methods) operating on those elements. Objects from different classes communicate with each other only through simple messages to request that the receiving object carry out the indicated method and return the result of that action. Thus they can be mutually protected from corruption by others, while protecting others from being affected by details that might change within a class. Prototype programs for specific computing needs may be constructed by combining objects from different classes to simulate the real world process that submits the computation problem. This paradigm then successively modifies and refines a mode of combining objects from classes by trial and error, while enriching classes of objects by adding newly redesigned elements. Since objects hide implementation details behind a common message interface, the object-oriented technology allows new kinds of objects to be added to enhance the complexity of a system without rewriting existing procedures as was necessary in old conventional paradigms.

This evolutionary construction of a new program thus has a close analogue in the innovative process operating under information-encapsulation cum product-modularization. However, there is one important difference between the two. Classes of objects in object-oriented programming are collections of software packets that are superior to the human mind in processing digitalized data faster and precisely but is mindless itself (it does not modify programming by itself because it is tired or excited). In the innovative process under information encapsulation, we have units of human agents (entrepreneurial firms), rather than objects, who have their own "principles of motion" (Adam Smith). How are the entrepreneurs motivated to contribute to the library of objects, even if there is a large chance that their products may not be used? How is the VC (program designer) motivated to bear the costs of enhancing a library of objects in the library? This is the question of the institutional-ization of the Silicon Valley model, which is the subject of the next section.

14.2 The VC Governance of Innovation by Tournament

In the previous section we dealt with the information-systemic architecture of the Silicon Valley model. However, we have not yet explicitly dealt with the incentives that support this information-systemic architecture. The present section tries to explore in a game-theoretic framework what kind of governance mechanism can complement this architecture by generating the particular expectations among the VC and the entrepreneurs that are conducive to the resolution of the potential incentive problems inherent in it.

The Structure of the VC Tournament Game

As background for the model below, imagine that time consists of an infinite sequence of stage games, each played over three dates between venture capitalists and entrepreneurial firms. The venture capitalists live permanently, competing with each other to nurture valuable firms, and entrepreneurial firms start up at the beginning of date 1 of a stage game and exit by the end of date 3, either by going public, being acquired by other firms, or being terminated. When terminated, entrepreneurs can come back to the next stage game as new start-up firms. In this section we do not explore the impacts that the repeated nature of the game have on venture capitalists' reputations, nor its impacts on the risk-taking traits of would-be entrepreneurs. We concentrate instead on the analysis of the single-stage game between one venture capitalist and multiple start-up firms embedded in the repeated game. We call the stage game the *VC-tournament game*. We take up the possible impacts of the repeated nature of the game and competition among venture capitalists in the next section.

We assume that before date 1 starts (and thus outside the model), a venture capitalist, denoted by VC, has screened many developmental projects proposed by cash-constrained, would-be entrepreneurs and selected some of them for start-up funding (ex ante monitoring). For simplicity, there are only two types of projects (design tasks, in the terms of the previous section) and the VC has selected two proposals for each.[4] The start-up firms are indexed by subscript ij, where $i = a, b$ denotes a project type, and $j = 1, 2$ distinguishes entrepreneurs. Hereafter we use a "start-up firm" and its "entrepreneur" as interchangeable terms. The entrepreneurs are ex ante symmetric in their parametric characteristics except for project type in which they are engaged.

At date 1, each start-up firm, ij, funded by the VC is engaged in development efforts, which amount to observing a parameter in the respective engineering environment, E_i, with some noise.[5] The choice of entrepreneurial effort level (investment in knowledge) at start-up firm ij is denoted by e_{ij} and its cost by $c(e_{ij})$, with the usual increasing marginal cost property, $c'(e_{ij}) > 0$ and $c''(e_{ij}) > 0$. The actual levels of effort implemented by the start-up firms are not observable so that they are not contractible. The engineering environment E_i is representable by a one-dimensional parameter and the development effort by entrepreneur, ij, generates noisy one-dimensional observation, ξ_{ij}—research results—with precision $\Pi_{ij}(e_{ij})$. The higher his effort level, the higher the precision of his posterior estimates regarding the engineering environment which he faces. Each entrepreneur also generates a tentative conjecture regarding the systemic environment E_s as a by-product of his own development effort without additional effort cost. The fixed amount of funding provided to each entrepreneur by the VC only covers the cost of information processing (including wages) at this date and is not enough for further product development of start-up firms.

At the beginning of date 2 when uncertainties regarding the environment still persist, on the basis of research results obtained at date 1, the entrepreneurs tentatively specify product-design attributes, y_{ij}, from a one-dimensional set, $\mathcal{Y}_i$ ($i = a, b$), with observable interface properties and performance characteristics; let us call this observable portion of the design the external design specification. Besides information obtained at date 1, each entrepreneur needs to take into consideration in his own design of how industrial standards are evolving. In order to obtain information regarding others' choices, entrepreneurs engage in communication through the intermediary of the VC, using the external design specifications of products as messages with the internal workings of the products hidden. Implicit in external design specifications are the tentative conjectures of entrepreneurs regarding the systemic environment.

The VC aggregates the entrepreneurial messages and combines them with his own assessment of the emerging industrial framework to generate a one-dimensional parametric message drawn from the space of the systemic environment E_s. In other words, the VC generates an estimate of the systemic environmental parameter with some noise. The entrepreneurs successively revise their design attributes, internal and external, in response to the VC's message. Communications and design revisions continue until the aggregate estimate of the systemic environmental parameter converges to an equilibrium value of the systemic, ξ_{Es} (we assume it does so within date 2). Suppose, for simplicity, that the precision of the aggregated information is a function, $\Pi_{vc}(.)$ of the VC's mediating effort, e_{vc}. The cost of the VC's mediating and monitoring efforts are represented by $\kappa(e_{vc})$ with the usual increasing cost property. Suppose that the precision of the VC's information is observable to the entrepreneurs (but not court-verifiable). At an equilibrium, entrepreneur, ij, specifies his product design attribute, y_{ij}, as a combination of the VC-mediated assimilated information, ξ_{Es}, and his own research results, ξ_{ij}, with respective weights equal to $\Pi_{vc}(e_{vc})$ and $\Pi_{ij}(e_{ij})$.[6]

At the beginning of date 3, the VC estimates which combination of product designs from each type is expected to generate a higher value, if the respective firms are offered to the public or acquired by an existing firm at the end of the date. By this judgment, the VC selects one proposal from each type of project for implementation and allocates one unit of additional funds to each of them for the completion of the project. We may call this VC's ad interim selection. The VC's decision is represented by $x = (x_{a1}, x_{a2}, x_{b1}, x_{b2})$, where $x_{ij} = 1$ if the ij product is selected for financing and $x_{ij} = 0$ if it is not. If $x_{ij} = 1$ then $x_{ik} = 0$ for $k \neq j$. The firms that are not selected by the VC exit.

At the end of date 3, the selected projects are completed and the VC offers the ownership of these firms to the public through a IPO market or sells to an acquiring firm. At that time all environmental uncertainty is resolved and the total market value, $V(x_{a1}y_{a1}, x_{a2}y_{a2}, x_{b1}y_{b1}, x_{b2}y_{b2} : E)$, is realizable, contingent on the state of the environment, $E = (E_s, E_a, E_b)$, prevailing at that time. The realized value is distributed among the VC and the entrepreneurs. Let us denote the distributive share of the value to the ij firm by α_{ij} and that of VC by $\alpha_{vc} = 1 - \sum_{ij} \alpha_{ij}$. The payoff of each firm is then $\alpha_{ij}V - c(e_{ij})$ $(i = a, b; j = 1, 2)$ and that of the VC is $\alpha_{vc}V - \kappa(e_{vc})$, assuming there is no discounting over dates within a SV-tournament game. Before the beginning of the SV-tournament game, the VC and the entrepreneurs have to agree on the way in which realized values are to be distributed at the end of date 3 (we will specify this momentarily). The incentive of each agent is to maximize his or her own expected payoff according to that agreement. The time line of this VC-tournament Game is summarized by figure 14.2.

Institutional Benefits and Costs of the Silicon Valley Model

Suppose, for a moment, that development expenditures have been made by the agents and that information regarding the engineering environment has become available to them with some imprecision. At that moment both the entrepreneurs and the VC are interested in utilizing their respective information for making decisions so as to maximize the total value, V, expected at the end of the V-tournament game, because the larger the total value, the larger their incomes with respect to ex ante agreed-on shares. We assume that the expected total value is a separable function of

	beginning of the game	date 1: development	date 2: design specification	date 3: refinancing selection	end of the game
entrepreneurs	contract agreement:	development effort	design specification	exit or project implementation	value realization
venture capital	start-up financing		information mediation	selective final-stage financing	and distribution

Figure 14.2
Time line of the VC-tournament game

efforts by players:

$$E[V] = H\Pi_{vc}(e_{vc}) + x_{a1}Z(\Pi_{a1}(e_{a1})) + x_{a2}Z(\Pi_{a2}(e_{a2}))$$
$$+ x_{b1}Z(\Pi_{b1}(e_{b1})) + x_{b2}Z(\Pi_{b2}(e_{b2})),$$

where H is a positive constant and $Z(.)$ is a monotone-increasing, positive-valued function. Information encapsulation among entrepreneurs warrants the assumption of separability.[7]

It was assumed that the contributions to the expected value by individual entrepreneurs would become estimable with some noise to the VC at the start of date 3, after observing the external attribute specifications of the proposed design. Suppose that the entrepreneurs believe that the VC chooses winning entrepreneurs with an error specified as follows: the VC's measurement of entrepreneur $i1$'s potential contribution equals $Z(\Pi_{i1}(e_{i1})) - \zeta/2$, and that of $i2$'s equals $Z(\Pi_{i2}(e_{i2})) + \zeta/2$ with $i = a, b$, where ζ is a random variable representing the observation error that is symmetrically distributed around zero with density function $f(.)$ and a cumulative distribution function $F(.)$. If $f(.)$ is tightly distributed around zero with less spread, that means the judgment of the VC is more precise and accordingly more sensitive to the entrepreneurs' actual effort levels. Suppose that the VC chooses entrepreneur j vis-à-vis k for refinancing and project implementation if and only if $Z(\Pi_{ij}(e_{ij})) - \zeta/2 > Z(\Pi_{ik}(e_{ik})) + \zeta/2$ $(i = a, b; k = 1, 2; k \neq j)$. That is, the VC selects only those entrepreneurs who are expected to yield higher values according to her judgment for the refinancing necessary for the completion of their proposed designs at date 3.

Suppose that an initial contract is such that at the time when winners are selected, a share $\alpha_{ij} = \alpha_i > 0$ is vested with the winning entrepreneur $(i = 1, 2)$ and the unfunded entrepreneur forfeits any share. We refer to this scheme as *VC governance by tournament*. Expecting such selection criteria, entrepreneur ij's objective function at date 1 is to choose e_{ij}, so as to

$$\max_{e_{ij}}[\alpha_i F((Z(\Pi_{ij}(e_{ij})) - Z(\Pi_{ik}(e_{ik}))))(Z(\Pi_{ij}(e_{ij})) - c(e_{ij}))], \qquad i = a,b; j = 1,2; k \neq j.$$

Since two entrepreneurial firms in the same project are assumed to be exactly alike in their characteristics and the probability density function of ζ is symmetric around zero, they are expected to choose the same effort level, ceteris paribus, and have equal chances of being selected ex ante. So the entrepreneur's choice must satisfy the following first-order condition:

$$\alpha_i[F(0) + f(0)Z(\Pi_{ij}(e_{ij}))]Z'(\Pi_{ij}(e_{ij}))\Pi_{ij}'(e_{ij}) = c'(e_{ij}),$$

where $i = a,b$, $j = 1,2$, $k \neq j$. Here we assume that efforts are not mutually observable (encapsulated) among entrepreneurs so that strategic interactions in effort choices among them are absent. Each entrepreneur equates his marginal expected private benefit of additional effort with its marginal cost. The marginal expected private benefit (the left-hand side of the equality above) is composed of two parts: its share times the probability of being selected for refinancing times its marginal expected value contribution, and its share times the marginal increase in the probability of being selected for refinancing times its expected value contribution. From the way F and f are constructed, the value of $f(.)$ viewed as a function of e_{ij} for a given level of e_{ik} is regarded as the marginal winning probability due to j's extra effort. Let us refer to the second term as the "tournament effect."

Let us examine this choice vis-à-vis the following alternative taken as a comparative benchmark. Suppose that the financier selects ex ante (i.e., before date 1 begins) only *one* proposal from each project and promises each of them will be entitled to the same share α_i in the value V as the one that the winning entrepreneur in the V-tournament game is entitled to. Otherwise, the financier neither mediates information assimilation across entrepreneurs nor selects/rejects projects ad interim. He might as well sell his own share ad interim to any buyer in the market. Let us call this scheme the *arm's-length financing contract*. Since their effort levels are not observable, the entrepreneurial effort choice in project i would be described by $\alpha_i Z'(\Pi_i(e_i))\Pi_i'(e_i) = c'(e_i)$.

Therefore, if

$$1 - f(0) < f(0)Z(\Pi_{ij}(e_{ij})),$$

that is, if the entrepreneurs believe that the VC's refinancing selection is without much error so that the marginal winning probability due to extra effort is high (which is implied by a higher value of the elasticity $f(0)/[1 - f(0)]$), and if the total value that the winning entrepreneur can produce is expected to be very large relative to the marginal effort value, then the governance by tournament may elicit a higher development effort than under the arm's-length financing.

Let us take the balance obtained so far from the viewpoint of the VC. The VC's benefit from running a tournament is her share in the additional gains from the tournament effect. Her costs are (1) duplicated start-up funding at date 1, and (2) intermediating and monitoring effort costs at dates 2 and 3, which will have impacts on entrepreneurial confidence in the VC's ability to choose value-enhancing winners. Thus we submit:

PROPOSITION 14.1   If the total value created by entrepreneurial development efforts is expected to be high, and if the venture capitalist's selection of winning entrepreneurs is believed to be precise by the entrepreneur, then it is possible that even for the same share allocation between entrepreneurs and financiers, the VC governance by tournament can elicit higher development efforts from entrepreneurs than under arm's-length financing, and that its effect on the final total value can compensate venture capitalist's duplicated start-up financing and interim monitoring costs. Conversely, if the entrepreneur's confidence in the venture capitalist's competence in selecting value-enhancing projects for refinancing is low, the venture capitalist cannot adequately elicit the entrepreneurs' developmental efforts.

There are unique social costs and benefits arising from venture capitalist governance by tournament that institutionalizes the ad interim selection of modular product designs. One cost is that of the duplication of research and development efforts by entrepreneurs that are sunk at date 1. The effort costs of entrepreneurs who do not win the tournament become deadweight losses. As just mentioned above, there is also the sunk cost of the initial funding to them by the VC. The social net balance between the deadweight losses and the benefits from increased effort by the entrepreneurs is not clear without a further parametric specification of the model. It might be negative. Nevertheless, even in such a case venture capital financing may be institutionalized by the VC as the preceding proposition indicates. If entrepreneurs are risk-lovers who place a high utility on an uncertain high value obtainable as the prize of the tournament, then venture capital contracting may be preferred to arm's-length contracting by entrepreneurs as well, despite the possibility of ex post bearing of the deadweight loss. The next section will show how such risk-taking traits may be endogenously formed when governance by tournament is institutionalized.

As already argued, however, there is a unique social benefit from venture capitalist governance because of the possibility of the ad interim selection of projects, particularly when engineering environments involved in modular product developments are highly uncertain and statistically less correlated among design tasks and attribute complementarity between modular products are made low.

PROPOSITION 14.2   The VC governance by tournament generates deadweight losses of the loser's development efforts and duplicated financial costs. On the other hand, it can configure ad interim a system of product design in response to the emergent state of highly uncertain systemic and engineering environments, and this possibility may create unique system benefits in the absence of strong attribute complementarity and strong correlation in developmental environment among design tasks, with complementary supports of ad interim venture capitalist's monitoring.

14.3   Norms and Values in the Silicon Valley Model

The Market Reputations and Club Norms of Venture Capitalists

We now turn to the venture capitalist's incentives. In the model of the previous section, the venture capitalist's net payoff within a stage game—a VC-tournament game—is $\alpha_{vc}E[V] - \kappa(e_{vc})$. If the VC maximizes the payoffs only within the horizon of the current V-tournament game, the static Nash-equilibrium condition would be $\alpha_{vc}E[dV/de_{vc}] = \kappa'(e_{vc})$. However, the optimal level of effort by the VC requires that the following condition hold: $E[dV/de_{vc}] = \kappa'(e_{vc})$. Thus an undersupply of effort by the VC would occur if she is myopic, since her private marginal benefit from her effort equals only her share in her marginal contribution to the total value.

At this point it becomes necessary to make the repeated nature of venture capital financing explicit, albeit vis-à-vis a different set of entrepreneurs in each stage game, and to make explicit the role of reputation and competition among multiple venture capitalists. Venture capitalists are financial intermediaries who manage venture capital funds contributed by other investors such as wealthy individuals, banks, portfolio funds, foundations, and the like, that lack knowledge and expertise in administering the system of governance by tournament. Venture capitalists compete with each other in securing those funds for the formation of successive venture capital funds over time. At the same time, they often co-invest in entrepreneurial start-up firms, while reciprocating the role of leading financier (see the appendix). In such situations reputation mechanisms that operate in markets for the supply of funds, as well as among venture capitalists, can play an important role. If a venture capitalist fails to deliver a high value to her own investors at the contractual end of a fund, she will have difficulty in raising future funds. If she fails to do the same for the other venture capitalists who have delegated monitoring to her, she may be ostracized from future joint financing through a "club norm" regulating reciprocal delegation of monitoring (see chapter 3.1 for a club norm).[8] The benefits for the venture capitalist from pursuing the value maximization of current funds are not limited to a one-time share in the current venture capital funds that she manages but include the avoidance of losing her reputation in the market and the club. Suppose then that the venture capitalist chooses her effort level in each period to maximize her own continuation value in the face of this possibility of punishment for underperformance. However, note that the effect of the venture capitalist's effort is hidden behind the state of the environment so that investors and other venture capitalists can observe only the realized value at the end of each period, but not her effort level.

To see more formally the impacts of market competition and a club norm on venture capitalists' incentives, let the cumulative probability function of value V created at the end of date 3 when her effort level is e_{vc} be written as $F(V : e_{vc})$. Suppose that if the value of a venture capital fund at the end of date 3 falls short of a threshold value $\underline{V}$, then the capacity of its manager (VC) to raise further funding, as well as to join profitable co-financing led by other venture capitalists, is weakened from the next stage game on so that her future earning ability is lowered by J in flow terms. In a repeated game context with stationary environments, the VC chooses the same effort level if she can raise the same quantity of funds. Then her problem of choosing e ought to be

$$v = \max_{e}(1 - \delta)(\alpha_{vc}E[V] - \kappa(e_{vc})) + \delta[(1 - F(\underline{V} : e_{vc}))v + F(\underline{V} : e_{vc})(v - J)],$$

where v is the present value of her future income in equivalent flow terms, and δ is the time discount factor. In the current stage game the VC receives the contracted share in realizable value $\alpha_{vc}E[V]$ and incurs effort cost, $\kappa(e_{vc})$. If the VC can raise funds in the next period with probability $1 - F(\underline{V} : e_{vc})$, she receives flow value v at the end of the period. If she fails to raise adequate funds for the next stage game on, because the value falls below $\underline{V}$ with probability $F(\underline{V} : e_{vc})$, she expects to receive only $v - J$ in each future period. The weights in the equation on the present and future payoffs are $1 - \delta$ and δ respectively. The weighting expresses the present value of incomes in equivalent flow terms v. The corresponding stock value can be found by dividing it by $1 - \delta$.

The Nash equilibrium effort level of the VC is then given by

$$\alpha_{vc}E\left[\frac{dV}{de_{vc}}\right] - \frac{\delta}{1 - \delta} \times \frac{J\,dF(\underline{V} : e_{vc})}{de_{vc}} = \kappa'(e_{vc}).$$

Evidently the fear of a loss of reputation on future earnings provides greater incentives for the VC than in the case of myopic maximization because of the second term of the left-hand side of the equation: the reduction of continuation value due to a loss of reputation. Suppose that the investors can locate a threshold value $\underline{V}$ just below the expected optimal value, for which the probability of failure $1 - F(\underline{V} : e_{vc})$ can be dramatically reduced by an increasing effort. Then a Nash equilibrium strategy of the venture capitalist under the reputation mechanism can approximate the first-best solution.[9]

PROPOSITION 14.3 The decision of suppliers of funds regarding whether or not to renew partnership contracts with a venture capitalist on the basis of his/her previous records of capital gains realization, as well as a club norm regulating venture capitalists reciprocal delegation of monitoring, can elicit higher monitoring and governance efforts from the venture capitalists. This reputation effect becomes stronger if the probability distribution of funds' outcomes is not wide-spread when the venture capitalist's effort is near the first best.

Other Institutional Ramifications of the Silicon Valley Model

An Element of Gambling and the Social Cost of the VC-Tournament Game If venture capitalists remain active over multiple stage games, they will be able to accumulate knowledge and expertise in administering governance by tournament, such as mediating information exchanges among entrepreneurs, and judging the potential values of modular product designs in a systemic context, hence helping a complex system to configure in an evolutionary way. As a by-product of this process, the venture capitalists accumulate knowledge about development environments as well as the engineering competence and the entrepreneurship of founders of start-up firms, partially independent of the success or failure of their product-design projects in a particular tournament game. The failure of an entrepreneur to win a design tournament in one round of a stage game may not necessarily be due to his/her incompetence but might have been caused by bad luck, lack of a fit of an inherently good design with an evolving system, a slight lag in design completion, and so forth. Therefore the entrepreneur may be judged to be qualified to enter another tournament. Making such judgments (ex ante monitoring) is another important function of venture capitalists. The tacit knowledge about entrepreneurs obtained on site from past stage games may be helpful for selecting new competitors for subsequent stage tournaments. Thus venture capitalist's ad interim monitoring is complementary to her ex ante monitoring in the next round of financing. The view often prevails abroad that the Silicon Valley model is successful in generating innovation because of the ease with which a one-time failure is provided a second chance. But this view is not entirely precise as it is, without the qualification that the endogenously created VC's competence to judge a failure's real potential is essential in the process.

On the other hand, if potentially capable entrepreneurs can have reasonable expectations of being allowed to participate in subsequent tournament rounds despite past failures, their risk-taking attitudes can be endogenously enhanced despite possible losses of effort costs. In other words, even if there is a chance of losing in a tournament, one could be tempted to repeatedly mount a challenge in new tournaments in the hope of getting a large prize someday. However, possible asset-value inflation in the market for initial public offering in the formative stage of an innovative technological product system may enhance the expectation of a winner's prize beyond its potential social value. Then social losses from the multiplication of development efforts and financing may become aggravated.

CONJECTURE 14.1   The repeated play of the VC governance by tournament may endogenously shape the risk-taking trait of entrepreneurs, entailing an element of gambling in the VC-tournament.

Complementarity between VC Governance and the Engineer's Labor Markets   We have assumed that the venture capitalist has the ability to select a modular product from each project that fits to constitute a new technological product system. But, the VC's expertise and knowledge in judging the technological potential of entrepreneurial firms may actually be limited. However, such shortcomings are compensated for by the mobility of engineers across entrepreneurial firms. Ambitious and competent engineers may be constantly looking for a "cool" technology. If the research and development of a new entrepreneurial firm at date 1 is not generating a satisfactory outcome, and/or it turns out to be incompatible with emergent technological standards at date 2, it may be the engineers in that firm who can recognize it first. If other entrepreneurial firms are continually being organized to search for "cool" technology with the aid of VC financing, those engineers may then exit the soon-to-be-unsuccessful firm and move to a new firm. The heavy reliance on stock options as a form of compensation may in general slow the mobility of engineers, but it cannot serve as a blockage of outflow from the soon-to-be-unsuccessful firms. This outflow of engineers provides negative momentum to the process of research and development of the slowed-down firm and signals its losing status in the tournament to the VC.[10] Thus we submit:

CONJECTURE 14.2   The limited technological ability of venture capitalists to judge winners of a VC-tournament ad interim may be compensated by the signal given by engineers who exit from soon-to-be-unsuccessful entrepreneurial firms. On the other hand, the mobility of engineers is aided by the repeated play of the VC-tournament game. Thus the VC governance and the highly mobile engineer markets are institutionally complementary.

Concluding Remarks

In this chapter we have argued that in order to understand the unique governance role of the venture capitalists in the Silicon Valley model, it is not enough to take a look only at the relationship between a single entrepreneurial firm and a single venture capitalist. Neither is it appropriate for regarding the role of the venture capitalist as simply the supplier of risk capital. Since the truly revolutionary nature of the Silicon Valley model lies in its ability to generate innovative technological product systems through the evolutionary selection of modular products generated by entrepreneurial firms, it is crucial to take a look at the multifaceted relationships between the venture capitalists, on one hand, and the cluster of entrepreneurial firms, on the other. In this chapter we have focused on the information-systemic and governance-structural relationships between the two in an integrative way, and tried to identify the social benefits and costs of the Silicon Valley model.

One important insight of the analysis is that venture capital governance by tournament can elicit higher efforts from entrepreneurs only if the amount of the total prize for winners is very high. Therefore the application of the Silicon Valley model may be limited to domains in which successful developmental projects are expected to yield extremely high values in markets, somewhat as in a lottery. At the same time, however, the identification of conditions for the information efficiency of information encapsulation may have broader implications for corporate organizations in general. Because of the development of communications and transportation technology, even mature products (e.g., automobiles) are being increasingly decomposed into modules, whose production and procurement become less integrated in comparison to traditional hierarchical firms (as represented by traditional American firms of a decade ago) or relational contracting (as represented by Japanese *keiretsu*). This tendency renders compact modular organizations (in independent firms or subsidiaries) increasingly efficient and viable. Various innovations in corporate governance appear to be evolving even within traditional firms in ways somewhat reminiscent of the Silicon Valley model. Some aspects of the organizational-based contingent governance referred to in chapter 11.3 could be considered such an example. In this structure, operational business units are modularized as relatively autonomous subsidiaries and the information processing necessary for their operation tends to be encapsulated. Parent organizations (holding companies or management partners) are less intervening in their operation, but organizational modularization helps them to pursue strategic reconfiguration of business units in response to rapidly changing market and technological environments.

Appendix: The Stylized Factual Background for Modeling[11]

From the purely financial point of view, venture capital funds are intermediaries, channeling large sums of investment funds from other financial intermediaries, such as pension funds (45 percent in 1996), insurance companies, and banks (6 percent), together with those from foundations and universities (20 percent), wealthy individuals and families (7 percent), corporations (18 percent), and foreign investors (4 percent), to mostly start-up entrepreneurial firms.[12] As an intermediary the venture capital process is unique in its legal structure. It is a system of partnerships in the venture capital funds in which there are two classes of partners: general and limited. The general partners act as organizers of the fund, accepting full personal responsibility and legal liability for fund management. Limited partners supply most of the capital but are not involved in the management and investment decisions of venture capital funds, which allows them to enjoy limited liability status as well as the advantage of avoiding double taxation.[13] General partners receive an annual fee of a few percent (2–3 percent) of the total capital committed and receive 15 to 25 percent of the realized capital gains for their much smaller contribution to the funds. Funds are set up for a fixed period of time, say ten years, but in many cases management companies are formed and run by general partners to provide management continuity. Thus there can be the usual principal-agent problems between limited and general partners, which we discuss at the end of this chapter. This chapter does not explicitly differentiate between venture capital funds and venture capital companies but simply refers to them as venture capitalists.

Venture capitalists seek promising investment projects, while potential entrepreneurs with planned projects, but insufficient funds, seek venture capital financing. There are more than two hundred venture capital companies in Silicon Valley alone, but experienced venture capitalists are said to receive several hundred applications a year. Screening and searching are not easy for either side, but suppose that a promising match is found. Unless the reputation of an entrepreneur is already known to a venture capitalist and a proposed project is judged to be certainly sound and promising, the venture capitalist initially provides only seed money to see if an entrepreneur is capable of initiating the project and possibly extending aid to help his/her start-up (the so-called seed stage). When a venture capitalist decides to finance a start-up, elaborate financing and employment agreements are drawn up between the her and the entrepreneur (start-up stage).[14] These agreements specify the terms of financing and employment of the entrepreneur as a senior manager (Testa 1997; Hellman 1998).

Start-up financing may involve co-financing by several venture capitalists with one of them acting as a leading financier and manager, although this practice has recently become less common.[15] Among experienced and mutually known venture capitalists, the position of leading manager is rotated over different projects. This arrangement serves not so much as a mechanism of risk-diversification than one of reciprocal delegation of monitoring among a group of venture capitalists. The reciprocal delegation not only avoids the duplication of intense monitoring but also functions as a device to control possible shirking of monitoring by venture capitalists (Lerner 1994; Fenn, Liang, and Prowse 1995). If a leading venture capitalist shirks ex ante monitoring or is incompetent, and more than a normal number of entrepreneurial projects monitored by him/her fail, his/her reputation will be tarnished. Then the venture capitalist will lose opportunities for raising additional funds and participating in potentially profitable future projects organized by others. This aspect of venture capital financing is analyzed in the last section of this chapter. Otherwise, we abstract from this reciprocal relationship among venture capitalists, and regard the relationship of an entrepreneur with venture capital funds as if it were with a single venture capitalist.

At the time of start-up the venture capitalist commits only a fraction of the capital needed for the ultimate development of a project, with the expectation that additional financing will be made stepwise, contingent on the smooth proceeding of the project which may not be contractible—a process that Salman (1990) called "staged" capital commitment. Recently there is an increasing tendency for the financing of different stages to be specialized by different classes of venture capitalists.[16] However, in modeling we ignore this and assume as if staged financing were performed by a single venture capitalist. Venture capital financing normally takes the form of convertible preferred stocks, subordinated debt with conversion privileges, or combinations of multiple classes of common stock and straight preferred stock (Fenn, Liang, and Prowse 1995; Gompers and Lerner 1996; Gompers 1998; Kapalan and Stromberg 2000). In any case, venture capitalists are protected from downside risk because they are paid before holders of common stock in the event of project failure. Also they retain an exit option exercisable by refusing additional financing at a critical moment when a start-up firm needs the infusion of new funds to survive or to proceed to the next stage of development. Nevertheless, a typical shareholding agreement allows an entrepreneur to increase his ownership share (normally in common stock) at the expense of initial investors if certain performance objectives are met. Fired entrepreneurs forfeit their claims on stock that has not been vested.

The venture capitalists, leading as well as nonleading, are well represented on the boards of directors of start-up firms. For example, Lerner (1994a) reports that venture capitalists hold more than one-third of the seats on the boards of venture-backed biotechnology firms—more than the number held by management or other outside directors. Kaplan and Stromberg (2000) also report a similar finding (the venture capitalist has the majority of the board seats in normal states in 26 percent of their 190 samples), noting that venture capitalist control tends to increase with a number of financing rounds. In addition to attending board meetings, leading venture capitalists often visit entrepreneurs-cum-senior-managers at the site of venture-funded firms ("stay close"). They provide advice and consulting services with the senior management, such as helping raise additional funds, reviewing and assisting with strategic planning, recruiting financial and human resource management, introducting potential customers and suppliers, and providing public relations and legal specialists. They also actively exercise conventional roles in the governance of the start-up firms, often firing the founder-managers when needed. According to the *Stanford Project on Emerging Companies* (SPEC) which collected panel data on 100 high-technology start-up firms in Silicon Valley, the likelihood that a nonfounder will be appointed as CEO in the first twenty months of a company's life is around 10 percent; this likelihood increases to about 40 percent after forty months and to over 80 percent after eighty months, to say nothing of companies going out of business that are not included in the sample (Baron, Burton, and Hannan, 1996; Hannan, Burton and Baron, 1996).

There are many business failures among entrepreneurial start-up firms.[17] Many failures crop up early, usually in the first one or two years. Frequent failures may be caused not only by overzealous competition among ambitious entrepreneurs but also because the venture capitalist himself may contribute to it. For example, Salman and Stevenson observed the following phenomenon in an emerging segment of the computer data storage industry in the mid-1980s. "In all, forty-three start-ups were funded in an industry segment that could be expected in the long run to support perhaps four." Thus "'failure' is at the very least endemic to the venture capital process, an expected commonplace event; in some cases, the process itself may even promote failure." (Gorman and Sahlman 1989:238) In casual conversations in Silicon Valley, venture capitalists normally regard three successes out of ten initial fundings as successful and two successes as acceptable.

If the project is successful, the relational financing terminates, either with an initial public offering (IPO) or buyout (acquisitions) by other firms. It used to take five to seven years for the start-up firms to be able to go to the IPO market. Recently there has been a tendency for this period to be shortened (even two years). However, the shortening of the period may have been partially induced by the stock market boom, as were the cases in the past. Another reason could be that early-marketed firms of recent vintage aim at business applications of more-or-less known technology so that the development time can be shortened.[18] Venture capitalists decide when to go to the IPO market with marketing expertise. When an IPO exceeds a prespecified performance criteria (e.g., designated stock price), the securities held by the venture capitalists, such as convertible stock and debt, automatically convert into common stock. Capital gains are distributed among the venture funds and the entrepreneur according to their shares at that time. Experienced venture capitalists can time the IPO to occur when the market valuation of portfolio firms is particularly high, while less experienced and less reputable venture capitalists are found to be eager to bring a portfolio firm to market prematurely (Lerner 1994; Gompers 1995).

Some authors argue that the presence of active IPO markets is an essential element of the success of venture capital financing and the resulting product innovation, and that their absence may be responsible for the fact that other economies have a difficult time emulating the Silicon Valley phenomenon (e.g., Bankman and Gilson 1996). Although there may well be an element of truth in this claim, it is also important to note that recently successful start-up firms have increasingly become the targets of acquisition by leading firms in the same market rather than going to IPO markets (Hellmann 1998b). These firms are often themselves grown-up entrepreneurial firms that have been successful in assuming leadership in setting standards in their niche markets. They aim to acquire successful start-up firms, either to kill off potential sources of challenges to their set standards, or to further strengthen their market positions by shortening the period of in-house R&D by the so-called A&D (acquisition and development). These leading firms are said to have an influence on venture capitalists in guiding their activities.

From the viewpoint of start-up entrepreneurs, they are said to prefer buyouts to IPOs, particularly when they have only a single innovative product line (Hellmann 1998b), but competition among them for a buyout is keen.[19] By bundling complementary technology the acquiring firms may be able to establish monopolistic positions in respective markets. However, since this bundling occurs ex post (after the development of products), their monopolistic positions cannot be taken as the inevitable outcome of technological increasing returns but as those of a marketing strategy. As discussed in the main text, the innovative nature of the Silicon Valley model lies in its ex post flexibility in the reconfiguration of innovative technological product systems. Its important public policy implication can then be that any bundling of modular products by a leading firm that is not technologically imperative but serves primarily as a deterrent to innovative re-bundling (e.g., the bundling of the OS and the internet browser by Microsoft) ought to be regulated.

The venture capitalists perform the functions of ex ante monitoring (screening of proposed projects to cope with the possible adverse selection problem), ad interim monitoring (preventing shirking and wasteful, private use of resources that do not yield economically valuable technology, selection of ongoing projects for staged refinancing), and ex post monitoring (the verification of project results and the controlling decision as to which exit strategy is to be exercised) vis-à-vis venture-funded firms, although these functions tend to be specialized by different classes of venture capitalis. Ex ante monitoring, and ad interim monitoring to some extent, of an entrepreneurial project requires professional engineering competence in specialized fields, while ex post monitoring requires financial expertise. The venture capitalists meet such needs and tend to focus on companies in specific industries. Although the venture capitalists play a dominant governance role in venture-backed firms, their property rights arrangements have complex elements of joint-ownership with the provision of bilateral option rights: the venture capitalists' rights to exercise an exit option against the entrepreneur's interest in bad times (liquidation rights), and the entrepreneur's right to the issued options to be vested contingent on subsequent performance. Control rights are voluntarily relinquished ex ante by the entrepreneur, particularly if he is liquidity-constrained at the outset (Hellmann 1998a). But as the project moves ahead successfully, he can regain control rights and the venture capitalist will relinquish liquidation rights. As stated in chapter 11.3, this mechanism is reminiscent of relational contingent governance (see also Black and Gilson 1998; Kaplan and Stromberg 2000).

15 Epilogue: Why Does Institutional Diversity Continue to Evolve?

The major purpose of this book has been to construct a conceptual and analytical framework for understanding the role of institutions in the economies—both historical and contemporary—in a unified way. We defined institutions as self-sustaining systems of collective beliefs and examined the ways in which they form a coherent overall arrangement. Our emphasis has been the diversity of viable institutional arrangements as is implied by the multiplicity of equilibria in the presence of strategic complementarities. In section 15.1 we put together the pieces analyzed and used as illustrative examples throughout the book, into some important theoretical and contemporary models of the overall institutional arrangements.

Any institutional arrangement, regional, national, or local, can be thought of as having the emergent state of technologies and global market institutions as its environment. Institutional arrangements may then be regarded as potentially linked with each other through technologies and markets. We are witnessing that this linkage is becoming ever more extensive as well as intensive because of the remarkable progress of information and communications technologies (ICT) and the increasing global integration of markets. So we need to examine some interesting questions: How do national and other local institutional arrangements adapt themselves to the forceful impacts of these ongoing environmental changes? Despite various institutional complementarities that tend to make institutional arrangements endogenously robust and inertial, are they compelled to respond to these changes in an identical manner? In other words, do they tend to become more or less alike? As a result, will the overall global institutional arrangement become, and should it perhaps become, uniform and monotone, dominated by transnational organizations and global rules, regardless of whether or not we wish such world? Section 15.2 presents some skeptical conjectures on these questions as a way of summarizing the arguments that we have developed. We will argue that institutional diversity in the overall global arrangement will remain despite the closer linkage of national markets and the development of ICT.

15.1 Some Stylized Models of Overall Institutional Arrangements

Equilibrium institutional arrangements across domains can be suboptimal in the presence of institutional complementarities. They are also partially shaped by types of embedding social-capital distributions, as well as the abilities of agents (internal or third-party) that bundle various games across domains in pursuit of entrepreneurial rents through the creative destruction of old bundling. The synchronic structure of overall institutional arrangement can therefore be multiple and diverse (chapter 8). Indeed, we observe a remarkable diversity, even though there is a tendency for some aspects of national institutional arrangements to converge under the influence of globally integrated markets and ICT. Before examining the latter tendency, we summarize below some prominent models of institutional linkage across domains.

In figure 15.1 several models of overall institutional arrangements are represented in terms of mutually interdependent constituent institutions that arise in and across domains, such as organizational fields; corporate governance; financial, labor, supply, and product transactions; property rights definition and contract enforcement; social exchange; and polity. They may be classified into three subgroups. The first is comprised of two models of pure theoretical construct that can serve as a benchmark for the analysis of institutional complementarities: the Walrasian neoclassical model and the property-rights model due to Grossmann, Hart, and Moore. The second includes some representative models derived from stylized observations of advanced national economies such as those of the United States, Germany, and Japan, prior to the recent breakthrough in ICT. (It omits some other models, reflecting the stylized characteristics of French, Italian, and Scandinavian economies, etc. However, these omissions are not because of their lesser relevance or importance, but only because we lack adequate knowledge to analyze them beyond casual observation.[1]) The third subgroup comprises two important models—global (transnational) and local (Silicon Valley)—emergent in the age of the ICT revolution. Whether these models are going to dominate the models in the second class, or whether the second will pursue their own courses of evolution in response to the competitive challenge posed by the models of the third class, is a subject of great current debate. Before trying to answer this question in the next section, however, we first need to recognize the essential systemic differences existing among the members of the second class.

The following discussion does not cover two other important classes of overall institutional arrangements, that is, those found in developing and transforming economies. For the latter we have made some succinct references in chapters 6.2 and 10.3 (example 10.11). The variety in developing economies is so rich that even primitive subclassification is far beyond our present expertise. But often in these models such institutional phenomena as classical hierarchies, government-controlled or relational banking (chapter 12), diversified business groups (example 8.10), underdevelopment of specialized supplier-firms, social and family networks (example 10.2), market-enhancing or degenerate developmental states (chapter 6.3), repressed labor movement or strong labor organizations, and weak third-party legal enforcement are found to cluster. Whether or not the coexistence of these phenomena can be explained by some kind of complementarities relationships, under what conditions they can or cannot contribute to economic development as a system, or in what sequence they may be reformed, and the like, will undoubtedly constitute the most important research agenda for comparative institutional analysis.

domain / model	convention of organizational architecture	corporate governance	financial institutions	labor and employment institutions	product market/ industrial institutions	supply relationships	property rights rules and enforcement	social embeddedness/ norms/values	state
W	technological black-box	entrepreneurial control	auctioneers	auctioneers	auctioneers		exogenously set and enforced	utilitarianism	liberalism
HM	functional hierarchy	owner control (H-M firm)	active capital asset markets	efficiency wage		integration of complementary physical assets	incomplete contracts/ residual rights of control		(liberalism)
A	functional hierarchy	managerial control	securitization (markets of corporate control)	employing bureaucracy, job-control unionism	regulated oligopolistic competition	vertical integration	interpreted and enforced by the court	various communities	representative democratic
D	participatory hierarchy	co-determination	committed stockholders	corporatist regulations	enabled trade associations	autonomous suppliers	associative regulations	industrial citizenship	social-compact corporatism
J	horizontal hierarchy	relational contingent governance	main bank system	companywide personnel control	industrial associations	supplier keiretsu	repeated ex post renegotiation	social status gradation	bureau-pluralism
SV	encapsulated diversity	VC-governance by tournament	venture capital staged-financing, IPO markets	high mobility due to short life cycle of start-up firms	clustering, standard-setting associations	fabless-firms	lawyers' contract design and deal-making	professional communities, entrepreneurial tournament	entrepreneur-friendly
GL	network integrated f-hierarchies	market monitoring	global corporate assets markets	cross-border competition	strategic alliance, e-commerce	A&D, b2b e-commerce	"contract as products"	diverse NGOs	multi-layered states

Figure 15.1
Some models of institutional linkages

Models of Theoretical Reference

W-Model   This is the Walrasian neoclassical model used in pre-game-theoretic, neoclassical comparative economic systems as the yardstick for measuring efficiency of (non)market economies (e.g., see Bergson 1964). The model is built on the premise that property-rights arrangements implicit in the initial distribution of endowments of capital, labor, and land are predetermined and enforced outside the model, presumably by the nonintervening liberal state.[2] It is also assumed that all goods and services are marketed and their prices are competitively adjusted by the auctioneers and known to everybody. The firm is taken as a technologically determined black box run by the entrepreneur who commits to the utilitarian value of profit maximizing and combines factors of production, such as services of labor, capital, and land, as well as intermediate goods, to achieve that objective. This model is assumed to adapt to changing technological environments smoothly through the adjustment of competitive prices and entrepreneurial responses to them. The auctioneers and the entrepreneurs may be considered as representing the personifications of quintessential institutions, markets and capitalist firms, operating according to very definite rules understood and expected by every agent. However, we may consider that one of the utilities of the Walrasian model is to suggest a value of nonmarket institutions by making clear how "the real economy differs from [it] in significant ways" (Arrow 1998:39) especially in the incompleteness of markets. Nonmarket institutions coordinates expectations of the agents in situations where markets fail to exist.

HM-Model   This model, based on the contributions of Grossman, Hart, and Moore, is considered to be an important modification of the W-model, explicitly taking into account the role of property rights in physical capital goods.[3] The essence of this model has already been discussed in chapter 4.3. The HM firm is run by the owner-manager who controls a functional hierarchy through the residual rights of control over assets, both physical and human. Such rights associated with the ownership of physical assets can fill the gap left by incomplete employment contracts. Applying the same logic used for explaining the integration of ownership and management, it can be shown that the owner-manager expands the boundary of the firm up to the point where complementary physical assets are fully integrated.[4] Since the workers are not provided with sufficient incentives for accumulating and efficiently using organization-specific human assets, the owner-manager may be interested in adopting and developing technologies in which reliance on workers' information processing is minimized. Therefore this model may be less relevant in places where the production of alienable information assets takes place with the use of nonphysical, information assets, alienable and human (chapter 4.3).

Some Traditional Models of Advanced National Economies

A-Model This model is based on the stylized traditional features of oligopolistic corporate firms and the surrounding institutional environments prevailing in the American economy prior to the ICT revolution. These firms were organized according to the legal tradition of "public corporations," providing the board of directors with somewhat autonomous internal control rights.[5] These firms internalized nested functional hierarchies to coordinate the activities of managers and employees at various levels (chapter 4.1).[6] The information-processing role (job description) of each node of the hierarchy was clearly articulated and demarcated, while the employment contract for an occupant of the position was set according to its job contents (required skills and experience, responsibility, hazards, etc.) and the level of his/her ability to perform the job. These practices were institutionalized through the bureaucratization of personnel management by the "employing bureaucracy" (Jacoby 1975) and the countervailing "job-controlled" unionism.[7] No obligations were expected by either side of the contracting partners beyond a contractual agreement. The collective interests of the working class were partially represented by the Democratic Party competing in the framework of a two-party, representative democratic state (chapter 5.2).

Residual revenues after contractual payments to employees accrued to the corporation. If the payments to the employees and other product factors reflect their marginal value contributions through competition in external and internal markets, residual maximization can be theoretically consistent with internal efficiency. The traditional view has been to regard the board as owing fiduciary duties to the stockholders when evaluating management policy and/or selecting top management.[8] The existence of a competitive market for corporate valuation (and corporate control rights) can theoretically provide effective external discipline on residual maximization of the board (Manne 1964). Thus, at a theoretical level, the coexistence of competitive (internal and external) job markets and stock markets are mutually complementary to the efficiency of the stock-price maximizing of the corporate firm internalizing a functional hierarchy.

As the HM-model above suggests, residual rights of control over physical assets, downstream and upstream, benefit the top manager of functional hierarchies by enhancing his bargaining power vis-à-vis other managers using those assets, when they are not mutually concerned with building cooperative reputations over time. Therefore there are incentives for the top manager to integrate both backward and forward.[9] Thus, up to the 1970s, the representative American firms tended to comfortably operate in oligopolisitc product markets under the price leadership of dominant firms. Because of their market positions these firms were able to afford a certain degree of internal inefficiency due to the growing rigidity creeping into their organizational architecture. The rigidity expressed itself in ever-longer lines of managerial coordination. Also the job-controlled unionism, which had originally developed to curve the arbitrariness, nepotism, and favoritism in the hierarchical control of foremen, began to deter flexible job assignments in response to changing technological and market environments. This observation indicates that the competitive product markets is complementary to the market for corporate control. That is, the disciplinary effect exercised by the market for corporate control on the management may be diminished (resp. enhanced) by decreased (resp. increased) competitiveness in the product market.

D-Model   This model is derived from stylized facts about the German economy before the ICT revolution and the unification of Germany after the demise of the East German communist state. We have already seen in chapters 4.2 and 6.2 that the organization convention prevailing in this model is characterized as participatory hierarchies internalizing work councils as a constituent element and embedded by the social-compact corporatist state. The government "enables" (Streeck) trade associations and industrial unions to develop their own governance in the labor transaction domain. Their bargaining outcomes can be legally extended to nonmembers. Combined with social norms of social solidarity and "industrial citizenship" (Marshall 1964) that affords various socially recognized rights to workers distinct from formal political and civil rights, it entails remarkably compressed wage differentials among individuals, industrial sectors, and small and large firms.

At the level of the corporate-governance domain, the matching structure is provided by the statutorily stipulated codetermination scheme. Many German firms are still individually owned and/or relate to a few universal banks that own significant share of equity and debt contracts and serve as share custodians for individual shareholders as well as board membership.[10] In chapter 11.2 we provided a formal reasoning of institutional complementarity between national social-compact corporatism, on one hand, and codetermination, on the other.[11] For this complementarity to hold, it appears to be essential that the stockholding structure is relatively stable, either through closed ownership or the majority voting rights of committed stockholders such as universal banks, so the *Aufsichtsrat* (supervisory board) is not under strong stock market pressure.

Some argue that a fundamental change is occurring in this respect, because both D-firms and universal banks are shifting toward more market-based financing and operations (e.g., Edwards and Fischer 1994). However, this argument should be heeded cautiously. German universal banks, even in the new emergent market environment, are undoubtedly in an advantageous position for sustaining relational financing to the D-firm in the form of investment banking. In contrast to Japanese city banks until the mid-1990s, they have not been hampered by regulations from developing expertise in market-based financing, which can be beneficial to the D-firm as well.[12] Further the development of securities markets for corporate financing and the development of markets for corporate control are not the same thing, and the former will not necessarily be accompanied by the latter. Although American business-school-trained managers are increasingly active in corporate asset markets for restructuring, there is no sign yet that markets for corporate control are emerging as an institutionalized corporate governance environment of the D-firm.[13] However, a recent regulatory change regarding the reduction of capital gains tax from sales of stock may provide incentives for banks to reduce their equity ties with client D-firms. The prospect of the increasing transferability of shareholding through the projected growth of private pension funds may also affect the coherence of the D-model more than anything else.

J-Model This is a model derived from stylized facts about the Japanese economy as observed in the period from 1960 through the early 1990s. We have discussed in various places institutional complementarities involving organizational conventions of horizontal hierarchies, the main bank system, and the bureau-pluralist state (chapters 6.2, 11.3, 12.2, and 13). In this model organizational and various economic transaction domains, as well as political economic domains, are embedded by a web of social exchange domains through which nontangible, symbolic social capital (prestige, esteem, social approval, etc.) are distributed among the members—organizational or individual—in a gradational manner, according to competence, achievement, reputation, contribution to collective goods, and so forth, depending on context (e.g., examples 8.1 and 8.2). The high density of social embeddedness have helped sustain an income disparity reduced as has been the case under social-compact corporatism and the D-model. However, it also means that a safety net was often provided in the form of ex post renegotiations among relational partners (e.g., between financially distressed firms and their main banks, or depressed industries and relevant government bureaus). Such a renegotiation possibility might have helped social stability and institutional coherency in fairly stable environments, but when the risks involved were systemic, it could create systemic moral hazard problems. In chapter 13.3 we saw how the globalization of financial markets and the development of ICT created a crisis of shared beliefs in Japan in the late 1990s through the web of institutional complementarities and linkages across various domains. In response, the institutional framework described by this model has begun to undergo significant modifications, although the process is gradual and its road map has not been clearly depicted yet (chapters 10.2 and 13).

Emergent ICT-Driven Models

SV-Model   This model is derived from stylized observations of the Silicon Valley phenomenon. The fascinating story of the Silicon Valley phenomenon all began at a place where a small number of risk-taking venture capitalists and a small number of entrepreneurs started to meet. The venture capitalists started to experiment with a new strategy in the domain of financial transactions—the "venture capital financing" strategy characterized by staged, relational financing (chapters 8.2, 12, and 14). Similarly the entrepreneurs started to experiment with a new strategy in the domain of the organizational field—the "information encapsulation" strategy characterized by independent, modular development projects outside the context of traditional corporate hierarchies (chapters 4.2 and 14.1). As analyzed in detail in chapter 14, both strategies are potentially complementary, but for them to co-evolve, they need to be backed up by "institution-relevant" policies, competence, and other parameters. Important parameters were as follows:[14]

• The presence of a research university and other educational institutions in the neighborhood having a culture of open intellectual communications and capable of supplying risk-taking engineers as well as technicians with a broad range of expertise.

• The presence of competence in machinery manufacturing, partly inherited from the defense industry, facilitating the fast fabrication of customized pilot products.[15]

• The government policy of deregulating the portfolio selection of pension funds in risky investments in venture capital funds, lowering the capital gains tax, and liberalizing the immigration of technologically qualified foreigners.[16]

Once all these factors were put to work together in one place, the experimental strategies became increasingly viable. Learning from doing, combined with an inherent complementarity between the two strategies, have provided a momentum, further attracting relevant resources from outside. Both strategies became established as mutually supportive equilibria and thus as an overall institutional arrangement in the local domain, whose impact could start to propagate beyond the region and the high-tech industry.

Entrepreneurial firms in this model are more or less specialized in the design of modular products of potential product-systems and the fabrication of their products are often contracted out (thus "fabless" firms, i.e., devoid of fabrication facilities).

In-process information generated by the inventive activities of entrepreneurs can be potentially valuable to other entrepreneurs as well, but at the same time the economic value of this information can depreciate very quickly in the age of rapid technological progress. It has made a legalistic approach to intellectual property-rights definition and enforcement rather difficult and costly, unless processed information can be made into patentable commercial output. Indeed, postemployment covenants not to compete became legally unenforced in California, on the basis of a statutory stipulation dating back to the last century (Gilson 1999). Thus intellectual property rights became somewhat diluted.[17] Accordingly the boundary of the firm based on property rights over physical assets à la the HM firm became blurred.[18]

Entrepreneurs are then forced to encapsulate inventive activities from each other by enclosing employees with stock option plans and other benefits, while communicating unpropriety information mutually beneficial to them in specifying their product performances and interfaces. The entrepreneurial strategy of this dualistic characteristic is facilitated by being embedded in various open-ended professional communities formed by school and professional ties, ethnic backgrounds, and so forth (chapter 2.3). These communities ease the fast and dense exchange of technical knowledge and ideas. Often these communications are done only in face-to-face contacts and by providing high social esteem and iconic status, as well as pecuniary rewards, to the most able and successful. At the same time they facilitate flexible combinations and recombinations of their members to form new start-up firms.

GL-Model This is the model formed by stylized observations of emergent practices of global corporate firms, typically of American origin but not necessarily limited to it, and their surrounding institutional environments in the age of ICT. The A-firm of the pre-ICT vintage started to face increasing competition from the D-firm and J-firm after its golden age in the 1960s, having the access to oligopolistic profits increasingly encroached. The relative decline of those oligopolistic firms led to the gradual unbundling of business activities traditionally integrated within the old corporate form, and as a result a loose re-bundling emerged on the periphery of traditional industrial America, such as Silicon Valley, and started to threaten the innovative capability of the traditional A-firms from inside as well (Baldwin and Clark 2000; see also example 10.9). Thus they were forced to restructure to survive.

There were two important parametric factors that facilitated this change: one is the burst of ICT development, and the other is the accumulated competence conducive to the efficient operation of financial markets. The development of ICT has made some large competitive firms—GL firms—extend their activity globally without increasing hierarchical layers. Their organizational architecture can be characterized as a network-integrated, functional hierarchy as conceptualized in chapter 4.2. In using ICT-based information networks, the GL-firms are reorganizing and extending the scope of functional hierarchies. On the other hand, the same ICT development, together with the rise of institutional investors (pension and mutual funds) induced by demographic change (the prospect of longer life), has enhanced competition in financial markets operating on codifiable information (e.g., financial data of portfolio firms), while pressing more transparent corporate information disclosure and share-value maximization on the GL-firms. In response, the GL-firms focused more on value maximization through such means as competitive outsourcing of modular parts and internet procurement of standardized supplies (the so-called b2b e-commerce), as well as the acquisition of successful entrepreneurial firms (A&D) and cross-market strategic alliances with other firms on both the upstream and downstream sides (chapter 14, appendix).

The increasing globalization of GL-firms also poses interesting questions in commercial exchange and other domains. Economies where governments impose higher regulation may be bypassed as possible production bases by such firms, which will reduce the ability of governments to tax. Still the traditional international regulatory architecture may not necessarily fit well with unprecedented increases in commerce, communications, and transportation on a global scale. Facing such situations, GL-firms seek to protect their own property rights partially by technologically designed mechanisms of contract enforcement, such as in the use of cryptology, "contracts as products" (Radin 1999; see chapter 3.5). In lieu of retreating national governments, these firms are beginning to be embedded by diverse communities, not only geographically defined ones, but also cross-border nongovernmental organizations (NGOs) bound by various professional standards, ethics, and value commitments. Although influential and internally embedded in corporate culture of respective national origin, the GL-firm may not secure its position in product markets if it ignores the possible impacts of these organizations and communities.

15.2 Self-organizing Diversity in the Global Institutional Arrangement

The state as an equilibrium of the game in the polity domain constitutes an essential element of any overall institutional arrangement, while the polity domain is often structured with the national government as a focal agent. The nature of institutional arrangements may accordingly appear to be largely characterized nationally. However, in the face of the increasing integration of national economies into globalized markets, some political economy theorists and others contend that nation-based comparative analysis is losing relevance. For example, after arguing that the accelerated technological progress has made it more efficient for firms to operate beyond the narrow confines of national borders, and that organizational differences have consequently become greater across (oligopolistic) sectors than across nations, the late Susan Strange asserted:

> There are three further reasons for thinking that the approach of most comparativists greatly overstates the role of national institutions and national policies. One is the general decline in the ability of governments to manage their national economies as they might like . . . . Second is the growth in transnational regulation of capitalist behaviour, by means of which national regulation is steadily supplanted and national differences eroded. Third is what could be described as the denationalization of firms, the loss of identity between the location of the firm's headquarters and its behaviour in the world economy.   (1997:188)

While this view captures certain aspects of emergent phenomena, it seems nevertheless one-sided to regard the world economy as heading toward a monotone, uniform state dominated by integrated international markets and transnational firms, with national institutions in retreat—a view that may be referred to here as transnationalist for convenience. Our approach, and thus its implications as well, differs from the ones that either national comparativists or transnationalists pursue. What are the major differences?

First of all, note that the unit of our analysis is a (transactional) domain described by a set of agents and sets of their action choices. The characteristics of the domain, together with a rule (the consequence function) that assigns a consequence for each profile of agents' action choices, constitute the "exogenous" rules of the game (or, a mechanism). An institution is then conceptualized as a summary representation of one out of the game's possible many equilibria that would emerge in the domain (chapters 1 and 7). A domain may be identified with a national economy (as the comparativists do), but it also may be subnational or supranational (as viewed by the transnationalists). Thus, for example, a convention of organizational architecture can evolve in an organizational field of national scale (e.g., the A-firm, J-firm, D-firm), but also at a subnational level (e.g., the Italian industrial districts or the SV-clustering in chapter 4.2) as well as at the supranational level (e.g., the GL-firm). We have also tried to understand why different organizational conventions have evolved in practice, and can be viable theoretically as multiple equilibria, in domains with the same technological characteristics. This is what "comparative analysis" means to us. We do not need to limit ourselves only to the comparison of national systems, although it is admittedly an important and relevant research focus. On the other hand, there is no compelling reason why there will eventually be only one equilibrium in organizational fields as would be embodied in the GL-firms. Even if homogeneous denationalized firms appear dominant in certain markets, in other markets the organizational architecture of local, national, or regional origins can evolve in path-dependent ways and their interactive dynamic can have important implications for understanding future trajectories of the world economy.

As we emphasized in chapter 1, we cannot start our analysis with a domain characterized by completely institution-free, completely technology-determined, exogenous rules of the game. The rules of the game given in any domain have already been more or less characterized by some humanly devised mechanisms (rules). Thus some transactions may take place in the trade domain in one place during some period of time, but in the organizational domain in other places in other periods of time (Williamson 2000). Likewise some other transactions may take place either in the polity domain or the trade domain, depending on the historical path. From this perspective the transnationalists can be interpreted to contend that national mechanisms, be they polity, organizational, social-exchange, or trade, are being, and will be, encroached and replaced more and more by corresponding transnational mechanisms and that prevailing institutions will thus be of a transnational nature (although they are not clear about the distinction between a mechanism and an institution evolving as an equilibrium therein).

However, the prospect of such linear development cannot be taken for granted, even if the impacts of globalizing markets are undoubtedly significant. There are at least two reasons for this. One is the paradoxical increase in the relative value of tacit knowledge despite, or rather because of, the developing ICT (chapter 12.1). Because of the value of this knowledge, institutions that are "local" in the sense of natural geography, cultural heritage, or communications purview, are bound to keep evolving, side by side with transnational institutions. Second is the systemic nature of institutional arrangements. Throughout the book we have emphasized the interdependencies and linkages of institutions across domains, synchronic and diachronic. Such interdependencies have often evolved with nation states as one of their important focal points. By this we do not mean that policies and organizational designs of national governments have dictated the evolutionary paths of the overall institutional arrangements of national economies. Rather, we have conceptualized the state as an equilibrium of the game in the polity with institutions in other domains (including international trade domains) as environments (data). Conversely, institutions in other domains evolved as equilibria with a state as an environment (data). Thus a state and other institutions are codetermined. Since the international trade domain (global markets) is one of the important environments of nation states, institutions will certainly adapt themselves to impacts of globalizing markets and transnational firms. But this will not imply that all the differences across national domains will disappear and the world economy will be governed by uniform, transnational institutional arrangements. We need to understand how institutions at the transnational level and those at national and other levels interact and co-evolve. In this process transnational and regional institutions (global markets, property-rights enforcement in cyberspace, governance of global financial markets, supranational federalism such as EU, etc.), on one hand, and national and subnational institutions, on the other, may well complement each other rather than act merely as substitutes.

This book is an attempt to prepare a framework for analyzing such complex institutional interdependencies on a global scale. Admittingly the book does not attempt to provide comprehensive treatment because it omits models of developing and transforming economies. Nevertheless, some important implications and possible conjectures about the evolving global institutional arrangements can be derived from the preceding pages. A summary of the possible impacts of the global integration of markets, the preeminence of transnational firms, and the development of ICT[19] would take into account the following points:

1. *Regarding organizational fields and organization domains:*

a. The development of ICT should make the transnational, or global firm (GL-firm) viable, whose organizational architecture is characterized as a globally extended, network-integrated functional hierarchy (chapter 4.2). However, as we saw in chapter 12.1, economically valuable information cannot be digitalized in real time. Some economically valuable information is processed and utilized only tacitly on spot. The other side of ICT development is that it facilitates small firms to be able to efficiently encapsulate information processing leading to the development of a unique (module) product in niche markets (chapter 14.1). Thus, while the GL-firm is becoming increasingly prominent in global markets, small firms, such as observed in the Silicon Valley clustering of firms and in the Italian industrial districts, will likely remain active in niche markets.

b. The efficiency of encapsulated information processing by small organizational units, either small firms or subunits of larger firms, does not lend itself to the unconditional superiority of any organizational architecture to be deployed *within* those units. Comparative-informational efficiency of types of organizational architecture depends on such factors as microtechnology, organizational history, types of available human assets in local markets, and the surrounding institutional arrangements including social norms (chapters 4.1 and 5). Thus organizational diversity will remain, even if there is organizational learning from better practices elsewhere.[20]

c. When small (modular) organizational units are linked into an effective system, various new intermediating and consulting organizations may arise. One example that we have discussed at some length was venture capitalists in Silicon Valley clustering (chapters 4.2, 12, and 14).[21] Also we indicated that the role of management and holding companies, which do not intervene in the operational decisions of constituent units but are active in re-configuring them, can be interpreted from this perspective (chapters 10.3).

2. *Regarding financial transaction and other trade domains:*

a. As discussed in chapter 12.1, some types of tacit knowledge is economically valuable in some financial transaction domains. While (crony) relational financing governed by industrial interests involves a high risk of moral hazard and the financial restraint and entry control by national governments becomes less viable in the environment of the globalizing financial market, the value of relational financing based on economically valuable, uncodifiable knowledge should not be entirely dismissed. Also we showed the theoretical possibility that such relational financing may remain viable even under the global integration of securities markets (proposition 12.3), although its emergence may initially require some kind of protection by national governments (financial restraint, entry restriction, control of short-term capital flows, etc.).

b. Global financiers may be superior in their engineering capability to align efficient portfolio selections and hedge risks based on digitalized information communicated through globalized markets. However, they may lack the ability to directly monitor final borrowers and delegate that function to other types of financiers (e.g., venture capitalists and indigenous bankers in the so-called emergent markets). If an interface between international financiers and indigenous financiers in emergent markets is not well designed and regulated, and if the monitoring competence of the latter is not reliable, instability of the inter-financiers markets may result (chapter 12.2). However, the design of governance rules for international capital flow to emergent markets may not be simply reducible to the requirements of information transparency, prudent regulations, and third-party contract-enforcement on the side of borrowers alone.[22] The East Asian financial crisis occurred because of the symmetry in the inability of making good use of uncodified knowledge on both sides of global and indigenous financiers. The expectation that countries in a currency-crisis will be bailed out by international organizations such as the IMF may leave the moral hazard behavior of lenders unchecked.

c. The development of e-commerce through global cyberspace may genuinely link trade domains globally. However, as we saw in chapter 3, any trade domain cannot function without a credible mechanism of governance for protecting property rights and enforcing contracts. Certainly the role of national governments in this function may recede if there are inconsistencies of property-rights definitions and enforcement rules designed by national governments. Just as the development of markets at the early stage of capitalist development was complemented by the ability of emergent national governments to enforce contracts, further development of e-commerce may call for the harmonization of national laws and cooperation of national governments in contract enforcement, protection as well as control of abusive use of intellectual property rights, and so forth (Radin 1999). But also we should note that even in the domain of e-commerce, third-party enforcement mechanisms need to be, and actually are, replaced or complemented by other mechanisms, such as a multi-party reputation mechanism (e.g., auction Web sites), as well as technology-based digital enforcement mechanisms (chapter 3.5).

3. *Regarding polity domains:*

a. In considering the possible adaptation of nation-states to changing environments, the distinction that we made in chapter 6 between the government as a player in the polity domain and the state as an equilibrium becomes highly relevant. We have seen in chapter 13 a case in which a national framework of government regulations became inconsistent with the increasingly globalized environments, culminating in an institutional crisis (the Japanese banking crisis). Such an inconsistency can be more acute for national economies where political institutions (states) are nonliberal (in the sense defined in chapter 6.1) and constructed with specific domestic interest groups as essential constituents (e.g., national labor unions in social-compact corporatism, industrial associations in bureau-pluralism). These states may thus be forced to adapt themselves to increasingly global environments. As we saw in the example above, this adaptation may not be so easy and thus be only gradual, because the states and other institutions are more tightly linked in those economies.[23] Differences in the characteristics of nation-states as identified in chapter 6.2 will continue to be important factors in determining ways by which they adapt to changing environments.

b. National governments may respond to increasing tensions between national regulations and globalizing markets by forming a supranational, organizational arrangement that overrides national regulatory frameworks. This move may be easier among nations with closely interconnected transaction domains. The formation of supranational federalist arrangements, such as the European Union, is an example (chapter 6.2). On the other hand, for the same reason that small organizational units become viable in organizational fields, certain functions of the government, such as regulations or the provision of safety nets and public goods, environmental protection, may be performed more efficiently in a narrower jurisdictional scope with the participation of local communities and NGOs than that of an entire national economy. The decentralization of the government through market-preserving federalism may be more incentive-compatible in regulating the government's soft-budget constraint tendency (chapter 6.2). Thus evolving political institutions tend to become multi-layered, overlapping structures rather than composed of mutually exclusive Westphalian nation-states that has never been the case even up to now (Krasner 1999).

c. The globalization of markets and the development of ICT makes the global polity domain increasingly relevant. Existing international governance architectures (e.g., UN, IMF, and WTO, and the International Court of Justice) were designed before the globalization era and were based on the exclusive membership of national governments. It is beginning to be debated whether these organizations are capable of resolving emergent international issues, such as the assignment of environmental rights, regulatory inconsistencies, governance of financial markets and trade disputes, the provision of the infrastructure for global markets and protection of property rights in e-commerce, and North–South conflicts, or whether a new global governance mechanism is needed. But, given the differences in nation-states (interpreted as a system of collective beliefs) across North and South, as well as across East and West, combined with the diverse political, social, and moral causes of international nongovernmental organizations (NGOs), it is doubtful that a "global" state (as a system of globally shared beliefs) could emerge and override nation-states in near future.

4. *Regarding social exchange domains:*

a. One of the paradoxes of globalization is that norms that are generically thought of as more or less of localized origins still embed and constrain globalized transactions. We referred to cases where the norms prevailing among professional (and ethnic) communities contribute to the development of software technology in cyberspace and international linkages of high-technology centers (chapter 2.3).

b. The possibility of fast communications in cyberspace and easier physical mobility has given rise to global networks of NGOs for various causes (environmental protection, safety, various human rights, etc.). Transnational firms, nation-states, and international organizations now face the scrutiny of their activities by these networks where the moral causes of their political and social objectives are diverse and sometimes conflicting.

Clearly, the evolving overall institutional arrangements on a global scale are far from a monotonic, uniform state where the transnational firms and globalized financial markets alone dominate and override various national and other local institutions. The global environment has evolved into a complex structure in which various institutions intermesh and interact in a competitive or complementary manner. Because of the fast globalization of markets and the development of ICT, this structure is often in flux, although, as is always the case with any institution, there are elements of inertia and robustness. If this were not the case, the world economy would be neither stable nor viable. Overall, we can expect that as national institutions continue to adapt to the changing global and technological environments, they will do so in path-dependent ways. Then we will continue to see dual tendencies of global institutional arrangements toward the rising importance of supranational institutions, on one hand, and the evolving diversity of regional, national and local institutions, on the other. We believe, however, that it will be the diversity that will make the world economy more robust to unforeseen shocks and its innovative adaptations to its changing environments possible. Since we never know an a priori ideal model of global institutional arrangement, what will allow us to be creative in responding to unfolding environments will be mutual learning, experiments, chance events, and the like, that come from the diversity.

Notes

Chapter 1

1. Greif (1994, 1997b, 1998b), Aoki (1995/2000, 1996), Aoki and Okuno-Fujiwara (1996), Okazaki and Okuno Fujiwara (1999[1995]). Greif calls the approach Historical and Comparative Institutional Analysis (HCIA).

2. For Durkheim, social institutions are composed of symbolic systems—systems of knowledge, beliefs, and the collective ideas. These systems are a joint product of human interactions, but they are experienced by individuals as objective and "coercive" (Durkheim, 1901[1950]).

3. The definition of institutions by Veblen was "settled habits of thought common to the generality of man." (1909[1961]:239).

4. Ostrom is another notable advocate of this view (1990:51).

5. Although enforcement of formal rules is made exogenous to the game by a "third party," the performance of the game would depend upon the effectiveness of monitoring and sanctions. North asks: "What happens when a common set of rules is imposed on two different societies?... The results, however, are not similar.... Although the rules are the same, the enforcement mechanisms, the way enforcement occurs, the norms of behavior, and the subjective models of the actors are not. Hence, both the real incentive structures and the perceived consequences of policies will differ as well. Thus, a common set of fundamental changes in relative prices or the common imposition of a set of rules will lead to widely divergent outcomes in societies with different institutional arrangements" (1990:101). North therefore invokes a more comprehensive notion of an institutional framework that includes "legal rules, organizational forms, enforcement, and norms of behavior" (1991:33. See also 58, 101). Elsewhere he uses the expression "institutional scaffolding" (North 1998) to refer to a similar set.

6. The range of the outcome function is the space of physical outcomes rather than that of utility payoffs. Hurwicz considers that players' utility functions are not part of the rules of the game. Thus he uses the term "game-form," rather than "game," to refer to the triplet of the set of players, their choice spaces, and the outcome function.

7. Strictly speaking, such a parametric representation may be too restrictive and narrow for identifying the institution of a price ceiling, however, as the government may have discretion on the actual level of the price ceiling. Therefore Hurwicz allows for variations in the parameter value and derives the concept of an institution as a family of mechanisms (e.g., a range of ceiling prices) rather than a single mechanism (e.g., a particular ceiling price).

8. Schotter defined a social institution as "a regularity in social behavior that is agreed to by all members of society, specifies behavior in specific recurrent situations, and is either self-policed or policed by some external authority" (1981:11). In this conceptualization, as in the second view, institutions are regarded as rules of conduct. However, instead of being given exogenously by the political or legislative process, such rules are assumed to be endogenously created within the economic process as a solution to the game.

9. A general overview of evolutionary thinking on institutional economics is given by Hodgson (1993) although it does not adopt an explicitly game-theoretic framework.

10. A sociological equivalence of a comprehensive plan of actions may be found in the notion of "script" introduced by Schank and Aberson (1977), which describes behavioral patterns and sequences called up by specific roles or situations.

11. For a more recent conceptualization and its ramification, see Greif (1998b). One subtle difference between his and our conceptualization that will be made clear in this book is our explicit treatment of the cognitive mechanism in the process of institutionalization and its implication for institutional evolution (see particularly chapters 5.2, 7.2, and 9.2).

12. We will argue in chapter 7 that alternative notions of equilibrium, particularly classical and evolutionary, are not necessarily mutually exclusive but may be complementary. Also, depending on the level of specification of domain characteristics, the appropriate equilibrium concept may differ.

13. This aspect is consistent with the phenomenological view of institutions initially developed in sociology of knowledge by Berger and Luckmann (1966). According to these authors, "institutionalization occurs

whenever there is a reciprocal typification of habitualized actions by types of actors" (1966:54). But this "institutional world is experienced as an objective reality" (ibid.:60).

14. In a comprehensive survey of social scientific approaches to institutions, Scott (1995) argues that although different disciplines and schools of social sciences focuses on the regulative, normative, and cognitive aspects of institutions, they may be all present in any institution. Our scheme may also be thought of incorporating the three aspects: an institution is regulatory in that it constrains the choice of the individual agents, it is normative in that it prescribes certain action choices for all the agents through shared beliefs, and it is cognitive in that it is constructed as shared beliefs.

15. Thus Searle, the author of *The Construction of Social Reality*, states that" [a]ll institutional facts are ... ontologically subjective, even though in general they are epistemically objective" (1995:63). However, Berger and Luckmann, the authors of *The Social Construction of Reality*, emphasized that "[the institutional world] does not ... acquire an ontological status apart from the human activity that produce it" (1966:60). Our equilibrium-oriented approach admits that both human activities and beliefs are mutually constitutive as institutions (see figure 1.1).

16. This may be considered as an economist's way of looking at the cognitive aspect of institutions referred to by Scott (1995) in note 14 above.

17. Arrow submits: "Expectation *per se* can be thought of as an element of individual psychology, but in practice social institutions play a major role in guiding and forming expectations. There are ... understandings that others will not exploit every possible short-term profit opportunity, and elaborate financial services networks to provide forecasts and to smooth out temporary difficulties" (1997:6).

18. Later I will make this robustness property a requirement of an institution. In that sense the price vector as a summary representation of tastes and technology cannot be an institution, as it adapts in response to changes in these parameters. Therefore the analogy stops here. However, beliefs that one can buy goods by paying agreed-upon prices and have them delivered as promised can be an institution.

19. The following points have evolved from my own writings (see Aoki 1994a, 1995/2000, 1996). Also Greif have developed the same ideas based on his original research (Greif 1989, 1994, 1998b) and presented them in succinct form in (Greif 1997, 1998a). His influence on my thinking is clear from the next statement. Also, contributions to the third point by Milgrom and Roberts (1990a, 1992, 1994), and my indebtedness to them, need to be noted.

20. For the latter approach, see Reiter and Hugh (1981) and Hurwicz (1996). At one point Young adopts this approach from the evolutionary game perspective (1998:ch. 9).

21. Basu (1997b) provides an interesting parable indicating this point. Compare two games. One of these games—call it "the law"game—has law and the public officials, while the other—call it "the anarchic game"—does not and thus is institution-free. However, suppose that these two games do not differ in terms of the available strategy sets or payoffs to the agents and in any other respects because any action available to an agent labeled the "public official" in the former is available to the same agent (without that name) in the anarchic game. Suppose that we can identify the equilibrium in the former as "lawful equilibrium" and in the latter as "anarchic equilibrium." Then it may appear that legal rules are simply equilibrium. However, the question remains as to what factor would make the "lawful equilibrium" chosen in the former rather than the "anarchic equilibrium." There must be some extra-technological situation that has an effect on the choice of the equilibrium. In this case the law constitutes such a "focal point" (Shelling 1960).

22. The multiplicity of equilibrium as an requirement of a convention is emphasized by Sugden. He submits that "[a] self-enforcing rule ... could be regarded as a convention if and only if we can conceive of some *different* rule that could also be self-enforcing, provided it once become established" (1986:32).

23. This is discussed in more detail in chapter 10.3.

24. For their own contributions to the comparative analysis of institutions and organizations, see Milgrom and Roberts (1990b, 1992, 1994), as well as Holmstrom and Milgrom (1994). Also Pagano (1993) and Pagano and Rowthorn (1994) are two of the earliest analytical contributions to institutional complementarity.

25. Transaction cost economics regards the transaction as the basic unit of analysis as opposed to the agency theory which regards the individual agents as such (for the comparison of the two approaches, see Williamson 1996:ch. 7). In that sense the approach of transaction cost economics is similar to ours which regards the domain of the game as the unit of analysis. Williamson, an authority on transaction cost economics, makes explicit the institutional nature of the environment of the transaction: "[t]hese definitions of institutions [such as by North, Schotter, and others] mainly operate at the level of the institutional environment, the so-called rules of the game. The second, more microanalytic, level at which institutional economics works is at the level of institutions of governance. This book is principally concerned with the institutions of governance (markets, hybrids, hierarchies, bureaus)" (1996:4–5). See also Williamson (2000).

26. Bhagwati et al. (1984), Basu (1997a), Calvert (1995), and Weingast (1995, 1997).

27. Greif (1998a, b), Basu (1997b, 1998), and Kornhauser (1999a, b).

28. Greif (1998a, b).

29. North (1990, 1995) and Basu (1997a).

30. Later, in chapter 9, we deal with the case where agent's subjective perception defines his or her activated set of action choices.

31. The notion of common resources here is close to that of "common-pool resources" used by Ostrom (1990). We include collective goods or bads, such as environmental pollution, from (negative) common resources as long as the sets of actions are qualitatively symmetrical across the agents in the domain. When the common resources are unilaterally provided by the public authority, we call them public goods and relegate their analysis to the polity domain discussed below.

32. We are primarily concerned with the coordinating aspect of the organization here, although the organization may have other aspects as mentioned momentarily. From this perspective, even organizations that are egalitarian or collectivist from the governance perspective may be viewed as having the focal agent (the management).

33. This is regarded as a defining characteristic of organizations by a classical treatise on organizations by Barnard (1938).

34. By distinguishing the government as an autonomous player of the game, our approach in this book is in accordance with lines of thought developed by political scientists such as Skocpol (1979, 1985), Krasner (1978, 1984), and Weingast (1997). However these authors refer to governments (sovereigns) by "state" rather than as an equilibrium state in the polity. For various concepts and approaches to "state" in political science, see Krasner (1984). For the game-theoretic literature, see note 26 above.

35. This type of domain has been the object of institutional study by diverse schools of sociologists, such as the social exchange theorists (e.g., Blau 1964; Homans 1961), phenomenological theorists (e.g., Berger and Luckmann 1966), new institutional sociologists (e.g., Meyer and Rowan 1977; Zucker 1977; Meyer and Scott 1983; DiMaggio and Powel 1983), social embeddedness theorists (Granovetter 1985), and rational choice theorists (e.g., Coleman 1990). For a survey of sociological and other social scientific approaches to institutions, see Scott (1995).

36. In that the exchanges of symbols and languages directly affect the payoffs of the agents, they are distinguished from the so-called cheap talk in game theory. As a survey of the cheap talk for general readers, see Farrell and Rabin (1996).

Chapter 2

1. So we have $u(x : y') = u(x : y'')$ for all x, y', and y'' whenever $x + y', x + y'' \leq 100$ and $v(y : x') = v(y : x'')$ for all y, x', and x'' whenever $x' + y, x'' + y \leq 100$.

2. Here is a sketch of the proof. Take for simplicity only the case where $k(A) = k(B) = k$. Suppose that during the periods between 1 and k, A and B always pick up the same samples composed of catches in the

preceding periods between $-k + 1$ and 0 (this is possible because $2k < m$) and therefore always catch x and y respectively. Suppose that in the following periods between $k + 1$ and $2k$, A and B always pick up the samples composed of the observations from the preceding periods between 1 and k so that the optimal catches of A and B are always $100 - y$ and $100 - x$. Next assume that in the period $2k + 1$ the samples of B contain only observations from the periods between 1 and k and those of A from the periods between $k + 1$ and $2k$. Then their catches are x and $100 - x$, respectively. Assume that at period $2k + t$ ($1 < t \leq k$), the samples of B contain observations from the periods between $2k + 1$ and $2k + t - 1$ and between t and k, while A derives samples from the period between $k + 1$ and $2k$. Then their catches are always x and $100 - x$ respectively. Finally, assume that from $3k + 1$ to $3k + m$, both samples contain only observations from the k immediate past periods. The combination of catches x and $100 - x$ are then repeated. Therefore from the period $3k + m + 1$ on ward, the optimal catch of A and B will be always x and $100 - x$, respectively, which implies the establishment of a convention. Since the choice of k samples from m records are random, the described situation will occur with a positive probability $p > 0$. Therefore the probability that a convention will not be established over the $T(3k + m)$ periods is $(1 - p)^T$, which approaches to zero as T gets infinitely large.

3. Here is a sketch of the proof. Suppose that a convention $X = (x^*, 100 - x^*)$ is established. Let us conceptualize the cost of the transition from x^* to $x^* + 1$ as the minimum number p of experiments that player A needs to make in order for player B to accept $100 - x^* - 1$ as the best response—player A (or B) refers to individual A (or B), and his or her ancestors. This happens if player A makes p successive experimental catches of $x^* + 1$, and player B includes this information in its sample $k(B)$, so that $v(100 - x^* - 1 : x^* + 1) \geq (1 - p/k(B))v(100 - x^* : x^*)$. Rearranging obtains $p \geq k(B)[-v(100 - x^* - 1 : x^* + 1) + v(100 - x^* : x^*)]/v(100 - x^* : x^*)$. By ignoring the integer requirement, approximate the right-hand side by $k(B)v'(100 - x^* : x^*)/v(100 - x^* : x^*)$, and define it as the cost of transition from x^* to $x^* - 1$. Symmetrically the cost of transition from x^* to $x^* + 1$ may be defined as $k(A)u'(x^* : 100 - x^*)/u(x^* : 100 - x^*)$. Imagine that random experiments drive the convention in the direction where the transition cost is smaller. Repeat the same reasoning. Though somewhat lacking precision, we may conjecture that the long-run stochastic process marked by random mutation tends to be stabilized in the long run with a higher probability around a convention at which the costs of transition in either direction are the same. Dividing by m the balancing condition, $k(A)u'(x^* : 100 - x^*)/u(x^* : 100 - x^*) - k(B)v'(100 - x^* : x^*)/v(100 - x^* : x^*) = 0$, we have $d[(k(A)/m) \log u(x : 100 - x) \times (k(B)/m) \times \log v(100 - x : x^*)]/dx|_{x=x^*} = 0$. This is equivalent to the condition $x^* \in \text{argmax } u(x : 100 - x)^{k(A)/m} \times v(100 - x : x)^{k(B)/m} = \text{argmax } u(x : 100 - x)^{I(A)} \times v(100 - x : x)^{I(B)}$. See Young (1993) for a detailed proof.

4. One may contend that the assumption of complete ignorance of the risk preference (utility function) of the other party may not be a reasonable one in a situation where games are played repeatedly while risk preferences remain stationary. Suppose that each party comes to correctly conjecture the other's preferences. Then the cost of transition from x^* to $x^* + 1$ defined above divided by $k(A)$ can be interpreted as player A's assessment of player B's "boldness" (Auman and Kurz 1977) or "local bargaining power" (Harsanyi 1977); that is, it can be interpreted as the maximum probability of the conflict situation (zero utility situation) that player B can tolerate at x^* to withstand player A's aggressive demand toward $x^* + 1$. Then, if we assume that the bargaining outcome is pushed in a direction that favors the agent having higher local bargaining power, the process is stabilized at the point where the local bargaining power is equilibrated. At equilibrium we have the ordinary Nash bargaining solution: $x^* \in \text{argmax } u(x : 100 - x)v(100 - x : x)$. Aoki (1984:part II) gives a full discussion of this idea and its application to the bargaining theory of the firm, where the employees are regarded as stakeholders of the firm together with the stockholders.

5. See De Alessi (1980), Libecap (1986), Eggertsson (1990), and Platteau (1999) for historical survey of the development of property rights.

6. This is the point emphasized by North (1990).

7. See the proof in note 2. As the agent's information-processing capacity measured by $I(.)$ exceeds one-half, convergence to a convention becomes problematic.

8. In a book based on field work investigating neighborhood dispute settlement in Shasta County in California, Robert Ellickson found that landowners settle most of their disputes (e.g., those over border fence financing or damages caused by highway collisions involving stray livestock) without any recourse to, and

sometimes even inconsistently with, legal codes. He claims that "neighbors achieve cooperative outcome . . . by developing and enforcing adaptive norms of neighborliness that trump formal legal entitlements" (1991:4). From this viewpoint, he criticizes the "legal centrism" of the so-called Coase theorem on social costs. According to him, the theorem took the legally defined entitlements as initial starting points for dispute settlements and "failed to note that in some contexts initial rights might arise from norms generated through decentralized social processes, rather than from law." (1991:138–39).

9. See Black and Baumgartner (1983).

10. For a recent approach to regard law as the codification of a custom, see Schlicht (1998:ch. 12).

11. From one perspective, the distinction between *nomos* and *thesis* may be thought of as corresponding to the distinction between the endogenous and the exogenous rules of the game that we have already considered in chapter 1.3. The latter specifies the game form in terms of the consequence function (defining sanctions placed on the agents—the citizenry and public officials—depending on actions chosen by them), while the former refers to an equilibrium order chosen under a specific game form. If we interpret law narrowly as codified text (thesis), it may not qualify as *nomos* in the sense of Nash equilibrium. Some laws are duly enacted and, on occasion, enforced. Yet it may not be the case that everybody conforms to it as he or she believes that almost every other member conforms to it (e.g., jaywalking laws in New York City). See Kornhauser (1998a, b).

12. For a discussion of various factors determining the selection of privatization versus the commons, see J. P. Platteau and J.-M. Baland (1998). However, we will see later in chapter 9.3 that the selection may not be completely determined by technological factors alone.

13. References to this topic are numerous. See, for example, Ostrom (1990, 1992), Ostrom and Walker (1994), Bardhan (1993), Platteau (1999), and Baland and Platteau (1996) for comparative perspectives.

14. For a succinct historical survey of the Tokugawa period, see Hall (1991). Ikegami (1995) provides a noteworthy historical and institutional analysis of the role of the *samurai* from sociological perspective.

15. The Tokugawa government set up a rigorous demarcation between towns and villages for political expediency. It classified only castle towns where lords of Han governments resided as official towns (*machi*) and the rest as villages (*mura*), including population centers that had previously developed as towns at strategic crossroads of transportation, market places, and temple towns. Even in such quasi-villages, regular taxpayers were classified as farmers (*hyakusyo*) and their tax obligations were fixed in terms of quantities of rice, even though the substance of their occupations might be merchants, craftsman, and the like. (Amino, 1997:127–28) This chapter deals only with ordinary villages inhabited mostly by land-holding peasants who owe collective tax obligations to a government, although they gradually got involved in the production of commercial crops, such as raw silk, cotton, and rape seeds, as well as in non-farming activities, such as spinning, weaving, and brewing. We consider the commercial and industrial activities of peasant families and their implications to the transition to the market economy later in chapter 10.1.

16. See S. Hayami and M. Miyamoto (1988).

17. The concept of "social capital" originates with Coleman (1990). He defines it as follows: "I will conceive of these social-structural resources as a capital asset for the individual, that is, as social capital. Social capital is defined by its function. It is not a single entity, but a variety of different entities having two characteristics in common: They all consists of some aspects of social structure, and they facilitate certain actions of individuals who are within the structure. . . . Unlike other forms of capital, social capital inheres in the structure of relationships between persons and among persons. it is lodged neither in individuals nor in physical implements of production" (p. 302). Coleman makes no explicit reference to a game situation, although he invoked analogous argument (1990:1). However, there is no explicit contradiction between his and my definitions.

18. For other applications of linked games, see Fudenberg and Kreps (1987), Bernheim and Whinston (1990), and Spagnolo (1999).

19. For the evolutionary selection at the supra-individual, group level in general, see Field (2001).

20. For example, toward the end of the Tokugawa period, village families started to exchange scattered paddies and build small ditches and ridges separating individual paddies to attain a certain degree of individual control over water supply and drainage (Nagata 1971:34–56). Individual rights of water control

within the village eventually came to be codified by a statute enacted some twenty years after the Meiji restoration (1887), although rights to water intake from a larger water supply system (e.g., river) remained collectivized and endowed to the village-based water-use union which operated formally on a majority voting rule.

21. See note 35 in chapter 1.

22. Although not in linked game modeling, a notable earliest treatment of norms in the game-theoretic framework is Ulmann-Margalit (1977).

23. The role of a community norm for market development is the unifying theme of a collective project, *Communities and Markets in Economic Development*, sponsored by the Economic Development Institute of the World Bank and the Stanford Institute for Economic Policy Research. The fourteen papers contributed to this project have been assembled in Aoki and Hayami (2001).

24. To my knowledge, the relationship between linked games and social embeddedness was first pointed out in an earlier version of Spagnolo (1999) dated back to 1994.

25. Later in chapter 9 and 10, we will broaden the notion of linked games beyond the commons domain to understand the nature of diverse institutions as outcomes of such games.

26. For this example, I owe a great deal to Ikeda (1997, 1999) and to conversations with him.

27. It is also possible to do business with OSS. Linux derives profits by the provision of user support services for commercial packages.

28. Since I am not an economic historian by training, the following historical interpretations are highly speculative and conjectural. In writing this section, I benefited from conversations and instructions about facts and the literature by Professors Hiroshi Miyajima and Meredith Woo Cummings. But the interpretations described below are mine.

29. See Palais (1975:chs. 1, 4; 1996:ch. 6) and Wagner (1974). I rely more on Miyajima (1995) as sources of my own interpretations.

30. The Choson Dynasty appointed central bureaucrats as magistrates for a limited period of time. However, they were prohibited from residing in their assigned localities (thus city *yangban*), so they lacked the ability to govern effectively. They delegated tax collection and other local administration to local clerks, but the latter were, in effect, controlled by the local *yangban* whose ancestors had once been central bureaucrats. See Palais (1975:ch. 7) for the grain loan system.

31. Widely quoted is an historical estimate by Hiroshi Shikata, a Japanese scholar who studied the registration records of the Choson Dynasty during his tenure as professor at Seoul Imperial University during the colonial period. In 1690 the proportions of *yangban*, commoners, and *nobi* in the population of Tegu province were 7.4, 49.5, and 43.1 percent respectively. The 1858 record provided a remarkably changed picture: 48.6, 20.1, and 31.2 percent respectively. His study was later criticized for its narrow coverage and methods of classification (e.g., Palais 1996:251). However, the critics seem to be more concerned with the political characteristics as classification criteria, such as eligibility for the central bureaucracy, but less with its social characteristics. The overall picture presented by Shikata seems to be in accord with the generally held view among Korean scholars.

32. Such theory finds its way into the official history textbook in the Korea Republic (Cho and Sung 1995[1997]). James Palais, an American authority on the Choson Dynasty, seems to fundamentally subscribe to such thesis as well. An alternative view held by some Korean scholars is to emphasize the significance of managerial farmers who started to become entrepreneurial in response to increasing marketization in the nineteenth century.

Chapter 3

1. In chapter 1.3 we refer to the exogenous rules of the game as the game form, or equivalently as a mechanism. Here we visualize a governance "mechanism" as an institution, or equivalently as endogenous rules of the game, that would yield stable expectations among traders for sustaining honest trades. We

derive the endogenous rules of governance as an stable equilibrium of repeated plays of the trade game. Once they are established as an institution, however, the rule may effectively govern each individual play of the trade game.

2. As discussed afterward, the basic feature of a bazaar as a meeting place of many mutually unknown traders is encountered on a much larger scale in the present-day e-commerce domain in cyberspace.

3. Denote the payoff matrix as represented in figure 3.1 by M and a possible mix strategy for an agent by $x = (x_1, x_2)$, where the x_1 is the probability of playing H and x_2 that of playing C. The elements of x can also represents the fraction of agents in the domain employing respective each available strategy. Then the evolutionarily stable strategy is x^* such that for all possible x, where $x^* \neq x$, either (1) $x'Mx^* < x^{*'}Mx^*$ or (2) if $x'Mx^* = x^{*'}Mx^*$ and $x'Mx < x^{*'}Mx$ (i.e., x^* is a better response vis-à-vis x).

4. If the exchange of language does not affect the agents' payoffs directly (even if they do strategies), their exchange (cheap talk!) ought to be made distinct from social exchange. See note 36 to chapter 1.

5. Robson describes the requirement of a mutation, whereby inefficient equilibrium, in the present case no trade, can be upset, as follows: "[The] mutants must involve more than simply a different choice from the original set of strategies. Indeed, the mutants here entail the possession of a signal, that is an observable characteristic which can be taken to have zero inherent cost." Robson makes an analogy with a game among the Harris sparrows which mutually differentiate their behavior against opponents according to the color of plumage.

6. The reason Carmichael and MacLeod had to use the concept of neutral stability is that the ESS (evolutionarily stable strategies) concept requires local uniqueness. Their model, and similar models that use communication, face the problem that there are many Nash equilibria that cannot be invaded, corresponding to different gift levels and different "languages."

7. Consistent with the game-theoretic prediction, Geertz submits: "Clientalization represents an actor-level attempt to counteract, and profit from, the system-level deficiencies of the bazaar as a communication network—its structural intricacy and irregularity, the absence of signaling systems and the underdeveloped state of others, and the imprecision, scattering, and uneven distribution of knowledge concerning economic matters of fact—by improving the richness and reliability of information carried over elementary links within it" (1978:31).

8. An important point of the model of Carmichael and MacLeod (1997) is that equilibrium existence requires gift exchange to occur before or at the same time as communication. If communication occurs before the gift exchange, then there is again nonexistence. This is interesting not only because we observe gifts being given at the beginning of a relationship, but also because it highlights the importance of protocol in ensuring efficiency. I owe this point to personal communication with Macleod.

9. See, for example, Calvo (1979), Solow (1980), Shapiro and Stiglitz (1984), and Bowles (1985). The structure of the exchange game that Greif considered was asymmetric in that the possibility of dishonest behavior exists only on the side of agents (employees). However, in reality employment contracts may involve the possibility of dishonesty on both sides. For example, if a contract specifies performance-related payments such as bonuses or piece rates, and if the performance is hard to verify to a third party, then there is a temptation for the employer to default on the contract. The essence of the individualist strategy in Greif's model was to create endogenous gains—the efficiency wage ω_I—for the agent to be honest so that the contract becomes self-enforcing. Is it possible in a symmetric prisoner's dilemma situation to employ a similar device to make performance-related employment contracts self-enforceable so that productive relationship can be sustained? An affirmative answer can be given. See, for example, MacLeod and Malcomson (1989), and Levin (2000).

10. To prove this claim, we only need to check, as before, whether any one-time deviation in the trader's action from the prescribed strategy can raise from the present-value sum of his expected payoffs, given the prescribed beliefs. If not, then by the optimal principle of dynamic programming, there is no other point at which a more complicated deviation will be profitable. Let us check, for example, whether it benefits a dishonest trader not to pay the penalty. If he does not pay, he can save J in the current period and will get zero payoffs in each of the future periods, since his default will be recorded with the LM. If he pays, he will be able to get $\Gamma/2 - Q$ in future periods, of which the present-value sum is $\delta(\Gamma/2 - Q)/(1 - \delta)$. If this sum

is greater than J, it will never be profitable for the trader not to pay the penalty. Likewise one could check that there is no other situation in which any other one-time deviation from the prescribed strategy is beneficial for a trader. Thus mutually shared beliefs that dishonest trading will be penalized by a judgment against the trader and an LM record may deter any dishonest cheating by traders provided that the LM acts neutrally and honestly.

11. If a trader deviates once by paying a bribe even though he has never paid a bribe before, the resulting payoff is $\alpha - Q - B$ this year and zero in the future, since his name will be on the LM's list (note that the LM is assumed to be honest after taking a bribe this year). If he refuses to pay a bribe instead, then his expected payoff is that of the one-shot Nash equilibrium outcome, meaning no exchange this year and $\Gamma/2 - Q$ in each of the future years. Therefore, if it holds that

$$\alpha - Q - B < \frac{\delta(\Gamma/2 - Q)}{1 - \delta},$$

it is not beneficial for the trader to bribe the LM. If a trader has ever paid a bribe before and a bribe is requested again this year, then the net payoff from the prescribed strategy is $\alpha - Q - B$, while not paying leads to zero payoff. Therefore it is profitable to pay the bribe, if $B \leq \alpha - Q$. To maximize his payoff, the LM will then set the level of bribe requested at $B = \alpha - Q$.

12. The example was improvised when I was engaged in a seminar discourse with Stephen Krasner. Later I learned that this contrasting example is parallel to the recent theorizing and empirical findings of cultural psychology on moral judgment and emotions. An authoritative survey of the state of cultural psychology and its implications to social psychology, in general, states that until very recently almost all psychological research on morality and the development of moral reasoning was rooted in the "justice tradition," but this paradigm is specific to the Western (cultural) system, based on the individualistic notion of personal liberty and social contract. 'This tradition judges individuals according to whether their actions violate the 'rights' of others. . . . [H]elping them is not a moral requirement, because given the particular individualist focus of the justice perspectives, people are not entitled to aid; thus helping them . . . is discretionary, not a moral requirement" (Fiske et al. 1999:940). On the other hand, "in interdependent cultures [as found in East Asia], the emphasis is on . . . living up to social-relational standards: inadequate performances leads primarily to shame" (ibid:943). In short, the manner by which people judge morality is not rooted in the invariant human nature but constitutive with a collective reality that cultural psychologists call a cultural system or a local cultural model (meanings and practices), although our focus is on economic systems as a part of collective realities.

13. J.-P. Platteau (1994) calls the game with this payoff structure the *Assurance Game* and discusses links between it and moral norms.

14. For example, see Landa (1994:ch. 6).

15. The enhancement of market exchanges in present-day developing economies seems to be dependent on such institutional development. Marcel Fafchamps and his coauthors have done extensive comparative field studies in contemporary Africa on the use of exchange credit. They summarize their findings as follows:

> In Ghana first time customers are virtually never offered exchange credit from the date of their first purchase. The normal way of accessing supplier credit is to build up a relationship by buying cash for six to twelve months. In contrast, many Kenyan firms get exchange credit from the date of their first purchase. One Nairobi respondent, for instance, was able, at start up, to fill his shop with goods on credit because he was recommended to his new suppliers by friends and relatives. Only the members of the Kenyan-Asian community seem to benefit from this system, however. Other entrepreneurs, as in Ghana, have to buy cash for a while. Zimbabwe offers yet another picture. The presence of a credit reference bureau, combined with informal information sharing, enables suppliers to screen new clients more effectively than in Kenya or Ghana. As a result, established firms find it easy to switch suppliers. New firms, however, especially those headed by blacks, appear to be left out of the system.   (1996:4)

16. To be sure, real estate transactions are usually more complex than the simple model outlined above. Frequently a loan agreement from a lender such as a commercial bank is sent to the escrow agent in lieu of direct payment. Further the instructions given to the escrow agent—which outline the requirements for each party to fulfill before the transaction to be completed—can be fairly complex; the transaction will not be complete until the parties have met these requirements.

17. Escrow has developed organically over the past century. In an 1928 article of *T.I. News*, L. J. Benyon, the Vice President of Title Insurance and Trust Company, relayed the story of the first escrow in Southern California:

> One day in 1895, a man came into the office of Title Insurance and Trust Company and left an order for a Certificate of Title. He said he was obligated to leave town for a few days and asked the order clerk if he would, as a matter of convenience, take his executed deed, deliver it to the buyer together with the Certificate, and collect and send him the sum of $1000. That was our first escrow,—and thus originated the escrow as we know it today.   (Title Insurance and Trust Company 1977:11)

Demand soon increased. People went into escrow if they couldn't meet the other party at a convenient time or had trouble working out all the details of a deal. Title companies soon were not able to keep up with the number of requests for escrow services. Banks began to offer escrow services as well. As housing sales kept climbing in southern California, the "independent escrow company organized for the express purpose of handling escrows evolved naturally" (Reyburn 1980:5).

18. In the first three months of the year 2000, eBay held 53.6 million auctions on which $1.15 billion worth of goods were traded.

19. For a seminal treatment of this, see Dunlop (1958/1993).

20. See Suchman (2000) and Johnson (2000).

21. In chapter 6 we will further argue that the form of a state may be endogenously codetermined with the degree of market development, mode of architecture of organizations as agents in the market domain, and the associated structure of economic classes.

22. It is well known that during the great real asset price bubble of the late 1980s mafia-like organizations were active behind scenes in facilitating real estate transactions.

23. For a persuasive argument on the need for international contract and property-rights laws, see Radin (2000).

24. The patenting of the "one-click" order method by Amazon.com as a business model incited a barrage of e-mail protests organized by Richard Stallman, who called for a boycott of Amazon.com. Jeff Bezos, the president, had to respond quickly by proposing reform of the business model patenting (e.g., shortening the patentable period) while claiming that there was no abuse of patent's rights on their side. This episode suggests that traders in the e-commerce domain are subject to the monitoring of numerous anonymous traders and their reputations could be damaged instantaneously if they misbehave.

25. Jones (1976) provides a framework for discussion of money commodities that will circulate as media of exchanges. Matsuyama, Kiyotaki, and Matsui (1993) presents an interesting evolutionary model of international currency in which multiple equilibria exist.

Chapter 4

1. For example, the merchant can economize on transaction costs through scale effects in transportation, storage, resolve the problem of absence of coincidence of wants (see the appendix of the previous chapter and Rubinstein and Wolinsky 1987), localize external diseconomies that the failure of a contract may propagate through the chains of contractual relationships (Landa 1994:ch. 3), as well as reduce information asymmetry between individual sellers and buyers (see chapter 8.2).

2. The property-rights theorists argue that writing complete (long-term) contracts for all possible contingencies is not possible in a complex environment, so residual rights of control in unspecified contingencies is better when assigned to the owner of physical assets (Grossman and Hart 1986; Hart and Moore 1990). Transaction-cost economists, such as Williamson (1975, 1985), focus on hierarchical-discretionary control over assets—human and physical—that mitigate the opportunistic behavior of contractual partners when the assets are transaction-specific. Contractual theorists, such as Milgrom and Holmstrom (1994), examine complementarities among fixed-wage, long-term contracts, the hierarchical direction of human assets, and the employer's ownership of physical assets as efficient responses to the risk-averseness of the workers and the uncertain market environment, as well as for ease of monitoring. Finally game theorists, such as Kreps (1990b), remind us of the importance of the corporate culture identified as generally shared expectations regarding the pattern of entrepreneurial choices in uncontractible events. We discuss some of these theories in this and later chapters.

3. See, for example, Nelson and Winter (1982), Dosi and Marengo (1994), and Dosi (1995).

4. I use the words "organizational-coordination mechanism" and "organizational architecture" interchangeably, although I use the former when a contrast with mechanisms operating in domains other than organizations (e.g., price mechanisms) is at issue. The latter is appropriate for referring to the basic structure of information-connectedness among organizational units without necessarily specifying the content of the (nonprice) messages between them.

5. For a more technical treatment of this subsection, see Aoki (1995a).

6. The described situation may be simply formalized with the following quadratic payoff function:

$$V = V^* + (\gamma_s + \gamma_1)x_1 + (\gamma_s + \gamma_2)x_2 - \tfrac{1}{2}[G(x_1 + x_2)^2 + H(x_1 - x_2)^2]$$
$$= V^* + (\gamma_s + \gamma_1)x_1 + (\gamma_s + \gamma_2)x_2 - \tfrac{1}{2}(G + H)(x_1^2 + x_2^2) - (G - H)x_1 x_2,$$

where γ_i denotes the stochastic parameter representing the state of the i segment of the environment, E_i $(i = s, 1, 2)$. We assume that it is ex ante expected to be normally and independently distributed with mean zero and variance σ_i^2. This payoff function may be thought of as a second-order Taylor series approximation of a general cost function around the optimal values (standard values) of x's ($= 0$) with respect to the prior distribution of the stochastic parameter (therefore the expected payoff is V^* when there is no ex post information other than the priors). Parameter G measures the magnitude of resource-constraint and/or diversity-requirement between the two tasks, while parameter H measures the degree of technological and/or attribute-complementarity. As is easily seen, if $G - H < 0$ (respectively > 0),

$$\frac{\partial^2 V}{\partial x_1 \partial x_2} = -(G - H) > 0 \qquad \text{(respectively} < 0).$$

Clearly, the marginal payoff of one unit in adjusting its choice variable in the positive direction increases (respectively decreases) if the choice variable of the other unit is adjusted in the same direction. When $G - H < 0$ (alternatively, > 0), we say that the two tasks are complementary (respectively, competitive).

7. We adopt the following measure of precision of an observation in this book (this chapter and chapter 14) according to the Bayesian theory of inference. Suppose that the prior variance of the observed environmental parameter is σ_i^2 $(i = s, 1, 2)$ and the variance of observation error (data-generating process) of task unit i is s_i^2. Then the precision of its observation is defined as $\Pi_i = \sigma_i^2/(\sigma_i^2 + s_i^2)$. Π_i is an increasing function of the precision of the i's ex post observation (the inverse of s_i^2) relative to the precision of its prior estimate (the inverse of σ_i^2) and assumes a value between zero and one. In Bayesian language, we perceive the situation as follows. At the beginning of production, each agent draws a sample of the environmental parameter with a data-generating error distributed normally with a fixed variance. Then he or she revises the prior distribution of the parameter on the basis of observation (sample means) using the Bayesian rule. The precision of the posterior distribution measured by the inverse of the posterior variance improves linearly with an improvement in the precision of the observation measured by the inverse of the variance of the data-generating process times the number of samples.

8. If the objective function (payoff function) is quadratic as given in note 6, we know that the "second-best" choice rules are linear functions of observations of environmental parameters. The second-best choice rules for information assimilation and encapsulation respectively are given by

$$x_i^{\text{IA}} = \frac{1}{2G}\Pi_{1 \oplus 2}\xi_{s,1 \oplus 2} + \frac{1}{G+H}\Pi_i\xi_{i,i} \quad \text{for } i = 1, 2,$$

$$x_i^{\text{IE}} = \frac{1}{(G+H)+(G-H)\Pi_i}\Pi_i\xi_{s,i} + \frac{1}{G+H}\Pi_i\xi_{i,i} \quad \text{for } i = 1, 2,$$

where $\xi_{j,i}$ is the observation (sample means) of the j segment environment by i agent in each mode ($\xi_{s,1 \oplus 2}$ represents the common observation error of T_1 and T_2) and Π_i is the information-processing capacity of the task unit i as defined in note 7. The second-best choice rules for hierarchical decomposition are approximated by

$$x_1^{HD} = \frac{(G+H)-(G-H)\Pi_2}{(G+H)^2-(G-H)^2\Pi_2}\Pi_1\xi_{s,1} + \frac{1}{G+H}\Pi_1\xi_{1,1},$$

$$x_2^{HD} = \frac{2H\Pi_1}{(G+H)^2-(G-H)^2\Pi_2}\Pi_2(\xi_{s,1}+\varepsilon_{c,2}) + \frac{1}{G+H}\Pi_2\xi_{2,2},$$

where $\varepsilon_{s,2}$ is a transmission error from T_1 to T_2, and Π_2 is defined as $(\sigma_s^2+s_1^2)/(\sigma_s^2+s_1^2+s_2^2)$ with s_2^2 being the variance of transmission error from T_1 to T_2. The latter can be thought of as measuring the relative precision of hierarchical communications.

By substituting these second-best rules into the payoff function and comparing their expected payoffs under different modes, we can derive the propositions in the main text regarding their comparative information-efficiency properties.

9. Assuming the same magnitude Π of information processing capacities of constituent units across encapsulated and assimilative modes, substituting the respective second-best decision rules derived in the previous note into the payoff function, and taking the difference of its expected values between the two modes, we get

$$E[V^{\text{IE}}] - Ex[V^{\text{IA}}] = \frac{(G-H)(1-\Pi)}{2G[G+H+(G-H)\Pi]}\Pi\sigma_s^2.$$

Since Π is less than one (see note 7), $E[V^{\text{IE}}]$ is greater than $E[V^{\text{IA}}]$ if and only if $G < H$. This proposition was first proved by Cremer (1990) in the absence of the idiosyncratic segment of environments. See Aoki (1995a) for an extension. Prat (1996) extended Cremer's proof to a general case where the payoff function is not approximated by the quadratic form and can be nondifferentiable.

10. This assumption may be warranted in the Bayesian context provided that each of the task units spends one-half of the information-processing time in drawing samples from the environment independently, and the rest in pooling their observed samples and constructing a common posterior distribution of the environment as a basis for individual decision choices.

11. Alternatively, an intermediate unit specialized in the information processing of the subsystem environment can be inserted between T_1 and T_2. Then this unit sends a message combining the superordinate decision, as well as its own observation, to the subordinates. Thus a three-level hierarchy (HD–HD) ensues with additional communication costs.

12. See, for example, Simon (1951), Williamson (1975, 1985), Geanakoplos and Milgrom (1991), Radner (1992, 1993), and Hart and Moore (1999).

13. See Williamson (1985:ch. 9). Also see Aoki (1988:ch. 2) for more on functional hierarchies from a comparative perspective.

14. The reports of these delegates were reprinted with N. Rosenberg's introductory remarks (Rosenberg 1969). See also Pine (1993:ch. 2).

15. Qian and Xu (1993) applied the *U*-form and *M*-form distinctions to a difference in national economic planning architecture between the USSR and China before their transitions to market economies. See note 26 of chapter 10.

16. Some aspects of a successful development team in the automobile industry, conceptualized as the one led by the "heavy weight" manager by Clark and Fujimoto (1991) and Fujimoto (1999), and discussed further in chapter 14.1, shares a modicum of commonality with this organizational architecture type.

17. See Aoki (1986, 1988:ch. 2, 1990).

18. See Monden (1983), Aoki (1988:ch. 2), Womack et al. (1990), and Fujimoto (1999).

19. For work councils, see Streeck (1997b). An intersting field work study about hybid firms created by the transplant of Japanese factory system into Germany; see Sako (1992).

20. For the Japanese *keiretsu* in the automobile industry, see Aoki (1988:ch. 6), Asanuma (1984, 1989), Nishiguchi (1994), and Fujimoto (1999). Also see Wormack et al. (1990) for an American interpretation of the system. Japanese suppliers contrast sharply with the integrated functional hierarchies of American firms. Williamson (1985) and Hart (1995) both used an anecdote first given by Klein, Crawford, and Alchian (1978) about the acquisition of Fisher Body by General Motors in the 1920s as an important piece of empirical evidence motivating and supporting their transaction-cost and property-rights theories. Prior to the acquisition, Fisher Body supplied car frames to GM as an independent supplier. However, it failed to respond to the increasing demands of GM by investing in transaction-specific equipment because of fear of ex post appropriation of the surplus by GM. They argued that integration with GM was an efficient solution because it provided GM management with hierarchical control over Fisher Body's management (transaction-cost theory) or residual rights of control over physical assets (property-rights theory). However, these theories cannot explain why a different organizational architecture emerged in Japan. Some economists attributed the lower rate of integration of the Japanese automotive industry to the preceding capital scarcity that core manufacturers had faced. But this explanation is flawed, not only from the cost-of-capital point of view (if the assemblers faced capital scarcity, why not the suppliers?); it also fails to explain why integration did not subsequently increase as those core manufacturers accumulated their own capital. Further a recent historical study based on a detailed examination of GM documents reveals that the holdup problem described by Klein et al. did not disappear after integration (Freeland 2000).

21. Thus Clark and Fujimoto (1991) characterized the *keiretsu* supplier relationships as "black box parts" transaction system and Asanuma (1984, 1997) as the "approved drawing system" (the drawing provided by the supplier and approved by the core manufacturer) in contrast to the "provided drawing system" (the drawing provided by the core manufacturer). The idea is that the suppliers has much autonomy in design specification of modular parts within the framework of systemic information-sharing and the core manufacturer does not intervene it.

22. See Piore and Sabel (1984), Pyke, Becattini, and Sengenberger (1990), and Ogawa (1998).

23. It is said that there are as many as 1,000 converters in Como with in a population of 85,000, ranging from individual firms to larger-scale firms owning equipment for certain work processes. See Ogawa 1998.

24. This characterization seems to correspond closely to what Baldwin and Clark (2000) call "Modular clusters."

25. Based on panel data compiled through interviews of 100-odd entrepreneurial firms in Silicon Valley, Baron, Burton, and Hannan identified three types of work coordination and control of the founders' model in their sample cluster (Baron et al. 1996:251–52, Hannan et al. 1996:512–13): (1) managerial control with monitoring, (2) peer and cultural control where the employees have extensive control over the means by which work gets done but do not control the strategic directions of the firm or the kinds of projects pursued, and (3) delegation to professionals of the right to influence how the work gets done and shape the larger strategic directions of the firm. They refer to the last mode as the star model, since it relies on finding potential stars when they recruit and select employees. The coordination characteristic of model 1 roughly corresponds to the functional hierarchy, that of model 2 to horizontal or particpatory hierarchies, and that of model 3 to the star-led, hierarchically-controlled teams. In Silicon Valley model 1 is rather scarce relative to model 2 or 3, although the latter are relatively unstable and experience more changes. Despite their

instability, these two models form the blueprints in the early evolution of the firms, and such firms have had higher success in initial public stock offerings.

26. Hart and Moore (1990) describe this as the manager being indispensable to physical assets, but I adopt the terminology in Hart (1995).

27. It is easy to see that the model above can be extended to the case of a two-tier functional hierarchy where there are multiple workers specializing in decomposed tasks under the direction of a single manager. In this case the manager's human assets are indispensable in his/her role in organization-specific hierarchical coordination. As the operating tasks in a functional hierarchy are divided in a mutually independent manner, the managerial function becomes indispensable.

28. See Brynjolfsson (1994:1654) for a similar proof and interpretation from the Taylorist perspective.

29. Here the owner-cum-manager may be interested in the development/adoption of technology that requires a lower human assets investment. The notion that property rights and the power relationship shape technology and the organization of labor has long been stressed by Marx and radical economists (e.g., see Marglin 1974; Bowles 1985; Bowles and Gintis 1986). See also Pagano (1993).

30. This assumption is represented mathematically by the condition where the density function satisfies the monotone likelihood ratio property (MLRP). Namely $f_i(y, e)/f(y, e)$ is monotone increasing in y for every $\mathbf{e} = (e_m, e_w)$, where $f(y, e)$ is the probability-density function of F and $f_i(y, e)$ is the partial derivative of f with respect to e_i.

31. Rajan and Zingales (2000) make the same point.

Chapter 5

1. Contract theory poses some related questions, such as whether multi-tasks are jointly or separately assigned to workers, as basically answerable depending on technological parameters. For example, if technological interrelatedness among tasks, in the sense of statistical correlation, is high (alternatively low), it is incentivewise preferable to separately (respectively jointly) assign workers to those tasks (Holmstrom and Milgrom 1991; Itoh 1992). Transaction cost theory submits that if the specificity of physical assets is reduced, a nonhierarchical governance mechanism may be adopted to mitigate its inherent disincentive impacts, but outside of the organization as relational-contracting (Williamson 1985). See Williamson (1995) for a defense of the one-dimensional transaction cost criteria.

2. Pagano (1999a, b) applies the biological concept of "allopatric speciation" to account for such phenomena.

3. For example, see Aoki (1986, 1990), Dosi, Pavitt, and Soete (1990), Saxenian (1994), and Teece et al. (1994).

4. The notion of an organizational field is due to new institutional sociologists. By this term they refer to "those organizations that in the aggregate constitute a recognized area of institutional life" (DiMaggio and Powell 1983:143). More specifically, they mean "the existence of a community of organizations that partakes of a common meaning system and whose participants interact more frequently and fatefully with one another than with actors outside of the field (Scott 1994:207–208). We will use the term to stand for a domain in which a convention in organizational architecture may be formed as an outcome of an evolutionary game. For a sociological model of the evolutionary approach to organizational population dynamics, see Carroll and Hannan (1989) and Hannan and Carroll (1992).

5. The underlying framework is Bayesian. Agents form posterior beliefs on the state of the environment by revising prior beliefs on the basis of observed samples containing certain errors. Then the agent's information-processing capacity is defined as the ratio of the prior variance of observed variables to the variance of sample error.

6. As for analytical works dealing with the co-evolution of the social order and individual preferences, see Kuran (1991) and Bowles (1996). Also Pagano (1993) and Pagano and Rowthorn (1994) analyze the codetermination of property rights arrangement (capitalist vs. labor rights regimes) and technology (easy-

to-monitor capital vs. easy-to-monitor labor) as "organizational equilibria" (Nash equilibria) under strategic complementarities, where "production managers" choose that technology that maximizes profits given the existing property rights system and "financiers" arrange that property rights regime that maximizes ownership rent given the existing technology. Then they argue that the simultaneous "homogenization" (i.e., conventionalization) of property rights and technology regimes occur because of "network externalities" (i.e., economywide strategic complementarities).

7. We will propose in chapter 9 a more complex mental model called the "subjective game model."

8. Thus defined, mental programs or human assets in this chapter are a close analogue of the "mental models" in Denzau and North (1994). The connections between them will be explored in chapter 9.

9. As noted below, recent theoretical and empirical achievements in cultural and social psychology provide ample support for the distinction made here. For example, Peng and Nisbett (1999) demonstrated through their experimental studies that when presented with contradictory accounts of a situation, Chinese subjects attempted to find a "middle way" in which both accounts had some validity, whereas American subjects tended to reject one side entirely in preference to the other. See Fiske et al. (1998) for a survey of recent psychological studies on analytic versus holistic modes of thought.

10. However, when the state of the environment becomes volatile and highly uncertain, the cognitive representations of agents do not easily converge. In such a situation the information-assimilation mode may not function efficiently. We consider this issue and its implications in chapter 9.

11. For example, Markus and Kitayama summarize their work in a series of attempts to integrate cross-cultural differences in numerous psychological domains, such as cognition, emotion, and motivation, as follows:

> Western, especially European American middle class cultures are organized according to meanings and practices that promote the independence and autonomy of a self that is separate from other similar selves and from social context.... Those in Western cultures may then be motivated to discover and identify positively valued internal attributes of the self.... In contrast, many Asian cultures do not highlight the explicit separation of each individual. These cultures are organized according to meanings and practices that promote the fundamental connectedness among individuals within a significant relationship (e.g., family, workplace, and classroom). The self is made meaningful primarily in references to those social relations of which the self is a participating part. Those in Asian cultures may then be motivated to adjust and fit themselves into meaningful social relationships. (Kitayama, Markus, Matsumoto, and Norasakkunikit, 1997:1247)

12. This and next sections draws on Aoki (1998). For proofs to the propositions, the reader is referred to the article. These sections are relatively technical, so those readers who are not concerned with the formalization of the evolutionary thinking beyond what was stated in section 5.1 may choose to skip the rest of this chapter.

13. An alternative modeling strategy would be to consider a matching game defined on two populations instead of one: the population of entrepreneurs whose strategy is composed of the choices of organizational architecture and industry, and the population of workers whose strategy set is composed of human asset types and industry choices. As realistic as this alternative modeling may appear, doing so will add little substance to the results obtained in this chapter. Also, in assuming that the matching of individuated human assets will lead to a functional hierarchy, I do not treat explicitly the disparity of information-processing capacity between them which is an essential characteristic of a functional hierarchy (recall proposition 4.3). However, this "quantitative" disparity within the class of individuated human assets is of secondary importance in comparison to the qualitative difference between individuated and context-oriented human assets in the current context. So it is ignored.

14. Recall propositions 4.1 to 4.5.

15. In the setting of the current model, any evolutionary equilibrium is evolutionarily stable strategies (ESS) in the sense of M. Smith (1982). See note 3 to chapter 3 for the concept.

16. For evolutionary models dealing with interactions of different economies and their consequences, see Boyer and Orlean (1992) on firms, Matsui and Okuno-Fujiwara (1997) on culture, and Matsuyama, Kiyotaki, and Matsui (1993) on currencies.

17. Specifically we assume that $b_{II} - b_{IC} = d_{CC} - d_{CI}$, $b_{II} - b_{CC} = d_{CC} - d_{II}$ and $\beta = \Delta = \frac{1}{2}$.

18. These conditions are stated more rigorously as (1) the smaller that $b_{IC} - b_{CC}$ is relative to $b_{IC} - b_{II}$, (2) the smaller β is, (3) the smaller γ is, and (4) the greater $b_{CC} - d_{CC}$ is, the lower will be the cost of transition.

19. In terms of figure 5.3, this specification implies that the evolutionary dynamics of the population distribution among human assets types and industries, $(0, m_{CD}, m_{IB} + m_{ID})$, is represented on the segment between I and D—that is, on a one-dimensional simplex.

20. See Krugman (1991) and Matsuyama (1991).

21. This condition is specified as $d_{IC} + d_{CI} - d_{CC} - d_{II} > \rho/4\lambda$.

22. See, for example, Okazaki (1993, 1997), Aoki (1996b), Okazaki and Okuno-Fujiwara (1998), Moriguchi (1998), and Fujimoto (1999).

Chapter 6

1. According to Williams (1976/1983) the English word "institution" is also ultimately traceable to Latin word *stature* ("to establish").

2. The original model of Weingast is primarily devoted to understanding the nature of the democratic state and the rule of law. However, it also provides a useful comparative analytic framework by which various types of states can be derived as equilibrium phenomena. A somewhat similar game theoretic approach to the role of the government is taken by Sened. But I do not agree with his "polity-centrism based on "the premise that our most basic property and human rights are the result of a political process" (1997:83) nor with his rule-of-the-game conception of institutions (ch. 3).

3. Bhagwati et al. (1984), Basu (1997a), and Calvert (1995), among others, treat the government as a player of the game.

4. For a comparative institutional analysis of the government as an organization, see Medina (2000). He analyzes game-theoretic implications of organizational differences in the legislature (the closed vs. open systems) and in political parties (opportunist vs. activist dominated) and their institutional complementarities.

5. Theoretically the concept of "anonymity" of markets has been formulated as the case where no traders have identifiable impact on the terms of exchange. Following Gale (1986), consider the case where the number of goods is limited but the number of traders is very large. Traders are classified into finite types by kinds of initial holdings and preferences, but contrary to our supposition the type of each trade is assumed to be common knowledge. Gale has analyzed a market exchange game with such a structure without assuming a Walrasian auctioneer who sets prices. In his game a trader of one type is randomly matched with one partner of another type at one time to bargain over the terms of exchange until he/she comes to an agreement with some partner. Bargain partners are forced to separate if they do not reach an agreement, and once separated, there is zero probability that they will meet again, even if they remain in the market. This is his conceptualization of "anonymous markets." Gale showed that there is something like a sub-game-perfect market equilibrium in this game whereby, whenever players meet opponents from the other type, they propose a Walrasian allocation—a point on the contract curve in the Edgeworth box diagram at which the common tangent of the indifference curves for each type passes through the point representing the initial distribution of commodity bundles—or accept it, if proposed. The playing of these equilibrium strategies will lead the final outcome of the game to a Walrasian allocation with probability one, which is Pareto-efficient.

6. See Luebbert (1991).

7. The remaining of this subsection heavily relies on Luebbert (1991), Lehmbruch (1999), and Streeck (1995, 1997).

8. Also see Streeck (1995:22), who argues: "Devolution of governance from the state to associations, giving the latter self-governing autonomy in return for responsible behavior, has a long history in Germany, and is reflected in ideological traditions as different as Social Catholicism, with its emphasis on "subsidiarity";

Hegelian organicism, in which "corporations' figure as one of the "moral roots" of the state; and democratic socialism with its idea of *Verbändedemokratie*, or associative democracy."

9. For a seminal treatment of corporatism, see Schmitter and Lehmbruch (1979).

10. Weingast (1995) arguably submits that the state that emerged in England after the Glorious Revolution can be also understood as de facto federalism.

11. The main opponent of the First Bank of the United States—James Madison—questioned "the constitutionality of such a bank" (Timberlake 1978:7). He felt that "a national bank issuing notes on a national basis would directly interfere with the right of the states to prohibit as well as to establish banks, and [it would also interfere with] the circulation of [state] bank notes" (ibid.). Alexander Hamilton, on the other hand, relied upon Adam Smith's classical economic theory and pushed for a national bank that could influence the national economy.

12. The federal government tried to further centralize the banking industry by taxing wildcat currency at 10 percent. Since the state banks were financed by the seniorage that they gained by issuing currency, this tax made their operation unprofitable: "it was hoped that the state banks would liquidate and take out national charters. In fact it was stated in Congress at that time the bank note tax measure was introduced that the intention was to have national banks exclusively, a unified banking system" (Clark. 1935:6). Indeed, the tax did force the closure of many state-chartered banks. However, in the 1880s deposit banking became more widespread and state banks were again able to generate profits. So a dual system of banking emerged. Each of the state governments had regulatory control over the state-chartered banks in their respective jurisdictions, while the federal government regulated another system of nationally chartered banks.

13. The consumer price index appreciated at rate 14.7 percent in 1993, 24.1 percent in 1994, 17.1 percent in 1995, but then declined to 8.3 percent in 1996 and 2.8 percent in 1997.

14. There are other aspects of the decentralization of government control in China, where the retreat of the government bureaucracy from centralized planning has proceeded more gradually through a spontaneous transfer of the authority for defining ownership rights to lower levels of government. The lowest levels of the administrative apparatus, township and village governments, became active in creating new enterprises under their ownership (the so-called TVEs) and were effective as intermediaries for restraining possible predatory behavior of the central government (Che and Qian 1998; Li 1996). They functioned as de facto holding companies of TVEs and were mutually engaged in fierce competition for markets and possible imports of foreign capital. The TVEs have been the major vehicle of the remarkable growth in GDP for almost two decades since the late 1970s.

There has also been the spontaneous evolution of de facto fiscal federalism in Russia (OECD 2000). However, haggling between the central government and local administrations regarding the collection of taxes appears to have had dire consequences on economic organizations. In order to circumvent the predation of the central government, the regional administrations avoid the use of bank accounts and accept settlements of tax arrears in noncash payment, which also facilitates the de-monetization of transactions wide-spread in interbusiness transactions and wage arrears in labor exchange (Gaddy and Ickes 1998, 1999; OECD 2000). The situations in Russia do not satisfy the first and second conditions for the market preserving federalism. (We will discuss this issue more in chapter 10.2.)

15. For a comprehensive treatment of corporatism in Latin America, see Berins Collier and Collier (1991).

16. The Japanese state that emerged after the Meiji restoration in 1867 may also be considered an example of the developmental state as conceptualized below. However, it subsequently evolved into what we conceptualize as a bureau-pluralistic state in the next section.

17. It has been widely recognized that taxing agriculture in order to extract resources for industrialization has been a common strategy among developing economies as well as communist-led planned economies. See, for example, Anderson and Hayami (1986) and Krueger et al. (1991).

18. See Ranis and Orrock (1985), Oshima (1987), Bates (1981), Hayami, and Ruttan (1985:ch. 13).

19. See Aoki et al. (1997) for the concept of rural-inclusive developmentalism and Hayami (1998) on a related concept of "peasant fundamentalism" in East Asia. One of possible factors that may make the emergence of rural–inclusive developmentalism can be the lack of exportable natural resources on which

the government may be able to rely as a source of the extraction of resources for development and/or rent-seeking. Japan, Korea, Taiwan, Singapore, Hong Kong, and China are all devoid of such resources. Indonesia is a notable exception in East and Southeast Asia. But because of rich endowment in natural gas, Indonesia has had to maneuver its developmental strategy on the edge between the degenerate developmentalism (crony capitalism) and rural-based, market-enhancing developmentalism. See Thornbeck (1998) on this.

20. Such a model is constructed and analyzed by Ichiishi (1993).

21. I use the word "bureau" as a generic word for any bureaucratic unit that has autonomous jurisdictional domains. It can refer to a ministry or agency, such as the Ministry of Agriculture, the Agency for Small and Medium Enterprises, or the Ministry of Welfare.

22. See Okuno-Fujiwara (1997) for lower-tier bargaining in bureaupluralism and Aoki (1988:ch. 7) for upper-tier bargaining.

23. Toya (2000) makes this point in examining the role of the permanent bureaucracy in the introduction of the so-called financial Big Bang in the mid-1990s. See chapter 13.3.

24. See Aoki (1988:ch. 7).

25. We will discuss this example in the context of finance industry (the so-called convoy system) later in chapter 13.3.

26. Thus Okimoto (1989) characterizes the Japanese state as a "network state."

Chapter 7

1. The expression "game form" is due to Hurwicz (1993, 1996). It is "game form" rather than "game" as it does not include information regarding the "subjective" utility payoffs to the agents. It is useful to introduce the former concept as it captures the concept of "exogenous rules of the game" as distinct from that of "endogenous rules of the game" to be introduced later. My approach differs from Hurwicz's, however, in treating the sets of actions as being only technologically constrained. Hurwicz regards the sets of actions and the consequence function as "institutionally designed." I submit that "legally designed" rules can be represented by the consequence function, for example, that assigns the "punishment according to law" to any technologically possible, "illegal" action. Implications of the difference will become clearer in the discourse of this chapter. But this difference is noteworthy at the outset.

2. More generally, action choice may depend on a longer history of consequences. Let the history of length τ at time t be described by the τ-tuple: $h(t; \tau) = (\omega(t-1), \omega(t-2), \ldots, \omega(t-\tau))$, and ω^0 is null history. Let $\mathscr{H}^t$ be the set of all lengths of τ histories. Then a private action choice rule may be given by a function: $s_i(.) : \mathscr{H}^t \to \mathscr{A}_i$ that assigns $a_i(t+1) = s_i(h(t))$ for $h(t)$ in $\mathscr{H}$.

3. For simplicity we confine our attention to the steady-state equilibrium by excluding the possibility of cyclic equilibrium state.

4. As noted, readers familiar with the subgame-perfect equilibrium conception of repeated games may skip this section. For a more rigorous treatment of the concept and related discussion, see representative textbooks on game theory, such as Fudenberg and Tirole (1991), Osborne and Rubinstein (1994), Gibbons (1992) or Gintis (2000).

5. We can extend this solution concept easily, only at the cost of notational complexity, to cases where the sequence of changing environment, $e = \{e(t), e(t+1), e(t+2), \ldots\}$, is expected.

6. For a textbook on evolutionary game theory, consult Weibull (1995). For varius institutional applications of evolutionary game theory, see Young (1998), Bowles (2000) and Gintis (2000). Matsui (1996) provides an interesting survey of institution-relevant discussions of the evolutionary game approach.

7. We require the two properties on F: (1) $\sum_j F_j(\hat{a}) = 0$ for all $\hat{a} \in \mathscr{A}$, and (2) $\hat{a}_j = 0$ implies $F_j(\hat{a}) = 0$, where subscript j refers to the jth choice in the choice set. These two conditions ensure that the frequency distribution of the agents never gets negative and their sum is always equal to one.

8. See Damme (1987), Friedman (1991), and Kandori (1997) for relationships among various equilibrium concepts in evolutionary games.

9. Take the set of four absorbing states, P, H, F, and L, of the model in chapter 5 and consider all possible "trees" among them. The tree is a half-order relation on the set of states such that: (1) each element except one has only one immediate successor, and (2) there is only one element which is a (immediate or indirect) successor to all the other elements in the set. The last element that is excepted in (1) is called the root of the tree. For each tree calculate the aggregate costs of transition, as defined in the text, and identify the minimum aggregate cost tree from all the trees having an absorbing state, say S, as the root. Refer to the minimum aggregate cost as the "cost of transition to S." Finally, compare the costs of transition to all four absorbing states. The root of the minimum cost tree among the four absorbing states (conventions) is P in our model. According to the reduction theorem of Young (1993), the root of the minimum cost tree is indeed the unique stochastic stable equilibrium of evolutionary dynamics in which agents from a finite population mutate with a very small probability at a discrete time interval. In some games the stochastically stable equilibrium may not be efficient, but the one called a risk-dominant strategy profile. See Kandori, Mailath, and Rob (1993).

10. An interesting example of the role of random element (mutants) is provided by Fudenberg and Maskin (1993). They constructed a dynamic process in which two agents, randomly matched from a large population, play symmetric games with finite memory and mistakes having some positive probability. At discrete intervals this population is invaded by mutants playing a strategy different from the prevailing strategy as some incumbents exit. For this dynamic process they conceptualize the notion of an evolutionary stable strategy, immune from mutants, inspired by the static notion of evolutionarily stable strategies due to Maynard-Smith (1982). Then they show that under some conditions an evolutionary stable strategy will survive with high probability, once it is established as the prevailing strategy, and it approximates an efficient outcome. In this case too mistakes ensure that an efficient outcome evolves.

11. Suppose that the payoff functions of agents are private information so that their believes regarding other choices can not be formed by deductive reasoning but inferred only by relying on observable states in past. Then the question is whether there exists any inference rule under which both beliefs and choices of all the agents converge and become consistent with each other in the limit, starting from any initial beliefs and choices. However, it is not generally known that there exist inference rules that guarantee such stability. For example, if we assume the agents have complete memory and the beliefs of each agent are the empirical frequency distribution of actions taken by the others through time $t - 1$, such a learning process is called fictitious play. For many games, fictitious play does not converge either in beliefs or in action profiles. Indeed, Foster and Young (1998) have proved a kind of impossibility theorem: without any randomness, a reasonable learning process does not converge either in beliefs or actions, unless the initial beliefs of the agents are very close to a pure, isolated Nash equilibrium and the initial uncertainty about the others' strategies can be resolved in a finite period of time. Generally, it is necessary to have some randomness either in action choices (mistakes) or in beliefs formation (e.g., "haziness" introduced by Foster and Young) for the process to converge to an equilibrium (quasi-stability). However, note also a contribution by Milgrom and Roberts (1990). They showed for a certain particular class of games called supermodular that if the agents take the best response against beliefs that are revised adaptively, only Nash strategies will survive. Supermodular games will be introduced in the next chapter and many interesting games in comparative institutional analysis can be included in this class.

12. See Scott (1995:ch. 3).

13. For a survey of the literature on how various rational solution concepts can be justified by the evolutionary approach, see M. Kandori (1997:254–58).

14. See note 3 of chapter 6 regarding an important contribution by Gale (1986) that shows the emergence of the Walrasian prices as an equilibrium outcome of a trade game.

15. As hinted earlier in chapter 1, our definition of equilibrium–summary-representation, Σ^*, may be regarded as analogous to the concept of sufficient statistic in statistical inference theory. The statistical concept is defined as the minimal summary of data for the purpose of statistical inference having certain properties (such as unbiasedness). However, note that we describe here that the price vector is sufficient for the individual agent to make the corresponding equilibrium choice. In contrast, some neoclassical econo-

mists, such as Koopmans (1957) and Hurwicz (1960), who were interested in the informational efficiency property of the perfectly competitive price mechanism, asked whether prices could be sufficient statistics for the purpose of achieving Pareto efficiency. However, markets cannot be complete. Further markets cannot be sustained without costs necessary for running the proper mechanisms of governance. More fundamentally, we may not even take the individual preferences for goods as fixed and given. Rather, an economic institution and ways in which economic agents evaluates the outcome of the economy may co-evolve in tandem (e.g., Bowles 1998). By these reasons, saying that prices are "sufficient" for the achievement of the Pareto efficiency may lose a meaning, although it can be admitted that the price mechanism is a relatively more informationally efficient institution wherever it works competitively under effective governance mechanisms.

16. This distinction between an institution and a set law may be considered to roughly correspond to the distinction between "institutional constraints" and "social constructs" made by Greif (1999). By "social constructs," he refers to organizations and coordination mechanisms, while "institutional constraints" are regarded as "endogenous in the sense that they are a product of the interactions among members of the society, yet they are exogenous to an individual member in the sense that they constitute the exogenous, salient features of the society from the individual perspectives" (1999:14).

17. North makes a distinction between "informal rules" (norms, customs) and "formal rules" (contracts, property rights, constitutions) from the rules-of-the-game perspective of institutional analysis. His "informal rules" correspond to the construct of autonomous institutionalization in our sense. However, we do not regard the formalization of laws themselves as institutionalization. They have to be implemented and may have unintended outcomes via the strategic interactions of the agents inclusive of the enforcer.

18. The other side of this spiral process is the "infinite regression" of the origin of institutions into historical past (chapter 1.3). This spiral aspect of institutionalization process is elaborated in Greif (1998).

Chapter 8

1. As pointed out in chapter 2, such concept of "social capital" originates with Coleman (1990).

2. Formally, let there be a social-exchange domain, $\mathscr{D}_s$, and a domain of another transaction type, $\mathscr{D}_t$, with an identical set of agents $\mathscr{N}$. Denote the product of the agents' sets of action-choice rules—the set of choice profile in short—in each game by $\mathscr{S}_s$ and $\mathscr{S}_t$. Suppose that the environment is stationary and S_t^* is the set of equilibrium choice profiles of $\mathscr{D}_t$ when this game is played independently. Suppose that $\mathscr{D}_s$ and $\mathscr{D}_t$ are played "simultaneously" by the agents who coordinate their own strategic choices across the games. Let $S^*(s \cup t)$ be the set of equilibrium choice profiles of the linked game, and $S_t^*(s \cup t)$ be its projection onto the set of choice profiles of game $\mathscr{D}_t$. Suppose that there is a choice profiles $\{s_t^*\}$ such that $\{s_t^*\} \cap S_t^* = \varnothing$, but $\{s_t^*\} \cap S_t^*(s \cup t) \neq \varnothing$. This means that although the choice profile $\{s_t^*\}$ is not self-enforceable when D_t is played separately, it becomes so and becomes institutionalizable, if $\mathscr{D}_t$ is embedded in $\mathscr{D}_s$. For example, the irrigation game $\mathscr{D}_i$ has the choice set {Work/shirk} for each village family, and the social-exchange game $\mathscr{D}_s$ has the choice set {Contribute to/defect from social goods production, Socialize/ostracize}. If D_i is played in isolation, the only equilibrium is $\{s_t^*\}$ = {Shirk, Shirk, Shirk, ...}. Suppose that the two games are linked. Then there can be an equilibrium $\{s^*(s \cup i)\}$ = {Work, Contribute and Ostracize any defector; Work, Contribute and ostracize any defector; Work, Contribute and Ostracize any defector; ...}. So the projection of $\{s^*(s \cup i : e)\}$ onto the strategy space of $\mathscr{D}_i$ is {Work, Work, Work, ...}.

3. See, for example, Ostrom (1990, 1992), Ostrom and Walker (1994), and Bardhan (1993).

4. For a pioneering economic analysis of the role of exogenously given unequal distribution of social capital in the emergence and reinforcement of a norm (rather than its simultaneous determination with a norm as we do), see Akerlof (1976).

5. One could say that individual competition is potentially detrimental to resource conservation, but, with some exceptions, the authors' interviewees did not see the situation that way.

6. Holmstrom and Milgrom (1991) showed that multitask assignment requires less emphasis on piece rate payment as an incentive device.

7. For the workings of the Japanese ranking system and its theoretical analysis, see Aoki (1988:ch. 3) and Itoh (1994).

8. Recall the discussion in chapter 4.3 on the problem of controling shirking under a share contract and the suggested solution of an external imposition of a large penalty given a poor outcome. The following idea of linked contracts aims to endogenize such penalty by contract design.

9. For a survey and collection of works on the subject, see Bardhan (1980), Binswanger and Rosenzweig (1984), and Bell (1988). Kingston (2001) developed a model of linkages across the intracommunity social-exchange domain, the intercommunities trade domain, and the public domain in which public goods are allocated by a public official across communities. He investigated how "market" corruption—bribery of public officials in order to obtain a favorable treatment in public goods allocation—may or may not be controlled through such linkages. He showed that the control of market corruption may crucially depend on the market development path across communities.

10. To give a theoretical rationale for the findings in the West Bengal villages, the credit–labor linkage model does not need to include a sharecropping or bonded labor service clause (Bardhan 1984, 1989). The laborer pays for the consumption credit in the lean season (borrowed at the landlord's cost of raising money) by working for him at below the market wage rate in the next season, and this transaction is repeated through agricultural cycles. This way the credit-constrained peasant gets loans at a lower cost (for him) and the landlord gets labor at the peak season at a lower cost (for him).

11. Formally, let there be two games, $\mathcal{G}_1$, $\mathcal{G}_2$, defined on domains of the same type with respective sets of agents, N_1 and N_2, where $N_1 \cap N_2 \neq \varnothing$. Assume, for simplicity, that the environment is stationary. Suppose that S_1^* and S_2^* are the sets of equilibrium choice profiles of $\mathcal{G}_1$ and $\mathcal{G}_2$, when those games are played independently. Suppose that $\mathcal{G}_1$ and $\mathcal{G}_2$ are played "simultaneously," and let $S_i^*(1 \cup 2)$ be the projection of the set of equilibrium choice profiles of the linked game onto the set of choice profiles of game i ($i = 1, 2$). Suppose that there are two choice profiles s_1^* and s_2^* such that $s_1^* \cap S_1^* = \varnothing$ and $s_2^* \cap S_2^* = \varnothing$, but $(s_1^*, s_2^*) \cap \{(S_1(1 \cup 2), S_2(1 \cup 2)\} \neq \varnothing$. That is, although the choice profiles s_1^* and s_2^* are not self-enforcing if $\mathcal{G}_1$ and $\mathcal{G}_2$ are played separately, they become so and thus institutionalizable if the two games are bundled.

12. The structure of this example is homomorphic to the government–business relationship in the developmental state as discussed in chapter 5.2. In the developmental state model, the threat of termination of a subsidy by the government is not sufficiently credible to induce the industrialist to make an effort if there is a certain collusion between the government and a monopolist. However, if the government chooses to continually threaten the firms with termination in the event of a poor performance record, it could elicit higher effort from the firms.

13. For this hold-up problem, see note 20 to chapter 4.

14. Formally, let there be m identical, and independently played, games $\mathcal{G}_1, \ldots, \mathcal{G}_i, \ldots, \mathcal{G}_m$ ($i = 1, \ldots, m$) in a stationary environment. The number of agents, their strategic choice sets, and the consequence functions are identical across the game domains, but the sets of agents do not overlap. Let the equilibrium choice sets of these individual games denoted by S_i^* ($i = 1, \ldots, m$). Suppose that a single agent v with his own set of choices $\mathcal{S}_v$ is added to all these games to form an augmented game G_i^{+v} ($i = 1, \ldots, m$). Suppose that the additional player can coordinate his choices across all augmented games to form a linked game $\bigcup_i \mathcal{G}_i^{+v}$. Let the set of equilibrium choice profiles of the linked game be S^{+v*} and its projection on the sets of agents' choices in the original i game be S_i^{+v*}. Suppose that there exists an equilibrium choice profile $\{\prod_i (s_i^{+v*}, s_v^*)\} \in S^{+v*}$ in the linked game such that $\{s_i^{+v*}\} \cap S_i^* = \varnothing$. That is, the choices, s_i^{+v*} ($i = 1, \ldots, m$), which are not self-enforceable in the original individual games, become self-enforceable in the bundling of the games by the augmented third-party agent and thus institutitonalizable.

15. In this simple example, the character of the federal government as a strategic player is not explicit. Also the total budget of the government in the original political economy domain is assumed to be fixed, so hard-versus soft-budgeting is referred to only with respect to the SEO. However, the budget can be softened by the creation of money at the cost of inflation. Then an interesting game situation is created between the governments of the original game and the federal government having control over monetary quantity and seigniorage revenues at the social cost of inflation. The game situation may become even more complicated

when each government has access to monetary financing through a state banking system. See Qian and Roland (1998) for such a model.

16. An early contribution along this line of thought is by Leff (1976, 1978).

17. The study of the Chilean group by Khanna and Rivkin (1999b) provides evidence that the returns of group affiliates covary even after the portion of the covariation due to equity cross-holding is removed, which shows the economic impact of social ties.

18. There are some indications that Korean *chaebol* are responding to the so-called IMF shock by substituting mutual stock holding among member firms for the traditional centralized control by the family-controlled business holding companies.

19. A game $\mathscr{G}$ satisfying the following conditions for each agent $i \in \mathscr{N}$ is called a supermodular game:

• (A1) The choice set of each agent $\mathscr{S}_i$ is a complete lattice in the following sense: it is a partially ordered set with the transitive, reflexive and antisymmetric order relation $\geq$, and for any two elements x and y in it, the least upper bound denoted by $x \vee y$, as well as the greatest lower bound denoted by $x \wedge y$, exist and are included in the set. The set represented by a regular cubic in the t_i-dimensional Euclidean space $(a_{i1}, \ldots, a_{ij}, \ldots, a_{it_i})$ or by an ordered pair $\{a_{i1}, a_{i2}\}$, is an example of complete lattice.

• (A2) The payoff function $u_i = \times_{p \in \mathscr{N}} \mathscr{S}_p \rightarrow \mathfrak{R}$ converges along any ordered subset of $\mathscr{S}_i$ for fixed $a_{-i} \in \times_{p \in \mathscr{N} - \{i\}} \mathscr{S}_p$, and along any ordered subset of $\times_{p \in N - \{i\}} S_p$ for fixed $a_i \in S_i$, and it has a finite upper bound.

• (A3) The payoff function $u_i(a_i, a_{-i})$ is supermodular in $a_i \in \mathscr{S}_i$ for fixed $a_{-i} \in \times_{p \in \mathscr{N} - \{i\}} \mathscr{S}_p$; that is, for any a_i, a_i' in $\mathscr{S}_i$, $u(a_i \wedge a_i', a_{-i}) - u(a_i', a_{-i}) \geq u(a_i, a_{-i}) - u(a_i \vee a_i', a_{-i})$. If the payoff function is twice differentiable, this is implied by $\partial^2 f_i / \partial a_{ij} \partial a_{ik} \geq 0$ for all $1 \leq j < k \leq t_i$;

• (A4) The payoff function u_i has an increasing difference in a_i and a_{-i}; that is, for all $a_i \geq a_i'$ in $\mathscr{S}_i$ the difference $u(a_i, a_{-i}) - u(a_i', a_{-i})$ is nondecreasing in a_{-i}. If the payoff function is twice-differentiable, this is implied by $\partial^2 f_i / \partial a_{ij} \partial a_{lk} \geq 0$ for all $i \neq l, 1 \leq j \leq t_i, 1 \leq k \leq t_l$.

(A3) implies that increasing any subset of an agent's choice variables raises the incremental payoffs associated with increases in others. (A4) implies that when an agent increases (decreases) his choice variable(s), marginal returns to other agents' choice variables increase (decrease). This is the assumption of *strategic complementarity*. If (A1) to (A4) are assumed, then there exist the largest and smallest pure Nash equilibria that are componentwise the largest or smallest (they are identical if the equilibrium is unique). In addition suppose that all the payoff functions u_i have a parameter τ in some partially ordered set T and satisfy the following condition:

• (A5) The payoff function u_i has an increasing difference in a_i and τ; that is, for all $a_i \geq a_i'$ in $\mathscr{S}_i$ the difference $u(a_i, \tau) - u(a_i', \tau)$ is nondecreasing in τ. For a smooth function this is implied by $\partial^2 f_i / \partial a_{ij} \partial \tau \geq 0$ for all i and j.

Then we have the following lemma due to Topkis (1978). We will make good use of this lemma in the next part.

LEMMA (Monotone comparative static property) The largest and smallest pure Nash equilibria of the supermodular game are nondecreasing functions of τ. In other words, all the components of the largest and smallest Nash equilibria co-vary in the same direction in response to a change in the parameter value of τ.

For supermodularity analysis under uncertainty, see Athey (2001a, b).

20. See the note above.

21. To see this, suppose that $u(\Sigma^*; \Lambda^{**}) > u(\Sigma^*; \Lambda^*)$; namely with Σ^* being institutionalized in domain $\mathscr{D}$, the agents in that domain are better off if their institutional environment of $\mathscr{G}$ is Λ^{**} rather than Λ^*. The supermodularity conditions that are concerned with the property of incremental payoff gains does not preclude this possibility. But move from $(\Sigma^*; \Lambda^*)$ to $(\Sigma^*; \Lambda^{**})$ cannot be realized as the Nash condition requires that $v(\Lambda^*; \Sigma^*) > v(\Lambda^{**}; \Sigma^*)$. On the other hand, the Nash equilibrium condition at $(\Sigma^{**}; \Lambda^{**})$ states

that $u(\Sigma^{**}; \Lambda^{**}) > u(\Sigma^*; \Lambda^{**})$. Therefore, if the preceding condition holds, $u(\Sigma^{**}; \Lambda^{**}) > u(\Sigma^*; \Lambda^*)$. Likewise, if $v(\Lambda^*; \Sigma^{**}) > v(\Lambda^*; \Sigma^*)$, then $v(\Lambda^{**}; \Sigma^{**}) > v(\Lambda^*; \Sigma^*)$. Thus, if the two assumed conditions hold simultaneously, then $(\Sigma^*; \Lambda^*)$ is a Pareto-inferior institutional arrangement.

22. This presumption seems to bear a resemblance to the increasingly influential view in evolutionary and cognitive psychology that the information processing program in the human brain (i.e., the mind) is composed of a complex set of modules specialized for reasoning in different domains of social exchange. See, for example, Barkow, Cosmides, and Tooby (1993), Pinker (1997), and Field (2001).

Chapter 9

1. See Matsuyama (1996) for a forceful argument on this point from the viewpoint of information processing difficulty in the presence of multiple equilibria.

2. See also North (1990), David (1994), and Thelen (1999).

3. A related but somewhat different approach is pursued by Kaneko and Matui (1999) in their "inductive game" model. Also, albeit not formulated in terms of game-theoretic frame, the "mental model" discussed in a pioneering paper by Denzau and North (1993) is an important predecessor of the model developed below. However, a major difference between my approach and theirs is noted in note 7 below. Dosi, Marengo, and Fagiolo (2000) presents a similar conceptual framework for dealing with "open-ended evolutionary dynamics" involving not only adaptation but also discovery and emergence of novelty as ours, surveys the related literature, and submit thought-provoking, unresolved research agenda.

4. According to the notation used in chapter 7.2, $I_i(s) = \Sigma_i^*(s) \sim \Sigma^*(s)$.

5. More generally, it may be assumed that each agent assigns a probability distribution over the consequence space $\Omega(T)$ for each combination of own strategic choice and private information.

6. More generally, and realistically, over time agent will acquire multiple rules of inference and prediction that are mutually competitive in some respects but complementary in others. Then, given a continually changing institution, agents will experiment and choose the rules that they consider appropriate under the given circumstances (see Holland et al. 1986). They develop meta rules regarding which rules are to be triggered depending on circumstances. However, when a fixed set of multiple rules is retained as a useful tool by an agent, we still say that inductive subjective game model is reproduced.

7. In Denzau and North (1994) institutions are treated as "the external (to the mind) mechanisms individuals create to structure and order the environment." (1993:4) In our framework which regards institutions as systems of shared beliefs, they are the endogenous element of the subjective game model, although they may be perceived as the objective by individual agents once established.

8. An important work of Kaneko and Matsui (1999) may be interpreted as inquiring in a particular game context if subjective models, in our sense, can be inductively constructed by players of a game who lack the complete knowledge about the objective structure of the game in a manner consistent with their past experiences. They showed that a particular form of summary representation of an equilibrium strategic profile—ethnic configuration in their model—becomes sufficient for the existence of a best-response rule that supports the equilibrium.

9. External shocks, such as the defeat of war, are highlighted as a major cause of institutional change by some political scientists. See also Olson (1982) and Barca et al. (1999). War may certainly be regarded as an exogenous shock to economic transaction domains taken in isolation. However, if we consider overall institutional arrangements in an economy, there may be elements of endogeneity to a war. For example, the authoritarian states in Germany and Japan emerged in the 1930s as a preposterous "solution" in the polity domain, from many possible others, to institutional misfits evolving between emergent market relationships in economic domains and traditional social structure. The Second World War was an endogenous, albeit not inevitable, outcome of such a solution.

10. In evolutionary biology mutations at the molecular level are normally neutral for evolutionary selection or slightly suboptimal under the stable environment. See Kimura (1983).

11. The competing systems of predictive and normative beliefs may be regarded as akin to "ideologies" in Denzau and North (1994), who define ideologies as "the shared framework for mental models that groups of individual possess that provide both an interpretation of the environment and a prescription as to how that environment should be structured" (ibid.).

12. As noted in chapter 5, Denzau and North (1993) also refer to this analogy. As far as I am aware, one of the earliest social scientific references to this analogy is by Krasner (1988). Also see Hodgson (1991) and Mokyr (1990).

13. Recall that even for the simple evolutionary game model of chapter 5.2 in which, being far from equilibria, branching out along multiple paths was possible depending on the emergent beliefs of the entrepreneurial agents (proposition 5.5).

14. For a persuasive argument on the complementarity between the juncture theory and the equilibrium theory, see Fujimoto (1999). Thelen (1999) provides an excellent survey on historical institutionalism in comparative politics in an attempt to draw together insights from the critical juncture literature and the literature on path dependency and policy feedbacks. The evolutionary psychologist Pinker also considers that natural selection and developmental constraints are both important and answer different questions. He suggests that "[n]atural selection presupposes that a replicator arose somehow, and complexity theory might help explain the 'somehow'" (1997:161). Our argument in this and next chapters is an attempt to explain the "somehow" in a modified game-theoretic framework.

Chapter 10

1. In contrast, Bowles (1996) focuses on the influence of market institutions on the evolution of culture defined as "learned behaviors," or "the beliefs, values, and other learned or imitated aspects of individuals which durably influence their behaviors."

2. I owe Krasner for personally pointing out the relevance of the political theory of the Bali state by Geertz (1980) to the current context. See Krasner (1984).

3. The Geertz description of the ecological-sociological conditions of Bali's irrigation system has a striking similarity to that of Tokugawa Japan (chapter 2). However, one notable exception between the Tokugawa village and the Bali state was that the former got involved in trade with outside markets on the basis of the existing community-embedded norms, which eventually weakened the social cohesiveness of the village. See example 10.5.

4. At the beginning of the second half of the Tokugawa period, it was indeed widely observed that the village headmen (*shoya*) exchanged cash crops with specific outside merchants on behalf of village families (e.g., Shinpo and Hasegawa 1998:257). They thus emerged as embryonic indigenous merchants. However, being themselves peasant farmers, they originally were nothing more than agents of village families and their conduct was under the social control of the village.

5. The collective control of the quality of goods is instrumental for the village families to strengthen their bargaining power vis-à-vis outside merchants, and therefore it is in their mutual interest. In a situation where the adverse selection problem of product quality is severe, dishonest merchants could claim that the goods supplied to them are of lower quality, even if it is not always true, and thus take advantage of innocent village families lacking alternative trade opportunities. To prevent merchants from taking this strategy, village families must be able to unambiguously control and prove the quality of the goods they supplied. In the Tokugawa period, peasants' tax obligations were defined and fulfilled in terms of the bulk quantity of paddy rice first and processed brown rice later, rather than using paddy panicles. Its purpose was to leave as little room as possible for peasants to manipulate the delivered bulk quantity by compromising on quality (e.g., not remove immature grains, straw, or increase the moisture content). An unintended consequence of this obligation was that they accumulated the ability to control the quality of supplies (Koga 1982). If exchange in rice had been made in terms of paddy panicles as in most monsoon Asian economies, merchants might have been able to adopt the opportunistic strategy just mentioned. Village families continued to cooperate in improving postharvesting processing technology through the col-

lective ownership of equipment and exchange of information, etc. to strengthen their collective bargaining power.

6. My emphasis here is the emergence of the middleman indigenous to the rural community but instrumental in enhancing trade with outside agents (e.g., the village entrepreneurs who subcontract with fellow village families). Note that they differ from the middlemen who share an identity or norm and trade with each other (e.g., "ethnically homogeneous middlemen group" in Landa 1995:ch. 5) or a "cultural broker" who mediates between traders belonging to different tribes that do not trust each other but mutually trust the middleman because the latter has money/reputation (Landa 1995:201).

Although the parable in this subsection is constructed as a sequel to the one in chapter 2.2 and partially inspired by some historical reality of the late Tokugawa period, a homomorphic parable may be narrated with respect to other communities as well. For example, Hayami and Kawagoe (1993) challenge a famous anthropological thesis by Geertz (1963) that the entrepreneurship for modernizing, nonfarm business activities cannot emerge endogenously from within the village. They looked at the emerging Indonesian vegetable market in which village-based traders act as the intermediaries, delivering the produce to towns. For this operation to be effective, credit must be advanced by the traders in exchange for the promised amount of daily supplies by villagers, which induces moral hazard problems. However, community norms—and not any legal system—enforce these contracts and countervail against the temptation of farmers to cheat. Further traders are compelled to give farmers a fair price, since there is symmetric information in the village on the market prices. Thus the market and community norms act in concert to prevent trader cheating.

7. See Hayami (1998).

8. There was an attempt by the government in the early Meiji period to transplant Western-style textile factories and employ the daughters of urban ex-samurai. But their management attempts were a complete failure, and the factories were quickly privatized through fire sales of assets to private capitalists. Newly established private factories recruited female workers from rural localities and put them in dormitories. Some paternalistic capitalists even provided middle-school education, flower arrangement, and sewing classes at the dormitories to promote a community atmosphere.

9. A good survey on this situation in English can be found in U.S. Strategic Bombing Survey (1946).

10. The most common contractual forms were beneficial leases or copyholds for life recorded in the court of the manor. Both were long-term agreements in which the yeoman made a substantial payment at the outset and only nominal payment thereafter. The peasant thus received any extra income from improved productivity for the duration of the agreement. The peasant also had to save money to renew the contract at its termination. This combination of carrot and stick helps explain the productivity growth achieved by open-field farmers in the seventeenth century. (Allen 2001)

11. In contrast, the transfer of quasi-property rights in taxable lands in Tokugawa Japan was legally prohibited by the *Baku-Han* governments. Toward the end of the Tokugawa period, peasants who were increasingly involved in monetary exchanges were engaged in loan contracts with outside merchants or inside wealthier families, with land held by borrowers as collateral. When they were unable to repay debts, contractual agreements were executed, but bankrupt farmers normally kept cultivating the same land as lease holders. As a result the concentration of farming management as seen in England did not emerge.

12. The only exception that the detailed micro research by R. Allen in the south midlands found was that the installation of hollow drains in the heavily arable district usually followed enclosure. In this district the open fields were usually drained by the furrows between the strips, but these were not always cleaned. "Enclosure awards [in this district] often empowered a group of landowners to maintain the main drains and finance the cost by levying a rate on all the property owners in the parish." (Allen. 1992:121) This improvement contributed to a productivity increase to some extent.

13. Over 5,000 parliamentary acts were adopted between 1700 and 1850 by local parliaments to allow the landlords to proceed with enclosure. There were regional differences in the progress of enclosures that cannot be attributed solely to differences in technological or market developmental conditions. For example, Yelling found that in the midlands, where the wide scattering of individual holdings was the norm,

open and common fields survived well into the second half of the eighteenth century, even though the region was considered to be under no less pressure from market relationships than other regions. Thus he argues: "[T]he organization of a general enclosure was a difficult political step and it raised the problem of individual interests in an acute form. In particular, conflicts of interest between large and small landholders must be stressed, and it is the resistance to enclosure by the latter group which explains much of the survival of the system." (1982:414)

14. Between 1902 and 1911 the textile industry produced about one-quarter of the total industrial output and generated about 50 percent of exports. According to a recent estimate by M. Tanimoto (1998), the proportion of textile workers employed in the putting-out system was more than 70 percent of those in the industry in 1905, while the corresponding figure employed by the factory system was only a little more than 10 percent.

15. For mutually beneficial contracts to be implemented without the support of effective third-party mechanisms, mutual trust (reputations) had to have developed, thus sustaining relational contracting. Theoretically this requires two things: the credible threat of terminating relational contracting in the event of a partner's default, and the dissemination of information regarding any contract default throughout the relevant trade domain. Evidence indicates that many indigenous merchants competed in the same locality so that it was possible for peasant families to switch contracting partners if necessary. On the other hand, some peasant families served only as buffers against fluctuating demands but were potentially capable of replacing relational contractors. This situation might satisfy the first condition. In fact the problem of embezzlement was controlled by experienced indigenous merchants, while the contracting periods tended to extend over years with core contractors (Tanimoto 1998) Since the merchants had community roots, information regarding any misconduct on either side would have been quickly disseminated among themselves as well as among the villagers. Thus the intravillage information infrastructure that supported the preceding community norm also enabled the second condition to be fulfilled. However, the way in which contracts were made self-enforceable differed substantially from the traditional community norms; the expected penalty imposed on deviants was exclusion from contractual relationships rather than from the traditional network of social exchange.

16. Major analytical results obtained by Holmstrom and Milgrom (1994) in the context of the modern franchising system versus integrated firm may be rephrased as in the text in the context of the putting-out contracting versus the factory system.

17. For example, see Fujimoto (1999) for insights on the impacts of the rural-based textile machinery industry on the later-day Toyota system.

18. The rise of small entrepreneurial firms in the American information industry was largely facilitated by the massive exits of engineers from the giant corporation IBM through voluntary defections first and then layoffs later. They took the initiative of forming their own firms or joining smaller firms that could utilize their competence and knowledge. Baldwin and Clark (2000) provides an excellent description of the process as well as an analytical explanation on how the process initially evolved.

19. As documented and analyzed by Chandler (1977) and Williamson (1975), the emergence of the M-form (multi-divisional corporate firm) in early twentieth-century America was a quintessential example of organizational innovation by a new type of bundling: bundling through the internalization of capital markets.

20. See Aoki (1988:ch. 3, 1990, 1994a) for the complementarity between the horizontal hierarchy (contextual information sharing) and the centralized personnel administration.

21. As is evident from the discussion of complementarity, the encapsulation of contextual information-sharing cannot be achieved without also decentralizing the personnel administration. One way to do this is to transform the integrated corporate form into a pure holding company form. This way both personnel administration and information processing are decentralized to constituent subsidiary units, while the holding company concentrates on governance role. The decentralization allows diversity in organizational architecture and employment contracts to be accomplished. Also, as will be discussed in chapter 11.3, the pure holding company form provides a partial solution to the corporate governance problem created by the weakened governance capability of the bank. I discussed these and other implications of the pure holding company form in details in chapter 8 of Aoki (1995/2000).

The pure holding company form was not permissible until recently because of a legal ban instituted during the postwar reform years. This regulation was repealed in 1998, but as of the year 2000 it has not yet had visible impacts on corporate restructuring in the J-firms. Partially this was due to a delay in implementing the consolidation tax complementary to the scheme. Without the consolidation tax the spin-off of business divisions as subsidiaries under the holding company scheme would imply an increase in corporate tax when a division has negative corporate income.

22. We can extend the following analysis to the case where each domain is peopled with agents having different preferences, as we did in chapter 8.2.

23. Qian and Xu (1993) contrasted the difference between the pre-reform planning apparatus in the USSR and China as the U-form versus M-form. (A somewhat similar distinction in corporate internal organizations was made by Chandler 1977 and Williamson 1975.) Under the U-form, industrial activities (factories) were bundled according to the functional line of industry and placed under the control of industrial ministries at the national. In China, they were bundled according to the functional line of industry at local geographical levels. Geographic-based bundling was further re-bundled at higher geographical levels up to the national level. The latter's organizational strategy was adopted by the Chinese government to make the national system of production less vulnerable to outside shocks (e.g., nuclear attacks). Theoretically, depending on whether shocks to industrial activities are correlated more along industrial or geographical lines, either the U-form or M-form is efficient. See Maskin, Qian, and Xu (2000). An earlier analysis in a generic context is found in Cremer (1980). The differences between the planning apparatuses of the two economies constitute an important initial condition that can significantly affect their transformation to market-oriented economies. See Qian (1999).

24. I owe this point to conversation with J. Touffut.

25. Braguinsky and Yavlinsky (2000:45) argue that the industrial ministries, together with the SOEs under their jurisdiction, formed powerful industrial pressure groups.

26. By November 1993, 91 percent of the privatized enterprises had adopted the so-called type II privatization program, in which employees and mangers could buy up to 51 percent of shares at the pre-inflation book value. See Aoki (1995b) and Akamatsu (1995) for the legal aspects of the program.

27. Braguinsky and Yavlinsky (2000:121–22) submit a new criterion for distinguishing between so-called insiders and outsiders. They see, insiders as those who derive their incomes from the former SOEs in question, often in the form of malfeasance and rent-seeking. Thus insiders come formally from outside the firm, as representatives of key suppliers or lenders, members of regional and local governments, and also as outright gangsters, whereas workers who suffer wage arrears are classified as outsiders. Although the substance of my argument below does not differ much from theirs, from the game-theoretic analytical point of view the insiders in their interpretation may be interpreted as agents in collusion with the manager of the firm while the workers under wage arrears may still be taken as inside collusive partners, with whose association the manager can derive continuation value. Gaddy and Ickes (1999) point out the symbiotic relationship between the workers and directors: "Workers need the director to keep the unviable enterprise afloat. Directors need the enterprise in order to exploit their relational capital [vested in relationship with primarily directors of other enterprises]."

28. The term "virtual economy" was used in the December 1997 report of the Karpov Commission. The report concluded that barter, by its use of "nonmarket or 'virtual' prices, [created] illusory or 'virtual' revenues, which in turn led to unpaid, 'virtual,' fiscal obligations." Gaddy and Ickes (1998, 1999) and Ericson and Ickes (1999) analyze the phenomenon of the virtual economy as an equilibrium. OECD (2000) provides useful supporting evidence as well as acute analysis on complementary relationships between the use of money surrogates and fiscal federalism. Also, while not explicitly game-theoretic, Branguisky and Yavlinsky (2000:pt. II) give a related analysis.

29. OECD (2000) estimates that 70 percent of interfirm transactions and 40 percent of tax payments were demonetized in 1998. Also noncash receipts as a share of federal and consolidated regional tax revenue were close to 50 percent in 1997.

30. The energy sector accounts for almost half of Russia's industrial output in the late 1990s.

31. OECD (2000:155) reports that additional transaction costs of over 20 percent associated with barters are commonly cited by mangers in surveys of enterprises. Although I am not aware of any work dealing with the historical origin of such intermediaries, their role is obviously reminiscent of the *torkachi* (pusher) in the era of the USSR who were employed by the SOEs as merchants of material goods and intermediate goods in black markets.

32. Accompanying nonmonetization are widespread arrears in wage and tax payments. See Earle (2000) and Earle and Sabirianova (2000).

Chapter 11

1. Later Berle conceded to Dodd and admitted that the modern directors act de facto and de jure as administrators of a community system, although he remained rather cautious about admitting this as the "right disposition." (Berle 1959:vii)

2. Another related definition of corporate governance is given by Zingales (1998) in the spirit of Hart-Moore. He defines a "governance system as the complex set of conditions that shape the outcome of ex post bargaining over the quasi rents that are generated in the course of a relationship." For recent treatments of the stakeholder society view, see Berglöf and von Thadden (1999) and Blair (1995). My early treatment of the comparative corporate governance from the bargaining-game perspective is Aoki (1984a).

3. For example, any minority stockholder who owns at least 1 percent of the total stock or 300 unit shares of a corporation can propose a slate of directors and the replacement of a director without cause at the shareholder meeting. However, this statutory provision only provides incentives for the managers to devise countermeasures to preserve their own autonomy: such as to implicitly collude among themselves to hold shareholder meeting in the same day of each year (the last day of the accounting year), bribe implicitly or explicitly professional troublemakers, called *sokaiya*, who collect minority shares.

4. As noted in chapter 4.3, this second-stage moral hazard problem is assumed away by Hart and Moore.

5. In contrast to the Hart-Moore approach which postulates the equal division of the organizational quasi-rents à la Nash-Shapley, we leave the division of expected rents unspecified in this section.

6. To implement this arrangement, for example, the entrepreneur may issue a level of short-term debt greater than the low first-stage profit (low-effort signal) but smaller than the high first-stage profit.

7. See the lemma in note 19 of chapter 8.

8. I owe this observation to von Thadden. Actually the return curve for the worker may become strictly concave if implicit values from job security, working conditions, training opportunities, and so on, are included.

9. The Co-determination Law in Germany stipulates that every company with more than 2,000 employees must install a supervisory board that is entitled to vote on major corporate decisions as well as select the management board. It is required that one-half of the seats on this board are to be held by employees' representatives and the rest by shareholders' representatives. When votes are equally divided, the chairperson, selected from among the shareholders representatives, is allowed to cast a decisive vote. However, in practice, this provision is seldom invoked and decisions by the board are normally made unanimously or without a substantial block of opposition. This may be interpreted as indicating that an agreement is normally sought and becomes an equilibrium, as unanimous opposition by either side can be expected to destroy the effectiveness of a decision, which implies that both sides have de facto veto power.

10. We formulate the specified technology as follows. Let $F(V : e)$ be the cumulative distribution function of the value of one-period team output V on the closed, finite support $[V_{min}, V_{max}]$ and conditional on a vector of efforts e undertaken by the N insiders. F is independently and identically distributed for all periods, and is symmetric and differentiable in e. The probability density function associated with F is denoted by $f(V : e)$. We assume that team output is observable but that an individual member's effort supply is not observable to anyone else. We assume that the density function satisfies the monotone likelihood ratio

property (MLRP), namely $f_i(V : e)/f(V : e)$ is monotone increasing in V for every e, where $f_i(V : e)$ is the partial derivative of f with respect to e_i.

11. In maximizing the present value of expected current and future flows of utility, each insider chooses the same effort level as long as (s)he stays in the H-firm, if the environments are stationary. The flow value to the insider of remaining in the H-firm will then be constant, say at U. Therefore, given a contractual wage schedule $w(V)$ as well as contractual $\underline{b}$ and $\bar{b}$, the insider's problem of choosing the optimal e_i in each period can be expressed as

$$U = \max_{e_i}\{(1 - \delta)(E[w(V((e)) - c(e_i)) + \delta[(1 - F(\underline{b} : e))U + F(\underline{b} : e)(U - J)]\}, \qquad i = 1, \ldots, N,$$

where δ is the time discount factor. In the current period the member receives the income $w(V)$ and incurs effort cost $c(e_i)$. If the H-firm continues to the next period, which occurs with probability $(1 - F(\underline{b} : e))$, the insider receives value U in the future. If the H-firm terminates because the output value level falls below $\underline{b}$, with probability $F(\underline{b} : e)$, the insider receives $U - J$ in all future periods. The weights in the equation on the present and future payoffs are $1 - \delta$ and δ respectively. This weighting expresses the present value of incomes in equivalent flow terms U. The corresponding value as stock can be found by dividing through by $1 - \delta$. The solution to this problem is given by the following condition that constitutes the insider's incentive compatibility constraint:

$$\int w(V)f_i(V : \mathbf{e})\, dV - \frac{\delta}{1 - \delta}J\frac{\partial F_i(\underline{b} : \mathbf{e})}{\partial e_i} = c'(e_i). \tag{IIC}$$

12. Consider the maximization of the organizational quasi-rents:

$$S = E[V(e)] - Nc(e) - \gamma F(\underline{b}, e) - \rho - M,$$

subject to the participation conditions for the R-monitor [RMPC: $B = E[s^{RM}(V)] - M = 0$] as well as for the investor [IPC: $F(\underline{b} : e))\bar{s}^I + F(\underline{b} : e)\underline{s}^I = \rho$], the H-firm's budget constraint [BC], the insider's incentive compatibility condition [IIC], and the renegotiation proofness condition [RNP: $s^{RM}(V) - s^{RM}(\underline{b}) \geq \gamma$ for $V > \underline{b}$], where $\gamma = [\delta/(1 - \delta)]NJ$. Form the Lagrangian function with λ, μ, $\xi(V)$, and η as multipliers for [RMPC], [IPC], [BC], and [IIC] respectively. It is immediate that $\mu = \lambda = 1$ and that $\xi(V) = -f(V : e)$. Therefore the pointwise differentiation of the Lagrangian function with respect to $w(V)$ yields $\eta f_i(V : e) - Nf(V : e)$. By the monotone likelihood ratio property (MLRP) for the density function f, this is negative on $V \in [V_{\min}, \bar{b}]$ and positive on $V \in (\bar{b}, V_{\max})$ for $\bar{b}$ satisfying $\eta f_i(\bar{b} : e)/f(\bar{b} : e) = N$. Therefore w needs to be minimized on the former domain and maximized on the latter domain in ways consistent with other constraints: $w(V) = w_{\min}$ for $V \in [V_{\min}, \bar{b}]$ and $= \max_{\bar{s}^I, s^I}[V - s^I(V) - s^{RM}(V)]$ for $V \in (\bar{b}, V_{\max}]$. The latter maximization can be accomplished by the following two devices: first let $s^I(V) = \underline{s}^I = \rho - \gamma[1 - F(\underline{b} : e)]$ for $V \leq \underline{b}$ and $s^I(V) = \bar{s}^I = \underline{s}^I + \gamma$ for $V > \underline{b}$ so that (RNP) is satisfied. Next choose $\bar{b}$ (in terms of η, e) so that $E_{V \leq \bar{b}}[V - s^I(V) - Nw_{\min}] = M$. Differentiating the Lagrangian function with respect to $\underline{b}$ and setting it equal zero yield determines $\underline{b}$ (in terms of η, e). By MLRP, it is implied that $\underline{b} < \bar{b}$. The value of e_i $(i = 1, \ldots, N)$ in terms of η is determined by (IIC).

13. The mechanism of relational-contingent governance was derived above as a second best solution to the conventional constrained maximization problem. However, an alternative way of characterizing the same solution in a way more consistent with our conceptualization of institutions as an equilibrium phenomena is to derive it as an outcome (an equilibrium) of a game. Such a game is constructed as a supermodular game (see chapter 8.3) played between the fictitious governor of the H-firm and its insiders. For simplicity we ignore the presence of investors (i.e., the H-firm does not need any capital input from outside) and suppose that a game is played between the representative insider and the governor, with the R-monitor as an automaton.

The representative insider strategically chooses his own effort level e_i to maximize the present value sum of expected current and future utilities, $U = \int_{V \geq \bar{b}}(V/N)f(V : e)\, dV + w_{\min}F(\bar{b} : e) - \gamma F(\underline{b} : e) - c(e)$. The governor forms conjectures regarding the unobserved effort levels of the insiders and strategically chooses the termination point $\underline{b}$ so as to maximize the H-firm quasi-rents, $S = E[V(\hat{e})] - \gamma NF(\underline{b} : \hat{e}) - Nc(\hat{e}) - M$, given her conjecture on the insiders' choices $\hat{e}$. The R-monitor is an automaton that adjusts the control-transfer point $\bar{b}$ so as to satisfy its own budget constraint, $B = E[s^{RM}(V)] - M = 0$ with her conjecture on the insiders' choices, $\acute{e}$.

Then the payoff functions of both strategic players and the budget surplus function of the automaton can be proved to be supermodular in $(e, \underline{b}, -\bar{b})$ for given conjectures of the governor as follows: given $(\bar{b}, \underline{b})$, the representative insider can maximize its payoff by choosing e_i satisfying $\partial U / \partial e_i = 0$. Straightforward calculation shows that $\partial^2 U / \partial e_i \partial \bar{b} = \{(\bar{b}/N) - w_{\min}\} f_i(\bar{b} : e) < 0$ and $\partial^2 U / \partial e_i \partial \underline{b} = -\gamma f_i(\underline{b} : e) = 0$. Therefore the function U is supermodular in $(e, -\bar{b}, \underline{b})$. Because of the complementarity between $\underline{b}$ and e shown above, it is assumed that the governor forms "rational" expectations such that $\acute{e}_{\underline{b}} = 0$, with second derivatives being of negligible lower order. We can then prove that the objective function of the governor is also supermodular. The R-monitor's budget constrain is trivially supermodular, as it is constant with respect to e and $\underline{b}$.

Thus the game is supermodular so that there exists a pure strategy equilibrium (see note 8), for which the following conditions are met: (1) the insider's choices, e_i^*, are optimal given the R-monitor's and governor's choices $(\bar{b}^*, \underline{b}^*)$; (2) the governor's choice $\underline{b}^*$ is optimal given her conjecture and the R-monitor's choice $(\acute{e}, \bar{b}^*)$; (3) the R-monitor's choice $\bar{b}^*$ is in equilibrium given its conjecture and the governor's choice $(\hat{e}, \underline{b}^*)$; (4) the R-monitor's and governor's conjectures are correct so that $\acute{e} = \hat{e} = e^*$. This equilibrium is equivalent to the mechanism of relational-contingent governance.

One advantage of this approach is to facilitate comparative static analysis of the fairly intricate model. The supermodularity of the game implies that the highest-equilibrium values of the endogenous variables covary in response to changes in any parameter value in which U, S, and B have increasing differences (lemma 8.1 in chapter 8.3). Suppose that $NF_i(\underline{b} : \hat{e})\hat{e}_{\underline{b}} + f(\underline{b} : \hat{e}) < 0$ for any $\hat{e}$, which implies that the insider's incentive response to a higher termination point $\underline{b}$ is sufficiently sensitive so that the governor conjectures that the higher termination point will decrease the probability of an actual occurrence of termination. Then it holds that $\partial^2 U / \partial e_i \partial \gamma = -F_i(\underline{b} : \hat{e}) > 0$, $\partial^2 S / \partial \underline{b} \partial \gamma = -NF_i(\underline{b} : \hat{e})\hat{e}_{\underline{b}} - f(\underline{b} : \hat{e}) > 0$, and $\partial B / \partial \bar{b} \partial \gamma = 0$. Thus U, S, and B have increasing differences in $(e, -\bar{b}, \underline{b})$ and J. By applying the lemma in note 8.19, they have increasing differences in $(e, \underline{b}, -\bar{b})$ and J. Therefore, the lemma in the text holds. Likewise we can prove that $(e, -\bar{b}, \underline{b})$ covary with $(-M, \delta, -w_{\min})$.

14. Further, if the dense communications within the H-firm entails the spontaneous formation of social exchanges domains among its members, their separation will destroy the value of their social capital, aggravating the effect of penalty by termination. See chapter 8.1.

15. Banks that play the role of relational monitors may not necessarily be limited to commercial/long-term credit banks but may cover investment banks. For example, Franks, Mayer, and Runneboog (1998) present evidence that in the United Kingdom the discipline-cum-rescue of poorly performing management is often done through board turnover accompanied by new equity issues arranged by investment banks rather than by a hostile takeover or by inside blockholders. Although it is not clear whether such firms significantly relied on context-oriented human assets, this system implies that it is possible for informed investment banking to simulate the function of a relational monitor in relational-contingent governance.

16. See Aoki, Sheard, and Patrick (1994) and Aoki (1994c) for a systematic description of the main bank system as a whole.

17. Jensen used this word with respect to LBO (leverage buyout) associations. He commented "LBO partnerships act much like the main banks (the real power center) in Japan's *keiretsu* business groups.... Ironically, even as more U.S. companies come to resemble Japanese companies, Japan's public companies are becoming more like U.S. companies of 15 years ago.... In short, Japanese managers are increasingly unconstrained and unmonitored" (1989:73). See Baker and Smith (1998) for a discussion of how LBO associations create value. Khanna and Palepu (1999c) makes an interesting point that business groups in India have an aspect of LBO associations as well as that of conglomerates, because they may internalize some of missing market-governance institutions such as contract enforcement mechanism, and various market intermediaries. From this perspective, they argue that focused strategies may be wrong for emerging markets and that the right way to restructure conglomerates is to reform their corporate governance structure rather than de-bundle them (Khanna and Palepu 1997, 1999a).

18. In the model developed there, the termination of an entrepreneurial firm is supposed to occur when it is judged by the venture capitalist to be behind a competitor in a competition (tournament) for the development of a product in a niche market; the entrepreneur forfeits all rights in this event.

19. Che (2000) argues that an abrupt transition from centralized financing to decentralized financing is not productive in the transition economy because of the latter's excessive short-termism syndrome. However, a transition to a "financial dual structure" is efficiency enhancing. In this system, budget constraints are soft in the centralized financial sector but induce macro stability. The resulting improvement of input quality enhances the disciplinary effect of proper hard-budget constraint in the decentralized financial sector. This view shows that the soft-budget constraint syndrom in the state sector may be complementary to the productivity growth of the nonstate sector as observed in China.

20. See Bernake (1983) and Petersen and Rajan (1994).

Chapter 12

1. This definition of "tacit knowledge" in the current context is consistent with its original, generic conceptualization by M. Polanyi who sought an understanding of the phenomenological and ontological structures of "the fact that we can know more than we can tell." (1966:4). Also see M. Polanyi (1958).

2. Cowan, David, and Foray (2000) developed their taxonomic framework for classifying knowledge related to research and development, as well as production technology, and examining its implications to public policy regarding R&D. A major difference between their framework and the one adopted here lies in the definition of "tacitness." Although we follow the original definition of Polanyi more closely, they refer to "uncodified" knowledge as "tacit." Thus our northeast cell is absorbed into their southwest cell. Instead, their northeast cell (latent-codified case) represents the type of knowledge based on highly developed codification but with the "code book–displaced" because of a common understanding within the group, and the like. This knowledge constitutes the distinctive regions occupied by normal science. However, we presume that scientific knowledge has less importance, if any, in the financial transaction domain. It is the distinction between "codified" and "uncodified" knowledge in the class of "codifiable" knowledge that weighs more heavily in financing domain, as we will see.

3. In response to my question, "If you name only one important quality of the venture capitalist, what would it be?" Arthur Rock, one of the pioneers of venture capitalists who funded Intel, Apple, Scientific Data Systems, among a number of other successful firms, replied simply, "Judgement of the people."

4. This and the next subsections draw on Aoki and Dinç (2000).

5. Rajan's analysis of the robustness of information rents to increasing external competition is not restricted to commercial banks. But many investment banks have the ability to acquire tacit information and negotiate with firms—these are the functions that characterize the entities Rajan calls "banks."

6. See note 3 to chapter 11 for a proof. The described situation corresponds to the lowering of M, which is complementary to the insiders' efforts in the mechanism of relational-contingent governance. Analogous to lemma 11.2, it holds that

LEMMA 12.1   The lowering of the lending rate by the main bank makes the simultaneous hardening of the firm's ex post budget constraint the second-best arrangement. These two factors together strengthens the effectiveness of the relational-contingent governance of the firm by the main bank, inducing the insiders of the firm to make higher efforts.

7. Total borrowing from abroad by Korea increased from 65.4 billion U.S. dollars in 1993 to 112.1 billion U.S. dollars in 1996. The share of the banking sector in 1996 was about 60 percent and that of short-term debts about one-half. Similarly the total international borrowing by Thailand in 1997 was 91.8 billion U.S. dollars, in comparison to 52.6 billion U.S. dollars in 1993, of which about 40 percent was in short-term debts. Public borrowing from abroad was relatively low in both economies (5.6 billion U.S. dollars in Korea and 2.2 billion U.S. dollars in Thailand).

8. McKinnon and Pill argue that the established preference for a flexible exchange-rate regime should not be taken for granted. They argue that a "good" exchange-rate fix to the U.S. dollar—one that is credible and close to purchasing power parity—may well reduce the foreign exchange risk premium. If the first-best solution to fully control banks' moral hazard behavior is not possible, then short-term capital controls that

prevent banks from taking an open position in foreign exchange markets may be a second-best, transitory policy. But if banks and other firms are restrained from doing so, a flexible exchange regime is not possible and the government has to take the position of a market maker.

9. The introduction of substantial capital reserve requirements on competing banks imposes a debt-contract type of discipline on the banks not to engage in overly risky behavior (Dewatripont and Tirole 1995). A violation of the minimum capital requirement can automatically trigger the intervention of a regulatory agency. One drawback of such rule-oriented regulation, however, is that banks may be made subject to regulatory control in the event of a large systematic shock (e.g., general depression) for which the individual banks may not be responsible. The theoretical analysis of contingent governance suggests that bailing out banks in a critical event of capital shortage (e.g., through temporary nationalization or capital infusion) should not be excluded in order to control external diseconomies of a systemic credit crunch, as well as to preserve tacit information assets (other than top management) that might have been accumulated within the banks. See Stiglitz (1999).

10. However, the number of foreign banks allowed to enter should be neither too small nor too large. If the number of banks is too small, excessive monopolistic rents will accrue to them, depriving them of incentives to develop monitoring expertise tailored to local needs. On the other hand, competition among too many foreign banks will wipe out rents (franchising values) compensating them as well as domestic banks for being engaged in monitoring based on the processing of tacit information. See proposition 12.2 below.

11. Suppose that it is publicly known that a certain proportion of firms—"good" firms—have investment opportunities as described above, while the remaining firms are bad ones whose investment projects always fail. Suppose that each bank obtains a signal in the beginning of a period that conveys imperfect information regarding the quality of a firm's project and bids the premium rate R it wants to charge depending on this signal. Firms select those banks who offer the lowest rate. Then this bank competition process is essentially a sealed-bid, first-price, common value auction (see also Riordan 1993). There can be multiple equilibria to this game: one is a static Nash equilibrium of one-shot lending: In this equilibrium, if a signal is good enough, a bank bids an interest rate with no commitment to rescue; if a signal is bad enough, no loan is offered. The expected rate of profit of each bank at date 0 is positive, but it decreases with the number of banks. We may refer to this equilibrium as an arm's-length banking institution. Provided that the number of banks is more than a certain number, there can be another subgame perfect equilibrium in which banks' equilibrium strategies have a three-tier structure as follows: they lend with commitment to rescue to those firms whose signals exceed a high-threshold value; they do not lend to those firms whose signals fall short of a low-threshold point. In between, banks make loans without commitment with a lower interest rate than in the case of loans with commitment.

12. Suppose that bond holders do not by themselves have the ability to screen firms, so they form beliefs regarding a firm's type by observing the kind of loans made to it by banks and make competitive zero net profits. Evidently the possibility of bond issues enhances a firm's profitability in comparison to a case where its only financiers are banks, whether relational or arm's-length, who are making positive profits. Suppose that firms can issue as many bonds as are profitable for financing their investment, which diminishes the expected profit of banks. Then, if the bond markets are fully developed, the minimum discount factor (the right-hand side of the inequality) that can sustain relational financing may go up and the feasibility of relational banking could disappear (Dinç 1996:prop. 6).

13. Schumpeter (1934) regards that as it is the carrying out of new combinations that constitutes the entrepreneur, many 'financiers,' 'promoters,' and so forth that are not connected with an individual firm, may still be entrepreneurs in this sense. (1934:75)

Chapter 13

1. See chapters in Aoki and Patrick (1994) for comprehensive descriptions and analyses of the Japanese main bank system as well as discussions of its relevance to developing and transforming economies.

2. Financial *keiretsu* is to be distinguished from suppliers *keiretsu* introduced in chapter 4.1.

3. This framework generated a tendency toward a kind of overborrowing syndrome, both in the industrial sector as well as in the banking sector. Undercapitalized industrial firms competed for bank loans to expand shares in respective markets within the protective framework of the bureau-pluralist state. Credit conditions were differentiated by banks according to the ranking of firms in terms of market shares and the length of their mutual relationships. This mechanism reinforced the dependence of firms on banks. Banks in turn relied on borrowing from the Bank of Japan (BOJ) for their supply of growth money. The BOJ was engaged in delicate money-supply engineering for meeting the active demands for growth money, on one hand, while restraining overlending that might lead to the overheating of the economy. One difference from the overborrowing syndrome observed in East Asian economies during the post–Miracle phase was that the BOJ was able to retain a fairly firm grip on the quantity of money through the so-called window guidance policy (administrative guidance on bank lending policy) in the context of insulated domestic financial domain.

4. The value of assets destroyed by the earthquake was estimated to be more than 20 percent of the GDP. JOB's refinancing was made through re-discounting of commercial bills issued by earthquake-stricken companies.

5. They were Dai-ichi, Mitsui, Mitsubishi, Sumitomo, and Yasuda.

6. The first-tier *zaibatsu* firms relied more on internally generated funds. For example, in 1930 one of the largest banks, Mitsui Bank, extended only 10 percent of its loans to member firms, mostly second-tier member firms except for Mitsui Bussan, which as a trading company had very large financial needs (Teranishi 1990:325). Also in the 1920s the major sources of funds for major firms were corporate bonds (33.6 percent in 1920–1925 and 25.5 percent in 1926–1930) and equity issues (46.4 percent in 1920–1925 and 20.4 percent in 1926–1930) rather than bank loans (−0.3 percent in 1920–1925 and 13.0 percent in 1926–1930) (Matsumoto 1986:101). In 1928 the number of corporate bond issues (1,205 million yen) reached more than double that of previous years (584 million yen in 1925 and 627 million yen in 1926).

7. Between 1928 and 1931 the price index was lowered by 23 percent, while the GDP growth rate stagnated slightly above zero percent. The slowdown of growth rate was not as severe as in the United States, which experienced about a 40 percent decline in GDP between 1929 and 1931.

8. See Kindleberger (1986).

9. See Gordon (1985).

10. See Teranishi (2000).

11. The price index of farm products declined by 40 percent between 1928 and 1931. The peasant farmers were estimated to have on average debts equivalent to the two-year wage incomes of the farm laborer (Okazaki 1997:98).

12. The takeover of the government by the military bureaucracy was essentially achieved on the basis of a tactful interpretation of the constitutional rules. The military establishment enhanced their political influence on the basis of, but by suppressing, the uprising of radical officers who advocated an anticapitalist symbolic system. The latter were mostly rural recruits, but there was no direct political mobilization of the landed class or the peasantry to support the military takeover.

13. See Okazaki (1993) and Okazaki and Okuno-Fujiwara (1999) for descriptions of policy changes and organizational designs under the military regime.

14. See Teranishi (1994) and Okazaki (1994) for bank consortia.

15. Before the opening of the Pacific war, Japan relied on the United States for more than seventy percent of its crude oil supply.

16. See Gordon (1985) and Moriguchi (1998).

17. No individual was allowed to purchase more than 1 percent of the stock of any firm: 29.3 percent of workers of affected firms purchased 38.5 percent of the total stock sold by the government. See Aoki (1988:124–27).

18. Barca et al. (1999) pinpoint the institutional shocks in the aftermath of the defeat of the war as a decisive determinant of the postwar evolution of the Japanese corporate governance structure and thus

its bifurcated evolutionary path from the Italian corporate governance structure. While admitting their significant impacts, we rather emphasize the pre-war changes in institution-relevant policy parameters as factors triggering the diachronic complementarity between the relational-contingent governance and horizontal hierarchies.

19. The size of the business losses from the repudiation is estimated at almost 20 percent of the GNE in 1946.

20. For statistical evidence, see Aoki (1984b).

21. See Horiuchi (1994), Yoshitomi (1998), Hoshi and Kashyap (1999), and Miyajima and Arikawa (2000).

22. Banking and securities supervision was detached from the MOF and absorbed into the newly created Financial Supervisory Agency (1998) and eventually into the Financial Agency (2001).

23. See Toya (2000) for the description and analysis of the Big Bang from the comparative institutional analytic perspective. Hoshi and Kashyap (2000) predict that as a result of the Big Bang there will be a massive contraction in the size of the banking sector. However, they seem to identify the banking sector with traditional commercial banking. Under the deregulated framework it is expected that banks will expand their activities in investment banking and security-related businesses.

24. This political process may be divided into the two phases: phase I (up to mid-September 1998) in which the Young Turks in the LDP and the Young Democrats with financial expertise dominated policy debates, pushing the scheme to temporarily nationalize failed banks (the so-called revitalization scheme); and phase II in which, with the shift of the U.S. policy stance toward consenting to the injection of public funds to the banking sector, the LDP mainstream regained the initiative (with the involvement of the MOF no doubt behind it), turning some of the opposition to switching sides into acceptance of the "recapitalization" scheme. The resulting legislative package contained both schemes. See Toya (2000), particularly chapter 7, and Sakakibara (2000).

Chapter 14

1. Even a most authoritative account of the influential property rights approach argues that both the increasing importance (technically speaking, indispensability) of human assets and the increasing flexibility of technologies (the reduction of complementarity) make it an optimal arrangement for property rights to physical assets to be held by an individual entrepreneur—that is, "de-integration" (Hart 1998:53–54).

2. This standard-setting may be considered as corresponding to "design rules" in a conceptual framework developed by Baldwin and Clark (2000). An early draft of this chapter was written in the fall of 1997 and has been circulated through the Web site of the Stanford economics department since early 1999. However, I was not aware of their exciting work until their publication in 2000. Their work and this chapter are highly complementary and partially overlapping. They provide a rich analysis of the evolutionary process starting from the design of IBM 360 in the 1960s to the emergence of the Silicon Valley model in the late 1970s—"modular clusters" in their word. However, as the immediate object of their study is the computer industry, their analysis does not explicitly involve a kind of comparative assessment of alternative R&D organizations ("design rules") as I do in this chapter and chapter 4. They argue that the Silicon Valley model ("modular clusters") is intrinsically superior to the centralized design rule setting as observed in the era of IBM 360, to which I agree regarding the computer industry. I clarify later some conditions under which the Silicon Valley model may be Pareto superior, which may not necessarily be satisfied in other industries, for example, arguably in the auto industry. The evolutionary nature of the technological product system innovation in the Silicon Valley model (discussed below) is the focus of analysis in both their and our works. The complementary nature of analytical contents between the two works is mentioned in endnote 4 below.

3. Also it is interesting to note that this software development paradigm corresponded to a similar hierarchical paradigm in hardware design: the IBM 360 was run by a centralized OS, and researchers were able to access computer resources only through "dumb" terminals that merely received data inputs and gave computed outputs. See Ikeda (1997).

4. Baldwain and Clark (2000:ch. 11) explicitly deals with the problem of ex ante choice of the number of start-up firms (i.e., experiments) to be financed per project type. By assuming a normal distribution (with the mean normalized to zero) of the value outcome of each development and design effort ("experiment" in their word), they showed that the option-value benefit of having k firms in the design of a single modular product is proportional to the standard deviation of the value outcome of a development effort (i.e., the degree of uncertainty in design outcome) times the expected value of the best k trials drawn from a standard normal distribution. Thus the higher the uncertainty, the better it is to have more entrepreneurial firms. They treat the cost of experiments parametrically given. In contrast, while we treat the number of experiments per project type parametrically given, we analyze a situation in which actual opportunities costs of experiments by individual entrepreneurial firms become endogenous to the mechanism of governance and examine its welfare implications. Thus our approach and their approaches are complementary.

5. We follow and extend the formulation and notations developed in the notes to chapter 4. Also, from discussion in the previous section, in places where the Silicon Valley architecture is applied, the systemic segment E_e of the engineering environment is less important relative to the idiosyncratic segment E_i, so modeling subsuming the former to the latter may be warranted.

6. See note 8 to chapter 4 for a rationalization of the linearity assumption.

7. Substituting the optimal decision rule for x_i^{IE} in note 8 to chapter 4 into the quadratic approximation of the value function given in note 6 to the same chapter will yield the separable value function.

8. Established venture capitalists in Silicon Valley cluster in a rather small office complex located on Sand Hill Road between Stanford University and Route 280. They know each other well and form a type of professional club.

9. Let e^* be the first-best effort, and for fixed $\underline{V}$ choose J so that the Nash equilibrium condition in the text is satisfied at $e_{vc} = e^*$. Let $\Delta = (\delta/1 - \delta)J[dF(\underline{V} : e^*)/de]$. Then, the expected penalty in flow terms is given by $\Delta\{F(\underline{V} : e^*)/[\partial F(\underline{V} : e^*)/\partial e_{vc}]\}$. If the V-distribution at $e_{vc} = e^*$ is tight in the sense there is a $\underline{V}$-value for which $-[\partial F(\underline{V} : e^*)/\partial e_{vc}]$ is large while $\{F(\underline{V} : e^*)/[\partial F(\underline{V} : e^*)/\partial e_{vc}]\}$ is small, then the expected penalty becomes very small, which implies that the first-best condition is approximated by a Nash equilibrium strategy of the venture capitalist. This roughly corresponds to the situation where investors can find a threshold value $\underline{V}$ near $\int V \, dF(V : e^*)$ for which the probability of failure can be dramatically reduced by an increasing effort. The proof follows Holmstrom (1979).

10. I owe this point to Thomas Hellmann. Using the SPEC data analysis, Baron, Hannan, and Burton (2000) also find that changes in the employment models or blueprints embraced by organizational leaders increase turnover of the most senior employees, which in turn adversely affects subsequent organizational performance.

11. For relationships between venture capitalists and entrepreneurial firms in general, see Salman (1990), Admati and Pfleiderer (1994), Bygrave and Timmons (1992), Gompers and Lerner (1996), Florida and Kenney (1998), and Kaplan and Stromberg (2000).

12. Figures in 1978 give a much different picture. In that year individuals and families are the largest contributors to venture capital funds (32 percent), while the share of pension funds was 15 percent. During the last twenty years the so-called institutionalization of venture capital funds has proceeded.

13. It is known that the flow of funds into this organizational arrangement was given impetus by various tax measures which were enacted between the late 1970s and early 1980s (the relaxation of the so-called prudential rules on pension fund management, the reduction of the capital gains tax in 1978 and 1981, deregulation of initial public offerings in 1978 and 1979, etc.).

14. In 1997 more than 3,500 companies were newly registered in Santa Clara County, even if not all of them were venture capital financed firms.

15. The decline of the practice of co-financing may partially reflect the stock market boom that has made more funds available to competing venture capitalists and partially the reduction of technological uncertainty involved in venture capital financing. Thus it is not yet clear whether joint financing will entirely disappear if the venture capital boom subsides and/or investment is directed to very uncertain projects.

16. According to the definition by the National Venture Capital Association, there are following developmental stages of venture capital financing:

- Seed stage (before the establishment of a corporation) mostly financed by the so-called angels who are experienced in venture business.
- Start-up (development stage).
- Early stage (preparation of product development, production, and marketing).
- Later stage (after product shipment).
- Mezzanine stage (six months to one year before initial public offering).

17. Between 1990 and 1997 about 21,000 new businesses were registered in Santa Clara County. About 7,000 entrepreneurial firms are said to currently exist (Joint Venture 1998).

18. For example, many firms that recently went to IPO after a short period introduce new business models in the Internet industry, but the technology involved is not considered strikingly innovative. Basic analytical algorithms of Internet auction sites and other e-commerce businesses have been long-known in experimental economics. On the other hand, in the biotechnology industry where R&D uncertainty is still relatively high, the shortening of the period needed for the recovery of venture-capital investment returns is not as dramatic.

19. For example, Cisco Systems, a start-up firm itself a decade ago but now close to the top-ranking corporation in terms of stock value, has grown by acquisition. They acquired some fifty companies in the last seven years. They are said to select from about fifteen companies for acquiring one technology (Senior Vice President Volpi).

Chapter 15

1. For alternative classifications of advanced market economies based on somewhat different approaches from ours, see Amable, Barré, and Boyer (1997), Boyer (1999), and Boyer and Hollingsworth (1997). Our approach is different from theirs in that the nature of institutional dependencies in each model is captured in explicitly game-theoretic ways.

2. It is well known that Walras himself advocated the public ownership of lands as a solution to what he regarded as the social injustice caused by rising rents and price of land, with limited supplies relative to the growing population and social wealth accumulation. One could even say that his major theoretical treatise (Walras 1926[1954]) was written for a theoretical justification of such a social reform program (Misaki 1998:111). Walras also conceived the possibility of the "collectivist" regime in which the government monopolized the function of the entrepreneur. He anticipated the market-socialism algorithm proposed by Barone (1908/1935) and Lange (1936, 1937), insofar as the state-cum-entrepreneur acts as a price-taker and follows the rule of adjusting a production plan to equate marginal costs with output prices. There is nothing against "liberty, equality, order, and justice" in this scheme. Walras considered that the essential difference of his scheme from the Marxian communist scheme was that prices for labor services were determined in markets (Walras 1898[1992]:251).

3. See Grossman and Hart (1986), Hart and Moore (1990), and Hart (1995).

4. The Hart-Moore setting used in chapter 4.3 can be applied to the situation where there are two managers engaged in different projects operating with different physical assets. For example, read subscripts, w and m, as referring to the development projects of word processing software and multi-media communications software instead of the worker and the manager, respectively. By applying the same logic, we can see that the boundary of the firm, as defined by the ownership structure of assets, is determined by the complementarity/independence relationship of the physical assets that the managers use in their respective tasks. If these assets are complements (alternatively, independent), the integration of the tasks in a single firm (respectively, disintegration into two independent firms) should ensue (Hart 1995). Then, as the characteristics of the particular transaction for which the physical assets are employed change, the ownership of the physical assets ought to change as well. The property-rights approach of Hart and Moore then anticipates the existence of an active market in physical assets.

5. Casual references are often made to the so-called Anglo-American firms, reminding one of British-American types of firms rather than those based in English-speaking North America. However, American corporate law evolved from the tradition of state statues for chartering the public corporations in public utilities and transportation that required large amounts of capital from the outset. On the other hand, English company law originated in a common law tradition regulating private partnerships. For implications of the legal tradition of "public" corporations, particularly regarding the emergence of the securities markets in the late nineteenth century and the subsequent path-dependent capital market development and corporate firms; see Rosenberg and Birdzell (1986).

6. As documented and analyzed by Chandler (1977) and Williamson (1975), the emergence of the so-called M-form (multi-divisional corporate firm) in early twentieth-century America was a quintessential example of organizational innovation by a new type of bundling of business units: bundling of multiple quasi-independent hierarchies through the internalization of capital markets.

7. See Dunlop (1958/1993), Jacoby (1985), and Baron et al. (1986).

8. An alternative, unorthodox view held that the board of directors (ought to) function as the trustee of the corporation rather than as the agent of stockholders. In strictly legal terms, the board is indeed not the stockholders' agent, since it can neither be replaced at the will of stockholders without cause during its term nor can it act according to their concrete instructions. This alternative view has been presented by many authors in various versions since Dodd in the 1930s in his debate with Berle. But a generic theme appears to be that the board is not obliged to single-mindedly maximize the stockholders' immediate wealth, but it may be subjected to other considerations relevant to the long-run viability of the corporation (e.g., relationship with the society and community, long-term interests of other stakeholders such as employees, consumers, and suppliers as constituents of the corporation). Chapter 10 revisited the debate between the stockholder-sovereignty versus stakeholders' views. See Blair (1995) for a recent exposition of the stakeholder's view.

9. The court interpretations of the Sherman Antitrust Act held that "loose combinations" (e.g., "gentlemen's agreements, pools and other types of cartels") were illegal but that firms could not be held in violation of the law simply because of their size. A long-term consequence of the Act was thus to induce the manager to enhance market power through the development of large integrated nested hierarchies.

10. For detailed information regarding share holding and custodial relationships between banks and enterprises, see Baum (1994).

11. See Hellwig (2000) for the role of government in preserving the non-market-oriented corporate governance structure in Germany.

12. For a comparison of corporate governance structure and its institutional complementarities between Japan and Germany, see Jackson (1997).

13. The recent well-publicized episode of the hostile takeover of Mannesmann AG by U.K.-based Vodafone AirTouch PLC appears to be an exceptional event since Mannesmann's widely dispersed ownership structure was rather unique among D-firms before the takeover.

14. Based on a statement by Gordon Moore and James Gibbons at a Center for Economic Policy Research conference in 1997 at Stanford. For historical development of Silicon Valley phenomenon, see also Florida and Kenney (1998) and Lee, Miller, Hancock and Rowen (2000).

15. For the role of the defense industry in general in the emergence of the Silicon Valley phenomena, see Florida and Kenney (1998).

16. For the role of liberal immigration policy, see Saxenian (1999).

17. However, lawyers play very important roles on Silicon Valley in designing self-enforcing contracts between venture capitalist and entrepreneurs, preparing prospectus for IPOs, striking deals with acquiring companies, and the like. See Suchman (2000) and Johnson (2000).

18. See Rajan and Zingales (2000) for a similar argument.

19. The other important factors that would affect making institutional arrangements on a global scale would include demographic change and the impacts of economic activities on global natural environments.

20. The discussion of organizational "bio-diversity" by Pagano (1999) is highly relevant here.

21. Law firms and accounting firms also play important roles in Silicon Valley; see Suchman (2000).

22. The view that the stability and efficiency of the financial system can be restored and supported only by these market-oriented measures is dubbed as the "market fundamentalism" by Sakakibara (1999, 2000). As suggested in chapter 12, however, in order to nurture market-relevant competence in emergent markets, some kind of control over volatile, unproductive short-term capital flow may be one option. See, for example, Stiglitz (1999) and Sakakibara (1999).

23. Freeman (1995) and Freeman, Topel, and Swedenborg (1997) observed that greater costs of adjusting to changes in the economic environment or specific policies would occur in "tightly linked economies" such as in the "welfare-state-as-system." The reason that they gave for it is strong institutional complementarities.

References

Admati, A. R., and P. Pfleiderer. 1994. Robust financial contracting and the role of venture capitalists. *Journal of Finance* 49:371–402.

Aghion, P., and P. Bolton. 1992. An incomplete contracts approach to financial contracting. *Review of Economic Studies* 59:473–494.

Aghion, P., and J. Tirole. 1994a. Formal and real authorities in organizations. *Journal of Political Economy* 105:1–29.

Aghion, P., and J. Tirole. 1994b. The management of innovation. *Quarterly Journal of Economics* 106:1185–1209.

Akamatsu, N. 1995. Enterprise governance and investment funds in Russian privatization. In Aoki and Kim (1995):121–183.

Akerlof, G. 1970. The market for "lemons": Qualitative uncertainty and the market mechanism. *Quarterly Journal of Economics* 84:488–500. Reprinted in Akerlof (1984):7–22.

Akerlof, G. 1976. The economics of caste and of the rat race and other woeful tales. *Quarterly Journal of Economics* 90:599–617. Reprinted in Akerlof (1984):23–44.

Akerlof, G. 1982. Labor contracts as partial gift exchange. *Quarterly Journal of Economics* 97:543–569. Reprinted in Akerlof (1984):145–74.

Akerlof, G. 1984. *An Economic Theorist's Book of Tales.* Cambridge: Cambridge University Press.

Akerlof, G., and W. T. Dickens. 1982. The economic consequences of cognitive dissonance. *American Economic Review* 72:307–319. Reprinted in Akerlof (1984):123–144.

Alchian, A. 1950. Uncertainty, evolution, and economic theory. *Journal of Political Economy* 58:211–21.

Alchian, A., and H. Demsetz. 1972. Production, information costs, and economic organization. *American Economic Review* 62:777–95.

Allen, R. C. 1992. *Enclosure and the Yeoman.* Oxford: Clarendon Press.

Allen, R. C. 1998. Agricultural output and productivity in Europe, 1300–1800. Mimeo. University of British Columbia.

Allen, R. C. 1999. Tracking the agricultural revolution. *Economic History Review*, 2nd series, forthcoming.

Allen, R. C. 2001. Community and market in England: Open fields and enclosure revisited. In Aoki and Hayami (2001):42–69.

Amable, B., R. Barré, and R. Boyer. 1997. *Les Systèmes d'innovation: À l'ère de la Globalisation.* Paris: Economica.

Amino, Y. 1997. *Nihon Shakai no Rekishi* (A History of Japanese Society), vol. 3. Tokyo: Iwanami Shoten.

Amsden, A., and T. Hikino. 1994. Project execution capability, organizational know-how and conglomerates corporate growth in late industrialization. *Industrial and Corporate Change* 3:111–148.

Anderson, K., and Y. Hayami with G. Aurelia. 1986. *The Political Economy of Agricultural Protection.* Sydney: Allen and Urwin.

Aoki, M. 1984a. *The Co-operative Game Theory of the Firm.* Oxford: Clarendon Press.

Aoki, M. 1984b. *The Economic Analysis of the Japanese Firm.* Amsterdam: North Holland, pp. 193–224.

Aoki, M. 1984c. Shareholders' non-unanimity on investment financing: Banks vs. Individual Investors. In M. Aoki (1984b):193–224.

Aoki, M. 1986. Horizontal and vertical information structure of the firm. *American Economic Review* 76:971–83.

Aoki, M. 1988. *Information, Incentives, and Bargaining in the Japanese Economy.* Cambridge: Cambridge University Press.

Aoki, M. 1990. Toward an economic model of the Japanese firm. *Journal of Economic Literature* 28:1–27.

Aoki, M. 1994a. The Japanese firm as a system of attributes: A survey and research agenda. In Aoki and Dore (1994):11–40.

Aoki, M. 1994b. The contingent governance of teams: Analysis of institutional complementarity. *International Economic Review* 35:657–76.

Aoki, M. 1994c. Monitoring characteristics of the main bank system: Analytical and development view. In Aoki and Patrick (1994):109–41.

Aoki, M. 1995a. An evolving diversity of organizational mode and its implications for transitional economies. *Journal of Japanese and International Economies* 9:330–53.

Aoki, M. 1995b. Controlling insider control: Issues of corporate governance in transition economies. In Aoki and Kim (1995):3–29.

Aoki, M. 1995/2000. *Keizai Sisutemu no Shinka to Tagensei.* Tokyo: Toyokeizai Shinposya. Translated into English by S. Gehrig as *Information, Corporate Governance and Institutional Diversity: Competitiveness in Japan, US and Transition Economies.* Oxford: Oxford University Press.

Aoki, M. 1996. Towards a comparative institutional analysis: Motivations and some tentative general insights. *Japanese Economic Review* 47:1–19. Reprinted in Aoki (1995/2000):159–180.

Aoki, M. 1998. Organizational conventions and the gains from diversity: An evolutionary game approach. *Industrial and Corporate Change* 7:399–432.

Aoki, M., and S. Dinc. 2000. Relational financing as an institution and its viability under competition. In Aoki and Saxonhouse (2000):19–42.

Aoki, M., and R. Dore, eds. 1994. *The Japanese Firm: Sources of Strength.* Oxford: Oxford University Press.

Aoki, M., and Y. Hayami, eds. 2001. *Communities and Markets in Economic Development.* Oxford: Oxford University Press.

Aoki, M., and H.-K. Kim, eds. 1995. *Corporate Governance in Transitional Economies: Insider Control and the Role of Banks.* Washington, DC: World Bank.

Aoki, M., H.-K. Kim, and M. Okuno-Fujiwara, eds. 1997. *The Role of Government in East Asian Economic Development: Comparative Institutional Analysis* Oxford: Oxford University Press.

Aoki, M., K. Murdock, and M. Okuno-Fujiwara. 1997. Beyond the East Asian miracle: Introducing the market-enhancing view. In Aoki, Okuno-Fujiwara, and Kim (1997):1–37.

Aoki, M., and M. Okuno-Fujiwara. 1996. *Keizai Sisutemun no Hikaku Seido Bunseki* (Comparative Institutional Analysis of Economic Systems). Tokyo: University of Tokyo Press.

Aoki, M., and H. Patrick, eds. 1994. *The Japanese Main Bank System: Its Relevance for Developing and Transforming Economies.* Oxford: Oxford University Press.

Aoki, M., H. Patrick, and P. Sheard. 1994. The Japanese main bank system: An introductory overview. In Aoki and Patrick (1994):3–50.

Aoki, M., and N. Rosenberg. 1989. The Japanese firm as an innovating institution. In Shiraishi and Tsuru, eds., *Economic Institutions in a Dynamic Society.* London: Macmillan, pp. 137–54.

Aoki, M., and G. Saxonhouse, eds. 2000. *Finance, Governance, and Competitiveness in Japan.* Oxford: Oxford University Press.

Aristotle. 1955. *Ethics,* trans. by J. A. K. Thompson (rev. trans. by H. Tredennick). Penguin Classics. London: Penguin.

Arrow, K. J. 1962. Economic welfare and the allocation of resources for invention. In National Bureau of Economic Research, eds., *The Rate and Direction of Inventive Activity: Economic and Social Factors.* Princeton: Princeton University Press, pp. 609–25.

Arrow, K. J. 1967. The place of moral obligation in preference systems. Reprinted in *Collected Papers of Kenneth J. Arrow,* vol. 1. Cambridge: Harvard University Press, pp. 78–80.

Arrow, K. J. 1969. The organization of economic activity: Issues pertinent to the choice of market versus nonmarket allocation. In *The Analysis and Evaluation of Public Expenditures: The PPB System,* vol. 1. A Compendium of Papers Submitted to the Subcommittee of Economy in Government of the Joint Economic Committee, U.S. Congress Washington, DC: Government Printing Office, pp. 47–63.

Arrow, K. J. 1970. Political and economic evaluation of social effects and externalities. In Margolis (1970):1–23.

Arrow, K. J. 1974. *The Limits of Organization.* New York: Norton.

Arrow, K. J. 1998. The place of institutions in the economy: A theoretical perspective. In Hayami and M. Aoki (1998):39–48.

Arthur, W. B. 1989. Competing technologies, increasing returns, and lock-in by historical events. *The Economic Journal* 99:116–31.

Athey, S. 2001. Monotone comparative statics under uncertainty. *Quarterly Journal of Economics,* forthcoming.

Athey, S. 2001. Single crossing properties and the existence of pure strategy equilibria in games of incomplete information. *Econometrica,* forthcoming.

Asanuma, B. 1984. Jidosha Sangyo niokeru Buhin Torihiki no Kozo (The structure of parts transactions in the automobile industry). *Kikan Gendai Keizai* (Summer):38–48.

Asanuma, B. 1989. Manufacturer-supplier relationships in Japan and the concept of relation specific skill. *Journal of the Japanese and International Economies* 3:1–30.

Aumann, R., and M. Kurz. 1977. Power and taxes. *Econometrica* 45:137–60.

Baker, E. 1998. Institutional barriers to technology diffusion in rural Africa. Mimeo. Stanford University.

Baker, G., and G. D. Smith. 1998. *The New Financial Capitalists: Kohlberg Kravis Roberts and the Creation of Corporate Value.* Cambridge: Cambridge University Press.

Baland, J.-M., and J. P. Platteau. 1996. *Halting Degradation of Natural Resources: Is There a Role for Rural Communities?* Oxford: Oxford University Press.

Baldwin, C. Y., and K. B. Clark. 1997. Managing in an age of modularity. *Harvard Business Review* 75:84–93.

Baldwin, C. Y., and K. B. Clark. 2000. *Design Rules: The Power of Modularity,* vol. 1. Cambridge: MIT Press.

Bankman, J., and R. J. Gilson. 1996. Venture capital and the structure of capital markets: Banks versus stock markets? *Journal of Financial Economics* 51:289–303.

Bankman, J., and R. J. Gilson. 1999. Why start-ups? *Stanford Law Review* 51:289–308.

F. Barca, K. Iwai, U. Pagano, and S. Trento. 1999. The divergence of the Italian and Japanese corporate governance models: The role of the institutional shocks. *Economic Systems* 3:35–61.

Bardhan, P. 1977. Variations in forms of tenancy in a peasant economy. *Journal of Development Economics* 4:105–18.

Bardhan, P. 1980. Interlocking factor markets and agrarian development: A review of the issues. *Oxford Economic Papers* 32:82–98.

Bardhan, P. 1984. *Land, Labor and Rural Poverty: Essays in Development Economics.* New York: Columbia University Press.

Bardhan, P. 1989a. A note on interlinked rural economic arrangements. In Bardhan (1989b):237–42.

Bardhan, P., ed. 1989b. *The Economic Theory of Agrarian Institutions.* Oxford: Clarendon Press.

Bardhan, P. 1993. Symposium on management of local commons. *Journal of Economic Perspective* 7:87–92.

Bardhan, P. 1998. The nature of institutional impediments to economics development. Mimeo. University of California, Berkeley.

Bardhan, P., and A. Rudra. 1978. Interlinkage of land, labor, and credit relations: An analysis of village survey data in East India. *Economic and Political Weekly* 13:367–84.

Barkaw, H., L. Cosmides, and J. Tooby, eds. 1993. *Adapted Mind: Evolutionary Psychology and the Generation of Culture.* New York: Oxford University Press.

Barnard, C. 1938. *The Functions of the Executive.* Cambridge: Harvard University Press.

Baron, J. N., M. D. Burton, and M. T. Hannan. 1966. The road taken: Origins and evolution of employment systems in emerging companies. *Industrial and Corporate Change* 5:239–75.

Baron, J. N., F. N. Dobbin, and P. Devereaux. 1986. War and peace: The evolution of modern personnel administration in US industry. *American Journal of Sociology* 92:350–83.

Baron, J. N., M. T. Hannan, and M. D. Burton. 2000. Labor pains: Change in organizational models and employees turnover in young, high-tech firms. Mimeo. Stanford University.

Barone, E. 1908/1935. *Il ministro della oroduzione nell stato collettivita, Gionale degli Economisti.* Trans. in Hayek (1935):245–90.

Barry, C. B. 1994. New directions in research on venture capital finance. *Financial Management* 32:3–15.

Basu, K. 1997a. On misunderstanding government: An analysis of the art of the policy advice. *Economics and Politics* 9:231–50.

Basu, K. 1997b. The role of norms and law in economics: An essay on political economy. In J. Scott, ed., *25 Years: Social Science and Social Change.* Princeton: Princeton University Press, forthcoming.

Basu, K. 1998. Social norms and the law. In P. Newman, ed., *The New Palgrave Dictionary of Economics and the Law.* London: Macmillan, pp. 476–80.

Bates, R. H. 1981. *Markets and States in Tropical Africa: The Political Basis of Agricultural Policies.* Berkeley: University of California Press.

Baum, T. 1994. The German banking system and its impacts on corporate finance and governance. In Aoki and Patrick (1994):409–449.

Bell, C. 1988. Credit markets and interlinked transactions. In H. B. Chenery and T. N. Srinivasan, eds., *Handbook of Development Economics.* Amsterdam: North-Holland.

Berger, A. N., and G. Udell. 1995. Relationship lending and lines of credit in small firm finance. *Journal of Business* 68:351–81.

Berger, P., and T. Luckmann. 1966. *The Social Construction of Reality: A Treatise in the Sociology of Knowledge.* New York: Doubleday Anchor.

Berglöf, E., and E.-L. von Thadden. 1999. The changing corporate governance paradigm: Implications for transition and developing economies. Mimeo. World Bank.

Bergson, A. 1964. *The Economics of Soviet Planning.* New Haven: Yale University Press.

Berins-Collier, R., and D. Collier. 1991. *Shaping the Political Arena.* Princeton: Princeton University Press.

Berle, A. 1931. Corporate powers as powers in trust. *Harvard Law Review* 63:853–70.

Berle, A. 1959. Forward to E. Mason, *The Corporation in Modern Society.* Cambridge: Harvard University Press, pp. ix–xv.

Berle, A., and G. Means. 1932. *The Modern Corporation and Private Property.* New York: Macmillan.

Bernanke, B. S. 1983. Nonmonetary effects of financial crisis in the propagation of the Great Depression. *American Economic Review* 73:257–76.

Bernheim, B. D., and M. Whinston. 1990. Multimarket contact and collusive behavior. *Rand Journal of Economics* 21:1–26.

Bhagwati, J. R. 1982. Directly-unproductive, Profit-seeking (DUP) activities. *Journal of Political Economy* 90:988–1002.

Bhagwati, J., R. Brecher, and T. N. Srinivasan. 1984. DUP activities and economic theory. In D. Colander, ed., *Neoclassical Political Economy.* Cambridge, MA: Ballinger, pp. 17–32.

Binswanger, H. 1991. Brazilian policies that encourage deforestation in the Amazon. *World Development* 19:821–29.

Binswanger, H., and M. R. Rosenzweig, eds. 1984. *Contractual Arrangements, Employment, and Wages in Rural Labor Markets in Asia.* New Haven: Yale University Press.

Black, B., and R. Gilson. 1998. Venture capital and the structure of capital markets: Banks versus stock markets. *Journal of Financial Economics* 47:243–77.

Black, D., and M. P. Baumgartner. 1983. Toward a theory of the third party. In K. O. Boyum and L. Mather, eds., *Empirical Theories about Courts*. New York: Longman, pp. 84–114.

Blackburn, J., S. Kozinski, and M. Murphy. 1996. Symantec Corporation acquiring entrepreneurial companies. Graduate School of Business, Stanford University.

Blair, M. 1995. *Ownership and Control: Rethinking Corporate Governance for the Twenty-first Century*. Washington, DC: Brookings Institution.

Blanchard, O., and M. Kremer. 1997. Disorganization. *Quarterly Journal of Economics* 112:1091–1126.

Blau, P. 1964/1998. *Exchange and Power in Social Life*, with new introduction. Brunswick, NJ: Transaction Publishers.

Bolton, P., and M. Dewatripont. 1994. Firms as networks of communications. *Quarterly Journal of Economics* 109:809–39.

Boot, A. W., S. I. Greenbaum, and A. V. Thakor. 1993. Reputation and discretion in financial contracting. *American Economic Review* 83:1165–83.

Bowles, S. 1985. The production process in a competitive economy: Walrasian, neo-Hobbsian, and Marxian models. *American Economic Review* 75:16–36.

Bowles, S. 1996. Markets as cultural institutions: Equilibrium norms in competitive economies. Mimeo. University of Massachusetts.

Bowles, S. 1998. Endogenous preferences: The cultural consequences of markets and other economic institutions. *Journal of Economic Literature* 36:75–111.

Bowles, S. 2001. *Economic Institutions and Behavior: An Evolutionary Approach to Microeconomic Theory*. Princeton: Princeton University Press, forthcoming.

Bowles, S., and H. Gintis. 1986. *Democracy and Capitalism*. New York: Basic Books.

Bowles, S., H. Gintis, and B. Gustafsson, eds. 1993. *Markets and Democracy: Participation, Accountability, and Efficiency*. Cambridge: Cambridge University Press.

Boycko, M., A. Shleifer, and R. W. Vishny. 1993. Privatizing Russia. *Brookings Paper on Economic Activity* 2:139–92.

Boyer, R. 1999. The variety and dynamics of capitalism. In Groenewegen and Vromen (1999):122–140.

Boyer, R., and J. R. Hollingsworth, eds. 1997. *Contemporary Capitalism: The Embeddedness of Institutions*. Cambridge: Cambridge University Press.

Boyer, R., and A. Orléan. 1992. How do conventions evolve? *Journal of Evolutionary Economics* 2:165–77.

Braguinsky, S., and G. Yavlinsky. 2000. *Incentives and Institutions: The Transition to a Market Economy in Russia*. Princeton: Princeton University Press.

Braverman, A., and J. Stiglitz. 1982. Sharecropping and the interlinking of agrarian markets. *American Economic Review* 72:695–715.

Brynjolfsson, E. 1994. Information assets, technology, and organization. *Management Science* 40:1645–62.

Burawoy, M. 1979. *Manufacturing Consent*. Chicago: University of Chicago Press.

Bygrve, W. D., and J. A. Timmons. 1992. *Venture Capital at the Crossroads*. Boston: Harvard Business School Press.

Calvert, R. L. 1995. Rational actors, equilibrium, and social institutions. In Knight and Sened (1995):57–93.

Calvo, G. 1979. Quasi-Walrasian theories of unemployment. *American Economic Review* (Papers and Preceedings) 69:102–107.

Canzoneri, M. B., V. Grilli, and P. Masson. eds. 1992. *Establishing a Central Bank: Issues in Europe and Lessons from the US*. Cambridge: Cambridge University Press.

Carmichael, H. L., and W. B. MacLeod. 1997. Gift giving and the evolution of cooperation. *International Economic Review* 38:485–509.

Carrol, G. R., and M. T. Hannan. 1989. Density dependence in the evolution of populations of newspaer organizations. *American Sociological Review* 54:524–48.

Chambers, R. 1988. *Managing Canal Irrigation.* New Delhi: Oxford and IBH Publishing.

Chandler, A., Jr. 1977. *The Visible Hand: The Managerial Revolution in American Business.* Cambridge: Harvard University Press.

Chandler, A., Jr. 1992. Competitive performance of US industrial enterprises since the Second World War. *Business History Review* 68:1–72.

Chandler, A. 1992. Organizational capabilities and the economic history of the industrial enterprise. *Journal of Economic Perspectives* 6:79–100.

Che, J. 1997. *Local Governments and Corporate Governance in Transition Economies.* Ph.D. dissertation. Stanford University.

Che, J. 1999. Organizing market transactions. Mimeo. Stanford University.

Che, J. 2000. Soft budget constraints, pecuniary externality, and the dual track system. Mimeo. Stanford University.

Che, J., and Y. Qian. 1998. Insecure property rights and government ownership of firms. *Quarterly Journal of Economics* 113:467–96.

Cho, C., and Y. Sung. 1995[1997]. *A History of Korea* (Japanese trans.). Tokyo: Akashi Shoten.

Clark, K. B., and T. Fujimoto. 1991. *Product Development Performance: Strategy, Organization, and Management in the World Auto Industry.* Boston: Harvard Business School.

Clark, L. E. 1935. Central banking under the Federal Reserve System. New York: Macmillan.

Clower, R. W. 1967. A reconsideration of the microfoundations of monetary theory. *Western Economic Journal* 6:1–8.

Coase, R. 1937. The nature of the firm. *Economica* 4:386–405.

Coase, R. 1960. The problem of social cost. *Journal of Law and Economics* 3:1–44.

Coleman, J. 1990. *Foundations of Social Theory.* Cambridge: Harvard University Press.

Commons, J. R. 1934. *Institutional Economics: Its Place in Political Economy.* Madison: University of Wisconsin Press.

Coriat, B., and G. Dosi. 1998. The institutional embeddedness of economic change: An appraisal of the "evolutionary" and "regulationist" research programmes. Mimeo. International Institute for Applied Systems Analysis, Vienna.

Cowan, R., P. A. David, and D. Foray. 2000. The explicit economics of knowledge codification and tacitness. *Industrial and Corporate Change* 9:211–54.

Cremer, J. 1980. A partial theory of the optimal organization of a bureaucracy. *Bell Journal of Economics* 11:683–93.

Cremer, J. 1990. Common knowledge and the co-ordination of economic activities. In M. Aoki, B. Gustafsson, and O. E. Williamson, eds., *The Firm as a Nexus of Treaties.* London: Sage, pp. 53–76.

Van Damme, E. 1987. *Stability and Perfection of Nash Equilibria.* Berlin: Springer.

Dasgupta, P., and J. Stiglitz. 1980. Uncertainty, industrial structure, and the speed of R&D. *Bell Journal of Economics* 11:1–28.

David, P. 1985. Clio and the economics of QWERTY. *American Economic Review* 75:332–37.

David, P. 1994. Why are institutions the "carriers of history"?: Path dependence and the evolution of conventions, organizations and institutions. *Structural Change and Economic Dynamics* 5:205–20.

Davis, L., and D. North. 1971. *Institutional Change and American Economic Growth.* Cambridge: Cambridge University Press.

De Alessi, L. 1980. The economics of property rights: A review of evidence. *Research in Law and Economics* 2:1–47.

Demsetz, H. 1967. Towards a theory of property rights. *American Economic Review* 57:347–59.

Demsetz, H. 1969. Information and efficiency: Another viewpoint. *Journal of Law and Economics* 12:1–22.

Denzau, A. T., and D. North. 1994. Shared mental models: Ideologies and institutions. *Kyklos* 47:3–31.

Dewatripont, M., and E. Maskin. 1995. Credit and efficiency in centralized and decentralized economies. *Review of Economic Studies* 62:541–55.

Dewatripont, M., and J. Tirole. 1994. A theory of debt and equity: Diversities of securities and manager-shareholder congruence. *Quarterly Journal of Economics* 109:1027–54.

Dewatripont, M., and J. Tirole. 1995. *The Prudential Regulation of Banks*. Cambridge: MIT Press.

Diamond, D. 1984. Financial intermediation and delegated monitoring. *Review of Economic Studies* 51:393–414.

DiMaggio, P., and W. Powell. 1983. The iron cage revisited: Institutional isomorphism and collective rationality in organizational fields. *American Sociological Review* 48:147–60.

DiMaggio, P., and W. Powell, eds. 1991. *The New Institutionalism in Organizational Analysis*. Chicago: University of Chicago Press.

Dinç, S. 1996. *Bank Competition, Relationship Banking and Path Dependence*. Ph.D. dissertation. Stanford University.

Dinç, S. 2000. Bank reputation, bank commitment and the effects of the competition in credit markets. *Review of Financial Studies* 13:781–812.

Dodd, E. M. 1932. For whom are corporate managers trustees? *Harvard Law Review* 45:1145–63.

Dosi, G. 1995. Hierarchies, markets and power: Some foundational issues on the nature of contemporary economic organizations. *Industrial and Corporate Change* 4:1–19. Reprinted in Dosi (2000):669–87.

Dosi, G. 2000. *Innovation, Organization and Economic Dynamics*. Cheltenham, UK: Edward Elgar.

Dosi, G., and L. Marengo. 1994. Some elements of an evolutionary theory of organizational competence. In W. England, ed., *Evolutionary Concepts in Contemporary Economics*. Ann Arbor: University of Michigan Press, pp. 157–78. Reprinted in Dosi (2000):211–35.

Dosi, G., L. Marengo, and G. Fagiolo. 2000. Learning in evolutionary environments. In K. Dopfer, ed., *The Foundations of Evolutionary Economics*. Cambridge: Cambridge University Press.

Dosi, G., K. Pavitt, and L. Soete. 1990. *The Economics of Technical Change and International Trade*. Oxford: Harvester Wheatsheaf.

Dunlop, J. 1958/1993. *Industrial Relationship Systems*, rev. ed. Boston: Harvard Business School Press.

Durkheim, E. 1901[1950]. *The Rules of Sociological Method*. Glencoe IL: Free Press.

Edwards, J., and K. Fischer. 1994. *Banks, Finance and Investment in Germany*. Cambridge: Cambridge University Press.

Earle, J. 2000. Equilibrium wage arrears: Institutional lock-in of contractual failure in Russia. Mimeo. Stanford University.

Earle, J., and K. Z. Sabirianova. 2000. How late to pay?: Understanding wage arrears in Russia. Mimeo. Stanford University.

Eggertsson, T. 1990. *Economic Behavior and Institutions*. Cambridge: Cambridge University Press.

Eichengreen, B. 1992. Designing a central bank for Europe: A cautionary tale from the early years of the Federal Reserve System. In Canzoneri (1992):13–39.

Eldredge, N., and S. Gould. 1972. Punctuated equilibria: An alternative to phyletic gradualism. In Schopf (1972):82–115.

Ellickson, R. C. 1991. *Orders without Law*. Cambridge: Harvard University Press.

Elster, J. 1989a. *The Cement of Society: A Study of Social Order*. Cambridge: Cambridge University Press.

Elster, J. 1989b. Social norms and economic theory. *Journal of Economic Perspectives* 3:99–117.

England, W., ed. 1994. *Evolutionary Concepts in Contemporary Economics*. Ann Arbor: University of Michigan Press.

Epstein, J. M., and R. Axtell. 1996. *Growing Artificial Societies*. Cambridge: MIT Press.

Ericson, R. E., and B. W. Ickes. 1999. A model of Russia's "virtual economy." Mimeo. Columbia University.

Eswaran, M., and A. Kotwal. 1984. The moral hazard of budget breaking. *Rand Journal of Economics* 15:578–81.

Fafchamps, M. 1996. Market emergence, trust, and reputation. Mimeo. Stanford University.

Farrell, J., and M. Rabin. 1996. Cheap talk. *Journal of Economic Perspective* 10:103–18.

Fenn, G. W., N. Liang, and S. Prowse. 1995. *The Economics of the Private Equity Market*. Staff Study 168. Board of Governors of the Federal Reserve System.

Field, A. J. 1979. On the explanation of rules using rational choice models. *Journal of Economic Issues* 13:49–72.

Field, A. J. 1981. The problem with neoclassical institutional economics: A critique with special reference to the North-Thomas model of pre-1500 Europe. *Explorations in Economic History* 18:174–198.

Field, A. J. 2001. *Altruistically Inclined? Evolutionary Theory, the Behavioral Sciences, and the Origin of Complex Social Organization*. Ann Arbor: University of Michigan Press.

Fiske, A. P. 1991. The cultural relativity of selfish individualism: Anthropological evidence that humans are inherently sociable. In M. Clark, ed., *Review of Personality and Social Psychology: Altruism and Prosocial Behavior*, vol. 12. Beverly Hills: Sage, pp. 176–214.

Fiske, A. P., S. Kitayama, H. R. Markus, and R. E. Nisbett. 1998. The cultural matrix of social psychology. In D. Gilbert, S. Fiske, and G. Linzey, eds., *Handbook of Social Psychology*, 4th ed. New York: McGraw-Hill, pp. 915–81.

Florida, R., and M. Kenney. 1988. Venture capital-financed innovation and technological change in the USA. *Research Policy* 17:119–37.

Foster, D., and P. Young. 1990. Stochastic evolutionary game dynamics. *Theoretical Population Biology* 38:219–32.

Foster, D., and P. Young. 1998. Learning with hazy beliefs. In W. Leinfellner and E. Koehler, eds., *Game Theory, Experience, Rationality: Foundations of Social Sciences, Economics and Ethics*; Amsterdam: Kluwer, pp. 325–35.

Franks, J., C. Mayer, and L. Renneboog. 1998. Who disciplines bad management? Mimeo. Catholic University of Leuven, Belgium.

Freeland, R. F. 2000. Creating hold-up through vertical integration: Fisher body revisited. *Journal of Law and Ecomics* 43:33–66.

Freeman, R. 1995. The welfare state as a system. *American Economic Review* 85:16–21.

Freeman, R. B., R. Topel, and B. Swedenborg, eds. 1997. *Reforming the Welfare State: The Swedish Model in Transition*. Chicago: Chicago University Press.

Friedman, D. 1991. Evolutionary games in economics. *Econometrica* 59:637–66.

Friedman, M. 1953. *Essays in Positive Economics*. Chicago: University of Chicago Press.

Fudenberg, D., and D. M. Kreps. 1987. Reputation in the simultaneous play of multiple opponents. *Review of Economic Studies* 56:541–68.

Fudenberg, D., and E. Maskin. 1986. The folk theorem in repeated games with discounting and with incomplete information. *Econometrica* 54:533–54.

Fudenberg, D., and E. Maskin. 1993. Evolution and repeated games. *Nobel Symposium on Game Theory.* Karlskoga, Sweden.

Fudenberg, D., and J. Tirole. 1991. *Game Theory.* Cambridge: MIT Press.

Fudenberg, D., and C. Harris. 1992. Evolutionary dynamics with aggregate shocks. *Journal of Economic Theory* 57:420–41.

Fujimoto, T. 1997. The Japanese automobile supplier system: Framework, facts, and reinterpretation. *Proceedings of the 3rd International Symposium on Logistics.* Padova: SGE-Servizi Grafici Editoriali.

Fujimoto, T. 1999. *The Evolution of a Manufacturing System at Toyota.* Oxford: Oxford University Press.

Fukao, M. 1995. *Financial Integration, Corporate Governance, and the Performance of Multinational Companies.* Washington DC: Brookings Institution.

Gaddy, C., and B. Ickes. 1998. A simple four sector model of Russia's "virtual economy." *Post-Soviet Geography and Economics* 40:79–97.

Gaddy, C., and B. Ickes. 1999. Stability and disorder: An evolutionary analysis of Russia's virtual economy. Mimeo. Brookings Institution.

Gambetta, D. 1993. *The Sicilian Mafia.* Cambrdige: Harvard University Press.

Gale, D. 1986. Bargaining and competition, Part I: Characterization. *Econometrica* 54:785–806.

Garfinkel, H. 1967. *Studies in Ethonmethodology.* Englewood Cliffs, NJ: Prentice Hall.

Gande, A., M. Puri, A. Saunders, and I. Walter. 1997. Bank underwriting of debt securities: Modern evidence. *Review of Financial Studies* 10:1175–1202.

Geanakoplos, J., and P. Milgrom. 1991. A theory of hierarchies based on limited managerial attention. *Journal of Japanese and International Economies* 5:205–25.

Geertz, C. 1963. *Peddlers and Princes.* Chicago: University of Chicago Press.

Geertz, C. 1978. The bazaar economy: Information and search in peasant marketing. *American Economic Review* 68:9–32.

Geertz, C. 1980. *NEGARA: The Theatre State in Nineteenth-Century Bali.* Princeton: Princeton University Press.

Ghemawat, P. 1998. *Games Businesses Play: Cases and Models.* Cambridge: MIT Press.

Ghemawat, P., and T. Khanna. 1998. The nature of diversified groups: A research design and two case studies. *Journal of Industrial Economics* 46:35–62.

Gibbons, R. 1992. *Game Theory for Applied Economists.* Princeton: Princeton University Press.

Gilson, R. J. 1999. The legal infrastructure of high technology industrial districts: Silicon Valley, Route 128, and covenants not to compete. *NY University Law Review* 74:575–629.

Gintis, H. 2000. *Game Theory Evolving: A Problem-Centered Introcduction to Modeling Strategic Behavior.* Princeton: Princeton University Press.

Gintis, H., and T. Ishikawa. 1988. Wage, work intensity, and unemployment. *Journal of the Japanese and International Economies* 1:195–228.

Gompers, P. 1995. Optimal investment, monitoring, and the staging of venture capital. *Journal of Finance* 50:231–48.

Gompers, P. 1998. An examination of convertible securities in venture capital investments. Mimeo. Harvard Business School.

Gompers, P., and J. Lerner. 1996. The use of covenants: An empirical analysis of venture partnership agreements. *Journal of Law and Economics.*

Gordon, A. 1985. *The Evolution of Labor Relations in Japan: Heavy Industry 1853–1955.* Cambridge: Harvard University Press.

Gorman, M., and W. A. Sahlman. 1989. What do venture capitalists do? *Journal of Business Venturing* 4:231–48.

Gould, S. J., and N. Eldridge. 1977. Punctuated equilibria: The tempo and mode of evolution reconsidered. *Paleobiology* 3:115–51.

Granovetter, M. 1985. Economic action and social structure: The problem of embeddedness. *American Journal of Sociology* 91:480–510.

Granovetter, M. 1994. Business groups. In N. J. Smelser and R. Swedberg, eds., *Handbook of Economic Sociology*. Princeton: Princeton University Press, pp. 453–75.

Granovetter, M. 1992. Economic institutions as social constructions: A framework for analysis. *Acta Sociologica* 35:3–11.

Groenewegen, J., and J. Vromen, eds. 1999. *Institutions and the Evolution of Capitalism: Implications of Evolutionary Economics*. Cheltenham, U.K.: Edward Elgar.

Greif, A. 1989. Reputation and coalitions in medieval trade: Evidence on the Maghribi traders. *Journal of Economic History* 49:857–82.

Greif, A. 1994. Cultural beliefs and the organization of society: A historical and theoretical reflection on collectivist and individualist societies. *Journal of Political Economy* 102:912–50.

Greif, A. 1997a. Microtheory and recent developments in the study of economic institutions through economic history. In D. Kreps and K. Wallis, eds., *Advances in Economics and Econometrics: Theory and Applications*, vol. 2. Cambridge: Cambridge University Press, pp. 79–113.

Greif, A. 1997b. Self-enforcing political system and economic growth: Late medieval Genoa. Mimeo. Stanford University.

Greif, A. 1998a. Historical and comparative institutional analysis. *American Economic Review* 88:80–84.

Greif, A. 1998b. *Genoa and the Maghribi Traders: Historical and Comparative Institutional Analysis.* Book manuscript.

Greif, A. 2000. Impersonal exchange and the origin of markets: From the community responsibility system to individual legal responsibility in pre-modern Europe. In Aoki and Hayami (2001):3–41.

Greif, A., P. Milgrom, and B. Weingast. 1994. Coordination, commitment and enforcement: The case of the merchant guild. *Journal of Political Economy* 102:745–76.

Grossman, S., and O. Hart. 1986. The costs and benefits of ownership: A theory of vertical and lateral integration. *Journal of Political Economy* 94:691–719.

Hadfield, G. K. 2000. Privatizing commercial law: Lessons from the middle and the digital ages. Mimeo. University of Toronto Law School.

Hall, J., ed. 1991. *The Cambridge History of Japan*, vol. 4. Cambridge: Cambridge University Press.

Hamilton, G., ed. 1996. *Asian Business Networks*. New York: Walter de Gruyter.

Hannan, M. T., M. D. Burton, and J. N. Baron. 1996. Inertia and change in the early years: Employment relations in young, high-technology firms. *Industrial and Corporate Change* 5:503–36.

Hannan, M. T., and G. Carroll. 1992. *Dynamics of Organizational Populations: Density, Legitimation and Competition.* Oxford: Oxford University Press.

Hannan, M., and J. Freeman. 1977. *Organizational Ecology*. Cambridge: Harvard University Press.

Hansmann, H. 1995. *The Ownership of Enterprise*. Cambridge: Harvard University Press.

Hardin, G. 1968. The tragedy of the commons. *Science* 162:1243–48.

Harsanyi, J. 1977. *Rational Behavioue and Bargaining Equilibrium in Games and Social Situations*. Cambridge: Cambridge University Press.

Hart, O. 1995. *Firms, Contracts, and Financial Structure*. Oxford: Clarendon Press.

Hart, O., and J. Moore. 1990. Property rights and the nature of the firm. *Journal of Political Economy* 98:1119–58.

Hart, O., and J. Moore. 1999. On the design of hierarchies: Coordination versus specialization. Mimeo. Harvard University and LSE.

Hayami, A., and M. Miyamoto. 1988. Gaisetsu: Juhichi-hachi Seiki (An overview: the seventeenth to the eighteenth century. In A. Hayami and M. Miyamoto, eds., *Keizai Shyakai no Seiritsu (The Establishment of an Economic Society), Nihon Keizaishi (A History of Japan)*, vol. 1. Tokyo: Iwanami Shoten, pp. 1–84.

Hayami, Y. 1994. Peasant and plantation in Asia. In G. Meier, ed., *From Classical Economics to Developmental Economics*. New York: St. Martin's Press, pp. 121–134.

Hayami, Y. 1998. Toward an East Asian model of economic development. In Hayami and Aoki (1998):3–35.

Hayami, Y., and M. Aoki, eds. 1998. *The Institutional Foundations of East Asian Economic Development*. London: Macmillan.

Hayami, Y., and T. Kawagoe. 1993. *The Agrarian Origins of Commerce and Industry: A Study of Peasant Marketing in Indonesia*. New York: St. Martin's Press.

Hayami, Y., and M. Kikuchi. 2000. *A Rice Village Saga: Three Decades of Green Revolution in the Phillipines*. London: Macmillan.

Hayami, Y., and K. Ohtsuka. 1993. *The Economics of Contract Choice*. Oxford: Claredon Press.

Hayami, Y., and V. W. Ruttan. 1985. *Agricultural Development: An International Perspective*, rev. ed. Baltimore: Johns Hopkins University Press.

Hayek, F. A., ed. 1935. *Collectivist Economic Planning*. London: Routledge.

Hayek, F. A. 1945. The use of knowledge in society. *American Economic Review* 35:519–30.

Hayek, F. A. 1973. *Law, Legislation, and Liberty: Rules and Order,* vol. 1. Chicago: University of Chicago Press.

Hayek, F. A. 1988. *The Fatal Conceit*. Chicago: University of Chicago Press.

Hellmann, T. 1998a. The allocation of control rights in venture capital contracts. *Rand Journal of Economics* 29:57–76.

Hellmann, T. 1998b. Teaching note for Symantec Corporation. (S-SM-27). Stanford Business School.

Hellmann, T., K. Murdock, and J. Stiglitz. 1997. Financial restraint: Toward a new paradigm. In Aoki, Kim, and Okuno-Fujiwara (1997):163–207.

Hellmann, T., K. Murdock, and J. Stiglitz. 1998. Financial restraint and the market enhancing view. In Hayami and Aoki (1998):255–279.

Hellman, T., and M. Puri. 1998. The interaction between product market and financing strategy: The role of venture capital. Stanford University Graduate School of Business.

Hellwig, M. 1991. Banking, financial intermediation and corporate finance. In A. Giovannini and C. Mayer, eds., *European Financial Integration*. Cambridge: Cambridge University Press, pp. 35–68.

Hellwig, M. 2000. On the economics and politics of corporate finance and corporate control. In X. Vives, ed., *Corporate Governance: Theoretical and Empirical Perspectives*. Cambridge, U.K.: Cambridge University Press, pp. 95–136.

Hicks, J. 1969. *A Theory of Economic History*. Oxford: Oxford University Press.

Hirschman, A. O. 1970. *Exit, Voice, and Loyalty: Responses to Decline in Firms, Organizations, and States*. Cambridge: Harvard University Press.

Hodgson, G. M. 1988. *Economics and Institutions: A Manifesto for a Modern Institutional Economics*. Philadelphia: University of Pennsylvania Press.

Hodgson, G. M. 1993. *Economics and Evolution*. Ann Arbor: University of Michigan Press.

Hodgson, G. M. 1998. The approach of institutional economics. *Journal of Economic Literature* 36:166–92.

Holland, J. H., K. J. Holyoak, R. E. Nisbett, and P. R. Thagard. 1986. *Induction: Processes of Inference, Learning, and Discovery*. Cambridge: MIT Press.

Holmstrom, B. 1979. Moral hazard and observability. *Bell Journal of Economics* 10:74–91.

Holmstrom, B. 1982. Moral hazard in teams. *Bell Journal of Economics* 10:324–40.

Holmstrom, B., and P. Milgrom. 1991. Multi-task principal-agent analysis. *Journal of Law, Economics and Organization* 7 (special issue):24–52.

Holmstrom, B., and P. Milgrom. 1994. The firm as an incentive system. *American Economic Review* 84:972–91.

Homans, G. 1961. *Social Behavior: Its Elementary Forms.* New York: Harcourt Brace Javanovich.

Home, W. S. 1952. *Escrow and Land Title Procedure.* Los Angeles: Olin W. Smith.

Horiuchi, H. 1994. The effect of firm status on banking relationships and loan syndication. In Aoki and Patrick (1994):258–94.

Hoshi, T. 1995. Cleaning up the balance sheet: Japanese experience in the postwar reconstruction period. In Aoki and Kim (1995):303–59.

Hoshi, T., and A. Kashyap. 1999. The Japanese banking crisis: Where did it come form and how will it end? Working Paper 7250. NBER, Cambridge, MA.

Hoshi, T., A. Kashyap, and D. Sharfstein. 1993. The role of the banks in reducing costs of financial distress in Japan. *Journal of Financial Economics* 27:67–88.

Hume, D. 1739[1992]. *Treatise of Human Nature.* Buffalo: Prometheus Books.

Hume, D. 1777[1985]. *Essays, Moral, Political and Literary,* posthumous edition, ed. by T. H. Green and T. H. Grose. London: Longman, Green.

Hurwicz, L. 1960. On the dimensional requirements for non-wasteful resource allocation systems. In K. J. Arrow, S. Karlin, and P. Suppes, eds., *The Mathematical Methods in the Social Sciences 1959.* Stanford University Press. Reprinted in K. J. Arrow and L. Hurwicz. 1977. *Studies in Resource Allocation Processes.* Cambridge: Cambridge University Press, pp. 413–24.

Hurwicz, L. 1973. The design of mechanisms for resource allocation. *American Economic Review* 63:1–30.

Hurwicz, L. 1987. Inventing new institutions: The design perspective. *American Journal of Agricultural Economics* 69:395–402.

Hurwicz, L. 1993. Toward a framework for analyzing institutions and institutional change. In Bowles et al. (1993):51–67.

Hurwicz, L. 1996. Institutions as families of game forms. *Japanese Economic Review* 47:13–132.

Ichiishi, T. 1993. *The Cooperative Nature of the Firm.* Cambridge: Cambridge University Press.

Ikeda, N. 1997. *Jōhō Tsūshin Kakumei to Nihon Kigyō* (The Digital Revolution and Japanese Firms). Tokyo: NTT Publishers.

Ikeda, N. 1999. *Internet Shihon Shugi Kakumei* (Explosion of Digital Capitalism). Tokyo: NTT Shuppan.

Ikegami, E. 1995. *The Taming of the Samurai: Honorific Individualism and the Making of Modern Japan.* Cambridge: Harvard University Press.

Itoh, H. 1992. Cooperation in hierarchical organizations: An incentive perspective. *Journal of Law, Economics and Organization* 8:321–45.

Itoh, H. 1994. Japanese human resource management from the viewpoint of incentive theory. In Aoki and Dore (1994):233–64.

Iwai, K. 1993. *Kaheiron* (A Theory of Money). Tokyo: Chikuma Shobō.

Jackson, G. 1997. Corporate governance in Germany and Japan: Development within national and international contexts. Mimeo. Max-Planck Institut für Gesellschaftsforschung, Köln.

Jacoby, S. 1985. *Employing Bureaucracy: Manager, Unions, and the Transformation of Work in the American Industry, 1900–1945.* New York: Columbia University Press.

Jensen, M. 1989. The eclipse of the public corporation. *Harvard Business Review* 67:49–74.

Jensen, M. 1993. The modern industrial revolution, exit, and the failure of internal control systems. *Journal of Finance* 48:831–80.

Jensen, M., and W. Meckling. 1976. Theory of the firm: Managerial behavior, agency costs, and capital structure. *Journal of Financial Economics* 3:305–60.

Jevons, W. S. 1875. *Money and the Mechanism of Exchange.* London: Appleton.

Jin, H., Y. Qian, and B. Weingast. 1999. Regional decentralization and fiscal incentives: Federalism, Chinese style. Mimeo. Stanford University.

Johnson, C. W. 2000. Advising the new economy: The role of lawyers. In Lee et al. (2000):325–41.

Joint Venture. 1999. *1998 Index of Silicon Valley.* Palo Alto, CA.: Joint Venture.

Jones, R. 1976. The origin and development of media of exchange. *Journal of Political Economy* 84:757–75.

Kandori, M. 1992. Social norms and community enforcement. *Review of Economic Studies* 59:63–80.

Kandori, M. 1997. Evolutionary game theory in economics. In D. Kreps and K. Wallis, eds., *Advances in Economics and Econometrics: Theory and Applications.* Cambridge: Cambridge University Press, pp. 243–77.

Kandori, M., G. Mailath, and R. Rob. 1993. Learning, mutation, and long run equilibria in games. *Econometrica* 61:29–56.

Kaneko, M., and A. Matsui. 1999. Inductive game theory: Discrimination and prejudices. *Journal of Public Economic Theory* 1:101–37.

Kaplan, S. N., and P. Strömberg. 2000. Financial contracting theory meets the real world: An empirical analysis of venture capital contracts. Mimeo. University of Chicago.

Khanna, T., and K. Palepu. 1997. Why focused strategies may be wrong for emerging markets. *Harvard Business Review* 175:41–51.

Khanna, T., and K. Palepu. 1999a. The right way to restructure conglomerates in emerging markets. *Harvard Business Review* 77:125–34.

Khanna, T., and K. Palepu. 1999b. Policy shocks, market intermediaries, and corporate strategy: The evolution of business groups in Chile and India. *Journal of Economics and Management Strategy* 8:271–310.

Khanna, T., and K. Palepu. 2000a. Is group affiliation profitable in emerging markets?: An analysis of diversified Indian business groups. *Journal of Finance* 55:867–91.

Khanna, T., and K. Palepu. 2000b. The future of business groups in emerging markets: Long run evidence from Chile. *Academy of Management Journal* 43:268–85.

Khanna, T., and J. W. Rivkin. 1999a. Estimating the performance effects in emerging markets. *Academy of Management Best Paper Proceedings*, forthcoming.

Khanna, T., and J. W. Rivkin. 1999b. Ties that bind business groups: Evidence from Chile. Mimeo. Harvard Business School.

Kimura, M. 1983. *The Neutral theory of Molecular Evolution.* Cambridge: Cambridge University Press.

Kindleberger, C. P. 1975. *World in Depression: 1929–1939.* Berkeley: University of California Press.

Kingston, C. 2001. *Essays on Social Structure and Corruption.* Ph.D. dissertation. Stanford University.

Klein, D. 1990. The voluntary provision of public goods? The turnpike companies of early America. *Economic Inquiry* 28:788–812

Klein, S., and N. Rosenberg. 1986. An overview of innovation. In R. Landau and N. Rosenberg, eds., *The Positive Sum Strategy: Harnessing Technology for Economic Growth.* Washington, DC: National Academic Press, pp. 275–305.

Kitayama, S., H. R. Markus, H. Matsumoto, and V. Norasakkunikit. 1997. Individual and collective processes in the construction of the self: Self-enhancement in the United States and self-criticism in Japan. *Journal of Personality and Social Psychology* 72:1245–67.

Kiyotaki, N., and R. Wright. 1991. A contribution to the pure theory of money. *Journal of Economic Theory* 53:215–35.

Knight, F. 1921/1971. *Risk, Uncertainty and Profit*. Chicago: University of Chicago Press. Originally published in 1921 by Houghton Mifflin.

Knight, J., and I. Sened, eds. 1995. *Explaining Social Institutions*. Ann Arbor: University of Michigan Press.

Koga, Y. 1982. Problems in the post-harvest processing of rice in southeast Asian countries. In N. S. Scrimshaw et al., eds., *Nutrition Policy Implementation—Issues and Experiences*. New York: Plenum Press, pp. 385–417.

Koike, K. 1984. Skill formation systems in the U.S. and Japan: A comparative study. In Aoki (1984b):47–76.

Koike, K. 1988. *Understanding Industrial Relations in Modern Japan*. London: Macmillan.

Koike, K. 1994. Learning and incentive systems in Japanese industry. In Aoki and Dore (1994):41–65.

Koopmans, T. 1957. *Three Essays on the State of Economic Sciences*. New York: McGraw-Hill.

Kornai, J. 1980. *Economics of Shortage*. Amsterdam: North-Holland.

Kornhauser, L. W. 1999a. Excerpt from three roles for a theory of behavior in a theory of law. Mimeo. New York University.

Kornhauser, L. W. 1999b. The normativity of law. Mimeo. New York University.

Koumakhov, R., and B. Najman. 2000. Labor hoarding in Russia: Where does it come from? Mimeo. Ecoles des Hautes Etudes en Sciences Sociales.

Kranton, R. E. 1996. Reciprocal exchange: A self-sustaining system. *American Economic Review* 86:830–51.

Krasner, S. D. 1978. *Defending National Interest: Raw Materials, Investments and the U.S. Foreign Policy*. Princeton: Princeton University Press.

Krasner, S. D. 1984. Approaches to the state: Alternative conceptions and historical dynamics. *Comparative Politics* 1:223–46.

Krasner, S. D. 1988. Sovereignty: An institutional perspective. *Comparative Political Studies* 21:64–94.

Krasner, S. D. 1999. *Sovereignty: Organized Hypocrisy*. Princeton: Princeton University Press.

Kreps, D., P. Milgrom, J. Roberts, and R. Wilson. 1982. Rational cooperation in the finitely repeated prisoners' dilemma. *Journal of Economic Theory* 27:245–52.

Kreps, D. M. 1990. *Game Theory and Economic Modelling*. Oxford: Claredon Press.

Kreps, D. M. 1990b. Corporate culture and economic theory. In J. Alt and K. Shepsle, eds., *Perspectives on Positive Political Economy*. Cambridge: Cambridge University Press, pp. 90–143.

Krueger, A. O. 1974. The political economy of rent-seeking society. *American Economic Review* 64:291–303.

Krueger, A. O., M. Schiff, and A. Valdes, eds. 1991. *Political Economy of Agricultural Pricing Policies*, 5 vols. Baltimore: Johns Hopkins University Press.

Krugman, P. 1991. History versus expectations. *Quarterly Journal of Economics* 56:651–67.

Krugman, P. 1996. *The Self-organizing Economy*. Cambridge: Blackwell Publishers.

Krugman, P., and M. Obstfeld. 1994. *International Economics: Theory and Policy*, 3rd ed. New York: Harper-Collins.

Kuran, T. 1991. Cognitive limitations and preference evolution. *Journal of Institutional and Theoretical Economics* 147:241–73.

Landa, J. T. 1994. *Trust, Ethnicity, and Identity: Beyond the New Institutional Economics of Ethnic Trading Networks, Contract Law, and Gift-Exchange*. Ann Arbor: University of Michigan Press.

Lange, O. 1936/1937. On the economic theory of socialism. *Review of Economic Studies* 4:53–71, 123–42.

La Porta, R., F. Lopez-de-Silanes, and A. Shleifer. 1999. Corporate ownership around the world. *Journal of Finance* 54:471–517.

La Porta, R., F Lopez-de-Silanes, A. Shleifer, and R. Vishny. 1998. Law and finance. *Journal of Political Economy* 106:1113–55.

Lee, C., W. F. Miller, M. G. Hancok, and H. S. Rowen, eds. 2000. *The Silicon Valley Edge: A Habitat for Innovation and Entrepreneurship*. Stanford: Stanford University Press.

Leff, N. 1976. Capital markets in the less developed countries: The group principle. In R. MacKinnon, ed., *Money and Finance in Economic Growth and Finance*. New York: Dekker, pp. 97–122.

Leff, N. 1978. Industrial organization and entrepreneurship in developing countries: The economic groups. *Economic Development and Cultural Change* 26:661–75.

Lehmbruch, G. 1999. The rise and change of discourses on "embedded capaitalism" in Germany and Japan and their institutional setting. Mimeo. Universität Konstantz.

Lerner, V. J. 1994. The syndication of venture capital investments. *Financial Management* 23:16–27.

Lerner, V. J. 1995. Venture capitalists and the oversight of private firms. *The Journal of Finance* 1:301–17.

Levi, M. 1988. *Of Rule and Revenue*. Berkeley: University of California Press.

Levin, J. 1998. Relational incentive contracts. Mimeo. Stanford University.

Li, D. 1996. Ambiguous property rights in transition economies. *Journal of Comparative Economies* 23:1–19.

Libecap, G. D. 1986. Property rights in economic history: Implications for research. *Exploration in Economic History* 23:227–52.

Litwack, J. 2001. Central control of regional budgets: Theory with applications to Russia. Mimeo. OECD.

Luebbert, G. 1991. *Liberalism, Fascism, or Social Democracy: Social Classes and the Political Origins of Regimes in Interwar Europe*. Oxford: Oxford University Press.

Luhmann, N. 1979. *Trust and Power*. New York: Wiley.

McKinnon, R. 1997. Market preserving fiscal federalism in the American monetary union. In M. Blejar and T. Ter-Minassian, eds., *Macroeconomic Dimensions of Public Finance: Essays in Honor of Vito Tanzi*. London: Routeledge, pp. 73–93.

McKinnon, R., and H. Pill. 1999. Exchange-rate regimes for emerging markets: Moral hazard and international overborrowing. *Oxford Review of Economic Policy* 15:19–38.

MacLeod, W. B., and J. M. Malcomson. 1989. Implicit contracts, incentive compatibility, and involuntary unemployment. *Econometrica* 57:447–80.

Manne, H. 1965. Mergers and the market for corporate control. *Journal of Political Economy* 73:110–20.

March, J. G., and J. P. Olsen. 1989. *Rediscovering Institutions*. New York: Free Press.

Marglin, S. 1974. What do bosses do? *Review of Radical Political Economy* 32:60–112.

Margolis, J. ed. 1970. *The Analysis of Public Output*. New York: Norton.

Markus, H. R., and S. Kitayama. 1994. Culture and the self: Implications for cognition, emotion, and motivation. *Psychological Review* 98:224–53.

Marschak, J., and R. Radner. 1972. *The Theory of Teams*. New Haven: Yale University Press.

Marshall, T. H. 1964. *Class, Citizenship, and Social Development*. Garden City, NY: Doubleday.

Maskin, E., Y. Qian, and C. Xu. 2000. Incentives, scale economies, and organizational forms. *Review of Economic Studies*, 67:359–78.

Matsui, A. 1996. On cultural evolution: Social norms, rational behavior, and evolutionary game theory. *Journal of the Japanese and International Economies* 10:262–94.

Matsui, A., and M. Okuno-Fujiwara. 1994. Evolution and interaction of cultures. Mimeo. Universities of Pennsylvania and Tokyo.

Matsumoto, K. 1986. *Kigyo Syueki to Kigyo Kinyu* (Corporate Earnings and Corporate Finance). Tokyo: Nihon Keizai Shinbunsha.

Matsuyama, K. 1991. Increasing returns, industrialization, and indeterminacy of equilibrium. *Quarterly Journal of Economics* 56:617–50.

Matsuyama, K. 1996. Economic development as coordination problems. In M. Aoki et al., eds. (1997): 134–60.

Matsuyama, K., N. Kiyotaki, and A. Matsui. 1993. Toward a theory of international currency. *Review of Economic Studies* 60:283–307.

Maurice, M., F. Sellier, and J.-J. Silvestre. 1986. *The Social Foundations of Industrial Power: A Comparison of France and Germany*, A. Goldhammer, trans. Cambridge: MIT Press.

Mayer, C. 1988. New issues in corporate finance. *European Economic Review* 32:1167–89.

Maynard-Smith, J. 1958. *The Theory of Evolution*. Cambridge: Cambridge University Press.

Maynard-Smith, J. 1982. *Evolution and the Theory of Games*. Cambridge: Cambridge University Press.

Medina, L. F. 2000. *Essays on the Formal Theory of Parties and Elections*, Ph.D. dissertation. Stanford University.

Mendels, F. F. 1972. Proto-industrialization: The first phase of the industrialization process. *Journal of Economic History* 32:241–61.

Menger, C. 1883/1985. *Investigations into the Method of the Social Sciences with special reference to Economics (Untersuchungen über die Methode der Sozialwissenschaft und der Politischen Oekonomie insbesondere)*, F. J. Nock, trans. New York: New York University Press.

Meyer, J., and B. Rowan. 1977. Institutionalized organizations: Formal structure as myth and ceremony. *American Journal of Sociology* 83:340–63.

Milgrom, P., D. North, and B. Weingast. 1990. The role of institutions in the revival of trade: The law merchant, private judges, and the champagne fairs. *Economics and Politics* 2:1–23.

Milgrom, P., Y. Qian, and J. Roberts. 1991. Complementarities, momentum, and the evolution of modern manufacturing. *American Economic Review* 81 (Papers and Proceedings):84–88.

Milgrom, P., and J. Roberts. 1990. Rationalizability, learning, and equilibrium in games with strategic complementarities. *Econometrica* 59:1255–77.

Milgrom, P., and J. Roberts. 1990b. The economics of modern manufacturing: technology, strategy, and organization. *American Economic Review* 80:511–28.

Milgrom, P., and J. Roberts. 1992. *Economics, Organization, and Management*. Englewood Cliffs, NJ: Prentice-Hall.

Milgrom, P., and J. Roberts. 1994. Complementarities and systems: Understanding Japanese economic organization. *Estudios Economicos*:3–42.

Misaki, K. 1998. *Warurasu no Keizaishisou: Ippan Kinkou Riron no Shakai Bijon* (Economic Thought of Walras: The Social Vision of the General Equilibrium Theory). Nagoya: University of Nagoya Press.

Mishkin, F. S. 1995. *The Economics of Money, Banking, and Financial Markets*. New York: HarperCollins.

Miyajima, Hideaki, and Y. Arikawa. 2000. Relationship banking and debt choice: Evidence from the liberalization in Japan. Institute of Fiscal and Monetary Policy Ministry of Finance, Japan.

Miyajima, Hiroshi. 1983. Richo Kōki no Nōgyō Suiri (Agricultural irrigation in the late Yi dynasty). *Toyoshi Kenkyu* 41:645–95.

Miyajima, H. 1995. *Yangban* (in Japanese). Tokyo: Chuō Kōron.

Miyajima, H., T. Matsumoto, Y. Yi, and S. Chang. 1992. *Kindai Chōsen Suiri Kumiai no Kenkyu* (Studies in Irrigation Associations in Modern Korea). Tokyo: Nihon Hyoronsya.

Mokyr, J. 1990. Punctuated equilibria and technological progress. *American Economic Review* (Papers and Proceedings) 80:350–54.

Monden, Y. 1983. *Toyota Production System*. Atlanta: Industrial Engineering and Management Press.

Montinola, G., Y. Qian, and B. Weingast. 1995. Federalism, Chinese style: The political basis for economic success in China. *World Politics* 48:50–81.

Moriguchi, C. 1998. *The Evolution of Employment Systems in the United States and Japan: 1900–1960: A Comparative Historical and Institutional Analysis*. Ph.D. dissertation. Stanford University.

Moore, J. 1992. The firm as a collection of assets. *European Economic Review* 36:493–507.

Moore Jr., B. 1966. *Social Origins of Dictatorship and Democracy: Lord and Peasant in the Making of the Modern World*. Boston: Beacon Press.

Murdock, K. 1996. *The Role of Institutions in Enforcing Implicit Contracts: Analysis of Corporate and Government Policy*. Ph.D. dissertation. Stanford University.

Nagata, K. 1971. *Nihon Nōgyō no Suiri Kōzō* (The Structure of Irrigation in Japanese Agriculture). Tokyo: Iwanami Shoten.

Nash, J. 1951. Non-cooperative games. *Annals of Mathematics* 54:286–95.

Nash, J. 1953. Two-person cooperative games. *Econometrica* 21:128–40.

Nelson, R. 1994. The co-evolution of technology, industrial structure, and supporting institutions. *Industrial and Corporate Change* 3:47–63.

Nelson, R. 1995. Recent evolutionary theorizing about economic change. *Journal of Economic Literature* 33:48–90.

Nelson, R., and S. Winter. 1982. *An Evolutionary Theory of Economic Change*. Cambridge: Harvard University Press.

Neumann, J. von, and O. Morgenstern. 1944. *Theory of Games and Economic Behavior*. Princeton: Princeton University Press.

Nishiguchi, T. 1994. *Strategic Industrial Sourcing*. Oxford: Oxford University Press.

Noguchi, Y. 1995. *1940-nen Taisei* (The 1940 Regime). Tokyo: Toyokeizai Shinposha.

Noguchi, Y. 1998. The 1940 system Japan under the wartime economy. *American Economic Review* 88:404–16.

North, D. C. 1961. *The Economic Growth of the United States, 1790–1860*. Englewood Cliffs, NJ: Prentice-Hall.

North, D. 1990. *Institutions, Institutional Change and Economic Performance*. Cambridge: Cambridge University Press.

North, D. 1995. Five propositions about institutional change. In J. Knight and I. Sened (1995):15–26.

North, D. 1998. A summary evaluation. In Hayami and Aoki (1998):552–60.

North, D., and R. Thomas. 1973. *The Rise of the Western World: A New Economic History*. Cambridge: Cambridge University Press.

North, D., and B. Weingast. 1989. Constitutions and commitment: The evolution of institutions governing public choice in seventeenth-century England. *Journal of Economic History* 49:803–32.

Nozick, R. 1974. *Anarchy, State and Utopia*. New York: Basic Books.

Oates, W. 1972. *Fiscal Federalism*. New York: Harcourt Brace Jovanovich.

OECD. 2000. *OECD Economic Surveys: Russian Federation 2000*. Paris: OECD.

Ogawa, H. 1998. *Itaria no Chūshō Kigyō: Dokusō to Tayōsei no Network* (Small and Medium-sized Enterprises in Italy: Networking for Creativity and Diversity). Tokyo: JETRO.

Okazaki, T. 1993. The Japanese firm under the wartime planned economy. *Journal of the Japanese and International Economies* 7:175–203. Reprinted in Aoki and Dore (1994):350–378.

Okazaki, T. 1995. Dainiji Sekai Taisenki no Kinyuseido Kaikaku to Kinyu Sisutemu no Henka (Financial institution reforms and changes in financial system during the Second World War). In A. Hara, ed., *Nihon no Senji Keizai* (The War Economy in Japan). Tokyo: University of Tokyo Press, pp. 107–139.

Okazaki, T. 1997. *Kōgyōka no Kiseki: Keizai Taikoku Zenshi* (A Trajectory of Industrialization: Prehistory of an Economic Power). Tokyo: Yomiuri Shinbunsha.

Okazaki, T. 2000. Role of holding companies in prewar Japanese economic development: Rethinking *zaibatsu* in perspectives of corporate governance. Mimeo. University of Tokyo.

Okazaki, T., and M. Okuno-Fujiwara. 1998. Evolution of economic systems: The case of Japan. In Hayami and Aoki (1998):482–521.

Okazaki, T., and M. Okuno-Fujiwara, eds. 1999[1995]. *The Japanese Economic System and Its Historical Origins*. Oxford: Oxford University Press. Trans. from *Nihonteki Keizai Sisutemu no Rekishiteki Kigen*. Tokyo: Nihon Keizai Shinbunsya.

Okimoto, D. 1989. *Between MITI and the Market: Japanese Industrial Policy for High Technology*. Stanford: Stanford University Press.

Okimoto, D., and Y. Nishi. 1994. R&D organization in Japanese and American semiconductor firms. In Aoki and Dore (1994):178–208.

Okuno-Fujiwara, M. 1997. Toward a comparative institutional analysis of the government-business relationship. In Aoki, Kim, and Okuno-Fujiwara (1997):373–406.

Okuno-Fujiwara, M., and A. Postlewaithe. 1995. Social norms and random matching games. *Games and Economic Behavior* 9:79–109.

Olson, M. 1982. *The Rise and Decline of Nations: Economic Growth, Stagflation, and Social Rigidities*. New Haven: Yale University Press.

Olson, M. 1993. Dictatorship, democracy, and development. *American Political Science Review* 83:567–76.

Olson, M. 1997. The new institutional economics: The collective choice approach to economic development. In C. Clague, ed., *Institutions and Economic Development: Growth and Governance in Less-Developed and Post-Socialist Countries*. Baltimore: Johns Hopkins University Press, pp. 37–64.

Osborne, M. J., and A. Rubinstein. 1994. *A Course in Game Theory*. Cambridge: MIT Press.

Oshima, H. 1987. *Economic Growth in Monsoon Asia: A Comparative Survey*. Tokyo: University of Tokyo Press.

Ostrom, E. 1990. *Governing the Commons*. Cambridge: Cambridge University Press.

Ostrom, E. 1992. *Crafting Institutions for Self-Governing Irrigation Systems*. San Francisco: Institute for Contemporary Studies Press.

Ostrom, E., and J. Walker. 1994. *Rules, Games, and Common-Pool Resources*. Ann Arbor, Michigan: University of Michigan Press.

Pagano, U. 1993. Organizational equilibria and institutional stability. In Bowles, Gintis and Gustafsson (1993):86–114.

Pagano, U. 1999. The origin of organizational species. In A. Nicita and U. Pagano, eds., *The Evolution of Economic Diversity*. London: Routledge and Keganl Paul.

Pagano, U. 1999. Information technology and the "Biodiversity" of Captalism. Mimeo. University of Sienna.

Pagano, U., and R. Rowthorn. 1994. Ownership, technology and institutional stability. *Structural Change and Economic Dynamics* 5:221–42.

Palais, J. B. 1975. *Politics and Policy in Traditional Korea*. Cambridge: Harvard University Press.

Palais, J. B. 1996. *Confucian Statecraft and Korean Institutions*. Seattle: University of Washington Press.

Pareto, V. 1916[1935]. *The Mind and Society*, 4 vols. English trans. of *Trattato di Sociologia generale*, A. Bongiorno and A. Livingston, trans. New York: Harcout, Brace.

Parsons, T. 1951. *The Social System*. New York: Free Press.

Peng, K., and R. E. Nisbett. 1999. Culture, dialectics, and reasoning about contradiction. *American Psychologist* 54:741–54.

Petersen, M. A., and R. G. Rajan. 1994. Benefits from lending relationships: Evidence from small business data. *Journal of Finance* 49:3–37.

Petersen, M. A., and R. G. Rajan. 1995. The effect of credit market competition on lending relationships. *Quarterly Journal of Economics* 110:407–43.

Pinker, S. 1997. *How the Mind Works*. New York: Norton.

Pine, B. J. 1993. *Mass Customization: The New Frontier in Business Competition*. Boston: Harvard Business School Press.

Pinker, S. 1997. *How the Mind Works*. New York: Norton.

Piore, M., and C. Sabel. 1984. *The Second Industrial Divide*. New York: Basic Books.

Platteau, J.-P. 1994. Behind the market stage where real society exist, Part II: The role of moral norms. *Journal of Development Studies* 30:753–817.

Platteau, J. P. 2000. *Institutions, Social Norms and Economic Organization*. Amsterdam: Harwood.

Platteau, J.-P., and J.-M. Baland. 1998. Dividing the commons—An assessment of the new institutional economics of property rights. Mimeo. University of Namur.

Platteau, J.-P., and Y. Hayami. 1998. Resource endowments and agricultural development: Africa versus Asia. In Hayami and Aoki (1998):357–410.

Platteau, J.-P., and E. Seki. 2000. Community arrangements to overcome market failures: Pooling groups in Japanese fisheries. In Aoki and Hayami (2000):344–402.

Polanyi, K. 1944. *The Great Transformation*. New York: Farrar Rinehart.

Polanyi, M. 1958. *Personal Knowledge: Towards a Post-critical Philosophy*. Chicago: University of Chicago Press.

Polanyi, M. 1966. *The Tacit Dimension*. London: Routledge and Kegan Paul.

Porter, M. 1998. Clusters and the new economics of competition. *Harvard Business Review* 76:77–90.

Prat, A. 1996. Shared knowledge versus diversified knowledge in teams. *Journal of the Japanese and International Economies* 10:181–95.

Putnam, R. D. 1993. *Making Democracy Work*. Princeton: Princeton University Press.

Pyke, F., G. Becattini, and W. Sengenberger. eds. 1990. *Industrial Districts and Inter-firm Cooperation in Italy*. Geneva: ILO Publications.

Qian, Y. 1999. The institutional foundations of China's market transition. Presented at the World Bank's *Annual Bank Conference on Development Economics*, April 1999.

Qian, Y., and G. Roland. 1998. Federalism and the soft budget constraint. *American Economic Review* 88:1143–62.

Qian, Y., and B. Weingast. 1997. Federalism as a commitment to preserving market incentives. *Journal of Economic Perspectives* 11:83–92.

Qian, Y., and C. Xu. 1993. Why China's economic reforms differ: The N-form hierarchy and entry/ expansion of the non-state sector. *Journal of Economic Transition* 1:135–70.

Radin, M. J. 1999. Retooling contracts for the digital era. Mimeo. Stanford: Hoover Institution.

Radin, M. J. 2000. Humans, computers, and binding commitment. Mimeo. Stanford Law School.

Radin, M. 1994. Cognitive dissonance and social change. *Journal of Economic Behavior and Organization* 23:177–94.

Radner, R. 1992. Hierarchy: The economics of managing. *Journal of Economic Literature* 30:1382–1415.

Radner, R. 1993. The organization of decentralized information processing. *Econometrica* 61:1109–46.

Rainis, G., and L. Orrock. 1985. Latin American and East Asian NICs: Development strategies compared. In E. Duran, ed., *Latin America and the World Recession*. Cambridge: Cambridge University Press, pp. 48–66.

Rajan, R. G. 1992. Insiders and outsiders, the choice between informed and arm's-length debt. *Journal of Finance* 47:1367–1400.

Rajan, R. G., and L. Zinglaes. 1998. Which capitalism? Lessons from the East Asian crisis. *Journal of Applied Corporate Finance* 11:40–48.

Rajan, R. G., and L. Zingales. 2000. Governance of new enterprises. In X. Vives, ed., *Corporate Governance: Theoretical and Empirical Perspectives*. Cambridge: Cambridge University Press, pp. 201–32.

Ramseyer, J. M. 1990. *Hou to Keizaigaku—Nihonhou no Keizaibunseki* (Law and Economics: Economic Analysis of Japanese Law). Tokyo: Kōbundō.

Remseyer, J. M., and M. Nakazato. 1999. *Japanese Law: An Economic Approach*. Chicago: University of Chicago Press.

Reyburn, S. S. 1980. *California Escrow Procedure: A Blueprint for the Nation*. Englewood Cliffs, NJ: Prentice-Hall.

Reiter, S., and J. Hugh. 1981. A preface on modeling the regulated United States economy. *Hofstra Law Review* 9:1381–1421.

Riordan, M. 1993. Competitin and bank performance: a theoretical perspective. In C. P. Mayer and X. Vives, eds., *Capital Markets and Financial Intermediation*. Cambridge: Cambridge University Press, pp. 328–43.

Robson, A. 1990. Efficiency in evolutionary games: Darwin, Nash and the Secret Handshake. *Journal of Theoretical Biology* 144:379–96.

Rogers, J., and W. Streeck, eds. 1994. *Works Councils: Consultation, Representation and Cooperation*. Chicago: University of Chicago Press.

Romer, P. M. 1986. Increasing returns and long run growth. *Journal of Political Economy* 94:1002–37.

Rosenberg, N., ed. 1969. *The American System of Manufacturers: The Report of the Committee on the Machinery of the United States 1855 and the Special Reports of George Wallis and Joseph Whitworth 1854*. Edinburgh: Edinburgh University Press.

Rosenberg, N., and L. E. Birdzell Jr. 1986. *How the West Grew Rich*. New York: Basic Books.

Royce, J. 1901/1959. *The World and the Individual*. New York: Dover.

Rubinstein, A. 1982. Perfect equilibrium in a bargaining model. *Econometrica* 50:97–109.

Rubinstein, A., and A. Wolinsky. 1987. Middlemen. *Quarterly Journal of Economics* 102:581–93.

Sahlman, W. A. 1990. The structure and governance of venture capitalist organizations. *Journal of Financial Economics* 27:473–521.

Sakaibara, E. 1999. The end of market fundamentalism. Speech delivered at the Foreign Correspondent Club in Tokyo.

Sakakibara, E. 2000. *Nihon to Sekaiga Furueta Hi* (Days When Japan and the World Trembled). Tokyo: Chuō Kōronsha.

Sako, M. 1994. Training, productivity, and quality control in Japanese multinational companies. In Aoki and Dore (1994):84–114.

Salmon, L. M., and H. K. Anheier. 1996. *The Emerging Nonprofit Sector: A Comparative Analysis*. Manchester: Manchester University Press.

Salmon, L. M., and H. K. Anheier. 1996. *The Emerging Nonprofit Sector: An Overview*. Manchester: Manchester University Press.

Saxenian, A. 1994. *Regional Advantage: Culture and Competition in Silicon Valley and Route 128*. Cambridge: Harvard University Press.

Saxenian, A. 1999. *Silicon Valley's New Immigrant Entrepreneurs*. San Francisco: Public Policy Institute of California.

Saxenian, A. 1999. The Silicon Valley-Hsinchu connection: Technical communities and industrial upgrading. Mimeo. Stanford University.

Schank, R. C., and R. P. Abelson. 1977. *Scripts, Plans, Goals, and Understanding.* Hillsdale, NJ: Lawrence Erlbaum.

Scharpf, F. W. 1997. *Games Real Actors Play: Actor-Centered Institutionalism in Policy Research.* Boulder: Westview Press.

Schelling, T. 1960. *The Strategy of Conflict.* Cambridge: Harvard University Press.

Schlicht, E. 1998. *On Customs in the Economy.* Oxford: Clarendon Press.

Schmitter, P. C., and G. Lehmbruch, eds. 1979. *Trends Toward Corporatist Intermediation.* Beverly Hills, CA: Sage.

Schopf, T., ed. 1972. *Models in Paleobiology.* San Francisco: Freeman, Cooper.

Schotter, A. 1981. *The Economic Theory of Social Institutions.* Cambridge: Cambridge University Press.

Schumpeter, J. 1934. *The Theory of Economic Development.* Cambridge: Harvard University Press.

Schumpeter, J. 1947. The creative response in economic history. *Journal of Economic History* 7:149–59.

Schumpeter, J. 1952. *Capitalism, Socialism and Democracy,* 5th ed. London: George Allen and Unwin.

Scott, W. R. 1994. Conceptualizing organizational fields: Linking organizations and societal systems. In H. Derlien, U. Gerhardt, and F. Scharpf, eds., *Systemrationalität und Partialinteresse.* Baden-Baden: Nomos Verlagsgesellschaft, pp. 203–21.

Scott, W. R. 1995. *Institutions and Organizations.* Thousand Oaks, CA: Sage.

Scott, W. R., and J. Meyer. 1983. The organization of societal sectors. In J. Meyer and W. R. Scott, eds., *Organizational Environments: Ritual and Rationality.* Beverly Hills, CA: Sage, pp. 129–53.

Seabright, P. 1993. Managing local commons: Theoretical issues in incentive design. *Journal of Economic Perspectives* 7:113–34.

Searle, J. 1995. *The Construction of Social Reality.* New York: Free Press.

Sened, I. 1997. *The Political Institution of Private Property.* Cambridge: Cambridge University Press.

Shapiro, C., and J. Stiglitz. 1984. Equilibrium unemployment as a worker discipline device. *American Economic Review* 74:433–44.

Sharpe, S. A. 1990. Asymmetric information, bank lending, and implicit contracts: A stylized model of customer relationships. *Journal of Finance* 45:1069–87.

Sheard, P. 1994. Main bank and the governance of financial distress. In Aoki and Patrick (1994):188–230.

Shinpo, H., and A. Hasegawa. 1988. Shōhin Seisan, Ryūtū no Dainamikkusu (Dynamics of commodity production and distribution). In S. Hayami and M. Miyamoto, eds., *Keizai Shakai no Seiritsu:17–18 Seiki* (The Establishment of an Economic Society: 17–18 Centuries). *Economic History of Japan,* vol. 1. Tokyo: Iwanami Shoten, pp. 217–70.

Shleifer, A., and L. Summers. 1988. Breach of trust in hostile takeovers. In A. J. Auerbach, ed., *Corporate Takeovers: Causes and Consequence.* Chicago: University of Chicago Press, pp. 65–88.

Shleifer, A., and R. W. Vishny. 1994. Politicians and Firm. *Quarterly Journal of Economics* 109:995–1025.

Shleifer, A., and R. W. Vishny. 1997. A survey of corporate governance. *Journal of Finance* 52:737–87.

Simon, H. A. 1951. A formal theory of the employment relationship. *Econometrica* 19:293–305.

Simon, H. A. 1957. *Administrative Behavior,* 2nd ed. New York: Free Press.

Simon, H. A. 1982. *Models of Bounded Rationality: Behavioral Economics and Business Organization.* Cambridge: MIT Press.

Simon, H. A. 1991. Organizations and markets. *Journal of Economic Perspectives* 5:25–44.

Skocpol, T. 1979. *States and Social Revolutions.* Cambridge: Cambridge University Press.

Skocpol, T. 1985. Bringing the state back In: Strategies of analysis in current research. In P. B. Evans, D. Reuschemeyer, and T. Skocpol, eds., *Bringing the State Back In.* Cambridge: Cambridge University Press, pp. 3–37.

Smith, A. 1759[1976]. *The Theory of Moral Sentiments.* Oxford: Oxford University Press.

Smith, A. 1776[1991]. *The Wealth of Nations.* Buffalo: Prometheus Book.

Smith, T. C. 1959. *The Agrarian Origins of Modern Japan.* Stanford: Stanford University Press.

Solow, R. 1980. On theories of unemployment. *American Economic Review* 70:1–11.

Sorge, A. 1991. Strategic fit and the societal effect: Interpreting cross-national comparisons of technology, organization and human resources. *Organization Studies* 12:161–90.

Spangnolo, G. 1999. Social relations and cooperation in organizations. *Journal of Economic Behavior and Organization* 38:1–26.

Stiglitz, J. 1999. The global financial crisis: Perspectives and policies. Mimeo. World Bank.

Stiglitz, J., and A. Weiss. 1981. Credit rationing in markets with imperfect information. *American Economic Review* 71:393–410.

Stopford, J., and S. Strange. 1991. *Rival States, Rival Firms.* Cambridge: Cambridge University Press.

Strange, S. 1996. *The Retreat of the State.* Cambridge: Cambridge University Press.

Streeck, W. 1992. *Social Institutions and Economic Performance.* Newbury Park, CA: Sage.

Streeck, W. 1995. The German social market economy: External competitiveness and internal cohesion. Mimeo. Max-Planck Institut für Gesellschaftsforschung, Köln.

Streeck, W. 1996. Lean production in the German automobile industry: A test case for convergent theory. In B. Berger and R. Dore, eds., *National Diversity and Global Capitalism.* Ithaca: Cornell University Press, pp. 138–70.

Streeck, W. 1997a. German capitalism: Does it exist? Can it survive? In C. Crouch and W. Streeck, eds., *Political Economy of Modern Capitalism.* London: Sage, pp. 33–54.

Streeck, W. 1997b. Citizenship under regime competition: The case of the "European work councils." European University Institute.

Streeck, W. 1998. The internationalization of industrial relations in Europe: Prospects and problems. Mimeo. Max-Planck Institut für Gesellschaftsforschung, Köln.

Stuart, L., and R. Kargon. 1996. Selling Silicon Valley: Frederick Terman's model for regional advantage. *Business History Review* 70:435–72.

Suchman, M. C. 2000. Dealmakers and councelors: Law firms as intermediaries in the development of Silicon Valley. Mimeo. University of Wisconsin.

Sugden, R. 1986. *The Economics of Rights, Co-operation and Welfare.* Oxford: Basil Blackwell.

Sugden, R. 1989. Spontaneous order. *Journal of Economic Perspectives* 3:85–97.

Sugden, R. 1995. A theory of focal points. *Economic Journal* 105:533–50.

Swidler, A. 1986. Culture in action: Symbols and strategies. *American Sociological Review* 51:273–86.

Tadelis, S. 1999. What's in a name? Reputation as a tradeable asset. *American Economic Review* 89:548–63.

Tamaki, A., and I. Hatade. 1974. *Fūdo:Taichi to Ningen no Rekishi* (Cultured Landscape: A History of Land and Human Being). Tokyo: Heibonsha.

Tamaki, A., I. Hatade, and N. Imamura, eds. 1980. *Suiri no Shakaikozo* (The Social Structure of Irrigation). Tokyo: United Nation University.

Tanimoto, M. 1998. *Nihon ni okeru Zairaiteki Keizai Hatten to Orimonogyo* (Indigenous Economic Development and the Textile Industry in Japan). Nagoya: University of Nagoya Press.

Teece, D., R. Rumelt, G. Dosi, and S. Winter. 1994. Understanding corporate coherence: Theory and evidence. *Journal of Economic Behavior and Organization* 22:1–24.

Teranishi, J. 1990. Financial systems and the industrialization of Japan:1900–1970. *Banca Nacionale del Lavoro Quarterly Review* 174:309–41.

Teranishi, J. 1994. Loan syndication in war-time Japan and the origins of the main bank system. In Aoki and Patrick (1994):51–88.

Teranishi, J. 1997. Sectorial resource transfer, conflict, and macrostability in economic development: A comparative analysis. In Aoki, Kim, and Okuno-Fujiwara (1997):279–311.

Teranishi, J. 2000. The fall of the Taisho economic system. In Aoki and Saxonhouse (2000):43–63.

Testa, R. 1997. The legal process of venture capital investments. *Pratt's Guide to Venture Capital Sources.* Wellesley Hills, MA: Venture Economics.

Von Thadden, E. L. 1995. Long-term contracts, short-term investment and monitoring. *Review of Economic Studies* 62:557–75.

Thelen, K. 1999. Historical institutionalism in comparative politics. *Annual Review of Political Science* 2:369–404.

Thornbeck, E. 1998. The institutional foundations of macroeconomic stability: Indonesia vs. nigeria. In Hayami and Aoki (1998):106–38.

Tiebout, C. 1956. A pure theory of local expenditures. *Journal of Political Economy* 64:416–24.

Timberlake Jr., R. H. 1978. *The Origins of Central Banking in the United States.* Cambridge: Harvard University Press.

Title Insurance and Trust Company. 1977. *Escrow Procedure Book I.* Los Angeles: Title Insurance and Trust Co.

Tirole, J. 1988. *The Theory of Industrial Organization.* Cambridge: MIT Press.

Tirole, J. 2001. Corporate Governance, *Econometrica* 69:1–35.

Topkis, D. 1978. Minimizing a submodular function on a lattice. *Operations Research* 26:305–21.

Topkis, D. 1998. *Supermodularity and Complementarity.* Princeton: Princeton University Press.

Toya, T. 2000. *The Political Economy of the Japanese Financial Big Bang: Institutional Change in Finance and Public Policy Making.* Ph.D. dissertation. Stanford University.

Veblen, T. B. 1909[1961]. The limitation of marginal utility. Originally published in *Journal of Political Economy*, vol. 17. Reprinted in *The Place of Science in Modern Civilization and Other Essays.* New York: Russell and Russek, pp. 231–51.

Ullmann-Margalit, E. 1977. *The Emergence of Norms.* Oxford: Oxford University Press.

U.S. Strategic Bombing Survey. 1945. *The Effects of Strategic Bombing on Japan's War Economy.* Pacific War Report no. 53. Washington DC: U.S. Government Printing Office.

Wade, R. 1990. *Village Republics: Economic Conditions for Collective Action in South India.* Cambridge: Cambridge University Press.

Wade, R. 1990. *Governing the Market: Economic Theory and the Role of the Government in East Asian Industrialization.* Princeton: Princeton University Press.

Wagner, E. W. 1972. The ladder of success in Yi dynasty Korea. *Occasional Papers on Korea* 1:1–8.

Walras, L. 1926[1954]. *Elements of Pure Economics or the Theory of Social Wealth,* W. Jaffe trans. definite ed. London: Urwin.

Walras, L. 1898[1992]. Etudes d'économie politique appliquée: Théorie de la production de la richesse sociale. In *August et Léon Walras, Oeuvres économiques complétes.* Paris: P. Dockès. Economica.

Weber, M. 1998. In R. Swedberg, ed. *Essays in Economic Sociology.* Princeton: Princeton University Press.

Weibull, J. 1995. *Evolutionary Game Theory.* Cambridge: MIT Press.

Weingast, B. 1993. Constitutions as governance structures: The political foundations of secure markets. *Journal of Institutional and Theoretical Economics* 149:286–311.

Weingast, B. 1995. The economic role of political institutions: Market-preserving federalism and economic development. *Journal of Law, Economics and Organization* 11:1–31.

Weingast, B. 1997. The political foundations of democracy and the rule of law. *American Political Science Review* 91:245–63.

Westney, D. E. 1987. *Imitation and Innovation*. Cambridge: Harvard University Press.

Wiener, N. 1966. *God and Golem, Inc.* Cambridge: MIT Press.

Williams, R. 1976/1983. *Keywords: A Vocabulary of Culture and Society*, rev. ed. New York: Oxford University Press.

Williamson, O. E. 1975. *Markets and Hierarchies: Analysis and Antitrust Implications*. New York: Free Press.

Williamson, O. E. 1985. *The Economic Institutions of Capitalism*. New York: Free Press.

Williamson, O. E. 1995. Hierarchies, markets and power in the economy: An economic perspective. *Industrial and Corporate Change* 4:21–50.

Williamson, O. E. 1996. *The Mechanisms of Governance*. Oxford: Oxford University Press.

Williamson, O. E. 1999. Human action and economic organization. Mimeo. University of California, Berkeley.

Williamson, O. E. 2000. The new institutional economics: Taking stock, looking ahead. *Journal of Economic Literature* 38:595–613.

Womack, J. P., D. T. Jones, and D. Roos. 1990. *The Machine That Changed the World: The Story of Lean Production*. New York: Rawson Associates.

World Bank. 1996. *World Bank Participation Book*. Washington, DC: World Bank.

Wrege, C. D., and R. G. Greenwood. 1991. *Frederick W. Taylor, the Father of Scientific Management: Myth and Reality*. Burr Ridge, IL: Unwin.

Yasuda, A. 2001. *Three Essays on Relationships and Imperfect Competition in Corporate Banking Industry: An Empirical and Comparative Analysis*. Ph.D. dissertation. Stanford University.

Yelling, J. A. 1982. Rationality in the commons fields. *Economic History Review* 35:409–15.

Yoshitomi, M. 1998. *Nihon Keizai no Shinjitu* (The Truth of the Japanese Economy). Tokyo: Toyo Keizai Shinposha.

Young, H. P. 1991. An evolutionary model of bargaining. *Journal of Economic Theory* 59:145–68.

Young, H. P. 1993. The evolution of conventions. *Econometrica* 61:57–84.

Young, H. P. 1998. *Individual Strategy and Social Structure: An Evolutionary Theory of Institutions*. Princeton: Princeton University Press.

Zingales, L. 1998. Corporate Governance. In *The New Palgrave Dictionary of Economics and the Law*. London: Macmillan, pp. 497–503.

Zucker, L. G. 1977. The role of institutionalization in cultural persistence. *American Sociological Review* 13:443–64.

Index

Printed in the United States
by Baker & Taylor Publisher Services